1968

This book may be kept

FRENCH INDO-CHINA

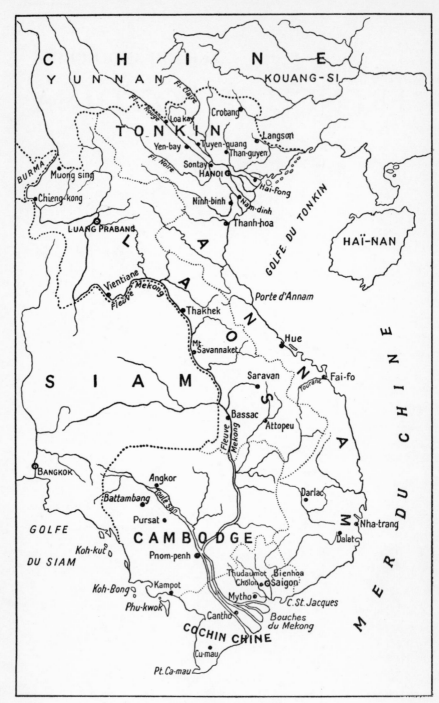

FRENCH-INDO CHINA

FRENCH INDO-CHINA

by

VIRGINIA THOMPSON

1968

OCTAGON BOOKS, INC.

New York

Originally published in 1937 by The Macmillan Company
for the American Council, Institute of Pacific Relations

Reprinted 1968
by special arrangement with Virginia Adloff and
George Allen & Unwin Ltd.

OCTAGON BOOKS, INC.
175 FIFTH AVENUE
NEW YORK, N. Y. 10010

LIBRARY OF CONGRESS CATALOG CARD NUMBER: 68-17756

Printed in U.S.A. by
NOBLE OFFSET PRINTERS, INC.
NEW YORK 3, N. Y.

TO

V. B.

PREFACE

CONSIDERING the recency of French colonization in Indo-China, it has given birth to an unusually rich and vast literature of more than three thousand books in French. Works in other languages are few and negligible. Lost between the more stimulating and turbulent countries of India and China, and boasting an almost wholly peaceful development for the last seventy-five years, Indo-China has been largely lost to view. But since the War the growth of Chinese Communism, the growing recognition of the importance of the Pacific, and the more recent sop to Cerberus in the form of African colonies proffered to Hitler have all given new significance to the lands bordering upon it. French Indo-China deserves to be better known, not only in France itself, but also in those countries which have a stake in the Far East. In spite of its latent wealth, Indo-China lies too far off the main scene of action to play any but a secondary role in the Pacific drama. Yet in its local problems and in its reaction to a Western civilization it has had to accept, this colony deserves serious study. The process of amalgamation, flux, and interpenetration not only of two widely opposed Oriental cultures, but in their reactions to an Occidental power which forces them into new channels of thought, action, and feeling, offer a fascinating field for observation.

To the wealth of available written material there are a number of excellent guides. Of these the two most important are H. Cordier's *Bibliotheca Indosinica*, which includes works on all the countries of the peninsula up to 1912, and the continuation of this great bibliography ably carried on by P. Boudet and H. Bourgeois. In Indo-China a Library and Archive Service was created in 1917, and the following year a catalogue for the Central Library was begun. The excellent collections of the *Ecole Française d'Extrême Orient* and of the colony's Buddhist Institutes deserve special mention. Outside of the colony, Paris is naturally the richest field. The libraries of the *Agence Economique de l'Indochine*, the *Ecole Coloniale*, the *Bibliothèque Nationale*, the Ministry of the Colonies, the Colonial Museum, and the Archives of the Society of Foreign Missions and of the Grand Orient are valuable in the order of their sequence. Official documents are conspicuously unavailable, excepting for statistics and popularization purposes, for the study of a colony of such comparative importance.

The excellence, variety, and quantity of printed material on Indo-

China makes the student's task one of difficult choice rather than a mosaic patchwork of archive scraps. From 1908 to 1930 there appeared in the field of imaginative literature alone ten times as many books as from 1886 to 1908. About a third of the books on Indo-China are novels. Some of the earliest works written on the colony are still the best, because the writers were for the most part officers who lived in direct contact with the people. They brought zest and scholarship to their writing, which was, moreover, a self-imposed task apart from their official routine. The work of Luro, Schreiner, Philastre, Lagrée, Garnier, Pouvourville, Dumoutier, Cadière, Briffaut and Silvestre are outstanding for Annamite culture, as are the books of Aymonier, Mouhot, Groslier, A. Leclère. Meyer, Cabaton, Coedès for Khmer civilization. Laos has been studied thoroughly by Pavie and his collaborators, and the art of Champa by Parmentier. Very little has been written on Indo-China's primitive tribes.

Criticisms of the administration have been both numerous and witty, as, for example, the work of the journalists Ajalbert, Dorgelès, Bonnetain, Bourde, Roubaud, Durtain, and Viollis. To savour the colonists' viewpoint one should read the bitter books of Jung, Bernard and Bonnafont: for the military campaigns, Lyautey's letters, Galliéni's and Famin's narratives. For the functionary viewpoint one should consult Garros, Morel, and the different Governors-General. Excellent general studies are to be found in the two series edited by Lévi and G. Maspéro, and in the economic treatises of Boudillon, P. Bernard, and Y. Henry. Malleret's guide to Indo-Chinese literature indicates the value of the novels of Boissière, Daguerches, Marquet, Louba, and Nolly.

No attempt, except in the outline offered in the opening chapters, has been made in this volume to give a chronological story, nor has the same organization of material been used for all the countries studied. Rather, the aim has been to present cross-sections of the problem as a method of studying mutual influences and reciprocal reactions. The study of cultural interpenetration involves necessarily a certain amount of repetition at those places where the lines of thought intersect.

It will be noted that the word "colonial" is used for all the French residents in Indo-China, and "colonist" applied to those engaged in agricultural or industrial production. "Métropole" has been appropriated from the French to indicate Paris's uniquely dominant position in colonial government, and to differentiate between the French of France and those in the colony.

PREFACE

Although the author has visited Indo-China, she cannot offer years of residence nor knowledge of the native languages there as a basis for this study. The printed word and conversations with men and women versed in the colony's history and actuality have been the data from which conclusions were drawn. This volume does not pretend to be the fruit of personal experience, but an effort to lay before the English-reading public a background for the general problems in French Indo-China to-day.

Special thanks are due to M. Bauduin de Belval and Professor Violet Barbour for their kindness in reading and criticizing the manuscript; to the Librarian of the *Agence Economique de l'Indochine* for her astonishing and amiable resourcefulness in finding material; and above all to the American Council officers of the Institute of Pacific Relations. The author would also like to express appreciation of aid to Mesdames Gauthier and Viollis, and to MM. Ajalbert, Bouvier, Demiéville, Dennery, Dufresne, Gauthier, Gourdon, Le Fol, Lévy, Maspéro, Meyer, Ng. V. Tuong, Père Sy, and Comte A. de Vogüé.

CONTENTS

13

CONTENTS

"L'Indochine est, à tous les points de vue, la plus importante, la plus développée et la plus prospère de nos colonies."

Sarraut

FRENCH INDO-CHINA

CHAPTER I

ANNAMITE CIVILIZATION

"Jamais, à aucune époque de l'histoire, un peuple colonisateur n'a rencontré un aussi grand nombre de conditions favorables. Un pays riche et d'une infinie variété, un peuple déjà unifié, une administration régulière, des habitudes studieuses. . . . De toutes les institutions annamites il n'en est pas une dont on ne puisse tirer parti."   *F. Bernard*

THE HISTORY OF ANNAM

BEFORE their contact with the Chinese, the Annamites were but one of the many nomadic peoples of the Far East. Originally they probably came from Thibet, but only legends from this period have survived showing that the Annamites possessed a language of their own, along with assorted rites and superstitions. Since they were bounded on the east by the sea, and to the south and west by foreign peoples of like force and degree of civilization, conquest or cultural stimulus could only come from their neighbours to the north.

The Annamites would never have left their nomadic life in the forest and high mountains to settle as farmers on the delta land, had it not been for China's physical and moral domination. It cost the Chinese a great military effort to tame and teach this vagrant people, and for the Annamites it was far more helpful than harmful to be subordinated to an infinitely more disciplined and cultured nation. The Chinese invasions began about 213 B.C. This military period ended in A.D. 186, when the moral conquest of Annam, or the Pacified South, began. At the outset the Chinese followed no plan of colonization, but after the second century A.D. they used all their consummate art to assimilate this people whom they contemptuously called the Giao-chi. In four centuries of effective domination the Annamites forgot their own past and adopted Chinese civilization in the fullest sense.

In the seventh century, the southern fringe of Annamites was troubled by Cham invasions, and China, preoccupied with internal difficulties, did nothing to protect her vassal. The Annamites, however, proved to be by now such apt pupils that they not only drove back the Chams—eventually exterminating or forcing them into the mountains—but threw off the Chinese yoke as well, in 931. This brought to an end China's political domination, though five centuries later for a brief interval of fourteen years (1414–28) China regained control. In their life as a nation and as individuals, the Annamites to this day bear the indelible print of Chinese culture left by the first conquest.

The conquest of the Chams was but the first step in that *drang nach dem Süden* which was to characterize Annamite expansion for the next thousand years. Under their irresistible drive, the frontiers of the south gave way and the old kingdom of Champa vanished, leaving only traces of its admirable architecture and ephemeral splendour. This first Annamite conquest was typical of the future: the Annamites in their violent wake left only ruins. Unlike the Chinese, they did not educate and assimilate the vanquished, but pushed back into the mountains the remnants which they had unwittingly spared, so as to clear the ground for their own agricultural colonization. The same methods characterized their later wars with the Khmers and Laotians. Not even reconquest by the Chinese nor the internal strife by which Annam was ceaselessly rent could arrest this dynamic southward push.

The internal history of modern Annam was equally dominated by dynastic struggles. By the end of the sixteenth century the reigning family of Le had become decadent. The power that was slipping from their hands was disputed by three great rivals who, for the next few centuries, fought for it among themselves and with the nominal sovereigns. In the seventeenth century the Mac family experienced a transient triumph, only to disappear before an insurrection that occurred a little more than a hundred years later. A parallel to the Le–Mac rivalry has often been drawn with that of the Merovingians and their Mayors of the Palace in Frankish times, only the Les had definite revivals of strength. To this day their name, like that of the Stuarts formerly in England, serves as a rallying-cry for rebellion in the north. In general, the Macs depended for support upon the Chinese, and the Les upon popular affection. This northern drama paled in the seventeenth and eighteenth centuries before the destructive struggles of two other families—the Nguyens of Cochin-China, as modern Annam was formerly called, with the Trinhs of Tonkin. Though the Nguyens were greatly helped by the Portuguese, this put no immediate end to the turbulent and bloody warfare of the next centuries—in fact, the Cochin-Chinese king, Nguyen Anh, was driven into exile in Siam in the late eighteenth century. But the presence of the Portuguese was significant of the entry of a new factor upon the scene—European imperialism.

While the Arabs jealously guarded the secret of the sea route to the East, an occasional European succeeded in getting there by the overland route. Of these the most famous was Marco Polo, who wrote of Champa and Annam though he may never have visited either kingdom. Not until the fifteenth century did the Portuguese begin to trade along the Annamite coast and as far inland as Cambodia. It was at the mouth of the Mekong River that the famous Camoens was shipwrecked. Portuguese missionaries explored Angkor in 1570, a discovery which sank into oblivion until the nineteenth century. Portugal was not officially interested in Indo-China, but her soldiers and missionaries went there freely from neighbouring Macao, as did the Spanish priests and adventurers from Manila. Nowadays, after three centuries of mingling with the Cambodians, descendants of these early Portuguese have retained their names, customs, and religion.

By the opening of the seventeenth century, the Annamites were engaged in a brisk foreign commerce. At Fai-fo the Chinese and Japanese had long had trading posts, and it was to this market that the Portuguese first sent their ships. The Dutch East India Company was founded much later, in 1602, but it was not long before these formidable rivals of the Portuguese and Japanese made commerce there almost impossible. The Dutch began gradually to take the side of the Tonkinese in the North–South struggle, as a natural consequence of the Portuguese support of the Nguyens, but this did not increase their profits. In Cambodia, too, they suffered cruelly from the jealousy of the Portuguese, who managed to arouse even the tolerant Khmers to massacre the few Dutch who had penetrated as far as their Court. The Governor of Batavia was strong enough to exact a money indemnity for this outrage but no commercial concessions. No European power could for long play an important role at the Khmer Court because Cambodia's perpetual warfare with Siam and Annam was too all-absorbing.

The English, at this time weak in comparison with the Dutch and Portuguese, were hunting trade in the Far East. A massacre of British merchants at Fai-fo in 1613 was not a propitious beginning, nor were they more successful in getting established in Tonkin. The rapacity of the Annamite mandarins, who either stole goods outright or set their own prices for what they took, forced them to close down their posts in 1697, three years before the more persevering Dutch. An attempt in 1702 to transfer their headquarters to Poulo Condore was likewise a failure. All the European nations recognized the trade possibilities with Annam, but the mandarins' exactions, the people's lack of purchasing power, the incessant local warfare, and the destructive mutual jealousy of all the European traders there contributed to making it an unprofitable and hazardous venture. India, China, and Java offered a far greater reward in proportion to the obstacles encountered.

The French came to Indo-China long after the Dutch and Portuguese. At first only missionaries were sent there who worked on the foundations laid by the Portuguese and Italian Jesuits, who came there after they were expelled from Japan. These Jesuits had founded in 1608 a Mission at Fai-fo, and later spread to Tonkin, whence they were driven out twenty years later by Emperor Trinh Trang. Among those exiled then was the famous Père Alexandre de Rhodes, the first Franco-Annamite scholar and creator of the country's native clergy. His subsequent attempt to win the Pope's consent to naming special bishops for Annam was foiled by the machinations of the Portuguese, who were as jealous of their evangelical monopoly as of their commercial control. In 1658, however, the Pope's consent was finally obtained: one of his nominees was François Pallu, who later became one of the most famous bishops of Annam. That same year at Paris was founded the *Société des Missions Etrangères*, which was to send forth numerous missionaries to Annam.

The Annamite emperors were no religious fanatics, but they were wise enough to recognize in the missionary a precursor of European political penetration. Commerce and missions with both the French and the Portuguese went hand in hand, in spite of Papal Bulls forbidding missionaries to indulge in trade. One English captain reported that a French missionary was in charge of his country's trading post in Annam, and each nationality thoughtfully denounced to the native authorities the infractions of its European rivals. The native government, therefore, was well aware of the dual role of merchants and missions, and they carefully searched all commercial ships entering Annamite ports for the missionaries who were usually hidden on board.

The French East India Company had for years been interested in trading with Annam. Dupleix himself tried to get a foothold there by working through the missionaries established in the country. But the Company distrusted his motives, ignored his advice, and despatched their own emissary, Pierre Poivre, to make for them a survey of Annam's economic resources. Local opposition and the Company's financial status, however, annulled the commercial efficacy of his task, but not the general usefulness of the information he gathered. It was Poivre who later became Pigneau de Behaine's champion, by getting for him what slight recognition that famous missionary received, when he returned to France to put through an alliance with the exiled king of Cochin-China. The paper treaty with Nguyen Anh which Louis XVI made he later rescinded, after Pigneau had sailed away fondly believing his mission to have been successful. When he got to Pondichéry not only was he not aided by the Governor there, as he had been led to expect, but his project was definitely opposed. After heartbreaking delays, Pigneau was force to recruit, as a private enterprise, as many of the young Frenchmen in Pondichéry as were willing to risk their lives and fortunes in the dubious venture of placing Nguyen Anh upon the throne of Cochin-China. With these reinforcements Pigneau was able to obtain for Nguyen Anh an eventual triumph in 1802, which made him Gia-long, emperor not only of his patrimonial estates but of all the Annamite-speaking peoples. Gia-long received the imperial investiture of China, treated with Siam as an equal, and reduced Cambodia and Laos to the position of semi-vassal states. In regard to internal administration, the French officers helped him to build up a dynasty and an organization so remarkable that it is still partially in active use.

Gia-long was agreeably conscious of the non-official character of the aid he had received from the French. His benevolence towards the individual officers who had been instrumental in winning his victory was unbounded, but he made it clear that such awards were for their personal use and not to serve as an opening for their country's commerce. Upon his death, his son Minh Mang politely asked these officers who were still living in Annam to leave the country. He marked their departure by beginning a persecution of their compatriot missionaries and of their native converts. Worse violence was done them by the Emperor Thieu-Tri (1841–47), to be followed by even greater excesses on the part of Tu-Duc, his successor. Ironically enough, it was this effort to rid the country of missionaries that precipitated the French conquest—exactly what these emperors had been trying to avoid.

During the Second Empire, France sent warships to Annam upon several occasions to protest the treatment of her missionaries, but the concessions wrung from Hué merely meant the renewal of persecutions as soon as the fleet had sailed away. The number of French and Spanish missionaries put to death in the 1850's led both governments to lodge an official protest at Hué. When no response was forthcoming, the French Admiral, Rigault de Genouilly, was ordered to bombard the forts of Tourane (1858). Spain, making common cause with France, joined in this attack. The forts were quickly demolished, but trouble began when an expeditionary force was attempted on the mainland. The Annamites, retreating before the French advance, left their country to inflict a defeat, through the lack of supplies and the presence of tropical germs, which they were impotent to do by force of arms. After some hesitation, the Admiral decided to shift his attack elsewhere. He chose Saigon rather than Tonkin—a move that was subsequently severely criticized—because of its accessibility, and because it was one of the rice granaries of the Far East. After he had captured the Saigon citadel the Admiral returned to Tourane where the same circumstances continued to hold him in check.

In November 1859, De Genouilly was replaced by Admiral Page, who was instructed to make a treaty with Annam that involved no territorial concessions, but only a guarantee of religious liberty and the privilege of having French consuls in the main Annamite ports. Hué did not seize upon such liberal conditions with sufficient alacrity, believing that a policy of interminable delays and contradictory interviews, in the best Oriental manner, would discourage the French into a permanent withdrawal. But before Admiral Page could force through the issue, he received orders to take part in the current Chinese campaign. When he sailed away to the North, he left a garrison of only one thousand men at Saigon. They were almost immediately besieged in the citadel by Annamite forces numbering twelve thousand men—at a conservative estimate. This siege lasted from March 1860 to January 1861, and was withstood by the small garrison cut off entirely from the outside world. When the war in China came to an end, Admiral Charner was despatched to their relief with a strong force of three thousand men. In addition to a hard-fought campaign, which won for France the delta provinces, Charner had to organize a new administration in Cochin-China since all the Annamite officials had withdrawn, to a man, as the French approached. The Court of Hué was exceptionally resourceful in stirring up revolt in these new French possessions, and it required repeated military victories as well as a simultaneous revolt in Tonkin to make the Emperor Tu-Duc sue for peace. In 1863, just before he was replaced by De la Grandière, the Admiral succeeded in forcing through a treaty with Annam that legitimatized the French

24

conquest of the three Cochin-Chinese provinces and the payment of a money indemnity. This did not, however, end the matter, for the continued success of the revolts he stirred up encouraged Tu-Duc to send an embassy to Paris offering to buy back his lost possessions. The fate of Cochin-China hung on such a slender thread that if Tu-Duc had been more swiftly conciliatory, and if Chasseloup-Laubat, then Minister of the Navy, had been less strong in insisting upon the retention of the new conquest, Indo-China might not to-day be a French colony.

THE CENTRAL GOVERNMENT OF ANNAM

The Emperor is the absolute sovereign of—politically—the most democratic of peoples. He is the pivot around which the administrative machinery rotates—in modern times very creakily. Legend relates him to the Emperor of China, of whom he is at least spiritually the descendant. The fact that succession to the throne is not invariably fixed by primogeniture has fomented innumerable palace revolutions. Only royal blood is essential and a ceremony by which the reigning sovereign designates his successor.

It is the Emperor's religious character that makes his power absolute and any disobedience to it a sacrilege. The mark of his supreme authority is his exclusive right to make the Sacrifice to Heaven: he calls himself the Son of Heaven, not in arrogance as it sounds to Western ears, but in token of filial submission. The imperial will is, therefore, above law, of which it is the fountain-head and by which it is subsequently safeguarded. Respect for authority is a fundamental concept in Sino-Annamite belief. There is no contractual element in this imperial absolutism, indicating that it originally emanated from popular consent, but it is regarded as a mandatory delegation of power from the supreme celestial authority. The Annamites, ever copying the Chinese, have surrounded their sovereign with mystery and divinity. The emperor, quasi-divine, formerly remained hidden in his palace—an inviolable sanctuary. Ceremonials in which he figured were regulated to the minutest detail. His real name might never be pronounced. Responsible only to Heaven, he is on earth the living symbol of his people's unity.

Confucianist principles so inculcate filial piety that even the Emperor must listen respectfully to his mother's advice. Tu-Duc, powerful as he was, never dared tell his mother of the loss of Cochin-China. But

25

there existed only one effective counterpoise to his absolute and sacrosanct authority—the possibility of losing Heaven's mandate. In his
paternalistic role, as head of the hundred families which make up
Annam, the Emperor is responsible for the welfare of his subjects. Only
if he succeeds in making his people happy does he justify the supreme
authority conferred upon him by Heaven. By further delegation of this
power and to the same end, the mandarins and heads of families participate, in varying degrees, of this same authority. As part of the
principle of balancing privilege by duty, which permeates the whole
system, the Emperor must serve as an example of virtue to his subjects:
he is the first scholar of his kingdom, the Complete Observer of Confucius's precepts. Thus in cases of public misfortune, the Emperor
casts up his spiritual accounts, humbly confesses his unworthiness at
Heaven's altar, and asks for a renewal of the celestial mandate. If the
sovereign is persistently evil or unjust, he is regarded as having forfeited his right to rule. Then, and only then, have the people a right
to revolt, and they are even authorized to do so by divine law. This
limitation of the imperial power is, however, purely theoretical, for
in practice the Emperor can dispose of his kingdom and people virtually
as he pleases. The mandarins, the imperial aides, are raised from the
masses to which they can be returned if they prove unworthy of their
trust. Like the small unprivileged and transient aristocracy of Annam,
they remain prostrate at the foot of the throne and in no way endanger
the absolute central power. By an organization that gives a religious
basis to all existing institutions, the Annamites have been forcibly
moulded into a united and stereotyped people. Up to very modern
times any other form of government would have seemed to them
anarchical, so firmly did they believe in the Confucianist adage that it
is beneath human dignity for men to be without a leader.

The mandarinate was recruited from the masses but, when constituted as a group, formed a distinct body of officials. The poorest boy
was eligible for such a career provided that he could master the knowledge required for the mandarinal examinations. Although education in
Annam was neither free nor compulsory, the civil service system itself
was the epitome of democracy. The tutor hired by a rich family would
always accept additional pupils for a nominal fee, and a promising
student always found a financial sponsor. To be sure, this saddled the
successful mandarin with such debts that he had to profit by any opportunity in his later career to defray his early expenses. The subjects on
which he was examined were purely literary, philosophical, and moral,

with no direct bearing on the office in view. It took a lifetime's efforts of memory to retain the Chinese classics and their commentaries. This system was borrowed from the Chinese and introduced in all its elaborate detail into Annam in the twelfth century. It consisted of three progressive degrees culminating, by a process of ferocious elimination, in the triennial examinations held at Hué over which the Emperor himself presided. Out of twelve hundred candidates only two hundred and fifty could become Bachelors of Arts, and from twelve to fifteen Masters of Arts. The many who failed to qualify swelled the ranks of the malcontents who were always ready to revolt against the existing order. This system had many admirable features: it was democratic in selection and rationally tolerant in subject matter. But Confucianist education ignored the world and bred in its students a verbose formalism and complacent pedantry akin to that of the mediaeval scholastics. Absolutism in the government was paralleled and upheld by an intellectual despotism exercised from birth, by and through the educational system, upon administrators and people alike in support of the existing order. The lack of a vital national culture resulted in a complete spiritual stagnation, which was the heavy price paid by Annam for China's moral domination.

Military mandarins were not chosen in the same way since their eligibility depended upon physical prowess and a vague knowledge of Chinese military tactics. But a literary examination was also required for the highest ranking officers. The Confucianist ideal was perpetuated in Annam that the military were inherently inferior to the civil authorities, so that the latter took precedence over their military colleagues of even the same rank. Both civil and military mandarins were divided into nine classes of two degrees each. The basic characteristic of the whole mandarinate is the exercise of all powers without specialization because, by delegation, they partake in varying degrees of the Emperor's universal authority. This sacred origin makes the mandarin's person inviolable: his miniature seal of state is the symbol of his authority. These privileges, as ever, breed certain obligations: the mandarin may never leave his official residence or district, nor may he acquire property or marry therein. Decapitation, exile, or demotion were the different penalties he might pay for the abuse of his large powers. On the rare occasions on which the mandarin was visible to his people, he was accompanied by an awesome retinue, preceded by a guard of elephants, and sheltered in a palanquin by parasols, his badge of office. He could not be approached without ceremonial prostrations, or *lays*, and gifts appropriate to his station. To retail the mandarin's powers is not to know the respect he inspired, based on a religious authority profoundly different from Western functionaries. Oriental respect is recommended by morality, fortified by tradition, and maintained by the practice of rites. The mandarin is no administrative cipher who may be replaced by a secretary or an interpreter, but an awe-inspiring representative of the Emperor, the indispensable intermediary between the central government and the people. The mandarinate represented the highest aspiration of an ambitious Annamite youth.

The Annamite aristocracy is a small ever-changing group of infinitely less importance than the mandarinate. Titles are conferred by the Emperor upon members of the royal family, meritorious mandarins, and singularly deserving citizens. They do not involve office-holding nor any but honorary privileges. Five titles existed which might be inherited, but with each generation the degree of nobility diminished in such a way that by the sixth generation the family was once more reabsorbed into the people. Gia-long created four Chancellors who were called the Pillars of the Empire. They, with a host of minor officials, were in charge of the royal household, executed the Emperor's will both during his lifetime and after his death. Two councils of state existed: the Comat was a secret group which dealt with all important questions of government; the Ministerial Council discussed agrarian law, justice, rites, and the framing of imperial edicts. There were six Ministers in charge of the departments of Justice, Interior, Rites, Finance, War, and Public Works. A corps of inspectors comprised a permanent official control over the whole administrative machinery.

State revenues were handled by the Minister and department of Finance, as if they belonged to a single proprietor, and one who was neither very meticulous nor scrupulous. The Annamites servilely copied the excessively centralized Chinese system, where the theoretically uniform treatment of different localities was supplemented by no more equitable a basis for taxation than the government's good pleasure. Taxes were both upon persons and on the produce of the soil. The land belonged to the Emperor who, excepting for quarries and mines, gave it to his people to cultivate. The non-cultivation of this land or failure to pay taxes for more than three consecutive years automatically broke this tacit agreement. Lands were classified according to crops—the place of honour going naturally to rice-fields. This tax varied from year to year, according to the harvest which was recorded by the provincial authorities in the commune's land register, the *dienbo*. All the male citizenry, between the ages of eighteen and sixty, were divided into those who did or did not pay taxes. The latter group formed the communal proletariat who must do military service for the state, and *corvée* duty for the village, as substitutes for a financial contribution. Only the taxpayers were listed in the local register: they formed the leisure class, from and by which communal officials are chosen. Theoretically a census was taken every five years, a task which involved not only great expense but an enormous amount of initial labour and verification. Moreover, the results were highly inaccurate. It was the village which kept the register, and it was obviously to its advantage to pay as small a tax as possible. It has been estimated that these communal registers dissimulated about two-thirds of their cultivated lands, so neither the population statistics nor land survey can be accurately derived from these records. Annam was never rich : its agents were venal and its communes dishonest. Probably only about a fifth of its legitimate revenues ever entered the imperial treasury.

Legally the communes were responsible for the collection of taxes. Although fiscal leniency was shown to newly colonized territory, the principle of communal tax responsibility was steadily maintained. Village Notables must make up for any deficiency caused by bad harvests or individual delinquency. Taxes were paid sometimes in specie but usually in kind. Other revenues were obtained by small and variable taxes like those on navigation. A prohibitive export tax on rice was the Emperor's paternalistic way of preventing rice speculation in famine years. There were also the Farms of Opium and Gaming, but this source of income was decried by the moral Annamite legislator. A small tax was derived from men enrolled in the trade corporations, but this varied widely from province to province, depending on the local prosperity of each guild. Minh-Mang abolished these corporations. The period of expansion had come to an end in his twenty-one year reign, and he needed the military and *corvée* service from which these guild members were exempted. Chinese merchants paid a special and heavier tax. In theory these taxes were everywhere uniform, but in reality they differed from one province to another. So much inequality existed that the treasury never knew from one year to another upon what it could count. Irregular and arbitrary as they were, these taxes were light. The principle of equality in taxation was unknown: the fundamental conception of taxation was that of a rental of land rather than of contributions to public services.

Public works, in the Western sense, were little known in old Annam.

Such as they were, agriculture was almost the sole benefactor. There was only one real road in the whole country, the Mandarin Route, which was barely distinguishable from the adjacent uncultivated fields. Elsewhere there were only narrow paths, dangerous bamboo bridges supplemented by river craft. The *mémoires* of great mandarins recall how uncomfortable, costly, and dangerous such travel used to be even for persons of consequence. In general, however, the mandarins opposed improving the means of communication, since it would mean a tightened control over them by the central government. A postal service, the *tram*, existed, but exclusively for official use. Such relays were placed along the major river routes and paths at intervals of nine kilometres. The code decreed penalties for damage and delay of official communications. Unofficial news travelled with even greater speed. Those who have lived in Annam are impressed by the incomprehensible swiftness of rumour.

Government service left its deepest imprint in the domain of agriculture through dyke-building and canal dredging. In this the Annamites were the Dutch of the Far East. They showed the same extraordinary courage and perseverance in contending with a nature which was, however, far more violent than in Holland. The Tonkinese character shows the marks of this struggle: their industry contrasts with the more easy-going southern Annamites. Annam's imperial annals reveal a constant preoccupation with the problem of dykes. Mandarins who built dykes were rewarded, those who neglected them were punished, and the death penalty merited by those who wantonly destroyed them. The actual work of building was done by local *corvées* under government supervision. The methods used were so primitive that the results obtained are all the more admirable.

Next to dykes and canals, public buildings were a very secondary effort. Labour was furnished by the village *corvée* system, so that the state had only to confiscate a desirable site and supply the materials and direction. Only the most urgent repairs could be undertaken without preliminary authorization, and all construction had to conform to a standard model. The Imperial tombs at Hué are examples of the Annamites' building prowess. They reveal a colossal effort and a sure artistic taste.

THE LOCAL ADMINISTRATION

The empire was divided into thirty-one provinces, each under its governor. The selection of provincial names was the object of imperial solicitude: Hanoi indicates a province surrounded by rivers; Haiphong, the sun sinking into the sea; Thai Binh, profound calm. Small provinces have the same type of administration as the big, only the rank of the head mandarin differs. A provincial governor, or *tong doc*, has the rank of a Minister. Under him are three very important officials: the *quanbo*, or head of the administration; the *quan-an*, or judicial mandarin; and the *lanh-binh*, or military commandant.

The canton is important only as a buffer state between the people, whom it represents, and the provincial administration. It is the highest form of self-elected government whose officials are not mandarins imposed by the state. The canton has a head but no headquarters, for aside from the provincial capital there are really no important towns, only market places. Nor does the head of a canton necessarily live in the largest of his villages. The canton has nothing like the importance of the commune: its suppression would not disturb society, and its very existence seems in many ways artificial. But as a practical link between the independent commune and the autocratic central government, it serves to oil the wheels of the administration. When the French deprived the head of the canton of his elective character, they did not realize that by reducing him to the status of a state functionary they were destroying his essential usefulness. For all these officials, promotion came very slowly and always in the province to which they were originally assigned. Like all Annamite officialdom they were venal and arbitrary, but Confucianist ideals of high thinking and enforcedly plain living, as well as long contact with the people they administered, gave them a benevolent and paternalistic character. Reproduction of the identical organization throughout the whole administration, in greater or lesser degree, gave to the empire an unusual uniformity.

Proceeding from the base of the Annamite social pyramid, the commune reproduces the family organization. The cult of the village genii parallels that of the family's ancestor worship: the authority of the communal Notables is analogous to that of the head of the family. The Annamite commune is not only a fiscal and an administrative unit, but a self-conscious city-state with its own history, its social and economic life, its own gods, politicians, and priests. Excessively jealous of its independence, the village has always tried to escape official notice. Markets are never held within its walls. The visiting mandarin finds himself in deserted streets and is never taken beyond the communal house where he does business. The basic fear, of course, is that official knowledge will mean an increase in taxation. The commune is the embodiment of the Sino-Annamite dream of houses, fields, and ancestral tombs. Because it was such an excellent instrument for expansion, the state was willing to stay its centralizing hand and to leave it largely alone.

The internal development of communal organization has had a most interesting history. The commune is a miniature state which is governed oligarchically by self-elected Notables. "If the king makes the law, the commune makes custom," says an Annamite proverb. In Indo-China, as in so many parts of the East, the clan preceded the family, and to this day many Annamites still live under the clan régime. This is shown in the legislation which imposes responsibility for crimes and taxes upon the group rather than upon the individual. The clan probably gave way to a gradually forming communal life, when the Annamites ceased their nomadic existence and became established as farmers or fishermen. At first the Chinese merely perfected the rudimentary Annamite political organization, but gradually they fashioned the embryo commune after their own image. This evolution was cut short by the loss of China's political control, so the Annamite commune was not modified by the changes subsequently wrought in Chinese village organization by the Manchus and Mongols. To this day the names of certain Annamite communal officials can be traced to obsolete Chinese institutions.

Chinese legislation has had an enormous influence upon the growth of the commune. Pre-eminently concerned with the cultivation of virgin soil and the expansion of frontiers, the Chinese-inspired code taught the Annamites new agricultural methods and moulded the commune to this purpose. The result was an ideal combination of local initiative and governmental support. Possibly it was the old nomadic impulse rather than official encouragement that gave to this expansion its driving force. When the head of the commune-clan felt that the soil was becoming exhausted for his ever-increasing population, he chose the most ambitious and able man of the younger generation to direct the task of colonizing a new territory. The young leader called to his aid any who showed conspicuous courage and initiative. Among those who took part in the exodus were naturally the resourceless and the malcontents, of whom the old commune felt itself well rid. The new villages, founded usually along the river banks, were like so many frontier citadels. They were the advance guard of an expanding civilization in which the ownership of property was thought to be the best guarantee against lawlessness—no matter what the origin or character of the new colonizers. The possibility of colonization by enterprising individuals, in the Western manner, was unknown to Orientals, who can conceive of no action outside the group.

Local initiative had for psychological and practical reasons to be supplemented by official support. The mother commune, through its rich and influential members, created a kind of patron-client relationship with the new-found community—a policy dictated by immediate necessity but the source of future discord. The central government, too, was glad to empty the state prisons and to force out erstwhile malefactors to colonize new lands—a purging of the body politic akin to disposing of the commune's undesirables. For two thousand years the Annamites had all the land they wanted at their easy disposal, so naturally they took the best ground first, swarming loosely over its surface and leaving great gaps of wasteland in their successive waves of expansion. Here the state stepped in and tried to regulate, by military and penal colonization, the filling in of these voids, especially around the frontier region. The incorporation of these new communes into the great Annamite family came with the official recognition of their utility. As a special mark of his benevolence the Emperor himself would select the name and site of the infant commune. In this way the whole movement was harmonious: it was a spontaneous expansion from within the old commune, and it was officially regulated from without by a government eager to push back its frontiers and also to dispose of anti-social elements which threatened its internal tranquillity.

The quiet industry with which this colossal colonizing effort was accomplished detracted from the dramatic quality of this struggle to reclaim land from a violent nature, and from enemies both internal and external. So vital to the state was the function performed by the expanding commune that the central government did not interfere in its political or economic life, providing taxes were paid, military recruits selected, and the socio-religious order maintained. Within this orbit the commune could govern itself. Despite a certain diversity caused by varying local conditions, the internal organization of Annamite communes shows an underlying uniformity. The commune named its own administrators, it could borrow or sell at will—all but its inalienable lands—carry out public works, police its own territory, and care for its own poor and infirm. On certain salient points, the commune showed its independence of the central government. The state did not know what its population was nor the amount of land under cultivation, nor what assessment each citizen paid as his share of the taxes. The com-

33

mune selected as its soldiers the most undesirable of its citizens and with them the state had perforce to be content, imposing upon the commune only responsibility for their good behaviour. In all such ways the commune slipped through the imperial hands and treated with the central power as one state to another. If such a system was a salutary check upon *étatisme* and the autocracy of an Oriental government, there was no redress for the masses within the commune itself. The Notables made the laws and executed them, and there was no check upon their power. In theory it was age and ability, but in practice solely property, which qualified them for this office, so naturally they governed in the interests of their own class. These Notables, whose number varied with the importance of their commune, were subdivided into the leaders who directed general policy, and their subordinates who carried out their decisions. Their meetings, which took place in the pagoda or communal house, dealt with the cult of the village genii, the settlement of local disputes, the requisitioning of labour, the voting of the communal budget, and the recruiting of soldiers. Neither the number of taxpayers nor the amounts they paid could vary because of harvest conditions. It is an Annamite axiom that a taxpayer never dies. The *dienbo* was drawn up as a guarantee of property titles, as an aid to assessing the taxes, and as a method of permitting the sovereign to control the amount of land under cultivation in his empire.

Just as the young commune can never break away from the mother commune and the central government, so the individual can never loosen himself from the hold of his family and native village. Not only is he called back by the imperious ritualistic demands of the ancestral cult, but he is also drawn by the security which the commune offers to its own. Communal lands nourish even the village paupers. This feeling of an ever-present refuge and shelter is, as a by-product, a main cause of Annamite irresponsibility and lack of altruism. The state encourages these ties. Criminals are returned to their commune after they have served their sentence, or their bodies are sent back there for burial if they have been executed. Exile is a more severe penalty than death. The code, too, made every effort to reincorporate the vagabond into his own community. If severe disaster forced villagers to take flight the government temporarily remitted taxes, sent food to the dispossessed, and helped to repair the damages. Special laws were made to insure village tranquillity during the harvest season. Changing communes was impious enough but changing countries, even temporarily, was treason, because it meant shirking the fiscal and social obligations into which one was born. It might also mean a return to the nomadic existence—the ultimate betrayal of the Chinese agricultural ideal. Law and religion combined to reinforce the links between family and commune, and of both together with the state. Immutability, isolation, and stagnation were, however, the price paid by Annam for social harmony and political tranquillity.

Annamite law, in appearance only, is a masterpiece of incoherence, for underneath it has a fundamental unity. Unlike Roman law, it is not grouped around certain abstract ideals, but is inspired by daily living, with the result that it is over-detailed and lacking in clarity and order. One may recognize in it the various stages through which Annamite society has passed, for the code represents a continuous judicial effort covering more than four thousand years. Under the Chinese impetus, this code has passed through several degrees of civilization at a single bound, acquiring perhaps too easily the results of an experience which had cost other peoples centuries of struggle.

The sources of Annamite law are legion. *The Five Kings*, China's classical or canonical books, contain moral precepts which are a kind of non-codified law. There are also the statutes of the empire, the rulings of the six Ministries, the code of penalties and prohibitions, and the collection of rites. Custom is another great source of law, especially in a country where tradition has always been respected. The Annamite legislator, desirous of dealing with every possible case rather than to lay down general principles, naturally overlooked or could not foresee certain situations where custom-law must necessarily fill in. Knowing the Annamite flair for contending every issue, the code has tried to place all possible disputes under family or communal arbitration, leaving the intervention of formal law only for those cases in which the social order is at stake. Because custom is inspired by the identical Confucianist precepts which are embodied in the code, there is no conflict of ideas in the settlement of civil or penal suits.

Legislation is the exclusive prerogative of the sovereign, who exercises it in an absolute albeit paternalistic fashion. No latitude is left to the magistrate, who has nothing to do but apply the specific penalty allotted to each crime, and who is himself punished for showing any initiative in interpreting the law. No one dreamed of modifications or commentaries. The emperors were too sure of their authority to conceive of criticism, let alone correction. When they recommended to their subjects the study of law, it was solely to learn its dictates—an attitude that made it impossible for Annamite jurisprudence to be born. Since the sovereign's authority was derived from Heaven, it could not be discussed dispassionately as if it were based on ordinary equity. As mandatory of celestial justice, the sovereign owes justice to all and must himself be the embodiment of this ideal. Thus, at the apex of the pyramid, as throughout all of Annamite society, privilege entails a corresponding discipline and responsibility. The Emperor's first duty is to make the code known to all: neither the judge nor the judged should be justified in pleading ignorance of the law. Methods for giving publicity to new laws were prescribed. Functionaries must be questioned annually to see that they are kept up to the mark. As the father of his people, it is the Emperor's duty to bring straying members back into the fold: as head of the state, he must prevent infractions of his supreme and beneficent powers. The right to punish is not only the sovereign's privilege, but his duty as well. In the worst cases, extenuating circumstances may not be considered lest leniency encourage another assault upon society, whose welfare must eclipse every other human sentiment.

The Annamite code idealizes the rural village life in which virtue is tantamount to good citizenship, and vice to any disturbance of the social order. This point of view explains the almost exclusively penal character of Annamite law. The Sino-Annamite code is unique in being made up of penal sanctions of the existing socio-political system, and consequently there is no room for growth and change. What does not concern the social order is left to the arbitration of the commune and family, who use custom, tradition, and conscience to the same end—their own protection from internal discord and disintegration. The result is equivalent to a religious sanction of the *status quo*. The law punishes immediately and efficiently, leaving nothing to negligence or divine vengeance. There must be no vagueness in defining the duties and responsibilities of every group in the hierarchy. To call this code only a *tarif de coups de bâton* is a superficial judgment of its worth. It embodies, rather, a complete conception of life. By specifying penalties for shirking the carefully defined duties of all classes of people, the code hoped to maintain them in the active respect and practice of virtue.

The preface to Gia-long's code states that the laws contained therein are for the instruction of his people, so that eventually all penalties may be replaced by education. This conception of punishment as an instructive medium is finer than the Occidental idea of penal law as, ultimately, an act of society's vengeance upon its enemies. It must be admitted that the Annamite ideal has in many cases miscarried, for some of their severest penalties betray an element of revenge.

Social utility is the yardstick by which penalties must be appraised: their severity is apportioned to the harm done to the nation. Guilt is gauged partly according to circumstances but more to the rank, age, and sex of both the victim and aggressor, as well as the amount of damage done. Whereas Western law is divided into afflictive, infamous, and correctional penalties, the Annamites classify them as atrocious crimes, which cannot be pardoned, or as serious misdemeanours, whose punishments can be commuted to a money payment, and lesser delinquencies. There is far less concern in the mind of the Annamite legislator as to whether or not the delinquent was responsible for his actions. One may be punished for crimes committed by others, and also even if one is admittedly insane. It is true that varying degrees of guilt among the accomplices of a crime are more finely gauged than in Western codes, but the Annamite magistrate is not allowed to use his judgment, as in the West, in applying a sliding scale of maximum and minimum penalties. Only the Emperor has the privilege of mercy, for the legislator has more confidence in the impartiality of his code than in that of the judges. In its concern to uproot anti-social designs, the code punishes the criminal's family, confiscates his possessions, and occasionally even disciplines his commune. Those who have prescience of a crime, which they do not report, are also penalized. Crime is treated like an epidemic which must at all cost be stamped out. This is why espionage and mutual denunciations were encouraged, and they still disfigure Annamite society.

The corporal punishments in the Annamite code revolt the Westerner. Though it is true that many of the worst of them had disappeared, long before the French conquest, the principle of corporal punishment was still admitted. One must also remember that because of his totally different conception of death, the Oriental prefers strangulation to decapitation. In this he considers not the physical pain involved, but the preservation of his body in order to facilitate the soul's passage into the spirit world. Exile, a penalty introduced by the French, is far worse to them than any form of death. Moreover, the slow deaths enumerated in the Annamite code, as punishment for treason and patricide, show certainly no more barbaric state of mind than that of the seventeenth-century French gentlemen who were pleased to witness the agonies of Ravaillac. Assorted penalties for crimes of a lesser nature were hard labour, the pillory, caning, and fines—each with varying degrees of severity. Time, the treasury's needs, and judicial venality, all combined to develop more and more the money commutation of almost all penalties. The very fact that a case could not be settled by arbitration automatically placed it in the penal category, for one of the parties was considered guilty of disturbing the public peace by wrongfully bringing suit. Penalties have no defamatory character as they have in the West. Once the criminal has served his sentence he is received back wholeheartedly into society's bosom. Punishment, thus, has far more the character of an expiation which generously wipes out the fault and leaves the offender as he was before.

If penalties are the extraordinary means used by the sovereign to teach his people virtue, rites are the normal method. To insure social harmony, the Annamite code prescribes rules for every sentiment upon all occasions. These innumerable ritual regulations show the inseparability of ceremonial from religion in the Annamite mind. Unlike the more negative Occidental conception of punishment only for infractions of the moral code, the Annamite legislator used rites as a positive means of making ethical practices obligatory. Basically it was believed that rites would foster appropriate moral sentiments and a feeling of unity in the people. Rites gave force to Confucius' teachings, and his precepts, in turn, enforced ritual. They also gave, to an ethical system, an outward expression to what would be in the West solely a matter of conscience. Such was the positive psychology of the Annamite legislator that he punished far less the intention behind the action than its social consequences. Thus, too, sumptuary laws enforced external submission to the social hierarchy rather than real humility. By making everyone's place immutable and known to all, it was hoped to remove all impulse to foment discord. Clothes, utensils, and houses for each class of persons are fixed by law. Failure to mark one's respect for superiors is punished as irreverence and presumption. The irony and caustic wit, which have always characterized Annamites, is obviously a reaction and an outlet for centuries of enforced, daily acknowledgment of one's place in a rigid hierarchy, both in this world and in the next. So all-absorbing was this preoccupation that the law dared to interfere in communal and family life to regulate the ancestral cult or that of the village genii, in regard to rules about mourning, the upkeep of tombs, and the inalienability of the *hung-hoa*.[1]

Etiquette forms an important part of the legislation concerning rites,

---

[1] Cf. below, p. 39.

especially in relation to the Emperor. Mentioning his real name, appearing in his presence with any but the prescribed costume and ceremonial, speaking out of hierarchic order, are but a few of the many errors into which one could fall. There were penalties for entering the imperial palace, for failure to follow the proper forms regarding the cortège, lodging, and care of the imperial suite when the Emperor travelled. Sins of omission were punished with as much severity as those of commission. Honours and precedence are regulated with a minutia startling to the more spontaneous Western mind. The fact that laws on rites dominate all of Annamite legislation shows how important a place they held as a symbol and cohesive force in Annamite society.

Inspired as always by Confucius, the Annamite civil code has allowed public utility to dominate all other relationships. Individuals are important only in so far as they constitute one of the three main social groups—family, commune, and state. The family is the basic social unit and the law never interferes in its internal affairs. The *état civil* of its members has never been publicly recorded. Birth, marriage, and death are strictly family matters which are legally regulated only when they take on a wide social significance. Grounds for divorce, the time and categories of persons one is forbidden to marry, the periods of mourning, the imperative adoption of male heirs—all are fixed by strict rules. Children and grandchildren cannot without special permission set up a separate establishment so long as their parents live, nor can they possess property of their own. In the same way the state considers the commune as an extension of the family, and will tolerate no change in its domicile lest it be only a means of escaping communal burdens. In the division of property, all the children have equal rights, no matter what their sex or the legal status of their mother. Only the oldest son is given a larger share since he becomes the head of the family and, therefore, administrator of their joint property or *hung-hoa*. There is great variety in the rank of wives, and the husband is severely penalized who undermines his first wife's status by elevating a concubine. The first wife's place in the home is an honoured one: she can choose the successors to her husband's favour—who unlike herself have a negligible legal and social status—and bring up their children as her own. If the first wife does not remarry after her husband's death, she becomes a life beneficiary of the family property.

The code upholds the authority of the head of the family, originally the absolute master whose despotic hand time and custom have tempered. Nowadays the father's rights over his family are those of correction but, like the Emperor himself, he has duties corresponding to his authority. He administers the family property, nominally in the interests of all, but his children have no protection against his poor judgment or wastefulness. They may not bring suit against their parent nor even remonstrate with him, even on the score of gaming, the chief dissipator of Annamite family property. All that a wife can do is respectfully to call the mandarin's attention to the illegally established gaming houses which her husband has the weakness to frequent. In the final analysis, however, the really important personages in the family are the ancestor who has just died, and the grandson who will carry on the cult. The father is but the living link between the two: the mother, only a means of perpetuating the family. Filial piety is the rock upon which the Annamite social edifice is reared. Sons owe obedience, respect, and submission until they themselves become heads of their families: a woman is always under male authority, first as a daughter, then as a wife or concubine. Only as a mother has she any real authority. Their exclusion from the ancestral cult is the basis of this unfavoured position, though in practice their status is higher than that designated by law, and distinctly above the position of Chinese women. Certainly women are the hardest workers in an Annamite family and the only members who have any commercial ability. The average Annamite's attitude towards women is uncomplicated by love—which is a theme of literature that seems to be confined to written expression. A wife is a "younger sister" to her husband or "elder brother," the classical expressions of Annamite conjugal affection. Emotions are confined principally to parents and children who are spoiled when they are young, treated severely as adolescents, and regarded with indifference when they become adults. A wife is her husband's inferior and she merits his affection only when she cares suitably for their home, and has presented him with the male offspring indispensable to insuring his comfort in the spirit world. Love is frowned upon like any other folly that brings disorder into one's life. Rice-fields are almost the unique occupation of the Annamite family. A proverb expresses this domestic ideal:

If you wish to live happily, stay well within your house in the bosom of your family, and avoid like the plague any indiscreet visit or the profaning glance of the curious.

In property regulations the legislator is solicitous of both parental and imperial authority. As usual, the Emperor's authority is balanced by an obligation to assure his people protection. State granaries in time of disaster, the remission of taxes for just cause, the building of dykes and dredging of waterways, the prevention of theft, are all measures designed to strengthen family and communal property. Yet the state has constantly to fight against the commune's encroachments, and in this subtle duel it is the commune that usually wins. The state for all its judicial rights loses out in the actual control of property.

The unit of ownership is as ever the family, not the individual. Perhaps because group interests invariably dominate, the character of Annamite property has not the absolute and egotistical character given it in France by the Napoleonic Code. Property, like imperial authority and indeed the individual's life on this earth, has kept its character of stewardship. It is a temporary delegation upon good behaviour, and the Emperor is the intermediary by Heavenly dispensation. The payment of taxes and the cultivation of the land, as requisites for ownership, have created in Annam a tradition of industriousness which contrasts with the lethargy of most Oriental peoples. If the conditions of occupancy are not fulfilled, the state simply takes back its own and cedes it once again to a more worthy tenant. The state may, on the grounds of public utility, confiscate property without indemnity. The fear that large properties might constitute a danger to the state has made Annam, like France, a country of small proprietors. In Annam's political economy the word capital is synonymous with work and savings: ownership of land does not constitute capital, since in the final analysis all belongs to the Emperor. Although Annam is the incarnation of Proudhon's dream of a country where capital belongs to the worker—for property was land with the exception of a few slaves—the needs of the people have not been completely satisfied. Usury for centuries has had a noxious grip upon the country. No banks existed, no large-scale industries or commercial operations. A fourteenth-century attempt to introduce paper money into the country failed. The patriarchal simplicity of Annam's economy might be theoretically enviable were it not for the widespread usury and misery, extreme to the point of starvation.

In an abstract appraisal of Annamite legislation one must remember that social utility is the point of departure and not the guarantee of individual rights. What most offends the Westerner—the confusion not the separation of powers; the principle of collective responsibility; the bolstering of arbitrary authority within the family, commune, and state; an inequality before the law that is translated into the most complete hierarchy; the binding of the individual to his predestined place spiritually in the ancestral cult, and physically to the family and commune—all these means are used by an enlightened despotism to insure immutable social harmony. It is an immense gamble upon the value of Confucius' precepts which show a touching belief in pure virtue as a panacea for human ills. So long as outside influences could be controlled—and witness the code's efforts to keep out foreigners and to prevent Annamites from having any communication with neighbouring countries—this unyielding mould could be maintained. In return, it offered the individual a protection, security, and the minimum of emotional problems, by regulating every possible contact within the home, and between inferiors and superiors. An assurance of comfort in the next world was also thrown in. The balancing of duties by privileges enforced a universal *noblesse oblige*, and bred in the Annamites a faith in earthly justice. In this confusion of law and morality, in this paternal despotism of Heaven's mandatory, the dynamic force latent in a living society was ignored. If the whole system were to prove unsuitable with time, there was no room for change. But it never occurred to the Annamites to question the absolute wisdom of these principles. Too much domination and foresight on the part of the state has bred in the people a dangerous irresponsibility and trickiness. Adults are kept in a state of perpetual tutelage under a patriarchal absolutism which makes them automata or dishonest schemers. In the end the people lose all desire for change: if they rebel against a bad sovereign they merely raise up a replica in his place. Moreover, carefully conceived and harmonious as is the whole body politic of Annam, the system presupposes too much idealism on the part of those in authority. The venality of judges, and the commutation into fines of almost every penalty, has with time made a travesty of justice. In theory the simple and expeditious pyramid of legal procedure should enable the monarch to hear every subject's appeal, but in practice he came to hear only those cases which his Ministers cared to lay before him. It is true that the law made every effort to circumvent the miscarriage of justice, but Confucianist virtue offered too barren and austere a consolation for human nature to resist even relatively unattractive temptations.

ANNAMITE PSYCHOLOGY

Europeans who have lived long in Annam claim that the difficulties experienced in understanding Annamites are caused by approaching an Oriental problem from a wholly Occidental viewpoint. The Annamite seems enigmatic because he is perfectly natural—a phenomenon so unusual that it appears complicated. There is no such thing as privacy in the Far East. The Annamites live in the fields all day, and at night their houses cannot be closed against intrusion or even the gaze of the passer-by. Moreover, years of Confucianist training and pruning have resolved the Annamite into a type character. If one succeeds in understanding a single *nhaqué*, or peasant, one understands them all.

Geographic and historical factors have been, as always, the two major influences on native character. The climate exhausts the nerves and stimulates the circulation of blood in such a way that the Annamites age more quickly than men who dwell in temperate zones.[1] Few Annamites live to be more than sixty years old: they are adults at the age of thirteen, fathers at sixteen, and old men at fifty. The Tonkinese, thanks to their invigorating climate, show more energy and initiative than the other Annamites. The Annamite nervous system is certainly less sensitive than that of Occidentals. There is a significant lack of comfort in even the homes of the wealthy. Clothes reveal the same disdain. Their colour is drab at the outset, and their general negligence is increased by layers of dirt and betel-chewing. Native methods of eating show a similar indelicacy. There is absolutely no thought of the body's beauty, and they have a great shame of the nude. Exercise is scorned as a sign of poverty: it is inconceivable to them that anyone who might ride would walk for pleasure. This apathy, insensitivity, and placidity are certainly forced on them by the climate and under-nourishment. Their extraordinary resistance to suffering, their endurance bred by hard work in the rice-fields, their cruelty and their fatalism—all are attuned to a belief that self-control is the highest expression of human dignity. They lack the driving power given by strong desires and needs. Generous impulses have been reduced by the climate, by social discipline, and by a paternalistic state to an exclusively family and local egoism. The famous tolerance of the Orient is largely dislike of effort. Love is nothing beyond sensuality and the begetting of children. There is no compassion for those outside the groups to which one belongs, and even within them those who have contagious diseases are mercilessly driven out. They accept the principle of authority and group responsibility so completely that they never even question, or try to mitigate, the most cruel of legal penalties. The indifference of the Annamites to their compatriots' sufferings is unbelievable.

[1] Cf. Paul Giran, *Psychologie du Peuple Annamite* (Paris, 1904), p. 25.

43

A more subtle effect of the climate upon Annamite psychology is their inability to receive sharp, clear-cut impressions. Perhaps it is the brilliant sunshine that has weakned their sensory reactions along with their will power. The Annamite dreams in a perpetual melancholy reverie uncontrolled by any critical faculty. His thinking is confused and indecisive: he cannot distinguish between people and things. The animal, vegetable, and mineral kingdoms are thought to share the same feelings as humans. Proclamations are read to trees threatening to reduce them to kindling wood if they are not more productive. Annamites will reason politely with the tiger who is about to spring on them, telling him of their poverty and dependent families. Life flows indiscriminately into every object and being about man. Thus the individual is merged with the group and his physical environment: the property of one's neighbours has no clear-cut boundary from one's own. The living are barely distinguishable from the dead. Annamite folklore is rich in such magical metamorphoses of ladies into fox, and conversely of fish into men. Their cleverness in detecting human foibles is far above the Annamites' objective observation of nature. Similarly, in their work there is no division of labour, just as there is no specialization of function among the mandarins. In eating, the Annamite starts with a foundation bowl of rice, to which he adds what pleases him from the many ingredients that lie at hand. It is impossible to get precise information from an Annamite. Not that they are incurious—they will insistently put questions of the most personal nature—but their replies are notoriously inaccurate. If one asks the age of a man obviously tottering, they will solemnly reply that he is over forty. Rites and myths with their interminable detail reveal a chaotic state of mind which is incapable of separating the essential from the trivial. The most original of Annamite intellectual contributions are their terse and pithy maxims. These sayings show the ritual mind at its best. They constitute the wisdom of a race that has found and accepted formulae and ready-made solutions, possible only in an immutable society.

The Chinese domination, the development of their own paternalistic autocracy, and southward expansion were the other great influences in shaping Annamite character. The forced acceptance of cruel Chinese governors and, morally, of Confucianism's consecration of social inequality paved the way for their own despotic sovereigns. All effort became futile when rapacious mandarins took over one's savings, or requisitioned men who showed conspicuous talent. Nature was abundant especially in the South, and there was no need and certainly no stimulus to exert oneself beyond subsistence needs. Games of chance nicely took care of any surplus one might have accumulated.

Though the Annamites accepted the Chinese disdain for armed force, the old nomadic instincts, as well as a vital need for expansion, forced the Annamites into bitter fighting with their neighbours. Nevertheless, the *nhaqué* has a profound love of peace and security—as the essential conditions of a farming life. They named their villages Profound and Intense Peace, Crystal Purity, Canton of Love and Calm Contentment, Tranquil Constancy and Heart of Jade. Their unequal, life-long struggle with a violent nature, destructive diseases, and an autocratic theocracy, has created an apparent acceptance of superior force which covers a perpetual inward rebellion. The perennial role of underdog has developed in the Annamites endurance and a passive courage, but also some disagreeable characteristics. Ruse and intrigue are esteemed more highly than honesty and courage because they are more effective. Hypocrisy and irony are certainly the compensations of a weak vanity wounded by unending and forced admissions of inferiority. The intelligence is keen but the character weak when faced with superior force. Death is a release and a repose which is accepted with indifference, where there is no escape, and with contempt because it is the supreme manifestation of force. In battle a European fights better if he thinks he has a chance, but an Annamite will show less fortitude than when he knows that death is certain. Physically they shrink before violence: spiritually they neither admire nor accept it. Pride is the great sustaining force, but too often with the Annamites it degenerates into puerile vanity.

ANNAMITE CULTURE

In spite of centuries of Chinese domination, the Annamites managed to retain their own language. Unfortunately it is a poor intellectual heritage. Not only is it the most difficult spoken language in the Far East, because of the rules of intonation, but it is pronounced differently in the three Annamite countries, varying even from province to province. In construction it is simple enough, and adapted to the mentality of a primitive people. The vocabulary is limited and lacking in words to express the major emotions. Love, in Annamite, is the object one loves; hope, that which awaits; courage, the animal with a liver and stomach. The language materializes and analyses everything it touches. Words classify chronologically objects as they appear to the speaker.

45

A cow is not simply a cow, but successively designated as a bovine, female and a living being. Annamite formalism can also be neatly expressed: there are three or four different ways of saying "yes," depending upon the relative social status of the persons speaking. The words themselves must contain all shades of meaning, for Annamite training is strongly against letting emotion appear in either voice or gesture. The essential poverty of this language as a vehicle for expressing complex ideas has been shown in Cochin-China when it was transposed for official usage into *quoc-ngu*. Since Chinese has always been the language of cultured people and Annamite only the vernacular used by the masses, it is natural enough that the latter was never developed into a rich medium of expression.

The Annamites, as well as the Japanese, have taken over Chinese characters for their official written language. But the Annamites have also their own written language, *chu-nom*, culled from among the simplest of Chinese characters. This dual use of characters has led many Europeans to confuse Chinese and Annamite literature, or to think of the latter as only a dialect. Defective as it is in many ways, the Annamite language both written and spoken makes up in conciseness for what it lacks in suppleness and delicacy. Minute rules govern the composition of poetry. *Tho* is the name given to the lyric, ode, epigram, and song: *van* includes long compositions like history, philosophy, or the drama. It is not known when *chu-nom* originated, but by the thirteenth century it was in current use, especially for poetry which eventually absorbed this medium completely. Sino-Annamite characters were used for the scholarly work of which very few examples have survived. The climate and constant warfare have combined to destroy them. They were written by and for a very limited group, and never held in high honour. Printing never developed so vigorously in Annam as it did in China, Japan, or even Korea. To encourage local printers, one of the Le sovereigns in the eighteenth century tried unsuccessfully to prevent the printing of Chinese editions. A few Annamite works went through one edition but the majority have remained precariously in manuscript form, in spite of the fact that the Annamite emperors themselves were scholars and poets. It is a curious fact that the majority of those Annamite writings which have survived were found in China.

Popular literature in *chu-nom* took the form of songs, proverbs, and legends, and from the beginning was never abundant. It is unfortunate that Annamite scholars never felt that a collection of such works was worthy of their efforts. Chinese, like Latin in the Middle Ages, was the only proper medium of expression. Fear of being discredited by their *chu-nom* productions made these writers chary of revealing their identity or the circumstances of their composition. Some poets won celebrity for only a few verses written in characters, while the masterpiece *Kim-van-Kieu* was long ignored simply because it was composed in the vernacular and for the amusement of the author and his friends. This poem was barely mentioned by the Court Annalist when he sketched the biography of the high mandarin who was its dilettante author. Such inattention naturally resulted in a neglect of style, so that the value of these works lies much more in the originality and finesse of their writers' observations.

Luc-van-Tien is the most popular work in Annamite literature. Characteristically its author is unknown. The hero is a simple man of the people whose sole ambition is to better his estate through the study of philosophy. He must pass through a series of physical and moral ordeals but is never vanquished by evil passions. His virtue eventually wins him the royal crown and Heaven's mandate. Embodied in this poem are three fundamental Annamite beliefs—filial piety, fidelity to the emporor and his mandarins, and the devotion of pupil to teacher. The hero's disdain of wealth, the attribution of unhappiness to immoderate desires, contentment with one's lot—with virtue being rewarded and vice punished—have made this poem dear to every Annamite heart. *Kim-van-Kieu*, its rival in popular affection, is not an epic but a lengthy novel both naturalistic and licentious. For more than a century it has served in Annam as the touchstone of linguistic elegance. A strong Buddhistic strain underlies its thought: our present misfortunes are but the expiation of faults in a former existence. In all of Annamite literature there is a conspicuous absence of epic virility akin to that of the *Chanson de Roland* and the *Niebelungen Lied*.

Popular songs and legends allow free scope for the Annamite love of the ironic and the marvellous. Every event of any importance has its legend, which may be gross or tragic, but which has also a naïve charm. They are quite typical of the Annamite mind which basks in a chaos of supernatural events, and loves gratuitous complications. Genii abound, occasionally benevolent but usually ferocious, who interfere interminably in human affairs. These legends glorify craft, ruse, and lies—anything to circumvent brute force, be it exercised by the Chinese or tigers. They needs must bow to it, but they can and also do ridicule it. Stupidity is the only serious fault. One may add that the ladies play a stellar role in this type of tale. The Annamites have also another side.

When by themselves they are inclined to dreamy melancholy, and this sentimentality dominates even the caustic vein in certain popular songs.

Music is handed down by oral tradition. The method of notation is imperfect, and the air may be embroidered *ad infinitum*—just as the time and words are left to the singers' and orchestras' good pleasure. The few musical rules that exist, as well as the official Department of Music under the Minister of Rites, are copied from the Chinese. But the Annamite songs themselves are a spontaneous outburst, beloved of the people.[1] They claim that so great is their power that not only do songs soothe the savage breast, but they can make peace to reign even among functionaries. Annamite music is subordinated to the singers, usually women, who are required to have beauty and a colossal memory, as well as a voice trained through a long and painful apprenticeship. Misery alone will make parents dedicate their daughters to such a calling, for while music may be highly appreciated on its artistic merits, its purveyors are thought to be addicted to immorality, from whom the code advises all respectable men to flee. The gestures and discreet pirouettes that accompany these long, monotonous, and unintelligible songs are as minutely regulated as the singer's conduct and costuming. The best singers and orchestras serve as entertainers at rich men's banquets, but those of inferior ability wander from village to village earning a precarious living as street musicians.

It is through the theatre, even more than in song, that most of the historical legends percolate into popular consciousness. The drama is a diversion which even the poorest can afford. Every important town, as well as provincial capitals, has its regular theatre. Travelling troupes go through the villages playing at the communal house dramas which often last two or three days. Tradition insists that the impresario himself be a scholar, so as to have authority over the actors. Theatres are especially numerous in Cochin-China—ten for a public of one hundred thousand—and each has its own clientele. Actors are paid in proportion to their renown, but only about three out of a troupe of twenty are rated as stars. As is the case with musicians, it is hard to get players from good families, so much is the profession held in disrepute. Merely to frequent the company of actors endangers one's morality.

The Annamite theatre is exclusively traditional in presentation, and historical in dramatic material. Plot has none of the importance given

---

[1] The first written collection of many of these songs was made by Dumoutier in 1886.

to it in the West, and no effort is made to achieve a realistic presentation. Old names and places are used to depict current events. All this is but a part of the Annamite belief that civilization is immutable, so modern acting of obsolete scenes is not considered an anachronism. The Chinese Annals are the material upon which the Annamite drama draws. It is curious that peace-loving peoples like the Chinese and Annamites should revel in such blood-curdling drama. What they go to see in the theatre is a portrayal of historical events which they already know by heart, and which are most disdainful of their own country, aping as they do the Chinese viewpoint. Interpretation of these legends is fixed with such precision that the slightest infraction of tradition is penalized. There is no room for individual interpretation. The drama is a synthesis of Annamite life with eleven type-characters: the king, princes, dignitaries, civil and military mandarins, warriors, and finally men and women of honourable and of servile condition. Likewise the hierarchal spirit world is synthetically represented. The value of the performance is social: its symbolism makes of it an allegory in which the traditional costumes and stereotyped gestures at once permit the spectator, forearmed with knowledge and in spite of sketchy scenery and props, to assign to every performer his role. This effort to depict the universal and the abstract in human life, rather than the local and realistic, in the theatre makes the Annamite drama akin to the Greek. It is typical of Annamite theatre-going that only a few scenes are in the Annamite language, whereas the rest are in an archaic Chinese incomprehensible to audience and actors alike. The strained voice, which must be forced for days to carry over the tumult, and the crashing music, complete the setting in which the Annamite heart rejoices as in nothing else, despite its lack of repose or of melancholy relief.

ANNAMITE ART

Ritual dominates Annamite art as it does every other form of national expression. The perennial need felt by the Annamites for protection against hostile forces is translated into their art as a religious obsession. Since both Chinese rites and rules prevail, the artisan naturally becomes the slave of a rigorous taskmaster who keeps him copying his predecessors and away from the direct observation of nature. So faithful is he, that in some Annamite pictures one sees the vegetation of China totally unknown in Indo-China. The necessity for seeing everything in the light of the past gives a curiously archaic character to Annamite art. Warriors are still represented with ancient lances, and philosophers wear throughout the ages the same consciously inscrutable expression.

Although the code prescribes the size, style, and colour of houses and even of clothes, the *motifs* used by Annamite artists have undergone an interesting metamorphosis—their only concession to the diverse and the unforeseen in life. But many generations ago they became crystallized into hierarchic form, few in number and symbolic in meaning. The *sapèque* and piastre came to represent wealth; the tiger, force—though fear always prevented the artist from getting near enough to make an accurate drawing. No picture is complete without its wish for happiness. Flora and fauna, even colours, came to assume a rigid formalism and to attach themselves to specific members of the Annamite hierarchy, once again affirming the essential unity of Annamite society.

Cleverness and ingenuity, as well as a slavish imitation of the Chinese, were shown by these Annamite artists. Their predilection for monotonous repetitions is a national characteristic. When one has seen a single pagoda one has seen them all. The Annamites are as garrulous in their art as in their conversation. They are digressive, and in a mass of incoherent lines, they are unable to concentrate upon the essential. There is, too, a wilful absence of symmetry and perspective in the Western sense. The Annamite artist rejoices to represent groups of five or seven but never six. In statuary they can only conceive of the monotonous or the grotesque. Because of this refusal to seek inspiration in nature, their art betrays a certain lack of virility. They are at their best in the conscientious execution of detail and when they are unimpeded by tradition and rites—which unfortunately is very occasional. The lack of names, schools, and styles is a hindrance to classifying and analysing Annamite art. It is a phenomenon which can be traced to Buddhism's encouragement of the artist's anonymity, and its discouragement of any expression of personal emotion.

In addition to being monotonous, Annamite architecture is impermanent. This is partly due to the materials used. The country has much wood, but in Tonkin no stone. The Annamites have only a very limited knowledge of the use of bronze and iron. Buildings were necessarily small and easily destroyed by fire, and by persistent tropical insects as well as the perennial wars which ravaged the country. What has survived is relatively modern. Conservation of their work is not an Annamite, Chinese, or even a Khmer characteristic. No effort is made to keep up buildings since there is more merit acquired in constructing a new pagoda than in repairing an old one. Moreover, it gives greater scope to the artist's talent and is more pleasing to the divinity who does not in the least mind his using materials taken from an older temple. Horizontal lines are favoured especially for pagodas. The Annamite does not look up to a divinity but renders a cult to the dead: he is perennially bent over his rice-fields or his family's tombs, so that his whole life is rooted in the ground. Pagoda roofs are only slightly upturned to indicate a transient rupture with this perpetual preoccupation with the soil. The rigidity and omnipresence of death are betrayed in the inert quality of his architecture.

The Annamite code has regulated the type of dwelling appropriate to each social group. Only mandarins might use durable materials and large dimensions, or indulge themselves in interior decoration. But little outwardly distinguishes their homes from those of poor people. Rich or poor, the Annamite consults a sorcerer as to the site of his home and a favourable day on which to begin building. As an additional precaution he will hang a rhinoceros' horn inside. Windows are unknown, and the few tiny grilled openings allow little air to enter. The Annamite prefers it this way, for he believes that the wind is disease-ridden. Nor does he mind the smoke-laden atmosphere, for it preserves the wood of his house and keeps away a multitude of hungry mosquitoes. Most of the houses are infested with rats and snakes of a harmless albeit ubiquitous character. Personal cleanliness is no greater than that of the house itself, where animals and humans live side by side. Stagnant pools abound in the villages, and buffaloes rejoice to lie all day long in these fetid waters. Such unhygienic conditions are the delight of epidemics which spread with abandon throughout town and country.

Painting is almost wholly the province of professionals. Perspective and proportion are regulated entirely by the whim of the artist. Unlike the Chinese they paint little landscape, but prefer as in the theatre a legend or military exploit in which tradition rather than improvisation invariably dominates.

The love of ceramics is universal in Annam, but little such work is now done there. The famous *Bleus de Hué* came from China, as did the Annamites' potter-teachers, and their art unfortunately disappeared when they returned to their native land. Pottery is made by all Annamite families, but the best professional work comes from Tonkin. Bronze and brass were little used and only for cannon, bells, and urns, but work in the precious metals has always flourished. Jewellery is the most prized possession of an Annamite woman: it forms the bulk of her wedding gifts, and is the ultimate stake laid on the gaming table. Embroidery on silk or on cotton is a contemporary art which can be traced back to the sixteenth-century Chinese who taught the Annamites. Originally embroidery was used only as temple decoration, but in recent years it has served to brighten the sombre interiors of Annamite homes.

Beautiful craftsmanship makes the work of the Annamite artisan more successful than that of his artist colleague. Working in wood, either in sculpture, lacquer, or incrustation, brings out his best qualities—the patient, faithful, and delicate execution of detail. Artisans are organized into a kind of guild system whose tangible expression is shown by their grouping together in certain streets of every town. Contrary to the Western conception of the artist working independently of his fellows and following his own inspiration, he is in Annam the servitor of his work and his colleagues. Their life in common standardizes and perpetuates certain models and methods which have resulted in machine-like uniformity. The peculiar history of Annamite artisanship has warped its development. Any worker showing conspicuous talent aroused the covetous interest of the Court, who requisitioned his services for the palace. Unfortunately this often meant forcing the artist into a line of work for which he was not fitted, at starvation wages and under a rigid military discipline, with the possibility that he would in time be dismissed without compensation. Such a system naturally destroyed any progress in the arts. Many potentially gifted artists took up another profession or hired a salesman to put on their work a foreign trade mark for protection.

MEDICINE

Annamite medicine is purely empirical and based upon no knowledge of anatomy or physiology. Religious beliefs curtail any surgical interference, notably autopsies, lest the soul of the deceased become malevolent. Evil spirits, as well as the elements, are regarded as purveyors *par excellence* of disease. For different reasons the ancestral souls are discontented, and choose sickness as an effective way of tormenting the survivors. The sorcerers share with so-called doctors the task of dispelling disease by propitiating the spirit with incantation or herbs.

Chinese medicine was introduced into Annam in the sixteenth century, and has always kept its place of honour. It was easier to become a doctor in Annam than in Molière's plays, for it sufficed to give oneself a diploma. There was, however, a single school of medicine at Hué, directed by the royal doctors who had studied Chinese medical lore. More usually, professional knowledge was handed down from father to son by oral tradition. Unfortunately it is a point of honour in Annam that a doctor never ask any information from his patient. He may only feel his pulse but this process will probably take hours, for it gives the doctor time to make up his mind about the malady. Since he can have no idea of the real nature of the disease, the doctor is necessarily bound to be at least half charlatan. If he guesses right, the doctor is treated like a scholar: if wrong, he is completely discredited. Suggestion is his most effective remedy. Annamites have little confidence in their physicians. First a price is bargained for that will guarantee a cure, but the sum is paid only when the patient recovers. Annamites want quick results, and if the medicine prescribed is not immediately effective they change doctors. In this way the list of local and even ambulatory physicians is quickly exhausted. Their reaction is based on the firm belief that nature has supplied a remedy for every disease, and so a trial-and-error method is used until it is found. They believe that there are five organs in the human body which are interrelated, like a family, and which have affinity with the five elements and planets. Certain days and seasons, and even colours, are therefore propitious for treating their related diseases.

The Annamite doctor must needs be an apothecary as well, for his name means literally the master of remedies. Annamites specialize in herbs whereas the Chinese have more animal and mineral concoctions. Horses, for instance, are highly serviceable, in the moral as well as in the physical sphere: their bones are good for bile, women's diseases, fever, and eye trouble; their powdered teeth cure fear; the mane and tail protect youth. Dogs and pigs are almost equally valuable, not to mention deer and serpents. When the Sino-Annamite pharmacy has been exhausted in vain to effect a cure, the sorcerer is called in, or the family carries to him a piece of the patient's clothing. After invoking favourable spirits, the sorcerer consults his book for the right remedy and then tells on what day the cure will take place. If this does not work the sorcerer then goes to the patient's house and performs a sacrifice to induce the malignant spirit to leave the sick body. As with doctors, suggestion is often the most effective cure.

It is principally under-nourishment and the amazing lack of hygiene that causes the majority of Annamite ills. Nervous diseases are almost unknown. Ritual and group life have removed any crushing sense of responsibility or of pressure. The few cases of insanity that exist are treated with barbaric cruelty: the victim must be chained in one room even for years after he is, to all appearances, cured. Imbeciles are not regarded as insane or as a social menace, and they may marry and inherit property like anyone else. There is no legislation regarding the treatment of lepers or the infirm.

The religions of Annam have been compared to a tropical forest where no one tree can live isolated. There is no clear-cut boundary between them, and one person may hold simultaneously and without friction a half-dozen beliefs. The Annamites work on the principle that if one religion is good, three are better. If the result is chaos, there is at least a comforting absence of fanaticism. Both this tolerance and the all pervading formalism of Annamite religions, which are Chinese in origin, cover a multitude of indigenous beliefs that have never been eradicated. Even Buddhism which came into Annam from China and Thibet had not only been distorted *en route*, but was profoundly modified after it arrived in the country by the ancestral cult and government opposition. The bonzes' celibacy and their exemption from ordinary fiscal and social responsibilities made Buddhism the object of official opprobrium. In spite of the fact that they figure at every public and family ceremony, Annamite bonzes have merited and acquired nothing like the prestige they enjoy among the Khmers.

Taoism in Indo-China is on an even lower plane. It is an extraordinary metamorphosis of a religion born of one of the greatest of Chinese philosophers, whose priests in modern Annam are only miserable sorcerers. The earth and sky are Ministers of Tao, or the Way of Life, which permeates and transforms everything, but under the Annamite touch this concept has degenerated into magic. From Taoism comes the Emperor of Jade, whom almost all Annamites worship. Taoism lives side by side with Buddhism on the best of terms, and their priests are called along with bonzes for every public and private ceremony.

Confucianism has so far outdistanced both Buddhism and Taoism that it dominates every phase of Annamite life. The confusion of cults in Annam so shocked the fifteenth-century scholars that they attacked all disorderly superstitions and reduced them soon to a legal uniformity. Their official version was distributed by the Minister of Rites throughout the villages so as to suppress the numerous local variations. A hierarchy of genii was also created, in imitation of the Chinese, whose brevets were renewed annually, with promotion or demotion by the Emperor on the basis of merit acquired during the past year.

Confucianist doctrine is set forth in the four classical books, composed by the master's disciples, and in the five canonical books written by Confucius himself. There is no first cause: force and matter have existed throughout all eternity, with the former steadily gaining ground at the expense of the latter. This action of force upon matter, akin to the active or masculine element upon the feminine or passive element, has produced heaven and earth, and from their union came mankind. This celestial origin has endowed man with an essentially good nature. But to preserve it intact he must sharpen his reason so that its clarity may not be obscured by his emotions. Heaven has endowed each person with a conscience that permits him to distinguish good from evil. Virtue, through the tranquillity it assures to the soul, is—familiarly enough—its own reward. For some scholars virtue has also meant more material advantages, like the trio of happinesses—fortune, longevity, and male progeny. Confucianism would have remained a purely ethical system in Annam, had it not been for its union with the old Annamite spirit world whose constant intervention has made life so complicated and uneasy. Confucianism did successfully regulate the relations between people,[1] and gave harmonious unity to the body politic and social. But it also grafted on to an exaggerated respect for tradition innumerable superstitions which have become hopelessly enmeshed with the original doctrine. Confucius himself has become a deity.

The cult of the dead had long existed in Annam before Confucianism adapted and laicized it. A rigid and immutable character was infused into this cult by placing it among the sacrificial rites. In trying to cleanse it of superstition and magic, so as to make of it a suitable instrument for good government and social order, filial piety was made the central pivot of this heavy pseudo-religious mechanism. The ancestral cult became the regulator of family unity and morality. The finer points of Confucianism, as shown in its innumerable commentaries, were appreciated exclusively by the scholar class who scorned the popular forms of Buddhism and Taoism.

Confucianism, as it filtered through to the masses in the form of rites, has a social value. The cult of the dead aims to affirm the immortality

[1] The relation of subject to sovereign, son to father, wife to husband, younger to older brother, and friend for friend.

of the group, a solidarity of souls both living and dead. Thus death strikes a more severe blow at the group than at the individual most closely related to the deceased. In an Annamite funeral it is the commune, not the family, which plays the major role. Custom forces all male adults, on pain of fine, to attend the funeral of a co-villager. Non-taxpayers, like women and children, are for the same reason given very inferior burials. Because death has weakened the community, it is a defiling stain which the deceased's family must wipe out and expiate by burning everything that has touched the corpse, by rigid rites and rules of mourning, and by offering the soul every facility in food and transportation into the spirit world. Decomposition alone releases the soul from the body. Its final burial, at the end of three years, marks the end of society's repugnance. A tablet with a brief biography of the dead is placed on the family altar, from which it may be removed only after the fifth generation. Time has modified the severity of some of these practices, but even nowadays Annamite society seems very harsh towards those whom death has touched. It forces upon them a temporary ostracism, symbolic of the soul's long exclusion from the spirit world before it may enter upon the ten thousand generations of peace. Just as the cult of the family dead binds together all its members, living and deceased, so the communal cult of the common ancestor unites by an unbroken chain the larger social group. The family ceremonies of offerings and periodic celebrations at the tomb have their replica in general communal festivals.

Under the official cult of Heaven and Earth, and of the agrarian deities and communal genii, lies an enormous mass of popular beliefs regarding the spirit world. Not only have the dead a potentially harmful influence on the living, but rocks, trees, and animals—particularly in the mountains—harbour a flock of malevolent spirits. Many of these wandering immortals are the souls of those without tombs and offerings, and it is from this host that the sorcerers recruit their spiritual servitors. Much of the magic common to all primitive peoples makes up those beliefs. *Tinh* is the name which Annamites give to the *virtus* inherent in all forms of nature. Life is inconceivable without it, but it is not life itself—rather its essence which forms the basis of the soul. *Khi* is a secondary abstract force, a subsidiary condition of existence. It is, in nature, light, heat, cold, and wind: in humans, it cannot act independently of *tinh*. The union of these two forces parallels that of the universal male and female elements.

With time a conception of deity slowly emerged from this inchoate mass of spirits. Annam, like all theocratic countries, has clothed its sovereign with divinity. The Emperor belongs to the dragon race and he has a controlling power over all genii. His sacred person is surrounded by innumerable taboos because the enormous quantity of *tinh* he possesses makes him dangerous to approach. Similarly in the animal world, the tiger—and to a lesser extent the whale and the dolphin—are full of *tinh*. The tiger is so fearsome that one cannot pronounce his name without risking invoking his awesome presence. As with the Emperor, a whole vocabulary of indirect references to him has grown up. If a man-eating tiger is trapped, a sacrifice is offered to him before he is killed, and in certain regions his permission is asked before chopping down a tree. In general, what is most intimately concerned with life—like sex, birth, marriage, or death—has acquired the greatest quantity of taboos. Sorcerers' power, like their amulets and incantations, is based upon the optimistic belief that they know the rules that govern the spirit world. Certain places, like the hearth, are known to be their favourite haunt, and have in consequence a cult of their own. Cannon are believed to be the favoured residence of warriors' souls, so military rations are placed beside them. During the French attack on Hué one of the cannon refused to work until it was given its regular repast which had been forgotten during the heat of battle. The relations of these spirits with mankind are usually unpleasant. They show a remarkable ingenuity in assuming disagreeable and Protean forms, but they are puerile and easily duped. Though they are more powerful than the living, they are even less intelligent. To outwit them successfully requires the aid of magicians and a lifetime's attention to the appropriate rites.

It is their hierarchical organization that is the Annamites' most original religious contribution. Hierarchy serves to clarify, to a slight degree, the numerous and ubiquitous deities of the Annamite pantheon. A vague unity of command over them is given to the Emperor of Jade who exercises dominion over the three worlds of earth, sky, and sea. Each of the male spirits in these worlds has a feminine counterpart, who in recent years have been receiving more worship than the male contingent. This is primarily due to the attraction of this cult for women who find compensation in it for their exclusion from the ancestral cult. These worlds are minutely organized in the same way as the empire of Annam itself. The large percentage of magic and the low standing of its priestesses have forced this cult of the three worlds into grave disrepute.

57

CHAPTER II

THE FRENCH ADMINISTRATION OF INDO-CHINA

"Je définis ainsi le droit de conquête: un droit nécessaire, légitime et malheureux, qui laisse toujours à payer une dette immense pour s'acquitter envers la nature humaine."   *Montesquieu*

WHEN Admiral Charner came to Cochin-China in 1861, his instructions were of the vaguest. The desirability of a French military post in the Far East had been apparent to the July Monarchy, but it became an imperious necessity under Napoleon III, who involved himself in Chinese campaigns. Nothing beyond this skeleton idea, however, had been evolved, so that the Admiral's administration was not according to preconceived principles but born of current circumstances.

Annamite civilization was an unknown quantity to the French. Only missionaries, and the natives trained in their schools to speak a deformed Latin, could serve as intermediaries. All clues to the old administrative system had disappeared with the mandarins who had destroyed their records—of which the most important were the tax registers—before they took flight. Not only were the French officers who tried to replace them unfamiliar with administrative work in general, but without any previous experience of the Asiatic mind. They were given small garrisons at strategic points and told to maintain order as best they might. Since slow and circuitous waterways were the sole means of communication, they had to contend with regional independence as well as isolation from Saigon.

Admiral Bonard's title, Governor of Cochin-China, mildly indicated a different official conception of his role. He had had previous experience as colonial administrator and was familiar with the current Algerian theories of a Protectorate. But the flight of the mandarins made such a government almost impossible in Cochin-China. Native administrators had to be artificially created from very inferior material. Over them were placed French officers, as Inspectors of Native Affairs, who, like the mandarins, their predecessors, exercised all powers indiscriminately. They were offered inducements in salary and promotion to stimulate their learning of the native language. In spite of Bonard's attempts to introduce the Protectorate form of government, the periodic renewal of hostilities throughout the country forced him more and

58

more into direct administration. The governors after Bonard had too short a tenure of office to do anything but perpetuate this "temporary" arrangement, and the modifications that they made were in detail rather than in principle.

La Grandière's five-year administration was by far the most important. His was a curious combination of the Protectorate ideal with a military régime. This Admiral's extensive powers included nominating his subordinates, assessing taxes, drawing up the budget and a public works programme, and creating a school for interpreters. A strict training was given to prospective administrators in the *Collège des Stagiaires* at Saigon, which now opened this career to other than military men. Their number was increased and their new functions assigned on the basis of experience. Naturally a conflict ensued between the three Inspector-Officers in charge of each province. Theoretically they were equals, but in reality the Class I Inspector dominated his disgruntled colleagues. That the government functioned as well as it did was due to the remarkable talents of the men who were Cochin-China's first Inspectors. Daily contact with new experiences served to limber up the usually unsupple military mind.

With the establishment of the Third Republic there was naturally a return to the assimilationist principles of 1789.[1] When the new government had had time to realize that the military were still in control of Cochin-China, there was an immediate move to replace them by a more democratic régime. Their choice of a civil governor fell, characteristically, upon an ex-prefect, Le Myre de Vilers, who had had, however, some Algerian experience. The very precise instructions with which he was saddled showed a total lack of understanding of the Annamite mind and of the preparation it would need before ideas of French liberty, equality, and fraternity could be absorbed. Le Myre was fortunately able enough to give an elastic interpretation to the orders of an uninformed bureaucracy, anxious to shape the colony after its own image.

Application of the principle of the separation of powers, as a means of controlling the colony's governor, was the chief object of Le Myre's reforms. He created the Colonial Council as a further check to gubernatorial irresponsibility. It was also to serve as a representative organ for the French of the colony, and to a lesser extent of the native Notables. Time was to show that this Council's control of the budget was a serious defect: their selfish disposal of the colony's revenues

---

[1] Cf. below, p. 399.

was quite contrary to the taxpayers' interests. Ultimately, this change simply meant a new division of spoils among the conquerors. Such, fortunately, was not the fate of Le Myre's judicial reforms.

Le Myre's initial distress at the confusion of powers was soon followed by a more real appreciation of the difficulties which a fundamental reorganization would entail. To begin with, the cost of establishing nineteen courts was prohibitive. Moreover, in the colony's unsettled condition, a brusque withdrawal of judicial powers from the administrators would be dangerous to their prestige as well as to the general security. Le Myre's position was that of the Admirals: circumstances had forced them to retain a military government when they would have much preferred a Protectorate. A judicial compromise was finally reached in 1864. Native law was to be retained for suits between Asiatics, with the governor's approbation essential for imposing severe penalties. Under the Admirals, justice had been rendered theoretically according to the Annamite code, but in practice arbitrarily, at the Inspectors' good pleasure. Crimes of a political character were still tried before the War Council. The principle of two judicial systems, based on nationality, was established by the Admirals, who had neither the time nor the opportunity to work out the details. Le Myre, however, was not, like them, faced with constant revolts, but he lacked money and most of all trained collaborators to put his republican ideas into practice. So he, too, retained the existing organization, trying only to check its worst abuses. He created a Court of Appeal, tried to clarify the native code and to modify its penalties along the lines of French penal law. The whole judicial reform was a compromise and a breach in the assimilationist creed.

The newly created magistracy at once encountered opposition from the administrators, who brooded jealously over their shorn judicial attributes. There was on both sides a great showing of ignorance and tactlessness. Despite the practical obstacles encountered, contemporary French opinion showed unabated zeal for assimilation. The natives, on their side, were bewildered by an administration that lacked the power to punish infractions of its own regulations. The host of new functionaries needed to carry out these reforms descended in a swarm upon the colony. Annamites found themselves judged by Hindu magistrates, who enjoyed the privileges of French citizenship simply because they belonged to France's old colonies. All foreigners, but especially judges, were at the mercy of their interpreters. If it was true that the Inspectors had only had local experience as an asset and no knowledge of French law, it was no less true that the new magistrates with a better legal equipment knew nothing about the country, and, what was worse, made no effort to learn. The evils engendered by their mutual jealousy were aggravated by the premature retirement of Le Myre. After him there were many modifications in personnel and legislation, but always along the line of increased assimilation. As they worked out, Le Myre's reforms proved to be too hastily applied and, above all, too theoretically conceived. The judicial reform was his most important contribution, though Le Myre regarded it only as the corollary of his administrative changes. In an over-zealous moment he suppressed the *Collège des Stagiaires*, so as to create a carefully regulated bureaucracy, but the salary inducements were not great enough to lure able men from France, nor were the local premiums sufficient to stimulate functionaries already in the country to learn such a difficult language as Annamite.

Economically the French were making little impression on the country. In conquering Cochin-China they had simply acquired one of the world rice reservoirs, already well organized by the Chinese. Without planning and without effort, revenues poured into the treasury, yet the populace remained as miserable as before. Le Myre tried to ease the tax burden, to strengthen small property owners so as to decrease the growing proletariat, and also to protect the peasant against the ravening Notables. Although the French facilitated the growth of these Notables' fortunes, by permitting the free exportation of rice, nevertheless their simultaneous reform of *corvées* deprived this class of free labour. Their irritation naturally took itself out on the peasants, who no longer had even mandarinal protection, for the French administrators were inaccessible and ignorant of local affairs. By a fairer division of the taxes, by a prolonged peace, and by improvements through public works, the population increased rapidly and a few fortunes grew apace. The drawbacks to Le Myre's work were: the unnecessary multiplication of officials, which drained the budget; a policy of assimilation, which meant the dissolution of the Annamites' communal and family life; the régime of the interpreter through the application of inappropriate legislation; the diffusion of garbled French to a few Annamites in the place of widespread Confucianist education; an expensive native army to replace an economical militia; and some superficial administrative changes designed solely to check a military régime, and which only transferred to the French electorate ever greater powers for them to abuse. It has become the fashion to blame

Le Myre for representing really only what was the spirit of his times. Assimilation, by any other hand, would have been as bad. In fact, Le Myre's four years of titanic labours show what a capable interpreter can do for a bad idea. The worst breakdown came in the educational field, where assimilation succeeded in being unmitigatedly destructive.

Prosperity made Cochin-China very arrogant. The Colonial Council, with its vast financial powers, came under the control of a clique, the Blanchy régime, which regularly voted to increase its own salaries and did nothing at all for the country. De Lanessan,[1] despite his extensive authority, was blocked by this faction from creating an Indo-Chinese Union, lest it mean Cochin-China's underwriting the Tonkinese deficit. Rousseau, his successor, wrestled with the recalcitrant colony, whose arrogance and secessionist spirit had grown with its victory over De Lanessan. In addition, Blanchy had the ear of the Minister of the Colonies in Paris, which added to the trials of Rousseau, already sufficiently absorbed by troubles in Tonkin. It took the strong hand of Doumer to bring Cochin-China to terms, but that colony has always resented having to subsidize its weaker neighbours, and has regularly displayed a *frondeur* spirit in its relations with the Governor-General.

TONKIN

When Jean Dupuis sailed up the Red River, in 1873, to sell firearms in Yunnan, he proved the navigability of Garnier's river route into China's southern provinces. Although Dupuis was only an enterprising trader without official backing, his presence in Tonkin was contrary to the current Franco-Annamite treaty, and it elicited a protest from Hué to Admiral Dupré, then Governor of Cochin-China.

Dupré's attitude in this affair was extremely complex. He had been struggling for five years to get a treaty from the Court of Hué, and now he seemed further than ever from his goal, so low had French prestige fallen even in Asia since the Franco-Prussian War. Dupré had always been a partisan of forceful action as the only effective policy with the eel-like Annamite government. Moreover, at this time, Hué was having serious difficulties with a widespread revolt in Tonkin. Like all his French contemporaries, Dupré feared English intervention. British control of Tonkin would mean their holding the key to Southern China and imperilling France's position in the peninsula. For years

[1] Cf. below, p. 75.

he had begged Paris to let him close Tonkin to foreign aggression, promising that it would cost nothing if he were given a free hand. Psychological defeatism in France, since the war of 1870, made the government chary of even the display of force. In addition, Hué had sent ambassadors directly to Paris to plead the return of Cochin-China, and this also served as a check on the Admiral.

Dupré was beginning to be discouraged when he heard of Dupuis' successful navigation of the Red River, but the Métropole, with its congenital fear of complications, at once formally ordered him to abstain from armed intervention there. Dupré was, however, determined to do so, and to use Dupuis as the opening wedge. In looking about for a leader for this delicate mission, Dupré's first choice was Francis Garnier.

Garnier's career had been amazingly full for so young an officer. He had participated in the Chinese campaigns, and he had conceived the Mekong exploratory expedition, although he had been thought too young to be given its command. When Lagreé's death left him in charge of it, he gave a political character to what had hitherto been solely a scientific and commercial expedition. Returning afterwards to Paris, he distinguished himself during the siege and the Commune. Once again in the Far East, he was planning an exploration into Yunnan from Shanghai, when he received an urgent message from Dupré asking him to return to Saigon for an important piece of work —nothing less than the conquest of Tonkin.

When Garnier and Dupré talked over the situation, they found themselves only in partial agreement. Garnier wanted no armed expedition: he thought that Tonkin was tired enough of Hué's administration to submit spontaneously to him. Both agreed, however, as to the importance of opening the Red River to commerce. Finally Garnier agreed to take two hundred French soldiers and a few Annamites, and to sail at once for Hanoi. There is ample proof that it was the force of circumstances which gave a military turn to the expedition, and against Garnier's expressed wishes.

The open distrust of the officials at Hanoi was shown by their military preparations and a stream of aggressive proclamations. Garnier replied with an ultimatum, threatening to storm the citadel if the town were not immediately disarmed and the Red River opened to commerce—and incidentally to Dupuis. Their failure to reply brought about an amazingly rapid capture of the Hanoi fort without the loss of a single French soldier. Equally swift successes were repeated throughout the delta until, on December 25th, envoys brought word of Hué's orders to make peace. Just prior to this event, a new complication—the Chinese Black Flags—had entered upon the scene. Garnier was fatally interrupted in a campaign he was planning against them by the arrival of Hué's envoys. In the midst of negotiations with them, he heard that the Chinese were marching on Hanoi. Leading a sortie from the citadel in person, Garnier became separated from his men and was killed by the Black Flags at the Paper Bridge, just outside of the city. Although the attack was a failure, his death was an irremediable loss, for it delayed by ten years the conquest of Tonkin.

The fright of the Annamite Court was only exceeded by that of Paris and Admiral Dupré. Mindful that he had gone counter to his instructions in a policy which only success would have justified, Dupré disavowed Garnier in order to avoid being himself recalled. The Métropole, believing that Garnier's death had fatally jeopardized the whole undertaking, peremptorily ordered him to negotiate with Annam, and to give up the idea of a Tonkinese conquest. Dupré's choice of a conciliatory negotiator was also in accordance with Paris's instructions. He chose Philastre, a man of encyclopedic learning in regard to Annamite affairs and of long local experience. Dupré had already used him in his Tokinese project without, however, having taken him into his full confidence. Dupré now only persuaded Philastre to negotiate with Hué by saying that Garnier had exceeded his instructions. When he learned the whole truth, Philastre was greatly embittered, and the treaty which he made was his attempt to make amends to the Annamite civilization which he sincerely admired. In reality, no side had the monopoly of righteousness, for it was a duel of mutual duplicity.

Philastre's work destroyed the vestiges of Garnier's achievements. France was recognized as legal sovereign of Cochin-China, thus merely registering the accomplished fact. Religious liberty was also guaranteed, but this had already been done in 1862. Three new ports were opened to commerce, as well as the Red River. While this was a technical advantage, the river was never more closed in actuality than when it had legally been opened. Annam was officially dispensed from paying its old indemnity, on which no payment had ever been made, and in addition Annam received from France five warships, one hundred cannon, and the loan of some officers. to instruct the Annamites in their use. The French also promised to aid in maintaining peace, which meant that they must turn on their erstwhile partisans, the native

Christians, now delivered over to the mandarins' sweet revenge. The only Annamite concession, in an otherwise benevolent treaty, was the promise to conform her foreign policy to French guidance.

The decade, 1874–1884, was to reveal the impracticability of this treaty. To the Emperor Tu-Duc, it conclusively proved that France's timidity would permit him to get rid of her by a policy of vexations and by the renewal of his vassal relationship with China. The French, on their side, found the treatment to which their consuls in the treaty ports were subjected impossible, and their position altogether too anomalous. To the other Europeans in Annam, they were responsible for maintaining order, yet they could not do so without Annamite co-operation. Annam further violated the treaty by persecuting native Christians, and by maintaining tariff barriers along the Red River. When finally Hué forbade the exportation of rice from the treaty ports, it spelled ruin for the local European merchants. These numerous vexations elicited protests on all sides, which determined the French to take a stronger course of action.

When a French engineer, in 1882, was captured by bandits in Upper Tonkin, in spite of the French and Annamite passports he carried, attention became focussed on the troubled condition of that region. The Court of Hué had long encouraged these bandits as a counterpoise to the French, even at the risk of their gaining control of the whole country from Laos to the Chinese frontier. These bandits were the remnants of the Taiping rebellion, who were overrunning the country even at the time of Garnier's explorations. Tu-Duc had called upon the Cantonese viceroy to stop them by sending some regular troops, but they only added to the general confusion by joining the rebels once they had got into Tonkin. Eventually two mutually antagonistic bands were formed—the Black and Yellow Flags, whose names were taken from the colour of their standards.

The Gulf of Tonkin had long been famous as a pirate stronghold. Ships plying between India and China could be neatly waylaid there, and even easier loot was furnished by the many wrecks which took place in those treacherous waters. The natives there were terrorized into submission by the pirates' brutal treatment of any who resisted them, and this fear made them refuse to give evidence against their tormentors. The Chinese in the country protected the pirates, since they supplied them with cheap contraband goods. By the 1860's, this crime-worn gulf had become the centre of a flourishing trade in women and children, destined for sale in Chinese ports. The best French achievement in this generally ineffective decade was to clean up the Gulf of Tonkin. Again, in this instance, the Court of Hué proved itself helpless. In dealing with these pirates they admitted them to be invincible, although they were only increasing the anarchy in the country. In 1878, a third element of disorder was added by the revolt of the Le partisans in Tonkin, supported by the local bandits. This did, however, give Tu-Duc the opportunity of calling upon Chinese aid, contrary to his treaty obligations to the French. The position of the Emperor was indeed curious. On the one hand, he subsidized these bandits to spread death and destruction in his own country, and on the other he asked China for aid in suppressing them as the sole means of ousting the French.

By 1881 the French government realized that it must act, or that all its influence would be annihilated by Annam's subtle policy. Ten years had passed since the Prussian War, and there was still great fear of England's getting a foothold in Southern China through Tonkin. So the deputies finally voted credits for an expeditionary force to establish a Protectorate over Annam. Secrecy and vacillation, however, still characterized this second Tonkinese expedition. Commandant Henri Rivière was sent to the Far East in charge of these forces, without being told of their exact destination. When Le Myre confided to him his mission, in January 1882, he showed himself anxious not to err as Dupré had done: Rivière was not to conquer Tonkin, but to act "pacifically, politically, and administratively" to extend French influence there. But before Rivière could set sail, he got word of Gambetta's fall, and it was not known till the following March whether or not the Tonkin expedition had been forgotten in the shake-up of Ministries. Finally, in April, Rivière was despatched to Tonkin, on the ground that the Black Flags there menaced the Hanoi garrison and the safety of French citizens in the country.

The Tonkinese authorities naturally concluded that Rivière was going to be a second Garnier. And for a time the resemblance was marked. Rivière felt compelled to take the Hanoi citadel, and this act was disavowed by Le Myre. The Paris press and Ministries, however, showed themselves favourable to Rivière's action, and little attention was paid at the time to the protests of the Chinese ambassador. All would have gone smoothly had not the Egyptian crisis just then distracted Paris, and forced a temporary return to the 1874 frame of mind. Party warfare was bitter then in France, as a consequence of Arabi's revolt and England's action, so Tonkin was totally eclipsed.

In fact, the confusion was so great that Le Myre was recalled by the Minister of the Navy without even notifying the Minister of Foreign Affairs.

As a result of the secret negotiations between Hué and Peking, the confusion in Paris was more than matched by that in Tonkin. Chinese troops arrived in the delta, officially to drive out the bandits, but in reality to co-operate with them against the French. Rivière was finally aroused to action, and began in March 1883 to conquer the delta, just as Garnier had done before him. Two months later he was killed in a sortie against the Chinese, on almost the identical spot where Garnier had met death some nine years before. But this time Paris was aroused. By a big majority in the Chamber, credits were voted for military action. The French bombardment of Hué's forts forced Tu-Duc to sue for peace. On August 25th a temporary treaty was signed in which the Emperor finally recognized a French Protectorate. Slowly the delta towns were taken in the spring of 1884, despite the frequent changes in the French command. Now only the Chinese remained to be dealt with.

While the delta was being conquered, French diplomacy was active in Peking. Due to acute jealousy, there was the most amazing lack of co-operation among the French officials there. Fournier, a personal friend of Ly Hung Chang's, without the knowledge of the French chargé d'affaires, the Comte de Semallé, was preparing an agreement which he thought would put an end to the hostilities (May 1884). Another entirely separate negotiation was being conducted by Patenotre at Hué. Further confusion was added by wire-pulling in Paris, which led to the recall of certain of these diplomats for personal or political motives, and this lightly jeopardized the outcome of the war. Ferry's diplomacy had succeeded, however, in bringing hostilities to an official close when the famous Bac-Le incident occurred. In conformity with China's promise of evacuation, French troops were occupying the post of Bac-Le when they were attacked by the Chinese, whom they thought had withdrawn. Opinion in France was so stirred by this time that the deputies were willing to carry the action into China. But war was never officially declared, for fear of antagonizing the other Powers. France was long afraid to shell Chinese ports lest this alienate England, upon whom the French fleet in the East depended for supplies. In August, however, Admiral Courbet did destroy the forts along the Min River, and in October attempt, with only partial success, to occupy Formosa, and later the Pescadores Islands. These achievements were largely fruitless: Peking was too far away to be very much affected, and distant victories were lost to sight in the meanderings of high diplomacy.

In Tonkin, General Brière de l'Isle was ordered to march on Langson and to lift the blockade at Tuyen Quang. Peking seemed to be on the point of yielding, and Ferry hourly expected word of peace when, by an amazing stroke of bad luck, came the cabled news of a French defeat at Langson. Then followed a terrific explosion of French public opinion. When Ferry went to the Chamber, on March 30, 1885, a crowd surged about the Palais Bourbon, and he was thrown from office in one of the most stormy sessions on record. Next day, by an ironic sequence of events, came the news that Peking had signed the peace and that the army's defeat had been exaggerated beyond all recognition. As a matter of fact, the Chinese themselves had taken flight at Langson, thinking that their attack upon the French had failed.

THE PROTECTORATE OF ANNAM-TONKIN

Annam is *par excellence* the country of scholars, yet the vast majority of its miserable inhabitants, wedged in between the Annamite Range and the three hundred miles of rocky coast, offer a marked contrast to the scholar-aristocracy. There is no spiritual or geographical cohesion in the country. The inaccessibility of Annam has a replica in its capital, Hué, whose site was chosen for its very isolation. The Emperor, who lived there, shared its inviolability. When for the first time he had to receive a French envoy face to face, his mandarins forced him to commit suicide.

The centuries of warfare between North and South bred in these Scholars of Annam a contempt for the Tonkinese, whom they tried to dominate culturally as well as politically. Tonkin, a country of dense population and traditional loyalty to the defeated Le dynasty, was more and more saddled with functionaries from Hué, who left to the local officials only such places as they themselves could not fill. The obvious differences between the two countries were exploited by the French missionaries. The mandarins of Tonkin had always been their implacable enemies and the persecutors of the native Christians. Garnier and his successors, new to the country, naturally adopted the missionary viewpoint. They translated this belief in the innate hostility of the Tonkinese for their "foreign" mandarins into a policy of suppressing these mandarins in order to win popular support. So convinced were they and the Métropole of the gulf between them, that a totally different administration was evolved for the two countries. At one time France even contemplated sacrificing Annam to keep Tonkin. But this project was nipped in the bud by the realization that some foreign Power could drive a wedge between the two French colonies of the peninsula, and that an independent Hué would always stir up trouble in Tonkin. For many years this initial error kept the French from appreciating the cultural unity of the three Annamite countries, and they tried by different administrative methods to sunder what history had knit together throughout twenty centuries of common traditions.

In the new-born Protectorate of Annam-Tonkin, it was soon obvious that the storm centre would be Hué. Tu-Duc died in July 1883, but the course of the Protectorate ran no smoother for the death of its most implacable enemy. His demise, rather, opened the way to the mandarin-Scholar party, who, thanks to a series of ephemeral emperors, were soon able to dominate the situation. The Bac-Le episode was to this group the joyous confirmation of French impotence, so they proceeded to crown and depose monarchs without even consulting the French Resident Consul. Finally a French battalion had to be called in to reduce the Scholar party to a humbler state of mind. It was hoped that this advantage would be permanently confirmed by the stationing of French troops in the Hué citadel.

Temporarily thwarted at the capital, the Scholars turned their activities to the provinces. There their venom was exercised principally upon the native Christians, for, said they picturesquely, without them the French would be like crabs without claws. Throughout 1883-84 only the vigilance of the French kept these reprisals from materializing. The situation was still fundamentally the same when General de Courcy took over the command, in June 1885.

De Courcy's incompetence and foolhardy behaviour precipitated the Scholars' long-maturing plans for a general massacre of the French and of their Christian supporters. This attack failed, but due to no foresight on the part of De Courcy. The Regent Thuyet fled to the mountains, taking with him the twelve-year-old Emperor, Ham Nghi. Since the Protectorate needed a sovereign to protect, the French at once cast about for some harmless substitute. Their choice finally fell on Dong Khanh, brother to the Emperor-in-flight. The Comat was next reconstituted with more obliging Ministers. Popular resentment of this policy was shown by the outbreak of a general revolt, which

69

took many years to burn itself out. Even after Ham Nghi was captured, months of campaigning were needed to force the country to accept the new government: even after De Courcy's recall the whole country remained as troubled as ever.

Public opinion in France was alternately enraged and perplexed by the turn of events in Indo-China. Smaller and smaller majorities voted credits for the war: once the colony was saved by a slim majority of four votes. The situation called for a radical solution. In January 1886, it was found when Paul Bert was named Resident General of Annam-Tonkin. Bert's friendship for Gambetta, his distinction as a scientist, and his marked anti-clericalism were of long standing, but he had only recently developed an interest in colonial expansion. Paris received word of his nomination with mixed surprise and dismay. His motives were generally suspect, as voiced by one anonymous letter he received: *"Eh bien, mon ami Paul, auras-tu bientôt ton petit million?"*[1]

Despite this discouraging send-off, Bert's achievements were remarkable for so short a tenure of office. His principal reform was a return to the Protectorate ideal in Annam, by governing through the Scholars and the Emperor, whose prestige and power he partially restored. In Tonkin, however, he favoured direct administration. He did not break with French policy in this matter, and by transferring the imperial power to a viceroy, the *kinh-luoc* of Tonkin, he completed the administrative break between the two Annamite countries. Bert's motive in severing ties with Hué was to cut the subsidies given by that Court to the Chinese bandits in Tonkin. Without this support he thought that the disorders there would automatically collapse. But in his calculations Bert had overlooked a new and profitable three-cornered trade which these bandits had recently organized in Tonkin, with themselves as intermediaries between the Annamites of the delta and their compatriots in Yunnan. These bandits ransomed compliant villages, or sacked those which resisted, quite in the traditional manner. But they exchanged their booty in the form of Tonkinese women, children, and livestock, for opium, arms and munitions from China. At the time that Bert came to the colony, this traffic was steadily increasing, for its success attracted new recruits, especially from among the criminal elements. But the whole issue in Annam-Tonkin was far from clear-cut. Along with free-lance adventurers there were some sincerely patriotic groups, fighting for the dethroned Emperor. There were also Mans and Thos struggling for their independence

[1] Chailley, J., *Paul Bert au Tonkin* (Paris, 1887), p. 10.

from the Annamites and for the opium monopoly. The various motives of this widespread revolt were as tangled and confused as the mountainous brushland through which the French were fighting. Putting down banditry in the interest of general security was an obvious military duty, but to stamp out a national movement went strongly against the republican fibre.

Bert's policy as educator and conserver of Annamite traditions was a more congenial role, and one in keeping with the principles of '89 as well as his belief in France's colonizing mission. He was the first organizer of Indo-Chinese education, with the double aim of training men to replace interpreters and of spreading among the people a working knowledge of French. Replacing the Hué mandarins in Tonkin was his greatest administrative problem, since it was almost impossible to find men who were both trained and loyal. To this end he founded the Tonkinese Academy. In the meantime he had to use the old mandarinate, but he made them as harmless as possible by cutting all their ties with Hué. A Council of Tonkinese Notables was another of the republican ideas which Bert introduced into the government, to the universal disapproval of his colleagues. It was part of his programme to do away with intermediaries between the government and the people, but he died before this idea was carried out. Like so much of his work, it had to wait years before his successors actively appreciated his wisdom and foresight.

In the financial realm, Bert's pioneering was far less effective. He was hampered by the knowledge that at all costs he must not call on Paris for money. Any public works that he might undertake must come from new resources within the colony itself. Although he strictly regulated forced labour, and wiped the slate clean of arrears in back taxes, yet transmutation of taxes into money payments was a burden on an already miserable population. In the long run, however, although the dykes and hospitals which he constructed proved to be a wise investment, his work in the economic field was sketchy and in no way really resolved the problem. It was left to Doumer to put the colony —somewhat brutally—on a paying basis, and to make it permanently independent of the Métropole's reluctant subsidies. It was chiefly in his native policy that Bert was most revolutionary. He laid the foundations for associationist principles, which his premature death unfortunately left in an embryonic condition.

Through a policy of stupid violence, Bert's numerous and short-lived successors prolonged the revolt in Annam-Tonkin, which had been calmed under his régime. The larger and larger budgetary deficits proved to the Métropole, more eloquently than anything else, the error of such ways. Business in the colony was paralysed by uncertainty: capitalists were afraid to invest in a country which had not yet found a stable administrative formula. De Lanessan, who had previously been sent there on a mission of inquiry, found himself named Governor of the colony with the opportunity of putting the theories he had evolved into almost immediate practice.

De Lanessan's arrival stirred the slumbering colony into life. His obvious ability, but even more his vibrant oratory, aroused new hopes for Annam-Tonkin. Nor was the new Governor himself the least insensitive to the inebriating quality of his own eloquence. In spite of an undeniable charm, De Lanessan's personality was too dictatorial. He kept an iron grip on all branches of the administration, and broke with his ablest collaborators. Sterile personal struggles eventually wore De Lanessan out and hurt a work which had already encountered enough other obstacles.

It was in his administrative policy that De Lanessan cut loose from the Bert tradition. He was unwilling to retain mandarins in Annam, and simultaneously to dispense with them in Tonkin. He found them everywhere indispensable, for they had a moral authority over the people which French functionaries could never acquire. They formed an integral part of the Annamite social structure, and one which must stand or fall with it. In his devotion to the Protectorate ideal, De Lanessan was one with Paul Bert, but he wanted it for Tonkin as well as for Annam. De Lanessan's further efforts to strengthen the Governor-General's powers at the expense of the local administrators did not increase his popularity with his compatriots. Paris had only been willing to give De Lanessan very extended powers provided that Indo-China would no longer be a drain on French resources. A deficit of 12,000,000 francs in the Tonkinese budget made this task enormously difficult. De Lanessan attacked the old problem from a new angle—that of credit. He lured capitalists to invest in Indo-China by a public works programme—chiefly improving the means of communication—that would justify the bright future he painted for the colony. Although taxation was more efficiently handled under his aegis, De Lanessan's economic contributions were rather more in developing the country's productivity than in improving its immediate revenues.

The flare-up of an old struggle between the civil and military French of Tonkin, dating from Bert's régime, underlay much of the hostility to De Lanessan, both in Paris and Tonkin. At that time, only the delta was held by a few garrison posts, while the mountain country was given over entirely to anarchy. Budgetary exigencies had forced the French to repatriate some of their forces at this crucial moment, and out of this mistaken economy grew the rift between the civil and the military. Rumour had it that Bert's marked preference for the military lay at the bottom of this rivalry. Bert, temperamentally and politically, loved the army, but his emotion could not be fully reciprocated, for was he not a civil governor who had displaced a military régime? To the military, it was ridiculous for a civil official to be responsible for keeping order when he had only the legal authority and no practical means of doing so. The army had conquered the country, but to others was going the power and the glory. To the premature intrusion of the civil government, the military attributed the contagion of revolt which was spreading from Annam to the Tonkinese delta. The rub between these two elements was much worse in the north, where the unpacified state of the country necessarily left a larger role to the army. Since Bert had used as civil administrators those ex-Officer-Inspectors who had done such admirable work in Cochin-China, a colonel or a general in Tonkin would often find himself under the orders of a former lieutenant.

If the military had been mildly dissatisfied with Bert, the civil were downright hostile to De Lanessan for having delivered over Upper Tonkin to the army. It was worse than his reinstatement of the mandarins in the delta. They could not deny that the great run of civil administrators were a motley crew, of far from uniform ability, whose capacities did not usually correspond to the extensive powers they wielded. Poverty and inefficiency revealed in France were too often thought to qualify a man for a colonial post. To find places for this host of incompetent newcomers, the provincial organization had to be expansively and uselessly subdivided. This period of civil supremacy culminated in a ridiculous military expedition, led in person by one of the civil residents in command of the militia, his infantry. He had been roundly beaten by the bandits, to the mirth and general satisfaction of the regular army. In order to keep their remunerative positions, many of the civil officials insisted that the country was pacified. Governor Picquet was one of the worst offenders in distorting such facts in his reports to the Métropole—notably in suppressing news of the ambush at Cho-Bo (January 1891), which had been partly due to his negligence. Since Paris paid the military expenses of Tonkin, and since at the time there was an hysterical fear of military *coups d'état*, Parliament naturally favoured the continuance of a civil government in Annam-Tonkin. Delcassé saved De Lanessan in order to save the civil government. Both he and the Chamber were willing to tolerate De Lanessan's new policies lest his recall make him more dangerous as Minister of the Colonies.

Since the Cho-Bo disaster coincided with De Lanessan's arrival, it was natural that he should begin his reforms by restoring their shorn powers to the military. The civil government was replaced along the frontier by four military Circles which have survived to this day. This partially salved the pride of the military, who had too long been sulking in their tents. The civil guard was reorganized and relegated to policing the delta, still under the authority of the Residents. The business of pacifying Upper Tonkin was once more in the hands of the regular army, and it remained to be seen if they would be more equal to the task than the civil authorities, whom they had so ridiculed.

De Lanessan was fortunate in having at hand two remarkable officers, Galliéni and Lyautey. Galliéni's original policy consisted of arming loyal villages so that they could defend themselves against the bandits. He built a series of blockhouses along the frontier, drew the country together by a network of roads, and inaugurated an administrative framework as far as this *tache d'huile* policy of pacification would permit. The people, whose confidence was restored by the protection Galliéni assured them, were beginning to return to regions long deserted. Tax exemptions and state aid also speeded up the work of reconstruction. The government was so pleased by the success of these operations that for the second time the country prematurely was declared pacified. The bandit groups still existed: they had only been displaced by the military activity of 1892.

A distinct change in bandit tactics was soon apparent. They seemed to be giving up the pillaging of villages for the ransoming of European captives. This gave them the maximum of profit for the minimum of danger. The administration, hypersensitive to the Metropolitan injunction of *"pas d'histoires,"* preferred coming to terms with these bandits rather than to conduct costly campaigns against them. For home consumption, the bargains thus arranged were euphoniously called submissions. One Chinese chieftain, Luong-Tam-Ky, received in 1890 a monthly pension of 3,000 piastres and a tax-free estate in Tonkin, where he ruled like an independent autocrat. This pleasant policy gave banditry a new lease of life, from 1893 to 1895. The money

74

so liberally given them went into purchasing firearms superior to those used by the French army itself. Ten more years of effort were needed to put an end to this anarchy in Upper Tonkin.

The military, whom De Lanessan had restored, showed themselves not wholly worthy of the charge. The Legionaries were the martyrs of the regular army, largely because they lacked influence at home. These soldiers bore the brunt of bandit warfare in Upper Tonkin. Left for months without relief in the unhealthy garrison posts of the Tonkinese mountains, they succumbed to the climate more than to the bandits' attacks, while the rest of the army remained securely in the relatively agreeable barracks of the delta. Fever and ambush made such ravages in the troops that the number of deaths was kept secret from public opinion at home. Only slowly did there grow an appreciation of the impossible conditions in these under-staffed and overworked mountain barracks, and of the unnecessary mortality they suffered through lack of proper care and their officers' ignorance of the local topography. The army had shown great heroism and devotion during the conquest, but their sterile struggle with the civil officials was leaving its mark on the general *morale*.

The indirect results of creating Military Circles were almost equally insidious. Many civil officials were displaced, only to return to Hanoi in desperate search of positions in an already over-staffed administration. Their salaries even then made the budget groan, and their presence only lengthened the already interminable red tape. The native government was also suffering. The new military zones were drawn arbitrarily across the old districts and across racial frontiers. These new territories were too big for the military personnel to handle. A single officer often had to replace several civil officials. Commerce, too, was victimized: merchants refused to go where they were not sure of having civil justice. The Residents found their powers much diminished, inasmuch as the military were responsible only to the head of the colony. It has taken years for the necessary adjustments to be made. Though their antagonism has died down, a certain rivalry between civil authorities and military still subsists.

THE INDO-CHINESE UNION

When Paris deputed extraordinary powers to De Lanessan, it was not meant as a permanent delegation of authority, but as a radical measure designed for a specific situation. His brusque recall revealed to the colony the Métropole's firm intention of keeping the reins of power in its own hands. A curt cable informed De Lanessan that his indiscretion in communicating state documents was unpardonable. That his sudden withdrawal at a crucial moment might imperil the future of a young country did not enter seriously into Parisian consideration. Good care was taken that his successors should have no such chance to initiate independent policies. Nor were the men selected as De Lanessan's successors of dangerous calibre.

Indo-China had, at this period, nothing but geographical unity. Cochin-China was a colony run by a corrupt machine which refused to co-operate with its neighbouring countries. Up to 1887, it had been administratively linked to Cambodia and placed under both a local governor and the Minister of the Colonies. Cambodia was nominally a Protectorate whose superficial Gallicization covered an essentially unchanged Indian feudalism. Annam-Tonkin formed a second group, each with its Resident Superior, who were in turn dependent on the Minister of Foreign Affairs. This Protectorate was quite absorbed in keeping down open revolt, and had made no attempt as yet to penetrate the internal administration.

In 1887, a first step towards unification was taken by the creation of a Governor-General and Council, still under the Colonial Minister. No federal budget existed to give force to its orders: finances were strictly controlled by the Métropole, as well as general policy. For a brief moment Paris had permitted the creation of an Indo-Chinese budget, but soon repented of its generosity. As was ever the case, it took an increasing budgetary deficit to wrench a permanent grant of power from Paris. Paul Doumer, a former Budget Reporter, was the man selected to initiate this new policy and to create a real Indo-Chinese Union.

Doumer's reorganization aroused great opposition in the colony from those whose interests he attacked, like the Blanchy group in Cochin-China, and also from those who disapproved of assimilation, centralization, and rampant *étatisme*. His essential administrative reform was a division between local and federal interests, and one which he carried into all spheres of the government. Heretofore the Governor-General had been too much absorbed by Tonkin: henceforth he was to govern everywhere but to administer nowhere.

The Central Services, with a uniform organization along Napoleonic lines, were to radiate federal influence throughout the colony. The most important among them was the Department of Civil Affairs, the only general non-technical service. Its octopus-like grasp soon made it so strong that it had to be suppressed; and while the technical services remained, they were profoundly modified. A resuscitated Superior Council, along with local Chambers of Commerce and Agriculture, completed the new federal framework. A reorganization of justice along federal lines strengthened the Union and also curbed Cochin-China's autonomous instincts. But the general budget was the backbone of the new system. It broke Cochin-Chinese resistance by canalizing and circulating its wealth throughout the whole Union. Its principal revenues were indirect taxes, or the famous monopolies of alcohol, opium, and salt. Though they were inherited from the Annamite government, the new form given to these revenues by Doumer made them of dangerous utility. They became in time the greatest single cause of native discontent. A public works programme that would develop the country economically and also strengthen federal ties took the form of extensive railroad construction. The loan of 200,000,000 francs which Doumer ably raised in France gave reality to his project and new life to the colony. Doumer was the first governor to stake the success of his whole work on Indo-China's economic development.

In his local reorganization, Doumer aimed to make the Protectorate form truly effective. Tonkin's ties with Hué had already been broken and the native organization simply existed side by side with its French replica. Unlike Bert and De Lanessan, Doumer saw no good in the mandarinate: he felt them to be the chief source of popular disaffection and corruption. By suppressing the office of kinh-luoc, Doumer gave still further impetus to direct administration in Tonkin. Since native justice still remained largely in their hands, he augmented the mandarins' salaries so as to counteract their inbred venality. Though he felt that the communal organization was theoretically undesirable, he was willing to retain it on the grounds of practical utility. By a further subdivision of provincial administration, Doumer hoped to restore to the civil service some of the powers it had recently lost to the military. An advisory committee, made up of a few hand-picked native Notables with a Resident Superior and his council, completed the new local set-up. Though still nominally a Protectorate, Tonkin was well launched on the way to direct administration.

Up to now, the French had been so absorbed by Tonkinese troubles that all they asked of Annam was to live in peace. The Protectorate was only a framework lightly imposed upon the existing organization, and its very inefficacy invited Doumer's reformatory attention. The Emperor Thanh Thai's coming of age was thought to be a propitious time to effect a change. The Regency Council was suppressed as well as many of its attributes. When French titles to property were recognized and the Emperor had renounced his rights over all unclaimed land, the way was opened for French colonization of Annam. The most important reform, however, was fiscal. Hitherto only the tariff and indirect taxes had been placed under the French: now in return for the annual payment of a fixed sum to the Hué treasury, France got complete financial control. Doumer was able to inaugurate a separate budget for Annam, which through more efficient methods of collection soon showed a gratifying increase.

Cambodia, like Annam, had been almost untouched, and the reforms which Doumer effected there showed a distinct parallelism. The Resident Superior presided over the Cambodian Council of Ministers. Khmer finances were taken over and a civil list given to the King. There was an important extension of French jurisdiction over the non-Cambodian Asiatics, and the legal abolition of serfdom and torture. The King protested at his declining juridical powers, but more so at the closing of his profitable gaming-houses. But there was none of the popular opposition in Cambodia at this time which had prevailed in the Annamite countries. What should have aroused royal resentment was the opening of the country to Annamite penetration. France had arrested their political expansion in Cambodia, but was favouring Annamite economic encroachment. With the local recognition of French land titles, as in Annam, the future of Cambodia's rubber plantations was assured and the control of the country's economy passed definitively into foreign hands.

In Cochin-China, little was done but to assert the power of the federal government and to curtail rampant regionalism. Administrative assimilation was running its course: functionaryism flourished, though not quite so lushly as of yore.

Laos offered a virgin field for Doumer's administrative experiments. In 1895, two years after its nominal occupation, Laos had been divided into two districts which corresponded to no geographic or economic reality. Moreover, the country was totally undeveloped, and Cochin-China, as usual, was called upon to subsidize the administrative expenses. In the final analysis, this country had administrators but no administration. It was rather vaguely hoped that the projected railroad system would eventually overcome Laos's geographical barriers and arouse the country from its economic lethargy.

Doumer's account of his work reveals, along with much self-satisfaction, a juggling of statistics that does not accurately reflect his achievements. In appraising Doumer, one must strike a balance between his own fatuousness and the violence of his detractors. Luck certainly favoured his work. Doumer's régime marked a period of profound peace coming after a prolonged struggle. The Chinese crisis of 1900 left Indo-China untouched, a tribute to the solidity of Doumer's work. A vital factor in his success were five successive years of good harvests, which in an Oriental country is the supreme proof of celestial approbation.

Doumer's greatest contribution was his freeing of the colony from Parisian supervision, by making it economically self-sufficient. He realized that Paris would be willing to sacrifice some of its sovereignty only provided it were assured that Indo-China would stand financially on its own feet. It had been Ferry's wish that the colony's Governor should have a mandate "to do and to dare," and Doumer was the first man to realize that ideal. Though the budget had still to be submitted to Paris for approval, this now became a mere formality. Doumer had permanently resolved the problem, and in 1911 even a further delegation of sovereignty to the Governor-General was made. A balanced budget and an active public works programme were a complete reversal of the former financial situation, and one that encouraged the development of commerce as well as the investments of capitalists. Doumer also extended French influence in the Far East, notably in the penetration of Yunnan. His strong federal framework checked Cochin-China's secessionist movement, and gave reality to what had hitherto been only a geographical expression. He had a vision of Indo-Chinese unity that is still in the process of realization, and the organization which he created has served as a model for other French colonies.

In the exercise of this new gubernatorial authority, practical difficulties were bound to arise. The power that had been wrested from the Métropole soon proved to be too great a burden for one man. A governor is naturally influenced by personal sympathies, and this too often made him clay in the hands of his friends. He was also the butt of his colleagues' attempts to acquire some of that independence from federal control which Doumer had won from the Métropole. The history of Indo-China's administration has been the struggle of the colony's executive for independence from Paris, and for control over his own subordinates. Doumer left too soon for this to become apparent: he could still play the autocrat and give orders through his bureaux in the Napoleonic manner. He used his personal authority to deprive the Minister of the Colonies of his attributes, and then to reduce the local Residents to simple agents. It was his successors who had trouble, less with Paris than with their unruly subordinates. A Governor-General was always between the upper and nether millstone: Paris, trying to regain the ground it had lost, and the local officials who used their distance and too loosely defined powers to have their own way. Far too much depended on the Governor's personality. If he were a strong man, he was apt to be despotic; if weak, it meant the reign of intrigue from top to bottom of the hierarchy.

The worst offenders, it soon became apparent, were the General Services. They did not satisfy even their creator, for they involved too real a parcelling out of sovereignty. So marked was their trend towards autonomy that they could not co-operate even long enough to get what they all wanted from the central government. The Director of Civil Affairs, for example, became a rival to the Governor-General, and his office had to be reduced, in 1902, to a minor secretaryship. Budgetary unity was a far better propagator of federalism. But it was only natural that such excessive centralization should provoke a reaction. By 1905, the trend towards decentralization was well under way. The local administration was to prove as successful in its contest with the Governor-General as the latter had been with the Métropole.

In his fiscal policy Doumer went too fast, and overburdened a poverty-ridden people. Pat projects were imprudently launched and every possible source of revenue forced to the limit. Taxes were increased without assuring their equitable assessment. Loans were raised for grandiose public works of doubtful utility, and then left uncompleted because too hastily conceived and too wastefully executed. Rigid formalism characterized the new organization. In a legitimate desire to break local selfishness, Doumer did not allow enough leeway for varying local needs. The new organization was arbitrary and the Union artificial: it meant a new reign of officialdom in an already over-administered colony. The state rode roughshod over the colonials' wishes, and there was no time to evolve a native policy—if such a thing was even thought of. Everything was subordinated to a flourishing budget: the success of colonization was appraised in terms of revenues.

Just as Doumer had been unusually lucky, so Beau was visited by three successive bad harvests and diminishing revenues with which to work out some of Doumer's unrealizable schemes. Resentment of fiscal injustice increased in Indo-China with the repercussions of the Japanese victory of 1905. For the first time under Beau there emerged clearly a native problem. The decline of the piastre was the final blow. To offset the disasters, Beau had only one solution to offer—the moral conquest of Indo-China by education and by medical service.

Beau's nomination was typical of Paris's concern for its colony. He was quite without colonial experience, and what interests he had were centred in China and Siam. Political motives played the primary role, for Indo-China was a plum for political merit or for dangerous Parliamentary ability. The frequent gubernatorial changes—and every new Governor brought his own satellites—made the pursuit of a regular policy impossible. Primarily it unsettled the natives, who could get used to anything provided it did not mean constant change. The only uniformity shown by Governors was their short tenure of office.

Beau bore the full brunt of the antagonism which Doumer's policy had aroused in the local services. Many of these men felt that their long years of service had entitled them to the highest position. So, out of jealousy, they presented the paralysing force of inertia to any changes inaugurated by the new Governor-General. Inevitably they won, for they were permanent and their opponent transient. The Federal Services loafed in non-splendid isolation. What contacts they had among themselves and with the central government were bellicose. They were particularly recalcitrant at any kind of financial control. The lesser functionaries, too many in number and too poor in quality, made little effort to learn the Annamite language and so dispense with the interpreters' noxious aid. The latter exploited their compatriots and misled French officials. Too often were their dubious services rewarded by a mandarin's brevet. Not only was this new native officialdom hated by the Scholars whom it had displaced, but despised by the masses who had been taught to reverence this office. Sometimes the people even selected a mandarin whom they were willing to obey, although he was without the legal investiture.

Beau's most original contribution was his native policy. He restored respect for native institutions, and to the mandarinate some of the attributes which had disappeared through the encroachments of direct administration. More government places were opened to the native intelligentsia, to win their co-operation. Beau also created provincial councils, and the first advisory chamber in Tonkin. His was the first definite attempt to prepare Annamites for participation in the government of their own country.

By developing secondary education and by organizing the medical service, Beau gave to his native policy a wider if indirect range. Promising students were sent to France or to the new ill-fated University at Hanoi. Councils for perfecting native education were founded in the different countries and placed under a federal board. Though the work of these councils was almost immediately eclipsed, the wisdom of their advice became apparent in the post-War period. The new medical services penetrated to the masses, just as the new educational opportunities won over the intelligentsia.

Beau's policy marked a turning point in Indo-China's administration, away from the conquest and towards native co-operation. The contemporary situation in the Far East made it apparent that the colony could never be defended against its rapacious neighbours unless the Annamites themselves assisted in its defence. And their co-operation could only be insured by a policy of mutual benefits. Though it is to Beau's credit that he actively appreciated the situation, his excellent intentions and industry were neutralized by the Russo-Japanese War, and by the obstinate abstention of his so-called collaborators. He also recoiled from attacking the monopolies and left the economic situation untouched generally—tasks which were taken up with gusto by his successor, Klobukowsky.

Like Beau, Klobukowsky suffered, and even more intensively, from a situation that was not of his making. He had to struggle with an increasing deficit, with native discontent, and with an autonomy in both the federal and local services. Again, like Beau, he was the opening wedge in a policy of which his successors were to reap the benefits, and without having to encounter the same obstacles. The violence of Klobukowsky's opponents conclusively proved the importance of the interests he attacked and the quality of his personal courage.

The lack of contact between French and Annamites permitted the former to live for long in blissful ignorance of the resentment which their conquest had inspired in the latter. Nascent Annamite nationalism was fanned into life by the Japanese victory of 1905. Three hostile manifestations, which antedated Klobukowsky's arrival, convinced the French that their protégés were no longer perennial minors.

Emperor Thanh Thai's sacrosanct character had not been safeguarded by his Protectors. He had become a tourist exhibit. He was forced to invite to his table guests selected by the Resident, without any regard for his feelings. Many puerile and grotesque incidents were the result of this violation of the traditions and rites. The Emperor's personality, always enigmatic and curious, became with time increasingly a prey to sadistic insanity. Unpleasant rumours circulated in Hué about the martyrdoms suffered by the ladies of his Court. Although unverifiable, they were thought to be sufficient ground for invading the sanctity of the palace. The French Resident forced through the Emperor's abdication in 1907, and Thanh Thai went to join the growing group of Annamite Emperors-in-exile. The Annamites were incensed at the French treating their Emperor first like a puppet and then like a child, and they claimed that he had been poisoned. Nor were their feelings soothed to learn of a stupid rifling of the imperial tombs, on the absurd charge that they contained firearms and hidden treasure. Such incidents aggravated their irritation and despair, already aroused by fiscal vexations, and resulted in the march of the *Cheveux Coupés*. This march, in the beginning, was an unarmed protest which soon became violent and was as brutally suppressed. The colonial government, fearing Parisian reaction, withheld the murderous statistics and claimed that the natives were protesting against mandarinal abuses and not against the French administration.

In Tonkin, the trend towards direct administration created friction between the traditional mandarinate and the juxtaposed French administration, which was steadily sapping their powers and complacently usurping their prestige. The mandarinate continued its pointless existence because the French administrators were too ignorant of the country and too inaccessible to the people to replace them effectively. Even the luxury of venality was no longer theirs but the interpreters', whose corrupt exploitation of their fellow countrymen went unchecked because they were indispensable to the unilingual administrators.

The decline of the ignored and underpaid mandarinate was most clearly seen in the law courts. Natives were encouraged to appeal directly to the Residents, without passing through the local native courts. Because the French magistrates were overworked and ignorant of native law, cases dragged on interminably, at great expense and to no equitable verdict. Tax collections and the military draft were also now handled by the French through responsible Notables, and this completed the undermining of that remarkable instrument of local government—the Annamite commune. The mandarins gave up the struggle and, in good Oriental fashion, played their trump card—

inertia. Anarchy reigned in the provinces, which were soon, and for a second time, to be devastated by the rebirth of banditry. The new administration, obviously riding for a fall, presented a curious political triangle: the Residents had the physical force, the mandarins the moral authority, and the interpreters the people's money. Moreover, troops had been rushed from Tonkin to Cap St. Jacques in an alarmist fright of Japan, leaving the North quite exposed to the tender services of banditry.

The situation in Cochin-China differed appreciably from that of the other Annamite countries. This fertile colony had been only recently an Annamite acquisition, and the mandarins had fled at the approach of the French, so there was no traditional administration and no class of discontented Scholars, no deeply rooted institutions, and no over-population. Direct administration there encountered no serious obstacle in completing the political and spiritual isolation of the Cochin-Chinese from their fellow Annamites. The French imprint was already deep-cut. But even in Cochin-China the situation was not without flaw. To begin with, there were entrenched the Chinese and their secret societies. Contacts between Annamites and French were confined to servants and prostitutes, neither of whom was the glowing personification of Annamite virtues. Certain natives were naturalized, but the number was strictly limited and the French unwilling to give naturalization its fullest political or social significance. Even the best of Annamites, it was clear, were to remain permanently subordinates.

Other causes of discontent, common to all the Union, could be traced to fiscal oppression. The miscarriage of justice was perhaps worst of all in Cochin-China because there were no native magistrates and they were not judged according to native law. Hindu judges from French India were resented by the Annamites as inferior to their own race and mandarins. Despite the swelling revenues, little was being done to improve the economic output of the country. Only a few railways had been constructed, some canals dredged, and the port of Saigon mildly improved. The country's income was swallowed wholly by the functionaries, yet the colony seemed prosperous because of the propitious climate, soil, and meagre population.

Klobukowsky's departure from France was hastened by news of the smouldering revolt in Indo-China. His first act, upon arrival, was to dissolve the Criminal Commission which the hysteria of the Hanoi French had instituted, as an extra-legal method of dealing with the rebels. When they had learned that an attempt had been made to

THE FRENCH ADMINISTRATION OF INDO-CHINA

poison the Hanoi garrison, the French civilians of that town had stormed the Governor-General, demanding severe measures of repression. A plot was simultaneously discovered in Cochin-China— Gilbert Chieu's—and an outbreak in Upper Tonkin, which were all linked to the main insurrectional movement. One good result of the repression was the final liquidation of Tonkinese banditry.

Klobukowsky's reforms showed an appreciation of the real roots of native discontent. He rightly believed that the monopolies had done more harm to the colony, in spite of their budgetary importance, than the costliest of wars. No immediate change was possible, however, since the colony was bound by a long-term contract, but Klobukowsky's campaign in the Métropole led directly to the reform of 1912. Although it was he who dealt the decisive blow, the fact that the monopolies did not at once melt away left the Annamites feeling very disillusioned. Their hopes had been falsely aroused once before when a faulty translation of Klobukowsky's first speech had made them think that all taxes were to be abolished. The truth not only disappointed the Annamites but made them thereafter distrustful of all French reforms. People attacked the agents of the Douane when they came to the villages, believing that their exactions were no longer legitimate. Klobukowsky, however, did succeed in mitigating some of the worst features of the monopolies. He suppressed the collective responsibility of the Notables in matters of contraband, and enforced a better control over agents.

The achievement of administrative decentralization was Klobu-kowsky's particular mission. The obstreperous General Services were to be drawn into hierarchic line. A decree was not sufficient to effect this change, for the trouble was too deeply rooted in the whole bureaucratic system. Klobukowsky's method was to encourage the Civil Services at the expense of the technicians, but after two years he was distressed to find that he had eliminated only two of the most inoffensive services—those of agriculture and education. Restoring the importance of the communes was another of his steps towards decentralization. Their old revenues from markets and ferries were given back to them, and a more careful regulation made for requisitioned labour.

In education, public works, and the judicial organization, Klobu-kowsky followed in Beau's footsteps, as far as his budget permitted. If his work was more courageous than effective, he was the first to attack seriously the evils which Doumer had allowed to take root in the colony. He was defeated by the powerful Monopolies Lobby in

Paris, and also by the functionaries in Indo-China who had been antagonized by his high-handed methods.

The popularity of his successor, Albert Sarraut, was largely due to Klobukowsky's able paving of the way. In the colonial budget report, the Métropole showed itself not a little discouraged, and somewhat half-heartedly despatched Sarraut to effect the decentralization attempted by his predecessor, to modify the legislative situation, and to pursue a policy of association and no longer one of assimilation.

In attacking the General Services, Sarraut lightened the budgetary strain by economizing on the personnel. For years it had been said that there was a plethora of functionaries in the colony whose salaries devoured the budget. They were too numerous for what they did accomplish, and too few for what they should do. Misery was the lot of most of them, especially since the decline of the piastre: 1905 had seen the last rise in salaries. The services they performed could have been done as well and more cheaply by natives. This white proletariat, in addition to its own discomfort, was the object of native scorn and a detriment to French prestige. Not only were natives now to be admitted to the first administrative rung, but the total number of offices cut, indemnities pared down, the retiring age advanced, and a general pruning effected all along the line. Functionaries had hitherto enjoyed a six months' leave of absence at the end of three years' service, with free passage home for themselves and their families, numerous sick-leaves, and additional travelling expenses. Already much had been done to improve their health by hospitals, city sanitation, and expensive mountain resorts. The rapid turnover in officialdom thus produced was extravagant, disastrous both to a fixed policy and to the budget. Sarraut's ideal was the British Civil Service—fewer officials better trained and better paid. Greater unity of policy and of action must be got by a strict budgeting of expenditures and by a discipline enforced throughout the hierarchy.

Insufficient and non-uniform training was the cause of many of these functionary defects. The closing of the Admirals' admirable training school at Saigon had been followed, in 1897, by the suppression of a serious civil service examination. Certain candidates, especially the military, were let in without the proper qualifications and placed on the same footing as the rest. Sarraut restored this examination because it required a needed background of general culture. The praiseworthy aim of the Colonial School, founded in 1889, had been to replace chance-made officials by men professionally trained. But on the occasion of the School's twentieth anniversary it was the object of violent criticism. Opponents claimed that its Director and teaching staff had never been nearer to Indo-China or Africa than their offices in the Colonial Ministry. Students fenced, swam, and rode horseback, as preparation for a career from which they could not be ejected even if they proved to be incompetent. Once in the colonies, these graduates formed a clique which scorned and was scorned by officials who had risen from the ranks, to the general detriment of the colony which they had been sent to serve. No one wanted the School to disappear, but only to mend its ways, which at the time seemed to be the last of its desires.

Competence in native languages was a most serious void in functionary training, even at the Colonial School. Beau and Klobukowsky had frequently denounced this defect, but not until it was voiced in the budget reports of Messimy and Violette did this criticism percolate into Metropolitan consciousness. The first Frenchman in the country had encountered almost insurmountable obstacles in learning the language without the aid of dictionaries, lexicons, and interpreters. The natives could say what could be pointed to, but did not grasp or indicate abstract ideas. Missionaries were the pioneers in this field, and their accomplishment showed what perseverance could do. The first governors realized how important were the contacts between races and the importance of language in this regard. But it was part of the assimilationist creed that it was easier for some millions of natives to learn French than for a few thousand Frenchmen to learn Annamite. Since the school system was unable to afford the native masses a chance to learn French, inducements were offered to functionaries to make some linguistic efforts themselves. This was quite ineffective, for the premiums were not large, and Annamite is one of the world's most difficult languages. Graduates of the Colonial School had been trained in the rudiments of Annamite, but practice was lacking. Those who studied Annamite might be assigned to Cambodia, or given office work that only required them to speak French, so the reward of such effort was negligible. Nor did magistrates who rotated from one colony to another, often at two-year intervals, find it worth their while to try dispensing with an interpreter's services. The trend towards decentralization threw an emphasis on provincial office-holding, which gave renewed life to the whole language problem. Saurraut's sincere efforts to stiffen the language requirements, for entry and promotion in the administration, were nullified by his colleagues' co-operation to disobey. His 1912 decree raised a storm of protest followed by an ominous silence. The friendship of an influential man was a very good substitute for struggling with Annamite syntax. From 1904 to 1909, Hanoi had only two magistrates who could speak the native language. This vital problem was not again seriously attacked until 1928.

After administrative decentralization, Sarraut's next most important reform was that of the judicial service. He insisted upon uniform justice throughout the Union, where there were as many variations as there were administrators. Justice ranged from applying the French civil and penal codes almost unmitigated in Cochin-China, through a mixture of French and Annamite law in Annam and Cambodia. Corresponding to this penetration of French justice was the degree to which the French ideal of the separation of powers had been effective in the different countries. Tonkin, as ever, represented middle ground which evolved more slowly and with slight modifications towards the status of Cochin-China. Specifically, Sarraut's reforms, besides that of legal procedure, were a revision of the codes with increased guarantees of native justice, the abolition of torture and corporal punishment in both Annam and Cambodia, with various minor rulings to control more strictly the Chinese secret societies, vagabondage, and the traffic in women and children.

Through his native policy, Sarraut became the successor to Bert, De Lanessan, and Beau, and was the first Governor-General to win native devotion. He spontaneously liked the Annamites, and was in turn beloved by them, for he represented to the intelligentsia all the liberalism of French republican ideals. Time was to show that Sarraut permitted himself to be carried away by his own eloquence, and to promise more than he could possibly fulfil. Yet his first governorship remains green in Annamite memory as that of the most popular man France ever sent to the colony.

Sarraut's first step was to raise the standard of native living through a new impetus to public works—also in education and medical service—and by higher salaries for native officials. Public works, though still too prone to develop the means of communication, were to be more closely allied to the natives' welfare. Education got a much larger slice of the colony's revenues. Like his predecessors, Sarraut could not resist the temptation to reorganize, but he did the work to good effect. A Normal School for bonzes was built at Pnom-Penh, and a badly needed pedagogical training was instituted for the Annamite countries. School curricula gave more place to the traditional culture, especially

Confucianist morality. Sarraut strengthened the link between education and administrative positions in native eyes by opening more posts to qualified Annamites. He also furthered the specialization of mandarinal functions. Native representation was reorganized along the lines Beau had projected. Countries which had no advisory Chambers were so endowed, and their attributes slightly enlarged. In Annam, provincial Councils were instituted. Tonkin's electorate was increased so as to be more representative of the people as a whole, and less of the administration.

New impetus was given to the work of the Medical Service. A network of hospitals and clinics, especially in the rural districts, crusaded against the epidemics which periodically devastated the country. Like the educational system, the Medical Service was understaffed, so Sarraut enlarged the Hanoi School of Medicine. His pioneer work consisted of building leper and insane asylums, and in improving city sanitation. Saigon itself had long suffered from a defective water supply. By 1913 there were 175 medical establishments in the colony, as against 69 in 1904.

Sarraut was studying reforms in land and labour laws, when a severe illness forced his return to France in 1914. His two-year governorship had marked a turning-point in Indo-Chinese history, notably in native policy. What his predecessors had only envisaged, Sarraut had succeeded in carrying out: he had been effective where they had been merely projective. The courage of his convictions was most clearly shown when he persevered in a liberal native policy even after the seditious manifestations of 1913. The most serious of these outbreaks occurred in Hanoi, where bombs thrown in a café killed two French officers, who happened to be, ironically enough, strongly pro-native. Though there had been sharp discontent at the renewal of the alcohol monopoly—albeit in a modified form—Sarraut was on the whole accurate in diagnosing it as an isolated instance, for which the cure was a native policy of more rather than less liberality.

During the War, Indo-China had three interim Governors, of none too brilliant a calibre. The first, Van Vollenhoven, was a victim to local press attacks, and felt compelled to return to France to vindicate his patriotism by being killed at the Front. His successor, Roume, was too ill to undertake the task effectively, and his place was assumed by Charles, who remained until he was replaced by Sarraut in 1917. In general, these three men pursued Sarraut's policy, as well as they could, but the War drained them of the men and money necessary for any real accomplishment. As was natural, the Métropole neglected Indo-China: the only resources at its disposal came from within the colony itself.

Very little news filtered through to France from Indo-China during the War. This silence was taken, somewhat erroneously, to indicate complete tranquillity, in spite of dark hints about German machinations in Siam and Yunnan. Two major incidents marked the War, but they were confined to the Protectorates where the forces of reaction were always strongest. In Annam occurred the tragi-comic plot of the child Emperor, Duy-Than, who was used by the Annamite nationalists to head their revolt. The conspiracy had a semi-religious coating: amulets, mystic initiations, and the usual blood oath. The French police knew of the plot's progress and what night had been set for the Emperor's flight. He was arrested two days later, for it became at once apparent that there would be no general uprising. The Emperor showed remarkable dignity, even when he was being scolded like a naughty child, and he was sent to join his father and brother in exile lest he serve as a focal point for future conspiracy. The 1917 revolt at Thai-Nguyen can hardly be considered a War manifestation, as it was directed against an individual Resident. In the Annamite countries the most important reaction was against forced recruiting.

By 1915, France decided to call on her colonies for aid, and about 140,000 Annamite soldiers and labourers were sent to Europe. Insufficient care was taken to control unscrupulous agents, who used terrorism to get the commission they received per recruit. Money subscriptions were subject to the same extortionate methods. Since these evils were after all temporary, and were offset by a general economic prosperity, far more important were the psychological effects of the War on Indo-China. Not only was the belief in European superiority given a shattering blow, but the liberal promises made in wartime emotionalism aroused ambitions which the disillusionments of the post-War period did not wholly obliterate. Minor rewards, like increased naturalization facilities and land concessions to veterans, left the heart of the problem untouched. Sarraut's name, however, was still magic, and when he returned in 1917 he kept peace in a country of 20,000,000 Asiatics with a French force of 2,000 men. For the first time in a public discourse, on April 27, 1919, Sarraut discussed the problem of Annamite emancipation, and envisaged the possibility of a colonial charter under French sovereignty. Cynics refer to Sarraut's governorship as the era of discourses, and it is true that both he and the Annamites were genuinely moved by his meridional eloquence. Despite certain accomplishments in the labour and educational fields, Sarraut sailed away, and little was ever heard thereafter of those liberal projects, even after he had become Minister of the Colonies. Like the Girondists, he was the first to recoil before the excesses of a nationalism which he had stimulated. As a result, both Annamite deception and nationalism grew apace.

Maurice Long came to Indo-China in 1920, qualified by a long Parliamentary career and a special knowledge of Morocco. The problems which he had to meet were mainly political and financial. A rise in the cost of living and the decline in the franc were creating budgetary trouble in Indo-China. This necessitated a readjustment of functionaries' salaries, involving bank operations for which Long was severely criticized both in the colony and in Paris. His greatest success was the raising of a loan for the first time within the colony itself—the vindication of Indo-China's claim to economic self-sufficiency. The growing prosperity of the War years, and the isolation which the War had forced on Indo-China, created a psychology of complacency and a separatist movement on the part of colonials as well as the natives.

Long was the last Governor-General to experience a period of political peace. None of the sporadic conspiracies that had characterized the pre-War years, and which were to flourish in the next decade, troubled his term of office. The importance of the Far East, as heralded by the Washington Conference of 1922, was already making the French appreciate their "balcony on the Pacific." The Marseille Exposition of 1922 reaffirmed in French minds the War lesson of the colonies' importance as sources of supplies and man power. When the Emperor Khai Dinh left his son in France to be educated, it was a public consecration of Annamite loyalty in Metropolitan eyes.

Like all his predecessors, Long reorganized the administration. His native policy had deceptive earmarks of liberalism, but he did not resolve the problem of native officialdom which Sarraut himself had merely brought to the fore. By creating what was termed *cadres latéraux* Annamites were admitted to offices parallel to the French bureaux in qualifications and in work, but not in salaries and promotion. This compromise was only a stop-gap that failed to satisfy native ambitions, and it was also an unnecessary and expensive duplication of office.

More successful were his reforms of native representation—another of the projects inherited from Sarraut. In Cochin-China, native political aspirations, as well as the general standard of living, had evolved more than in other Annamite countries, so a solution to native representation was the most pressing problem. The native electorate—one Notable from each village out of a population of four millions—was conservative and hand-picked by the administration. The French electorate, numbering ten thousand and in great majority functionaries, was numerically inferior to the natives and far more transient in the colony. Long was willing to enlarge the electorate, but not the attributes of the council, except in matters of optional advice. Here the French majority was still maintained, but not in such overwhelming proportion. The communal and provincial councils had long been criticized for their unrepresentative quality and for their excessive docility to the government. Long tried to increase their vitality by giving them budgets of their own, as part of a general decentralization policy. He realized that the whole representative system was outworn, so he widened the electorate but not the powers of these assemblies.

In Annam, representative government had been tried out, but none too successfully, in 1913. The country was so unprepared for such a Western institution that it was thought best to give a preliminary training in social and economic problems to the mandarins, who could later instruct their people. The usual advice on budgetary questions and prohibition of political discussion characterized these meetings. Long, seven years after their inauguration, decided that the time was now ripe to experiment with a representative chamber for the whole of Annam, analogous to those in the other Annamite countries.

In Tonkin, Long's régime was marked by restoring power to the communes, and by a prolongation of the codes whose revision had been begun by Sarraut. Similar work was under way for Laos, both in endowing that country with a revised code and by instituting provincial assemblies, so that now the most backward country in the Union was drawn into line with the others. In Cambodia, a reform of the administration, begun in 1919, was completed by a total separation of the administrative and judicial powers.

Long's work, in general, was but the fulfilment of Sarraut's programme, especially in the matter of decentralization. It is curious that he went to such lengths in revising the local administration and in endowing it with financial autonomy when he did nothing to improve the archaic machinery of the central government. In the financial field, Long made his most important contribution. His loan marked officially Indo-China's economic coming of age.

Martial Merlin, Long's successor, was thought to be qualified for any colonial post simply because he had been a successful Governor of West Africa. Unfortunately, experience proved him unsuited to Indo-China. He continued Long's revision of the local administration, by giving more powers and a wider representation to the *Conseil de Gouvernement*. Financial decentralization reached its nadir under Merlin. The federal budget ceased to devote itself to works of general interest, so as to become the subsidizer of the local budgets, which were constantly in arrears. In a period of obviously increasing prosperity, Indo-China presented the curious spectacle of state finances in ever-increasing distress. The growing importance of Indo-China in the Far East was shown by a tour made by Merlin in the neighbouring countries. At a banquet given for him in Canton, a bomb which was thrown for his special destruction by an Annamite nationalist succeeded in demolishing five of his compatriots. The financial deficit, as well as this evidence of Merlin's unpopularity, were the causes of his recall in 1925.

A Socialist deputy, Alexandre Varenne, in spite of colonial inexperience, was thought to be a happy successor to Merlin because of his liberal opinions and financial *expertise*. He succeeded admirably in pulling the colony out of its fiscal morass. The general budget was fed by economies and new taxes, though a projected assessment on income was howled down by Cochin-China. The reserve fund was filled once again and the local budgets forced to stand on their own feet. This policy, amounting virtually to financial centralization, was reversed when applied to the federal government, where Varenne continued the work of decentralization. He strove further to revitalize the commune and took up the crusade against Paris's encroachments on the Governor-General's independence of action. It was in the field of native policy, however, that Varenne's work was outstanding. Like Sarraut, his sincere desire to ameliorate native conditions won him great popularity.

The problem of native admission to government office was faced courageously by Varenne, by contrast with Long, who had really avoided the issue. Although a financial distinction was maintained, because of the essential difference in standards of living, Varenne cut the Gordian knot when he suppressed obligatory naturalization for natives. Henceforth they could qualify for administrative jobs on an equal footing with the French. Naturally French functionaries were alarmed by this increasing parity. No one could seriously cast doubts on the Annamites' intellectual attainments, but with far more justice their professional integrity and disinterestedness could be challenged. Although Varenne took steps to improve French functionaries' salaries, he could not appease their wrath, particularly when he did likewise for the mandarinate. Although his measures improved the status of native officials, they did not entirely satisfy their ambitions, for the highest offices were still closed to them. But the improvement was sufficient to assure Indo-China three more years of peace.

A liberal policy, that both enlarged mass education and improved the secondary schools, suffered somewhat from being a compromise. It was too radical for the colonials, and not generous enough for the native intelligentsia, who expressed their thwarted ambitions in a series of school strikes. One of Varenne's best measures was the organization of agricultural credit in a commendable effort to extract peasant farmers from the usurers' leech-like grip. With the introduction of Varenne's measures to insure the protection of workers, labour legislation was born in Indo-China, along with a revelation of the terrible conditions on many of the new-born plantations. Legal protection of Eurasians and the abolition of debt imprisonment for natives were other of Varenne's good works.

Naturally such a radical policy aroused a storm of opposition both in Paris and Indo-China. A speech which Varenne had made before sailing to the colony had already aroused Metropolitan fears. But when a few months later he was so imprudent as to speak publicly of the eventual independence of Indo-China, he unleashed an attack of unprecedented violence. The interests he had undermined were so important that his recall was only a question of time and of opportunity. This came, in March 1927, with a Parliamentary debate over land concessions in which Varenne was indirectly involved.

The nomination of Pierre Pasquier marks a turning-point in Paris's relations with Indo-China. For the first time not a politician but a functionary, whose thirty years of service had been spent in the colony, was appointed to be its chief executive. Pasquier's profound knowledge of the Annamite countries was shown by his book, *L'Annam d'Autrefois*, whose scholarship Annamites themselves could admire. Even Pasquier's personality bore the imprint of his years of association with the natives. Parisian indecision or negligence had made the colony wait ten full months for this nomination, and the sigh of relief that went up from French and natives alike indicated pleasure at terminating a paralysing uncertainty, and was a tribute to Pasquier himself.

A bad economic and psychological situation greeted Pasquier upon

94

assuming the reins of office. The low price of rice and the sensational drop in rubber—both antedating the depression—as well as fluctuations in the exchange, were vital factors creating suspense and uncertainty. Varenne's recall had been exploited by the colonial bloc as a victory over the pro-native party, and this feeling was to show itself in a recalcitrant resistance to any strong measure the new Governor might try to impose. Pasquier had been Varenne's chief collaborator, and many of the projects he sponsored had been initiated or conceived by his predecessor. This applied to a wide range of measures, including agricultural credit, labour legislation, the public works programme, his educational policy, and a strengthening of the provincial administration. The decentralization of local government was paralleled by a renewed autonomous movement away from Paris's interference. In ousting Varenne, his enemies had brought upon themselves intervention from a Parliament that only too accurately reflected the average Frenchman's indifference to and ignorance of colonial affairs. The rigours of the tariff of 1928, though it gave more place to Indo-China's special needs, was supplemented by the depression, and by a renewal of inter-colonial solidarity within the empire. Stabilizing the piastre by linking it to the franc further strengthened the ties between France and Indo-China. Circumstances beyond Pasquier's control, in these ways, countered his efforts to give to the colony more autonomy.

Among the thorny problems, which Pasquier had inherited from Varenne, was the rivalry between French and native functionaries. To offset the improved status of French officialdom, Pasquier raised the salaries of native functionaries and opened to them more widely the administration's doors. Such a policy put a sudden stop to inter-functionary quarrels: all the French now banded together to oppose their native competitors. But indignation against Pasquier was to know no bounds when he cut all functionaries' salaries in order to balance the depression-struck budget. Habit was too strong for the colonials, and they again called in the Métropole to bring pressure to bear upon their obstinate Governor. Very cleverly Pasquier replied that he would be glad to restore the salary cuts provided that Paris would underwrite his deficit. Pasquier had already added insult to injury by enforcing strict language requirements on French functionaries. In seventy years of colonization the functionaries had foiled the efforts of thirty Governors in this matter. It took an ex-functionary like Pasquier to put an end to the farce of an examination in which the ignorance of the candidate was only matched by the jury's indulgence. Pasquier did show himself lenient to those long in harness, and was strict only in requirements for newcomers. His efforts to diminish the number and to improve the quality of French officialdom bore fruit, but in the process Pasquier was treated like a traitor who had risen from the ranks only to turn and rend his former colleagues.

If, like Varenne, Pasquier took steps towards administrative decentralization, he also reversed this policy in the economic domain. From the ashes of the *Conseil de Gouvernement* sprang the *Grand Conseil des Interêts Economiques et Financiers*, an embodiment of the federalist principle. Such a project had long been brewing, but Pasquier first gave it life in 1929. It was to represent the colony as a whole and not just the bureaucracy. The essential differences between the various countries still required local media for expression, so the provincial assemblies and their budgets were retained. Though the *Grand Conseil's* function was advisory and only in the economic sphere, it represented the taxpayers as never before, and its advice was obligatory on certain matters. Opponents of the idea claimed that not fifty persons could be found in Indo-China capable of discussing the budget, but this was amply disproved by its first session. The Cochin-Chinese delegates, with their longer political experience, and a self-confidence born of their country's wealth, distinguished themselves from the outset. There was the usual incoherence in discussion, and the customary over-docility to government projects, which were railroaded through without healthy opposition. After 1931, a reform brought about by the Yenbay massacres removed the old numerical inequality between French and native representatives. Although still embryonic, the *Grand Conseil* promises well as a training ground in political education that may eventually be formed into the Parliament of Indo-China.

With the aid of the *Grand Conseil*, Pasquier was able to break the alcohol monopoly, which had been ingloriously immune to attack since the beginning of the century. A less successful modification of the salt and opium *régies* followed. Budgetary revenues, always delicate to tamper with, were rendered especially vulnerable by the depression, and by the sums needed for aid to planters. The trail, however, was blazed.

In Annam, a reform of singular significance was achieved by the Paris-educated Emperor Bao-Dai. Upon his return to Indo-China, in 1932–33, he took the initiative in cutting adrift from conservatism without forfeiting at the same time popular affection. A thoroughgoing purging of his Cabinet was followed by a reform to complete the separation of powers. Modernized legislation and an educational programme were likewise drafted. The 1925 Agreement, whereby Annam seemed to be moving towards direct administration, was thus given a different orientation. This arrangement, because of the outcry, had been immediately and officially announced as temporary. The Protectorate pleaded solely a desire to cut short the palace intrigues which were inevitable during any imperial minority. Nevertheless, it had left the Emperor with only the macabre privilege of promoting and demoting the dead. Bao-Dai, however, showed himself more concerned with the living, and his reforms have succeeded, in spite of the opposition of traditionalists, in forcing Annam faster along the road to Westernization.

The depression and native revolts had already forced Pasquier to swerve somewhat from his goal, and an aeroplane accident in the early months of 1934 brusquely cut short his remarkable accomplishments. Headstrong functionaries and smouldering native discontent required a strong man to be Pasquier's successor. He was found in the person of René Robin, also a functionary of long standing in the colony. His record as Resident Superior of Tonkin had shown great energy. He had promulgated a new civil code, pushed through a network of dykes, and actively suppressed the native uprisings. Whereas Pasquier's policy was characterized by *souplesse*, Robin's was marked by a taste for authority and action. Though his encouragement of the Legionaries' brutality at Vinh is an ineradicable blot in native eyes, Robin can point to the security and peace which Indo-China has since enjoyed as the best justification of his methods. In his official speeches, Robin reiterates his taste for clemency and the humanity of his native policy, yet his critics still keep green the memory of his share in the massacres in Annam.

The apparent swiftness with which the depression has lifted under Robin's magic touch is either miraculous or a tribute to his sagacity. But one must also add that if Indo-China has been able to survive the depression with flying colours it is due not only to her Governors-General, but also to M. Diethelm, the colony's financial director from 1928 to 1934. He heroically brought down the general budget from 108,000,000 to 55,000,000 piastres. Recognizing the vital necessity of exportations, Robin has fought to keep the French market open to Indo-Chinese rice, and to make commercial treaties with Far Eastern neighbours. Draconian measures of economy have succeeded in balancing the budget without devaluating the piastre, and Robin has even silenced the functionary group. Long-term credit and lowered interest on debts have relieved the agricultural crisis. The completion of Doumer's old railway programme may help the labour situation, and also finally give Laos an outlet. This achievement symbolizes the realization of the Indo-Chinese Union, and gives an iron framework to what had been since 1900 only a paper ideal.

In August 1936, Jules Brévié was appointed Governor-General of Indo-China. He is the fourth West African administrator to fill that post. This selection seems to deny the change of policy inherent in Pasquier's and Robin's elevation to power. The Métropole has preferred to ignore the several capable functionaries trained in the Indo-Chinese service in order to reassert the principle of unity in high colonial administration throughout the French Empire. Above a certain official level, specialization is not deemed essential, for fundamental French principles—so the theory runs—can be applied as well by an able administrator to one colony as to another. It is also rumoured, un-pleasantly, that Brévié's African post was coveted by another official whose suit won favour in the eyes of the government.

Brévié's utterances, on the eve of departure for Indo-China, empha-sized above everything else the human side of native policy. His swift promulgation of the labour code, which had so long hung fire, gives fair promise of such action. There is, among the reactions of some functionaries in the colony, fresh evidence of the perennial jealousy of that body of officialdom for "outside" aid. M. Brévié's importation of some of his African associates has given rise to criticism and nervous hostility in the colony.

INDO-CHINA'S FOREIGN POLICY

Prior to the French conquest, Annam had a clearly defined foreign policy: the destruction of weak neighbouring states, like the Cham's and Khmer's, and isolation from distant peoples of superior force, like China and France. The Emperors of Annam had an accurate appre-ciation of the role of missionaries and merchants as heralds of im-perialism.

The expedition against Annam in 1859 was undertaken jointly by Spain and France until the latter conquered Cochin-China. Then the Admirals insisted upon Napoleon III's forcing Spain's withdrawal from the enterprise—a concession that Spain long resented, and which marked the birth of Indo-China as a diplomatic personality.

THE FRENCH ADMINISTRATION OF INDO-CHINA

France's interest in the Far East, like her whole colonial policy, was made up of contradictions. A sentimental role as protector of foreign missions, particularly in China, was inherited from the Empire by the anti-clerical Third Republic, at the same time as an aggressive determination to share in England's trade profits and possessions there. France's situation in Europe, as well as her educational background, made for an indifference to Far Eastern affairs. The exotic tradition, however, had long looked upon the Orient as a continent filled with laborious peoples and great resources that offered remedies for all Europe's social ills. The surprising conquest of Saigon permitted many of these latent dreams to be fulfilled. Saigon would become a great port that would not only shelter the fleet in time of distress, but radiate French cultural and religious influence throughout the Far East. A fevered searching for a back door to China placed new importance on their acquisition and a new bitterness into Anglo-French rivalry.

England

England's alliance with Japan, and her activity in Siam and Burma, were all causes for alarm. She had long been seeking a trade route between India and Burma so as to cut down the distance between Shanghai and European markets. Moreover, Russia's intrigues and expansion in Asia caused great uneasiness. Three routes were possible: of these Assam seemed the most likely, but explorations soon proved the obstacles to be insurmountable. Another road lay between Rangoon and Yunnan through Szemao, but the extent and unhealthiness of those regions and the natural drawbacks offset the lack of political complications that such a route would encounter. This road was carefully studied in 1866, but abandoned because public interest had been aroused in favour of the Bhamo road to Taly. In 1868 exploration was started from both ends, but the murder of one member of the party, as well as the current Moslem revolt in Yunnan, led to the virtual abandonment of this idea. Although natural obstacles and local warfare were responsible for giving France a free hand in the Tonkin route, nevertheless relations with England remained strained for a number of years. About thirty years ago, Indo-China welcomed to Saigon a Burmese prince who sought the throne of his country, then under English control, and the English returned the compliment by harbouring at Singapore Prince Iukanthor, the recalcitrant heir to the Cambodian throne. It was the fear that England would acquire the Hongay coal mines that determined the vacillating French government on the Rivière expedition. Then it was England's backing of Siam in Laos, and of her claims in the Shan States, that brought the next wave of tension. Until the guaranty of Siamese independence, in 1896, and the *Entente Cordiale* of 1906, England was to France the arch-fiend of the Far East, just as France was England's great rival in South China and Siam. Books of this period[1] reflected the current nervousness. Since the World War, and particularly since the growth of Chinese Communism, relations between England and France in the Far East have been cordial and co-operative.

Germany

In 1890, many Frenchmen saw in the conquest of Tonkin only another of Bismarck's clever moves to divert French energies into colonizing channels and away from the Rhine, where he was plotting some nefarious scheme. The very absence of German monkey-wrenches in the way of French Far Eastern expansion seemed to them in itself suspicious. In the early years, Germany had a considerable commercial stake in Indo-China, but after 1918 this was all swept away. During the War, the old animosities reawakened. It was noted that the Annamite Pretender, Prince Cuong De, visited Berlin in the spring of 1914; that Annamite revolutionaries had been admitted to the German schools in Canton; that the German Consul whom the War had forced out of Hong-Kong had taken refuge in Siam, whence issued much Annamite nationalist propaganda. Yunnan, too, was a great centre for German agitation. The border incidents of 1915, as well as the Muong revolt, were thought to be German-incited. During the post-War years, however, fear of Germany was displaced by other hopes and alarms, so that by 1929 the German consulate was restored at Tourane.

China

By far the most important phase of Indo-China's Far Eastern policy is her relations with China, and particularly with Yunnan and Canton. Yunnan for years had maintained an obstinate independence from the Chinese, who had had to make several attempts before successfully colonizing that barren country. A series of revolts against the Chinese domination culminated in the Moslem insurrection of 1856–73. These Yunnanese Moslems traced their origin to the Arab traders of the seventh century who had settled in the country. They had suffered at

[1] Cf. J. G. Scott, *France and Tongking* (London, 1885), and C. B. Norman, *Le Tonkin* (Paris, 1884).

the hands of the Chinese mandarins, who, among other vexatious measures, forbade them freedom to worship. The atrocious struggle lasted sixteen years: it ravaged the country and decimated the population. It has been estimated that a million men perished on the Chinese side alone. The cruelty with which the war was conducted by both combatants has been noted by many eye-witnesses. In 1873 came the fall of Talifou, the last Moslem stronghold. The revolt was crushed, but Yunnan was left ruined. Jean Dupuis was not a little responsible for the ultimate Chinese victory by the arms and munitions he rushed through to them by the Red River route, for the Chinese government was badly handicapped by the simultaneous Taiping rebellion. The war left the Yunnanese with the habit of pillage, and this was incidentally responsible for prolonging Tonkin's pacification.

Ferry's war with China was an accident, the denial of France's traditional policy of reinforcing Chinese independence as a counterpoise to English and Russian expansion. Moreover, Chinese culture has always exercised a fascination over the French mind. Part of the confusion in the negotiations, and the mistakes which led up to the war, were due to a diplomacy between Paris and Peking that ignored Indo-Chinese officialdom. The latter were less influenced by Metropolitan politics, and also far better informed about Indo-China's best interests. A little later Galliéni was to prove, for the regulation of Yunnanese problems, the superiority of direct dealings with local officials.

With the termination of hostilities, both in China and Tonkin, a commercial interest in Yunnan was reborn. The axis of the mercantile world was shifting rapidly towards the Pacific. In 1897, the Lyon Chamber of Commerce, in conjunction with other French cities, sent a commission to study Yunnan, Kwang-Si, and Tonkin's commercial possibilities. Their report was the first authoritative account which exploded the legend of Yunnan's immediately utilizable wealth: the shortage of labour and general insecurity there prevented tapping that province's mineral resources. The Moslem revolt had revealed the progressive weakening of the Peking government, and had aroused the anti-foreign feeling which was to have repercussions all over the Celestial Empire. In June 1899, the French Consulate at Mongtzeu was burned, and a month later Europeans were forced out of that province for almost a year. This state of affairs greatly hampered Doumer's railway projects in Yunnan, for which France had got Peking's consent in the 1885 treaty. This railway was only a part of

Doumer's dream of extending French sovereignty and influence throughout the Far East by means of cultural penetration—an ideal that succeeded to the earlier goal of commercial profits in South China. Expansion of the French Legations in China, hitherto parsimoniously subsidized, as well as hospitals, schools and Missions, were to achieve this at Indo-China's expense. The general budget, as well as Annamite nationalists, has long groaned under this irrelevant burden. Doctors are sent to mitigate Yunnan's epidemics, and rice to solace its famine-ridden areas, when Indo-China itself is miserably in need of such aid. Cordial relations were cultivated with Yunnanese mandarins: Chinese sovereignty was to be maintained; the dismemberment temptation had passed. The cultural side of the expansionist programme survived, but political ambition had deflated.

The Metropolitan French sympathized with China's 1912 revolution. In Indo-China its first consequence was to bring to the fore the problem of the resident Chinese. Hitherto a weak central government in China had done nothing to support their demands; now it was hoped that the nationalist régime would and could better their status in Indo-China. The resentment of the Young Chinese over the Yunnan railway and France's extra-territorial privileges in China might itself prove a strong lever to change the treatment of their compatriots in Indo-China. The entrance formalities—medical examinations and finger-prints—they regarded as insulting; the high taxes on Chinese merchants they thought unjust; and, above all, they wanted Chinese consuls in the colony to protect their nationals. In addition, they complained of the high tariff and freightage on Chinese goods entering or passing through Indo-China. These pre-War grievances found a more powerful motor force in Communism and its support of Annamite nationalism. The fact that Beau had twice refused to extradite Sun Yat Sen, when he sought refuge in the colony, was only a slight factor in France's favour. The effervescent Cantonese offered shelter and instruction to anti-French elements, and even put up a monument to the Annamite who had thrown a bomb at Merlin while he was supposed to be enjoying that city's hospitality. Incidents on the Yunnanese railway and frontier, culminating in 1926 with the murder of the French Consul Robert at Longtcheu, showed an aggravation of the same hostile state of mind. In fact, it was remarkable that nothing worse happened, considering the unstable temper of the country and the impotence of the Chinese authorities. The frontier was carefully guarded by the French and neutrality strictly maintained, but it was significant that the Yenbay murders took place so near the Chinese frontier. All of these incidents, and the obvious link between Annamite nationalism and Cantonese Communism, delayed from 1930 to 1935 negotiation of the badly needed commercial treaty between China and France.

The Yunnanese are undeniably dependent on the French, but they do little to cater to their wishes. The cultural influence which France has exuded in that province has not been the success its sponsor anticipated. Yunnan's geographic and economic dependence on Indo-China has perhaps had a sobering influence on Soviet activities there, since the French controlled their only egress to the sea. But only recently Yunnan got an Italian to head its new hospital, in spite of the French hospitals which have functioned for many years in Yun-nanfou, Mongtzeu, and Canton. In 1920 an English company was given a ten-year monopoly of local aeroplane building. Yet in that same year eight hundred Chinese students went to study in France, and Peking considered asking Lyon to open a special Chinese University. In Yunnan and Kwang-Si, France has both technical and regular schools in the main towns, for whose graduates scholarships are reserved in the University of Hanoi. In 1929, there were about three hundred French in Yunnan and six thousand Annamites. If France is not popular in that province, no foreign power is, or even the Chinese government itself. Banditry and opium contraband are to-day probably the most tense practical problems along the frontier, but it is the recent establishment of soviets at Longtcheu, two days away from Tonkin, that has aroused the greatest concern in the colony.

Japan

The Russo-Japanese War alarmed French opinion for the safety of Indo-China. It marked the beginning of the Yellow Peril psychology in France, as well as a more serious appreciation of Japanese strength. The first reaction was to strengthen Indo-China's military defence. Any number of officers sprang forward to tell how vulnerable was the colony's undefended coastline. France's position, at this time, between her allies Russia and, more recently, England—herself the ally of Japan—was somewhat delicate. Peroz' contemporary book[1] tried to show the Japanese menace was based on land hunger. He was indignant at French public opinion that looked benignly on Nippon as a land of Mesdames Chrysanthèmes. Most of the Japanese ladies in Indo-

[1] Peroz, Lieut.-Col. Etienne, *France et Japon en Indochine* (Paris, 1906).

China were only prostitutes, who added espionage to their more strictly professional duties. Parliament and public opinion allowed themselves to be only temporarily moved by such alarmist considerations. A polemic about sending submarines to Saigon, the divulgence of a sensational Japanese document of doubtful authenticity, the anchoring of a Japanese cruiser off the coast of Annam, did excite public attention. No sooner had the first shots been fired at Port Arthur than a special committee was named to study the colony's defence, and troops were drained from the more dangerous Yunnan frontier to protect Cochin-China's Cap St. Jacques. But the excitement soon died down, and Japan once again became the land of poetry and flowers. In 1907, Russia and Japan signed their Asiatic agreement, in which France played the role of honest broker. That same year a loan was floated in France, and the two countries reached an understanding as to the integrity of China. It had also become obvious that Japan's predatory intentions were directed to the North. This and the Japanese war alliance dissipated the last of French fears. With the increasing disorder in China, these two powers have been drawn together by the feeling that they alone stood for law and order in the Far East.

Far more important than the 1906 military menace was the indirect effect of Japan's victory on Annamite youth. Japan became the leader of the Yellow peoples, replacing China as the cultural head of the Asiatic hegemony. Japan was ultimately responsible for turning the passive Annamite disdain of Western accomplishment into a feverish imitation. This spiritual leadership, however, did not long remain Nipponese. Japan's large share in war spoils, and her attitude towards China, Korea, and Manchuria, have pointed an ominous moral to Annamite nationalists: Russia and China have now become the lodestars.

Commercial relations between the two countries have been excellent. Unlike the innumerable Chinese, there are only about four hundred Japanese in Indo-China, because they acclimatize themselves with difficulty. Japan has always bought more than she sold there, so for long the colony put off all Japanese overtures for a commercial treaty. But the fall of the *yen* and the cutting of Indo-China's rice and coal exports, as well as increasing competition from Japan's cheap manufactures, have given Indo-Chinese industrialists pause. Japan's twenty-year pertinacity was finally rewarded by a temporary treaty in 1932, which at least succeeded in offending neither side. Politically, France finds Japan an ideal element in the Far East; economically, a dangerous rival.

Siam

Out of a heterogeneous collection of tribes an orderly Asiatic state has emerged. While its neighbours and fellow Thais have fallen under foreign domination, the Kingdom of the White Elephant has remained a sovereign state, due to the mutual jealousy of England and France, but also to the superior qualities of its people and princes.

Since the days of Siam's embassy to Louis XIV, relations between the two countries had been cordial. The government of Napoleon III stupidly lost the opportunity of creating a Protectorate over Siam. Only a commercial treaty favourable to the missionaries came out of these abortive negotiations. French diplomacy continued to be weak when it recognized Siamese sovereignty over the Cambodian provinces of Angkor and Battambang (1868). It was natural for the Siamese to conclude that France was thoroughly occupied with Annam and that Metropolitan indifference was tantamount to hostility towards any colonial expansion, so they encroached more and more along the Mekong valley. Garnier's warnings about an eventually Siamese Laos were taken up and amplified by Pavie's explorations and advice. Certain dramatic incidents, involving the inevitable insult to the flag, aroused French public opinion to support an aggressive policy in Laos, even at the risk of offending England, who was backing Siam's intransigeance. The Mekong, a French river, not a boundary, became the rallying cry of the opposing party. The traditional Anglo-French colonial rivalry was finding simultaneously different points of tension both in Africa and in Asia.

Friction with Siam developed almost immediately over the execution of the 1893 treaty. When Doumer in 1899 returned a visit made two years before by the King of Siam, relations were not in the least improved. The French complained that Siam was not only breaking the treaty, that she had not renounced her territorial ambitions in Laos, but that advisers of every other nationality than French were being called to Bangkok in the reorganization of Siam. The repercussions of a Kha revolt in 1902 served as the occasion for reopening negotiations for a new Franco-Siamese treaty, in which the pro-expansionists hoped to better France's Laotian position. Certain elements in France openly preferred a military to a diplomatic solution of the problem, and they loudly denounced the 1902 arrangement.

A slight rectification of the frontier was all that France got in return for renouncing her extra-territorial rights in Siam. French opinion was decidedly hostile: the publication of a Yellow Book was demanded, and this further strengthened the opposition. The government dared not ask Parliament for ratification, and so the negotiations were resumed. In February 1904, a new agreement was reached, only slightly more advantageous than the 1902 project. It was presented at the same time as the Anglo-French boundary agreement,[1] and both were rather carelessly ratified together. When application of its clauses was attempted, so many practical difficulties arose that both sides once more started to negotiate. The outcome, consummated in 1906, meant territorial advantages for France and diplomatic gains for Siam, who was willing to make sacrifices to get rid of foreign sovereignty on her soil. Indo-China found that diplomatic action through Paris was weak, uninformed, and subject to a thousand irrelevant considerations. The *Entente Cordiale* with England, however, made Siam more malleable, and Indo-China—now diplomatically of age—was able to exert direct pressure on the negotiations. The 1907 treaty that resulted, returned the two lost Cambodian provinces, and this settled the major issue on the French side. A commission was named by both powers to settle disputes that would arise in regard to the Mekong. Though the Chauvinists loudly bewailed this treaty, it laid an excellent basis for cordial relations in the Indo-Chinese peninsula.

Siam's mild but willing participation in the Allied fortunes during the War further cemented cordial relations with France. Their community of interests in the peninsula was not hampered by any commercial competition. Siam was slowly emerging from under English influence and making diplomatic overtures to Japan. The country had evolved so rapidly that France was now willing to relinquish a judicial protection of her nationals and protégés in Siam, and to co-ordinate her railway system with Siam's. In return, Siam gave France a larger share in her national development. French engineers constructed a bridge across the Menam, and locomotives were ordered by Siam from France. In the cultural sphere French was taught in Siamese schools, and France did much to reorganize Siamese justice.

In 1923 England approached France about joint negotiations for a new treaty from Siam. Naturally Siam was displeased by the prospect of solidarity between the two former rivals whom she had so cleverly played off against each other. So she offered France important con-

[1] Cf. below, p. 368.

cessions in return for a separate agreement. The ensuing Franco-Siamese treaty of 1925 was negotiated with the full knowledge of England. It marked the end of France's judicial rights in Siam, and it made the Mekong Commission a permanent institution, with a demilitarization of that river's banks. The juridical régime of the Mekong has proved to be a thorny problem, but the evident goodwill of both sides is the best guarantee for a satisfactory settlement. This treaty was also a triumph for the policy of direct negotiations between Indo-China and her neighbours. Relations between the two countries have steadily improved since 1907, despite the activity of Annamite nationalists there. Since the depression some Siamese students have found a European education prohibitively expensive, and have come instead to Hanoi University. A series of exchange visits culminated in the recent journey of the King of Siam to his erstwhile vassal and enemy, the King of Cambodia. Greater goodwill could not be shown by any nation.

France's Role in the Pacific

At the turn of the century, all but a few of the most ardent imperialists in France had renounced territorial expansion in the Far East, notably in Yunnan, and had turned towards a consolidation of what was already acquired. Indo-China was, by her admirable location, well suited to radiate French culture and commerce to the neighbouring countries. In such a role France never thought of her colony as a separate entity, but rather as an integral part of herself.

Up to 1922 Indo-China could not communicate with the outside world except through the English cable at Cap Saint Jacques. The post-War establishment of a French line had an obvious military and diplomatic significance. It was supplemented in 1930 by the installation of a telephone service to France. Aeroplanes, plying between France and Saigon, are still another more recent link in bringing Indo-China closer to Europe, and at the same time in developing her individuality. In 1936 a radio-telephone service was established from Saigon with Tokio and Bangkok.

A series of post-War visits to neighbouring countries, as well as a mutual fear of Communist agitation, has confirmed this development. Varenne, like Merlin, visited Java. He created a consulate there and a direct maritime service between Saigon and Batavia (1928). Indo-China participated in the Batavian Exposition, and Java reciprocated at the Foires de Saigon. In 1935, an advantageous commercial treaty sealed this economic *entente*. Much the same may be said of Hong-Kong and Singapore, where France and England's colonial interests find common ground, especially against Cantonese Communism. This is also true of the Philippines and of the United States, though the recent tariff barriers have choked off Indo-China's exports there. In 1921 the Pacific Mail line had to suppress its call at Saigon. The treaty signed on May 16, 1936, will affect, favourably, American imports into Indo-China—to what extent it is still too soon to tell.

American machinery and insurance companies have found Indo-China a good market for their wares. But in Indo-China there has been a good deal of indignation over American policy in China, where French missions have been losing ground to their more heavily endowed Protestant rivals. It is also felt that the United States has been encouraging Chinese arrogance and anarchy, and in particular has tried to replace France in Yunnan. Protestant missions have made no headway in French Indo-China. The administration sees in them no religious menace but the opening wedge of political activity. The post-War proposal to give Indo-China redlands in payment of the American debt met in the colony with outspoken hostility.

Another unpopular post-War proposal was the placing of Indo-China at the head of France's Pacific colonies. This idea, originally Sarraut's, was expanded by Archimbaud in Parliament and in the *Revue du Pacifique*. Indo-China resented this suggestion as part of the post-War revival of the old Colonial Pact, in which Paris high-handedly was disposing of her colonies in her own interests. There are, however, a number of arguments in favour of this idea. The Pacific Islands are forty days away from Marseille—there are no cable lines—and they are scattered over an area of 4,320 square kilometres. Only the Nouvelles Hebrides and Caledonie have extensive surfaces, and 56,000 out of a total population of 86,000. At first blush they would seem to have little interest for France, except in their forest and mineral reserves, but they have a definite strategic value. These Islands, with their declining population, need capital and labour. But the experiment of sending Tonkinese workers there has just met with bitter opposition by Annamite nationalists.[1] In this dream of a Pacific Federation, Indo-China sees only an onerous burden, which by right is not her responsibility but that of the Métropole.

[1] Cf. below, p. 163.

CHAPTER III

THE ECONOMY OF INDO-CHINA

"L'Indochine est comme la vigne de Naboth: si riche qu'elle ait été, elle s'est épuisée à force d'être pressée et grattée par tant de mains."
Pasquier

PRODUCTION: NATURAL RESOURCES

THE classical image of Indo-China as a pole balanced by two baskets of rice has a significance beyond that of the economic sphere. The pole which represents the Annamite Range is a spiritual as well as a physical barrier, for it separates the countries of Indian culture from those of Chinese civilization. While these mountains cut off the spring rains from the Mekong valley, they make possible a second harvest of rice in Tonkin and in most of Annam, whose southern-most region is climatically linked to the Mekong. Its deep valleys create a profound isolation that makes of Annam the most backward of the Annamite countries. Unfortunately, not only is its long coast inhos-pitable—particularly in harvest time—but the back country of dunes and wooded hills rises to inaccessibly high peaks which cut off Laos from the coast and orientate its economy towards Siam—political frontiers to the contrary. The plateaux of this range have a certain economic value as pasture land, forest, and redlands. But the hostile Moi tribes ensconced there, as well as the congenital Annamite hatred of the forest, have, up to now, prevented utilizing these resources. Two passes traverse the range. One of these, the Porte d'Annam, marks a cultural frontier between the North and South of Annam, and served formerly as an administrative division as well.

The baskets of rice are the two great deltas formed by the Red and Mekong Rivers. They support a very dense population, particularly in Tonkin, where there are five hundred inhabitants to the square kilo-metre, as against eighty-seven in the more recently colonized Cochin-Chinese delta. The narrow connecting strip of Annam's coastal plain supports an almost equally dense population.

French Indo-China's two mighty rivers are vital factors in the economy and culture of the peninsula. The Annamites have always used their valleys as channels of expansion, and even to this day they are pushing up into the underpopulated regions of Cambodia and Laos through the waterways. The Laotians and Khmers live in scattered hamlets along the Mekong, and present to the invader no compact towns wherewith to resist this aggression. The lack of a natural frontier to the West has had an importance which the Siamese invasions revealed.

The inundations of the Mekong are as beneficent to the local economy as those of the Red River are harmful to the Tonkinese. Cambodia is the country of *beng*, or characteristic depressions in the land surface, over which the rising Mekong gently flows. The great lake, the Tonlé Sap, covering 10,000 square kilometres at high tide, is a great source of Cambodian prosperity. Not only does it support a veritable city of fishermen, but when its waters have subsided rice can be cultivated all over its fertile bed. Rice can also be grown the length of the river banks, and many other crops all over Cambodia's non-inundated surface.

The Mekong's Nile-like utility as irrigator of the adjoining land is far greater than its value as a means of communication. Despite its appearance as a great waterway, its rapids, especially above Vientiane, make navigation impossible for a good part of the year. Great sums have been spent in improving its navigability, but the falls of Khone among other obstacles necessitate a parallel railway construction to supplement the steamboat service. The numerous tributaries of this great artery have a potential value as means of irrigation and of electrical power. Despite the adjacent thick forests, covering 40,000 square kilometres out of a total area of 173,000, Cambodia and Laos could support a far denser population than at present, especially on their fertile redlands.

The dominant characteristic of Indo-Chinese geography is the sharp contrast between the high region, with its wooded hills and scattered population, and the flat intensively cultivated delta lands. The mountainous chaos of Upper Laos and Upper Tonkin is cut by deep, narrow valleys, separated by high ranges which culminate in the Fan Si-Pam, 3,142 metres high. There are few arable valleys or extensive plateaux. Economically, this country can never be very interesting because of its inaccessibility and scattered population, which is infinitely subdivided. A certain livelihood can be gained from forest products along with animal raising, and specialized crops like opium and tea, notably on the Tran-ninh plateau.

Middle Tonkin extends from the Chinese frontier along the left bank of the Red River as far as the delta. Its mountains are more moderate, and have a wealth of minerals, as well as picturesque attractions for tourists. In Indo-Chinese literature this country is known as the *brousse*, and it supports a scattered and diverse population of about fifteen persons to the square kilometre. It also served as a very inauspicious region for military operations during the pacification. The great rivers of Tonkin are imaginatively called Red, Black, and Clear, and they are orientated towards Southern China, whose economy is linked by geography to Tonkin, just as Laos is soldered to Siam. The failure of geographical barriers to coincide with political frontiers has had an enormous influence on Indo-China's history. This factor has permitted the century-long infiltration of peoples into the peninsula, and accounts for the present jumble of ethnological groups. The diversity of peoples in French Indo-China is only matched by their uneven distribution over its surface.

The violence of the Tonkinese rivers is in keeping with the excesses of the climate. Typhoons and inundations from the monsoons alternate with droughts. In contrast with the greater regularity and mildness of the South, Tonkin and North Annam are a prey to incalculable natural forces which make human effort seem futile and unavailing. The stimulus of a colder climate, the competition of a denser population, the struggle with implacably hostile forces, have all left an imprint on the Tonkinese character, important in estimating that group's economic productivity.

Forests

Formerly forests covered the entire country's surface, but about half of them have been cut down in the most accessible regions. Natives have abused these forests since time immemorial. They cut down trees either to get new land for agriculture or simply for their immediate needs. The primitive mountain peoples have been the most destructive in burning the forests to fertilize the ground. After a few years they abandon the place and repeat the process elsewhere. An enormous grass, called *trann*, grows up in these abandoned *rays*, which is the bane of the farmers' existence. Animals, too, crop the young plants. Nowadays this lack of forest land is being keenly felt, for the new industries and towns have an ever-increasing need of wood.

The French were the first to take steps towards forest conservation. In 1902 a group was formed to attempt reforestation. This work was long hampered by local resistance and poverty of means. Even prior to this the Admirals in 1862 had forbidden the cutting of certain growths, and thirteen years later authorized the regular exploitation of Cochin-China's forests. At this time forest guards were installed, but not until 1897 was a real forestry service organized and extended to Cambodia as well. By 1900 it was also imperative to do something about the forests of Annam and Tonkin, so a general service was created two years later, at the same time as special services for each country of the Union. In 1913 this service was suppressed in favour of the local groups as part of the general decentralization.

Nowadays the Union has about two hundred Europeans in its Forestry Service, aided by native technicians and guards trained at the Forestry School of Hanoi. One of their most important contributions was a classified inventory of Indo-Chinese forests. Their work revealed that 16 per cent of these forests were in the process of disappearing, due to *ray* cultivation; that 17 per cent had been impoverished through deforestation; that 33 per cent were still intact but inaccessible, and only 34 per cent accessible and exploited. The present forest area of Indo-China covers 31,000,000 hectares, and it belongs almost exclusively to the state and to the communes. There are almost no private forests, since such land is never granted as a concession.

Fishing

Fishing is an important native occupation, since it furnishes one of the principal elements of native diet. The two greatest fishing areas are the lakes of Cambodia—notably the Tonlé-Sap which is one of the world's most productive regions—and the coast of Cochin-China. Indo-China's total annual catch in fresh fish amounts to about 260,000 tons, part of which is exported to Hong-Kong, Singapore, and even to France.

The colonial administration has wisely maintained a passive role in regulating this fishing industry. The natives have long assigned certain fishing areas to the various districts, and the government has respected these innumerable and detailed customs and local usages. In this they have resisted Metropolitan pressure to apply legislation, for example, forbidding the use of certain nets. For the fish on which many Anna-mites depend for their living could not be caught with other than the outlawed nets. The method of farming out fishing rights was originally used in Cambodia, where large-scale abuse led to its suppression in 1908. The allotment of specified areas was found preferable, since it eliminated the sub-leasing of privileges. Tonlé-Sap is unique at the time of the great inundations, and even the nearby forests furnish such

THE ECONOMY OF INDO-CHINA

remarkable specimens as to attract thither the Oceanographic Institute's researches.

The fishing banks off the coast of Cochin-China offer, in the not too distant future, a potentially thorny international problem. These banks have long been used by Cochin-Chinese fishermen without any particular rights. A bitter rivalry is imminent there unless a timely agreement first solves the problem, for the Pacific Coast suffers from a lack of fish.

Animal Husbandry

It is more than usually hard to get statistics of animal breeding because of the natives' perennial fear that their taxes may be raised if they do not underestimate their possessions. The most recent census (1931) gives 1,850,000 cattle, 2,070,000 buffaloes, 2,040,000 pigs, and 90,000 horses as the imposing array of the colony's animal wealth—but every writer on economics has his own figures. Impressive as it looks upon paper, these figures are very small for so thickly populated a country, since those regions which have the most inhabitants are the ones that are poorest in stock.

Climatic conditions, as well as the land's intensive cultivation, explain the lack of suitable pasturage in the deltas, but there is still much unused land in Upper and Middle Tonkin. Poverty and Buddha's injunctions against the killing of animals account for the incredibly low meat consumption—less than a kilo per person in the Tonkinese delta, and for the general undernourishment. Indo-China imports no meat so that the country may be said to raise—not all that it needs—but all that it consumes. An export trade could certainly be further developed.

Cambodia is the country best suited to cattle-raising, and possibly the Laotian plateaux. During the War Paris thought of developing the refrigeration of meat in the colony, and the idea has survived as a possible export trade with the Philippines. High freight rates and those Islands' prohibitive tariff have at least temporarily checked such a development. Leather, because of its smaller freightage, might become a more profitable export to France.

The climate of Indo-China is not conducive to sheep-raising. Attempts to acclimatize the Yunnanese sheep, even under analogous conditions, have been a failure in Tonkin. Experiments in Laos have been conducted more with the thought of wool than of nourishment, but as yet the results are of too poor a quality to bear exportation.

Indo-Chinese horses could be greatly improved by cross-breeding.

Their miniature proportions are always a subject for merriment to the newly arrived, and of humiliation to cavalry officers. Buffaloes and oxen are used for farm labour. They are brought to Annam from Siam or from Laos, and a group of poor farmers will often pool their resources for a joint purchase.

The obstacles to increasing animal husbandry, as an economic resource, are numerous and varied. Tiger raids have great importance, especially in the underpopulated mountain regions during the winter months when game is scarce. Natives are unwilling to kill the tigers unless they turn to a diet of human flesh. Animal stealing, too, has become a well-organized industry, especially with the introduction of French penal law. Napoleon could not be expected to have foreseen the special significance of such thievery in Indo-China. The greatest of all obstacles is the prevalence of the epizootic, against which the colony's veterinarian service has made but little headway. The Institut Pasteur has worked on this problem, but as yet it is one of the most neglected fields in French agricultural effort. Very recently, in 1936, the Strait Settlements prohibited the importation of Indo-Chinese meat because of the outbreak of a cattle pest in Cambodia.

Mines: Coal

Coal is the greatest wealth of Indo-China's mines, and one of the colony's principal resources. Coal, largely anthracite, is the most important mineral, and with zinc and tin form 96·5 per cent of the total production. Ninety per cent of these mines are situated in Tonkin, which the presence of an already dense population has marked for an industrial future. The principal deposits are along the Bay of Along, which enjoys certain advantages like proximity to deep-water ports. Other less important minerals are zinc, lead, tin, and phosphate, with still lesser quantities of gold and iron. Laos has almost all the tin, Annam the phosphates, Cambodia precious stones, and Cochin-China nothing. The Annamites and Chinese have mined from time immemorial, and their work has great value for the modern prospector. Almost no mines have been discovered by the French that were unknown to them. Most of them were abandoned, however, because of their primitive methods of surface exploitation.

Knowledge of the existence of these mines was one of the main causes of French intervention in Tonkin. In 1881 Le Myre de Vilers persuaded the government to send some French engineers to study the Tonkinese mines, which he hoped might rival Japanese production.

The mission was headed by the eminent Parisian scientist, Fuchs. Although his research was hampered by the uncomfortable proximity of Chinese bandits, he predicted great wealth for the nation who controlled these mineral resources.

After the capture of Hanoi, the French came upon some books in Chinese characters about these mines. Excellent studies of these and other archive material were made, which revealed that the Court of Hué had received revenues from 123 mines, of which all but six were located in Tonkin. This report showed the country's potential wealth, and about 1890 started the first mining fever that Indo-China was to know. Mining talk was in the air, and everyone was a potential prospector; but conditions were unfavourable to realizing these dreams of wealth. Lack of capital, and the unpacified state of the country, in addition to its inaccessibility, made prospecting almost impossible and led to a general disillusionment. Interest in these mines flagged, and by 1901 all that was left of the excitement was one active coal mine at Hongay. Even this one would have succumbed had it not been sustained by English capital from Hong-Kong. From 1901 to 1904 the number of Tonkinese mines under exploitation was very limited, and none at all was worked in other parts of the Union. One request for an iron mine had been conceded. Vague hopes were still entertained for gold and tin in Laos, but Tonkin was and continued to be the magnet for prospectors.

Although the Chinese were working the coastal mines at the time of the conquest, coal mining may be claimed as an exclusively French activity. Not only did persistent piracy make the early days very difficult, but there was a vital lack of markets. In 1888, the *Société Française des Charbonnages du Tonkin* received the anthracite concession at Hongay. High freight rates and inadequate capitalization kept this company long from getting on its feet. The same was true for the company exploiting the mines of Tourane. Imprudence in installing costly apparatus, as well as the cost of transporation, raised the cost price to unprofitable heights. There was a distinct lack of caution in adding to their activities the docks of Tourane, especially since no effort was made to conciliate the Chinese whom they had ousted and who refused to the new company their important patronage. A final effort to put life into this concession was to cede to it the tramline from Tourane to Faifo, but this only succeeded in absorbing the remnants of the company's capital. The shareholders' complaints resulted in forcing the Protectorate of Annam to purchase this enterprise, which it had never encouraged and the burden of whose failure it now had to bear.

Less *naïveté* but more guile was shown in the first catastrophic exploitation of the mine at Kebao. False despatches and enormous bluff in the best stock exchange manner resulted in pushing up the value of its stock in 1893 to 1,600 francs a share. This mine enjoyed a privileged situation along the Bay of Along, so it was hoped to induce De Lanessan to create there the colony's principal port, and to link it with the railroad to the Langson frontier. Large-scale waste was shown in developing the port of Tien Yen. A superb granite quay and a 14-kilometre railroad were duly and splendidly baptized by the Governor himself. In 1895 a Russian warship visited this port, and the ensuing festivities gave another opportunity for riotous expenditure. A few years later all illusions were shattered by the forced sale of the company's equipment. Thereafter the whole concession was abandoned to the jungle.

These two misadventures made French capital, ever skittish about colonial investments, more than ordinarily nervous about Indo-Chinese mines. Kebao, however, was to know after the War another and more successful exploitation. The pre-War mining efforts were not all failures because of dishonesty: the chief drawbacks were, rather, a lack of capital and ignorance of the technical difficulties and local conditions.

The post-War development of coal mines was sensational, especially after 1920. The War had given an impetus to production, until by the middle 1920's Indo-China had become the chief coal exporter of the Far East. Japan, whose production Le Myre had once hoped to equal, now became a client of Tonkinese coal. It was not Tonkin's unlimited production but that local industry was as yet so little developed, and the amount used for heating in a tropical country so negligible, that a very large percentage of the coal mined could be exported. In 1931 Indo-China produced 2,000,000 tons of coal. Although this forms only 2 per cent of the total production in Eastern Asia, by selling outside of the colony two-thirds of her production, Indo-China has become its greatest exporter.

Because of its almost exclusively export character, the depression has naturally affected this industry enormously. The currency situation of her two best clients, China and Japan, has aggravated these conditions. The 1928 tariff bill also caused Far Eastern countries to avoid buying Indo-China's products as much as possible, and to retaliate with high tariffs of their own. By 1932 these markets were virtually closed, and they were not re-opened until 1935 by Robin's special treaties. The Metropolitan market always remains, but the high cost of freight makes this an unsatisfactory outlet. Nor can compensation be hoped for through an immediate adjustment of the internal market, which, however, has not been so badly hit as that of metal mining. An effort has also been made to consolidate efforts and to reduce the cost price. By 1933 the Hongay *Société des Charbonnages* had absorbed its rivals, and the whole group now represents 78 per cent of the colony's total production. In 1936 the production of anthracite represented an increase of 30 per cent over 1935.

Almost all the colony's gold mines were known to the natives and the Chinese, but abandoned long before the French came. Although the French, too, have found them unprofitable to work, there has been inevitably a certain vogue in connection with gold mining. The Myden mine in Tonkin was the first to attract public attention, but it was located in an unhealthy region which also presented a complicated labour problem. The Attopeu mines in Laos have the same shortage of labour. This discouraged the company which had been working there, so it turned first to copper and later to tin. An exception to the general rule of the inaccessibility of the colony's gold is the Tourane mine of Bong Mieu. It has been markedly profitable because of its situation in a healthy, accessible region, where labour is available and nearby waterfalls supply the power.

Although gold in small quantities has been found in almost every country of the Union, its importance is not great, and it is usually too costly to extract. As with most mining history, it presents the drawbacks of inaccessibility, labour shortage, inadequate capital, technical ignorance, and extravagant expenditure. Moreover, the metal market is more precarious than that of coal because it is essentially artificial.

Indo-China belongs to the principal stannic regions of the world, but it is a small producer of tin. Up to 1922 Tonkin was the only place where tin mines were worked—ever since 1906. The extraction of tin was favoured by the high War prices, but this was partially offset by the scarcity and cost of freight transportation. Prices fluctuated during the post-War years until 1923, when the Laotian mine of Patnam was discovered and worked. The tin output was thereby increased, but it has remained practically stationary since that time. Although Laotian tin has to bear costly transportation charges before it reaches the sea, from which its Burmese and Siamese rivals do not suffer, this expense is not prohibitive in view of the value of the metal and the richness of these veins. The building of roads and an improved navigation of the Mekong have partially diverted it away from Siam and towards the Singapore market.

The year 1926 marked the highest price brought by tin, although the boom continued throughout the succeeding years, to be followed by a very abrupt decline. A study of the situation made by *L'Indochine* (1929) showed how much ignorance existed in France about the Indo-Chinese tin situation. The public should realize that tin is known to exist in only certain specified areas, and in only one province of Laos—that of Cammon. All other tin mines are uncertain, and especially hazardous for the investor since no control exists on the Bourse to prevent speculation. The existing Indo-Chinese tin mines have a real though limited importance from the world market viewpoint. The exaggerated hopes founded on the colony's tin, especially in 1929, when it displaced rubber in popular favour, have unjustly discredited the entire mining industry. In addition there are the customary drawbacks of difficult transportation and an unhealthy climate.

The international market will naturally continue to control Indo-Chinese tin. The future looks bright because of the relative scarcity of the metal. The chief tin-producing countries—Bolivia, Malaya, Siam, the Dutch East Indies, and Nigeria—control 90 per cent of the world output. In 1929, at London, they formed themselves into the Tin Producers' Association, and agreed to restrict their production. This arrangement was called the Byrne Plan, and it reduced tin output from 25 to 30 per cent. The result was fairly successful, and Indo-China has benefited by the ensuing rise in price without having curtailed her production. Tin mining has not ceased to increase despite the depression, for tin does not suffer from the same causes of permanent decline as does zinc. The restriction agreement was renewed in December 1936.

The zinc mines that were abandoned by the Chinese were situated on beforested and roadless mountains. Only in the twentieth century were they seriously exploited by the French. In 1902 the Mines Service was instituted, and two years later some important zinc mines were discovered.

Zinc has participated in two important booms, the first of which occurred during the War. Before 1914, what zinc was mined was shipped to Europe, where Germany was the principal buyer. The War, and in particular the freight situation, cut off this Western market, but the simultaneous creation of war industries in Japan opened up a period of prosperity for the colony's zinc. The 1917 Revolution in

Russia incidentally involved the ruin of Japanese metallurgy. The persistence of high freight costs, even after the War, reduced and finally stopped altogether the export of Indo-China's zinc. In 1920 the lowering of freight rates was offset by a decline in the world price of metals. The colonial government had to step in with premiums, and not until 1922 was the liquidation of the stock accumulated at Haiphong completed.

In 1915 a technical report on Indo-China's zinc mines was published in France by the head of the colony's Mines Service. Slowly it percolated into the industrialist milieu. This report called attention to the favourable conditions in Tonkin for establishing a zinc metallurgy. A group of French capitalists were thereby induced to buy the rich mines of Chodien, and then to build a zinc factory at Quang-yen. Simultaneously they profited by a rise in the world price of zinc. This increase in price culminated in 1926, and declined as steadily thereafter. This decline, preceding as it did the depression, had a technical cause— a new method of extraction that has permitted the working of mines formerly considered without value. This, along with the depression, will probably keep down the price of zinc for many years. All subsequent efforts to raise its price have failed. In 1928 an international cartel proved ineffective, and the group was dissolved in 1933. On the good side, the Far East is poor in zinc mines, and Indo-China's internal market is capable of much expansion—just as her mines are capable of a far greater development. Especially important was the fact that it then employed ten thousand coolies in a region where life had always been hard.

Indo-Chinese iron has the insurmountable drawback of inadequate quantity, but more important even is the absence of coke, without which the iron is unutilizable. The most important mines are situated in Tonkin, but there the exploitation is as yet unimportant. In 1929 the opening of a canal to the Song-Cau has made that region accessible and exploitation henceforth possible and profitable.

The Mines Service has long pointed out that metallurgy might well be developed in the colony. Local conditions are propitious, especially with coal mines so accessible. Markets are the most important single factor. China and Japan—especially the latter—are the best possibilities, and the quality of Indo-Chinese iron is good. In exportation it would have to compete with the Tata output from India, or else persuade the *Comité des Forges* to give up some of its markets in the colony's favour. It would also mean furnishing the colony with equipment and technicians, for it is estimated that at least twenty-five years would be needed to train a native personnel. Thai-Nguyen has an excellent location, but it would have to count on a steady internal market: a metallurgical factory is profitable only when it can dispose of a certain minimum daily output, which at present is far more than the colony could absorb.

THE GOVERNMENT'S POLICY AND ACTION

The development of Indo-China's mining industry has been more rapid than that of the colony's economy as a whole. Even before the depression the rashness of many hopes founded on these mines had been revealed. There was a boom during the War, followed by a decline; then a second rise to be succeeded by an even more vertiginous fall. Their principal drawback is inaccessibility, especially of the metal mines, so that when the intrinsic value of the output is slight—as in the case with tin—the transportation and labour charges make the cost price prohibitive. No matter how successful may be international measures of restriction, many Indo-Chinese mining projects can never be revived, nor the savings which they have swallowed up for ever. From 1920 to 1933 about 500,000,000 francs were invested in such hazardous enterprises.

During the mining rush of 1928–29 unpardonable excesses occurred. Eighteen thousand permits for prospecting were granted, covering a fourth of the colony's entire surface. Many of these mines existed only on paper. All capitalists were exposed to the dangers of ignorance, but the small investor was usually the hardest hit. In vain the colonial government denounced this danger to the Colonial Ministry.

Indo-China is filled with mines, but the search for them is difficult because of the natural formation. Brush covers many of the veins and makes them very deceptive. This facilitates fraud, for often a surface looks so promising that it deceives even experts. Nature seems to conspire with human weakness to exploit the ignorant.

An unpleasant by-product of prospecting is the profession of spying on prospectors by means of native agents. An enterprising prospector exhausts himself in searching for new mines. When he ultimately files his claim at the Mines Service Bureau he finds that a rival has got there ahead of him. Prospecting seems to attract the adventurer type whose honesty—but not his ignorance—is doubtful. This type of prospector hunts mines haphazardly, wandering across the *brousse*, asking natives for information. Others, less scrupulous and better informed, live by exploiting the discoveries of others.

Publicity, usually of an inaccurate kind, long served to keep public speculation at white heat. The smallest find was magnified by the local press. Petrol is a curious case in point. It had never been found in Upper Tonkin, but in the 1920's prospecting all over the world centred on petrol. In tropical forests spots are often found on the surface that were made by organic decomposition of a vegetable origin, but which were taken to indicate petrol. This was the origin of the wholly false legend, which grew up overnight, that Indo-China had a wealth of petrol resources.

The administration's role is very important in this business. Prospecting cannot be undertaken without a permit given out by the local officials for a restricted area. The fixed price is 500 francs, but with the inevitable formalities. By a 1912 decree perpetual possession of a mine may be granted but the owner must pay a 2 per cent tax on its produce. Certain regions are not open at all to prospecting, but these are very limited. The government's chief aim is to insure an exclusive right to search. Under Annamite law, the Emperor was sole proprietor of the soil and sub-soil. Severe punishments awaited those who tried to work mines, except that of Mong-Son which had been ceded to the Chinese. After the Protectorate was established the Emperor agreed to accept the French mining regulations. A prospector must indemnify the owner if he prospects on private property. For mines whose existence is already known, the government prefers disposal at public auction. Usually, however, the state takes a percentage on profits rather than work the mines directly.

Very early the government tried to prevent speculation by heavily taxing mines that were not being worked (1888). This long remained the régime until criticism became rife over the startling discrepancy between the number of prospecting permits issued and the number of mines under exploitation--1,224 to 215. This revelation led to a revision in 1912. With the completion of Tonkin's pacification, mining had taken on new life, and its growth would have forced a modification in the existing regulations. Mining products were reclassified. Foreigners were excluded from the ownership if not the benefits of Indo-Chinese mines. There was a restriction in the number of permits to be issued. Further regulations about the policing of quarries, safety rules, reports, and statistics from the Geographical Service, and analysis of minerals were forthcoming. In spite of the importance of the colony's mineral resources, mining legislation has encountered fewer difficulties than regulation of the land concessions.

Formerly Chinese were used as miners, but now they have been largely replaced by the less sturdy, but also less expensive, Annamites. There are very few miners among the mountain peoples. The Laotians and Khmers are too independent and nonchalant, and their best services to prospectors are as guides to the country. The Annamites much prefer their rice-fields to mines that are usually situated in the mountains which they hate and fear. They are not only cheaper as labourers, but they are more adroit and amenable to discipline than the Chinese, who, however, are more robust and who expatriate themselves more willingly. By 1931 the Annamites had replaced the Chinese in Tonkinese mines to the extent of forming nine-tenths of the labour. Their output is certainly small—about a third of that of French miners—but so are their wages. In 1931 men received from 3.50 to 4.50 francs a day; women 2.20 to 2.80 francs; and children from 1.80 to 1.50 francs for a theoretically ten-hour day. Specialized workers are still Chinese, though here, too, Annamites are being trained to replace them. As yet there are few Annamite engineers. The main problem, as ever with Annamite labourers, is to get them established in the place where they work. This largely depends on developing the means of communication so as to facilitate the periodic returns to the natal village, essential to Annamite life. The fact that towns are springing up in the mining regions serves to make the labouring population more stable.

Mining activity nowadays is not what it was ten years ago. In 1930 eighteen thousand prospecting permits had been issued, of which only nine hundred subsist to-day. This diminution is not to be deplored but, rather, is a cause for rejoicing. It indicates a promising convalescence, now that the mining fever has fallen—provided always that the lessons of the past are not forgotten.

With the exception of mining, Indo-Chinese industries began with the twentieth century. One group of factories transforms agricultural products, like the rice alcohol distilleries, silk and cotton spinning and weaving, and sugar refineries. Forest products are transformed into matches and paper, for which there is a good international market. Among the public works industries which have recently expanded, thanks to French capital, is that of electrical power, building enterprises, and transportation. Chemical industries are both numerous and financially unsuccessful—like those of glass, soap, and cement. French capitalists and technicians have shown far more interest in agricultural development, but even there they have not played the chief role in the colony's major product—rice.

AGRICULTURAL PRODUCTION

Rice

Rice plays such an important role in the colony's economy that it has made Indo-China a country of *monoculture*. Rice forms three-fifths of all the agriculture, four-fifths of the native diet, and 69 per cent of the export trade. For the vast native peasantry rice is the sole product, the only article for both consumption and as a medium of exchange, the condition of the country's prosperity, the keystone to Indo-China's economy. Indo-China has always been and will probably always be an essentially agricultural country, with the cultivation of its chief crop rice always in native hands. The many varieties of rice change with the soil and with the climate, and there are as many different methods of farming. In the North and in the South rice creates two entirely different problems.

In Annam and Tonkin the population is so dense that not enough rice can be raised for local needs. The amount planted would undoubtedly suffice, were it not for an unstable climate which alternates floods with droughts. Moreover, the population in the North is growing rapidly, and with it the need for greater production which has not proportionately increased. Public works, in the form of hydraulic engineering, have not kept pace with the need. Even more important will be the results of the completion of the Transindochinois Railroad, which should enable Cochin-China to sell her surplus in the North in an emergency. Tonkin, at least in the delta, has the advantage of two annual harvests. This is also true of certain parts of Annam, but the monsoon season along the coast of that country coincides with the harvests, and makes provisioning from the sea impossible in case of famine. The districts most exposed to disaster, particularly in the north of Annam, have for centuries coincided with the areas of political discontent.

In Cochin-China, the old provinces colonized by the Annamite government consume all the rice that they raise. It is only in the new under-populated provinces opened up by the French that rice can be grown for exportation. The amount of land devoted to rice-fields amounts to about 2,000,000 hectares in Cochin-China and to 700,000 in Cambodia. The fact that fifteen out of the twenty-two provinces of Cochin-China have no other crop shows its outstanding importance.

The three great rice-exporting countries of the Far East are Indo-China, Burma, and Siam. These countries have varying climatic conditions and currency problems, but they are alike in having had no over-production even during the depression. The relative position of these three rivals has been unchanged, but not so their clients'.

Japan has her own rice granaries in Korea and Formosa, so her demands on foreign rice are spasmodic and confined to emergencies. In 1931 Japan was even able to export rice herself. The little rice that she buys comes from Siam, because of their commercial treaty. Japan has, therefore, a negligible importance in the world rice market.

China protects her own rice-growers by a high tariff. In spite of this barrier, Indo-China's geographical proximity gives her a privileged position in supplying China's perennial rice needs. China is the greatest rice market in the world, both as producer and consumer. Her Western rice-fields are far from the sea, and without transportation facilities, and so her crops must be locally consumed. Under normal conditions, Indo-China sends more than half of her rice exports to China, so that that market dominates her economy. The large number of Chinese resident in the colony facilitate commercial relations, and cheap transportation is effected in large measure by junks. Although Indo-China has to compete with American wheat in China, as a rice substitute, the treaty of 1935 has ameliorated her position—at least temporarily. China's recent Ten Year Plan to effect a more self-sufficient economy will mean a gradual closing down of this market to the colony's rice. Since she is Indo-China's most important client, China's buying power in terms of silver has enormous influence upon the colony's prosperity. The recent depreciation of China's silver currency, because of internal strife, has had a great repercussion on Indo-China which has been on the gold standard since 1930. The Chinese rice market is the link between the present crisis in Indo-Chinese economy and the steady decline of Chinese money.

Of the other foreign markets, British India is naturally the client of Burma. Ceylon and Malaya have suffered, because of the rubber crisis, serious diminution of their buying power. This has, in addition, turned their attention to the raising of rice and other food products, with a subsequent decline in their importation of rice. Only very recently have new markets been opened in South Africa, the Philippines, Australia, and Java.

The Dutch East Indies are good clients of Indo-China's, especially since Robin's 1935 treaty. The rapid increase in the Javanese population is somewhat offset by the government's recent encouragement of rice-growing on the islands: at one time it was forbidden to import rice into Java.

The European market takes about one-fifth of the world rice output. The Burmese have captured the two most important Western clients— England and Germany, as well as the Netherlands. France and her African colonies are the only possible clients left for Indo-China. 1935–36 was so exceptional a year that France's rice imports from the colony almost doubled. But even here there are two obstacles. The most serious is the opposition of France's wheat-growers, who almost succeeded in limiting rice imports from the colony. The other drawback could be more easily overcome, since it is based on the inferior quality of Indo-Chinese rice. The French prefer a better grade of rice, so that when they buy their colony's rice it is solely because it is cheaper. China is a far better client, for she is concerned exclusively with the nutritive value of rice and not with its appearance, and in addition the freight charges are much lighter. Depending as she does at present almost exclusively on rice exports for her prosperity, Indo-China is indissolubly linked to Far Eastern markets, and in particular to that of China and its silver currency. It is a curious fact, in view of this situation, that the amount of rice available for exportation has only slightly increased, despite the new hydraulic works and the ever-larger amount of land devoted to rice-growing. This is partly due to the fact that rice exportation has grown much faster than the surface cultivated, and the same may be said of the 12 per cent population increase in the last fifteen years. Even the depression has caused a shrinkage of only 12 per cent in the amount of rice-land under cultivation from 1930 to 1933.

Indo-China's rice-growers and merchants in their methods have lagged well behind the international market. Up to the War it may be said that they made almost no effort to better the quantity and the quality of their rice, nor to remedy its lack of homogeneity by improved methods of seed selection or classification. The War brought up the problem acutely enough for a specialized service to be created, so as to select and propagate the finest varieties of rice. Insufficient fertilization and primitive methods of cultivation had resulted in the smallest yield per hectare of any country on the Pacific. Capital is available to the Indo-Chinese farmer only at usurious rates. There are, in addition, the hazards of inundation or inadequate irrigation—all of which makes the cost price almost prohibitive. The method of collection by Chinese middlemen who pick up the sacks of rice in their junks, as they go through the far-off *arroyos*, has also contributed to the lack of standardization.

The Annamite is a mediocre though hard-working farmer, and rice-growing requires great labour and patience. A level of ten centimetres' depth of water must be maintained in the rice-fields for a hundred days. An abundant water supply is the secret of success, and not the preparation of the soil, which is most elementary. The feet of the farmers and buffaloes are more effective in this respect than the plough. At the time of replanting, hard labour is required for a short period on the part of many workers. Even the children participate, and work must be done day and night. This spasmodic but intensive labour is well adapted to the family system of cultivation and to the structure of Annamite society. It also explains why machines have not been successful in rice-growing. The very nature of the crop means that rice will probably be profitable only when grown by native family labour.

A study of the rice production of Annam and Tonkin shows that their crops have not increased since the French conquest, and that there has been even a decline in exportation. This is caused by the rapid increase of the Tonkinese population. There is not enough rice raised locally to serve as the indispensable minimum per person. Only in Cochin-China has production increased, and even there it was more rapid from 1875 to 1900 than from 1900 to 1930, despite all the efforts made to force an increase. It has been, rather, enterprises like rubber and mines, created by French capital and technical knowledge, that have had an enormous growth in recent years. Purely native crops have not enjoyed a parallel expansion. The failure to increase rice production was long disguised by a rise in the price of paddy which was not immediately followed by an increase in the cost of living. The result has been that, excepting in Cochin-China, the purchasing power of the natives has remained virtually unchanged. This stationary quality of native production is even more clearly marked for products other than rice and corn.

The depression served to bring these problems to a head. There has not been a Governor-General since the War who did not make efforts to improve and to increase the colony's rice crop. The administration has failed through lack of a general plan and the necessary co-ordination. Laboratory experiments have not only remained too fragmentary, but their results have not been consistently applied. This is the inevitable result of allowing what should be the work of technicians, backed by individual initiative, to fall into the hands of the administration, whose policy inevitably changes with each of its numerous turnovers. For example, the hydraulic agriculture of Cochin-China is well ahead of that country's use of fertilizer and its selection of seeds and plants. Often the wrong regions have been chosen for experimentation, and colonists have individually had to learn at their own expense just what are the local conditions and the right plants for the appropriate place. To supply a consistency which government efforts have heretofore lacked, and to save the colonists many of the blunders which have too often consumed their resources, Pasquier created in 1930 his *Office du Riz*. The work of this Bureau and that of the *Institut des Recherches Agronomiques*, as well as the resolution of the 1935 Imperial Conference, have brought to light the amount of potential rice-land still unused. Heretofore there has been overmuch concentration on rich regions already under cultivation, rather than a development of new areas like the Plaine des Joncs, on the left bank of the Mekong. The effect of the depression on the export trade and the almost repulsively rapid growth of the Tonkinese population have forced these improvements on Indo-China. The drawbacks are naturally its expense and the great scope of the work to be undertaken, but the new wealth that is practically insured as a result of such effort, will probably more than repay the colony for its outlay.

The depression struck the Far Eastern rice market late, but with a force that was accentuated by local conditions. It naturally varied in time and severity in the different parts of the Union. Cochin-China, as the exporting country, was obviously the most seriously affected, and there the price of rice was driven down to approximately its cost. At the outset the depression hit the commercial organizations, but those groups which had good paddy supplies resisted as long as they could, selling only what was necessary and hoping for a rise in sales prices for what remained. Tonkin and Annam, which consumed what they produced, felt the crisis only a year later, and then in an attenuated form.

The first evidence of a breakdown in the powerful organization of rice merchants was the numerous failures among the Chinese houses. The Chinese purchasers of paddy, who had a seemingly unshakable hold on the rural districts, were steadily losing their grip, and their disappearance was making possible a reorganization or the substitution of a different system. For the Annamites this meant great rejoicing, inasmuch as they had long complained of the Chinese abuse of credit and their dubious methods, but it remains to be seen whether they are capable of taking their place. The Chinese breakdown seems to be one of capital and means rather than of methods, for they had admirably adapted their technique to local conditions. As is customary in Cochin-China, when circumstances are adverse, there is a general casting of the blame elsewhere. Certainly the responsibility is both Annamite and French to have become so dependent on the Chinese organization. The rice catastrophe has been particularly bad because it coincided with a decline in rubber. Both French and native agriculture were simultaneously struck by the rapid devaluation of their products and the scarcity of liquid capital. Indo-China's commercial balance was disrupted by a tightening of credit and of money—both of which have caused profound trouble.

The present crisis, for both producers and merchants, is fundamentally one of speculation. The imprudence of the planters is largely responsible for their troubles, and this makes their demands for relief unjustifiably vehement. The majority of them are heavily indebted. Encouraged by the easy profits of 1924–30, they borrowed freely to extend their crops, and at very high rates of interest. Now they hysterically demand aid of the state, claiming that their plight is the result of patriotic endeavour, and threatening social and political troubles if they are not granted relief. All the projects for devaluating the piastre and a general moratorium are based on a desire to make the public pay for the consequences of their greed. For the average native it is the fall in the price of rice, and not rubber, that brings home to him the depression.

Reaction to the situation is very different on the part of natives and Europeans. Native apathy and fatalism contrast with the disorderly violence of the French colonials, notably in Saigon, which has always been the nerve centre of the colony's economy. In May 1931 the Governor-General received a petition from 611 rice-growers, representing in Cochin-China about half of the land under rice cultivation, which showed the prevalent atmosphere of panic. Two months later the Syndicate of Cochin-Chinese Rice-growers voted to ask the government for an extension of credit and for the lowering of interest rates on debts. The "disastrous" prices they quoted were identical with those of the pre-War era, but their recent profits had made them forgetful. Loans had been made without adequate guarantee, and real estate values had risen abnormally. It was such speculation that had led to the cultivation of mediocre riceland and the storing of paddy against future profits.

Prices continued to fall in 1932, and this naturally increased the panic. A small group of turbulent rice-growers, egged on by the local politicians, were particularly vociferous. In January of that year they opened a campaign to devaluate the piastre, claiming that its stabilization, which they had asked for in 1929, was now the ruination of Indo-Chinese agriculture. Propaganda pamphlets were so widely circulated that the government undertook a counter-offensive. The agitation was taken up in the Colonial Council and later carried to France.

The noisy distress of Cochin-China aroused regional feeling in the colony, where the forces of reaction were represented by the Tonkin Chamber of Commerce. This body protested against the undue influence of the South, where there even existed a group of dissenting merchants who did not find their country in so deplorable a condition as pictured by the agitators. No doubt the declining prices had added to the debts of the planters, but the proportions as yet were not catastrophic.

Such resistance to their pressure only stimulated the agitators to further efforts. In July 1933 they telegraphed to the French Cabinet, demanding devaluation in the name of the rice-growers of the colony. Sarraut, who knew the situation, vetoed the suggestion. In the following October the agitation was renewed. The government, in a conciliatory mood, named a committee to study the problem. Their report did not find devaluation the panacea advertised by the agitators, but recommended a reduction of export taxes and a programme of public works. The agitators vented their anger at this outcome by attacking Pasquier and the Bank of Indo-China, but the Metropolitan government left their petitions unanswered. To show their disapproval, Saigon's shops were closed for a day and the local press attacks took on a fresh virulence. The government's viewpoint—that all the agitation was but the work of a handful of malcontents for political purposes—confirmed the general discredit into which the whole movement had fallen.

The administration was also constructive. In 1931 taxes were suspended on rice exportation, which resulted in lowering the cost of living, particularly for the native masses. To compensate for the budgetary loss involved, the government created in 1932–33 a new tax on sugar and mineral oil. Certain tax reductions, notably in Cochin-China, were also granted. On the positive side came the development of credit institutions and public works, and the policy of developing small properties. Technical improvements in rice cultivation were also encouraged.

During the 1920's Indo-China had presented an astounding example of prosperity: it was the child of post-War inflation. The depression brutally aroused the colony from a false paradise, but with unmeasured violence the colonials have renounced any feeling of responsibility, and turned to and against the government as one man. Their attitude during the depression has been symptomatic of a fundamentally false viewpoint. The colony's two syndicates of rice-growers have been absorbed by individual and immediate interests, and have paid but little attention to the criticism of their clients. Everyone—producers, merchants, and factory owners—have shifted the blame on to anyone but themselves. Indo-China must face the issue, and choose between getting only a mediocre revenue from her principal product, thereby leaving her national economy at the mercy of recurring crises, or of applying modern methods of production and salesmanship.

The depression showed more clearly than ever before the necessity for producing rice of a better quality, at a lower cost, for a better price, and adapted to specialized markets. These factors will be the determining elements in the struggle between the three great rice-producing countries for control of the Far Eastern markets. Rice exports from Indo-China did increase appreciably in 1935–36—20 per cent over the 1934 figures—but this was the result, at least partially, of an unusual number of favourable circumstances—a rise in the price of silver and China's purchasing power, the devaluation of the franc and consequently the piastre, and the Métropole's unusual demands in rice and corn.

Rubber

Unlike many other products in Indo-China, rubber is exclusively the offspring of European capital, initiative, and technical knowledge. It has now passed beyond the experimental stage, and has successfully established its potential parity with the Dutch East Indies and Malaya because of its special conditions of soil, climate, and labour.

Up to 1900 French agricultural colonization was primarily concerned with rice in Cochin-China; coffee in Tonkin; and in Annam, rice, tea, and coffee. But even before the War it became clear that the *hevea* plant could be successfully grown in South Indo-China. It was first introduced into Cochin-China, in 1897, by the Mission Raoul. Originally the plant had come from Brazil. In 1876 Wickham, an English botanist, succeeded in transplanting it to the Kew Botanical Gardens, and from there to Ceylon. From this modest beginning sprang the great rubber plantations of tropical Asia.

The colonial administration is credited with the first important effort to grow *hevea* in Cochin-China, but unfortunately they selected lowlands with soil of poor quality. The experiment was entrusted to the Forestry Service, which had neither the leisure nor the technical knowledge to direct such an enterprise. The results were discouraging, but the government organized a far better experiment station at Ong-Yem in Cochin-China. The first non-official effort was that of Belland at Gia-dinh. Although he had too little capital, he had the advantage of better labour conditions and of greater accessibility to his plantation. Unfortunately the growth of his crops was handicapped by faulty planting.

By 1906 the prosperity of Malaya and Java aroused new interest in Indo-China's rubber. The following year a group of Frenchmen in the colony subscribed enough capital to start two large plantations at Thudaumot and Bienhoa. This effort marked the beginning of capitalistic colonization in Indo-China. The results were so encouraging that public attention was drawn to Cochin-China's wealth in redlands. The government was even aroused to build roads into this potential rubber region. In 1910 began the rubber boom which led French capitalists to think that Indo-China might surpass Malaya, for it had cheaper labour, lower taxes, and suitable land of greater accessibility. But the Metropolitan French continued to prefer Malaya where, in 1910, their capital investment was valued at 100,000,000 francs. Only a few of Cochin-China's rubber companies were created by Metropolitan capital: the majority were founded with local savings. The six-year interval between the planting and tapping of rubber is too long for the impatient French investor, who wants an immediate return on his money. Three-fourths of the pre-War capital invested in tropical Asia was English.

From the beginning of the War England declared rubber to be contraband, and this meant the closing of an important market. In spite of this handicap, rubber sales increased during the War, due both to the needs of the belligerents and to the growth of the automobile industry. In Cochin-China the difficulties of this period were principally caused by the mobilization of its technicians, by the scarcity of freight, and by a rise in the silver piastre. Rubber went through a crisis in 1921–22, and the planters who had formed themselves into an association in 1910 appealed to the government for aid. The Bank of

Indo-China was induced to lend a third of the needed money on governmental guarantee. The state also gave money outright and as subsidies. Without this assistance the rubber-growers of Indo-China would undoubtedly have succumbed. By 1922 the price of rubber had fallen so low that many of the Singhalese and Malayan plantations had had to be abandoned. It was at this time that the British government devised the Stevenson Plan, whereby the export of rubber was restricted according to a shifting scale that was based on cost price.

The adoption of this policy synchronized with the end of one depression and with the rapid development of the automobile industry. Prices rose swiftly and plantations expanded. In 1923–24 the Indo-Chinese planters saw their financial situation so improved that they redoubled their efforts which—though on a much smaller scale—compared favourably with those of their rivals. In 1925 the prices had rocketed to profit levels so great that the period was known as the Rubber Era, and it so remained until about 1928 when the Stevenson Plan was abolished. But the great gains realized by the planters had finally excited French investors to back Indo-China's rubber—a tendency increased by the then current flight from the franc in Europe. The abandonment of the Stevenson Plan and simultaneous decline in the price of rubber caused their enthusiasm to abate, but so much money[1] had already been invested that there could be no general brusque withdrawal.

The Stevenson Plan had failed principally because it was a national solution to an international problem, although at the time Ceylon and Malaya controlled two-thirds of the world production. The Dutch had abstained, and Malaya bore the brunt of this experiment, while her neighbours profited without expense or self-sacrifice. Serious frauds were unearthed in Malaya, but much more important than this was an evolution within the industry itself. A process was discovered to regenerate rubber. Speculation was also an important factor. It was true that the boom of 1925 had far surpassed that of 1910, but by 1922 the price of rubber did not cover its cost. Profits could be sensational, but they were also very irregular.

From 1925 to 1932, prices dropped 92 per cent while world consumption declined only 20 per cent, and exports 6 per cent. The efforts of England and Holland, in 1932, to negotiate an improvement in the situation failed. One of the new aspects of the problem was the rapid development of native plantations. In Malaya and in the Dutch East

[1] The investment of French capital then in *hevea* is estimated at about 4,000,000,000 francs.

Indies they now represent two-fifths of the *hevea*-planted land in the world. Their strong position makes any restriction of output a very delicate business, for no matter how low the price of rubber may fall, if the native planter can still sell it at all, he will continue to plant *hevea* because it is much less trouble than rice. This does not mean, however, that these crops are mutually exclusive. Three years of depression have created a vicious and confused struggle for survival. All the rubber companies were threatened with indefinite production at a loss, and with an exhaustion of their capital. The situation became so bad that some natives replaced *hevea* with banana trees, which would give them at least the assurance of nourishment.

Indo-Chinese rubber planters enjoy a privileged position in the world—state aid in both the colony and France, while the governments of Ceylon, Malaya, and the Dutch East Indies impassively witness the agonies of their planters. It is interesting to note that the colonists who are loudest in their criticism of the evils of *étatisme* are the first to plead for state aid in time of trouble. The government granted tax exemptions and reduced the export tax, but the bad side of its paternalism is the cultivation of a careless dependency. A policy of drastic economy and cost prices pared to the bone can only be forced on the planters when they must depend on their own efforts for survival. In Indo-China the large proportion of small or middle-sized property is a cause for anxiety. The government cannot indefinitely continue to assure salvation to its rubber planters. It might also be better for them if their activities were co-ordinated and concentrated. The almost insuperable drawback to such a solution is the attitude of many of the planters who apparently do not appreciate the gravity of the situation, but continue their peevish demands for aid.

The great lack is a rubber policy, and this is the responsibility of government and planters alike. Neither of them has undertaken a consistent study, research, or experimentation, and such insouciance is conspicuous when compared with the patient investigations of Dutch and English planters who have organized to facilitate their work.

The Saigon Syndicate of Rubber Planters is a group of individual proprietors in which the big rubber companies have no representatives in spite of the fact that their concessions equal half of the total *hevea* surface under cultivation. The small planters recognize the importance of this omission, but fear to accept what might become an onerous tutelage by the big financial interests. In their turn the large companies equally fear that their interests might not be wholly harmonious. They

133

would agree to accept the principle of collaboration provided they could control the entire group's policy. In their nervous zeal for independence, both sides lose sight of their mutual interest in fighting high taxation, export duties, arbitrary decrees, and the concessions régime. Here is a conspicuous lack of professional solidarity.

Experimental stations could be developed with greater profit, and this has not yet been adequately done by the government. A planter named Perrin kept a record of the experiments he conducted over a twenty-year period, and this is the nearest approach to systematic research. One of the worst obstacles in developing rubber are the isolated efforts of amateur rubber planters, who frantically experiment to achieve instantaneous wealth. Effective experimentation can only be conducted by groups with adequate capital—which means either the administration or big companies. The small planters represent, in such projects, the element of routine, a spirit of mutual distrust, and a dispersed, unco-operative and undisciplined self-interest. In 1927, and again in 1929, two circulars of the Michelin Company produced a typical reaction. They theatened reducing their rubber purchases in the colony because of their inferior quality. The small planters were indignant but they did nothing to make their rubber of a better or more homogeneous character.

Government aid, that unique feature of French policy, is partly due to the general *étatisme*, and partly to a recognition of the evils of *monoculture*. It is also part of the trend to make France with her colonies a self-sufficient unit. Indo-China, therefore, is to produce rubber not primarily for sale in the world market but to supply France, who will thereby no longer be dependent on foreign resources. This is not only a precaution in view of future hostilities, but an insurance against the current tariff barriers. It was such considerations that induced the government to give direct aid to the planters whose products fell the quickest and lowest. The government extended credit to colonists who had been refused by the banks, and its aid was apportioned to the individual plantation's state of development. By 1935 the state aid to *hevea* planters amounted to 7,500,000 piastres, and a bonus was also given on rubber tonnage exported. Obviously such generosity was only a temporary measure, for the government had already paid a high price for saving French rubber.

The depression revealed a disparity between the amount of land conceded and what was actually under cultivation. Out of concessions totalling 126,000 hectares, only 32,500 were actually exploited. From

1924 to 1929 rubber plantations had—nominally—increased at the rate of 15,000 hectares per year. Only about a fourth of these concessions had reached the stage of being *en saignée*, realizing by 1931 only 12,000 tons of crude rubber. By 1940, under normal conditions, this amount should be more than trebled, but in 1936 Indo-China began restricting her rubber output. Indo-China is justly proud of so rapid a development, but the depression has caused most of the plantations to run at a deficit. The colony is, of course, only a small rubber producer in the world market, and so is proportionately far less affected than her southern neighbours. The depression has brought a 25 per cent shrinkage in the plantations as a whole. At the time the depression struck the peninsula, rubber played an infinitesimal role in the colony's prosperity in comparison with rice, but since then a general shake-up has occurred. Rubber, which formerly was Indo-China's second export, fell in 1932 to fourth place, behind coal and corn, but in 1935–36 was rapidly regaining its former status. The United States, its biggest client, was consuming less and less when formerly it had absorbed two-thirds of the world output. It was a curious paradox that the price of rubber and the amount of exports were decreasing at a time when its quantity was automatically increasing, due to state aid.

Indo-Chinese planters had long before carried their grievances to Paris, where they demanded protection against foreign rubber. Four times Parliament rejected such proposals (1911–22), and in 1930 did so again. The government, however, was willing to place a small temporary tax upon foreign rubber, so as to allow the planter to make up the deficit between the cost and the sale price. Planters also encountered opposition from French industrialists. A compromise was ultimately reached in March 1931 with a sliding scale of duty permitted in each colony which varied with market conditions. A reserve fund was created for each colony whose functioning was highly complex. France showed itself willing to go to a certain point but no farther in its quest for rubber independence. In 1935 the government pledged itself to restrict exportations of rubber beyond 30,000 tons, but this was not felt by the planters till 1936. This new effort at international restriction has since raised the price. Simultaneously exports have increased and the planters have cut down their cost price to an appreciable extent. Undoubtedly the government's announcement of an end to the bonus system in 1933, and the work of the Saigon Rubber Bureau founded in 1934 have had a great influence in obtaining this result. The 1934 census conducted by the Rubber Bureau shows that the total area then planted in *hevea* was 125,931 hectares, cut up into 815 plantations, of which 97,023 hectares lie in Cochin-China. The 1936 rubber output was 36,000 tons.

Cotton

This industry in all countries of the Union is exclusively in native hands. Moreover, it is a family industry which means that it is infinitely subdivided. Cambodian cotton is by far the best. Laos seems to be a hopeful ground for experimentation, if the fogs there can substitute for its inadequate rains. Annam could raise cotton but there is a general dearth of farming land, and the ground given to cotton could be more profitably used for food crops. The cotton trade is in the hands of the Chinese, and all attempts up to now to break their monopoly have failed.

Indo-China did not escape the cotton-raising fever which gripped the world during and after the War. There was a general belief in fantastically easy production. Of two possible methods only one interested the public at the time—the extension of the French cotton industry and not of native production. From 1917 to 1920 an intensive publicity was given to this idea in France and in the colony.

In Cambodia a first attempt was made by the *Comptoir de l'Industrie Cotonnière* in 1919. They acquired a large concession, and without adequate study or capital launched the enterprise in an effort to obtain quick results. The outcome, within a year, was the loss of their capital as well as of public confidence. The principal mistake that they and succeeding companies made was to think that just where a good quality of cotton grew easily an industry would necessarily flourish. They forgot that abundant and cheap labour was essential. In the redlands where the experiments were conducted, there was only a small population, and nothing could persuade the plainsmen to migrate there.

The present-day trend is to encourage native industry as the only profitable means of growing cotton. Indo-China, at present, raises only about 12 per cent of what is locally used—cotton crops have markedly declined since 1920—and imports the rest from India. France itself imports from América and Egypt. There is little hope of Indo-China's ever being able to provision France, although none of the present obstacles is irremediable. In the regions where there is enough labour for profitable large-scale enterprises, the land is taken up with food crops. In time, of course, the natives might be lured to the unpopulated regions, but the Annamites will always prefer to relegate cotton to land where rice is impossible. In addition, climatic hazards and the commercial squeeze of the Chinese take all profits from the farmer.

Silk

Until recently silk was a family industry in all countries of the Union Unlike cotton, this textile has since the conquest been the object of governmental solicitude. France now imports a great deal of silk, but from the sixteenth to the nineteenth centuries the Rhône Valley supplied the country's needs. With the opening of the Suez Canal and steam navigation, the French market was flooded first with Chinese and then with Japanese silk. Oriental silk industries have the insuperable advantage of cheap and abundant labour.

The Admirals in 1870 sent samples of Indo-Chinese silk to Lyon but without success. A system of bonuses was instituted in 1894, under De Lanessan, but were discontinued in 1900 because of Metropolitan protests. Only in 1929 were they once more renewed. Administrative encouragement, however, continued in other fields. Taxes were lowered on silk plantations and experiments were officially undertaken. Native silk had not the solidity of its European rivals, and Annamites did not take up technical suggestions nor—patriotically enough—the foreign worms which the government brought into the country. These early attempts to improve the local silk were a failure due to the high cost price.

In 1929 a contract was made between the Indo-Chinese government and thirty Lyon manufacturers. The colonial government was to supply a Metropolitan factory with 3,000,000 cocoons annually. The Lyonnais fulfilled their end of the contract and spent more than 18,000,000 francs. Trouble, however, occurred in the colony, where they were unable to supply the factory with enough work, and so it had to close down. The currency crisis also had its share in upsetting the commercial equilibrium. The government's budgetary situation prevented carrying out its schemes for bonuses to be distributed to native silk growers and spinners, and also the creation of a technical school at Pnom-Penh. Although soil, climate, and labour conditions in Indo-China are favourable to this industry, a psychology of discouragement about it has persisted.

The silk industry escaped the depression until 1930–31. Indo-China consumed far more silk than it raised, but it had to face competition from artificial silk, whose cost price was much lower. Moreover, the devaluation of silver money had made it far cheaper to buy real silk from China. Silk production increased appreciably in 1935.

Corn

Corn has long been cultivated in Indo-China, and holds an honourable place in native diet. It has the advantage of growing in places too dry for rice, with which it does not compete, and it can supplement that crop wherever it has a poor harvest. Recently corn has been planted along the banks of the Mekong, Cambodia, and especially in Laos where it requires less effort than rice—which endears it particularly to the Laotian heart.

During the depression corn rose rapidly as an article of exportation. 1933 was a record year both in regard to its value and the quantity produced, and in 1935–36 its sales price was still high. Unfortunately the Metropolitan corn market is very precarious, depending as it does upon duty on Argentine corn, which in general is much preferred by the French public, and to a tolerance that has lately worn thin on the part of French wheat growers. There is a possibility of selling Indo-Chinese corn to Japan, but as is the case with rice farmers must improve its quality and standardize their product if it is to capture a place in the world market.

Coffee

Seventy years ago coffee was introduced into Annam by the missionaries. Only recently has it been taken up by the colonists, and is now almost entirely in French hands. In 1930 the total coffee-growing area was 11,000 hectares, chiefly in Tonkin, which represents only 0·07 per cent of world production. Native crops have an even more negligible importance.

The Metropolitan market seems to offer a great outlet for Indo-Chinese coffee, but at present it absorbs only 3 per cent. Not that Indo-China exports coffee elsewhere—for the entirety of her exports goes to France—but the output is at present stationary. The quality of the colony's coffee and conditions of cultivation are very good in Annam and Tonkin, although the climate is obstreperous and the soil quite poor. But peculiar circumstances govern the coffee market and make that crop hazardous as an export. At present, however, because of the small quantity produced, Indo-China is only a mdoest spectator of the large-scale operations of Brazil in the international sphere.

Brazil's domination of the world coffee market puts other exporters at the mercy of her national caprice. An international coffee congress was held at Rio, in April 1931, in which Brazil vainly tried to come to an understanding with other coffee planters. Since Brazil produces 80 per cent of the world's coffee, she was quite able to pursue her policy single-handed. By means of a heavy export tax, the government bought up and destroyed enough coffee to absorb the annual over-production and reserve supplies. This drastic measure forcibly tied production to consumption. Plantations were restricted and new plants were taxed. In December 1932 an even stricter law forbade the planting of new trees for the next three years.

The Metropolitan market for Indo-Chinese coffee is still essentially unaffected, although Brazilian action may, independently, change the world price of coffee. The colony's coffee planters naturally want a guaranteed market in France, and insist upon higher protection against their foreign rivals. France long remained deaf to their appeals. The Minister of Commerce even claimed that Brazilian over-production made it wholly unnecessary for Indo-China to grow coffee. By 1931, however, Paris grasped the seriousness of the situation and permitted a bonus, albeit insufficient, to be offered to coffee planters in distress. The colonial government has been more solicitous, and through its efforts, Indo-Chinese coffee has weathered the storm. By 1932, the situation had definitely improved, although negotiations with Brazil since that time have deceived the hopes that were raised as to the achievement of price stability.

Tea

Unlike coffee, Indo-China offers a definite local as well as a Metro-politan market for her tea, and is the only French colony where a large-scale production is possible. Although the crop really began with the twentieth century, and its quality is in no way remarkable, it has attracted capital investment and has achieved a rapid increase in exportation. Modern methods could improve the output, since conditions in Indo-China are analogous to those of the Dutch East Indies, and even superior to Ceylon and India.

Native tea crops cover 25,000 hectares, and those of Europeans, situated mostly in the redlands, only about 4,000. Native tea has, for all but the Indo-Chinese, an unpleasant flavour, so it is only the industrially prepared tea, especially that of Annam, which has a future as an export Internal and external circumstances control this, however: the internal factor means improving its quality; and the external, conditions in the world market.

As to quality, Indo-China produces innumerable varieties, and the poor reputation which the colony's tea as a whole has acquired is due to the predominance of certain inferior brands. Others, on the contrary, compare favourably with the best Ceylonese. Like all Indo-Chinese products, it needs to be classified and standardized, with a strict elimination of fraud, especially in native teas. Favourable conditions, both as to climate and labour, mean a low cost price for a good quality tea, and this is particularly important in view of the fact that the world is flooded with tea of mediocre quality.

The fluctuations in the world tea market make for prudence in extending Indo-Chinese tea culture. World tea consumption, however, is increasing. France and her colonies, as well as local consumption, offer a protected market. But a surplus production is growing even faster, and this has naturally resulted in lowering the price. Indo-China's tea output has small importance beside that of the big tea producers—India with 40 per cent and Ceylon 27 per cent. China is a great producer and consumer, but as always statistics for that country are untrustworthy. In 1933 England and Holland came to an agreement, after initial failure. Restriction was to be based on 15 per cent of their 1929–31 output.

If Indo-China's tea plantations had reached their peak of development sooner they would have suffered far more from the depression. Even now the future of the colony's tea is highly uncertain. Its greatest hope lies in an improvement in quality, notably in that of green tea, which should enable it to conquer the local and North African markets. This goal means a deliberate adaptation of the output to a specialized market—that is, to Annamite and Moslem tastes. England controls 70 per cent of world consumption. When, in 1935, Indo-Chinese tea for the first time was on sale in London and Amsterdam, it was a flattering indication that the colony's tea might hope for a wider European market as well.

Sugar

Since Indo-China still imports much of its sugar, this would seem to be an excellent crop to develop in the colony. It is at present sporadically grown all over the peninsula, but especially in the Red River delta, where there are innumerable varieties.

Its future, from an industrial viewpoint, is very limited. From 1905 on there have been a series of abortive attempts to improve the quality of the colony's sugar by introducing new cane, notably from Réunion. Appropriate land and climatic conditions should make this crop most lucrative, especially in Annam, but the price of production is very high, notably when compared with the superior Javanese product. A serious study of local conditions means a likelihood of improvement, with the possibility of at least capturing the local market.

Tobacco

Until recently tobacco was almost wholly a family crop, raised by the natives for their own consumption. Even in areas where it was important, few farmers counted on it exclusively to assure their livelihood. Although production never filled the colony's needs, there was a little commerce in the tobacco crop.

Cambodia is the country most suitable for tobacco, although it is raised in all parts of the peninsula. With its good yield per hectare and its high sales price, tobacco should be highly remunerative for the producer. But it needs a great deal of water, abundant labour, and more fertilizer than the natives can buy. The majority of profits go to the middlemen, who are, of course, Chinese. It is still profitable enough, however, for tobacco to have ousted cotton in certain regions of Cambodia.

Indo-Chinese tobacco has the great drawback of a flavour which cannot compete, even in local favour, with the light tobacco from Java or the Philippines. The result has been that Indo-China every year was, until recently, importing more and exporting less tobacco. In the early 1920's the quantity sent to France made it appear probable that the colony would be that *Régie's* great provisioner. In 1908 the subject was first broached when an official mission drew France's attention to this possibility. Two years later some samples were sent upon request. The matter was dropped until after the War, when efforts were again made to tempt the *Régie's* jaded taste. It seemed at that time as if successive analyses would go on indefinitely. Unfortunately the *Régie* eventually selected a variety that was raised in a very underpopulated region, and which could only be produced in small quantities. Moreover, the price offered by the *Régie* for the product packed and shipped to Marseille was less than its value in Indo-China. Not discouraged, the colony asked for another local investigation, but the *Régie* preferred after reflection to buy elsewhere. It looked then as if Indo-China must needs be content with the local market, which the administration had indefatigably set about to conquer. In 1933 the consumption of foreign tobacco was forbidden, and three local factories set up. Pasquier aimed in this way to favour the local tobacco growers and to create a new industry, as well as new revenues, for the fisc. It is too early as yet to predict the results, but his experiment has aroused considerable interest in Indo-Chinese tobacco, as well as angry protests from Algeria, of whose product Indo-China was formerly a good client.

Pepper

This crop is unique in that it is exclusively cultivated by the Chinese in a limited area along the Gulf of Siam. It is entirely exported to France, where it demands high protection, despite competition there with the superior Malabar product from French Mahé, not to mention other foreign rivals. Paris has subjected Indo-Chinese pepper to alternating régimes of free trade and protection, with varying success and with much agitation in the colony. France accuses Indo-Chinese planters of not trying to conquer other markets, of demanding a protection which harms the budget, and of too poor a quality to justify so high a cost price. The planters, in turn, point to a retrogression in their crops due to Paris's refusal to give them the privileged position they require. This was especially true after the 1928 tariff went into effect, which made the Metropolitan treasury suffer so much that Indo-Chinese pepper was re-taxed. Planters complained bitterly of such Indian-giving, but by 1930 they consented to a slight renewal of the tax. Indo-China's pepper situation is undeniably unsatisfactory: the problem is really one of excessive production.

There are other miscellaneous crops which can be grown in Indo-China, but whose future is problematical. There are cocoanut, vanilla, cinnamon, and cardamoms. Certain crops have value as textiles, like ramie, but more especially jute. Rice sacks, which might be made locally and with great profit, are imported now in huge quantities from Singapore.

It is a long and costly process to get new crops to the point of competing in the world market. In 1931, 81 per cent of Indo-China's exports consisted of five articles, and the government's efforts to develop to the same point silk, cotton, and tobacco have had only mediocre results. Yet in 1936 the outlook was distinctly encouraging. There was a steady outflow of the colony's main exports—rice, corn, and rubber—at higher prices. Credit is easier than it has been, and moderate optimism is in the air. The import situation was practically unchanged, though the treaties with China and the Philippines will probably create a greater volume of trade in those directions.

Labour in the North

Indo-China, with its 23,000,000 population, numbers half that of France, in a country that is a third larger.[1] Although small by comparison with the average density per square kilometre of other Oriental countries, Indo-China has more of a population than the other French colonies. The wealth of the colony lies in its labour. Its great characteristic is its uneven distribution. Tonkin and North Annam are one of the most thickly populated regions of the world, whereas the mountain districts often have fewer than five inhabitants to the square kilometre. Three-fourths of the Indo-Chinese live on the plains near the sea—on a tenth of the whole country's surface. Ninety per cent of this population is rural, and only in recent years has there been a trend towards the colony's five large towns.[2] Of these 20,000,000 it has been estimated that 56 per cent form the active labouring class.

Landowning constitutes the sole Annamite capital. Almost all the big Annamite proprietors live in Cochin-China.[3] Tonkin has most of the others, then Cambodia follows, with almost none at all in Annam. The big bourgeoisie of Cochin-China, numerically fairly unimportant, enjoy a large percentage of that country's revenues. They are, in general, absentee landlords—only 64 per cent cultivate their own lands —who live in the towns, and who have the usual bailiff relationship with their peasants. Because of their official connections, it would be folly for one of their tenants to bring suit against these rich landowners, so the masses must resign themselves to being fleeced. Their profits do not come from their crops, because these landowners have high running expenses, but from lending money at usurious rates. In them the French have created not a bourgeoisie but a plutocracy. More than the French colonists, they have benefited by the colonial régime: for a dozen French fortunes in Indo-China, there are more than twenty Annamite and a hundred Chinese. This class constitutes a danger to rural economy, as well as to France's political sovereignty. During the de-

[1] 737,000 sq. km. to 550,000. The population is 27 to the square kilometre in Indo-China, as compared with 76 in France.
[2] Saigon-Cholon numbers 300,000; Hanoi, 120,000; Haiphong, 120,000; Pnom-Penh, 100,000; Nam-Dinh, 75,000.
[3] 6,300 out of 6,690, established by the 1931 Inquiry.

pression it was principally this group which tightened credit and provoked many forced sales.

The middling proprietors or their families do not themselves cultivate the soil, for this would be beneath their dignity. Being forced to hire labour, their property is proportionately less profitable to them than to their humbler colleagues. In turn, they resort to usury to augment their funds. Since this is the class from which town Notables are chosen, they are notoriously unscrupulous in abusing their position. They are also able, unlike the small proprietors, to use government credit facilities, and can pay much less than their legal taxes. By liberality on fête days, and by gifts to the communal cult, they acquire a certain popular standing. Their situation has been particularly good in recent years, when they have been able to sell at high prices their surplus paddy, and to use their income either in usury or in purchasing new land. This class forms about 10 per cent of the population.

Annam and Tonkin are *par excellence* the land of small properties. In the old provinces of Cochin-China property is much subdivided and consequently there is a larger class of small landowners. In Tonkin 98 per cent, and in Annam 89 per cent, of the proprietors cultivate their own land, in contrast with the situation in Cochin-China. The small landowners have very little capital. Some possess only seeds, and a few pigs or a cow. There is, too, a certain amount of mutual assistance at harvest time. These men are chronically in need of money to pay their taxes and to participate in the communal fêtes. So they are always appealing to credit which they cannot get directly but through the village Notables, who do not fail to take a big commission. Unlike the labourers, they cannot migrate if disaster overtakes the region where they live. Sometimes they run a small commerce on the side, and through family labour augment their resources. Their lack of reserve funds and their constant needs force this class of farmer to sell paddy at harvest time, or even to pledge it at a very low price. Later, to feed their families they must buy it back at a much higher figure. It is a curious commentary that as soon as this type of landowner has a spare ten piastres he hastens to lend it at the same usurious rate from which he has himself been suffering.

The situation in Annam is analogous to that of Tonkin, but is even more precarious because of the climatic conditions. Its proximity to the Annamite Range, however, makes it possible for the natives of that country to live through hard times by collecting wood and the forest herbs which grow plentifully there. Despite a perennial indebtedness, this class of proprietor has land with which to guarantee loans, and they form the stablest element of the population.

The poorest class, made up of farmers, *métayers*, and labourers, leads a very miserable existence, and has an exceptionally low standard of living. They can only satisfy their most immediate needs, and not even those in the frequent years of bad harvests. Since they are unable to offer security in land, the new credit facilities have not reached far enough down to relieve this class, and every unforeseen expense—like sickness, accident, and disaster—puts them at the mercy of the usurers. A very large rural proletariat has grown up, especially in the over-populated delta and coastal lands; here the food density is 678 to the square kilometre of rice-fields. Even in Cochin-China where there is a rice surplus, rural poverty is so great that this class not only is a political and a social danger to the state, but a living force in the country that is almost unutilized. In certain regions the situation is very critical. The misery is not due so much to low wages, as to the fact that in the present state of the colony's development, there is not enough remunerative labour to go around. The population lives in a chronic condition of part-time labour. There is no possibility for this class, even in the best years, to put any savings aside against the inevitable disasters that come from poor harvests. When misfortune occurs, there are temporary southward migrations. This seasonal displacement does not usually extend to the Western provinces of Cochin-China, where proprietors must pay high for their labour. The poor class of Indo-Chinese averages an income of 49 piastres a year, so that to live they must hire out their labour for some part of every year.

Indo-China has not only a diversity of peoples, but there are enormous differences in their productive capacity, and in the economic conditions which control this production. The labour problem takes on very different forms in the North and in the South. Even the misery of the over-populated delta region cannot force the Tonkinese to migrate in large numbers to the mountains. Nevertheless, the colonization of this region has found labour, usually in the form of *métayage*.

Métayage was at first hailed as the panacea for developing Upper and Middle Tonkin, and as a means for repopulating the country after the conquest. Unfortunately the administration, in its anxiety to develop this country so long a prey to strife, gave away land which had been only temporarily abandoned by its native owners. As banditry died down, the returning proprietors found French colonists on their lands. Not only did violence ensue in certain cases, but there was a shortage of labour since the ousted Annamites naturally refused to work for those whom they regarded as usurpers. The administration had dealt out the whole middle region of Tonkin in twenty concessions, regardless of whether or not this land could be developed by the recipients. Lack of capital and labour resulted in only about an eighth of these concessions being worked. Many had been deceived into dreams of rapid wealth: few roads, no irrigation facilities, and the climate's great hazards were obstacles, but it was the eternal instability of labour that was the worst handicap. And it grew steadily less reliable, for Doumer's public works programme gave higher wages to workmen, which made them desert the concessions in a body. During the pacification Annamites had been willing to work for Europeans simply to insure their own safety, but this was no longer necessary.

Métayage had been De Lanessan's formula for the fixation of labour. In his efforts to introduce poppy-growing for the opium *régie*, De Lanessan had thought that by giving the Tonkinese an interest in the land it might arrest their transient character, and that they would work better under European supervision. This experiment in *métayage* was successful because of the special conditions in the country at that time.

An increase in vagrancy since the beginning of the French régime had been due to the weakening of communal and parental authority. Under the Annamite government vagrancy had existed, but the state made consistent efforts to reabsorb the delinquent into community life. This was done by giving him land, on the principle that poverty was the cause of vagrancy and crime. Some of the numerous vagabonds could be absorbed as local labour, though the Annamite proprietors always preferred to hire the local villagers rather than the floating population.

The Annamite code, because it favoured small properties, did not envisage the renting of land. Capital was so scarce that money payments were exceedingly rare. Nor was *métayage*, with its fixed quota payments, an Annamite usage, so great was the fear of deception on the part of proprietor and tenant alike. Custom, under the French, grew into a compromise between tenant farmers and *métayers*. The total lack of legislation on the subject permitted the drawing up of any kind of contract, so that it usually followed local custom. The leases ran for about a year, and they were often renewed without the formality of a contract. The *métayer* can offer no guarantee, yet he must be given the indispensable equipment in advance. The instability of labour, as

146

well as the unscrupulous character of the *métayer*, makes this a very risky business. These loans are repayable at harvest time in kind, unless there is a poor crop, in which case repayment is delayed a year. The Annamite, like all farmers, invariably finds the weather intolerable and conditions impossible for repayment.

The early colonists had no appreciation of the labour problem. One author, in 1900, wrote to encourage colonization in Tonkin:

> As to native labour, it suffices to compare the number of taxpayers with the number of non-taxpayers who are from five to twelve times as numerous, to be sure that the latter will gladly accept hire.[1]

Good relations with the native officials would have solved some of these labour problems. The mandarins had means of coercing their compatriots that the French could never have at their disposal. Unfortunately certain French colonists only too often went out of their way to show disdain for native officialdom, and they, in turn, would refuse their aid, preferring not even to go near the European plantations.

Many colonists felt that the administration should supply them with labour, since the government had a political and fiscal interest in advancing French colonization. Edicts to insure the police a knowledge of what natives were employed on a plantation simply served to facilitate the tracing of criminals who often hired themselves out as a means of escaping detection. Measures designed originally to protect the employer, by forcing a labourer to have a card of identity, miscarried in practice. Employers strongly objected to having a servant extracted from their service simply to serve his term in prison, and they saw in the identity card a purely fiscal exaction. There was much red tape in connection with this card. And, in addition, the colonist, like the Annamite, preferred that the government should remain in ignorance of the number of his employees lest this knowledge be later related directly to taxation. When the colonist was made intermediary for the tax payments of his native employees, there was naturally a suspicion that he pocketed some of the proceeds. Employees easily escaped fiscal pressure by claiming that they had already paid taxes to their employers, who could as easily deny it without running any risk of verification. In either case the administration felt itself to be the loser. It must be remembered that the Ky-dong conspiracy[2] was conceived and almost succeeded under cover of the plantation system. One colonist gave more trouble than ten thousand natives, from the adminis-

[1] Greverath, A., *L'Agriculture en Indochine* (Paris, 1900), p. 48.
[2] Cf. below, p. 231.

tration's point of view. Had not the government given them free land and exemption from years of taxation? It was asking too much to require state-furnished labour as well.

The colonists' chief grievance was that the state did nothing to assure them a labour supply, nor to protect them from the malefactions of their employees. The crowning blow came in 1896, when French justice was largely substituted for Annamite in Tonkin. Corporal punishments were suppressed, and prison penalties commuted to days of forced labour. The lack of a native *état civil* made it impossible to trace a delinquent employee who had taken flight. All natives looked alike to Europeans, and a traffic in false names and identity cards flourished. Natives found, so colonists claimed, that the new code was much less severe than the old, so that they felt less than even their ordinary scruples about breaking a contract, when the spirit moved them to leave—which was often. Legal prosecution involved many formalities and the expenditure of time and money, for the plantations were always far from the courts. Wails of anger from the colonists found utterance in the desiderata of the Chambers of Agriculture. At the end of this period it was generally conceded that *métayage* had been a political success in aiding the pacification of the country, but that it was economically a failure. The natives have never recovered from their resentment at the usurpation of their land, and on those vast plantations there was no opportunity for amelioration through close contacts between planter and employer.

The necessity for sustaining French prestige makes it almost impossible for the state to prosecute colonists. Their constant interference in communal life made the planters far too powerful in administrative eyes. They could protect any malefactor they wanted. The state wished for no such intermediary between itself and the natives. The government's extraordinary timidity in regulating the triangular relationship of planter and labourer with itself characterized the early stages of colonial labour legislation.

In 1898, for the first time, the government occupied itself with contracts. The chief aim of this regulation was to force the employer to buy off his employees from *corvée* service: only a subsidiary clause regulated the deposit of a copy of the contract with the local administrator. The following year came a very important edict fixing conditions for labourers' contracts in Tonkin. The identity card regulation was retained. Contracts could not be made for less than a year. Imprisonment and fines attended the delinquent who broke his agreement. In

1902 this edict was extended to Annam, Cochin-China, and Cambodia, and up to 1910 was the charter of labour in Indo-China.

Métayage continues to be current on Northern plantations, but it is not widespread except on big properties. Labourers much prefer seasonal work, with periodic returns to their native villages. *Métayers* show negligence in caring for the animals entrusted to them—notably, working them too hard and not feeding them enough. Bitter experience has made money advances infrequent. The *métayer*, though he has enough capital to buy seed and fertilizer, is usually very badly off. His contract is not an easy one, and after he has lived up to its hard terms he must pay his taxes and his workers. A good harvest affects his status favourably, and his social position is decidedly above that of labourers. But for him to be really well off, he must own his own ploughing animals and not run into debt. The *cai*, or foreman-intermediary between *métayer* and employer, is the enemy of both in his harsh treatment of the former, and in his exploitation of the latter. *Métayers'* and labourers' contracts are usually made through the village Notables; individual contracts do not exist. When the Notables are the middlemen, one may be sure that the labour contracted for is involuntary. In the guise of a new tax or *corvée*, the Notables can force any member of the commune to work for themselves or for the colonists.

It was estimated in 1933 that two-thirds of the Tonkinese are salaried workers for at least a part of every year. Work is difficult, they live from day to day, and only enjoy release from hunger at harvest time. Seasonal migrations are the rule in over-populated districts, though in certain of the provinces which have two rice crops the workers sometimes stay longer. Such labour is difficult to stabilize, the best workers try never to hire out their labour far from their own villages, and prefer to eke out an existence near home through various minor industries, small commerce, and fishing. Colonists have tried higher salaries and a plot of ground as inducements to make this floating proletariat take root, but such a system merges into *métayage*. Salaries differ enormously, depending on the season, the region, the abundance of labour, and the kind of work. Workers by the year are treated as part of the family, and are paid partly in money and about half in kind. This arrangement is easier for the labourer, who is usually far from any other sources of supply. In his budget the worker spends about three-fourths for food, one-tenth for lodging, and about 4 per cent for clothes.[1]

[1] Dumarest, A., *La Formation des Classes Sociales en Pays Annamites* (Lyon, 1935), p. 159.

The earliest regulations of labour in the South dealt exclusively with the servant problem. The same requirements for identity cards were made in Cochin-China, but applied with greater strictness in Tonkin. But until the end of the century there was no real labour problem. Up to that time the natural growth of the population had sufficed for labour needs. The opening of Cochin-China's Western provinces to colonization precipitated the application of the 1896 Tonkin labour edict. As in the North, it was the first legalized punishment of workers breaking their contracts. In 1903 the worker was allowed to appeal against an employer's failure to fulfil his end of the contract. The planters, as usual, were dissatisfied with this impartial arrangement, and asked for severer regulations. In addition they wanted authorization to recruit groups of labourers for an indefinite term, through the village Notables and not by individual contracts. Their agitation was such that a committee studied these proposals, and ended by embodying, in a 1909 edict, a more concrete definition of employees' contractual duties.

The edict of March 6, 1910, constituted a working code in forty-nine articles for the whole Union. Permission to hire labour had to be got from the local administrator, and in this way state supervision was inaugurated. Contracts had to be registered at Saigon and then sent to the Resident of the province where the labourer lived. There were also special rulings for female labour. This edict represented the second step in the colony's labour legislation, and it was in force until the end of the War, when the return of workers from France necessitated making new measures.

The central problem in Southern Indo-China is the migration of labour. The very fertile redlands of Cochin-China and Cambodia badly needed workers. The natives of the South offer a very restricted labour. While the Cambodians and Laotians are physically robust, they are few in number and very reluctant to work. They also live scattered throughout the country, and are both unavailable and unstable. The mountain peoples are the most unreliable of all: they distrust foreigners and dislike regular work. Nevertheless the Muongs and the Mois will work at certain seasons, but never for more than a few days at a time, and only for the sake of getting certain indispensable articles. The Mois apply in groups for employment, and return every night to their homes. Planters will only hire them if they cannot get Annamites. They are good at wood cutting but show a marked dislike of road building, and a general reluctance to learn anything. They can be paid in kind and have a weakness for textiles, salt, and empty bottles. At best this labour is seasonal and nomadic.

Of all Asiatic labourers the Chinese are by far the most satisfactory, as is shown by the high prices paid to them, and to the agents who procure their labour. The Chinese are inexhaustible numerically and physically; they have no need to adjust themselves to the Indo-Chinese climate, they are industrious and sober, with an amazing adaptability to either farming or commerce. The drawbacks to their labour are the higher price they demand: their transiency in the colony; their tendency to leave farming for commerce, except in Cambodia; and their close-knit political organization that makes them feared by French and Annamites alike.

In 1928 a census of foreign labourers in Indo-China showed that a vast majority of twelve thousand were Chinese, and that the remaining few were principally Javanese. An article comparing Javanese labour favourably to the Chinese,[1] had early awakened the Cochin-Chinese planters' interest. The Javanese were good and steady workers, though less robust than the Chinese. Their labour output was smaller, but they attached themselves more to the soil, were more easily disciplined, and totally without that commercial aptitude that made the Chinese a problem. The Dutch government naturally opposed their wholesale migration. In 1906 Indo-China contrived to get official consent to importing Javanese labour under certain conditions. The experiment proved highly successful: 45 per cent of the first group, and 85 per cent of the second, renewed their contracts. Good agents were partly responsible for the outcome, as well as the co-operation of the Dutch government in matters of transportation. The War, however, changed the willingness of the Dutch to permit labourers to leave Java. The stricter conditions that were subsequently imposed, and for a more limited migration, made Javanese labour more expensive than Annamite. In addition, there were certain complications, notably in food preparation, which arose from the fact that many Javanese were Moslems.

The obstacles to transporting labourers from North Indo-China to the South were primarily psychological. The misery of the over-populated Tonkinese delta, the opportunities offered by the unoccupied, fertile lands of the South—all militated in favour of a large-scale emigration. In 1898 occurred the first unsuccessful attempt to send peasants from Annam to Cochin-China. At that time the government's public works programme had raised the price of labour and this helped to

[1] *Quinzaine Coloniale*, 25 juillet, 1903.

keep them in the North. Moreover, most of the coolies who came South at that time had never before tilled the soil. The results were so unfortunate that there was a marked though short-lived swing back to Chinese labour.

In 1907 the Governor of Cochin-China proposed measures to the Hanoi Chamber of Agriculture for the transportation of Tonkinese labour. Rather naturally this bore no fruit, since the Tonkinese colonists had every reason to prevent an exodus of workers that would raise the price of labour still more in the North. The success of the Javanese workers, until the War, allowed the problem to remain in abeyance. At the same time, however, a similar attempt was made in Annam to give such immigrants lands in the South, which might establish them permanently in the country. The Annamite government, which was charged with hiring this labour, proceeded to get rid of all the undesirable elements from its communes. The results were disastrous: crime flourished with abandon. Only about twenty remained out of the entire group. Feeling that the mistake lay in enlisting the services of the native government, which had no interest in the success of the enterprise, the planters organized the next attempt themselves. They could only use the isolated and ineffective efforts of native agents who received a commission for each labourer hired. The Tonkinese who came were very unhappy: very different climatic conditions and a feeling of isolation from their homes induced their wholesale flight, with the inevitable loss of all the money they had received in advance.

About 1910 the problem took on a more acute form with the sudden growth of French rubber colonization. Attention became centred now on Western Cochin-China, where no population was already installed, and hence no eviction problem existed. On the other hand, it was virgin land and required abundant labour to conquer the dense forest. From this development was born the Indo-Chinese labour problem, with its twin growths of an Annamite bourgeoisie and proletariat. The long administrative and agricultural period was giving way to an industrial and financial era, that took on its full proportions only after the War.

Labour in the South

At the outset there was little trouble between employer and labourer. No large groups of workers existed. The colonists had lived long in the country and the workers had still the traditional respect for authority. With the post-War development of big stock companies, these early personal contacts were lost. Absenteeism, ignorant supervisors, the changing native mentality, a decline in European prestige—all were reflected in the new labour problems. This change in attitude was less apparent among the agricultural than among the industrial workers. From 1920 to 1925 occurred the first serious conflicts: out of these, in turn, came government intervention and the beginning of real labour legislation.

In 1913 Sarraut had created an Inspection of Cochin-Chinese labour. By 1918 this was extended to the other countries, excepting Laos, and embodied in a code that is still the basis of the colony's labour legislation. The government's control was initiated from the moment the contract was signed and deposited in the presence of an official. The contract's duration was not to exceed three years of labour, and work was limited to a ten-hour day, with extra pay for supplementary work. The coolie had a right to lodging, care, and medical attention, and the non-separation of families. Fines and imprisonment were specified for failure to live up to these conditions. Desertion on the part of the labourer was defined as forty-eight hours' absence from the plantation, but there were also stricter penalties for defaulting employers.

This code proved fundamentally satisfactory, but it had inevitable gaps which the development of plantations made increasingly evident. There was a phenomenal growth in the number of coolies imported: 3,684 in 1925; 17,177 in 1926; 18,000 in 1927; with a drop to 7,428 in 1929. The administration tried both to simplify and improve the formalities of recruiting, but in view of the steady decline of contracts, the planters have more and more claimed the right to hire workers without preliminary authorization. The chief cause of friction between planters and administration is the restriction of the recruiting zones. North Annam and the Tonkinese delta are the regions most open, and eight thousand coolies might be transported annually from there to the South. Unfortunately the population is most scattered in the mountainous mining areas. The fear lest wholesale emigration raise to prohibitive prices the cost of Tonkinese labour is the basis of attacks on the government's policy, by colonists like De Monpezat.[1] The government points out with justice that the decline in contracts is due principally to the world depression, and that a rise in the cost of Northern labour has made for higher standards of native living in the miserable over-populated North.

The unscrupulousness of native labour agents is beyond dispute. Sorcery, the use of drugs, and a gross misrepresentation of the contract,

[1] Cf. below, p. 163.

are all devices used to persuade the miserable coolie to consent to what is really three years' slavery. The Southern plantation is represented as an earthly paradise with all the food one can eat, short hours of labour, and high pay. No mention is made of fines or corporal punishments, or that days out for sickness are not paid. These agents earn from ten to twelve piastres for each coolie hired. The work is particularly easy after a serious inundation. An armed guard is necessary to convoy to the boats the procession of coolies who have unwittingly consented to work in the South. Thousands of men by such trickery have been deprived of their liberty and many of their lives, due to conditions on the Southern plantations. The return of disgruntled coolies to the North, as well as Annamite nationalist propaganda, has made it increasingly difficult to hire more of such labour. The force of this reaction was shown in 1930 by the murder of Bazin, head of the Labour Bureau.[1]

The government soon attacked this labour-hiring problem. A first attempt to control native agents was through a system of licensing. Next the recruiting areas were restricted. The state tried to make the gullible peasant cognizant of the terms of his contract, to make the medical examination effective, to make the coolie realize that the money he was given must be paid back in labour, and that it was not simply a gift in return for his signature and the pleasure of taking his photograph. An attempt was also made to approximate accuracy in the declarations on labourers' identity cards. It has been calculated that through the connivance of the village Notables, about 30 per cent of them are false.

The conditions of labour on Southern plantations have been the object of a sensational literature, and have been ably exploited by the Nationalist party and by the Opposition in the Chamber of Deputies. The result has been much statement and refutation: every fact has been laid open to discussion. When all these remarks have been subjected to impartial scrutiny, certain facts seem to emerge. Coolies worked about ten hours a day or a night, for which they were paid about 2.50 francs, with their lodging and usually their food. Unfortunately this salary arrangement was not definitely regulated by the employer himself, but through a native foreman, or *cai*. The *cai* is indisputably the coolies' worst enemy. He collects a commission from each meagre salary, he forces the coolie to borrow money from him at fantastically high rates, and he realizes a profit on food and even medical supplies.

[1] Cf. below, p. 487.

154

The worker is a serf to this petty creditor and overlord, who in addition often subjects him to unfair and brutal treatment. The worst kind of torture has been administered, as many eye-witnesses have related, which makes sorry reading in propaganda pamphlets. Coolies are punished by fines and blows; their correspondence is brutally censored; they are cut off from their families and communes. Misery and brutality lead to wholesale desertions and suicides. Europeans may plead excuse in the effect of the climate upon them, and that misunderstandings are the result of ignorance of the country and its people, and of the inebriating effect of unlimited power—nevertheless the coolie is the sufferer. The inadequacy of police protection on these distant plantations, as well as the prevalence of theft among the Annamites, has led to the planters' meting out justice with an arbitrary hand. In the case of deserters punishment has been particularly inhuman.

Part of the coolies' misery is due to their physical condition. The majority of workers are in poor health when they arrive. Agents get mostly the worst elements, and native officials are glad to pack off the local dregs. Most contracts are signed because of a famine, since physical depletion alone makes the worker willing to migrate. And permanent under-nourishment leaves little resistance to disease. Medical examinations, despite governmental efforts, have not prevented the embarkation of sick coolies. In addition, the moral isolation of the South augments their poor health. Nor have they proper care on the plantations. The exploitation of virgin soil, especially the deforestation of redlands, is extremely unhealthy work. Malaria has been one of the worst local diseases. Quinine was distributed but in insufficient quantities, and often the coolies failed to take it, not appreciating its value. Béribéri, a malady to which the Annamites are prone, has increased with a poor rice diet. Cooking was left to the coolies themselves, but they were not given the proper facilities. Drinking-water in many cases was bad. Ritual burial was not assured to those who died. The families were not even notified so that they could perform the rites so important in Annamite belief. In 1927 the mortality on Southern plantations was from four to five times as great as Cochin-China's average death-rate. It was naturally worst among those workers who had not become acclimatized, and on the redland plantations where the supervisors were newcomers who know nothing about local conditions.

Labour represented 75 per cent of a big plantation's expenses. In 1924 a recruiting agent received 16 piastres per coolie. Passage cost

10 piastres, and a like sum was given to each coolie in advance. The total of 36 piastres for every worker, before he even got to the plantation, rose after 1926. It represented a big investment for planters—that of 7,000,000 francs for a plantation importing 10,000 coolies. The small planter who got labour from an adjacent commune had no such expense. Such an outlay means that the employer is going to take no chance of having his coolies decamp—which they do at the slightest pretext. Hence he must regard as desertion any mildly prolonged absence from the plantation, for it may jeopardize the whole enterprise's success.

Desertions are not caused exclusively by bad treatment or nostalgia. There is a certain natural resentment of native peoples at having to cultivate their soil for foreign usurpers. Also, a series of accidents can awaken a superstitious belief that the spirits are hostile to an undertaking, and this is enough to make a hundred coolies take flight overnight. Cham ruins, coming to light during one canal dredging, caused the immediate withdrawal of all the workers. Self-mutilation is a current Annamite device for ceasing to work. It may be motivated by vengeance, or fear, or plain laziness. Then they often claim that it was done by a brutal employer. Gaming is a native weakness that may so involve its victims in debt or in dispute that their only recourse is to take flight. Or coolies may be lured from one plantation to another. This has grown to be a regular profession, and a planter who has expended vast sums importing his labour may one day find that a neighbour has spirited his coolies away. Such losses of workers have reached serious proportions: in 1927 three thousand workers deserted. The lack of an *état civil* and the heavy traffic in identity cards make recapture virtually impossible.

Varenne was the Governor who, after Sarraut, left his mark on Indo-China's labour legislation. He filled in the gaps by creating a general Inspection of Labour, better recruiting formalities, and more protection for the worker in regard to sickness, accidents, and repatriation. By increasing these guarantees, Varenne further antagonized the planters. They were already irate at the higher price of labour in the North, and at the expense to which government regulations were already putting them. But they were most seriously offended by the insinuation that they were treating their coolies brutally. Their desire for more authority and initiative is part of their general reaction against *étatisme*.

The earliest form taken by government control of labour was increased medical care. In 1924 sanitary control was given to doctors of the Institut Pasteur to conduct research on malaria. Companies, in order to decrease coolie mortality, were willing to finance these efforts. Safe drinking-water, enforced vaccination, copious distribution of quinine, and plentiful supplies of drugs were part of the new regulations. The Bernard Commission in 1925 had studied improvement of plantation infirmaries. These medical requirements cost the companies an additional 140 to 258 francs per coolie, and naturally the planters resented what they termed excessive coddling. The government felt that it was not over-paternalistic in a country given to swift and fatal epidemics, and it had the satisfaction of having its work enthusiastically approved in 1927 by a delegate from the League of Nations. The experiments made on the Michelin plantation at Thuan-loi, in 1929, proved that these expensive hygienic precautions were more than repaid by increased production.

In preparation for his important edict of October 25, 1927, Varenne had long studied labour problems. Although, in general, the partisan of decentralization, he felt that a federal inspection of labour could cope far better with the increasingly difficult situation than the old local inspectors, because it involved more than one country. These officials were to be chosen from among the civil service, and in some provinces this resulted in a mixed political and labour control. Some planters refused to let their property be inspected, and accused the officials of giving political considerations an exaggerated primacy. Varenne was not discouraged, and further worried planters by increasing control of the recruiting system. He tried to soothe the Tonkinese colonists by pointing to the local 3 per cent growth of the population, so as to allay their worries lest all the labour be drained to the South. As for the big companies, this was the period of the rubber boom, characterized by the lush growth of speculation. These mushroom concerns often exploited their stockholders before their concessions, and were naturally less considerate of their employees than of those who had entrusted to them their savings.

Varenne worked out accident and sickness insurance when he laid down the principle of limited working hours. He instituted most successfully a system of workers' savings, as a way of keeping at least a nucleus of their wages from being dissipated. Guarantees as to housing, lodging, and salaries were also reinforced. Varenne left Indo-China before he could complete this work, but his projects were taken up by Pasquier. The malaria experimentation of the Pasteur Institute proved to be of great worth. Béribéri was cured by improving the coolie diet by adding to the traditional rice some fresh meat and vegetables. Comfortable lodgings and pure drinking water were used more as preventive measures than the curative type of medicine. Salaries were to be paid monthly: some employers had always delayed payments as long as they dared, because pay day was often followed by a wholesale decampment. Clothing and housing were minutely—perhaps too much so—regulated, and half-pay specified for sickness. A contract could not be made for more than three years with repatriation at its expiration, when the worker received his savings account.

A report by A. Thomas, of the League of Nations' International Labour Bureau, in 1929, called Pasquier's attention to working conditions for women and children, with suggestions that were later embodied as edicts. On the employers' side there were to be stricter enforcement of contracts. Although the legislation had decreased the number of desertions to 10 per cent, they were still much too frequent. Improved police technique had also resulted in bringing to justice about half of these deserters.

In general it may be said that this legislation was successful: there were many more renewals of contracts. 1929–30 was a year of acute agricultural crisis, and there were only six collective refusals to work on the Southern plantations, and in only one case did armed force intervene. The government showed itself willing to help planters provided they recognized the state's right to intervene and to control labour.

In 1930 the *Grand Conseil* adopted in principle the government's reforms, and capped them with a decree making the arbitration of differences between capital and labour obligatory. The debates leading up to these decisions showed the unconciliatory spirit of the employer group, especially *vis-à-vis* the administration. In 1928 the planters and companies formulated their grievances to the government. They pointed to the enormous cost of transportation, and to the obstacles in the way of hiring labour. Coolies often turned out to be dangerous agitators, and penalties were not severe enough against infractions of contracts. The state had forced planters to raise the coolies' salaries so high that the cost price of articles could not compete with their rivals'. The planters wanted the state to aid them in getting workers, and then to relapse into benevolent inaction. Inspectors, they claimed, visited only the French plantations, and never went near the Chinese or Annamites. Constant government intervention had not only raised prices, but the minute regulation of housing, for instance, meant great expenditure for what was unsuitable to the climate and to the coolies' needs. Tonkin colonials still resented the draining of workers to Southern plantations and to the Pacific Islands. Salaries in the South were from two to five times higher than those in the North.

The government's general policy, not directly concerned with labour legislation, tends to increase small properties as the best solution to the proletariat problem. The growth of Communism has precipitated this movement. The creation of big Annamite properties has, in many ways, been unfortunate, for the native bourgeoisie are the worst oppressors of their compatriots. Social service has been developed to alleviate misery: private initiative, it is hoped, will co-operate here, with and through public support. Medical service in this respect is especially important. Diet and exercise may improve Annamite stamina and resistance to disease.

From the native viewpoint migration to the South has every economic advantage. Higher salaries in the South drive out starvation wages in the North. Government inspection has done little or nothing for the Northern plantations, but it has improved matters in Cochin-China. The savings system organized by Varenne was originally misunderstood by the natives, as but one more skin game, but in 1931, when the first instalment was paid back,[1] there was a distinct change in their attitude. By this device the government may actually instil in the Annamites the habit of saving. The state also profits by having fewer emergency cases that require repatriation.

The whole labour problem is now in abeyance because of the depression. But even so the big-scale importations of contract labour seem definitely over. The problem of how to attach these immigrants to the soil seems also to have been resolved through the village type of labour colony. The expense this involves makes it feasible only for big companies. Formerly only men were imported, and they lived in a kind of barracks. The present trend is, rather, to bring whole families South. History has shown the expansion possibilities in the Annamite race, and these can be utilized by giving them the kind of life they want—a house, rice-fields, and a place for the family tombs. There are at present two outstanding villages of colonization. That of Ha-tien covers fifteen thousand hectares. An experiment is being undertaken there by a company with the Mission's co-operation. The Rach-gia village is about half of that size. There the natives after a trial period of six years become

[1] The employer places 5 per cent of the monthly wages to the worker's account.

outright owners of the land. The government there is trying to use Annamite methods of colonization. As yet it is too soon to foretell the outcome.

There is no immediate prospect of machines replacing human labour in Indo- China. Rice-fields, being under water, make the use of machinery impracticable. Moreover, the transplanting requires periodic, intensive labour, a type of work well adapted to family labour, for even the small children can help. Nor is the type of work on rubber plantations adapted to machines. Tapping rubber trees is delicate, and requires adroitness and finesse rather than brute force. Annamites are particularly fitted for this work. Now that the cost of wholesale labour transportation is over, and the difficulties of provisioning are lessened by the building of roads, and the new agreement limiting rubber production is in force, Annamite labour is definitely cheaper and more suitable. According to the latest report of Jean Goudal (1936), the worst conditions are definitely over.

Labour legislation in Indo-China grew spontaneously with the development of labour itself, but not out of it, as was the case in Europe. Being a colony, Indo-China was artificially endowed with a ready-made code. The first legislation was sporadic, but in 1927 it became systematic and general. In 1933 it was completed by regulating the status of free labour. Gaps, however, still remained, as, for instance, the failure to regulate contracts between natives. Nor has the farmer yet been rescued from the grip of the usurer. A more detailed accident legislation was also felt to be desirable.

During 1935 and 1936 important edicts increased labour protection by which contract workers are now really salaried workers who have appreciable advantages over free workers. The 1937 completion of the labour code begun by Varenne was inspired by the liberal laws of the Blum government. Women's labour has been regulated with prohibition of night work; children under twelve can no longer be hired as labourers; the former ten-hour day has been reduced to nine hours, and in 1938 will be further diminished to eight. One day's rest a week is obligatory, and the workers have a right to paid vacations. This will be completed by the fixation of a minimum salary for all workers, based on the local needs and conditions in each province. A minute inquiry was required to lay down rules for this last edict, and it was conducted by a Franco-native committee named by Robin. The multiple technical details involved delayed the promulgation of this code until January 1937. Further provisions rounded out Varenne's edicts in providing for a more complete accident and compensation insurance, and the arbitration of conflicts.

With the most humanitarian concepts possible, it has seemed to many premature to apply a European code to Annamites: for example, to give an eight-hour day to an Annamite who does not work steadily four hours out of twelve. A labourer walks off if he is asked to replace the tools he has been using. His leisure, it seems probable, would not be profitably spent. Annamites have not method or discipline in their work, probably due to the spasmodic if intensive labour demanded by the rice-fields.

The Annamites have distinct psychological as well as economic drawbacks as farmers. Their whole life is so impregnated with ritual and static Chinese philosophy that it makes antique methods meritorious simply because they are old. New crops, the regular care of animals, the use of fertilizers are all incurably repugnant to him. He is even suspicious of agricultural credit, that will extract him from the blood-sucking usurers. Rice-fields require hard work of a disagreeable kind, standing knee-deep in water and shooing off predatory animals for hours at a time—yet it lasts for only a brief while. This has developed the qualities of perseverance and industry, but it has done nothing to remedy the Annamite's total lack of initiative. The native farmer works within the strict orbit of his needs, which may be summed up in his philosophy that it is easier to do without something than to work for it. If his daily needs are satisfied, the Annamite takes no thought for the morrow. The historical explanation of mandarinal exactions may be brought forward, and the sumptuary laws that restricted display of possessions, but with the increase of security and needs this attitude should gradually break down. Varying the crops should stimulate exchange in regions that formerly raised all the same products, and had no means of communication by which to distribute their highly perishable resources. Education over a long period of years is needed as a parallel effort to extending agricultural credit, before the Annamite's mental set-up will permit him and stimulate him to become a good farmer and labourer.

Free rather than contract labour is in accord with French policy: and contract labour did drive out the worst form of requisitioned labour. It seems likely that free labour will soon supplant contracts, but this somewhat depends on the railway system's completion. It should in any case result in a more equitable distribution of the population. If labourers can return frequently to their native villages with savings and in good health, free labour will automatically flourish.

Corvées

In 1897 *corvées* in Cochin-China were fixed at thirty days, and of these the communes could use ten. Ten more had to be bought at fixed prices, and the remaining third were to be served out in public works. The next year an edict absorbed *corvées* into the personal tax, and the principle of purchasing exemption, instead of working off *corvée* service, was finally established. The other countries of the Union went through the same legislative process.

In studying requisitioned labour, the important differences between law and practice must always be kept in mind. *Corvées* were very soon legally abolished, but they were retained in practice, though increasingly restricted. With the difficulty of getting free labour, especially for public works, it was the only method of accomplishing a service of undoubted social utility, but naturally the whole system lent itself to abuse. A mandarin was the indispensable intermediary for procuring this labour, and he used it naturally to pay off old scores. The heavy mortality that ensued was an eloquent tribute to the lack of care, poor provisioning, and wholesale desertions that railway building, notably, involved. The difficult climate, the almost insuperable obstacles to any accomplishment in the absence of pack-animals and roads, as well as too unlimited authority, accounted for the overseers' brutality. It was legally forbidden to strike coolies but there were, according to eyewitnesses, undeniable reprisals when the coolies dared to complain of maltreatment.

Abuses were so flagrant that Violette complained of them officially in his famous budget report of 1910. The horror of burden bearing is profound in the hearts of all men. Even when they were well paid, requisitioned coolies did not emerge physically and morally unscathed. And sometimes force had to be used on them. Men were often taken from far more useful work in the fields. The colonial government had not shown the same consideration as had the Annamite régime for native customs. Village Notables arbitrarily selected their victims who were perennially the same. These men spent their lives perpetually in transit from one *corvée* to another, without fêtes or family life. Villages were deserted at the approach of a traveller who might have a permit to requisition assistance. It is true that penury of labour is one of the greatest colonial problems, and that coolies desert even when they are well paid and well treated. The perpetual need for labour is the unanswerable argument to humanitarian reproaches, and it explains the divergence between law and practice. It is certain that requisitioned labour has given way in large measure to contract labour, and in time both may decline before the prevalence of free labour. Emperor Bao Dai's Labour Charter of 1933 recognizes its inherent injustice, and its solely exceptional necessity. Only high state officials, with the consent of elected assemblies, may requisition labour, and then solely for emergencies of public necessity. Such service must be remunerated at fixed wages, and only used where free labour is not available. The 1937 Labour Charter abolished *corvées* unconditionally in the directly administered countries of the Union.

Labour in the Pacific Islands

In the last decade of the nineteenth century a group of French merchants recruited Annamites, through Chinese agents, for work in the Pacific Islands. All the phenomena of early contract labour, under the appearance of legality, characterized this abominable trade—the separation of families and deception about the work and its fabulous salaries. The first period, 1890–95, was the worst, and few lived to be repatriated. After this the government became somewhat stirred and ordered an inquiry. Nevertheless, Doumer reauthorized this trade, despite many strong remonstrances.

These circumstances were almost identically reproduced in the 1920's. The first detachment of workers was such a success that one French company created a direct boat service between Indo-China and the Islands. Seven ships between 1920 and 1928 carried 9,363 coolies, who were deposited in about equal proportions at Nouvelle Calédonie and the Nouvelles Hebrides. The former island possessed such raw materials needed by France as cotton, coffee, cacao, copra, nickel, and chromium, all concentrated in a relatively small area. A steady diminution in the number of natives necessitated this importation of labour, and the Annamites were very successful in supplying the need. The Islands experienced a revival. New colonists came and business began to flourish.

In 1927, when it was proposed to create a General Inspection of Labour, a scandal was aired in regard to this highly profitable labour venture. The missionary of reform was none other than that unscrupulous conquistador—the Marquis de Monpezat, colonist, official, and director of the *Volonté Indochinoise*. Monpezat's important interests in

Tonkin were being affected by the draining of labour to the Pacific Islands, and this most disinterested of motives lay at the bottom of his crusade. He showed up this twentieth-century business as a scandalous slave trade, and the patriotic motives evoked by its sponsors as nothing more than plain profiteering. The powerful *Société des Phosphates de l'Océanie* used its influence with the administration to procure, through the village Notables, more cheap Tonkinese labour, so as to save them from having to hire the more expensive Chinese. Monpezat, in his publicity, spared no detail of the terrible conditions, not only on the Islands themselves, but on the boats transporting the workers. The unhealthy climate, and the failure to take any medical care of the sick or legal care for the rights of the labourers, he also scored. Monpezat became the bane of the government's existence, but the facts that he brought to light could not be denied, notably in proving the administration's guilty knowledge of this terrible trade. After long hesitation the government sent an Inspector to the Islands. His report was not published, but it was said on the whole to be favourable. The conspiracy of silence and general inaction again aroused Monpezat to the attack. His revelations once more made a profound impression. The profits he showed to have been made by the Pacific Islands Companies would more than have covered the higher cost of Chinese labour. Nor did a kilogramme of the phosphates of these patriotic concerns go either to France or to her colony.

The attitude of the administration was simply a denial of these charges. Tonkinese labourers, they claimed, readily adapted themselves to the climate, as the numerous renewals of contracts testified, and they were much better off there than in the delta. Indo-China belonged to the French Empire, and therefore owed help to the less fortunate colonies. Moreover, these workers would create new consumers of Indo-Chinese goods, in the now under-populated Pacific Islands. Annamite nationalists were and still are strongly opposed to this labour exodus, but then they are against sending Annamites anywhere outside the country for either military or commercial motives. When it was rumoured, in 1929, that five hundred Annamites were to be sent as a labour experiment to French Equatorial Africa, the native press went into a frenzy of indignation. As may be imagined, the abuses of the Pacific Islands venture have been capitalized in Communist propaganda.

THE ECONOMY OF INDO-CHINA

The Chinese

When Annam had shaken off China's domination in the fifteenth century, the Chinese in the country became legally, though not spiritually, foreigners. Those along the Northern frontier turned bandit, while another group, former Minh partisans, asked the Emperor of Annam for refuge in Cochin-China, where they settled near the Gulf of Siam. These Southern Chinese participated, and with profit, in the interminable Annamite-Khmer wars, and founded along with the later flourishing ports of Hatien, Rach-gia, Caman, the most important rice market in the country at Cholon. It was the Chinese who first colonized the Mekong delta, for not until 1699 did the Annamites place there an administration of their own.

Under Gia-long, for the first time, the Chinese infiltration took on the proportions of a migration. Usually they came in groups and took up commerce in the towns. Because of the prestige they enjoyed, the Chinese had a very favourable position, contrary to the usual Annamite attitude towards foreigners. The Annamite reaction, in general, was more of admiration than of affection. He called the Chinese respectfully "my uncle," whereas the Chinese, in the imperial tradition, still thoughtfully referred to the Annamite as the tail of a rat. When the Emperor Tu-duc had to deal with the French and simultaneously with a Tonkinese rebellion, he gave the Northern provinces of Quang-yen, Sontay, and Thai-Nguyen over to the Chinese partisans from Yunnan who were, at least officially, helping him against the rebels. Thus in the North and in the South, as well as in the towns of Annam, the Chinese firmly entrenched themselves.

The Chinese infiltration into Cambodia was of long and indefinite standing. Unlike those who went to Annam to make money and then return to China, the Chinese who came to Cambodia remained there and mixed with the population, devoting themselves less to commerce than to farming. The Khmer code never especially favoured the Chinese, for Cambodia had never been a vassal state. Each foreign group had its leader, but his powers never exceeded those of police discipline. From other viewpoints, notably the fiscal, the Chinese were assimilated to the Khmers, and aside from minor restrictions they enjoyed the same civil rights. They live unevenly distributed throughout the country, and form about a tenth of the total population. About ten thousand of them live at Pnom-Penh, which has a large Chinese quarter. None of the antagonism which characterizes their dealings with the Annamites embitters Sino-Cambodian relations. The Chinese are the most active group economically in the country, and the Khmers are only too thankful to be relieved of such onerous tasks. A Chinese husband is considered an excellent match for a Khmer woman, and the ensuing race of half-breeds is superior to the pure Khmer brand in energy and initiative.

In both Annam and Cambodia the Chinese were allowed to yield to their natural propensity for group life, and to organize themselves into congregations, called *bangs*, according to province and dialect. The heads of these congregations were selected by them, and were responsible to the Annamite government for taxes and order. They enjoyed the same civil rights as Annamites and were, moreover, exempted from military service and *corvées*. The Annamite Emperors regretted their liberality, and from time to time tried to reassert their authority by expelling the Chinese implicated in commercial fraud or clandestine opium trade. Legally they were assimilated to the Annamites, and since the codes were Chinese-inspired, they suffered no legislative hardships. The congregation unit was only possible where the Chinese remained together in towns and were not scattered throughout the countryside. They farmed certain indirect taxes, like that of gaming, and they were the official distributors of opium and salt for the Annamite government. Later they temporarily performed the same function for the French, but were subsequently suppressed because their power was becoming too great. If the money which they made with such ease had remained in the country, the problem would not have grown so acute. But those who came to Annam rarely brought their families with them, and repatriated themselves and their money as soon as they had made a fortune. They did contract secondary marriage alliances with Annamite women, and thus formed a numerous group of half-breeds called *minl. huong*. Up to the reign of Minh-Mang they were regarded as Chinese, but a need to increase the population caused that Emperor to turn them into Annamites. He still, however, treated them as a class apart, until they were gradually absorbed into the native population.

Contrary to what happened in Cambodia, the Chinese lived side by side with the Annamites, and yet were never a part of them. It is impossible to tell, even approximately, the number of Chinese in Annam before the French conquest, but they were certainly most numerous in Cochin-China. Usually the Chinese disembarked without money, but with an ability that soon got him employment. By thrift he rose to the status of small trader. Sober, industrious, and tenacious, it was only a step to his becoming a big merchant or banker. The Annamites badly needed capital and credit institutions. Poverty, gaming, a lack of foresight and of perseverance and co-operation—these were all Annamite defects which the Chinese could exploit. The fact that the Chinese could wax rich by charging a 60 per cent interest rate is significant in itself. Thus the Annamites were drawn into an inextricable network of obligations, largely due to their own weakness and incapacity. The Chinese had lost their political control over Annam, but they had substituted a no less deadly hold on the country's economy. They had never relinquished their intellectual and artistic domination.

The superficial resemblance between Annamites and Chinese has been inevitably exaggerated, but not enough has been said of their mutual antagonism. The Chinese do not disguise their feelings of contempt for their former vassals. The Annamites, on their side, resent the Chinese as arrogant, perfidious, and leech-like—yet they admire them for their success. It is, however, the deadly hatred of the inferior for the superior. It is a curious fact that the sense of solidarity, whose lack was partly responsible for the Annamite downfall, should now be slowly forged through a hatred for their Chinese masters. For the French, Sino-Annamite hostility is the greatest guarantee against either group's becoming a political menace.

The Chinese, far from opposing the French conquest, aided and abetted it. The war was only a stupid accident, contrary to the traditional policy of both participants. The French attitude towards the Chinese has been almost as liberal as that of the Annamite government, and for the same reasons—that they are indispensable to the country's existence. A high head tax exempts them from *corvées* and military service. They know thoroughly the Annamites and the country, and far better than any Westerner ever could. They are the essential link between the victor and the vanquished. First as provisioners of the troops, then as Farmers of the indirect taxes, they secured an ever greater hold on the colony's commerce and banking. It is not the vocal Annamites who are, as yet, the rivals of the Chinese, but the French capitalists and bankers themselves. Juridically they are now under the French commercial code, and in criminal cases under French or native law, depending on whether the other litigant is Asiatic or European. In regard to civil rights, they receive fair treatment, and can acquire property and trade with perfect freedom.

Population statistics are one of the mysteries of modern China. It is curious that with their traditions of family life, deeply rooted in the native village, the Chinese emigrants have covered the earth. Natural cataclysms, oppressive administrators, the pillaging of soldiers and bandits, the indifference of the central government, have all encouraged this outflow. Once these exiles have become wealthy, the Chinese government shows for them a solicitude it never betrayed when they were poor and still in the fatherland. Unlike the mass emigration towards Manchuria, what is directed towards Indo-China represents a restricted *élite*. The Chinese come to the colony only in proportion as they are needed there, inasmuch as they are required to have a guarantor within the country to answer for their solvency and good conduct. This measure is less of a barrier to their entry than a turnstile regulated to the country's economy. In 1874 a Bureau of Immigration was founded at Saigon and linked to the congregation organization. In an excessive zeal to insure identification, the government took measures which aroused such Chinese resentment that its worst features were suppressed in 1907. Indo-China presents a remarkable picture of immigration, centuries old and unchanging. The groups within the country are steadily nourished and supplemented from identical groups from without. Their predominant situation is due to years of concentrated effort directed always towards the same goal. Their force comes not from their numbers—there are now about four hundred thousand concentrated principally in the South—for the heavy taxes they pay prevent the poorest class from seeking admission. This curtails the number of adventurers, and the so-called Yellow Peril psychology has little material on which to operate.

As landowning farmers the Chinese are important only in Cambodia; in Annam competition with the natives is unprofitably keen. As coolies they played an important role in the recent plantation development in the South. The Chinese have more endurance, intelligence, and industry than any of their Asiatic rivals. The higher wages they demand reflect an appreciation of their superiority, and this forces employers regretfully to substitute Annamite labour. The Chinese themselves prefer Malaya where they can buy land, for it is forbidden foreigners to own property in the Indo-Chinese redlands. Rice-growing does not offer the same prospect of rapid prosperity as does commerce.

The merchant is the traditional type of Chinese in Indo-China. They are in all stages of commerce, from the small shopkeeper to the great rice exporter. It is extraordinary that a Chinese who has ability as his only asset can get so far ahead. Chinese commerce is so grafted on to native production that it forms a double menace. Not a farmer himself, the Chinese controls farming—as is illustrated by the Chinese domination of rice, the colony's major export. An agent from one of the big Cholon firms, or even an independent speculator, goes from village to village in his boat, gathering in the sacks of rice and draining the harvest to the town. The same is true of fishing and other kinds of production. Western buyers have none of these direct contacts with the producers. The Chinese are able to exploit most cleverly the Annamites' lack of capital and perennial need of money. To get ready-money quickly, they are willing to pledge their daughters or the next rice harvest at a price much below their worth. In buying paddy the Chinese not only speculate on the solvency of the natives, but on the price it will fetch in the world market, for it is usually bought up some months before the harvest. Except for its actual growing, the collecting, husking, and exportation of rice is in Chinese hands. On the rare occasions when these clever creditors bring suit—they usually prefer to threaten debtors and thereby increase their hold—they invariably win, for they are careful to remain strictly within the law. All business to the Chinese is a vast gamble—speculation and long-term risks. They have no savings for they cannot bear to leave capital idle. They evince courage in supporting their numerous losses. If bankrupt, they cheerily disappear and begin again as soon as they can. This means that there is no Chinese bourgeoisie: they are either rich or poor, and not permanently either.

The Chinese are remarkably versatile, and excel equally as farmers, merchants, coolies, or bankers, with profit to themselves and to the administration to which they become indispensable intermediaries. They suffer from no capital-labour antagonisms. It is often a family affair, and the employees have a share in the profits. In time, by saving and by winning the confidence of an influential man, the employee will himself become an employer. Through a highly developed spirit of association, the Chinese enter into joint business operations with their neighbours, but each maintains his commercial personality, so the risks of competition are thereby minimized. No written contract exists. At New Years (*Tet*) the accounts are balanced and the profits shared.

The lack of individualism and the omnipotence of the group make for practical difficulties which the French, as well as the Annamites, have learned to their sorrow. In any Chinese company it is impossible to find out who are its real directors. Every individual changes his name more than twice to escape the evil spirits, as well as official investigation. It is literally impossible to lay hands upon a bankrupt Chinese. To begin with, in China there is no such thing as bankruptcy procedure. The custom of regulating debts at *Tet* cuts short long commercial agonies, and forces delinquents whose credit is exhausted either to take flight or to commit suicide. Due to the prevalent illiteracy, verbal contracts prevail, and they are therefore impossible to verify.

The first taste which the French experienced of these legal problems, presented by Chinese flights and bankruptcies occurred in 1889–90, and made the Saigon Chamber of Agriculture agitate for legal protection. In 1892 all Asiatic merchants were placed under the French penal code—the initial attempt to bring unity into the colony's commercial regulations. This decree forced Chinese merchants to declare the name, aim, and headquarters of their companies, so as to focus responsibility in case of bankruptcy. The plurality of Chinese names and the instability of Chinese orthography added to the ordinary risks. But the decree was not very effective. The Chinese continued to play on French ignorance of their language and methods, and to substitute for their own names such promising appellations as "unalterable loyalty" and "uncontrolled prosperity." When the French tried to bring pressure, the heads of the congregations threatened a boycott of European goods, and so succeeded in opposing and postponing application of any strict measures. Until the recent depression the Chinese were powerful enough to resist any profound change of their methods or release of their hold on the country's economy.

The political supervision exercised by the French over the Chinese is very strict. The congregation organization has been retained, and their heads, as responsible intermediaries, are chosen with great care from a list drawn up by the electors. Provided he keeps order and turns over the high taxes which Chinese residents pay, this congregation leader has all possible latitude in internal organization. This covers a multitude of sins, like graft and secret societies, but it is excellent as a practical working system. It serves as a form of mutual insurance, as a trade union, and as a form of judicial arbitration. Only in cases of crime does the congregation call in the administration. In many ways the congregation resembles the old Annamite commune. Each has its own hospital, pagoda, and cemetery. It is a state within a state, and in some ways a grave political danger. Secret societies are the cement of the congregation, and its real head, not the official figurehead, is unknown to the administration. This seems to the French especially dangerous since such groups, notably the Society of Heaven and Earth, are affiliated with the mother organizations in China.

Up to now the government has confined itself to watchful waiting, playing off the Annamites against the Chinese, and the chaos and uncertainty of contemporary China against the peace, order, and security of French Indo-China. In the powerful and closed milieu of the congregation, it is very easy for subversive ideas to flourish imperceptibly. Up to now, however, the sole preoccupation of the Chinese seems to be money-making, and not political theories. Cholon, the quintessence of Chinese life in Indo-China, offers only two occupations —business and pleasure. The Chinese there are uprooted from their best home traditions, which are lost in the brutal struggle for wealth and enjoyment. For this the Chinese need the peace and security offered by the French government, and in return they are willing to pay heavy taxes and extend courtesies to it. If a foreign potentate visits Cholon hundreds of the flags of his country are manufactured overnight to do him honour. Everything is subservient to being permitted unrestricted trade.

The 1935 Franco-Chinese agreement will radically alter the status of Chinese in the colony. Chinese nationals have now the most-favoured-nation treatment. The congregation organization was suppressed, and in 1936 Chinese consulates were established in Hanoi and Haiphong. That same year an air service linked Canton to Hanoi, thereby shortening the trip from Paris to Shanghai to ten days.

Certain French merchants, as well as Annamites, plead for a restriction of the present Chinese immigration. They claim that if China should succeed in reconstituting itself a powerful nation, she would find a foothold already prepared for her in Indo-China, and the present apparently peaceful influx is but the vanguard of a more aggressive conquest. Chinese home ties are too strong: they show no desire to become rooted in the colony. But the majority of French are inclined to think it alarmist to call the Chinese a viper that is being nourished in Indo-China's commercial bosom. China is in ferment, and the Sino-Annamite hostility a perennial trump card. The Chinese parasites are potentially dangerous but, far more important, they are economically indispensable, as was shown when the depression forced many of them to repatriate themselves. They were the first to give the country— albeit not from altruistic motives—the credit facilities it badly needed, and to endow the population wherever they went with new blood that has created a race of semi-Chinese, superior in almost every respect to the indigenous populations.

Hindus

Aside from minor activities as coachmen and merchants, the vast majority of Indians in the colony are usurers. As traders, they under-sell even the Chinese, who in turn are cheaper than European shops. Most of these Hindus come from the Malabar or Coromandel Coasts. Some of them are Catholics from the French towns of India. But the majority are Moslems or Hindus who, through a remarkable industry in counterfeit papers, pretend to be French citizens. This is the basis of their importance in Cochin-China, where they form a large slice of an exceptionally venal electorate,[1] and where they may hold office denied to the Annamites. Not only do the Annamites feel themselves racially superior to the Hindus, who are in some cases their judges, but they are outraged at being legally and economically inferior to them in their own country. Under the Blanchy régime in Cochin-China, this situation became patently ridiculous. Hindus were given full pay and regular leaves of absence, on the same basis as Europeans, to recover from the disastrous effects of an Asiatic climate upon their health. Certainly the privileged position of these Indians is not com-mensurate with their utility to the country, and is simply a practical joke unwittingly perpetrated by the French Revolution.

There is a significant saying in Indo-China that one cannot become a *chetty*, or Indian usurer, one must be to the profession born. Their sole thought is the piastre, and they give to it an attention bordering on worship. They lead a mysterious and destructive existence, given over completely to their avarice. No one knows the whole mechanism, but their enterprise seems to be directed from India. This is the only explanation for the inexplicable and brusque changes in the interest rates they charge. Since the country, especially the rural districts, is so much in their grip, these fluctuations spell disaster for large portions of the people. Where the money goes is also a mystery. The colony is bled white and the distant coffers of Bengal are presumably filled with the proceeds. There is certainly no group of people in the colony so heartily hated. Annamite and Cambodian resentment of Chinese usury is at least tempered by admiration, but there is no alleviating tenderness for the *chetty*. One Communist agitator exploited this general hatred by advertising the time and place of an official revenge upon a *chetty*

[1] In 1923 there were 700 Hindu voters in Cochin-China.

who, he averred, would be thrown to the lions for his iniquities. Needless to say a large and credulous crowd gathered to witness this pretty spectacle, and to them the Communist could expound as a substitute the gospel according to Karl Marx.

THE EXCHANGE OF PRODUCTION: COMMERCE

In the conquest of Tonkin two practical considerations dominated more emotional motives—the prospect of the Indo-Chinese as buyers of French goods, and of Tonkin as a back-door entrance to China. In neither case have these tempting prospects materialized.

Yunnan was first visited in 1870 by Emile Rochers, who was to return there twenty-five years later as head of the Lyon Mission. He studied in detail the mining situation and the means of communication. Obstacles to tapping the commercial wealth of Yunnan were both psychological and physical. The Chinese dislike of foreigners, the absence of security for life and property, arbitrary vexations and taxations, were chronic drawbacks, but in addition there was the destruction left in the wake of the Moslem rebellion. At that time, anyway, the famous southern provinces of China were not rich but a desolate waste, and the scattered population could not furnish labour to develop its latent wealth. Tin and opium were Yunnan's exports, but the latter because of its small bulk and great value lent itself more readily to smuggling than to commerce. Attention automatically turned from the vain glitter of Yunnanese commerce to the realities of Indo-China's wealth.

Few people realized the profound poverty of Tonkin. Such glowing prospects had been painted to justify the conquest that the French industrialists mistook potential natural resources for a ready-made native clientele. At a time when the country could barely support its teeming tax-ridden population, Tonkin's army of functionaries ate away like locusts at its slender revenues. What should have been spent in developing the native buying power was wasted in riotous administration.

One curious phenomenon of Indo-China's commerce is the slight apparent relationship between the country's productivity and the statistics of its commercial prosperity. For example, in the year 1887 a drought ruined the rice crop of Tonkin, yet exports increased appreciably. A rise in imports may simply mean that the number of functionaries has increased, or that the public works department has ordered materials which have been covered by a loan. An artificial swelling of statistics by Doumer, without reflecting a real economic development, did, however, create enough confidence in France to float a good-sized loan. Organizing fairs was another device for giving the colony favourable publicity. Bert held an exposition in 1887 at Hanoi, and organized Chambers of Commerce in the colony. He sent detailed information to France as to the colony's commercial needs—with no appreciable results. In his wake Doumer organized the Hanoi Exposition of 1902. It was a conspicuous failure in that some of the buildings fell down at once, and that the few natives who saw it were shocked by the nudes rampant in French art. It had, however, a certain publicity value.

The army of occupation brought with it a flock of French merchants who provisioned the troops with considerable profit. Independently of war supplies, they began to undertake regular commerce. This early rapid development was checked by the return of the Chinese after the country was pacified. French profits at once wasted away: they could never undersell the Chinese. The latter had long been established in Annam, and had a wonderful organization adapted to the country and its people. A simple system of barter exchange eliminated French banking procedure which frightened the natives away. The tariff that protected French industry was powerless before Chinese mastery which was a composite of adaptability, solidarity, and business intuition. They knew what the Annamites had to sell and to buy, and were willing to travel in the interior where Europeans never penetrated. They sold articles like swallows' nests, Chinese medicines, and joss-sticks, which only Asiatics manufactured. They even encroached on the European clientele. They could live cheaper than their French rivals, and so were willing to take less profit. The French merchant who was blessed with none too much capital, knew nothing about the people or the country, and was loaded down with European commercial theories was hopelessly outclassed by the Chinese, who everywhere absorbed the position of middlemen. It took the development of French colonization, with products like rubber, coffee, tea, and minerals, to revive French commercial houses. Before the depression a fair balance had been struck: the Chinese, in general, handled native imports and exports, while the French did the same for the Europeans.

Means of communication have naturally been another vital factor in the history of Indo-China's commerce, but it has been on the whole a curious revelation of the prematurity of building roads and railroads. Native needs are few, and Confucianist doctrines discouraged their development. Native products are also few, and it was futile to export to the adjacent province exactly what that province itself was producing. In Laos, however, the transportation problem is paramount. Siam, because of geographical unity, is the provisioner of Laos, and the Mekong's great length prevents establishing an effective tariff frontier. Connecting Laotian commerce with the rest of the colony is an artificial process, still largely in the imagination of the public works department, as it has been for the last forty-two years.

Indo-China's exports are few in number and almost entirely raw materials. Rice heads the list, and reveals Cochin-China's preponderate position. Lagging far behind come minerals, corn, fish, and rubber. The colony has always been fortunate enough to sell all of its exports. In spite of the rapid development of France as Indo-China's best client, the countries of the Far East, notably China, now rival France. Exportations to China have remained steadily about 40 per cent of the whole, whereas those to France have risen from 7 to 37 per cent. This stability is due to the relative steadiness of the rice exportations. The commercial balance has always been favourable to the colony, excepting in 1931.

There are several interesting facts covered by this blanket of prosperous statistics. Because native production has remained practically stationary, there has been far more progress shown in the exportation of French products. Yet even so, the chief export—rice—is far and away the most important of the colony's exportations, and French products form only a comparatively infinitesimal proportion. Moreover, the statistics indicating a rapid increase in commerce do not reflect an increasing productivity, for they are largely the result of a rise in the price of paddy, rather than an increased quantity in exportation, which was more marked in the pre-War era.

In considering imports, which come in great measure from France, one must keep in mind freight rates and the perishability of colonial articles. The principal imports are food and drink, perfume, textiles, medicines, machinery, and petrol. About half of these imports were destined for the French, the wealthy Chinese in the colony, and the Europeanized natives. The majority of imports do not reach the masses whose purchasing power is very limited, and whose tastes France makes no effort to satisfy. Cochin-China, with its rich Annamites and Chinese, is a great importer as well as exporter. It must, as with the budget, subsidize the unfavourable balance of trade which prevails in Annam and Tonkin. The tariff régime has succeeded, throughout its Protean

175

forms, in reserving whole-heartedly to France 58 per cent of the import trade of the colony. France sells much more to the colony than she buys from it. China, an equally important client, finds herself in exactly the reverse position. This significant economic situation revealed itself during and even prior to the depression. One encouraging indication for future production is the increase of agricultural machine importations. Articles of prime necessity for the masses as well as luxury wares have remained stationary. This reveals both the static purchasing power of the Annamites, as well as the hoarding propensities of the native bourgeoisie.

Because rice so dominates Indo-Chinese commerce, the fall in its price is the form in which Indo-China has most felt the depression. But the general decline in the colony's commerce preceded the depression by quite a few years. Saigon, the colony's economic nerve centre, experienced numerous bankruptcies from 1925 on.

Absenteeism, by the heads of the big commercial houses, was a contributing cause to their fall. Many of their founders, worn out or tired of exile, had returned to France and directed their efforts from afar. Their successor-representatives, newcomers to the country, mistook temporary for permanent markets, and permitted the abuse of credit. Prudence was sacrificed to the pleasure of sending flourishing statistics to Paris. Speculation was rife, and embarrassment caused by the fall of the franc was the first indication of trouble. From 1924 on, import houses had laid in many supplies at high prices, with little real plan as to how to dispose of them. They even borrowed heavily to buy merchandise rather than have what they feared might be worthless francs left on their hands. The 1927 rise in the franc, accompanied by a decline in the piastre, meant double disaster for them. They had either to sell at great loss, or else watch the daily decline in the value of their stock.

An inherent weakness, unlike the currency crisis, lay in the lack of solidarity among the French. Each house courted customers with a concentrated selfishness. They rejoiced in any discomfiture of their colleagues. Chinese *compradores* conspired to cultivate in these houses a blind faith in their Asiatic clientele. Terms of payment were made easier, fewer guarantees were asked or verifications made. The fraudulent side of this business was not apparent so long as prices rose and business grew in volume, but eventually the bankruptcy of some Chinese buyers involved their French creditors, the import houses. Instead of concerted action by French creditors to ascertain the status of their

Chinese clients, mutual jealousy prevented any basic understanding. There could have been no greater contrast than this to the Chinese idea of solidarity and association.

Export houses revealed the same symptoms. Their lack of solidarity made them victims of the better organized Chinese. The latter had a fine technique. Instead of buying merchandise with the money advanced to them they decamped, or they claimed to be opening a store so as to persuade the import houses to give them merchandise on credit. Then these same men would get money advanced to them by the export houses by promising to deliver an order for rice or pepper. Thus they had both money and merchandise without giving any serious guarantee for either. The Chinese have a talent for disappearing suddenly at convenient intervals. Enough Chinese have been eliminated in this way to cause a serious void. Their organization was invaluable for financing the crops and for getting the rice from the interior to Cholon. The Chinese who remained in the colony were driven more and more to speculation to try to recover their losses, so it was only a question of time before they went bankrupt. A sincere effort has been made by both the French and Chinese to cut down their expenses. Many costly French clerks have been repatriated, and the Chinese have done the same with their innumerable relatives.

The year 1928 marks the high point in Indo-China's external commerce. From that year to 1932 it diminished 63 per cent. The following year an improvement was noted, due to a mitigation of the tariff régime and commercial treaties made with Far Eastern countries.

The government's role in regulating Indo-Chinese commerce is twofold: in internal commerce the state does as it pleases; and in foreign commerce it can make treaties and wrestle with Metropolitan industrialists. Government control of internal trade did not become effective until fairly recently. For long, Asiatic merchants could keep their books as they pleased, and with the Chinese this meant accounts written in characters and in a form that defied examination by French officials. Their complaints, at the prospect of state control, evoked counter-complaints in the Chinese press, which claimed that the secrets of their compatriots' commercial success would be revealed by state inspections. *Chettys* produced the same objections, with the added argument that they were never debtors or bankrupt, but always creditors in the colony, hence an asset. A 1927 edict enforcing the keeping of commercial books in Latin letters and Arabic numerals was considered by the French colonials as not strong enough, and by the Chinese as highly prejudicial. A compromise was reached in 1930, which made these regulations strictly applicable only for big business, which must be officially registered. As was inevitable, neither side was satisfied.

The government had long and vainly yearned for the real names of a Chinese business's directors and those of the men who were nominally running it. This step was designed to eliminate the Chinese trick of using names like "Eternal Happiness" or "Springtime of Youth" to prevent prosecuting the real directors of a bankrupt enterprise, who could melt away under such joyous nomenclature. Chinese merchants henceforth were to report their business balance every six months, and if they planned to leave the colony they must announce their departure a month in advance. These measures may have been unduly severe, as the Chinese complained, but the real reform should have been a change in attitude on the part of the French merchants. They, like other colonials, preferred looking to the administration for their salvation, which lay, rather, in their own hands.

CHINA

The commercial treaties which the colonial government has made with its Far Eastern neighbours run counter to the artificial ties by which France has bound Indo-China to her economy. Indo-Chinese relations with Peking have been complicated by three issues: border incidents, commerce with China, and the problem of the Chinese resident in the colony. An agreement of 1886, with its supplementary clauses attached in 1887 and 1895, for many years regulated commerce with China, and French influence in Southern China. Even the protectionist rigours of the 1892 tariff were mitigated by an exceptions list that contained much Chinese merchandise essential to the Indo-Chinese. Such wares in no way rivalled French production, and the tariff on them had pointlessly raised the cost of living for the masses. The Washington Conference of 1922, in its recognition of China's tariff autonomy, forced the negotiating of a new treaty with Indo-China. A first snag was struck when France demanded in return for permitting Chinese consulates to be established in the colony, and for a diminished transit tax on Chinese merchandise, indemnification for the damage done to French lives and property in China, and a cessation of political agitation in Indo-China. The delay in ratifying this treaty permitted China to raise her tariff and to devaluate her currency—both of which measures made the treaty problem very acute, though little faith was put by the

French in the permanency of agreements with so unstable a government. Eventually Robin succeeded in getting the 1930 Agreement ratified, despite a widespread criticism that it was all to China's advantage. A reduction in freight transit rates, and permission to have consuls in Indo-China seems, on the whole, a small concession to the colony's best client who is absolutely essential to her economy and who buys more from her than she sells. It is still, however, a moot question as to whether Indo-China's high tariff or China's diminishing purchasing power is primarily responsible for the decline in this trade.

JAPAN

The history of Indo-China's commercial relations with Japan reveals twenty-five years' efforts to negotiate a treaty. This delay shows that for a long time neither country was vital to the other's economy. The 1907 agreement which France had made with Japan was not applicable to Indo-China. The War, for the first time, brought a basic commercial arrangement. Japan provisioned Indo-China and in return bought Tonkinese coal. Long's visit to Japan was to have had a treaty-making significance which his death cut short. Merlin's mission to Japan, and a return visit from a Japanese prince, were concerned with negotiating a commercial treaty, but Indo-China was coy about becoming involved, and Japan seemed resigned to a permanent refusal of her quest for a minimum tariff arrangement.

The main drawback was a fear of Japanese industrial competition. Through cheap labour Japan produces manufactured articles which almost the poorest Indo-Chinese can afford to buy. Not only does this hurt French rivals, but it ruins Indo-China's infant industries as well. For example, a packing-case factory was opened in the colony to make cases for shipping rubber. The identical article made in Japan was cheaper in Saigon, even after it had paid freightage and duty. Yet Japan was an excellent client of the colony, and like China bought more than she sold. A commercial treaty between Japan and Siam made Indo-China uneasy for her rice and coal exports. The 1928 tariff, the devaluation of the *yen*, the closing down of Chinese markets, made both countries more conciliatory. The prospect of tariff reprisals, when the depression was already cutting down Indo-China's exports, made the colonials—always more nervous than the Métropole—put aside their fears and come to an agreement in 1932. This was the laborious result of years of intermittent negotiations. Mutual concessions were made. Certain Japanese articles essential to the native population had their duty diminished in return for lowering the tariff barriers against Indo-China's raw materials. In 1936 the balance of trade was still favourable to Indo-China. The political role of Japan, as a force for order in the Far East, against the machinations of Chinese Communists, had its influence in forcing through this treaty.

SIAM

Commercial relations with Siam have always been of the slightest, for both countries have practically identical exports. Political goodwill, however, has made Siam, especially since the War, give France a larger share in her economic development. Siam for years has been the chief provisioner of Laos. Cheaper goods and cheaper freightage, as well as the impossibility of making the Mekong serve as a tariff frontier, have flooded Laos with German and Japanese goods via Bangkok. With the completion of both countries' railway systems, Laos will be cut off from Siamese supplies, and the country linked automatically with the Union.

THE DUTCH EAST INDIES

The only article of important exchange between Indo-China and the Dutch East Indies is rice. For the rest of her exports, Indo-Chinese products hold a mere twenty-sixth place in the Javanese market. Dutch exports are more varied: petrol, sugar, paraffin, machinery, coffee, and quinine. There is no fear of commercial rivalry between two such varied economies. The Dutch policy of free trade presents an equally great contrast with Indo-China's strong protectionism. Robin's recent treaty has created a larger place in Java for Indo-China's rice. Commercial relations between the two countries could be correspondingly stimulated by a more regular transportation service in which proximity should reduce freight charges. Indo-China thinks wistfully of the vacations which the nearly three hundred thousand Dutch of their East Indies might spend in visiting the colony's tourist sights, and probably Java reciprocally holds the same thought.

ENGLAND

After France and England had recovered from their mutual suspicions in regard to Southern China and Siam, they began to consider Indo-China's possible commercial interest for Great Britain. During the post-War period, when freight was dear and scarce, Indian cotton and jute began to capture the Indo-Chinese market. British India was naturally provisioned from Burma, but Robin recently succeeded in opening the Indian market, as well as South Africa, to Indo-China's rice. The colony's industrialists are as skittish of cheap manufactures from India as they are from Japan, and the Métropole sees in both the ruination of her own industrial exports. Indo-China, in turn, has the right to complain, for Indian woods have ousted Indo-Chinese wood from the French market. The situation is further complicated by the smuggling of opium, for the Indian brand is decidedly preferred by connoisseurs to the Yunnanese.

THE UNITED STATES

Commercial relations with the United States grew rapidly during the War, but were halted later by tariff barriers. The Philippines, as a market for Indo-Chinese rice and livestock, have a great interest for the colony. An exchange of friendly gubernatorial visits and the opening of a navigation service have been the preliminary to a recent and promising reopening of negotiations by both Pasquier and Robin. In May 1936 a trade treaty lowered duties on American imports into Indo-China, to what general effect it is as yet too soon to tell.

GERMANY

Germany's prominence in Indo-China's commerce naturally died with the War. By 1904 German trade with the colony was important enough to have a separate account in the Customs Records. A very important commercial house, named Speidel, had its headquarters at Saigon and branch officer throughout the colony. It used Chinese employees almost exclusively, and imported cheap manufactured goods and exported raw materials on a magnificent scale. In August 1914 it was reported that the head of this house carried a brevet from the Kaiser for the governorship of Indo-China. Engler was the name of Speidel's important German rival, but these firms had a solidarity that was in marked contrast with the mutual suspicion of the French commercial houses. Since the War Japan has captured the position formerly held by England and Germany.

So long as French industrialists prefer to rely on a high tariff protection rather than to make cheaper articles more suited to native tastes and purchasing power, they must always fear their more adaptable rivals, both in Europe and the Far East.

ECONOMIC EQUIPMENT: THE BUDGETS

The expense of the conquest as well as of administration forced the Admirals to take over the Annamite taxes. Unfortunately, for their accuracy, the old tax lists were not immediately discovered. In addition there was no survey of the country, and the expense that this would involve kept the project from being carried out. Besides the personal and land taxes, which were revised after a superficial inquiry—and it was an honourable tradition in Annam to dissimulate the amount of cultivated land—there were the Farms of Opium and Gaming. Additional revenues came from commercial licenses and ships entering the port of Saigon. The year 1864 was the first to have a regular budget which boasted an income of over three million francs. Taxes at this time began to be paid in money and no longer in kind. This constituted a more serious burden for the people, and in addition the Officer-Inspectors were poor book-keepers, and often inadvertently unjust. The taxes paid under the Admirals were excessive for a poor country without capital reserves, and with only one crop and a sparsely settled population.

Bert was sent to Indo-China with very few credits, and with the express understanding that existing expenses must be cut. What work he might do must be accomplished with the local resources. A deficit would hopelessly compromise his work, even though the unpacified state of the country made tax-collecting next to impossible. So hostile was Metropolitan opinion to Tonkin that there was insistence that the colony should not only pay for itself but for the army of occupation as well. This was but the first of a series of financial burdens with which Paris saddled the nascent colony.

The responsibility for Cambodia's uprising in 1884 can be laid at the same door of fiscal exaggeration. The assignment of a civil list to the King and the use of French tax collectors was so great a mistake that it defeated its own ends. In addition to restoring the native administration, the Protectorate had to pay for the military suppression. Later De Lanessan put through a single budget, under Franco-Cambodian auspices, using the King's Farms for revenues.

Cochin-China was the spoiled child of the Union. Its wealth was entirely absorbed by its functionaries, who were allowed to persist in their collective selfishness because they made no demands on France. What was extracted to help out the shaky Protectorate budgets was unwillingly conceded, and Cochin-China's loud complaints defeated the 1887 attempt to effect a financial union.

Annam escaped entirely French financial guidance until 1894, when De Lanessan succeeded in placing its budget under a nominal French control.

The Governors-General of this period suffered regularly from two financial handicaps: France's timidity or downright refusal to grant credits, and Cochin-China's resistance to subsidizing its neighbours. Tonkin continued to earn French opprobrium. From 1887 to 1891 its budget had to be subsidized to the extent of 168,000,000 francs. None of this money went to developing the country's economy. De Lanessan, by his conciliatory native policy, furthered the pacification and consequently cut down the expenses. He also economized by destroying some of the superfluous officialdom, and in this way he added to the enemies who brought about his downfall. After he was recalled the situation rapidly became worse. Expenses soared and the budgetary balance he had established was destroyed. Loans granted by France only served to liquidate the past, without achieving any constructive solution. The acquisition of impoverished Laos in 1893 only added another burden.

Doumer was selected primarily to make Indo-China independent of France, and he succeeded ably in so doing. The keystone to his reform was a division of the general from the local expenditures and revenues, by creating a federal budget with indirect taxes, and five local budgets from direct taxes. Up to this time Indo-China had been a fiscal mosaic, with a host of infinitely variable local taxes, which were now systematized and regularized. By creating an effective Union, even the recalcitrant Cochin-China was brought into line, and its wealth harnessed to its less fortunate colleagues. Economies supplemented these efforts. The most questionable of his reforms were the monopolies of salt, opium, and alcohol, as indirect taxes. His work had the advantage of being immediately effective and of changing France's attitude towards Indo-China to one of benevolent approval. But the reverse side of the situation was its evil repercussion on native policy. Doumer was blithely unconscious of having added burdens to an already tax-ridden people. He looked upon his work and found that it was good. Malevolence or ignorance alone, he averred, could make people say that the Indo-Chinese were overtaxed.[1] For the first time the colony as a whole was endowed with economic machinery. Unfortunately it took the form of railway construction, but the loan he raised on the strength of this policy gave an enormous impetus to the colony, and created

---

[1] Doumer, P., *Situation de l'Indo-Chine* (Hanoi, 1902), p. 9.

Indo-Chinese credit as distinct from the Métropole's. Doumer created the legend of the rich Indo-China. The colony began to assume more of its military expenses, and even to pay for French philanthropy in the Far East. Despite an excellent basic conception—that of making a reality out of the Indo-Chinese Union by a truly federal framework—Doumer's methods were too arbitrary, too fraught with political danger. His successors to this day are still carrying out his economic programme, but the means by which he set it in motion—the monopolies, highly centralized services, grandiose unproductive public works—have had to be discarded after painful experience.

The Monopolies

Indirect taxes have always been preferred by the French because of their unpleasant historical association with the *ancien régime's* direct assessments. On the contrary, the Annamites prefer direct taxes as something they are used to, and upon which they can count. Applying this French psychology to the problem of raising new revenues, Doumer created the triple-headed monster of the monopolies, and placed it under the Service of *Douanes et Régies*. To this day the Douanes furnishes more than half of the colony's revenues, and in its halcyon days, 1907, employed 3,341 agents.

Raw opium was bought from Yunnan or India, and prepared by the Régie for consumption. It was sold through licensed agents, usually Chinese, who paid high for the privilege. Originally a Chinese vice, it has now spread among the masses of the people. The rapid growth of opium revenues—they doubled from 1894 to 1907—testifies to its increased use. The profits of the Chinese intermediaries were so great that in 1881 the Cochin-Chinese Colonial Council voted for a direct government control. This move was motivated less by an effort to increase the revenues than to strike a blow at Chinese economic power. It was also partly due to the prevalence of contraband. Opium's small bulk and high value particularly favoured smuggling. A contributing factor was the failure of state-prepared opium to suit the popular taste. In setting a high price, the government was also trying to realize excessive profits. Contraband, as organized by the Chinese, was a fine art. Spying and denunciations flourished. The utilization of opium dross also complicated the problem, and this finally forced the Régie to buy up the opium residue. The state tried successively lowering and raising the prices, to improve the methods of preparations, and a system of paying licenses, in an unsuccessful effort to check smuggling.

THE ECONOMY OF INDO-CHINA

The history of the opium Régie in Tonkin is also very instructive. It illustrates the state's struggle with a badly drawn up contract. The Court of Hué had always exploited an opium monopoly. For long Tonkin was too unpacified to make a monopoly practicable there by means of a rigorous suppression of fraud. An experiment, made in 1887, proved this conclusively. Banditry and contraband went hand in hand, and the pacification problem involved suppression of the illicit opium trade. So the company which had received the Farm abandoned the unpacified upper country in order to concentrate on the delta. There, to realize all possible profits, it raised the price of opium, which in turn renewed contraband activity. The state was now between two fires. It was sustaining a company whose zeal was increasing a rebellion that it was simultaneously trying to calm. The company even tried to drag in the state to help in its repressions, and when refused carried the case to Paris so successfully that its contract was renewed for eight years. The state was thus saddled with a terrible moral and financial responsibility. De Lanessan made herculean efforts to cut the Gordian knot which tied the state to the company, and at last, in 1893, the Protectorate was freed. That same year the government took over a thoroughgoing monopoly on the Cochin-Chinese model, but De Lanessan purposely refrained from any rigorous measures that might delay the pacification. Doumer did not find the situation so delicate, and he was able to make this monopoly pay more and at the same time diminish the influence of the Chinese in the country. Doumer went far in his reversal of De Lanessan's gentle fiscal methods.

The history of the opium Régie in Annam is almost equally tormented. The state had the same struggle with the distributor, and popular discontent was shown by a decreased consumption and increased contraband. The subsequent attempt at direct administration suffered from the usual handicap of an insufficient and untrained personnel, which brought in small returns. But, on the whole, this method had fewer evil repercussions than a Farm.

Laos's opium Régie was always directly administered because it presented the unique feature of a soil suitable to poppy growing. The natives had always grown enough for their own needs, so the government subsidized local efforts for a large-scale production. The result was not without charm. Two colonists in different regions were given seed and piastres. After two years, officially given to ruthless labour, an Inspector was sent to report. One of the colonists claimed that the seed

185

he had sown never came up. The other was more cynical: "I am a remarkable man," he told the Inspector. "Potatoes grow where I sowed poppy seed."[1]

The moral factor in the opium monopoly has made the French position equivocal. In Indo-China the state encourages the natives to poison themselves: in France a man is imprisoned if opium is found in his house. International opprobrium has reached such proportions that all realize that the colony must seek some substitute budgetary resource. The Chinese and rich Annamites are still the chief customers, so it is not quite so acute as if the masses were the principal consumers. No voice has ever been raised in defence of the opium monopoly, but it needs no more eloquent defence than the revenues it brings to the treasury. At no time has the state made more strenuous efforts to suppress fraud than at present, so undoubtedly the Régie will persist in its evildoing until a substitute resource can be found to feed the inviolable budget.

Before 1898 alcohol was freely distilled by Annamite families for their own use, principally for certain rites. Chinese distilleries also existed. An important by-product was hog-raising, since pigs could be fed on the rice which has been used in the distilling, and whole villages lived off this subsidiary enterprise.

The history of the alcohol monopoly differs with each country of the Union. In Cochin-China and Cambodia there was a long experimentation. A system of licensing proved ineffectual, and contraband increased. In addition the agents required to suppress fraud were expensive and their methods exasperated the people. Doumer, in his effort to break Cochin-China's independence, did forge some unity out of its innumerable alcohol laws. A permit for distilling was the method that resulted, and this system served as a model for Annam and Tonkin.

In Annam and Tonkin the sale of alcohol was a monopoly, although its manufacture was free, but the distillers had to sell all their alcohol to the state at fixed prices. The next step was for the state to cede distribution rights to its agents. The aim of this measure was to stop family distilling and to concentrate the distillers in certain areas. Not only was the Régie's personnel increased, but, far worse, the communes were held responsible for fraud. Such severe edicts transformed what was originally an unburdensome source of revenue. The monopoly was not thoroughgoing, for the permit to distil could still be bought, but the state was very arbitrary about according such permission. The

[1] Salé, G., *Histoires Coloniales* (Paris, 1931), p. 84.

climax of injustice came in 1903, when the government signed a contract giving the sales monopoly in Annam-Tonkin to a French group, on such scandalous terms that they were never made public. By this means the state hoped to increase its revenues which had been steadily declining. The company at once raised the price of alcohol, and bottled it in a container that forced the price up still higher. Numerous complaints were unavailing. The company was omnipotent and unmoved. That same year another company got a manufacturing monopoly which involved a brutal closing down of the remaining native and Chinese distilleries.

Cochin-Chinese distillers were more powerful and more wary. The Chinese conducted a campaign in Paris that mitigated the grip which the same company had got in Cochin-China, so it did not succeed in wholly ousting the local distillers.

The results of the government's policy were a mistake from every viewpoint. The agents' methods of suppressing fraud included domiciliary searches—a pleasure hitherto unknown in Annam. Bonuses for denunciations led to hideous abuse and the conviction of many innocent people. Communal responsibility was a terrible burden. It also involved the spoliation of a large group of native distillers and hog-raisers, who received very inadequate indemnification for their losses. The price of alcohol was exorbitant, but the Annamites had to have it for their rites. In addition, the native alcohol, *choum-choum*, had a special taste that suited the native palate far more than the official brand. Forced sales were effected by threats to penalize communes that did not buy. Out of the whole business the state won only native hatred, and to the monopolists went all the profits. The alcohol monopoly was largely responsible for the political uprising of 1908.

Klobukowsky took a courageous stand against this monopoly by suppressing communal responsibility for fraud, and domiciliary visits without a search warrant. A campaign of slander in the local and Parisian press, financed by the monopolists, prevented Klobukowsky's work from being effective, but it paved the way for the breaking of the sales monopoly in 1911. This reform was rewarded by an increase in the alcohol sales.

Klobukowsky's declarations and the successive budget reports of Messimy and Violette brought pressure to bear on French opinion. The public was ready to demand the monopoly's suppression at any cost, because of its evil effect on native attitude. Better to have a subsidy that would make Indo-China unpopular in France, than a monopoly that was making France detested in the colony. The government had either to buy off the company at its own price or face a lawsuit in which it had always been unlucky. It was even more difficult to find a revenue substitute. Current budget reports showed that the government was hedging. The 1911 budget reporter had been indignant, the 1912 reporter silent, that of 1913 conciliatory. The chief concern seemed to be in removing the word monopoly, which had become odious to Parliamentary ears, rather than in attacking the evil at its root. Despite reiterated official promises, the monopoly was retained—in fact if not in name. Sarraut had prolonged the contract with the monopolist manufacturers for ten more years. It was argued, in justification, that the price was now reduced, that the official alcohol was healthier than the native, and that its flavour had finally been adjusted to Anna-mite taste. This did little to mitigate the discontent of the natives, both as consumers and as taxpayers. In addition, the government had deceived them. Far more than opium, the alcohol monopoly has been a source of political grievance.

Discontent, though less violent, continued to stir native opinion. The 1921 edict did little to alter the situation. Fraud and continued contraband both involved and caused vexations by the Régie's agents. The monopolies have formed one of the major grievances of the Nationalist party. In 1931 the *Grand Conseil* asked for the complete suppression of the monopoly in two years, with the expiration of the current contract. It is greatly to Pasquier's credit that he accomplished this much needed reform, in spite of all the pressure brought to bear upon him. Dividends of the Fontaine Distilleries had risen from 40 per cent in 1914 to 200 per cent in 1925. Thirty-five years of experience had finally convinced the government that the political aspect of the alcohol monopoly was infinitely more important than its fiscal signi-ficance. The general solution has been free distillation by licensed companies or individuals. This has not given entire satisfaction, as shown by Robin's recent complaints at the continuation of contraband, and of the necessity for a drastic reduction in the price of official alcohol, but it has broken the back of the opposition.

The salt monopoly probably touches more people than even that of alcohol, for children as well as adults live on a diet of salted fish and rice. All dishes are seasoned with a sauce called *nuoc-mam*, for which salt is a prime necessity.

Criticism of the salt monopoly is essentially the same as for the other two monopolies. It was too hastily established by Doumer, without the proper study of native needs and customs, or as to whether or not the state had the means of enforcing it. As with alcohol, it has resulted in ruining a large number of merchants and fishermen who need salt with which to preserve their catch. Its faulty distribution has prevented many people from buying this necessity, at even the exorbitant official figure.

Salt production areas are scattered all along the coast, especially in the South. Under the Hué government the sale of salt had fallen almost entirely into the hands of the Chinese, who used it as an article of exchange. They bought salt at varying prices, depending upon the region, quality, and consumption needs, and the producers' prosperity. The sums advanced to salt-workers were but one of the many usurious holds the Chinese had upon the Annamites. If the new Régie hurt the usurers, it dealt a mortal blow to the salt-workers, who could not live without borrowed capital, or at least an exchange in rice which the Chinese had been able to effect.

Doumer was, as ever, anxious to turn the benefits of the Chinese middlemen to the treasury's profit, so he forced the natives to sell all their salt to the Régie, which had replaced the Chinese organization, only not nearly so effectively. For the producer it was a disastrous change of masters. Some were forced out for lack of capital, and those who stayed felt resentful towards the administration.

For the consumer the change was even worse. The government had neither the facilities nor the money necessary for the transporation, stocking, and control of fraud. Salt regions were widely scattered and inaccessible. Poverty of resources compelled the state to farm out the monopoly, with the proviso, however, that the concessionnaire be a Frenchman. The company that took up the burden suffered, like the administration, from a lack of money and the necessary equipment to replace the Asiatic intermediary, so in turn it secretly leased its rights to the indispensable Chinese, who were once more in the saddle. Fraud flourished openly, and bred an orgy of mutual recriminations. The consumer paid an exorbitant price, for there were now two middlemen instead of one. Salt had been originally costly enough, but now its price was trebled. Since little attempt was made to provision the interior, salt was prohibitively high there, when available at all. It was cheapest in Cochin-China, where the concentration of salt areas was so great that little surveillance was needed. Abuses and speculation, however, were rife. Consumption dwindled greatly, as did the revenues, with bad effect upon the health of the natives, as well as their political viewpoint. The ignominious *gabelle* of the *ancien régime* had come to life once more in a French colony. Salt had to be imported from China, whither it had formerly been exported. The purchase price was so low that more and more salt-workers went bankrupt.

In general the sale of salt improved both in price and in quantity. The monopoly expired in 1910, and was thereafter sold directly. A rise in the purchase price further contributed to help the salt-workers. The modification brought about in 1921 did not effect any real improvement. The discussions of the *Grand Conseil*, ten years later, reinforced the complaints and the native preference for a direct tax to the monopoly. In 1929 the *gabelle* had brought 11,000,000 piastres to the budget, but the natives still suffered from defective provisioning.

In 1931 it was proposed to have the salt-workers pay a fixed annual sum to the fisc, after which they would be free to dispose of their salt, and the Régie would be liberated from a great expense. Robin's speech in 1935 showed that the salt Régie was still criticized, especially since the depression had affected the salt export trade. Too few stores are authorized to sell salt, and there is still faulty co-ordination between producer and consumer. It is certain that the Régie has not yet found a definite formula. If the depression lifts the government can try more radical experiments, but for budgetary reasons will not tamper with it now except to improve its working mechanism.

A total disregard of the colony's real needs and the native viewpoint has characterized the creation and persistence of the three monopolies. Long experience has finally impressed upon the government the priority of their political importance over their immediate fiscal interest. What profited the fisc a transient revenue if it cost French sovereignty over Indo-China? Monopolies were established by a Governor anxious, at all costs, to make Indo-China independent of the Métropole's subsidies. France was grieved at the revelations of her policy's abuse, but not to the point of underwriting the deficit that would result from its suppression. A monopoly of manufacture was destroyed first, then the attack shifted to the sales' monopoly, which is still sustained by a powerful financial lobby, albeit in modified form. The back of the monopolies has been broken by an economic cause—the vicious circle produced by personnel costs forcing up the sales price, which in turn makes contraband profitable, thus diminishing the revenue returns which are consequently unable to pay for an increased personnel to check fraud. The monopolies are still profitable in terms of piastres, and until the productivity of the colony has been radically increased so as to bring in new revenues, they must subsist—moral considerations to the contrary.

On the practical side, the state showed a blithe ignorance of such important factors as its poverty in men, money, and methods. Its insufficient study of the means of transportation, native psychology and customs, and the mechanism of its rivals, has weighed heavily upon the consumer. The ousted middlemen organized an opposition which soon proved that they did know their job in a way that the state could never equal. Secretly or openly there was perforce recourse to their services. The multiplication of middlemen raised prices, and in the confusion between alternating régimes the colony was not properly provisioned at any price. The profits went to the concessionnaire, and the blame to the government. The budget, for whose sweet sake the monopolies were created, groaned under the cost of its cumbersome functioning.

The effect on native economy, health, and good temper is incalculable. A permanent state of war existed between the Régie and the people which resulted in thousands of legal condemnations every year. Prisons are filled with unfortunates whose crime has been to prefer the cheaper and better contraband article, or to have had an enemy to denounce their fictitious guilt. The majority of real contrabandists are the village Notables whose position makes them immune. Annamite forbearance has been hard proven by the blundering of the Régie's agents, who themselves suffer from ignorance of the country, debility caused by the climate, nostalgia for France, and too much authority. Tact, the quality they needed most, has been conspicuously absent. The monopolies are less hated for themselves than for the men who vexatiously enforce them. The problem has not yet reached an ultimate solution. Only recently Robin with one hand reduced the price of monopolies, and with the other increased the Régie's personnel. An easily balanced budget is the secret of any permanent reform.

Local Budgets

Doumer's strong centralization policy of developing the general budget at the expense of the shrunken local budgets produced a reaction under his successors towards financial decentralization. The 1911 decree not only tried to undermine the exaggerated importance of the General Services, whose staff expenses were absorbing the budget, but at the same time to give more life to local provincial and municipal finances, whose minute subdivision, it was thought, was adding to the general disorder. The lack of system in provincial expenditures permitted a multitude of sharp practices and chaotic projects. For example, road-building in one province was undertaken without relation to the adjacent territory. Under Sarraut there was a simultaneous trend towards pruning local autonomy from beneath by the federal government, and controlling the independent services from above. In his reforming enthusiasm Sarraut lost sight of the value of provincial autonomy, as a training school in administrative methods, and as a means of showing to the natives to what use their taxes were being put.

The General Services, in their overweening superiority, had refused to budget their expenses. The Public Works Service was notably arrogant in refusing to adapt its grandiose schemes to the colony's needs. They worked with the maximum of fuss and with the minimum of accomplishment. Being unable to pay for qualified technicians, all the services suffered from a plethora of poor functionaries. In 1807 there had been 2,860 of these functionaries: in 1911, 5,683, to whom were paid 27,771,000 francs, without counting the innumerable supplements for travel and sickness. The French personnel cost the budget 25 per cent of all its revenues. Sarraut's economies included advancing the retiring age, and a general elimination of the dead wood. Reducing the administrative unit was a step towards decreasing the white proletariat. Natives who were clamouring for government jobs could easily and more cheaply fill clerical positions. It was both pointless and wasteful for a Frenchman to travel thousands of kilometres simply to sell stamps at the Saigon post office or to man the twenty-three lighthouses of the colony.

Direct taxes form the revenue of the local budgets, and they have the advantage of being the only taxes which the Annamites pay without too great repugnance. Great was the joy of the people, and incidentally the increase in revenue, when the markets and ferry licenses were taken away from the Farms and changed into direct taxation (1910).

Equitable assessment of direct taxes depends on two factors which until recently have been lacking—a land survey and a native *état civil*. Without such a scientific foundation, any tax assessment is bound to be arbitrary. The *dienbo* offered a certain clue, but it was hopelessly outdated and notoriously inaccurate. A revision was attempted unsuccessfully because the French were unable to afford it, and it was to native interest to perpetuate frauds. The mandarins offered no greater guarantee of truthfulness. That they always collect more than the state requires is a well-established fact. With the rapidly increasing cost of administration, the state simply raised taxes arbitrarily. From 1890 to 1896 they were doubled: from 1896 to 1898 they were again increased by half. The docility of the communes in responding to these measures made the government merely repeat this simple process. In certain provinces, like Nam Dinh, Annamites had to pay on rice-fields which did not exist. Not only have the amounts aggressively increased, but like the monopolies it is the vexations attendant upon their collection that constitute an even greater burden for the people.

Equality in taxation, that cherished republican principle, would never recognize itself in Indo-China. European exemptions and their payment of exactly the same head tax as the humblest coolie—who has no voice in their assessment—constitute the gravest injustice. Many complaints never reach the administrator because they must pass by way of the interpreter. The government mistook the unvarying Annamite tax returns—good harvest, bad harvest—as a sign that their amount was not exaggerated. The favourite official cable to Paris was: "Calm is restored; the taxes are coming in." Beau claimed that the Annamite was less burdened with taxes than his Siamese neighbour, but critics question the accuracy of his statement. The grip of usury had already gangrened the country, and heavier taxes intensified the evil.

France's false conception about Indo-China's wealth is partly responsible, because it was played up in France to seduce potential colonizers in 1884. Harmand, the following year, estimated that Annam-Tonkin could pay taxes of more than 2,000,000 francs. When this was not forthcoming, every means was used to force the revenues. The instability of taxes made them seem worse. Not only were they crushing in amount, but they varied from year to year, and clemency was not shown to inundated regions. The year 1897 saw a perfect hailstorm of new taxes—on stamps, cinnamon, wood-cutting, etc. Such instability was bad for the natives and for the undertaking of any important enterprise.

Direct collection of taxes by French officials was tried as one means of increasing the revenues, since it had been fashionable to blame mandarinal corruption for the mediocre tax returns. When this failed to accomplish a miracle, it was decided that the commune, and not the mandarins, were incorrigible frauds. So the personal tax was increased, and money payment for a nominal release from *corvée* service became obligatory. For the first time the former non-taxpayers were taxed. It was estimated in 1901 that the Annamite paid from nine to ten pre-War francs as a personal tax—a sum which represented the rice he would consume in three months. In a country which had barely recovered from the conquest and a prolonged banditry, the natives paid a higher tax than the Hindus, Malayans, Javanese, or Japanese.[1] Nor was the country's productivity improved proportionately by public works.

The land tax followed the same general trends. It was divided according to whether land belonged to natives or French, and what crops were grown upon it. No effort to classify the land seriously was made until 1910, when Cochin-China re-classified her rice-fields. By diminishing the traditional unit of measurement, the *mau*, the land tax was automatically increased by this juggling. No one thought of consulting the taxpayers: the arbitrary reigned supreme. An inelastic uniformity gripped the country's resources, as a result of the commune's life-and-death struggle with the state. Increasing the revenues became an end in itself, and not a means of developing the country's resources.

Varenne's proposal of an income tax, in 1927, was the first approach to real justice in the whole system. The Colonial Council of Cochin-China was so incensed at the suggestion that they, natives and French alike, refused even to consider the idea. They did not take seriously Varenne's assertion that the head tax, which fell alike upon all persons, represented a terrible sum for the poor and a ridiculous amount to the rich. The next year the government re-studied the problem. From 1913 to 1924, they found that with the *per capita* increase had come an almost equal rise in the cost of living—the growth in income averaged about 66 per cent—so that taxes are now a slightly less heavy burden than they were in 1913, though larger in amount. During the depression certain tax remissions were effected by Governor Pagès. In 1935, Robin finally succeeded in reducing some of the indirect taxes and in taxing incomes over 80,000 francs—a move that did not bring in much revenue, but which was important as establishing a principle.

Currency Problems

In 1873, Germany, followed by Belgium and France, suspended the free minting of silver. The decreased demand sent the price of silver rapidly down. In 1893 India followed suit, and several years later Siam and the Philippines did likewise. By 1902 the Indo-Chinese piastre followed the metal upon which it was based, with bad effects on the country's economy. The ensuing loss of capital was so great that French investors, naturally timid about the colony, felt the risks now to be insuperably great. Doumer's reform aimed to keep the

[1] Bernard, F., *L'Indochine: Erreurs et Dangers* (Paris, 1901), p. 119.

piastre for internal use and the franc for foreign exchange. The importation of foreign piastres was forbidden, as well as the exportation of
Indo-Chinese currency. This was thought to be a preliminary step to
stabilization, but just at that time, 1905, the price of silver rose, so
the reform was postponed. The Indo-Chinese piastre presented the
inconvenience of being unadapted to commerce with countries on the
gold standard—notably France. Till the War, Europeans in the colony
used francs as the medium of exchange among themselves, and even
the budget was drawn up in terms of that currency. Piastres were
based on the daily exchange rate against the franc, and since French
currency was far more stable, it held the ascendancy until the War.
The situation changed after 1914, with the franc's dwindling purchasing power, and the trend was reversed—away from the franc and
toward the piastre, which rose to unknown heights in 1920. The state
was forced to adjust salaries to the new situation, and the result was
a virtual abandonment of the franc as currency. The capital made
available in the colony, by the favourable turn taken by the piastre,
was partly responsible for the success of Long's loan in 1921 and the
beginning of Indo-China's financial autonomy.

Pre-War efforts at stabilizing the currency had been foiled by outside
circumstances—the War, and fluctuations in the price of silver. In
1920, the problem was re-studied but rejected. The rise in silver,
hence in piastres, had permitted Indo-China to survive the rise in
world prices. Uncertainty about French currency was also a vital
factor, and at the time it was thought fortunate that Indo-China was
not linked to the troubled franc. From 1924 to 1926 Indo-China was
regarded as a secure, albeit temporary, investment area by French
capitalists until their own currency should once more become stable.
When this capital began to be repatriated, the wave of speculation in
Indo-Chinese resources was already under way, so its loss was felt
less keenly than it might otherwise have been. But the colony consequently paid very dear for its financial vogue.

The late 1920's coincided with a steady decline in the piastre, as
always the chameleon of silver, and an increase in trade with the gold
standard countries. It was, therefore, only natural that Indo-China
should again consider stabilization. Everyone, including French investors, wanted more security for their capital in the colony, and joined
in the clamour that resulted in Pasquier's stabilization measure of
May 31, 1930. The great source of monetary malaise, however, was
still not conjured. Rice, the almost unique source of the colony's

wealth, still obeyed the law of silver, because China was Indo-China's best client. In short, Indo-China was selling in silver what she produced in gold.

The depression focussed attention upon this essential weakness. The very voices which had so heartily approved of stabilization in 1929 were the first to denounce it as the evil genius of the colony's decline. This agitation proved to be more noisy than widespread. Successive governors have studied the problem, but have felt that any such radical change would be more harmful to the country, as a whole, than justifiably beneficial to the aggressively indebted few.

An indirect solution to the problem was found by the involuntary devaluation of the piastre which followed the adjustment of the franc in October 1936. This has caused an increase in the general price levels, notably in the cost of French merchandise. The future is quite unpredictable in view of the new French social laws which have been taken over in modified form by Indo-China, for they will mean an increased production cost. The government has taken steps to stop speculation in stocks, especially those involving native necessities.

The Post-War Budget

Since the War, Indo-China has lived off its own resources without recourse to any but Long's loan of 1921, and the more recent loan of 1931 aimed to offset the depression. Under Long's successor, the revenues of the general budget were melting away, and that fact more than the Canton bomb led to Merlin's recall. No one could understand the curious contrast between the colony's undeniable prosperity and its budgetary misery. The decline was partly due to failing revenues, which were partially established in francs, a dwindling currency. More important were the growing subsidies to the local budgets, which formed, in 1925, a fourth of the federal revenues. There was, in addition, undeniable extravagance in the administration.

Varenne's reforms, like Doumer's, lay in making a clear-cut division between the general and local budgets, but with the difference of a marked financial decentralization. His financial reforms envisaged an income tax, but opposition to it was so lively that he had to substitute for it a less reviled tax on imports. By his economies and reorganization, Varenne cured the colony's financial anaemia and even partially filled the reserve fund.

From 1927 to 1930 the total budget was forced up rapidly from 80,440,880 piastres to 113,606,000. Even if the depression had not come, this movement would inevitably have been halted. The reserve fund was emptied, and there was a dangerous accumulation of deficits. It was true that Indo-China's contribution to French military expenses —17·40 per cent of the general budget—was exaggerated. The colony had long protested, but it took the depression to force a "gracious gesture" of renunciation from the Métropole. Pasquier achieved stabilization of the piastre, and at the time it met with a universal approval. There were more profound causes than the depression for Indo-China's financial malaise.

The budget has been criticized as being too inelastic, since it depends upon such fluctuating revenues as tariff and indirect taxes for its chief source of income. It had better depend upon more stable elements that would reflect the country's prosperity, like a tax on income or on stock companies. Fluctuations in the exchange were the chief cause of the inflation of budgets, notably during the War, and afterwards the equilibrium was never restored. Expenditures estimated in piastres were almost stationary, whereas those expressed in francs rose very rapidly. Moreover, these expenditures went far more into non-productive projects, like education and social service, than for public works that would have increased the colony's wealth. The result has been that the expenses, hence the burdens upon the taxpayer, have increased far more than the colony's productivity.

Assessment of taxes is unfair not only as between rich and poor, but also between the different countries of the Union. Cochin-China, with a population of four out of the colony's twenty millions, furnished 40 per cent of the revenues. When Cochin-China had budgetary autonomy, it did not use its resources to good advantage, but that seems to be no reason why, for thirty-eight years, it should be forced to subsidize the other four countries of the Union. The Cochin-Chinese taxpayer contributes 20 piastres to the fisc, as opposed to 6 piastres from the Tonkinese, 5 for the resident of Annam, and 8 for the Cambodian. It has been estimated that the proportion of the individual's income absorbed in taxes, both federal and local, is 35 per cent for the Cochin-Chinese, 17 per cent for the Tonkinese, 16 per cent in Annam, and 18 per cent in Cambodia.[1] Far too much of this heavy burden goes to paying functionaries. The public administration of the colony is extremely expensive compared with that of other states, and it is the golden calf to which all taxpayers are sacrified, particularly in Cochin-China. As a partial remedy for this condition, regional

[1] Bernard, P., *Le Problème Economique Indochinois* (Paris, 1934), p. 50.

budgets are being restored so as to show the taxpayers the utility of their sacrifice. This is a complete reversal of Sarraut's pre-War financial policy.

The year 1931 saw for the first time a deficit in the budget, which was aggravated the following year. Salary cuts ordered by Pasquier aroused the usual fulminations from the functionaries. Devaluation of the piastre and subsidies to planters were the only positive counter-suggestions they offered. An enormous loan was authorized in 1931, so that the public works programme should not suffer cuts, and the military subsidy to France was renounced. Draconian economies—there was a 29 per cent cut in personnel expenditures from 1931 to 1935—ordered by Pasquier and Robin, some slight tax reductions, the institution of a Colonial Lottery in 1936, and the mildest of income taxes, have retrieved, at least temporarily, a budgetary balance. For the first time since the depression in 1935 and again in 1936, the budget was balanced, and even a small surplus found its way into the reserve fund. This was as true of local, railway, and municipal revenues as for the federal income. The sum total of the General Budget for 1937 is only 61,661,370 piastres. This is small when compared with its pre-depression colleagues, and even so represents a substantial increase over the preceding year, due to the restoration of salary cuts to French and native officials. The 1937 budget indicates a greater sense of financial relaxation. The fundamental evils of an over-padded bureaucracy, unproductive expenditures, and fiscal interests that triumph over good native policy have, as yet, been only too lightly attacked.

The Tariff

When France conquered Cochin-China, tariff conceptions in France had just undergone a profound change. The Franco-British treaty of 1860, followed six years later by the *Senatus-Consulte*, had abrogated the last vestige of the Colonial Pact. The colonies of that period acquired the right of free export to foreign countries and free entry of their goods into France—with the exception of sugar and its derivatives. Cochin-China did not enjoy all these new privileges, but had for twenty years what amounted to free trade. Prosperity characterized this régime. Imports rose from five to twenty-seven millions in the years from 1867 to 1885.

Towards the end of the century Indo-China's tariff régime began to be severely criticized by French manufacturers, who felt that they did not enjoy a sufficiently privileged position there. The press played up their viewpoint, and many were won over to the Protectionist fold. The expense of the Tonkin campaigns and of the new organization of the colony aggravated the feeling that Indo-China should begin to pay for itself. The crisis of 1882, with its lowering of prices, in addition to the recent taxes placed on French goods by certain of the colonies, fanned an aggrieved Métropole's ardour for tariff protection. Certainly a change was inevitable, but Paris vacillated between decreeing a special tariff for Indo-China and applying the regular French tariff. The colony, when consulted, agreed to protection, but wanted a system of preferential tariff applied to French goods. The result was a compromise, with the Metropolitan régime prevailing, and mitigated only by a list of exceptions.

Errors were naturally rife in this exceptions list. Certain articles never made or even heard of in France were taxed from 10 to 23 per cent, like Chinese medicines and exotic foods relished by the Annamites. The first application was disastrous for the country. Imports fell swiftly and were very soon followed by exports. The number of bankruptcies was significant, and the local budget was threatened with a deficit. Unanimous protests arose from the colonials, which won a new tariff arrangement. Foreign products having no equivalents in French industry were exempted from duty, or had their rates radically reduced.

Though the situation was economically improved, relations between France and Indo-China were strained. The Métropole's obvious wish to reserve for itself the colonial market, and to bring in revenues that might offset the expenses of conquest, had resulted in increasing the cost of colonial living. A sad picture of Indo-China's economic plight was drawn at the Colonial Congress of 1889. There the colony voiced its wish for a return to free trade, as well as a realization of the futility of such a desire in the face of a ruthlessly protectionist Parliament.

About 1890, the world situation was such that France felt the need of a radical economic change. The rapid industrialization of Northern Europe and America contrasted with the growing weight of the French national debt and the obvious decadence of France's merchant marine. The result was business stagnation. At the same time, other nations were encircling their colonies with a tariff wall that closed those markets to French goods. The nervous haste evinced by France for some telling gesture that would ameliorate her situation is revealed in the tariff law of January 1892. It showed the current Parliamentary attitude towards colonials and natives as mere consumers, who must become the exclusive clients of France. The Algerian experiment, along the lines of economic assimilation, was deemed so satisfactory that it could be applied universally, on the principle that what was good for one colony must be just as excellent for another. Contemporary opinion was so unanimously protectionist that the law was voted by the Chamber without any discussion.

French products were now free to enter Indo-China without duty, whereas that colony's products were only awarded a tariff reduction upon entering France. In other words, the colony was wholly French, when a purchaser, and half foreign when trying to sell. Foreign goods having paid duty upon entering France could be exported with free entry to the colonies, but the foreign goods which had already defrayed colonial duties had to pay the full French tariff if re-exported to the Métropole. The obvious unfairness of this situation showed Parliament's sole preoccupation with bettering its own finances, and its total disregard of the effect on colonial welfare. Of course, there was always the exceptions list, supposed to temper the absolute quality of the French tariff, but many exceptions requests were either ignored or refused by Paris. In twenty years that list was revised only eight times. What modifications occurred were realized on Oriental goods, which the Annamites found indispensable, and those changes were only due to the persistence of the colony's Chambers of Commerce and the economic importance of Indo-China.

Colonial agitation gradually took the form of demanding a tariff personality for Indo-China. At the Marseille Congress of 1906 this idea was put forward, and systematic centralization by Paris denounced. France's real interest, it should be realized, lay in the prosperity and not the subordination of her colonies. The Bordeaux Congress, held the following year, again expressed itself as favourable to a policy of enlightened self-interest that would develop the natives' purchasing power. All the pre-War Congresses unanimously denounced the 1892 tariff, and the economic subordination of the colonies to Paris, as harmful to themselves and to France. A separate tariff personality was necessary to each colony. The Congresses did manage to stir public opinion by their insistence on these points. In 1908 the Colonial Minister for the first time consulted Indo-China about its reaction to the tariff régime, and did so again two years later. On both occasions the colony denounced assimilation.

A falling off in the colonial exports to France gave body to these theoretical reproaches, and the success of the tariff autonomy in French West Africa gave food for thought. In 1911, a feeble effort was made towards a modification of the current system which, although intended as a colonial pacifier, resulted only in intensifying assimilation, for it gave four Ministers the right to veto exceptions demanded by the colony. Nevertheless, before the War, the exceptions list, inadequate as it was, had made headway and already formed the nucleus of a tariff régime, individual to the colony. Export taxes, not found in France, were a characteristic of the Indo-Chinese tariff. They were not organized until 1898, and had a fiscal rather than a protectionist character. This delicate and difficult type of taxation has tended to disappear, for it had had a discouraging effect upon commerce, which even the Métropole noted, along with the local industrialists.

The War, with its persistent need of money, remitted indefinitely the reduction of Indo-China's tariff. But in 1916 a committee under Morel studied the problem for two years, when the possibility of a general revision of French tariff halted that committee's work. Post-War opinion reflected a changed attitude on the part of Paris, which had become painfully aware of the importance of raw materials. It was recognized that colonial output could not be artificially stimulated by a protection based on raising French tariff, since this would only stimulate reprisals from other countries. Far better would it be to increase systematically the colony's resources by a special programme of public works. Sarraut's plan to this effect had to be postponed because of post-War financial embarrassment, and except for some oratorical pyrotechnics the situation remained about as it was before 1914. More colonial congresses and new official inquiries had to re-arouse Parliament to action.

An official inquiry in 1925 published a report that harmed rather than helped Indo-China in its struggle for tariff liberation. The impression left by this report was that the colony favoured the current system with modifications, a curious conclusion to reach in view of reiterations to the contrary by colonial organizations. It was true that certain colonial reactions had not reached the Ministry when the report went to press, and this was particularly unfortunate since the report did much to influence the Parliamentary vote on the 1928 tariff.

Further evidence of the working out of tariff assimilation came to light at the colonial congresses held at Marseille and at Strasbourg in 1924–25. Statistics showed that French commerce had profited greatly by the 1892 tariff, but a close examination of the figures led to formulating important reserves. For one thing, the franc and the piastre had both changed enormously in value. Also the statistics were not free from padding. For example, the loans for Indo-China had specified that French materials must be used in the 1898 railway construction, and this had resulted in a rise in imports wholly independent of the tariff régime. Moreover, the rise in French imports was equalled by that of the foreign imports, since native needs had developed automatically with the French occupation. The 1905–07 agricultural crisis was also reflected in the depreciated buying power of natives in Oriental commodities.

It is impossible to be absolute in drawing conclusions as to the working out of the 1892 tariff, for all deductions hinge upon conjecture. French industrialists are notoriously unwilling to adapt their products to a specialized market, especially to an exotic clientele. They rely upon quality and fashion, and Annamite buying power is not only very limited but unmoved by either of those considerations. Without the stimulus of competition, the necessity to please customers naturally dwindles. Foreign competitors offer far cheaper articles, adapted to Oriental taste. Nor can France force these rivals out of the Indo-Chinese market, for when French cotton textiles are the only ones for sale the Annamites limit to the strictest necessities their purchases of that indispensable commodity.

The whole tariff issue has had a great effect on the cost of living and the government's native policy. Articles protected by the tariff cost 15 per cent higher in the colony, and the native taxpayer contributes annually the formidable sum of 12,000,000 piastres to reserve a privileged position for the Metropolitan exporter to Indo-China. From a budgetary viewpoint, the revenues from duty on goods entering the colony would have been especially vital to the treasury, at a time when the administration's expenses were increasing. The free entry of French goods necessitated higher taxes, and the creation of the disastrous monopolies was due to the lack of a more legitimate source of revenue. From 1899 to 1925 there was only a slight increase in tariff revenue, but a heavy yield from indirect taxes.

The protection of Indo-China's infant industries is the only point that can be clearly credited to the 1892 tariff. Even before the War colonials were vocal about the injustice of taxing their goods upon entering France, especially when French wares entered the colony duty-free. Moreover, Indo-China was gratuitously sacrificing her naturally advantageous position in the Far East, midway between the free ports of Singapore and Hong-Kong. Indo-China was protectionist as exporter, and free trader as importer, and in both cases she came out at the small end. Yet it cannot be denied that, on the whole, France was and is both the chief provisioner and client of her colony. The question, rather, is as to whether Indo-China's undeniably increasing prosperity could not have been better achieved without the handicap of the 1892 tariff. France can never furnish Indo-China with certain essential products. In addition, the distance that separates the colony from France means high freight costs, and the general necessity for limiting exports to objects of high value and small bulk. Only the fact that Indo-China was in herself a rich country, possessing minerals and labour sufficient to develop an industrial life of her own, saved her from the fatal consequences of the drastic ingrown economy forced upon her by Metropolitan selfishness.

Tariff reprisals from her Far Eastern neighbours were in the natural sequence of events. Indo-China's great export, rice, found by far its best market nearby. The colony was forced by the 1892 law to apply the high French tariff to her best clients, who should also logically have been her best provisioners. A host of Oriental articles, never dreamed of in France, are vital to Annamite happiness, and they can only be obtained in the Far East. The obvious and laziest solution to such omissions in the French tariff was to take the duty on the most analogous articles—a veritable *reductio ad absurdum*. Custom officials vainly mused on how to appraise powdered rhinoceros horns and the varying qualities of shark fins. The whole ridiculous situation was the result of the triumph of fiscal over protectionist ideals, else why should duty be charged on exotic articles which had no counterpart in French industry, and hence need no protection? In the pre-War days the predominantly agricultural economy of Indo-China made any tariff protection at all inherently absurd.

The law of April 13, 1928, was the next great landmark in Indo-China's tariff history. The discussions in the Chamber, preceding its promulgation, showed certain changes in viewpoint, despite retention of the principle of assimilation. Economically assimilated colonies, among which is Indo-China, are now the exception, whereas they were formerly the rule. This change in classification is significant of an evolution in French economic theory. Not that there has been an abandonment of economic integrity within the French Empire, but the principle of a tariff personality for each colony has been admitted.

All colonial products were thereby to have the same freedom upon entering France as French goods enjoyed in the colonies. Local colonial assemblies were permitted initiative in tariff legislation. The colony's exceptions list would automatically be granted if no Ministerial action occurred within three months after the list had been formally submitted. This practical measure effectively put an end to the abuse of silence by which Paris had heretofore indefinitely delayed action on exemptions.

The new tariff is an assimilationist compromise, not in principle but in a more supple procedure. Its development of the exceptions list is the equivalent of a new-born tariff personality which gives each colony its own tariff solution. These modifications, especially for the necessities of native life, are important, and show as well the trend away from a fiscal to a protective tariff for Indo-Chinese industries. The notable intensification of protectionism is not only a general post-War development, but one peculiar to Indo-China. The colony has used its new privileges not to reduce but to increase duty, notably in protecting the local industries of porcelain, silk, and paper.

The fact that the Far Eastern countries, which are Indo-China's chief provisioners and clients, continue to pay the high French tariff, while lesser clients only pay the minimum, is contrary to the colony's interests. Indo-China's commerce with her neighbours declined steadily from 1892 on, in proportion as it increased with France, and this unfortunate consequence of assimilation has been accentuated since 1928. The situation has, of course, been complicated by the depression. The protectionist principle, if judiciously applied, is justifiable for a young colony, but unfortunately in Indo-China its application is defective because it has been influenced by private interests. The current tariff is the result of pressure by individual industrialists for protection of their own products, rather than in the interests of the colony as a whole. The great body of consumers is sacrificed anew for a few local producers. The consequences are inevitably a rise in the cost of living and a new stimulus to contraband. In addition, retaliation is evident in the dwindling purchases of Indo-China's Far Eastern clientele. A temporary rise in tariff revenues was soon offset by a rapid slump. The depression exaggerated its severity, but showed up the essential flaw in Indo-China's whole tariff conception—the lack of balance between the colony's purchases and sales to her neighbours. Indo-China's economy is inextricably bound up with the Far East, and its rigid tariff ties with France are thoroughly artificial and unrelated to her vital needs. France controls almost 60 per cent of Indo-China's exports, and buys there, in exchange, 39 per cent of her raw materials. Economic common sense would indicate far greater advantages in a country's selling where it buys.

The Indo-Chinese are the worst sufferers in this arrangement. They are forced to purchase more expensive and—to them—less useful and appropriate articles, long before their taste for European merchandise has been properly developed. It is undeniable that France has benefited far more than her colony from the various tariff régimes.

The recent treaties made with her Far Eastern neighbours are a step towards reintegrating the colony in her natural economic setting. In addition, export taxes have been so reduced as to strike now only materials needed by local industries. The antagonism of the French producer to colonial rivals has forced the administration to temper its economic assimilation. The principle is still intact, and the recent Imperial Conference shows that the goal remains economic self-sufficiency within the French Empire. It took many years for the principle of political association to make any headway. In the economic field, as yet, the only important breach in the otherwise impregnable wall that encircles France and Indo-China is the development of a colonial tariff personality.

PUBLIC WORKS

Many writers on Indo-Chinese economy confuse the colony's economic development with its production. The public works undertaken by the administration, whether they be of direct benefit to the population, like hydraulic agriculture, or of indirect benefit, like developing the means of communication, form only the mechanical framework, and cannot serve as a touchstone of the country's prosperity. An analogous group of government enterprises which had a related, though not direct, effect on the country's economy are medical assistance and educational organizations, arising out of the government's social obligations. For thirty years M. A. Pouyanne has been the directing spirit behind the colony's public works programmes.

The Means of Communication

Development of the means of communication has been above all the object of governmental solicitude. From 1900 to 1930, 650,000,000 piastres have been spent on public works, of which 62 per cent went for railroads, roads, and bridges; 19 per cent were given to hydraulic agriculture; 7 per cent for maritime ports; 7 per cent for civil edifices; and 2 per cent for city sanitation. It is significant that the first public works loan, that of Doumer, was nothing more than a railway programme.

A 77-kilometre railway in the Cochin-Chinese delta was the first railway built in the peninsula (1881–86). It connected the port of Saigon with the delta network of rivers. A sceptical Ministry in Paris cut down Le Myre's elaborate plan, and subsequent pleas for its extension have never been granted. The fact that its passenger traffic far exceeds its commercial importance, as well as the cost of so much bridge construction, has prevented its accomplishment. The second railway was frankly military. Provisioning the troops in Upper Tonkin during the conquest was very difficult. The road, or rather path, went through an unhealthy region that was infested with bandits. The death toll in coolies and soldiers on this road was only equalled by the loss in provisions. De Lanessan decided to build a railway, but adequate preliminary study was impossible because of the unsettled condition of the country. In 1889, under terribly hazardous conditions, work was begun. It was hard to get labour and worse to keep it. Bandits regularly carried off Europeans for ransom. Only 101 kilometres long, this road took five years to build, and cost 20,000,000 francs. Its great expense and the complete absence of paying traffic led to strong criticism. The difficulties of its construction and its military, not economic aim, were forgotten. Governor Rousseau began, and Doumer finished, an extension to this road from both ends, so as to make it pay. Unfortunately it had no sooner been finished than the gauge was declared to be too narrow for use, and the Chinese market of Longtcheou with which it connected was found to be one of the poorest trading centres in China. Again preliminary study had been lacking. Poor materials were used, in a mistaken effort to economize, and even then their cost exceeded the original estimate. Furthermore, Metropolitan authorization as well as the labour had been hard to get.

Doumer's vast programme was based on the idea that railways, merely by their passage through a country, would create wealth. This was the glamorous idea that seduced the Métropole to authorize his large loan. No one foresaw that there was little to transport. Natives, in most parts of the colony, raised only enough for their own wants and did not exchange the surplus, if any, because adjacent districts produced the same things. Railways were only useful in a country that had already evolved economically. They were the means, not the creators of wealth. The period of waiting, essential to realizing profits, had not been anticipated, nor the capital required for the railways' upkeep, which represented a serious drain on the budget. Lack of means of communication had not been the great obstacle to the country's development. It was, rather, the uncertainty and violence of the climate, the primitive methods of cultivation, and *monoculture*.

Inadequate study of the projected lines, as usual, characterized the Doumer programme. Preliminary research for the Yunnan-fou Railway was done with vertiginous speed in only four months, in spite of the rainy season and the impenetrability of the country, intensified by the absence of good maps. Two engineers and their assistants drew up plans in less than a year. No one thought of malaria, though the whole region was renowned for its unhealthiness. There was a lack of technicians. The engineers who came out from France knew nothing about the country's special conditions, nor the people. Labour was almost impossible to get. Road *corvées* were still too green in local memory. The same inadequate housing, provisioning, and negligence in caring for sick coolies prevailed.

Military considerations played a certain role in determining this railway's construction. The fear lest England be the first to penetrate Yunnan was a constant nightmare of the period. There was also the Ferry-inspired wish to connect South China with Saigon, and to substitute railway communication for the defective water route.

To make the newly created Indo-Chinese Union a reality, it was to be endowed with a railway framework. The programme included a coast line connecting Saigon with Hanoi, to be known as the Transindochinois. The Yunnan-fou line was to traverse Tonkin from Hanoi, through the Red River valley. A transversal, linking the Mekong to the coast of Annam, would give Laos an outlet to the sea. Another line was to cross the South Annamite Range. Cambodia was to be tied up at one end to the Siamese network, and at the other end to Saigon, through Pnom-Penh. The total length of these lines was to be 3,200 kilometres. These railways were classified according to their supposed importance. It was indicative of contemporary thought that the Yunnan railway headed the list, and that the Cambodian and Laotian network was set aside as of less immediate importance.

The Métropole for a year withheld its consent for the Yunnan railway, fearing that the 1900 troubles in China might prove to be too serious. Simultaneously with its approval came word that the British had renounced their Yunnan-Burmese project. The railway built by the French to Yunnan-fou remains among the most costly and laborious feats of colonization. The government, the colony, and a private company combined to put through the project. A private company was essential because part of the line was to be built on foreign territory.

The negligence with which the route had been traced showed itself almost at once. At one place an engineer, far from the scene of action, had marked with his pencil a line on the map, and this was the casual origin of the unheard-of difficulties encountered in the Namti valley. Among other minor obstacles it created was the need for a new authorization from the French government, and new land as well as permits from the none-too-gracious Chinese. This valley became celebrated as the "mistake of 500 metres" and presented almost insurmountable engineering problems. This initial error involved still others: building on unstable ground, with rock falling from great heights. The pride of the responsible engineers kept them from acknowledging the error of their ways, and led them into further mistakes. In 1905 the company asked more financial aid of the colony. This was granted, but the following year the sum proved to be insufficient. By 1908 the company had to be dissolved and the railway taken over directly by the administration.

Labour was one of the chief difficulties, besides the technical obstacles. The country through which the railway passed was very sparsely settled. Coolies had to be imported from China at great expense, and Peking was far from co-operative. The Namti was so unhealthy that it was called Death Valley. No one was prepared to cope with this problem. A legend grew up that the railway had cost the lives of one hundred thousand Annamite and Chinese coolies, but facts do not support such figures. The total number of coolies hired was eighty thousand. Probably 30 per cent of them died—an enormous mortality, even without exaggeration. Nor were the Europeans spared: forty out of three hundred of them died. This marvellous railway escaped by a hair's-breadth from being abandoned at one time, but on April 1, 1910, the first locomotive reached Yunnan-fou. The line has proved to be a picturesque *tour de force* rather than an economic miracle. Not only was the original cost tremendous, but its upkeep is very expensive. The land is unstable, necessitating constant vigilance. Moreover, political excitement has resulted in frequent attacks on the Chinese end of the line. Five years before it was finished the rails from Hanoi to Vinh were laid down, and three years later, in 1908, those from

Tourane to Hué. The Saigon-Nhatrang line was not finished until just before the War.

These railway ventures profited their contractors and engineers, if not the colony. Contracts had been drawn up without care for Indo-China's interests. High interest rates, up to 12 per cent, added to this burden. It took the financial distress of 1908, and much violent criticism, to make the administration put in its contracts that interest would henceforth be limited to 5 per cent. As with the monopolies contracts, the colony was hopelessly bled, and always lost its numerous lawsuits with unscrupulous contractors. Fluctuations in the piastre accounted for some of the losses, but a criminal carelessness, a failure to distinguish essential from sumptuary expenditure, the multiplication of budgets—all were responsible for this terrific leakage. The cost often doubled the original estimate.

These graft scandals disgusted France with Indo-Chinese railways. They were only profitable for the men who built them. There was a marked reluctance, just before the War, to allow Sarraut to finish what had already been begun. Railway building clearly reflected this changed attitude. In twelve years, from 1898 to 1910, 2,000 kilometres had been constructed, and from 1911 to 1928, a period of seventeen years, only 350 kilometres. The War cut Indo-China off from supplies and materials, so that the public works of this period were principally roads. After the War, the rise in the piastre interfered with Sarraut's projects, and it was not until just before the depression that railway building was again resumed. The economic prosperity of the post-War decade gave an additional and more reasonable impetus to a resumption of railway construction. The need for labour on the Southern plantations meant importing coolies from Tonkin. Completing the Trans-indochinois would help enormously in solving the labour problem.

Siam's concentration on railway building was an additional stimulus, especially in the long-neglected project of giving Laos an outlet to the East. Siam, with half the population, had more railways than Indo-China, and they carried almost three times as much merchandise, which consequently brought in much greater revenues. There was a natural fear lest Siam, by its railway enterprise, tap the resources of Cambodia and Laos long before the French lines would be built. This idea stimulated the completion of the Battambang-Pnom-Penh line in 1933, to compete as well as to connect with the Siamese railway from Bangkok to the Cambodian frontier. The discovery of Laotian minerals has lent a new importance to correcting Laos's natural orientation towards the West. The customary difficulties were the railway's passage through an unpopulated country, and the fact that mountainous regions made the construction expenses enormous. The terrible famine of 1931 in Annam reawakened interest in finishing the Transindochinois. By 1932, out of all Doumer's programme, only 2,400 kilometres had been built, at a cost of 162,000,000 francs. The depression stimulated completing the original programme. The Transindochinois was finished in 1936, despite its almost prohibitive bridging and tunnelling, and the current year the Tanap-Thakkek line should give Laos an eastern outlet.

Unfortunately for railway construction, by the time interest was renewed in building new lines, motor competition had become very important. Motor-buses charged much lower rates than trains. Native travellers did not mind the discomfort, to the point of willingly riding on fenders and hoods. The numerous breakdowns that ensued meant nothing to the Indo-Chinese, who are never in a hurry. The government seemed astonished at the appearance of these rivals to the railways. For years roads had been built that paralleled the railways, and now there was great official surprise at the serpent that had been nourished in its public works bosom. A circulation tax on motor-buses aimed to revive the drooping railways, which at best were slow, expensive, and lazily negligent in their assured monopoly. Press campaigns had vainly tried to rouse railways from their irresponsible slumber, but it took the motor-bus competition to speed up railway schedules, to lower their rates, and to import a few new locomotives.

The completion of the Transindochinois lengthens the colony's total railways to 2,523 kilometres. The introduction of motor-rails has formed an entirely new clientele who are not insensitive to the recent reduction in fares. Fourth-class passengers pay nowadays about a third of what fares cost in 1925, and approximately half of the 1931 prices. These factors have induced a return to public favour of the railways. An agreement which became effective in 1935 laid the ghost of their rivalry with the motor-bus whereby these two transport systems redistributed their service on a co-operative geographic basis. The state has likewise profited, for the motor-buses have obviated subsidizing some of the river steamship services. Native passengers totalled 7,300,000 in 1935, as against 5,700,000 three years before. By 1937 the deficits of the last few years will have been almost wholly absorbed despite the recent opening of new lines.

Government control has been both the strength and the weakness of Indo-Chinese railways. On the good side, it has enabled them to be built when no private company would run the risk or survive the losses. Although they do not run at a loss, and there is a slight surplus to their credit, yet the profits earned by the railways of Java and Siam have no counterpart in Indo-China. The colony's railways have one of the smallest freight services in the world, and their running expenses are among the highest. Even out of the Yunnan railway, which is extremely profitable because of its heavy passenger traffic, the state gets only an infinitesimal share of the profits. Fortunately, in 1936, the state wound up the last lawsuits of the Yunnan Company. In addition, the colony's budget must pay interest on the railway loans, for the income from the railways is barely enough to pay for their running expenses. Many claim that when the whole network of lines is completed the railways will finally pay. This is problematical in that the railways, in most cases, follow the waterways, and are also paralleled by roads. The fundamental mistake seems to have been in laying down railways out of political rather than economic considerations. The regions having the largest population and the most developed production have been neglected, and the rails built through rather deserted country. Branch lines would permit the railway to put life into untouched regions, but all the lines are like the Yunnan-fou —frail ribbons without the vitality which a network of judiciously laid branch lines would give.

The expense of these railways does not permit releasing the natives from their life as burden-bearers. The Annamites have no aversion for the railway—on the contrary, they crowd the fourth class and furnish all the railways' meagre profits. Monopoly, graft, and a misconception of the railway's economic function have been the stumbling-blocks to Indo-China's railways. In its present state of development, railways are a luxury equipment, by which the natives have not as yet the means to profit. So much railway construction was a premature exaggeration of the means of communication before a corresponding development of the means of production.

Roads

The same criticism, in large measure, can be levelled against the orgy of road building which has been indulged in within recent years. Indo-China is naturally endowed with good waterways, and Cochin-China, characteristically, which is the country with the best network of canals, has also been given the finest roads. Tonkin's earliest roads had naturally a military origin, but their development suffered an eclipse when provincial budgets were abolished. Under Sarraut, Tonkin became the object of road solicitude, because of its dense population and insufficient waterways. Provisioning famine areas, and making mines accessible, furnished additional motivation.

Sarraut had a prophetic vision of the importance of motor travel at a time when railways, though unpopular, were still regarded as the best means of transportation. The 1913 loan was the first to allot credits to railway building. From 1900 to 1927, 44,000,000 piastres were spent on such public works. The War, by cutting off railway supplies to the colony, gave an additional stimulus. By 1931, about 25,000 kilometres of carefully classified roads had been built, of which more than half were paved in stone. It was a remarkable work for a very few years. Motor-cars showed a corresponding increase. Their number rose from 5,663 in 1923 to 17,200 in 1927. The classification of these roads was patterned after the French model. The chief artery was to link the four capitals to the Chinese and Siamese frontiers. In 1937, Colonial Route No. 13 will link Lower Laos to Cochin-China from Savannakhet to Thakkek, and from Vientiane to Paksane. There will be a further effort to improve the present road between Vinh and Luang-Prabang. Subsidiary roads were to penetrate the hinterland, with the special aim of connecting plateaux with ports. No one can deny the remarkable quality of this achievement, but doubt can definitely be cast upon its usefulness.

As with railways, political reasons have triumphed over economic considerations. Facilitating the work of the administration, not to mention the comfort of the administrators, is added to assuring the military security of the country. Unlike the railways, roads bring in no revenue at all, apart from the sale of petrol, and their upkeep is a terrific burden on the budget. The original cost of the roads is as nothing compared to the vigilance and expense required, at an annual cost of 6,000,000 piastres. The most inacessible regions and famine areas have been neglected for the sake of other roads, easier to build and designed to facilitate tourist sightseeing.

The French have inherited the Roman tradition of road building, to such a degree that it has been called *la folie des routes*. Roads appeal to the eye by their symmetry, and to the imagination by bringing to life whole regions that were formerly suspended in somnolent isolation. They could be built in places where railways would take too long or be too costly. The effect on the natives has been immediate and picturesque. Everyone uses the roads, from *bonzes* to peasants. The roads have quickened their feeling of life and power. It has sufficed only the briefest contact with the road to dissolve the tradition of centuries that made for inertia, isolation, and detached contemplation. If the Annamite is taken more swiftly from his native village, he can also return there more easily. He fears journeys less, and departure for him no longer means death. The whole country is united by this living cordon. Products hitherto deemed unsalable find purchasers. A new sense of human dignity comes from this conquest of nature which is shared alike by those who build and those who use the roads. Egalitarian sentiments flourish. The Siamese are astonished at Indo-China's vehicular democracy which allows carts and motor-cars to use the same roads.

Bridges

Bridges are an expensive corollary to road and railway construction. Like the roads, they have had an extraordinary influence on the natives. In 1897 the need was felt for a great steel bridge to span the Red River so as to connect Hanoi with the adjacent provinces. This bridge, the Pont Doumer, crossed 1,700 metres of a torrential river that made the construction both costly and hazardous. The natives, egged on by the *bonzes*, firmly believed that the Red River dragon would never permit this Occidental impiety, and the washing away of several stone pillars in the early stages of construction reinforced this belief. The achievement of this bridge greatly enhanced French prestige, and simultaneously lowered that of the local dragon.

A bridge at Hué, built at the same time, and another at Saigon were the main constructions of this kind during the early period. Railway and road building in the delta regions has been greatly complicated and made expensive by the amount of bridging required. The continued use of the old ferries and boat transportation would have served about the same purpose and freed some of the funds for more useful works.

Waterways

The Red River presents an almost hopeless navigation problem, except for native craft. Increased efforts, however, have been made towards improving the Mekong, especially since the French established themselves in Laos. Towards the end of the nineteenth century, two steamboats managed to make their way up the Mekong during the summer floods, and to reach the Sino-Burmese frontier. From 1903 to 1910, a series of experiments proved the feasibility of commercial steam navigation, at least as far as Luang-Prabang. This success incited the *Compagnie des Messagéries Fluviales* to open a service— of course, subsidized. But the rapids of the Mekong have never been completely vanquished in spite of the money and effort expended upon them.

The whole river is divided into three parts. The Lower Mekong, 700 kilometres long, extends from the delta to the falls of Khone. Work has made this navigable in all seasons. The Middle Mekong, 800 kilometres long, extends from Khone to Vientiane, the present steamship terminus. In 1929, work was undertaken on the Khemmarat rapids to make them navigable at all times. The Upper Mekong from Vientiane to the Burmese frontier, 900 kilometres away, has as yet no regular steam service, only native boats. The total record is highly honourable. Steam navigation has been made possible in all seasons throughout two-thirds of the river's course. Perhaps a special type of boat will have to be designed for the last stretch of river, but the expense of such work is not at present justified by the density of the population nor the importance of the commerce in the country near which these boats would pass. When the effort has been made, it may be found that the Mekong's great rival, the Siamese railways, will have already diverted commerce to Bangkok. The whole effort is linked to that of an outlet for Laos, and the draining of its resources away from Siamese markets and towards the French ports.

Aviation

Since the War, aviation pioneering in Indo-China has been almost entirely in military hands. It is a fairly easy problem for light aircraft, but more difficult for the powerful planes which need bigger and better equipped flying fields. Airports have already been created at Vientiane, Hanoi, Vinh, and Saigon, but these still need many improvements. The small amount of level ground in the peninsula is the greatest of all handicaps.

Up to 1927 there was no commercial aviation. The year before, an attempt had been made at postal aviation along the Mekong. Its failure was due to local conditions. Although, from 1925 to 1928, the number of aeroplanes had doubled, the lack of landing ground and adverse climatic conditions are still almost insuperable obstacles. Aviation is paralysed during the rainy season. Fogs in the Mekong valley and the mists of Tonkin make for difficulty in the dry season as well. Great variability from one region to another, even nearby, has made it hard to organize a service which would link all the countries of the colony. A meteorological service must first be developed, with a network of observation posts in order to lessen the numerous dangers.

Military aviation is the only branch that has made any real headway. These 'planes have been very useful to administrators, especially in Laos and Annam, where the distances are great and present communications inadequate. Even there, heavy clouds and uncharted mountain peaks make the trip hazardous. A notable flight of Lieut. Guillaumot, from Vientiane to the Sino-Burmese frontier, was accomplished in spite of great difficulties, to the wonderment of the natives. From this viewpoint, aviation has a distinct political importance in enhancing French prestige. Incidentally, the geographical service has profited by the photographic work of military aviators.

In addition to the local colonial aviation, there is an important international service connecting France with the colony. In 1931 the Marseille–Beirut line was prolonged to Saigon. This had an important effect in facilitating close relations with the mother country. That same year, 1930, a Bureau of Air Travel was created and placed under the Governor-General to co-ordinate all the governmental services allied to aviation.

Canals and Dykes

The discovery of the inadequacy of the Mekong and Red Rivers as water highways was one of the early disillusionments of the French in Indo-China. Both rivers flow from the high Chinese plateaux and share the characteristic common to all tropical rivers of alternating summer floods with periods of winter dryness. The gradient of the Red River is ten times that of the Mekong, so that it falls precipitously to the sea. This has created the imperious necessity, since time immemorial, of sheltering Tonkinese homes and rice-fields by means of dykes. The overflowing of the Mekong is, on the contrary, of a beneficent nature to local agriculture. The rich alluvial soil left by the Mekong cannot be duplicated by the torrential Red River, which must be held in check as the price of survival. The nature of these two rivers, therefore, has forced hydraulic agriculture to take the form of dredging in Cochin-China and of reinforcing the dykes in Tonkin. Both of these rivers must be utilized in relation to the local agriculture through different forms of irrigation.

The dredging of canals in Cochin-China represents the most continuous effort of French colonization in the peninsula. It has the double interest of being a creator of new farmland and of navigable waterways. The vast marshland found by the French on their arrival has been drained by a remarkable series of canals. This work in Cochin-China exceeds what was done for the Suez Canal, and covers more than 4,000 kilometres. The Admirals alone redeemed many hundreds of hectares, and the work has been steadily pursued ever since, over a period of forty-five years, and at the cost of more than 48,000,000 piastres. Almost 2,000,000 hectares of farmland has thus been created.

Despite the commendable continuity of this effort, too much has been left to chance without being regulated by a general plan. Instead of following the water slope and a general north-south direction, canals have been dug every which-way. The use of these canals as waterways has taken precedence over their utility for irrigation. Farmers complain that no new canal can be dug to the profit of one region without being simultaneously harmful to another. Defective upkeep and a failure to connect new canals with old is a further basis for complaint. The undeniably fertile land of Cochin-China could be made to yield far more than it now does. Further work could be profitably undertaken, since the government has been more than amply repaid for what it has already accomplished. The canal of Rach-gia-Hatien, completed in 1930, is a case in point. It marks the beginning of the ultimate control of the Trans-Bassac. It took four years to dig and it communicates with the sea through four rivers. Hydraulic agriculture in Cochin-China is the most popular form of public works. Up to 1875 it was done by *corvées*, but thereafter by paid labour. The growth of arable land there has been paralleled by a rapid increase in population, and it has made of Cochin-China one of the great rice granaries of the world.

The work in Tonkin has been divided into protection against inundations and against drought. Of the two possible solutions, either to improve the existing dykes or to try a totally new system, the former was chosen and placed on a scientific basis. The work suffered from the usual handicap of lack of money and technicians, the absence of accurate maps, and above all of a general plan. Despite the improvements realized over a period of forty years, it was only in 1927 that a methodical plan was drawn up and followed; 1926 had seen a particularly destructive inundation. The dykes, which covered 20,000,000 cubic metres, had, in 1930, been increased to 72,000,000, and the work has since continued on the same scale. The project that was begun in 1927 has finally been completed, and no break has yet occurred in this network of dykes. The state is now beginning to enforce the second line of dykes. In the near future Cambodia and Cochin-China will receive more hydraulic attention. In Annam, work on a small scale has been undertaken during the last two years, and it has added amazingly to the productivity of more than 36,000 hectares of rice-fields. An abundant local labour supply greatly facilitates such work.

In forty years the French have built forty times the number of dykes, at a cost of 42,000,000 piastres (1936), than the Annamite government had done, though it prided itself on such work. The climatic and local conditions generally have created difficulties which the dyke work on the Mississippi and on the Po did not encounter, and the Tonkinese dykes remain one of the greatest systems in the world. Despite a heavy initial expense, and the cost of 40,000 piastres in annual upkeep, this work will be more than repaid in time.

Drought is a far more serious problem in Annam and Tonkin than generally realized, because inundations are more sensationally reported. The extreme variability of the rains makes the harvest in Tonkin an agonizing problem. A system of methodical irrigation used in Java, through *casiers* artificially irrigated either by gravity or pumping, has been very effective in Tonkin. The expense of such work is its greatest drawback. Though the food output has been undeniably increased by 60 per cent in the irrigated districts, so has the population. Nevertheless, though they may only come out even, such works are enthusiastically received by the people. But the natives refuse to pay a special tax for water, preferring rather to do without. No private company would consent to undertake the work at such an evident loss, so it is but another drain on the state budget. But it is an unavoidable burden. A poor rice harvest can be survived in the South, but in the more densely populated North a drought or an inundation means widespread starvation. This type of expenditure is far more closely related to the needs of the population than railways. The increasing proportion of funds allotted to hydraulic engineering in the budgets of the last ten years show a better appreciation of this reality.

In Tonkin, irrigation is a prime necessity for the June rather than the November rice harvest. There is inevitably much experimentation, for the Tonkin situation is in direct contradiction to other Far Eastern enterprises. The Tonkin delta, though flat to all appearances, slopes towards the sea. This is a very important factor in irrigation, and it is the basis for the distinction which the Annamites make between high, middle, and low rice-fields. One of the government's most serious mistakes was to regard the rice-fields having two harvests as particularly rich land, and to tax them accordingly. Sometimes all three types of rice-fields will be found in one commune's lands, and this makes the irrigation problem very complex.

Chemical analysis has revealed the unbelievable poverty of the delta soil. Lime and phosphoric acid are almost completely lacking, and they must be artificially restored. Fertilizer is an expense to which the Annamites are not accustomed, and one which they cannot afford. Monoculture's great danger in exhausting the soil necessitates a varying of the crops. It is a mistake to think that irrigation could or should assure a double rice crop. To begin with, the Tonkinese have not enough animal labour to handle two crops, and the delta's soil—already poor—would be totally exhausted. It would also involve suppressing vegetable crops, and though this is secondary from the viewpoint of the farmers' income, it brings in food without exhausting the soil as would a second rice harvest. Irrigation could guarantee all the farmers at least one sure and easier crop a year, and would obviate their dependence on the whimsical monsoons and permit a rotation of crops.

The Tonkin peasant already irrigates on a minute scale with primitive means, but nowhere has he utilized the big waterways. The French contribution has been essentially that of making possible large-scale irrigation—in fact, at the beginning they erred on the side of the grandiose and the over-simplified. The Tonkinese delta is very complex from an irrigation viewpoint, and its solution is perforce multiple, not uniform. Large-scale irrigation is possible only in the North, and even there conditions vary enormously from one village to another.

Part of the expense is the need for a constant supervision of these dykes. All who have witnessed the anguished struggle of the Tonkinese peasant with the rising waters realize the importance to him and to the colony of this victory over the redoubtable Red River. Though the state has given to the delta villages a line of dykes equal to the strongest in the world, they have not resolved the problem of floods. But whereas inundations were formerly the rule, they are now the exception, and the country is less a prey to famine and epidemic. The greatest single achievement has been Pasquier's Songcau-Songthilong Canal (1929). This has the advantage of serving as a waterway to the mining regions, and it has effected the transformation of a poor country into a fertile one. In 1932, the Thuyhoa-Phuyen gravity irrigation works were a resumption, with scientific means, of a former Cham project. Labour difficulties in this unhealthy region held back progress on this work for six years. It was not completed until 1934, when the sterile plain of Thuyhoa was transformed.

Only now is the colony beginning to reap benefits from decades of hydraulic engineering. By 1928 the period of experimentation was definitely over. The only wonder is that it lasted so long. The 1931 loan permitted finishing the main part of Pasquier's programme. Such work has a political as well as an economic and social value. A map of the irrigation works, now being carried on, would be nearly identical with that of the regions that revolted in 1931. Such being the case, giving them a larger place on the budget would be justified, especially for Cochin-China, which pays the heaviest taxes and whose hydraulic engineering has been relegated to second place after that of Tonkin.

Cities and Civil Structures

The French have a great talent for city building, though they tend to reproduce French cities in the East, where they are not usually appropriate. The external elegance of their towns is unfortunately not always matched by their sanitation. Saigon for many years has had the best theatre in the Far East, but simultaneously suffered from a defective water supply. Hanoi, the City of Perfume, has, in addition to the picturesque native town, a European quarter lined with villas. Its avenues of flowering trees give to Hanoi its special character. Life in these Occidentalized towns is so agreeable, so reminiscent of France, that it makes resident functionaries unwilling to serve in the provinces.

The 7 per cent of the budget spent on public buildings, as opposed to the 2 per cent dedicated to the town's sanitation, is a commentary on the attraction which both kinds of activity have for the colonial French. The unnecessary prodigality and sumptuary nature of these buildings has aroused serious native and French criticism. Such expenditures bring nothing to the colony, and, moreover, are expensive in upkeep. Many of them are miracles of wastefulness. The opera house at Hanoi, for example, was built on the most imposing site in the town. It was begun in the era of the *folie des grandeurs*, and on such a scale that, had it been completed, it could have seated at one time the entire European population of Hanoi. It had the additional disadvantage of being ugly and expensive. Brieux, the Academician, said that it summed up all the French faults: love of pleasure, artificiality, unreflecting enthusiasm, and a wanton lack of foresight.[1]

The recent large-scale project for electrification by water power for the provinces links up with the irrigation system. Like other recent public works contracts, the 1931 electrical project laid down the principle of a financial partnership between the colony and the concessionnaire. It is hoped that the sanitation conditions, through better ventilation and food conservation, will be improved by this measure, as well as a more abundant water supply. The country is richly endowed from an hydraulic viewpoint, but the control and distribution of this energy has usually proved very costly.

CAPITAL AND CREDIT

Capital in Indo-China may be constituted by the savings of Europeans, Chinese, or Annamites, by money invested in the colony in public or private enterprises, and by the credit facilities offered by banks or by individuals.

The savings of Europeans in Indo-China are naturally related to the average income of the 38,500 French in the colony. By examining income taxes and functionaries' salaries, it has been estimated that the annual income of a French family in Indo-China averages about 5,000 piastres. As for native savings, only in Cochin-China do important Annamite landowners exist, estimated numerically at eight thousand out of the nine thousand Annamites forming the rich native class in the colony. Judging by the price their paddy brings, their average annual income is 6,000 piastres.[2] In the other countries of the Union, the natives are too miserable to have any savings that would constitute capital, properly speaking. This is true notably of Annam and Tonkin, where the growth of production has not kept pace with the increase in population, as is shown by the steady decline of the exportable surplus. Therefore, only in Cochin-China, and solely in exports like rice, have the natives realized profits which might constitute savings. Of European savings, a large amount is sent out of the country to France, as is revealed by the postal money orders statistics. Where native profits exist, they are almost entirely absorbed in purchasing articles for immediate use or for future production, and the surplus, if any, is eaten up in paying off interest on loans, so heavily indebted

[1] Brieux, *Voyage aux Indes et en Indochine* (Paris, 1926), p. 37.
[2] Bernard, P., *Le Problème Economique Indochinois* (Paris, 1934), pp. 18–19.

is the whole population. It has been estimated that for a normal year, like 1931, the country's possibility of self-enrichment could be valued at only 30,000,000 piastres.

Capital investment by the Metropolitan French in Indo-China has been much more closely studied since 1924. It has been estimated that eight billion francs were subscribed to companies in Indo-China; about half of that sum comes from the French in the colony. Of this, only half has been used for the development of the country; the other half being dissipated in commissions to middlemen, graft, and the waste perhaps inseparable from all operations in a new country. The selection of enterprises for French investment in the colony gives by far the largest place, in value, to real estate, then rubber, rice, mines, and electrical energy, in the order of their importance. As a corollary it is interesting to compare this with all-native investments, which give first place to agricultural crops, then real estate, animal husbandry, industry and commerce—amounting to 20,000,000,000 francs, or five times as much as the French investments.

Loans is another form of investment in Indo-China for Metropolitan savings. There have been five main loans which have left Indo-China with a relatively light public debt. Interest, too, on pre-War loans has benefited by the post-War devaluation. Statistics are not available which would indicate how much any but two of the colony's banks have lent. Indian bankers have loaned money to the extent of 50,000,000 piastres, and Annamite usurers have loaned their compatriots approximately the same. The vast difference between them is that the profits realized by the Annamites remain in the country, whereas those of the *chettys* are in large measure exported. Chinese profits have been mostly reinvested in the country, though the recent fluctuations in the exchange have given their transactions the character of speculation. Some capital is still exported to China, probably about 5,000,000 piastres annually. Profits by French companies are also inevitably repatriated to pay their stockholders. To this exportation of capital must be added state payments—albeit recently radically reduced— towards the military expenses of the Métropole. In a normal pre-depression year, 40,000,000 piastres were sent out of the country. Because of its political relations with France, and its economic ties with foreign creditors, Indo-China will permanently suffer a drain of capital. The colony, therefore, is forced to compensate for this loss by a favourable balance of trade.

Banks

The Bank of Indo-China was founded with private capital, but, in 1875, it received for twenty-five years the privilege of issuing paper money. Though it had the oligarchical character of the banks in the old French colonies, it enjoyed greater liberty of action, in spite of some state control. This bank grew with the prosperity of the colony, and soon became one of the leading colonial banks in the world, with branches all over the Far East. With the periodic renewal of its privileges, it was allowed to participate in state loans in the countries where it had branches. It enjoyed and used brilliantly privileges that were unusual for a private bank in a French colony, and became a discount and a commercial bank in addition to its offical function.

Such prosperity was not achieved without arousing resentment. Among the reproaches made to this bank was that of operating anywhere—notably in China, where it has a quasi-monopoly of French banking—without concentrating its usefulness in Indo-China. The rise of the piastre, especially in relation to the franc, as well as the growth of the colony's business, increased its prosperity as well as the blame. Many deplored the grip which this and other banks had acquired on the colony's economy, and especially in the 1920's, when the Indo-Chinese banks came into their own, and played a stellar role by selecting certain enterprises for their support. For many the prosperity of the post-War period was the triumph of the powers of darkness and finance. Dorgelès well named the key chapter to his *Route Mandarine* "Under the Sign of the Piastre."

From time to time the state threatened not to renew the bank's privileges, but in the 1929 shake-up, along with its new charter and the expansion of its capital, the government gained control of 20 per cent of the stock. A minimum annual revenue was to be assured to the state by the bank, as well as its backing of the official agricultural credit organizations at low interest rates. The *Banque Franco-Chinoise* and a few foreign organizations are its only rivals as discount banks.

The *Société Financière Française et Coloniale* is the most brilliant and youthful specialized commercial bank, notably in its acquisition of a virtual monopoly in the field of electrical energy. The *Société Financière des Caoutchoucs* is the only other organization that can compare with it, though Indo-China is only a part of that organization's broad interests. The *Société Indo-Chinoise*, called the SICAN, has taken a large share in developing the tea and coffee plantations. These three commercial banks have a capital of about 400,000,000 francs, of which approximately half is invested in Indo-China—a relatively small amount when compared with their total capital and with the economic importance of the colony. This unique organization of credit for production in Indo-China is now, due to errors in policy, struggling for its existence.

All of these banks, but especially the Bank of Indo-China, have been the object of violent criticism by natives, colonials, elected assemblies, and even of a former Governor of Cochin-China. In addition to the old grievance of prudent selfishness in abstaining from investing in the colony which gave it its name, and of following prosperity rather than creating it, the depression aroused more concrete reproaches against the high rate of interest, the exaggerated facilities for credit in prosperous times, an undue tightening of credit in adversity, and its merciless treatment of debtors. To this the bank replies that if rates on short-term loans are very high, it is due to the extreme hazards of most of Indo-China's commercial operations. Banks are not philanthropic institutions designed to dispense individuals from the consequences of their imprudence. The reproach of insufficiently guaranteed loans in times of prosperity is better founded, though the merchants themselves were the first to abuse credit. Shifting the guilt of speculation from one group to another is a futile pursuit. Banks, by their very nature, are the most obvious butt of attacks, which at some moments in Cochin-China have taken a very violent turn. Its parsimonious distribution of credit has indeed been the basis of the security enjoyed by the Bank of Indo-China, at the price perhaps of a failure to further the colony's productivity as it could and should have done. The establishment, in 1935, of a Colonial Credit Organization is an eloquent indication that the government has had to find an institution that could fill the role which the Bank had failed to do. Attached to a similar organization of National Credit in France, it is to be the informed intermediary through which capital may be invested in the colony, as well as serve as a committee to study the colony's programmes for loans.

Agricultural Credit

Before the French came, land was almost the sole source of wealth. Credit was extremely scarce, and the legal rate of interest, 3 per cent a month, was much higher in actual practice. Capital, where it existed, had little chance of being profitably employed, because commerce and industry were in such a rudimentary state. The sole reason for having capital would have been to keep a farmer from losing his property in time of disaster. Since he was perennially without reserves, credit was organized in a collective form by the state or commune in the form of rice granaries. The communal lands, by being inalienable, constituted an ultimate resource for poor people, and theoretically at any rate restricted the necessity for credit. One unique form of credit was the *vente à reméré*. It was in many ways highly disadvantageous to the borrower, but at least his rights were still retained on the tax lists. If he did not fulfil the terms of his loan contract, the loss of ownership became final. Private capital's function was never the development of wealth, which existed—if at all—in the land. The aid of public credit was never granted to the individual but to the collectivity. There was a total absence of industrial or commercial credit.

High taxes, mandarinal exactions, sumptuary laws, natural disasters —in short, the futility of effort, have all contributed to making Annamites *insouciants*. On the other hand, there is the Annamites' constant need of money: fêtes, taxes, famines, and family ceremonies. The man to whom he has therefore recourse is the usurer, either Chinese, *chetty*, or Annamite. To them he must pledge his crops in advance, at a sum notably below their real value. Moreover, every Annamite with a little spare capital is a would-be usurer, and even more pitiless than his larger-scale colleagues. The rates asked by these usurers are so high that they absorb all of the farmer's profits and energies. It is not uncommon for an ultimate payment to cover three times the original amount of the loan. Naturally, there is an exploitation of the peasant's ignorance of the law and of the new facilities for agricultural credit. Especially high rates exist in Annam, which is subject to the worst disasters. The usurers prefer not to bring suit, but to send a vagabond to create a scandal on the debtor's threshold, which involves the usual cursing of his ancestors. Only as a last resort will the creditor take up formal action, for if the debtor defaults, his creditor usually prefers to negotiate another loan until his victim's rice-fields, and often his daughter, fall into his usurious hands.

All farmers in Indo-China, it may be said, are indebted in varying degrees. Even the prosperous landowners, who do not cultivate the land themselves, have high running expenses which necessitate borrowing. At the beginning of the farming season there is a universal call on credit from the whole gamut of the population. The average farmer needs short-term loans which bring an interest rate of from 15 to 25 per cent a month. Big farmers, wanting to extend their activities, need long-term loans which are of a rarer, because of a less profitable, kind. Usury honeycombs the economy of Indo-China, and is a terrible factor that needs an immediate solution.

The *chettys* are the worst of a bad profession. For one thing, they are better protected by the courts because they are British or French subjects, and are also highly profitable to the colony's lawyers. Formerly they were confined to Cochin-China, but are now spreading all over the Union. Their holdings in Cochin-China are about a fourth of the rice-fields. Their original grip on the country came after the series of bad harvests of 1905 through 1907. Starting their operations in the urban centres, the *chettys* have extended their influence to the countryside along with the growth of state credit institutions. Peasants only have recourse to them when other sources of credit are closed, which is often the case in view of the heavily indebted state of most of the population. They have the advantage of lending money with a minimum of formalities and guarantees. They have almost no running expenses, a great solidarity among themselves, and they apportion the interest rate to the material status of the debtor. Up to 1920, the *chettys* cleared 10 per cent profits on their loans, but after that time the French credit organizations lowered their rate of interest and their income. It has been calculated that the Indo-Chinese, since 1900, have paid no less than 182,000,000 piastres to *chettys*, of which 42,000,000 were exported to India, and 40,000,000 reinvested in new loans in the colony.[1] Annamite creditors have been no less greedy, but they have inadvertently benefited their own country by reinvesting their ill-gotten gains there.

Usury was early recognized to be a great evil in the colony. The Admirals, by making property rights inviolable and by lowering the legal rate on interest, made really constructive though inadequate efforts. Although the French have increased the opportunities for making and circulating money, nevertheless taxes, tariff, currency fluctuations, and the disappearance of rice granaries, combined with the Annamites' usual aversion to saving, have more than offset the growth of credit.

Certain faltering attempts to extend credit, through private initiative, were made in the pre-War era. In 1907, a *Caisse de Prévoyance* was instituted. It failed through a lack of confidence, for the natives were sure that they would never again see the money they had confided to this institution. Next, an insurance company against cattle mortality was organized in Tonkin, on the French model, and native participa-

[1] Bernard, P., *Le Problème Economique Indochinois* (Paris, 1934), p. 114.

tion was encouraged. The mechanism of such an institution proved too complicated for the Annamites to grasp, and that precipitated its dissolution. *Sociétés Indigènes de Prévoyance* were attempted on the Algerian plan and under government control. The premium to be granted to any society having more than a hundred members was not enough encouragement to make it survive. The most successful of these attempts were the *Dongloi*, or co-operatives. The mother society still exists in Tonkin, though some of her offspring have come to grief. Annamites do not relish the notion of periodic payments. Also the natives in charge of some of these experiments have found it irresistible to imitate usurious practices with the society's funds. The failure of almost all of these efforts has been grist to the mill of those Europeans who claim that natives are incapable of either the use or the control of such organizations.

The oldest of the government's efforts to rout usury was the *Crédit Mutuel Agricole*, born in 1907. Its early development was as nothing compared with its present growth. From 1918 to 1926 fifteen *Caisses de Crédit* were founded. In 1929, the last three provinces of Cochin-China were each given a *Caisse*, so that there is now one for all twenty provinces. The whole group has about thirteen thousand members, and administers a capital of 12,000,000 piastres, at a low interest rate. The creation in 1918 of property guarantees was the real basis of its success. But it reaches only the middle and upper class of farmers who want to extend their crops, or after a disaster when it has made them less a prey to usurers. With the depression, these *Caisses* have been experimenting with small loans under a hundred piastres and against personal guarantee. If they are able to continue this work, it will be fortunate in reaching the most miserable element of the population, which has heretofore been too submerged to get help.

Government action was for too long confined to scattering small bonuses among native farmers. Important official credit establishments for rural economy have functioned seriously only since 1923, with the foundation of the *Crédit Foncier de l'Indochine*, and similar institutions. They have rapidly atoned for their initial slowness by the importance of their loans, both urban and rural. In the countryside, they have been invaluable as the first to invade a field hitherto the preserve of *chetty* usury, and where they have already succeeded in reducing the rate of interest. Delays and multiple formalities are the basis of a justified criticism of these societies. The depression has proved that, contrary to current attacks, they have lent too freely, and at a rate of interest not commensurate with the country's productivity. *Caisses Rurales*, established in 1915 to encourage native thrift, were enlarged by Varenne, who tried to stimulate deposits by giving interest on savings. The *Crédit Populaire Agricole* was also Varenne's achieve· ment, and it was based on the Dutch Javanese model. It meant a co-operation between communes and provincial banks, but it did not really get under way until 1929. They number now only seventeen: eight in Tonkin, seven in Annam, and two in Cambodia. They have avoided some of the snares into which other credit organizations have fallen, by a stricter state control and by relating loans directly to guarantees in their amount and duration.

In ten years this group of credit organizations has grown steadily, and with them the long-term indebtedness of the whole colony, and especially that of Cochin-China. During the same period production was marking time, contrary to the usual stimulus credit exerts upon output. The producer has seemingly abused credit until the annual interest he must pay has become a dead weight. It amounts to 4 to 5 piastres *per capita*, which means that the Annamites in 1931 had to dedicate 10 per cent of their annual incomes to paying interest on debts, and the burden has grown considerably since that time.

The depression has shown up startling weaknesses in these credit organizations, notably in Cochin-China, where there has been a dimi-nution in the repayment of loans, in the making of new loans, a very slight increase in these organizations' reserve funds, and a widespread appeal for state aid.

The failure to lift the masses from their laborious misery is the most serious criticism that can be levelled against these credit efforts. The well-to-do Annamite proprietor has been the great beneficiary of these loans to the exclusion of his needier compatriots. The Annamite bourgeoisie has taken the money from these credit institutions and lent it to the poor farmer at usurious rates—a fatal interposing of a parasite between the administration and the people. This is basically caused by the lack of guarantee offered by the great mass of the populace. Private capitalists and banks will not lend to collectivities, like the commune, whose lands cannot be staked because they are inalienable. Individual natives offer even fewer liquid assets. The French capitalist, bank, or individual, does not want to be saddled with parcels of dis-jointed land which he could never profitably exploit. The confusion of the tax registers, and the inadequacy of scientific surveying, offer no serious guarantee of property ownership to justify a private group in making loans. Only the well-to-do Annamites, who can offer serious assets, may reasonably serve as guarantors of a poor man's loan, and here is the beginning of their abuse of power and the perpetration of fraud. Being usurers themselves, they have no interest in aiding their victims to escape through easier credit facilities. A creditor who loans without security, or who is the victim of a fraud, is regularly out of pocket. Hence only credit organizations which have government backing can continue to lend under such hazardous circumstances. The state is, therefore, the great victim, for it must assume all the risks and get no share in the profits. This completely destroys the character of mutuality in those very organizations which bear that name.

In return for assuming all the risks, the state has not had sufficient control over operations. Credit societies, especially in Cochin-China, have been left too much to their own devices, and only in 1931 was there any attempt made to control them through a central organization. They have been too prodigal with government charity: there was no methodical investigation of the borrower's capacity to pay, and too great a disequilibrium between the loans and his capital. Even in prosperous times too few loans were repaid, and this tendency naturally grew more marked with the depression. There was a considerable and natural misunderstanding on the part of the natives about the philanthropic character of state aid. The whole situation showed a need to educate native opinion as to the real function of agricultural credit. The Notables have proven very untrustworthy intermediaries. There have also been too much red tape and delays, too little state control, and too much state risk. Despite recent measures to improve these conditions, the greater part of the money loaned has been hopelessly compromised. The aid, claimed so raucously from the ever-paying government, comes from a very small percentage of the population. The arrangements made to relieve the very ones who so shamelessly profited when they could by easy money, should keep in view the principle that the masses must not once again be sacrificed for the few.

THE LAND RÉGIME

It was natural that the underlying hostility between colonials and natives should first break out over the ownership of land. The government's position was delicate. If it protected native rights too zealously, it would discourage colonists who were of prime importance to the colony's development. Yet insecurity of ownership would compromise far more seriously the country's future and, incidentally, native loyalty.

The incomplete property regulations of the Annamite code, supplemented by customary law, aimed to extend agriculture. To this end penitentiary labour and military colonization had been used, and virgin land was allotted to new communes in proportion to their growth. The *dienbo* was then established to consolidate the results thus obtained. The French interpreted the code literally to mean that all the land really belonged to the Emperor, with the peasants as only imperial tenants, but they failed to realize that time had modified their status in the direction of outright ownership. In taking over land abandoned during the conquest, the French thought that they were acting in accordance with Annamite law that decreed property to be revocable if uncultivated for three years. The giving of this land to French colonists was, in native eyes, an act of spoliation which contributed to prolonging their rebellion. Historical events, due to the successive stages of conquest and to the retention of native sovereignty in the Protectorates, have made for a bewildering variety of regulations, differing not only in every part of the Union, but within the individual countries themselves.

The Admirals guaranteed property rights wherever they found them even partially established. This was not, however, the case in the three provinces conquered in 1867, where the country was largely inhabited by Cambodians. Official efforts to get the Annamites to exchange their old titles for new ones with surer guarantees was a failure. This was partly due, despite many reassuring decrees, to native distrust and to a lack of method in carrying out the project. In the confusion the records had disappeared, and numerous lawsuits were the result. Surveying the land, especially in the interior, was a crying need, yet the administration blithely went on allotting lands in unabated confusion. An 1874 decree initiated the régime of free concessions. He who asked was given free land, on condition that he cultivated it all within three years, and paid his land tax. This edict was considered too severe, and tax exemption for four years was later granted to budding concessionnaires. In 1880 the state's right to grant free land was restricted to 500 hectares, and more strenuous efforts were made to see that natives were not dispossessed. The administration was certainly trying to follow the Annamite code in developing agriculture, but it dealt out property with an over-liberal hand, and without adequate investigation of titles or the concessionnaire's resources—invariably too slim. Much land was left untouched, taxes went unpaid, evicted tenants were disgruntled, surveying was not done, and confusion reigned in spite of the best governmental intentions.

In Cambodia the problem was different, though here, too, the king was in theory the sole proprietor of his land. But his rights were directly exercised over only a limited portion. Up to 1884 the French left his local sovereignty untouched, but a treaty made that year was the opening wedge that permitted interference in land legislation. Royal land ceased to be inalienable, but it could only be disposed of jointly by French and Cambodian authorities.

Like the Annamite code, Khmer law had few land regulations. Property could be bequeathed but retained only by cultivation, registration, and the inevitable tax payment. Even slaves had the right to own property. Cambodian rulings had variety and precision, but, like the Annamite code, they lacked general principles and coherent organization. Measures were simply taken as each emergency arose. Private property had certainly evolved in the positive sense, and away from the Indian concept of the king as sole master of his kingdom. But the problem in Cambodia and Laos was nothing like so acute as in the Annamite countries, because the land available exceeded the population's needs. Many Cambodians and Loatians still retained nomadic habits. Those who lived by hunting and fishing readily and capriciously abandoned their land. The lack of Laotian property regulations showed the small importance they attached to land, for the spirit moved the Laotians to change residence frequently. The French, therefore, had a free hand in drawing up a civil code there, promulgated in 1908. Property could be had by any, at the price of cultivation within a year of its occupation. Though the French had to do far more extensive work in creating land legislation, the task was essentially simple because there were no previous laws to combat.

In Annam and Tonkin, successive treaties wrested from the Emperor all of his former prerogatives over land, excepting what affected native property. Existing titles were recognized, and an effort made to make the *dienbo* a more accurate record. Retention of the Protectorate form of government created even more difficulties in the North than in Cochin-China, but the same principle of expanding land cultivation was applied even to communal lands. These formed in Annam 26 per cent and in Tonkin 21 per cent of the total surface. There was an even greater, albeit unwitting, violation of native rights than in Cochin-China, and more bitter complaints from the colonists that the state was giving them no protection against the malignancy of the natives. In short, in the North, the whole problem was intensified. In Tonkin it took the form of a struggle between an agrarian democracy, passionately attached to the soil, fighting a foreign landed minority, in which the government more than once had to intervene. The administration pointed to the fact that the natives, as well as the French, could benefit by the régime of free concessions, and that outright ownership would emancipate them from the tyranny of the village Notables. Few natives had the capital necessary for such enterprises, and, moreover, preferred the security of the delta land.

Matters muddled along in this confused way until 1910, when the state suggested a more liberal land régime for natives. The colonists claimed that such a move would jeopardize French sovereignty, and pointed to the Kydong conspiracy[1] that had germinated on a native concession, and to the vast inviolable domains of bandits like the Detham. The government yielded and re-wrote the decree which was principally a return to Annamite legislation. More leniency was shown to all concessionnaires about tax payments. The state still granted huge domains, but refused to accept the responsibility of verifying land ownership or labour recruiting, and the red tape and delays in according concessions went unmodified. Most of the colonist's capital was consumed by the time he had got his land, so only about a fifth of the concessions were under cultivation. All the best land by then had been nominally conceded. Colonists only survived at all because the government was lax about enforcing its rules as to time limits for exploitation and tax payments. The result was fatal for the fisc, which had realized only losses and had got nothing for its generosity. The indemnities granted for floods, droughts and blights had even eaten into the colony's reserve fund.

From the viewpoint of native policy, such enormous grants to Europeans had been impolitic. Their hostility to these usurpers and to the arbitrary and ignorant action of the government was shown in varying degrees of violence. From the colonist viewpoint, the government had lured them to Indo-China, and once there gave them no assistance in acquiring land. Nothing was done to guarantee their ownership, nor to protect them from native violence, or to procure them labour. Colonists revenged themselves by running down the

[1] Kydong, the Annamite "miracle child" whom Doumer had sent to France to be educated, was given a large concession, which he used as a centre for his anti-French plot, about which the military authorities learned in time.

administration in speech and in the press, and by complaining to Paris that the colonial government was to blame for all their failures.

The need of a remedy for this state of affairs was shown by Sarraut's commissioning of an expert named Boudillon to study the concessions régime and to suggest a programme. Boudillon's report (1912–15) emphasized the evils of having such a variety of legislations. The same property might be successively or even simultaneously justiciable under two legislations, and sometimes even by two courts, according to the nationality of its proprietors. Property rights and publicity of ownership should have a uniform regulation. Boudillon also pointed out the need of surveying to validate property titles, the lack of co-ordination between the state's liberality and the concessionnaire's means, and the treasury's failure to insist on benefits from the whole régime. Although Sarraut's 1913 edict had tried to simplify procedure, the stiffening of the fiscal side to property rights, and the making of a regulation common to all Indo-China for the first time—only distinguishing between rural and urban concessions—was incomplete. The War interfered with the embodiment of Boudillon's suggestions in actual legislation, but his report served as the basis for innumerable post-War studies of the property régime. The then current economic prosperity of the colony necessitated further property guarantees, and the conservation of forests and the sources of hydraulic power. But in spite of unanimous agreement that the 1913 edict imperatively needed reform, nothing was done about it until 1927. The difficulties involved by such a reform were almost insuperable.

Surveying was perhaps the worst need. The most ancient surveying document in Indo-China, dating from the reign of Gia-long, was supplemented only by the obsolete *dienbo*. In neither of these documents was there any general plan, a uniform measurement, or attempt to keep information up-to-date, especially for alluvial land. Surveyors met with technical difficulties in the form of a great diversity in population, a different division of property in each country, and deliberate misinformation by the natives, who feared increased taxes. In addition, the surveyors were in many cases incapable and unsupervised. The competent part of the personnel was much too small, and it had been largely disseminated by the War. Tonkin, which has been the most completely surveyed, proved to be enormously expensive, and even before the depression economies had had to be made.

The colonial fisc had found land concessions anything but profitable. Experience showed free concessions to be a mistake, not solely in relation to the treasury's needs, but because they had been awarded on too large a scale and lay uncultivated for lack of funds. And this, furthermore, deprived the colony of any tax revenues. In order to encourage small-scale colonization, concessions up to 300 hectares might still be awarded gratuitously. A more equitable land tax was to be assessed on the basis of yield per hectare, and a fine was to be placed on uncultivated property. The state would be strict about enforcing cultivation within a fixed time limit. A very important principle was contained in the ruling that concessions must be, in great majority, bought. A more serious guarantee of native rights was to be made, and land sold only to such persons as offered serious proof of their financial capacity to cultivate their own concessions.

Varenne's regulations showed a distinct change in policy. Up to then the colonial government had considered the request for concessions as in itself a sign of prosperity. Henceforth the returns from those concessions to the treasury were to be the yardstick of the régime's success. The current rubber boom and flight from the franc made land concessions a burning issue. In 1926, the government received applications for 50,000 hectares. In its response, two seemingly contradictory trends were obvious: a recognition that large-scale capitalistic cultivation alone was profitable, and the state's desire to encourage small colonization. The government's efforts to keep a stricter control over the big concessions was a fiscal concern, so as to prevent huge properties from lying idle, or from being sold as a form of speculatory investment.

The trend towards small properties was another *volte face* in policy. Annamites as well as French had profited by the state's liberality in concessions, and a powerful native plutocracy was the result. The native government had never been so imprudent as to create an independent landed class. The danger does not lie solely in this class's relations with the state, but in that they are the worst exploiters of their poorer compatriots. Their oppression, which has taken the form of usury and of brutal ejections of peasants living on desirable land, has inspired a hatred that was shown by the damage done to their property during the 1931 insurrection. Property, in general, is not in good hands. It is unequitably divided and it is badly financed. The tenant farmer has two parasites between himself and the administration—the proprietor and the usurer, who may be one and the same. Varenne's effort to encourage small properties, so as to offset the rich Annamite proprietors, has been furthered by the Communist revolt and by the depression. The creation of a real bourgeoisie of small

proprietors, attached to the soil and loyally grateful to the administration, has become the ideal, for the French have come to realize that
a restless proletariat offers the best field for Communism. The completion of this reform has been the work of the *Office de Colonisation*,
created as a result of Raynaud's trip to the colony in 1931.

The contrary trend is evidenced in regard to French colonization.
Here large-scale, highly capitalized enterprises alone are successful. The
small colonist has proved to be a *frondeur* in spirit and unco-opera-
tively jealous in method—a born non-conformist, politically and
economically. The history of small French colonization has been a
hard one. Insufficient means, technical unpreparedness, and a recently
conquered country, without economic equipment or labour, have been
its obstacles. Many bones of ex-soldiers and ex-functionaries, turned
colonists, have been left to bleach on the sands of their concessions.
But it is to the honour of the few who succeeded, against terrible odds,
that this group was the first to cultivate successfully the *hevea* in Indo-
China. The post-War decade was definitely away from small-scale
operations, and big companies waxed and grew rich. Many still think
that small colonization was harmful to the colony because it slowed
down the whole tempo of its development.

At this point Paris took a hand in the proceedings. A long and
peculiarly violent campaign against Varenne culminated in an official
interpellation in Parliament on the land régime in Indo-China, on
March 18, 1927. Outrey, the deputy from Cochin-China, led the
attack, and deputies entered the lists to hurl enormous statistics at
each other so as to show up the ruthless greed of capitalism in the
colony. To this it was replied that sugar and rubber plantations
required many thousands of hectares for profitable exploitation. Much
ignorance as well as indignation was shown by Parliament, with the
result that all land concessions were ordered to be stopped until a
committee of inquiry should report. Indo-China's fury at this stupid
interference, which paralysed the country, was reflected in the colonial
press. But the colonists who had been willing to create a scandal about
the colony and drag in the Métropole, in order to be revenged on a
hated governor, were far more culpable. Even those who had been
Varenne's worst enemies were abashed at the consequences of Paris's
resumption of control.

The Métropole's first suggestion, requiring a presidential decree for
the simplest land grant, was so palpably absurd that it was soon
retracted. The ironic outcome of the whole affair was a decree which

practically reproduced Varenne's. It favoured small colonization, but the colonial government had already turned away from large-scale concessions. The Métropole had aroused itself when a would-be scandal was brought to its attention, paralysed the whole machinery in order to limit the power of the big companies, and then put its stamp on what had already been done. The resulting increase in red tape did not encourage further investments by French capitalists or potential colonists.

As there was no complete surveying service, the planter-elect had to be his own surveyor. This work often absorbed two or three months, after which he had to draw up an exact plan of the land he wanted. This, with a detailed request, was sent to the head of the province. The planter's *dossier* now rested idly in the administration's files, and he must needs harry officialdom if he wanted any action. The next step involved persuading the Committee of Inquiry to make a report, and this committee had first to accompany the planter to the site of his claim and then to verify his plan. The request for this land must next receive publicity, which was done by posting a notice at the provincial capital, on the prospective site, and in the neighbouring villages, in both French and the native language. Only now did his real troubles begin. Each administrative bureau filed its objections, which were peculiarly numerous if woodland or waterways were involved in the grant. The Mois and other primitive tribes were aggressive about asking high indemnities for their land. Through the publicity given to his claim, rival candidates knew of its desirable features, and without having done any of the preliminary work they could rise up and file a counter-claim. Moreover, if the concession was over 1,000 hectares, it had to be put up at public auction.

Up to this point the planter's work had taken from fifteen to eighteen months. Not only were his resources eaten into, but he was worn out by the hard physical work and nervous strain of fighting every inch of his way through the administrative morass, and by warding off rival claimants who, even at the last minute, might outbid him. The 1927 legislation, among other improvements, aimed to conserve superior rights for the original claimant. There has also been a definite improvement in method and form. The public now knows what lands are available for colonization. The greatest flaw in the present system is the government's persistent refusal to guarantee a concession. In turn, inevitably, this depends on the completion of the country's survey.

CHAPTER IV

THE CONTACTS OF CIVILIZATIONS

"Je ne crois pas à l'impénétrabilité de l'Asie. C'est souvent la paresse de l'esprit Européen. L'est et l'ouest se sont rencontrés, voilà le fait. Deux civilisations doivent se combiner et se combinent tous les jours, en voilà un autre."   *Raynaud*
"L'homme prudent et sage se fait comprendre à demi-mot. Le fou seul livre sa pensée. La parole a été donnée à l'homme pour déguiser la vérité.   *Annamite maxim*

THE EVOLUTION OF ANNAMITE INSTITUTIONS

The Commune

IN the welter of Chinese imitations in which Annamite civilization abounds, the commune stands out as one of the few indigenous institutions. Its utility was not confined to aiding the central government in despatching the work of state, but it was the instrument by which agricultural expansion was effected and new communes forged. It was not only the custodian of the traditional culture, but jealous of its legal and moral prerogatives in relation to the state. In return for its independence, which even the imperial agents respected, the commune cared for its own poor, recruited its quota of soldiers, assessed and collected taxes, policed its precincts, and to a certain extent administered its own justice.

The advent of the civil régime in Cochin-China meant the arrival of a highly centralized bureaucracy. Just as it had absorbed all local independence in France, so it set about in octopus-like fashion to kill the commune, for it abhorred a state within a state. Its attack was the more insidious for being indirect. Collateral institutions were placed in juxtaposition to sap the vitality of the commune, very much as the French administrative machine in Tonkin had undermined the parallel mandarinate. The first assault was made on the social edifice when children were permitted to bring suit against parents, and in so doing pass over the head of the native judiciary by taking their case directly to the Resident. The cause of justice was not only betrayed by that ignorant and overworked official, but a mortal blow was struck at parental and communal authority. Further inroads were made when the state stepped in to collect taxes, supervise the military draft, search houses for contraband, reorganize the office of Notable in village and canton alike. Shorn of its powers, the commune's burdens were simultaneously increased. Responsibility in tax collection was aggravated by the steady increase in assessments, by responsibility for frauds and contraband in the new monopolies. The Notables, on whom this principally devolved, were more and more unwilling to serve. Theirs was the onerous responsibility without any compensating prestige and with daily diminishing powers. Mediocre men alone were willing to assume the burden in the hope that they could wrest from the people more than the state demanded of them. In all this change it was the non-taxpayers in the village who suffered the most, because they had no recourse against the Notables' abuse of power. This had ever been the case, but with increased pressure from above the Notables put the screws more on those below them.

Since independence was the breath of life to the commune, increasing interference by the central power precipitated its dissolution. This was true in varying degrees throughout the different Annamite countries, but most completely so in Cochin-China. One of its most striking evidences was the growth of pauperism and vagrancy. Though the state and mission have gradually stepped in to replace communal charity, the substitution was, especially in the early stages, very incomplete. Public security became endangered by the growth of crime. It became evident to even the most rampant assimilationists that the disintegration of the commune involved the loss of a very useful and inexpensive instrument of local government. It had certain obvious flaws, but perhaps something could be salvaged from the wreck.

The irresponsibility of the Notables was the weakest point in communal organization. To counteract their traditional abuse of power a larger place was given to men trained in Franco-Annamite schools. The new agricultural credit institutions aimed to undermine the Notables' usurious grip. The electorate was widened to be more truly representative, and by 1920 the distinction between taxpayers and non-taxpayers was obliterated. An effort towards a more equitable and supervised tax assessment and a control of the *corvées* was designed not only to increase direct administration but to protect the poor villager. If more was demanded of communal Notables in the way of education and responsibility, on the other hand they received more legal and financial guarantees than the Annamite government had ever given them.

The incessant juggling of cantonal and communal boundaries was a less happy form of intervention. The over-minute regulations for elections and the rigid formalism, imposed by an unsupple bureaucracy, were less fortunate. Everyone agreed that the old commune was out-moded and needed to be brought more into line with current conditions, but the changes had aroused the opposition of the old Notable group. In 1921 and again in 1927 changes were made and the feeling of in-stability grew with the refusal of the village plutocracy to participate in the new organization with only a partial return of their powers. Intrigues multiplied and offices became a form of barter. The people suffered proportionately—exactly the contrary of the result intended. Tumultuous village meetings showed that the traditional respect for authority had evaporated. The new system had only served to whet individual ambitions. In 1930 a new reform was attempted. Mandarins with residential ratification were to name village and cantonal heads, but this was neither in accordance with the spirit of the Third Republic nor with Annamite traditions. Such a measure could only strengthen the hand of the central government and hasten still more the decline of communal autonomy.

The history of communal budgets paralleled that of their politics. First they were deprived of their revenues, which came from ferry and market licenses, then in the general decentralization these were restored, but state interference prevented their effective use. The various vacillations between centralized and localized finances have at present turned in appearance to the latter's advantage. Unfortunately much of the machinery installed through reinstating the communal budgets is to the Notables not understandable and unusable. The model budget introduced by the state proved too complicated and has been discarded for the former primitive book-keeping. This is symbolic of the whole reform.

In 1931 the situation inspired a new inquiry. All agreed that a reform must be effected, and one along Western lines. Indo-China had advanced too far towards Occidentalism to turn back. While it was true that the old commune had not yet expired, it was undoubtedly dying. Remarkable organization that it was, it belonged to other than a contemporary civilization. Individualism is a far more potent solvent than even a centralized bureaucracy. A few more decades will find the Annamite commune only an Oriental variation of the universal village type.

The Mandarinate

Annamite civilization reveals a wonderfully harmonious unity, built up through endless modifications, so old and so refined that it is inevitably somewhat decadent. Many centuries ago it ceased to be the transient civilization of nomads, warriors, and shepherds. Its evolution was characterized by a love of home and of village, by a respect for justice, and by a veneration for learning and the written word, and by an absolute obedience to unalterable divine law. Since it was not built by the sword but on a complicated moral scaffolding, it disdained not only the display of force but also of wealth, of suffering, and of death. Generations of practising these precepts have formed all Annamites into a mould—even the most humble, even the outcasts. They hate and flee those who exercise brute force; they refuse to share their convictions or aid in their projects. Under the sway of eternal forces, the Annamite counts for little his own lifetime, he is the enemy of all change, as sacrilege, he is the tranquil observer and defender of law and custom.

The conception on which Annamite institutions are based is excellent beyond dispute, but it is in their practical application that flaws begin to appear. The mandarinate, recruited from the people on a merit basis, had a democratic foundation which never degenerated into a caste system. Yet Annam was never democratic in the sense of having representative institutions or equality before the law. An unalterable spirit of legal and spiritual hierarchy pervaded the social structure, and was only mitigated by the fact that privilege was offset by duties and responsibilities. So important was this contractual element that an emperor who neglected his responsibilities forfeited his right to reign. Heaven's mandate descending through him to his agents wrapped the whole system in rigid sanctity; the father's power over his family was a miniature reproduction of heavenly and imperial authority. The difference between them lay in the degree of authority, but not in quality or kind.

Confucianist idealism is partly responsible for the defects by which time has altered the mandarinate. The self-effacing philosopher-official, devoting himself to study and to the welfare of his people, proved to be too austere an ideal. Gifts were acceptable and in time obligatory from litigants, or any person desiring favours. If, like the Emperor, the mandarin was "father and mother" of his people, he proved to be an expensive parent. Confucius' underpaid priestly mandarinate, consecrated to the community and serving as an example of a life above material things, suffered lapses in practical living. But the force of Confucian idealism was so great that the mandarins did not amass vast fortunes nor live in luxury. Although graft was restrained in this way, the mandarinate was undeniably venal when the French came to Indo-China.

Missionary antagonism to the mandarins painted the picture unnecessarily black. Mandarinal abuses of power were exaggerated; in Tonkin especially they were pictured as the cruel and rapacious oppressors of the people. Partly through well-intentioned humanitarianism, partly because of an assimilationist belief in direct administration, the French created a dual officialdom in Tonkin. Useless duplication of office prevented adequate salaries from being paid to either French or native functionaries, so the essential evil of venality continued to flourish. Rather, the coming of the French had created new sources of revenue and broke down the restraints hitherto imposed by Confucianist morality.

The people's ignorance and credulity place them at the mercy of the mandarins. Official taxes, already far too high, are in actual collection increased at the mandarin's will and to his own benefit. On the rare occasions when taxes have been reduced, it is a well-known fact that the majority of people never hear of their good fortune: the same sum continues to be collected and the mandarin pockets the difference. This state of affairs continued to exist because French functionaries found, much against their will, that mandarins were the indispensable intermediaries between them and the people. This hard lesson was learned when they had tried to get rid of them and raise up in their place a new mandarinate of serviceable interpreters and servants, whose only claim to such promotion was natural wit and a dependence upon their French benefactors. The people refused to obey these upstarts, for they had neither the learning nor the moral authority of imperial investiture, which would have entitled them to popular veneration. As De Lanessan insisted, both in his writing and his actions, mandarinal prestige must be restored by giving them back the powers of which they had been shorn. Without responsibility or initiative the mandarins washed their hands of the current troubles. The system had to be retained, but it also had to be improved. The mandarinate, one of the main citadels of Annamite civilization, thus successfully though not entirely intact, withstood the first assault of Westernism.

Reforms were pursued along a double track: the mandarinate must be modified, but so must French officialdom in order to insure its effective control, and not merely annoying interference. So long as French functionaries used interpreters instead of their own tongues, and so long as they remained in offices associating exclusively with their own compatriots, the best mandarinate would get out of hand. Something drastic, too, had to be done to modernize and win the honest co-operation of the old mandarinate, now sulking in their tents, and to improve the moral and educational quality of their successors.

As a weapon against venality, mandarins' salaries have been raised at different times. Unfortunately a simultaneous rise in the cost of living has largely neutralized this reform, and their salaries are still pitifully small. Nevertheless, the administration has persevered in this policy as the only way of eradicating venality. When mandarins have security of income, promotion, and pension, when graft becomes un-necessary for mere livelihood, the government can punish corruption with severity, and exact a conscientious performance of their duties. The evil is unfortunately of such long standing and so deeply rooted in native psychology that, as yet, little headway has been made. More-over it is still a current idea among some of the French that the man-darins are to this day their irreconcilable enemies, incapable of ever being moulded into efficient administrative instruments.

The Russo-Japanese war marked a turning-point in the attitude of the native *élite*. Instead of continuing to disdain the Western bar-barians and bury themselves ostrich-like in their literary past, the Annamites were thenceforth moved to emulate the Japanese example. Beau's acquiescence to their demand for Western education was equivalent in their minds to being offered positions in the administration at the presentation of their diplomas. So eager were they to learn the secret of Western power that the abolition of competitive examinations for the mandarinate in 1915 passed almost without protest. The Occi-dental ideal of education as an attitude of mind was and still is literally foreign to the Annamite conception. This fundamental misunderstand-ing is mixed with racial prejudices and the principles of '89.

The native intelligentsia has become embittered at being grudgingly received into the administration. The last thirty years has witnessed the uphill struggle of the natives for admission to the same posts, and on the same social and financial footing as the French. A high-ranking man-darin was received by a French Resident without outward marks of respect, who *tutoyer*-ed him with either condescension or a misplaced geniality that wounded to the depths his refined and haughty soul. That the insult was often unconscious did not affect native reactions. Disregard of hierarchy in speech and in action, the suppression of prostrations as contrary to the Rights of Man, a brutal directness of speech without the usual hours of conversational detours, both embittered and transformed the Annamite mind. The veneer of courtesy and restraint wore so thin that the French and native functionaries came to resemble one another, to the detriment of Oriental traditions. The situation was so confused by a mixture of humanitarian and egalitarian principles, with a life-and-death struggle for the same government posts, that the main issues were wholly lost to sight. In this human metallurgy the mandarin has emerged more or less— depending on whether he belongs to a Protectorate or to a directly administered country—transformed into a French functionary. The miracle has been effected by only a few years' contact with Western ideas and people. Unfortunately as yet the ideal of professional integrity has not kept pace with the other changes. Destructive contacts have worked faster than the constructive.

The 1929 reform of the mandarinate, now disciplined and homogeneous, was the culmination of a long process to effect the separation of powers. In the judicial more than in the administrative sphere, the mandarins were vital to the French. They were now formally specialized and had already been given a code modified by Western ideas. The division was as yet, however, not clear-cut: nominally the native administrators, the *phus* and *huyens*, still controlled the magistrates, as tradition demanded, because the people were used to them and a change would sacrifice administrative prestige. The separation of powers must be gradually effected, but under the surface, despite mandarinal dislike of whatever reinforces control, it moved steadily forward. This process is as true of Annam as of Cochin-China; there is only a difference in time and degree of penetration. The most important part of this transformation has been an incidental by-product: the mandarin has lost his sacrosanct character. Formerly the mandarin was simultaneously priest, magistrate, and administrator, an indispensable participant in the imperial rites. Rites are now reduced to merely picturesque customs with local colour. The loss of the spiritual and paternal element in the mandarinate means the decline of their moral authority over the people—the fundamental reason why they were retained by the French. The structure of the mandarinate has remained intact, but in their laicization, which was the inevitable corollary of the separation of powers, the essence of their authority has filtered away.

THE CONTACTS OF CIVILIZATIONS

The Protectorate

Indo-China has proved to be a great school in colonization, where France has tried successively and simultaneously all possible systems. In Cochin-China and Tonkin a military conquest has been followed by direct administration: in Annam and Cambodia France has suffered the inconveniences with the reality of annexation, and been frustrated in a policy of force so that, until very recently, a Protectorate existed in name only. The surface of Laos has, as yet, not really been scratched by administrative or economic penetration. The Indo-Chinese Union offers a unique field for study of the various stages of colonization, whose variety even includes different administrations for three countries of the same civilization.

These variations have not been intentional, but are the product of circumstances often contrary to the governmental will. Historical events permitted a fuller penetration of Cochin-China, for example, than of Cambodia, despite the latter's wish to have a Protectorate. And even in Cochin-China the Admirals wanted to install a Protectorate in the full sense of the word, but practical necessities arising from the withdrawal of the native mandarinate made a retention of the French Officer-Inspectors imperative. To be sure the force of these circumstances was abetted by the contemporary French trend towards assimilation. The rebirth of republican ideals after 1870 heralded a reassertion of the equality of man, despite apparent differences in colour and evolution; of the superiority of the civil over the military; and of the living unity of France with her empire. The respect for native institutions, which had been the costly lesson taught by the long war in Tonkin, was forgotten or ignored by the new civil government. Differences between an Occidental and an Oriental civilization were expected to melt away in the fires of brotherly love, and from their ashes would arise an Indo-Chinese phoenix fashioned in the image of the mother country. If the sincere idealism of the assimilationists had not been tempered by economic exploitation, the administrative results might have been less confusing.

The absence of a native government in Cochin-China and Tonkin positively invited direct administration. In Cochin-China the way was wide open. There were no mandarins except those created by the French, no Scholar class, nor deeply rooted traditions. A scattered population in a rich unexploited country made possible profitable agricultural colonization by not only the French and Chinese, but contributed to the growth of an Annamite plutocracy, which owed its power to the French régime. This economic development has caused the native standard of living to rise, not universally but surely, and has bridged the gap between the two civilizations, as no amount of legislation could ever have done. The psychology of men in a wealthy and newly opened country, in which there is room and profits for all, has done much to mitigate the racial antagonism usually engendered by colonization. Here Western education, violent politics, and untramelled journalism, with Occidental social and economic rather than racial class struggles, reproduce Europe and the Americas and not the Far East. The dissolution of Annamite institutions is almost complete: everywhere Westernism is in control, from the new economic equipment of the country to the Occidentalized viewpoint of the Annamite. Not that there are no longer miserable peasants who live immersed in their traditions, but they do not spiritually dominate the country where the imprint and outlook are now unmistakably Western.

In Tonkin the process has been more painful and far slower. If the Tonkinese had historic cause for grievance against Hué and loyalty to their own dynasty, they had also recent memory of the violence they suffered following Garnier's repudiation and throughout twenty years of banditry and its suppression. If they had reason to distrust Annam and its mandarins, they had also just cause to doubt the stability and intentions of the French. Bert and De Lanessan inspired belief in the sincerity of their Protectorate ideal, but Metropolitan interference and the reversals of policy, wrought by their rapidly rotating successors, only brought distress and confusion to a people who, above all, loved stability and order. Moreover, current psychology and circumstances as in the time of the Admirals had not permitted the creation of a real Protectorate in Tonkin. A belief in the fundamental antagonism of the Tonkinese for Hué and all its works, as well as the contagion of revolt which spread to the North, contributed to retaining a strongly centralized government. When the regional independence of a country is encouraged by its local organization and geographical inaccessibility, when totally unknown traditions and language encourage armed resistance, relying on the ignorance of the conquerors and the co-operation of the mandarinate, then the trend towards direct administration is irresistible.

Creakings of the French administrative machinery and dissensions within the ranks further encouraged centralization. The rift between the civil and military authorities, the antagonism between the colonists and the administration, the independentist struggles of the general services and local administrations, the secessionist movement in Cochin-China—all forced the Governors-General into strengthening the hand of the federal government as the price of survival. Metropolitan pressure, to be rid of subsidies to an unpopular colony, necessitated tightening the federal grip on the country's finances. It is not surprising that not only was the Protectorate ideal almost wholly eclipsed, but that the bureaucracy which sprang up in its place overstepped the mark. Its excessive centralization was the object of attacks not only by the French from within, but from the natives without. They criticized its omissions and commissions, its expense, its wastefulness, and yet wanted a larger share in its powers and direction. If and when they get control it remains to be seen whether the machine will not have gathered so much momentum that they will themselves be caught up and carried farther along the road to *étatisme*.

The poverty of Annam, more than respect for treaties or the presence of a recalcitrant traditionalism, is responsible for its relatively untouched administration. The French contented themselves with getting a grip on the country's finances and deposing rebellious monarchs, leaving the existing mandarinate almost wholly intact. Only a few feeble efforts were made to revise legislation and education. The country was too poor, too underpopulated, too inaccessible, and too hostile to justify the expense and effort required to make a Protectorate effective. The policy of dividing and ruling differently the three Annamite countries had clipped the wings of Hué's resistance, and given to France direct control over the two wealthier parts. Suppression of the office of *kinh-luoc* by Doumer consecrated this administrative surgery. Annam was cut adrift in stagnant waters, undisturbed by the programme of federal public works which busied itself by linking the richer countries of the Union.

Nevertheless, the famine area of North Annam, always a centre of defection, was the one region which claimed the administration's fitful attention. Whenever the starving peasants found leaders among the Scholars—those perennial malcontents—revolt flared up. Unpleasant was the publicity in the Métropole, and bloody and costly its suppression. The 1931 famine, coming on the heels of Yenbay, fomented disorders that have finally impressed the administration with the need for doing something about Annam. The recent move to finish the Transindochinois, to complete the network of dykes and hydraulic engineering, is evidence of this change in attitude.

The return of young Bao-Dai coincided with the movement towards reform. He instigated a modernization of his Cabinet that started the ball rolling towards revision of education and legislation, and the reorganization of the mandarinate generally. There is a certain originality in having Occidental reforms emanate from an Emperor whom custom regards as the conserver of traditions. Though the Emperor suffers from being looked upon as a puppet of the French by the nationalists, and has lost much of his sacrosanct character as the inaccessible high priest of his kingdom, yet the veneration he still commands among the masses is a definite asset for his reforms. The changes he inaugurated are an improvement over the 1925 move towards direct administration by the French. The upshot has been that what was a theocracy is now a constitutional monarchy, veering towards a separation of church and state. Although the Emperor remains the religious head and the French Resident at the head of the administration, the distinction is not yet clear-cut. In theory what the Emperor and mandarins have lost in power and prestige by being specialized and laicized has been compensated by a greater security. It is to their interest to cling to the Protectorate, and reciprocally against the rising tide of communism and nationalism. It is an unforeseen and ironical turn to the word Protectorate for a foreign conqueror to be the mainstay of the government it has displaced, and against the assaults of its own people.

In Cambodia, although the Protectorate was not imposed by the French, it was in native eyes only the lesser of two evils. Better to maintain national integrity in the framework of a Protectorate than to be ground to dust between the Siamese and Annamite millstones. A Protectorate was grudgingly accepted as the price of national salvation, so that when the French took the first steps towards direct administration they provoked a widespread rebellion—particularly significant on the part of a docile and resigned people like the Khmers. This outbreak, when quelled, taught the French not to tamper with the King's authority. Norodom of the Sacred Feet and seventy-eight offspring, Norodom who adored music boxes and practical jokes, was not the absurd, over-dressed, and under-developed caricature of a king in the eyes of his people as he was to the French. He was the embodiment of a sacred tradition, no matter how ingloriously he might live up to the awe and worship he inspired. The moral authority of the kings of Cambodia has not ebbed away as it has done in Annam.

During the War Sisovath was able to stop a revolt merely by requesting his subjects to lay down their arms, an achievement which the French with all their forces had not been able to effect. Finally, appreciating the value of this authority, the French have undertaken reforms under the royal aegis. Control of the mandarinate and finances was, as usual, the keystone of French effort, followed by modifications of the legislation, and a separation of the judicial and administrative powers.

What has made the Protectorates of Laos and Cambodia a striking success is essentially the sympathetic character of the peoples of those countries. If they lack Annamite industry, intelligence, and initiative, they are gentle, artistic, and loyal. The French who have served in Cambodia and Laos become deeply attached to the people, and reciprocally. This fundamental congeniality, which has never been marred by the violence of conquest, is responsible for the co-operation that has slowly made Cambodia and Laos permeable by Western ideas. There is only one obstacle, but it is a vital one: the Annamites are slowly but irrevocably filtering into those two rich and under-populated countries. In the contemporary rush to develop every source of economic independence within the empire, it is inconceivable that France will stop the Annamites, who are born colonizers, from exploiting the agricultural and mineral wealth, which the natives will not and cannot do for themselves. Inter-colonial solidarity and federalism in Indo-China will inevitably triumph over the Protectorate ideal, whose very name, from the Cambodian and Laotian viewpoint, is fast becoming a farce.

In reality the Protectorate has proven an impractical ideal: it has evolved and been transformed beyond all recognition. Originally it was developed by generous-minded statesmen who were revolted by the idea of domination, but who equally distrusted assimilation. Instead of bodily transplanting French institutions, advocates of the Protectorate form preferred to encourage native evolution within its local orbit. Not unmindful of the principles of 1789, the Protectorate glosses over the brutal fact of colonization. While good as a sugar coating to the initial military intervention, the Protectorate almost immediately strikes a snag in application.

Since it is inherently a flexible form, adapting itself to the character of each colony, the Protectorate becomes a chameleon to each new Governor's ideas. Since the chief executive in French colonies is prone to frequent change, the Protectorate has a Protean-like quality that is not only confusing to the natives, but bewildering to a student of political science. Then there are practical difficulties that would never be experienced in direct administration. Armed or passive native resistance, ignorance of the country and its people, Metropolitan or local interference—all force the Protectorate into one of two camps—either direct administration, or complete neglect. The latter solution is ideal in that it lives up to the Metropolitan motto of *pas d'histoires*, but it is worthless as a form of colonization. Super-posing, without real contact, one administrative machine on top of the existing organization amounts only to a nominal occupation. None of the interests, principally economic, which inspired the original conquest is satisfied. The country slumbers on in its traditional Oriental rut, and what changes occur are purely superficial. This form of a Protectorate is perfectly logical, but it permits a multitude of lazy officials and a nonchalant administration to do nothing but "respect native traditions"—which are no longer suited to the people who have evolved through contact with Western ideas. On the other hand, the usual solution is the opposite one. To exercise a control that is anywhere effective, it must interfere all along the line. Starting with the country's finances, there follows from top to bottom an inevitable tightening of French control. To salve its republican conscience, the Protectorate announces that these measures are only temporarily valid until the natives are educated to be collaborators. Private interests and Metropolitan selfishness are the reefs on which the idealism of the Protectorate founders. So conflict ensues, when the natives take the promise of collaboration seriously.

The development of the country has bettered the standard of native living, and has given an economic drive to native demands. This new force bridged the gap and gave reality to the issue, as no amount of dangling verbal promises indefinitely over native heads by one set of theorists and another could do. It was the natives' demands for civil liberties which have destroyed the deceptive tissue of the Protectorate, and brought to light the essentially hypocritical basis on which it rests. Natives, forcing every opening, have pushed their way gradually up, against the bitter opposition of the colonials who cling passionately to the profits and to the key positions. Each step forward has made the Protectorate machinery creak more ominously, and has increased the tension between colonials and natives. Convenient theories are forgotten in this struggle for concrete realities, and the government is left trying to straddle the widening breach in the name of a Protectorate which has never been based on reality but rather upon a desire to avoid it.

FRENCH INSTITUTIONS IN INDO-CHINA

Political and Civil Liberties

The separation of powers, universal manhood suffrage, the laicization of the state, liberty of press, speech, and assembly might be taken for the cardinal points of French administrative institutions. What has happened to them in Indo-China illustrates the devious workings of circumstance on the best of theories, and the special psychology engendered by colonization.

Separating the judicial and administrative powers, and laicizing the state have succeeded in dissolving Annamite institutions like the mandarinate and the commune. Yet they have also had an important effect in saddling the country with bureaucracy and *étatisme*. The autonomy which the Governor-General succeeded in wresting from the Métropole was barely salvaged from a parallel attempt at independence on the part of the local governments and federal services. In a colony the administration, ever in the presence of a potentially hostile population, must perforce dominate, and the mechanism by which this is accomplished is the régime of decrees. The result is almost despotic power for the central government, and this is as much resented by the colonials as by the natives. To be sure, the colonials are used to *étatisme* and rigid bureaucratic formalism in France, but in a new colony the development of commerce, industry, and even agriculture demand more supple and original solutions. The state, fearful of native hostility and nervous of colonial initiative, has also trouble in keeping discipline within its own ranks. There is intensified in a colony the French state's perennial anxiety to keep control of every activity, and its jealous husbanding of power. This explains the rarity of organizations to voice colonial opinion: until the recent creation of the *Grand Conseil*, the Chambers of Agriculture and Commerce were almost the sole vehicles of such expression. Such a bottling up of ideas is uncongenial to the French temperament, and it accounts for the violence of the Indo-Chinese press and the constant carrying of grievances to the bar of Paris opinion. The ghost of colonist-administration wrangling can only be laid when more opportunity is given to the colony for self-expression, if not for action.

The case for native opinion is both more and less acute. While they are not used to the exercise of civil liberties, contact with their foreign conquerors has developed Annamite nationalism. Subjects which are legitimately their concern, and money which is of their making, are removed from their control and administered by an irresponsible and constantly shifting administration. When the Métropole sends a Governor-General to Indo-China who knows nothing about the country, or which recalls him for trivial reasons, it paralyses the whole country by dissipating the state's moral credit, and it destroys confidence in the development of a coherent native policy. Then certain emotional Governors have been carried away oratorically to promise more than the Métropole would carry out, or their speeches have been mis-translated or misconstrued. All these things arouse native ambitions only to have them become embittered by non-fulfilment. The promise of collaboration, inherent in the Protectorate ideal, was as much responsible as the Japanese victory of 1905 for making Annamites turn their backs on their own culture in order to adopt that of the West. They are naturally the first to point out hypocrisy in the disparity between promise and accomplishment, and their specific insistence on civil rights has more than once forced the hand of the government. Native representation, naturalization—both political and personal liberties—were the realistic issues around which the struggle has been fought.

The idea of native representation was part of the baggage of the assimilationists, and when it was first introduced the natives were confused and dumbfounded. One Masonic functionary even went so far as to distribute throughout the country thousands of copies of the *Rights of Man.* When the Cambodians were told to send representatives to an assembly, they thought it was a new form of requisitioned labour: the Laotians resigned themselves to it as a novel tax. The exigencies of colonization, as well as the misunderstanding of the natives, resulted in only a partial application of this legacy from the French Revolution.

The *Conseil Supérieur de l'Indochine*, created in 1887, as an advisory board for the budget, originally had no native members, only high French functionaries. Six years later two native Notables were added. In 1905 the total number of members was increased but without adding more natives. The following year two more natives were added, but all were still named by the Governor-General. In 1911 it became the *Conseil de Gouvernement*, and had now five native members and a slight enlargement of attributes, but the numerous modifications that followed did not increase the number of native representatives. The *Grand Conseil*, a long-maturing project for a wider representation of French and native economic interests, finally materialized in 1928. Its advisory field was enlarged and also its power of initiative. It represented a step forward through an important increase in native members until, in 1931, after Raynaud's visit to the colony, their numbers equalled those of the French representatives. It was also a step away from a purely official body. Both groups deliberate in common, and while its political powers are nil it has the embryonic form from which an Indo-Chinese parliament might be developed.

The history of this federal Council is essentially that of the local assemblies. In Tonkin Bert's ideas of an advisory chamber of Notables died with him, but the country had its *Conseil de Protectorat* (1889) with the same functionary members, both native and French, and the same restricted electorate and subjects of discussion. Klobukowsky, Sarraut, and Pasquier widened the electorate slightly, and once its name was changed, but it remained fundamentally the same. Its most original feature was the representation in a third section of the non-Annamite peoples by a tripartite division into mercantile and rural groups.

No attempt was made to introduce native representation into Annam until Sarraut created provincial Councils, as the preliminary to a bigger assembly. This did not materialize until 1920. The electorate included mandarins and notables, graduates of the Franco-Annamite schools and licensed merchants. Its importance lay in the historic sense that it was the first time the people of Annam had been summoned to give their opinion, rather than in the value of the ideas they expressed. Annam was at least two generations behind Tonkin's evolution—in the Western sense—for there was neither press nor organ for forming or expressing public opinion. Sarraut was also the creator of the Cambodian *Conseil de Résidence*, which had the same character and attributes as the Annamite assemblies.

Cochin-China has the distinction of having the oldest Colonial Council and the only one of any real importance. It virtually controls the direct taxes of the colony. Its long tradition of independence has made it a formidable body to tackle, as Varenne discovered when he had the temerity to propose an income tax. Although there are native members—the French formed for long an overwhelming majority—they are functionaries and do not represent the taxpayers. They elect a deputy of a sort to represent their interests in Paris, which he faithfully does by never confounding for a moment their interests with those of the country as a whole.

Cochin-China also boasts the oldest provincial Councils of the colony which vote their own budgets, but their members are selected and not elected. Their meetings, unlike the Colonial Council, have the double disadvantage of being secret and of being presided over by the provincial administrator. Although the electorate has been slightly enlarged, their non-representative quality furnishes no guarantee to the taxpayer, for the choice of members has unfortunately been based more on their docility than on their ability. The Oriental has a natural tendency to say what is agreeable to his superiors, and the presence of the French administrator reduces them to automatic acquiescence to all government projects. The natives do not grasp the basic idea, or the method of procedure in Western representative institutions, and this often gives a farcical aspect to the meetings. One native newspaper was suppressed for caricaturing a session in which the sound of a tram outside the hall completely drowned out a translation of the chairman's speech. The Cochin-Chinese are not spontaneously interested in voting, except from a monetary viewpoint, since the mandarins control the elections at so many piastres a head. If the powers of these assemblies were extended appreciably they might arouse more interest, but as they stand they are only a deceptive façade of European institutions designed for home Republican consumption. Probably the cure is more rather than less native representative government, but to achieve this it must overcome native apathy and the colonials' hostility.

One of the best aspects of assimilation is the bestowal of French citizenship on the natives of the colonies. This generosity inspired the liberal legislation of 1881 for Cochin-China, and of 1887 for Annam-Tonkin. The general requisites were a knowledge of French or some form of distinguished service. In 1913 this same legislation was extended to Cambodia and Laos. The wording of these new laws sounded more liberal, but was less so in practice. Full naturalization was restricted to the individual and not to his children, so that a family might find itself living under two legal régimes. In 1919 Indo-China's services in the War inspired a return to the earlier liberal policy, but again in practice it worked out to be more restricted than ever. The Minister of the Colonies was to examine personally each application, and the result was interminable delays and arbitrary decisions. Even in Cochin-China the number naturalized was ridiculously small, and after the expressions of brotherly love to which the War had given birth this avarice came as a chilling surprise.

The Annamites' anxiety for naturalization was not due to regarding French citizenship as superior to their own, but rather to the practical advantages it entailed. Naturalized Annamites could compete with the

French for the same office and at the same salary. Unnaturalized Annamites were either in very subordinate positions or paid an inferior salary for the same work. There were, in addition, other legal and social advantages. Since the earliest assimilationist frenzy, there has never been any question of mass naturalization, for both French and Annamites alike recognized the disadvantages of being uprooted from one civilization without becoming part of another. But after the War a particularly bitter campaign for a more generous naturalization was waged in the French and native press, upon the occasion of an Annamite judge's admission to the Haiphong Tribunal. Fear keeps the attitude of the government and colonials alike uncompromising, lest the administration be swamped by native competition. The conservative, resisting French aver, and with reason, that the Annamites have not as yet given sufficient guarantee of professional integrity, and point to the thousands of piastres that are stolen annually from the Post and Telegraph Bureaux by native employees. Long's creation of collateral posts for natives did nothing but perpetuate the irritating inequality, and it was not until Varenne suppressed naturalization as a prerequisite to government office that the main difficulty was resolved.

While naturalization and native representation affect a wide proportion of the Indo-Chinese, there are certain other civil liberties which are demanded with violence, by a small group of natives. These are principally freedom of the press, assembly, speech, and travel. The government points out that freedom of assembly has existed in France only since 1901 and the *droit syndical* since 1884. Meetings can now be held, and native newspapers printed, only by making a preliminary declaration to authorities. Whether this is merely a formality or a serious restriction depends on the interpretation given it by the individual official. It is undeniably true, however, that the régime of the *indigénat*, the periodic creation of a Criminal Commission, the violation of private correspondence, the restricted assignment of passports, domiciliary search by customs officials and the police, indicate clearly that arbitrary measures are not always confined to emergency conditions. Personal liberties are practically non-existent in Indo-China. Though the colonial government may point with perfect accuracy to the severe discipline enforced in the old Annamite state and family, where far fewer individual liberties existed than nowadays, yet it cannot deny that the safety of the colonizing power is protected as completely as possible, and at the expense of those rights which the French Revolution declared to be the inalienable property of all

mankind. Whether the Annamites are prepared to accept the responsibilities, which are the corollary to increased civil liberties, is a practical
consideration which the history and theory of the Protectorate leaves
unanswered.

Formerly Annamite justice was administered by the regular hierarchy
of mandarins. Family and communal justice was essentially conciliatory: when it was appealed over them to the provincial court, its
character automatically changed to criminal justice, no matter what
the type of litigation. The most important loopholes in the code lay in
its failure to define relations between individuals and in the regulation
of commerce. The procedure was of the simplest; penalties were
applied immediately after the verdict was given by a single judge
without forensic battles. Justice was, in theory, gratuitous, though
highly venal in practice.

After the French had conquered Indo-China, fear of revolt made the
Admirals long retain martial law and a strong hand in cases with any
insurrectional flavour. Just as in the administration, the flight of the
mandarins forced a reorganization of justice with a premium on prompt
common-sense judgments. This was made easier by the fact that the
Inspectors of Native Affairs were officers with no special knowledge of
the law, either French or Annamite. The first real judicial organization
dates from 1864, when slightly modified French codes were promulgated in the country, and a system of dual legislation and courts was
instituted. Criminal cases automatically went to the French courts,
especially to that of Saigon, and even commercial and civil suits
between natives could be transferred to them from the native courts.
In 1868, when all non-Annamite Asiatics became justiciable by French
courts, judicial assimilation was well under way. While the Notables
continued to police the communes, and the Inspectors their provinces,
the French magistracy grew apace.

The decrees of the next decade linked Cochin-Chinese justice more
and more to that of France. It took the form of driving a wedge
between the administrative and judicial powers, and a curtailing of the
Admiral's extraordinary judicial authority. The institution of the civil
régime in 1879 was the culmination of this trend. It was only a matter
of time before the native courts were suppressed throughout the
country, but the subsequent creation of French civil and criminal
courts encountered unforeseen obstacles. Such an elaborate network

could only exist on paper, for it was too expensive and too extensive for the personnel available. The French magistracy rotated between the different colonies with such rapidity that it was not felt worth the effort to learn native languages and law. Moreover, these judges were few in number compared with the demand. Colonial careers did not offer the same inducements in salary or promotion as in France. All of these factors meant the malevolent reign of the interpreter, whose systematic corruption weighted the popular distress, already heavy with the expense and faulty justice of the new magistracy.

The Prosecuting Attorney's optimistic report of the pleasure felt by the Cochin-Chinese at the reform of justice was belied by the fact that many cases were settled out of court, because the verdicts were often so wide of the mark. An unforeseen difficulty arose within the ranks, owing to the jealousy of the administrators for the magistrates who had partially displaced them. There was a reciprocal refusal to carry out the others' orders, and threats of reprisals were made to natives who carried their cases to the rival's court. The issue was not thrashed out till 1903, when the *indigénat* was suppressed in Cochin-China, and the last link broken so as to give the magistracy full powers. The natives lost respect for administrators who could not penalize disobedience to their laws, or if the punishment followed it was accompanied by mystifying delays. The separation of powers in the colony was essentially an effort to protect civil liberties against the administration's encroachments. But it did nothing to help the natives who had no civil liberties, and it was felt to be dangerous since the French were no longer adequately protected against native uprisings.

The codes naturally did not escape modification. Changes were made in the criminal code (as translated by Philastre) by taking as a model French penal legislation, and adapting it in an orgy of circulars to Annamite customs in such matters as polygamy and property. The most important reform was the abolition of corporal punishment, always excepting the death penalty. The civil code remained essentially Annamite, but this proved equally unfortunate. The code of Gialong was no longer appropriate to a people who had forgotten its texts, based as it was on a now obsolete civilization. Cochin-China needed a legislation of its own, and it was given a penal code that was too Occidental, and a civil code that was now archaic.

Unlike Cochin-China, native jurisdiction was never suppressed in Annam and Tonkin. By the 1874 treaty French and Annamite justice worked side by side on a basis of equality, and it was not until 1884 that the French courts forged ahead. As in the South, cases of rebellion went to the French courts, and regular magistrates replaced the administrators as judges. An attempt was made to institute a Court of Appeal at Hanoi, but the expense and delays involved were so great, and its cases so few, that it was reabsorbed by its Saigon rival—until 1919. French justice became gradually the rule, however, and native justice the exception. The former steadily absorbed all cases, especially the appeals from native courts after 1901. The French Resident, notably in Annam, continued to exercise judicial powers—an offence to Montesquieu's principles which Doumer hastened to remedy. A more clear-cut separation of the powers was effected by a skeleton judicial organization for both Annam and Tonkin. The simultaneous creation of commercial courts in the colony was a tribute to its rapid economic development. The new organization had unfortunately attracted a group of shyster lawyers to Indo-China, and this necessitated disciplinary measures to keep them from stirring up trouble just to get business. Gialong had recognized and tried to restrain his compatriots' passion for litigation, which the introduction of French justice now unleashed. Almost all the judicial developments of Cochin-China were reproduced in the North, but at a slower tempo. In both parts of the colony the inefficacy of the new justice was marked by a decrease in security, and an increase in crime and vagrancy. Prompter and more equitable judgments by better qualified magistrates, and a less expensive and complicated procedure, were the crying needs. The only ones who benefited by the new system were the interpreters.

Sarraut's judicial changes were very timely, for even the most ardent assimilationists were begging for reform. He felt that the pendulum had swung too far backwards. A lack of balance had resulted from giving the magistracy too much power in an effort to curb administrative autocracy. The native revolts of 1908 and 1913 had given pause: security in a colony was, after all, different from France and the Governor's hands were tied in an emergency lest he interfere in the due course of justice. The separation of powers had led not only to bad feeling but to a confusion of powers. The codes needed a revision not only in point of uniformity and precision, but a fundamental adaptation to the colony's new needs. Sarraut reversed the old idea of using French law as a basis, with slight modifications for native taste, and made Annamite and Cambodian law the foundations to be adapted to a modern civilization. The elaboration of these codes along the lines laid down by Sarraut was not completed until after the War, and their subsequent frequent revision is proof of the delicacy of the task and the enormous study required. Sarraut retained the principle of separating the powers, but to have it effective a magistracy qualified by character, ability, and experience, and specialized in Indo-China, must be trained. In every way judges must offer more serious guarantees to the natives.

Penetration of French justice into Annam was slower than elsewhere in the colony. The introduction of mixed courts for brigandage had given the Residents a wider scope of action, yet the whole system was comparatively untouched. There was for long no separation of powers; the code used was that of Gialong, and the mandarins only referred their most important cases to the Emperor and to the Residents. The Residential courts were mainly those of appeal, and with the Criminal Commission they were the vanguard of French justice.

In a quarter of a century Tonkinese justice was revolutionized, and the French courts had woven an ever-growing judicial network over the country. The re-creation of two separate Courts of Appeal provided an organization for the Northern half of the colony, while Saigon's Court of Appeal served for the South. There were criminal courts in Saigon and Hanoi, commercial courts in the various capitals, courts of the first instance and second degree justice in the provincial capitals, and also justices of the peace with extensive powers. In the Protectorates, where the separation of powers was largely theoretical, there existed Resident Courts, and either courts of the first instance or justices of the peace—a much less complete organization, with French penetration comparatively light. The infinite variety of the Indo-Chinese peoples demands a complex judicial system, but it has a federal link in a general Direction of Judicial Administration.

Native justice, except in Cochin-China, is in the hands of mandarins, temporarily detached from the civil service to which they belong. They are competent only in cases where both parties are natives. In Tonkin the specialization of native judicial magistrates is the farthest advanced: like their French colleague they are under the Federal Director, but in the provinces under the Residents. In 1923 native justices of the peace were organized, but all native justice— according to Western ideas—leaves too much power to the single judge in charge. The French, in a spirit of unwise economy, allowed this Annamite organization to continue, and even themselves emulated it for some provincial justice. An advisory committee was instituted in

257

1927, at Hanoi, to keep the authorities there in touch with local customs and the natives' reaction to new legislation.

APPLICATION OF FRENCH PRINCIPLES AND ORGANIZATION

The separation of powers is the principle which, more than any other, has dominated the French reorganization of justice. The expense and personnel of a separate judicial system and the presence of a highly developed native justice have been the two factors which have slowed up its advance, but now even in the Protectorates its triumph is assured. The universal value of this principle has been so seriously questioned in modern times that it seems problematical whether the sacrifices made to apply it in Indo-China have been worth while. Practice has proven it clumsy and expensive.

Although the Indo-Chinese probably pay no more for justice than they did under their native governments, the money is entirely absorbed by the new procedure. If it no longer goes—officially at least—exclusively into mandarinal pockets, it makes justice no prompter or more equitable from the native viewpoint. If its efficiency as a governmental method is open to doubt, even more so is its value as a safeguard to native liberties. Certain civil liberties dear to the European heart mean nothing to the Oriental. Moreover, whenever there is a conflict between native and French interests, those of the former are invariably sacrificed to the latter. The separation of powers is a contradiction in terms to the principle of colonization, where a minority must use every means in its power to dominate a potentially hostile majority. The resulting compromise is hybrid and incomplete, and it rests on an essentially false basis. Although assimilation may be a dead letter, as official policy, nevertheless it is still very much alive as a fixed attitude of the French mind. The separation of powers belongs to that category of absolute principles, inherited from the eighteenth century, which are still felt to have an intrinsic universal value, independent of time and milieu. This attitude makes the differences between Oriental and Occidental only superficial. Such a principle could not be more contradictory to Indo-Chinese traditions: no native can respect an administration that cannot punish infractions of its laws. Then the unfortunate choice of magistrates, especially in the early days, further devaluated a principle which is questionable at best.

Annamite law is highly complicated. Philastre, in his original translation, said that the omission of a few texts distorted one's understanding of the whole. This is due to the fact that Annamite legislation is a code of specific penalties, and not general principles from which a particular verdict can be deduced. In a system where the magistracy is rotated from colony to colony, time and the stimulus are lacking to learn the code, or the complicated civilization on which it is based. Magistrates and litigants alike are at the mercy of an irresponsible interpreter whose miniature salary, if nothing else, inclines him to venality. Experience is the *sine qua non* of a magistrate's worth, and France persisted in sending to the colony inexperienced young men, fresh from their law studies. No matter how naturally brilliant they might be—and the most able usually remained in France—they were not equipped to give valuable judgments in Indo-China. The salary and promotion guaranteed there were so inferior to France that the colony perforce acquired a magistracy recruited from the old French colonies. While their status as French citizens placed them legally on an equal footing with French magistrates, the Indo-Chinese were incensed at being judged by Hindus and Africans. Moreover, penury of men and means did not permit the presence of three judges, as in French courts, but only a single magistrate aided by an interpreter. The injustice of their verdicts was not due so much to their inability or character as to their ignorance—but this made it no more acceptable to the Anna-mites, who are particularly sensitive to injustice. Nor did the quality of the colony's lawyers make up for the judges' mistakes.

The novel procedure introduced by the French was as much of a pitfall as the new codes themselves. Rigorous formalities were demanded in a scrupulous respect for individual liberties, but they were intro-duced at the expense of a simple and expeditious justice. The oath required of litigants and witnesses made no appeal to native honour, for lying does not trouble the Annamite conscience. Swearing on the Bible, with the right hand upraised, has for them a comic quality not conducive to increasing the court's prestige. The introduction of lawyers into the proceedings has created a new profession in the country and has added to the natives' expenses. Prisons, on the other hand, are more comfortable than most native homes; moreover, they offered special facilities as a school in crime. Considerations of economy shortsightedly mixed hardened criminals with men awaiting trial, so that the latter could easily and effectively learn the best way of getting around this strange new law. With a few piastres the accused could win over the guard, arm himself with a cloud of false witnesses, and learn a plausible story by heart.

Even a short sojourn in prison before the Inquiry makes eliciting a confession practically impossible. Reliable witnesses are hard to get. The best of them are often unjustly detained for days, so that blood relations are almost the only witnesses available, and they are naturally not disinterested. Acquittal is inevitable if the accused is wealthy, for even the parents of the injured party can be bought off, and the case be dismissed for lack of evidence. Facts make little impression on the Annamite mind at best, and he has also a flair for imaginative lying. This was recognized by the Annamite code, which devoted an entire book to circumventing prevarication. The only hope of foiling fraud is to bring the accused to an immediate trial, so that the chances for fiction and corruption are minimized. The prisoner is questioned successively by three or four different magistrates. The Annamite is mystified as to why they each ask him the same set of questions, and he gives to each different answers. He does not grasp the fact that his replies are taken down, and that his *dossier* accompanies him from one judge to another. Moreover, the Annamite expects punishment to follow immediately upon the verdict, and he is puzzled by the unaccountable delay. The whole mechanism of French justice, to insure every precaution against summary injustice, escapes the Annamite mentality.

Even before these other obstacles are encountered there is the initial difficulty of laying hands on the criminal. Although the *état civil* was established in 1887 in Cochin-China, and in 1916 for the other countries, it is as yet ineffective for the rural districts. Nor can satisfaction be obtained by taking over the delinquent's property, for it belongs collectively to his family, and it is in the form of isolated strips which are impracticable for profitable exploitation. Imprisonment for debts was abolished by Varenne, so that creditors feel as if their last resource had melted away. In Annamite law the punishment of a debtor extended to his family, and this offered a more serious guarantee. Moreover, in the whole problem of indebtedness the omnipresent factor of gaming has an importance hard to over-estimate in creating social and mental disequilibrium.

When the question arose as to which legislation should be applied in Indo-China, even the most fanatical assimilationists admitted that the French codes must be modified and Annamite customs serve, when unforeseen problems came to light. As it worked out, unfortunately, the French codes were applied, except in the Protectorates, almost in their entirety, for the moral evolution of the Annamites was slower than their legal assimilation. Even in the 1931 code many articles were suppressed dealing with family solidarity and the cult of the ancestors. Laicization of the code removed the religious foundation of the *paterfamilias'* authority. The individualism inherent in the French code has been the greatest solvent of Annamite society. For example, the French regard adultery with Gallic leniency and mirth: to the Annamite there could be no worse crime against the social order. The vital differences in Occidental and Oriental civilizations made for an entirely contrary appraisal of crime: in the Annamite code a child who strikes his parents or grandparents is decapitated. In 1883 French law forbade parents to sell their children, or to use them as legal guarantors, and even prior to this children had been permitted to bring suit against their parents. The establishment of the *état civil* was felt to be a further intrusion on family privacy and autonomy.

French land regulations have gone towards strengthening individual property rights, especially those of small holders. Formerly ownership by family or commune prevailed, and they served as stewards for the state and for posterity. Now property is divided and children are leaving the paternal land and village for more remunerative work in the towns. Women's property rights have been strengthened, and a stricter enforcement of contracts has further emphasized the relations between individuals rather than groups. Penalties are no longer based on the amount of damage done and the rank of the injured and offending parties. More emphasis has been put on equality before the law and on the individual's motives, and less upon the material harm done to society. The fundamental principle of French law is the respect and protection of the individual, considered as a free being and equal to other members of society. Annamite law was based on the respect and protection of family and state authority, before which every other right is effaced, and where the group—not the individual—is responsible.

The whole basis of the Annamite code was religious: crime approached sin, and its immediate expiation removed any sense of infamy. The abolition of corporal punishments in 1901 was based not only on humanitarianism but on the feeling that such penalties were degrading. This is traceable to the Occidental sense of individual dignity, unknown to the Annamite. The worst of Annamite corporal punishments had fallen into disuse before the coming of the French, and if some blood-curdling penalties remained many of them were reduced to canings of varying severity or else had become frankly purchasable. The French could substitute only one thing—deprivation of personal liberty, culminating in a retention of the death penalty. To both peoples the cause of moral suffering is not the same. Being in prison, better fed and better lodged than at home, is no deprivation to the Annamite. To him time means nothing, and he has practically no personal liberty at best. Very few attempts to escape from prison are recorded. The prisoner, returned to his village, has even acquired prestige among his compatriots. Being kept long away from the ancestral tombs is a far greater source of moral suffering to the Annamite, so that a sentence of exile is much more severe to him than the death penalty.

Annamite belief that a spirit existence is superior to this mortal coil makes him approach death with an indifference which only the threat of a non-ritual burial can shake. Bravery on the scaffold for an Occidental entails a vast effort of the will over a trembling body, quite the reverse of the Annamite's indifference to this momentary transition between two kinds of existence. During the conquest the death penalty was quite ineffective, but a threat to disinter and scatter the bones of their ancestors often brought bandits to terms.

The social consequences of this new justice were far-reaching. Imprisonment, prior to the trial and subsequent to the verdict, deeply affected the family of the accused by depriving them for long of their wage-earner. Contrary to the French individualistic concepts, this was unconsciously a return to the Annamite punishment of the guilty man's family, who might themselves be the innocent sufferers. Caning was the Annamite code's alternative, and it had the advantage of costing the state nothing, of being immediately applicable, and of inflicting only temporary pain while not permanently injuring the delinquent's capacity to work. It is true that the mandarins could apply the cane with dispassionate justice, but this was not true of the French, whose natural impatience was sharpened by a tropical climate. The cane became too dangerous a weapon for human passions, since a lack of moderation might easily degenerate into brutality. There is a subsidiary argument in favour of mild corporal punishments: a confession of guilt, which the French law requires, may be wrung from an Annamite by this means. Otherwise he would feel constrained to remain silent under pain of being regarded as a traitor. Native indifference to suffering is partly based on religious belief, and partly on a less highly developed nervous system. Those who are horrified by the idea of corporal punishments do not face the Occidental alternative of the third degree method which is ultimately no more humanitarian. The Annamite historically has always associated force with authority: although this attitude is gradually changing, it is none the less true that his mentality still responds more readily to that kind of punishment than to its Occidental variations.

The inappropriateness of French law is nowhere more clearly shown than in the regulation of vagrancy. In a highly organized society vagrancy is punished as a preventive measure. A resourceless man is almost bound to commit crimes when life is hard, his needs numerous, and the weather inclement. Such is not, however, the case in Indo-China where, for the most part, the climate is agreeable, native needs reduced to the minimum and easy to satisfy—in short, it is not likely that the vagabond will become a social menace. A handful of rice is enough for a native's subsistence, the rivers abound in fish, and a house is an unnecessary luxury. A little work keeps a man alive for six months without further effort. Saving is unnecessary when nature and the commune provide so abundantly. Natural laziness, combined with a love of gaming, keeps the Annamite in a state of chronic poverty and often vagrancy. The Annamite law punished vagabonds, not as individuals, but only when organized into bands. The vagabond was assigned to a penal colony where by work he might eventually own land. This was based on the theory that crime, being caused by poverty, would disappear if a man were given the means of rehabilitating himself. Though there are other supplementary political and economic causes, the introduction of the French code, which strikes at vagrancy with as much severity as in France, is one of the chief causes of its recent increase in the colony.

Delays, perhaps inevitable, in revising the codes have been a great cause of judicial instability and confusion. An Annamite has a different legal status in the five countries of the Union. Only in 1934–35 did Annam get a new code. A revision of Cambodian legislation was begun in 1891 and not completed until 1929: Laotian modifications were also strung out from 1908 to 1929. This was partially due to the varying speed with which each country was evolving away from its own outworn code, and partly to the different cultural strata within each administrative unit. The jurisprudence has often been contradictory: it is hard to build up a solid legal philosophy on the inconsistent decisions of the colony's Courts of Appeal. Though one may criticize the new codes, as lacking in elasticity, they are models of excellence when compared with the old native legislation that denied the dynamic forces in society. The new codes have laid down, not specific penalties for each and every case, but general principles which the individual magistrate may interpret.

In French law the initiative left to the judge is based on the optimistic assumption that he is impartial, disinterested, and equal to his task. Annamite law is founded on the contrary belief that every possible situation must be handled specifically by the law, so that the hopelessly venal magistrate has only the mechanical task of application. Though the French have raised the mandarins' salaries, their opportunities for graft are greater than ever before. Moreover, the French magistrates have not been renowned for their impartial judgments when dealing with cases between Europeans and natives. The prestige of the white race has been maintained to the detriment of abstract justice. The worst example of partiality is the Criminal Commission, but it has become a very useful institution resorted to by even the liberal-minded.

Upon his arrival in the colony, Sarraut was shocked to learn that when the public order was attacked, the Governor-General could choose between sending the case before a regular court or to the Criminal Commission. Contrary to his request, Paris refused to suppress the latter. The next year Sarraut himself used this Commission, and pleaded in the local press the reasons for his change of front—the Hanoi bombs of 1913. The same situation was reproduced after the Yenbay massacres, when Pasquier gave to the Criminal Commission its most prolonged period of activity, although it meant the reign of the arbitrary and the unjust. It countenanced—unofficially—anonymous accusations, the use of torture, and terrible prison conditions. Its worst excesses may be traced to the hysteria which prevails in a colony immediately following an uprising. This court is in flagrant opposition to the principles of French justice, yet its usefulness to the government has been so great as to resist, up to now, all liberal attacks.

When a reactionary Governor like Robin recognizes publicly that many of the courts' judgments have shown "incomprehensible clemency" to Europeans, and that the natives need more legal guarantees, one may realize to what lengths the miscarriage of pure justice has gone. The judicial organization is but part and parcel of colonization: almost any event that ruffles the surface shows up the fundamental inconsistency of applying principles like the separation of powers to a colony. Far more than the work of administration, the action of official justice is the nerve centre of colonization. Here contacts with the natives are at their most sensitive point. More even than education, the administration of justice is the measure and test of the value and depth of the penetration accomplished in the colony by the mother country.

THE CONTACTS OF CIVILIZATIONS

Explorations

In the middle of the nineteenth century Indo-China offered a fertile field for adventurous spirits who found Europe too tame or too routinized. In 1858 a French scientist, Henri Mouhot, was charged by the London Geographical Society with the study of the Mekong Valley. He had tried before to get a similar commission from a French Society, but their refusal illustrated the indifference of France at that time to the Indo-Chinese peninsula. In collecting scientific specimens, Mouhot did not ignore the beauties of the country, in spite of the terrible hardships he endured. There were no roads, and the transportation of himself and his equipment was an ever-present problem. He never slept in a bed, his diet was of rice and dried fish, the water was dangerous to drink. Any imprudence was rewarded by an attack of fever. His spiritual obstacles were loneliness and discouragement, yet the exhilaration he experienced at being a pioneer in a new land was such that never before had he known so much happiness. It was Mouhot who had the joy of re-discovering Angkor:

At the sight of this temple, the spirit is overwhelmed and the imagination stunned. One looks, one admires, and, overcome by awe, one cannot speak. Where could words be found to praise adequately a work of architecture which perhaps has never been, or can never be. . . .[1]

Mouhot was destined to die in the country which he had opened to his ungrateful compatriots. Ten days after he was attacked by fever he made the final entry in his diary: "*Ayez pitié de moi, O mon Dieu!*"— eloquent of the loneliness of a man conscious that he was doomed to die in a distant land.

The systematic study of the Mekong by Doudart de Lagrée was one of the major explorations of the century, as regards its economic, scientific, and political importance. Since France's primary interest in Cochin-China lay in its proximity to China's southern provinces, it was imperative to investigate the navigability of the great river that united them. The expedition was decided upon during Admiral de la Grandière's visit to Paris in 1865. The next step was to persuade Doudart de Lagrée, then French representative in Cambodia, to accept its leadership in view of his precarious health. He was well qualified by his knowledge of the country and his ability to command. His ten

[1] H. Mouhot, *Voyages dans les Royaumes de Siam* (Paris, 1868), p. 194.

companions included two later well-known names: Francis Garnier and Louis Delaporte.

The Mission was handicapped by a scandalous penury of means. Like Mouhot they encountered trouble in getting transportations, passports, interpreters, and coolies. Laos had the reputation of being one of the unhealthiest of countries. Navigating the great rivers of Asia has certain features which demand courage, patience, and perseverance: fighting currents and reefs, or equally dangerous waterfalls; sailing between banks covered with jungle or monotonous rice-fields under the rays of a murderous sun. From the outset the first rapids convinced Lagrée that the Mekong was a capricious river, completely unnavigable for half of the year. A supplementary railway paralleling its course would be the only practical solution. Disappointed in their primarily commercial interests, the members of the Mission consoled themselves by developing political and scientific aspects. Though they were well treated by the local peoples, the political disorder in the countries through which they passed was very apparent. Interminable delays were forced on them by the petty chiefs who, like mediaeval princelings, levied their own tolls and refused to honour the passports of their suzerains. Garnier in particular was oppressed by the expanding domination of Siam. Though France had never recognized her claims to Laos, Siam was quietly continuing her historic absorption of that country, while her old rival Annam was occupied with the French. The Mission brought to the fore the inevitability of a reckoning with Siam, if France intended to expand into north-western Indo-China.

Despite the discouragements and hardships of travel which threatened the mutual goodwill of the explorers, the Mission persevered in its hope of finding compensation to the North. Finally,

on the afternoon of October 18, 1867, five months after our departure from Luang-Prabang, and sixteen months away from Saigon, after crossing a high ridge, we came upon a great plain spread out before our eyes. Far away against a hill stood a town with red walls and brick roofs. We were about to set foot on one of the most ancient and least known lands in the world. Tears filled our eyes; all hearts beat with emotion. If I had been fated to die on this expedition, I should have liked to expire there, like Moses at Mount Nebo, gazing for the last time upon the land of Canaan.[1]

Lagrée and his companions were to cross the frontier of Yunnan which no European before them had done. They arrived exhausted, almost

[1] Carné, Louis de, *Voyage en Indo-Chine* (Paris, 1872), p. 303.

without shoes or clothing, and in a land where a man's importance was judged according to appearances. Fortunately their passports offset their poor apparel.

Yunnan was still ravaged by the Moslem revolt of 1855. By the time they reached Yunnan-Sen, Lagrée, who had long been ill, felt that he must rest and send Garnier on ahead to explore the Moslem stronghold of Tali-fou. Garnier and a few men set out against the advice of even the French missionaries, so determined were they to trace the Mekong to its Thibetan source. Arrived at the kingdom of Tali—of whose existence the Mission had been totally unaware when leaving Saigon—Garnier was warned by its Sultan not to try to see either the city or the source of the Mekong. In fact, after several dramatic incidents, the travellers barely escaped with their lives.

Upon their return to Yunnan-Sen they were overwhelmed to learn of Lagrée's death, in March 1868. Thus ended the exploration, and the Mission, now under Garnier's command, turned eastward towards Shanghai, exhausted in health and in funds. They had failed to find the juncture between the Upper Mekong and the frontier of Burma— only recently has the aeroplane filled in this void—yet they had accomplished one of the most remarkable feats of the century. Though their work had doomed Saigon as a world port, it drew attention to Siamese expansion in Laos, and to the Red River route into Yunnan. Garnier summed up the scientific and political contributions of the expedition in two volumes, and edited Lagrée's diary and reports, adding his own commentaries. The fateful end of Garnier's life was but the consummation of this Mission, for he proved the importance of Tonkin to France which he had been the first to recognize.

Louis Delaporte, another member of Lagrée's Mission, returned to Cambodia in 1875 to study Khmer art. The years that had elapsed did nothing to lessen the difficulties which all prior Missions had encountered. By Herculean efforts he collected and brought back to Paris twenty cases of Khmer sculpture. The Louvre and Palais d'Industrie would have none of it, so he placed them in the Trocadéro, where they were subsequently enriched. In 1935 they were combined with the collection of the Musée Guimet. Delaporte left one of his ablest collaborators, Jules Harmand, to continue his explorations in Cambodia. From 1875 to 1877, before he became absorbed by diplomacy, Harmand collected the Khmer inscriptions which Professor Kern later deciphered. Aymonier's simultaneous explorations and studies supplemented these efforts and initiated the study of Khmer writing.

Auguste Pavie's was the last of the great Missions, and it covered a long period of years (1875-95). Pavie's career began with infinite modesty. He was a functionary stationed at Kampot, where he became acquainted with a Cambodian bonze, who stimulated his interest in his people and their culture. He studied Khmer art, and began exploring as a vacation pastime. His professional career as an explorer began when he interested Le Myre de Vilers in prospecting for a Cambodian telegraph line. Siam's encroachments in Laos and England's interest in the Shan States proved to be Pavie's opportunity, and it gave to his work a scope of which he had never dreamed. With forty collaborators Pavie explored Cambodia and Laos methodically. The results of his prodigious industry, which included historical and literary studies, were published in eight volumes, of which the most important contribution scientifically was the map of Indo-China. Pavie subsequently became French consul at Bangkok, and commissioner in the boundary settlement with England.

Pavie's travels paved the way for French control of Eastern Laos. The Siamese showed that they were not deceived by the commercial colour given to his explorations when they refused him a passport. The most important of his expeditions linked Laos directly with Hanoi, by way of the Black River Valley. This country was nominally under Annamite suzerainty, but in reality it enjoyed as much independence as was compatible with the presence of innumerable bandits. The Chinese Hos periodically ravaged Upper Laos, and the King of Siam used this as a pretext to install a Siamese officer and troops at Luang-Prabang. His troops radiated throughout the country, and showed clearly Siam's intention of taking over Laos at the first opportunity. Pavie happened to be at Luang-Prabang during one of the Ho invasions. The Siamese officer who had hitherto effectively prevented Pavie from communicating with the Laotian king left the town for Bangkok just at the crucial moment. The King did nothing to protect himself nor his capital from the Hos who, he knew, were approaching nearer every day, and spreading terror throughout his land. Nor were the people any more enterprising: they covered themselves with amulets but could not boast a single firearm among them. They took to the woods as their sole protection, and left the Hos (with the resigned heroism of the peoples of Asia) to pillage as they pleased. Pavie helped the grateful and timorous king to escape at the risk of his own life, and he proved to himself that France could conquer the country, morally as well as physically, by protecting the Laotian people. Wandering barefoot year after year through the most isolated regions, Pavie was miraculously successful in making himself and his country beloved. The title of his book, *A La Conquête des Cœurs*, is no sentimental dream, but the substance and reality of his policy. In the fullest sense Laos was Pavie's gift to France.

Orientalism

Pavie's work ended the role of periodic scientific missions. Institutions of permanent scholarship henceforth replaced the work of transient individuals. In 1899 Doumer founded the *École Française d'Extrême Orient*, or the EFEO, on the models of the French Schools at Rome and Athens, which was to form the most important group of Orientalists in the Far East. Its double task was to conduct scholarly research in all the countries of the Far and Middle East, whose culture had contributed to the Indo-Chinese civilizations, and to conserve and classify the colony's historical monuments. The library of the EFEO at Hanoi has an invaluable collection, notably of Chinese manuscripts. Under its supervision are the Royal Institutes and Libraries of Pnom-Penh and Laos, and the colony's five museums.[1] A tri-monthly bulletin has been published since 1901, with monographs by scholars. Its most important inventories are of the historical monuments of the colony, especially of the Cham remains. The EFEO is under the French *Académie des Inscriptions et des Belles Lettres*, but is virtually autonomous. Permanent members are named for life, and all of the School's expenses are covered by the colony's general budget.

The tendency of this School has been to become absorbed in the past, at the expense of the present. This criticism was embodied in a violent newspaper attack in 1910. The occasion of this campaign was a claim made by Paul Pelliot, a scholar of the EFEO, to have found and bought priceless Chinese manuscripts in Turkestan. He prematurely published an enthusiastic account of his discovery, with a not too modest appreciation of his own activity. Orientalists, who were naturally eager to see these manuscripts, were repeatedly put off with the excuse that they were still being classified. The Bibliothèque Nationale would never let them be seen, and there was no inventory forthcoming. Jean Ajalbert, in the *Depêche de Toulouse*, irritated Pelliot by his embarrassing questions into making an injudicious and tactless reply. Thus

---

[1] EFEO at Hanoi, Musée Cham of Tourane (1918), Musée A. Sarraut at Pnom-Penh (1919), Musée Khai Dinh at Hué (1923), Musée Blanchard de la Brosse at Saigon (1929).

the Affaire Pelliot was born, and it came to rapid maturity in a scandalous campaign in the *Presse Coloniale*. The famous manuscripts were
proven to have been fraudulently misrepresented and Pelliot a gullible
purchaser. It gave the public a chance to protest against the excessive
expense of the EFEO. It was claimed that its professors could not speak
a word of Annamite even after long residence in Tonkin, and that they
travelled incessantly in India, Thibet, China, or even never left Paris.
In the colony it drew its material from the gratuitous labours of
scholarly missionaries[1] or studious officers. The initial mistakes seem
to have been in giving a false impression of its function by calling
the EFEO a school and not a research institute. Despite certain shortcomings, the EFEO has brought to light the art and civilization of Champa,
hitherto completely ignored, and done remarkable work in the restoration of Angkor and other colonial monuments.

Certain minor efforts to stimulate the study of Indo-Chinese culture
deserve mention. The Admirals, as early as 1865, were concerned with
amassing information about their new colony. They founded in Cochin-
China a Committee of Agriculture and Industry, primarily to study
economic questions. Science and the arts were added in 1883 to its
programme, and the name changed to the *Société des Etudes Indo-
Chinoises*. Like the EFEO, its interesting bulletin by preference published
articles dealing with the past rather than the present. Its library is
the second best in the colony. It gives courses in Annamite and enjoys
a government subsidy. Another effort of the Admirals, to stimulate
public interest in and authentic knowledge of Cochin-China, was a
series of subsidized volumes called *Excursions et Reconnaissances*. The
Amis du Vieux Hué (1913) has many native members, and so have the
Société de Géographie de Hanoi and Indo-China's Council of Scientific
Research. All have public bulletins and specialized libraries. Sarraut
reorganized the colony's libraries in 1917, of which there is now one
for every country of the Union. Two-thirds of their readers are natives.

THE PROPAGATION OF IDEAS
Missions
The history of Indo-Chinese Missions is inextricably bound up
with the conquest. The Annamite government recognized this, and

[1] Contributions by missionaries are the source of the earliest knowledge of Indo-
China. Pères A. de Rhodes, *Histoire du Tonkin*; B. Vachet, *Mémoire de la Cochinchine*;
P. de la Bissachère, *Notes Sur le Tonkin*; A. de Rhodes, *Dictionnaire*; Mgr. Tabord,
Dictionnaire. Franciscan documentation was more rich than accurate. The Dominicans
had a wider culture.

the tempo of its persecutions corresponded to its fear of European intervention. Unfortunately for the Emperor's efforts, they only resulted in a vicious circle: the more he persecuted, the more stimulus it gave to armed intervention, especially when the Mission-minded Empress Eugénie was at the helm.

In the days of the Admirals, the missionaries and their neophytes were invaluable as interpreters and guides. The role played by Mgr. Puginier, who acted as Garnier's adviser and intermediary with Hué, made him at one moment the arbiter of Tonkin's destiny. The French nobility, which furnished many officers for the Tonkin campaigns, was traditionally the ally of the Church, so it was only natural that under them the Mission waxed powerful. In the 1874 treaty the Court of Hué had been forced to recognize the Mission's right to acquire land, build churches, and open schools and hospitals. This had laid the foundation for the Mission's temporal power, which the anti-clericals later resented as a throttling grip on the nascent colony. The missionaries were, too, rather aggressive in the early days about using their great influence to undermine the mandarins, their inveterate enemies, and to push ahead those natives most amenable to their guidance. They cultivated official hatred of the Scholar group, and even protected certain malefactors from justice. The Mission also wanted the administration to increase the number of conversions by offering promotion and profit to native Christians. The Mission further took umbrage at Admiral Bonard's recommendation that Annamite religious customs must be respected, because the cult of their ancestors was almost as dear to the government as to the Annamites themselves. Puginier resented the state's asking the Mission to aid in getting coolies for the army as a misunderstanding of the fundamental function of the Mission:

We are not in the service of the Protectorate. We ask of it only to assure us the protection to which all Frenchmen are entitled. We love our country, which we serve best by spreading the Gospel, and by multiplying the number of native Christians. In this way, we penetrate pagan circles which would otherwise be closed to European influence, to our ideas and customs, to the faith, and to civilization. Let no one ask more of us, nor try to distract us from our task by trying to make of us political or commercial agents. Each has his own work.[1]

With the coming of the civil government there was a marked change in the French attitude towards the Mission. Aspersions began to be

[1] d'Allenjoye, C., *Un Apôtre Français au Tonkin: Mgr. Puginier* (Paris, 1896), p. 510.

cast on the role played by the Mission during the conquest. Puginier was denounced as a religious zealot turned politician through a wish to make the Church triumph at all costs. His hatred of the mandarins dragged the administration into a mistaken policy of direct government: he had even been willing to involve France in a civil war just for the greater glory of the Mission. Christian villages wanted tax exemptions, privileged positions everywhere, and persecutions of their erstwhile enemies. In short, the Mission had made every effort to have a directing hand in the state and to use it solely for its own ends. Body was given to this denunciation when the Mission took active steps to get the Emperor of Annam deposed in 1891, and to substitute for him a prince, one of their converts, who would exercise pressure on his compatriots to turn Catholic. When De Lanessan helped to restore pagodas that had been destroyed during the conquest, the Mission asked him to desist, and when he refused he was denounced in the Hanoi Cathedral. Thus put on the defensive, the Mission loudly proclaimed its patriotism. Had it not served the interests of colonization in founding schools and printing presses, and by initiating social service work in the colony? The Mission's aim was not only to make the Annamites Christians, but also to make them French.[1] The government at the time, however, refused to admit any identity in their interests.

Relations went along smoothly under Bert, despite his ferociously anti-clerical reputation, because he and Puginier held each other in mutual esteem. All the state demanded, according to Bert, was that the Mission comply with its laws and expect no special favours. When he put this into practice by taxing Church property the Mission protested, for it was the greatest landowner in Hanoi and in many of the provinces. Some of the more zealous anti-clericals of the time carried on a heated propaganda against Mission machinations. They taught Latin, not French, in their schools: in the provinces the Mission was undermining mandarinal authority and embarrassing the French Residents in order to regain the moral influence over the people which they had lost with the advent of the civil government.

Many Freemason pamphlets[2] described the insidious way in which the Mission got control of entire villages. Missionaries would concentrate on the conversion of the head of a family, and, if successful, would proceed to baptize the forty or fifty members under his authority. As if by enchantment, the village Council of Notables would suddenly

---

[1] Varet, P., *Les Dieux qui Meurent* (Paris, 1932), p. 177.
[2] Cf. Van Raveschot and C. Paris.

find that it had a Catholic majority who blindly obeyed the missionary's behests. Because they lived in direct contact with the people, they had, through the native grape-vine telegraph, an information service that was far better than the government's. By acquiring evidence of a mandarin's misdeeds, they could blackmail him into submission by threats of denunciation to the administration. It was far easier to control the natives through economic advantage, or through promises to intercede in their behalf with the authorities. In all these ways the power of the administration was nullified, especially in the provinces. In the towns the Mission controlled the colony's most important newspaper, *L'Avenir du Tonkin*, dictated to the loyal Catholics in the government bureaux so that all *dossiers* and officials hostile to the Mission were systematically suppressed. They had even formed an alliance with the powers of darkness, as represented by the Bank of Indo-China. But principally, according to the most belligerent Freemasons, it was the Mission's influence over the natives which was the secret of their hold over the administration.

This dread moral influence over the Annamites can be traced to that age-old bone of contention between state and Church—the latter's temporal power. Not only did the Mission antedate the administration but it had the advantage of being permanent, with allies among the good Catholic functionaries, whereas the Governors rotated vertiginously. The missionaries themselves admitted to using an economic lever as a means of conversion. The misery of the peasants made them subject to periodic migrations, and extracted them from Mission influence, often just at a time when their conversion hung in the balance. In many countries comparative misery is a means of conversion, for it turns the individual away from the fleshpots to spiritual considerations. But in the Orient misery is too near the subsistence level. A man cannot keep his thoughts on God when he is wondering if his family will die of starvation. If the wolf is kept from the door, along with the tax collector and the usurer, it is solely through his unremitting toil. If the Mission were to make any headway at all, it had to attach these people to the soil by offering them a means of livelihood.

The day of wholesale conversions had come definitely to an end with the conquest. When the natives had no longer to flee from bandits or mandarinal persecution to find their only refuge with the powerful Mission, there was not the same pressure for conversion. If the Papal Bull of 1774 had not refused to welcome the ancestral cult into the bosom of Catholicism, there would surely have been a more widespread acceptance of Christianity—at least it would have been welcomed apathetically on the same eclectic basis as Buddhism and Taoism. But the intolerance of Rome, its insistence on an uncongenial moral code, its disruption of the social edifice, its lack of ritual appeal for the intelligentsia—all militated against large-scale conversions. Utilitarian motives played the stellar role, so it was the poorest and neediest of the population who turned Christian—a fact that still further discredited the Mission in the eyes of the upper stratum.

The missionaries were fully aware of all these drawbacks, but the Lord moved in a mysterious way. By turning apparently away from its spiritual mission to the aggrandizement of its material possessions, the Mission might be serving the greater glory. The fact that the Mission accepted this material basis for its influence in Indo-China has made its position equivocal, but it also has effected an improvement in native conditions. Christian villages are markedly more prosperous than their pagan neighbours. The Mission is responsible for the first social service in the colony, just as it was the founder of the first schools and printing press. It has fought higher native taxes. Missionaries were the intrepid pioneers in fever-ridden districts: they taught scientific agriculture to primitive mountaineers, and improved native arts and crafts. They helped the administration by building roads in inaccessible regions, by sending Christian villages to colonize the new provinces of Cochin-China, and by getting Christian coolies to labour on public works. Turning Catholic is for the natives tantamount to acquiring a new profession. One Annamite informed his employer that he was no longer a gardener but a Catholic.

In building on the foundation of material advantages, the Mission has risked losing its native converts when they become prosperous, or when they see that the Mission is no longer useful to them. A wholesale defection was threatened when anti-clericalism raged in the colony, because it was apparent to the natives that the Mission no longer enjoyed its former power. It cannot be denied, however, that the missionaries offer an inspiring example of heroic self-abnegation and of courage in the face of hardships in climate and spiritual isolation. The natives are not insensible to this, but the devotion it inspires in them is more towards the individual missionary than to the cause he represents. A young priest, sent into the *brousse* with only a neophyte speaking a few words of French, who devotes his entire life to the native people, and their language and culture, is an example to the colonial of what human effort and courage can achieve. Just before the

conquest the average life of a missionary in Cochin-China was estimated at five years. Such sincerity and ardent faith, the example of
his life and his knowledge of native psychology, have made the missionary feared and respected by the administration. At his voice an
entire Catholic village will rise up and follow him. Might not such
power be used to foment a rebellion against a government which has
shorn the Mission of so much prestige and power?

The Freemasons were not content to point out the political danger
inherent in Mission control, they also denounced it as economically
harmful. Did they not own vast tracts of land which the missionaries
could not themselves cultivate, yet which were left fallow through
their selfish greed? Instead of living normally like the Protestant missionaries, they had adopted the native way of life and so discouraged
the Annamites from adopting European habits and—more important—
from becoming buyers of French goods. Instead of being proud of
France's traditional role as protector of Far Eastern Missions, it was to
her interest to reduce their noxious power. "Every convert is a citizen
lost to his country, and a labourer lost to the French colonist."[1] All
the well and ill-founded criticisms levelled at the Mission, in the final
analysis, amount to the fear lest it become a state within a state.

The extent to which these fears were expressed in actual legislation
varied with the individual Governor. Many of the highest officials were
Freemasons, who did not, however, let this unduly influence their whole
colonial policy. Thus Doumer and Klobukowsky were regarded as
regenerate backsliders in Masonic circles. Beau was more ardent.
Under him the schools were laicized, the nursing nuns ousted from
the hospitals, and a press campaign initiated against the Mission's
wealth. Yet hostility to the Mission had largely played itself out before
the War. Jules Ferry's hope that anti-clericalism would not become
an article for exportation was not wholly fulfilled. There was certainly
no place in a new and expanding country for such a sterile transplantation of European grouches. The futility of antagonism between the
few Frenchmen in the colony was becoming more apparent with the
growth of a native problem, but it took the War to remove the bitterness from the struggle, and to deal colonial anti-clericalism a death-
blow. The missionaries were mobilized like their lay compatriots, and
their ranks were thinned to the point of no longer being an object of
fear but of commiseration. Also the fidelity of the native Christians
who prayed daily for the Allied victory, allayed all fears of their

[1] Paris, C., *Le Colon et l'Administration* (Paris, 1896), p. 8.

disloyalty. Antipathy to them was melted in a common glow of patriotism.

Education of the native intelligentsia was the *leitmotif* of post-War missionary activity. Their efforts to reach a better quality and a more influential group of Annamites met with the obstacles of penury in men and money—just like lay education. But unlike the state, the Mission had no taxes but the tithe, no funds but what the faithful sent from France, and even that had to encounter an increasingly unfavourable exchange. By 1934 the Mission's revenues had been cut by a third. Many missionaries, too, had been killed in the War, and the religious vocation, perhaps due to the anti-clerical laws, seemed to be waning in France. Formerly from sixty to seventy priests came annually to Indo-China, now only twenty. Thus fewer teachers were available for the new educational offensive launched by the Mission, and in the government's educational reorganization of 1924 strict laws required as high a standard of diplomas in private as in state education. If the state had strictly enforced its own rulings, Mission schools would have had to close down.

The government's leniency, however, did not extend to taxes, and in the 1920's they were ever on the increase. The state, in these new regulations, was not animated by the old anti-clerical hostility, but stiffened by fiscal pressure and by the attacks to which its educational system was being subjected. On the contrary a new humility as to the merits of lay education seized hold upon the government: could it be ultimately responsible for the aggressive nationalism of the natives? The Mission had long run schools just to counteract this lack of religious and ethical instruction in state education. Now they aimed not only to keep their native Christians isolated and safe from contaminating paganism, but to reach out to the intelligentsia who badly needed rescuing from the burning fires of Communism and Caodaism.[1]

There was a little of the smugness of men who had accurately prophesied doom in the missionaries' reminders to the government that they had long seen the danger of tolerating and even cultivating native religions. Their Christian villages remained steadfast islands of loyalty in the encircling tide of Communism. The state could not acknowledge the error of its lay ways, but it did for the first time whole-heartedly admit the community of its interests with the Mission's. The latter tacitly did likewise. In the official account of the Mission's work not one voice is raised in protest against the violence of the state's

[1] Cf. below, p. 474.

repression of the Communist movement. The fact that a Freemason like Varenne asked for the Legion of Honour for Sœur Antoine, of the Order of St. Paul de Chartres, is significant of the new entente. Men like Monet and Roux may complain that the Mission has done everything to undermine lay efforts to aid the Annamites, that Père Robert of Shanghai was the arch-fiend behind Merlin's mistakes and vacillations, and the Lodges may report these evils to their brothers in France, yet these are only voices crying in the wilderness. The religious issue is dead. If the Mission was instrumental in keeping Protestantism out of Indo-China, it was the fact that its proselytizers were foreigners and not Presbyterians which carried its point with the government.

Social and Medical Service

Philanthropy is both the first and last work of colonization. It motivated the original penetration of the country by missionaries, and it was the ultimate form taken by that very colonization which was the consequence of missionary persecution. It is no wonder that the natives have a confused and distrustful reaction to an Occidental intervention which is, simultaneously and incomprehensibly, both altruistic and egotistic.

In the whole field of social and medical service, the Mission was a pioneer. It was the missionaries, and even more the nuns, who came originally to nurse the wounded of the army of occupation, and who remained to care for the natives, even after anti-clericalism had ousted them from the hospitals. In the Hanoi hospital an over-zealous doctor got rid of the nuns before he was in a position to replace them with lay nurses. Sœur Antoine was the shining example among the nuns who refused to be repatriated so as to care for her native sick. With a capital of eight piastres she founded a home for incurables. This flourished so mightily that it redounded more than ever to the credit of religious philanthropy. It even elicited a decoration from the very government which had so cavalierly dispensed with her services twenty years before. It was also Mgr. Puginier who introduced vaccine into the colony. But all this was essentially only a by-product of the Mission's main concern—the conversion and care of souls.

Time and means alike were lacking to carry out this work on an appropriate scale. Just as with Mission education, the government's method has been to subsidize, then place under regular inspection, and finally to supplant Mission's medical and social work. If the state had earlier been content to supplement Mission work by co-operation, the colony would surely have been the beneficiary. But a sterile jealousy of the Mission's influence over the natives led the state to force its rival virtually out of the field of philanthropy. Government subsidies were ever more grudgingly given; state supervision became ever stricter. The administration not the Church must get the credit and native gratitude—if any.

After the War the very same accusation of a jealous undermining of lay philanthropy was levelled at the Mission. The founders of the *Foyer des Etudiants* and the *Jardins d'Enfants* claimed that the Mission would permit no rival in such enterprises, other than the state which it must perforce tolerate. Mission opposition, as voiced in its press campaign, claimed that religious instruction was totally missing, or that Catholic prayers were said along with Buddhist invocations. The whole question unleashed severe attacks on the quality of the Mission's care of the sick. Statistics, revealing the heavy mortality in Mission hospitals, precipitated the campaign. Visiting doctors complained that the nuns would not carry out their orders. The government, when it had begun to encroach on Mission activity, had made the very same excuse—the high mortality in Mission hospitals and orphanages. It was claimed that once sick children were baptized and their salvation assured, the Mission took little care for their recovery. Or that the Mission told the parents that their children had died so as to avoid having to return them to a pagan upbringing. Criticism on both sides seems puerile and petty when it attacks the motives behind the rival's altruism. Much more serious criticism of the missionaries than their motives in caring for the sick was their lack of training. More zeal than knowledge, more kindliness than scientific discipline has undoubtedly characterized Mission institutions. But could not equally serious criticism be made of the state for its penury in endowing the colony with an adequate medical service?

Lyautey's dictum that a doctor is worth a battalion was illustrated amply in the Tonkin campaign where the troops fell victims to tropical diseases. With Mission aid, the military doctors founded a hospital, and from this it was only a short step to caring medically for natives. They, too, though not in the same way, were a prey to the climate. The excessive heat and humidity of certain regions, the penetrating cold of the Tonkin *crachin*, the fevers of the forest and marshland, undermined constitutions even long acclimatized.

When the government, in addition to Mission subsidies, began in a small way to organize the public services, it was done at local discretion and, as a consequence, it grew up in Topsy-like confusion. The great laicizer Beau, in 1903, first placed these embryonic departments under a Federal Director of Public Health, working through specialized local committees. Up to this time the doctors had been military: now a collateral civil group was formed to counteract the perpetual transfers to which army doctors were subject, and to form a group specialized in Indo-Chinese problems. As in all the services, getting good doctors from France and keeping them in the colony is an expensive business. Few French doctors are willing to expatriate themselves and their families for so paltry a salary, which is, nevertheless, a strain on the budget. That is why there are only two hundred European doctors in Indo-China for a population of over twenty millions. Moreover, the majority of these are attached to barracks, scientific institutions or hospitals, and the country districts are grossly neglected. In 1930 there were forty-five lay nurses and thirty-five nuns: the colony has benefited by the disorders in China, which have driven out a number of Nursing Orders.

The paucity of Europeans has, however, had the good effect of opening the medical career far more freely than other professions to ambitious natives. Moreover, the Annamites show a marked aptitude for this kind of work, which arouses in them none of the repugnance usually associated with anything involving manual labour. So it is only natural that the Hanoi School of Medicine should be both the best and oldest of the higher educational institutions. In 1930 it had graduated two hundred doctors and thirty-five pharmacists. During the War the Annamite doctors won much favourable notice. About four hundred midwives and fifteen hundred native nurses of both sexes serve the country districts, through travelling medical units. Asylums for the insane and for lepers are an innovation in Annam, which in former times alternated between neglect or cruel confinement as a way of dealing with these problems. Cochin-China has by far the best organization of medical and social service. This is due not only to its wealth but to the enterprise of one remarkable mayor of Cholon, Frédéric Drouhet. He built a model maternity building, *crèches*, hospitals with training schools, homes for the blind and aged, exclusively from voluntary contributions.

The colony's medical service is unique in meeting with wellnigh universal approbation. Humanitarians naturally approve, but in addition it is considered good policy to win native confidence, and—what is more important—to increase the population. The Annamite people are very prolific, but their susceptibility to disease neutralizes the very high birth-rate. Motives, ranging from philanthropic through imperialistic, to commercial and industrial, converge to support the work of the Medical Service, yet its scope could be greatly enlarged were it not for a lack of means. In the early unorganized days the situation was far worse. For example, there was the case of a Russian prince who was treated for liver trouble when he should have been operated on for gallstones. Eventually he died, despite the daily bulletins issued in the most optimistic vein. Criticism was rampant, and ranged from Saigon's defective water supply to the Medical Service's many projects and few accomplishments. Without trying to apportion the culpability properly, one may say that the hospitals for both Europeans and natives were inveterately dirty, and that the patients were promiscuously cared for. All the inmates left the hospitals almost exclusively for the cemetery. As elsewhere, this service was subject to bureaucracy. For years it had been generally agreed that a new hospital must be built at Hanoi: every year for five years there were sent to the Minister of the Colonies two official and contradictory reports regarding its site. The hospital finally succeeded in getting built, but, up to the very last, reports continued to be sent to Paris bewailing the injudicious location selected.

Of the colony's scientific institutions, the most important are the Pasteur Institutes. When Dr. Calmette was with the colonial troops he created at Saigon in 1890 the first bacteriological laboratory, where he experimented principally on animal pests. A branch of the Paris Pasteur Institute was founded at Nhatrang by Dr. Yersin, who likewise devoted himself to animal serums, along with experimental gardens for vegetables and plants. Yersin's life is a medical epic. As a pupil of Pasteur's he had long studied Oriental diseases, notably cattle pests and the bubonic plague. He chose Nhatrang for its isolation as a place in which to experiment without danger of contagion. He bought twenty horses and paid his first assistant solely in enthusiasm. His work was interrupted by a visit to Canton, where he was conspicuously successful in using a serum against the plague then raging there. It was Yersin who created the Hanoi Medical School. In 1905 the two Indo-Chinese laboratory units were linked to the Paris Institute, and they were very jealous of this independence maintained in spite of accepting state subsidies. They were so successful in combating malaria on Cochin-China's rubber plantations that the government selfishly protested when they went to work in regions which had no European enterprises that might profit by their efforts.

Scientific research in tropical diseases is quite as important for the natives as for the Europeans. Malaria indiscriminately attacks both, but the natives are more subject to cholera and the plague. Added to these, the Indo-Chinese are susceptible to leprosy, béribéri, trachoma, tuberculosis, smallpox, and venereal diseases. The regular under-nourishment of all the population is further aggravated by the famines which follow inundations. Both leave a naturally delicate frame an easy prey to epidemic. Despite its amazing fecundity, the Annamite population, before the French conquest, was declining slightly. When coolies were transported in droves to work on Southern plantations, the Annamites' physical weakness and susceptibility to disease was more clearly revealed than ever before.

Of the various epidemics smallpox still dominates all its rivals, despite the fact that more than five millions are vaccinated annually. Aviation has recently played a dramatic role in bringing vaccine to afflicted and hitherto inaccessible areas. The customs of the people make for contagion. About half of the rural population has had this disease, and for about half of these it was fatal. In trying to vaccinate the first efforts met with little success. The doctors had to combat popular distrust, which was increased by the warnings of bonzes and sorcerers. An edict of 1871 making vaccination obligatory remained a dead letter for lack of means to carry it out. To supplement their efforts, and to concentrate the few French doctors on more difficult tasks, vaccination was entrusted to certain native doctors who travelled from village to village. When it was revealed that they were charging high fees for what was officially gratuitous, the state tried to exercise an effective control, but there were not enough doctors. What was worse, native confidence had been greatly undermined. A new method was tried whereby the local administrator rounded up the children in his district for a bout of vaccination on certain days of every month. Rapidity and exactitude in keeping these appointments was essential, otherwise native zeal, never hot, was quickly chilled. The Mois proved the most intractable. They would literally take to the woods at the doctor's approach. The Khmers, with their traditional submission to authority, were the most docile. What vaccination has succeeded in doing is shown by the amazingly rapid growth of the population.

Europeans are less subject to cholera than the natives. In the Far East cholera is not a transient disease, but develops periodically and spreads rapidly, with a very high mortality rate. The great epidemic of 1927 counted twenty-five thousand victims. There was another particularly bad period from 1874 to 1877. Prisons were found to be excellent incubators, and the numerous canal population of Cochin-China were very efficient transmitters. Annamite villages are still pretty oblivious to hygiene, but the government is making more and more efforts to improve sanitary conditions. Training in hygienic measures is the most effective way of combating these epidemics.

Skin diseases and rheumatism come principally from working too many hours in the wet mud of the rice-fields. Béribéri, a disease caused by a poor diet, has been controlled by improving the method of husking rice. Leprosy is also more under control through the use of new methods: three thousand lepers are now cared for in thirteen asylums. But many such cases are never declared, since it means the enforced separation of families. More scattered, semi-normal leper villages would deal better with this socio-medical problem.

Improving sanitary conditions by an inspection of markets, ships, slaughter-houses, and drinking water in the towns has made more headway than in the rural districts. An insistence upon the immediate declaration of deaths helps trace the origin of disease swiftly. Free treatment of natives at clinics and migratory ambulance units encourage hygienic propaganda. In building emphasis has been laid on the importance of proper house sites. Marshy regions must be avoided, as well as river banks where the natives are prone to build, and the light and air in houses must be increased. The usual native home is small, airless, and filled with smoke to drive out the mosquitoes. The people are chronically under-nourished, and any calamity places them perilously near to starvation. The average rice diet is inadequate for men doing heavy labour, and the average Annamite consumes no more than a thousand calories a day. The mountain tribes are better off, since they raise corn and beans, and can get meat through hunting. What can be done to the dwarfed and emaciated Annamites by means of a scientific diet and hygienic practices has been shown in the army.

In Tonkin native clothing, too, is inadequate. The rain and cold find them almost unprotected, and it accounts for the frequency of lung trouble, especially among the children. All their clothes have the same weight, and when they are cold they simply add another identical garment—if they are fortunate enough to have more than one.

It is not to be expected that the Annamites would respond with immediate cordiality to the changes proposed by Occidental science.

There is, too, a certain irony in subsidizing services to improve native welfare by a government which simultaneously forces on them consumption of noxious articles like opium and alcohol, simply for their revenue-bearing qualities. Such inconsistency corroborates the distrust engendered by years of exploitation under the Hué government, and makes the natives more than ever suspicious and hostile to change. Annamites are especially distrustful as patients. They downright refuse to permit amputation, since it runs counter to their religious belief that the body must remain intact. They refuse to give their children the milk prescribed just because they have always held it in horror. The mountain tribes are even more superstitious and obstinate, especially about anything that threatens their independence. Those who allow themselves to be operated on leave the hospital the moment the stitches are taken out. There is a universal taking of flight when convalescence begins. But the famous ingratitude of Orientals is not axiomatic. Doctors in the colony testify to the touching if embarrassing gifts they received from those whom they have healed.

Annamites at best are never clean, but sickness shows up this trait in its most revolting form. To have his pulse taken, the patient clothed in be-vermined rags extends a grimy fist covered with layers of dust. Annamites have also a marked love for dramatizing themselves. Every illness is the scene of theatrical lamentation. Native doctors have the advantage over Europeans in knowing what superstitions they have to combat. A physician in Indo-China has to have more patience and perseverance than in Europe, and he is paid less well for his pains. Native assistants play ducks and drakes with laboratory experiments. Instruments and the animals which are being experimented upon suddenly disappear. Observation of experiments is notoriously inaccurate because their significance is not grasped. Also any course of action which demands the least exertion is adopted. Inertia is a redoubtable obstacle to medical work, for among the Annamites leprosy, for example, is now the equivalent of a social status, thus obviating the necessity for further exertion.

A European doctor must be ingenious in adapting his methods. One physician found that the only way he could treat the Khas for bronchitis was to paint a tiger in iodine on each expansive chest, with the explanation that it would eat the evil spirit that was causing the pain. The tiger was so universally admired and the cure so rapid that the doctor was thereafter compelled to design tigers indefinitely so as to retain his patients' confidence.

Education

Education is the most important single factor in colonization. For the colonizing country it may mean the moral conquest of the conquered, and a method of training them as collaborators. For the conquered, it is the means of understanding the civilization of their masters, and by it of eventually emancipating themselves. For both it may lead to mutual understanding or to ineradicable antipathy.

Under their own governments both the Indianized and Sinicized peoples gave to education a religious and moral significance that it has lost in the West. In Annam, moreover, it was linked to government office; it meant both a livelihood and a lifetime's prestige. Education to the Orientals meant emancipation from manual labour, as symbolized by their mandarins' long nails. This mental set-up has run counter to Western concepts at so many important points that a conflict of ideas was inevitable. Not only was it necessary to cope with heterogeneous native cultures, but the population's uneven distribution over the surface of the land added to the practical problems. There was, too, the major issue of varied and suitable curricula, in which three additional factors raised their disquieting heads—the language vehicle, the expense, and the paucity of teachers.

The language medium is still a moot question, though the most recent solution regards itself as definitive. Not only was it such a cardinal point in assimilationist doctrines that native education was long confounded with a knowledge of the French language, but there were practical difficulties in using the native languages to express with precision complex ideas or technical terms. The first step was to use *quoc ngu* in Cochin-China, where it became official for public documents. Missionaries in the seventeenth century had invented this transcription into Latin letters of the Annamite spoken language. *Quoc ngu* offered the enormous advantage of permitting a student to write Annamite in three months, whereas formerly the Chinese characters had required a lifetime's effort. *Quoc ngu* is, essentially, an instrument for mass literacy, and not for the expression of abstract ideas. Its inappropriate use has given rise to so much criticism that there has been a distinct reversion to favouring some more scholarly language, either Chinese or French, at least for secondary education. French cannot fail to triumph over Chinese in this duel. It is far easier to learn and has the political incentive of cutting the Annamites off from Chinese influence—both ancient and modern—and orientating their thought into Western channels.

THE CONTACTS OF CIVILIZATIONS

The early widespread use of *quoc ngu* had one important and totally unexpected consequence. The learning of Chinese characters in the traditional education meant a simultaneous absorption of Confucianist morality, and chief among its principles was respect for parental and governmental authority. By enforcing the use of *quoc ngu*, the French not only cut off the Chinese influence as they desired, but they undermined the natives' respect for their own authority. In place of a primarily moral education, they substituted a poor instrument, and almost no instruction. Recognizing their mistake, the French are gradually translating the Chinese classics into *quoc ngu*, but in the beginning they were non-existent, for the change had come too suddenly and too sweepingly.

Under the Admirals all the emphasis had been upon the Annamites' learning of French. In addition to abstract assimilationist theory, the practical need for training interpreters or government clerks made this imperative. The Admirals did not want to destroy Annamite culture—on the contrary. But there was no Scholar group left in Cochin-China, and they were, above all, absorbed by practical realities. Scholarships and premiums in a school founded in 1861 lured ambitious Annamites to study French so as to become interpreters, for those who were then serving in this capacity were former Mission pupils and spoke only poor Latin. The Admirals' encouragement of learning French was partly traceable to the current belief that the stagnation of Chinese culture had been due to its system of writing. They attempted to restore the traditional education, and did succeed in opening a few communal schools. Villages were asked to send pupils to these new primary schools. At first they did so, thinking it to be a new form of *corvée*, but when they grasped its purpose students came flocking. Missionaries and a few Annamites were the first teachers, but the result of their efforts was only a superficial knowledge of *quoc ngu*, in no way comparable to the traditional education which had died with the flight of the mandarins. A Normal School, founded in 1871, tried to remedy this defect. Schools for adults wishing to learn French were also created and placed under the Officer-Inspectors.

By the end of 1869 there were 126 primary schools, having 4,700 pupils out of a population of more than a million. The Mission schools continued their work in which, both in the elementary education and at the College of Adran, the three R's were mixed with the catechism and manual training. In 1874 private education was placed under government control.

The teachers were too few and too poorly prepared. The Normal

School had to be suppressed and replaced by the *Collège Chasseloup-Laubat*. The best of its graduates were to be sent to France, at the colony's expense. The French curriculum was used, and it proved to have little interest or value for the natives. There was no study of Chinese characters in either primary or secondary education, the French that was learned was archaic and barbaric—the language of Louis XIV was heard again—in the streets of Saigon. Contrary to their intentions, the Admirals had not solved the practical problem of training interpreters. They had unwittingly destroyed the traditional education and had replaced it with the dubious *quoc ngu*, and nothing more. The problem of mass education was totally untouched.

With the coming of the civil government, trailing clouds of assimilationist theories, there was pending in the air an important change in education. Le Myre was shocked by the poor material equipment. Buildings were small and unsanitary; textbooks non-existent or inappropriate. But as regards a clear-cut educational policy, Le Myre's contributions were not much more coherent than his predecessors. On paper schools were established in each village and canton, but by 1884 nothing had materialized, and the education that was offered was even in retrogression because no more teachers were being trained. The masses continued in their illiterate slumber. The few teachers who existed worked without supervision, left to their own poor, pedagogic devices. It was a sad record for a rich colony like Cochin-China, twenty-five years after the conquest, and for a people so zealous for education as the Annamites. Not content with an already inadequate teaching staff, anti-clericalism was undermining the Mission's hold on the colony's education. Cochin-China might possibly have found consolation, if she had only been aware of it, in her services as an experimental field for the other Annamite countries.

As was natural with a man of Bert's scientific training and pronounced anti-clerical views, he favoured lay education as the great medium of colonization. Bert's aim was to diffuse a working knowledge of French among the Tonkinese masses. In studying out his first educational programme, he was astonished to read in one of the textbooks then in use that:

the horse is the animal most useful to man; it draws wagons and bears burdens.
The cow gives him milk and sheep furnish him with wool.[1]

[1] Chailley, J., *Paul Bert au Tonkin* (Paris, 1887), p. 137.

This information was particularly useful in a country where no sheep exist, no cow gives milk to the natives, and horses do not draw wagons. In addition to the difficulties encountered in Cochin-China, through a penury of teachers and equipment, Bert had to deal with the hostility of parents who preferred Chinese education to his new schools. Unlike the South, traditional culture still flourished in Annam-Tonkin, but alongside of it had been placed French schools for training interpreters, and the Franco-Annamite schools which dispensed modern education in both French and Annamite. Bert was especially clever in winning over the natives to a modern curriculum, and in training teachers by salary and promotion inducements. Bert's death interrupted his plans for a Tonkinese Academy, where French and Annamite scholars would have had a chance for contact and co-operative study.

Doumer was too busy and too absorbed in the administration and economic life of the colony to alter the educational situation. Professional schools in the three Annamite capitals were his most important contribution. It was not until Beau's administration that the second phase of Indo-Chinese education began.

The Japanese victory of 1905 made the Annamites, heretofore hostile or indifferent, for the first time eager for Western education. Pham Boi Chau, the nationalist leader of the period, urged his compatriots to learn from the French, since Occidental learning had been the secret of Japan's success. In Cochin-China education due to governmental inertia or economy had been reduced to a mechanism for turning out interpreters and clerks; in the North, traditional education was firmly entrenched, and the French schools had made no real dent on the people. As it stood, the educational system was incapable of training enlightened collaborators, though the country was in increasing need of their services. It took the native demands for more and better education to break through the state's timidity and inertia.

Though Beau was obviously taking up Bert's ideas, his work was so original that he merits the title of innovator. His principal aim was to bridge the gap between the two parallel but independent systems of education. Scholars taught the traditional culture, without taking any cognizance of the modern world. Nor did the state try to exercise any control, and candidates continued to be prepared for the mandarinal examinations as of yore. The Franco-Annamite system paid almost equally scanty attention to the traditional culture. Both primary

and secondary curricula were almost identical with those of the Métropole. The language principally used was *quoc ngu* and a little French.
To cut the Gordian linguistic knot, Beau was willing to sacrifice *quoc
ngu* and to use Chinese as the vehicle of traditional education, with
French for the Franco-Annamite system. Not that he wanted them to
continue working in watertight compartments, but rather to fuse the
two systems, taking care to safeguard the position of Chinese characters
as indispensable to the Annamites' ethical training. He was not able
to effect this in Cochin-China, however, where assimilation was still
in the saddle.   But he did manage to add to the curriculum there
Western science which the natives were loudly demanding. The whole
system was unified under a Director of Public Education. In time this
proved to be over-centralized, so a local organization was set up for
each of the countries. The whole reform paralleled the administrative
trend towards decentralization. These changes were recommended by
the *Conseil de Perfectionnement de l'Enseignment Indigène*, made up of
French and native scholars under the chairmanship of members of the
EFEO.

In 1907 the second meeting of this committee took up the problem
of teachers and school equipment, in all other matters clinging to the
programme evolved in 1906. Teachers were the system's weakest spot.
Not only was their training imperfect, but they always had their minds
on a possible opening in the administration, and so never gave themselves wholly to teaching. The Scholars could see nothing but the
letter of their texts; respect for form had atrophied their thought and
made them uncompromising in their attitude towards everything
Occidental.   The native teachers in the Franco-Annamite schools
were poorly trained, and in the key positions there were the French
just out from the Métropole. There was no contact between them and
the Scholars.

Secondary education was the field where pedagogic flaws showed
up most flagrantly. Beau tried to remove some of the causes by raising
teachers' salaries, then away below their administrative colleagues', and
by giving private school teachers access to positions in the state schools.
To train instructors a section of pedagogy was formed at the new Hanoi
University, as well as a Normal School. New textbooks in three languages were prepared, and a better organization of examinations effected.
The work of the Committee has been vindicated by time, for its recommendations were very literally followed in the post-War period. Though
they met with enthusiastic approval by both natives and administration

alike at the time they were enunciated, yet the old handicaps of money and trained teachers prevented their becoming anything beyond a theory. Private efforts, both French and Annamite, continued to supplement the state's defective system.

The most ambitious educational move Beau made was the creation of the University at Hanoi. Japan had begun to attract Annamite students, who were also drawn to the University of Hong-Kong. Most Annamites found it far too expensive to send their children to study in France. Beau realized that if Indo-China did not provide higher educational facilities there would be an exodus of students who, by coming under foreign influences, might become a political danger for the colony. Attracting Chinese students to Hanoi would enhance the University's prestige in Annamite eyes. He in no wise wished a University in the Occidental sense of the word, only a medium for interpreting Western ideas to the Annamites. This project, improperly understood by colonials and natives alike, was received with unmixed hostility by the former, and with enthusiasm by the latter.

The colonials thought Beau's move to conciliate the native intelligentsia most ill-advised. They felt that the Annamites were seduced by the University's pretentious name, and that it was premature to teach them Western notions of political liberty. Beau replied that native education was no longer a purely academic question, and that the recent political events had forced it into the foreground. It would be better to permit the intelligentsia to evolve under the French aegis, with their traditional culture as the basis of education and as a break against an over-rapid transformation. The native uprisings of 1908 were interpreted by both sides as proof of their contentions. They were blamed on a variety of causes, ranging from the Russo-Japanese War to fiscal pressure, but some critics went below the surface to find that the educational system, notably in Cochin-China, was fundamentally culpable. What, after all, was the aim of education in a colony?

If it were granted that the aim of education was to understand and to be understood, little encouragement could be derived from the current results in Indo-China. On this basis, would it not be easier for a thousand Frenchmen to learn Annamite than for 23,000,000 natives to learn French? Even where the traditional education still existed, it did little to promote mutual understanding or even solve practical problems. The French had been pre-eminently utilitarian in reducing education to the training of minor government officials, but in efficient results these functionaries had been anything but fortunate.

The intelligentsia, who wanted a more general culture expected, in addition, to be entitled to high administrative office, just because diplomas in old Annam had been the guarantee of such positions. Literally in spite of themselves the Annamites were breaking loose from their old moorings and losing their attachment for a Chinese culture which gave them no solution for the world they lived in, but rather turned its back on all disquieting change. The government began to be accused of a parsimony in creating educational facilities by that very group which had, until only recently, held scornfully aloof.

Though the training of teachers and the compiling of textbooks needed more time, the change in native attitude was more immediately reflected in the much larger place education was being given in the federal budget. It was unfortunate that just at the time when Annamites were showing initiative in acquiring Western culture the enthusiasm of France to dispense such an education was being dampened by the political agitation of 1908. The ensuing retirement of Western pedagogy within its academic shell was symbolized by the shutting down of the Hanoi University, to the vast deception of the Annamite students. Many still believed, however, that the cure for the unrest lay not in more stringent laws, but in better education. In the orders given to Klobukowsky, France stressed the need for more primary and professional instruction, and pointed definitely away from secondary education on the ground that the Annamites were not yet prepared for it.

In 1910 the Committee on Native Education held its third session. Tension had by then sufficiently abated to take up the problem again dispassionately. There was, however, a marked shying off from higher education, and a concentration upon primary and professional training, and also on education for women. Even the traditional culture was not proof against censure. The mandarinal examinations revealed the horrid fact that many Annamites had been reading Chinese revolutionary tracts, so the study of elementary Chinese characters was henceforth to be confined to ethical works.

The Committee also pointed out two danger signals on the horizon: the bad feeling between the administration and the educational authorities, and the continued inadequacy of the teaching staff. This latter reproach applied as much to the teaching of French children as to native instruction. When children returned to France, they shocked professors there by their elementary mistakes in grammar. Moreover, Indo-China needed teachers of its own, and not those who came fresh from inexperience in France. A struggle was being carried on between the graduates of the Jules Ferry School in Paris and those of the St. Cloud Normal School for the best teaching positions in the colony. Instead of devoting themselves to internal wrangling for the key positions, the whole staff could have better occupied itself with evolving new methods and programmes adapted to the colony's needs. A movement was even set on foot in Paris against these sterile struggles. Aulard in 1912 resigned from the Presidency of the *Mission Laique* because the St. Cloud School had kept a ten-year monopoly of Indo-Chinese pedagogy.

Sarraut, in an effort to win over the native intelligentsia, opened more secondary schools to them, and in so doing he furthered Beau's project of fusing the two educational systems more completely. In Cambodia and Laos, he continued to work through the bonzes and pagoda schools, trying to modernize their methods and programmes. But he discouraged sending Annamites to study in France. He also tried vainly to instil in all classes of natives the realization that a diploma was not the equivalent of a position in the administration, and he further endeavoured to turn their activities into other channels. Sarraut was no innovator in the educational field. He followed prudently in Beau's footsteps, but he also represented the reaction in his emphasis on utilitarian forms of education. Although he tried to win back the alienated intelligentsia and to promote greater understanding between the two peoples, his conciliatory policy did not at the time go so far as to favour higher education for the Annamites.

Sarraut accomplished very little from the educational viewpoint, and even his mild moves to open more *lycées* to native students provoked new criticism. The Annamites complained that they paid all the taxes, and that the openings for them were only such places as were left open when all the French students had been taken in. They further criticized the inferior food and lodging given them. It was indeed a curious fact that where Sarraut in his administrative, economic, and judicial programmes was markedly liberal, he showed himself timid and ineffectual in the educational field.

In 1915 competitive examinations for the mandarinate were abolished, and this was the death-sentence for traditional culture. Henceforth Confucianism was bankrupt in Indo-China; the study of the Chinese classics became a private enterprise and an exercise in scholastic rhetoric, unrelated to obtaining government office. There was only a partial resurrection when Varenne reconstituted the communal schools. The decline of traditional culture—its slow decadence in Tonkin was unlike its brutal suppression in Cochin-China—meant the triumph of Franco-Annamite education, and of French as the language medium. It also meant new life for assimilationist theories in education, just when they were dying in the administration. It meant relegating the traditional culture to the role of a museum piece, and it meant destroying the foundation and cement of Annamite society.

Sarraut's most important contribution lay in the field of organization. He compiled the *Code de l'Instruction Publique* out of a vast morass of edicts and circulars. This charter of Indo-Chinese education was too hastily drawn up, and it showed almost immediately disquieting omissions. Its almost sole pedagogic principle was that French should be the vehicle of instruction, even for primary classes. This was part of the super-unification trend, which placed the whole system under a Higher Education Service. The practical difficulty of finding instructors to teach a foreign language to a predominantly rural people who, furthermore, would have little use for it, made for a very loose application of this ruling. This was thought, however, to be a purely temporary necessity, and the language principle firmly established. The absence of further pedagogic concepts was a serious handicap. The teaching staff, especially after the War, was increasingly imbued with French ideas and methods, and no effort was made to find new programmes adapted to the colony. The movement towards specializing administrative and judicial functionaries was not echoed in the educational field. Assimilation reigned there supreme, and the wise recommendations of Beau's Committees were forgotten.

The War forced many of these discrepancies into the foreground which might otherwise have taken years to be revealed. Sarraut returned for his second term, full of a desire to reward native aid to the mother country by better educational facilities. He reversed his former cautious policy *vis-à-vis* the intelligentsia, and re-opened the Hanoi University. The Schools of Medicine and Pharmacy had survived the previous holocaust, and now he created five new faculties of administration and law, forestry and agriculture, veterinary training, and public works. The 52 per cent increase registered from 1917 to 1921, in the total number of students was a tribute to Sarraut's activity, but even then they only numbered 150,000. The budget allotment had also risen from 2,000,000 to 4,000,000 piastres, yet the schools were still too few for native demands. On the whole Sarraut's work was undone by time and his collaborators. The teaching staff which he had tried to improve took the bit into its teeth and won for itself and its

Metropolitan methods autonomy from administrative control. The natives continued to think that diplomas entitled them to government office—a concept to which new life was given when Long opened *cadres latéraux* in the administration to French-educated natives.

The decade of the 1920's saw a radical change in educational policy. Part of Merlin's reactionary native policy—part of the general pulling in of liberal horns after the War—was what he termed horizontal education. This primarily expressed his rather negative dread of higher education for the native intelligentsia. In spite of his expressed desire to educate the masses, only 200,000 children out of 2,000,000 of potential school age received any instruction under his aegis. This meant literacy for only one boy out of twelve, or for one girl in a hundred. The Canton bomb designed for Merlin's demolition had the unexpected consequence of precipitating a change in his educational policy. Certain acute minds had begun to link the social and political unrest to the uprooting of the Annamite from his traditional culture effected by the Franco-Annamite schools. The student strikes of the next few years gave body to this reproach. Not only were the Annamite students guilty of indiscipline in the classroom, but also in the home. Parents imbued with Confucianist respect for authority were horrified at the impertinence and rebellion of their children trained under the new system. These students were in the unstable, transitional stage, unhappily suspended between two cultures to neither of which they definitely belonged.

When the Rector of a French University took over the direction of Indo-Chinese education in 1921 the break with traditional culture was complete. Programme and methods alike were wholly French and unsuited to an Oriental mentality. No matter how distinguished their academic record in France, teachers who knew nothing of the Annamites or of their civilization were not qualified to instruct them. In 1924, to remedy this pedagogic inadequacy, two Normal Schools for each country of the Union were prescribed. Aside from the psychological evils in the transplanted French system, their effect on the budget was equally lamentable. Importing almost all teachers from France was expensive and wasteful. Moreover, Paris got rid of its elderly instructors, nearing the age of retirement, on the colony. Another evidence of pointless waste was the creation of a School of Pedagogy, whose diploma was a snare and a delusion, for it was not the equivalent of the Métropole's. It had been created for the benefit of the new teachers, who could thereby earn additional income. Rank favouritism also presided over the nomination of the staff of the School of Decorative

Arts. An arbitrary selection of high-salaried teachers was not made on the basis of their diplomas. Students, too, could be coerced into taking extra courses, with additional tuition as a refined kind of blackmail practised by the teachers who controlled the distribution of degrees.

Although the earning capacities of these diplomas was being slowly improved by the admission of more educated natives to government office, their cultural and practical value was nil. For one thing, there was a lack of modern textbooks. Like much of Beau's work, his efforts to revise manuals had been still-born, and the beginning he had made was swept away in the rising tide of Metropolitan methods which had been transplanted to the colony. In elementary education the majority of Annamites could only afford, by the greatest sacrifice, to keep their children in school for three years. It availed them little to spend this precious time in learning, in garbled French, the names of a few objects which they straightway forgot. Obviously elementary education should use the native language as its instrument. The whole programme from top to bottom needed overhauling, and a general taking of stock.

Fundamentally there had to be a recognition that the Annamite's mental set-up is different from a European's. If the Annamite was to be brought up in total ignorance of his own language and literature, if he were to have substituted for the strong traditional moral discipline an analysis of the emotions, it could only be expected that he would grow up unstable and unbalanced. The traditional emphasis has always been upon a maximum of memorizing and a minimum of original thought, so it is no wonder that the reverse proved unnerving. An Annamite's cultural roots must be in his own country, hence elementary education had to swing back towards Chinese teachings. A mature student might safely be exposed to Western ideas if he were first orientated in his own civilization. Over-centralization and over-uniformity in a country of such diverse peoples was officially recognized to be an error. The Annamite had been educated too much to suit French needs, and not enough for his own development—although it must be admitted that since 1905 this policy had been aided and abetted by the natives themselves. On both sides there had been a deliberate burning of Annamite cultural bridges. If social and political discipline had suffered, and incidentally Occidental prestige, it had admittedly been caused by faulty education. Annamite youth was excitable enough without the additional inflammatory reading of French classical dramas and the history of the 1789 Revolution.

The trend towards developing mass rather than higher education was so strong that even Varenne—who favoured a liberal native policy—was swept along in the current. His educational programme was, in general, the fulfilment of changes inaugurated by his predecessors, but his own contribution was the revival of communal schools. He found that Annamite villages were willing to share the expense of buildings and instructors if they were aided by subsidies. This village co-operation with its restoration of communal prerogatives was excellent both psychologically and financially, and it made mass education for the first time feasible. The curricula were adapted to the particular group and language, and it was no longer the usual flight of theoretical fancy on the part of a distant Metropolitan mind.

Solving the problem of higher education was much more complicated. At the outset had come a series of student strikes, the first school strike had occurred at Hué in 1909, and at the time there had been no convenient Bolshevism on which to lay the blame. Probably only a small percentage of teachers had unleashed the hostility of their students, but it was enough to arouse the colonials' fears and to relate the problem of secondary education to the current political fermentation. Always in Annam discontent has been evidenced by collective rather than individual protests.

The treatment of the strikers in 1926–27 was anything but tactful. On the anniversary of Phan Chau Trinh's death, the students appeared in crape bands. Instead of ignoring it their professors took it as a symbol of revolt. The head of Hanoi's primary education violently tore off one of these bands and stamped on it. Strikes broke out everywhere in the colony, but the most important were in Cochin-China.

The Annamites complained that the *lycées*, in practice if not in principle, were closed to them; that French students had a disproportionate number of places; that their programmes were made for them and not for the Annamites. At the Sarraut *lycée* in 1927 there were only 341 Annamites out of 731 pupils. The Chasseloup-Laubat College had only 180 Annamites and Cambodians. They further demanded that the diplomas delivered in Indo-Chinese schools should be the equivalent of those in France, where students found that the colony's baccalaureate was not recognized. This perforce added several more years of study, and by the time they were prepared they often found themselves beyond the age limit for competitive examinations. The financial drain on their families' resources, already almost prohibitive, was thereby greatly increased. An end should be put to the hollow mockery of the Hanoi University: the façade was imposing but its classrooms were empty. The standards were low by comparison with French Universities, but even so appallingly few graduates were turned out. In 1925 there were only twenty-five Bachelors of Arts; and in 1926 only nine. Moreover, the quality of these chosen few was very mediocre. The lack of money and trained teachers was always cited to excuse these defects, but a little more activity on the part of the officials, and some of the money spent on unnecessarily elaborate buildings, might have wrought the needed change.

Varenne concentrated on improving the quality and preparation of Indo-Chinese teachers. He wanted a Normal School for every province, but his actual achievements fell well below that mark. He raised teachers' salaries, trying to attract better men from France, and yet not let them transplant, as they had been doing, the whole French system. Indo-China needed specialized teachers, just as it needed special programmes. Indo-Chinese diplomas must be made the equivalent of French Universities'. This could be done by raising the standards, which in turn depended on the quality of the teaching staff and the supervision of a corps of Inspectors. More place on the curricula was to be given to ethics and Chinese characters. In 1928 a new *lycée* was opened at Saigon, which immediately took care of six hundred students. Far Eastern humanities could more appropriately replace Latin and Greek. Efforts were being made to turn the intelligentsia to professional and technical employment, and away from the idealization of government employ as the sole occupation worthy of a cultured man.

The impetus given to this programme lasted through the régime of Varenne's successor. Even the heart-searchings that succeeded the Yenbay uprising did not fundamentally alter the principles of education, as it had been worked out in the late 1920's. The evils which were criticized then had not yet had sufficient time to be eradicated—the miscarriage of the education received in France, and the undigested and inappropriate curriculum offered in Indo-China. The revelation that the Communist movement was one of leaders, and not of the masses, led to a new stocktaking of higher education.

In 1930 the Indo-Chinese baccalaureate was made the equivalent of the French, and in the same year the teaching mandarins were specialized as a branch of the administration. Programmes were revised and adapted to the different peoples in the colony; the revival of Beau's Committees aimed to bridge the gap between administration and education authorities: mass education in village schools would keep children more under the authority of home and Confucius—in short, there was an attempt to put into practice the realization that administrators, pedagogues, and natives alike had the same fundamental interests.

A corollary to the whole educational problem lay in the dubious future in store for graduates of the colony's higher schools. Three hundred law school graduates annually for a country of 23,000,000 was a menace to the social equilibrium. The Beaux Arts School, an admirable attempt to rescue native art from its decadence, could offer its graduates nothing beyond the felicitous title of Drawing Professors. The Hanoi University, no more than a nursery for functionaries, had medical graduates who were not entitled to the rank of doctor, but were euphoniously known as Hygiene Officers. No two successive Governors could reconcile themselves to making a reality out of this so-called University. Merlin, for example, nullified the impetus given to it by Sarraut. Only his signature was needed, when he disembarked in Indo-China, to make Hanoi's diplomas the equivalent of the French, but Merlin suppressed the law school. He replaced it with an *école des hautes études*, which dispensed a very limited legal training along with Sino-Annamite humanities, to which students had already been exposed in secondary schools. Very few graduates could be taken into the administration, and the disgruntled majority who failed to be employed threw themselves into pugnacious politics—and this was especially true of those who had returned from study in France.

Very few Annamites had the means to supplement their meagre learning by a sojourn in France. Moreover, other obstacles, especially since 1924, have been increasingly put in their way. Not that the government gives an outright refusal, but it makes every step discouraging and difficult. In the early days it was principally royalty who went to France for study. So little was made of some of these princes that few others were inspired to do likewise. One uncle of the Annamite Emperor was sent to France in 1907, and after a few months shipped back again without even being allowed to see Paris.

Recent efforts, however, have been made—witness the attentions showered on Khai Dinh—to win Annamite students' devotion. It was part of Doumer's and Beau's programme to send promising young natives to France so as to make them radiate French culture upon their return. The Kydong fiasco was one of the first disillusionments. Beau was not discouraged, however, and widened the scope of his experiment by placing it on an academic merit basis. In the colony the *Alliance Française* and the *Société d'Enseignement Mutuel* co-operated with the *Comité Paul Bert*, in Paris, in the selection and care of students. But it has been the political activities of Annamite students, both in France and in the colony, that has made the colony so chary about sending more to France, and much more ready to improve the local educational facilities.

In 1930 various incidents which occurred in the Latin Quarter alarmed conservatives. Blood was shed at a café meeting of Annamites and French, discussing a proposed Annamite branch of the *Jeunesses Patriotes*. As a protest against the suppression of the Yenbay uprisings, and also against the monopolist-donor, Fontaine (at the dedication of the *Maison de l'Indochine* at the *Cité Universitaire* to which he had given 50,000 out of a total cost of 7,500,000 francs), tracts were thrown into the auditorium, and the Annamite who had risen gracefully to acknowledge the gift was called a yellow dog in the full richness of the Annamite tongue. The house was subsequently boycotted as a protest by almost all of the three hundred Annamite students then in Paris. An association of these students, formerly subsidized by the government, was now hastily dissolved. The remnants, however, formed themselves into two camps, paralleling the communist-nationalist split in Indo-China itself.

Alarmists regard Paris as the hotbed of radicalism which encourages the Annamites to turn and rend the country which has educated them. Others claim that it is only the non-serious students who occupy themselves with politics—*ceux qui font leurs études à la brasserie*, who waste their parents' money and who are stranded because they do not dare to return to the colony without those diplomas which they have been supposedly acquiring. There can certainly be no reflection made upon the quality of Annamite brains: it was an Annamite who recently won the highest honours in Latin and Greek at the *Ecole Normale Supérieure*. Others have distinguished themselves at the famous *Lycée Louis le Grand* and the *Ecole Polytechnique*. Indo-China has two *agrégés*: Pham Duy Khiem, former pupil of the *Ecole Normale Supérieure* (1934), and Hoang Xuan Han, formerly a student of the *Ecole Polytechnique* (1930). The colony can also boast a *chef de clinique* in the Paris Hospitals, Pham Huu Chu; two *docteurs ès lettres*, Nguyen Manh Tuong and Nguyen Van Huyen; two *docteurs ès sciences*, Mlle Hoang Thi Nga and Doan Khac Thinh. Those who succeed have given proof not only of superior intellectual ability, but of exceptional perseverance as well.

The necessity for learning *quoc ngu*, Chinese characters, and French has delayed the Annamite student in the colony so that he is about three years older than his French classmates. Because there are fewer openings in the colonial *lycées*, the competition among Annamite students is keener and the examination, in consequence, harder. Then the government may refuse to grant him a passport, if there is any reason to doubt his loyalty. Once in France he finds that—until 1930— his colonial baccalaureate is not accepted by the Universities there. The courses he must make up, in addition to his regular studies, keep him from arriving at the doctorate until he is almost thirty-five. Until recently little was done for the Annamite student in Paris. His health and moral code were both undermined by the brusque transplantation.

It seems unfortunate that the present trend, accentuated by the depression, is strongly against encouraging Annamites to go to France. They may absorb the superficial side of French life, they may waste their time and substance in riotous living or become blood-curdling revolutionaries—but they got a view of the world and an egalitarian treatment by the French of France which they never receive in the colony. Despite the number of scholarships granted, independent means are required to enjoy this privilege, and the result nowadays has been not a democracy of education, as in old Annam, but a practical limitation of the educated class to the plutocracy. It seems unfortunate that the French have preferred the alternative of improving the educational system in Indo-China, so as to obviate the necessity for completing training in France, to a more careful selection of those able to profit by Metropolitan culture. It may be safer, but the results are nothing like so rewarding.

The trials of the Annamite student are not over when he receives his hard-won diploma. He is treated with suspicion upon his return to the colony by the authorities and by his family alike. They fear him as a potential revolutionary or dislike him as a conceited prig— and both assumptions are often substantiated. But the searching of his baggage for seditious literature, and the general treatment he receives, as well as the difficulty he has in finding a suitable position, are enough to turn the mildest intellectual into a raging Communist.

Officials claim that the intelligentsia's complaints are unjustified. Robin's investigation of the unemployed University graduates—which may be official blarney—revealed only twenty-six without positions. There are many more who are less highly qualified but no more content with their lot. These men feel that they have spent much time and money for an education that has given no practical results. This is only natural in view of the traditional link between diplomas and the Annamite civil service, but it is not so simple as it appears. Many whose brilliant promise is revealed by their diplomas dissipate their energies in a thousand wild schemes that never come to fruition. Almost as many diplomas were acquired for reasons of social or intellectual snobbery—a good position or a brilliant marriage—and they do not represent a cultured mind or zeal for further knowledge. Often their studies are not related to their future utility to the colony or to the openings available. If the more practical and less tradition-ridden Cochin-Chinese have shown more interest in scientific studies, the Tonkinese still cling to literature and law.

ORGANIZATION

The organization of present-day Indo-Chinese education has been the result of many false steps and hesitations. It is too soon to pronounce it definitive, yet the hard school of experience in which it has evolved leads one to conclude that the framework has at last been made durable. The whole system is placed under a Director, the ex-Rector of a French University, who lays down the basic pedagogic principles, but who leaves the administration to his subordinates.

Primary education has finally had the courage to diverge radically from the French model; now in only higher education do the two systems resemble each other. Its basis is the three R's, taught in the native language, along with moral precepts, rules of hygiene, and an introduction to the history and geography of Indo-China, its agriculture, and history, with an optional course in the French language for pupils desiring to pursue their studies further. This course is limited to three years, for the very practical reason that the vast majority of children cannot give more time than that to education. At the close of the first year half of the children withdraw: half of the remainder do likewise at the end of the second year, so that if the time limit were extended there would be virtually no pupils. The teachers must have a certificate from the local normal schools and have served one year's probation, with frequent attendance at vacation schools to keep them up to standard.

Elasticity in primary education is best shown in the variations made for primitive peoples. The courses' duration is lengthened and the curriculum lightened: more place is given to manual labour. Because of the impossible variety in language, French has had to be used there as the vehicle of instruction, but even here room has been left for each milieu to fuse its own, as best it can, with Western education. Varenne's happy solution of having communal schools has gone far to solve the rural education problem. In Cochin-China elementary education was, ironically enough for the education-minded Annamites, made obligatory in 1927. This was a government pledge rather than an actuality. Yet in 1931 out of the 1,419 communes, there were only 115 without schools, representing a population of 100,000 without instruction.[1]

The Franco-native system is divided into primary, higher-primary, and secondary education. The name erroneously suggests the nationality of the pupils, when it only refers to the blend of two programmes of study. It is traditional in the sense that it teaches Far Eastern humanities, and French is the language of instruction. The primary stage occupies three years. It gives a more complete training in French and continues the elementary courses. Chinese characters are compulsory for the Annamite students, just as Pali is required of the Khmers and Laotians. Teachers are still natives, but fortified with a higher diploma. French superintendents exist in the urban centres, and French Inspectors make a regular tour of rural schools. A final competitive system rigorously eliminates about nine-tenths of those who enter this cycle, and there is yet another test before these survivors can move on to the next stage of higher-elementary studies. Strict examinations and a severe weeding out process have made the standard of the certificate for these studies so high that it has been given preference on the teaching staff over its Metropolitan equivalent. About half of the students in the ultimate stage are boarders, and about one-third of these receive state scholarships.

The excellence of Indo-Chinese secondary education received an eloquent testimonial when its diploma was made officially equal to its French colleague, and opened the door of French higher education without reservations. Native *lycées* exist at Hanoi and Saigon, and much more recently in Pnom-Penh and Hué; their teaching staff is made up of French Masters of Art or *agrégés*. The Annamites may choose between preparing for the local or the Metropolitan baccalaureate—the difference lying only in the choice of programme and not in standard. The French baccalaureate is prepared in three colonial *lycées*—Hanoi, Saigon, and Dalat. Of these Dalat is the only *lycée* exclusively for Europeans. Natives are still admitted only in proportion as vacancies

[1] Crouzet Report, 1931.

occur after the French pupils have matriculated, but the improvement in their standards has removed most of the bitterness and pressure there. In these *lycées* there are special courses for the foreign group, as represented by Japanese, Siamese, and Chinese, although there is a general desire to draw them all into the French higher education.

In the field of higher education all distinction between the two systems disappear. The School of Medicine and Pharmacy is incontestably the most important. Until recently its graduates had to go to France for their final examination, but now Indo-China, with Algeria, shares the distinction of being the only colony whose medical degree equals that of France. The only reserve is that medical practice must be confined to the colony: this is no reflection upon the standard of its diplomas, but an effort to have the colony profit by the education it has dispensed. The law school at Hanoi had its most recent incarnation in 1931. Law had previously been combined with literary studies. Raising that school's standards, as well as admission to the Bar, has given new stimulus to this ever-popular study. Abortive attempts were made in 1923–24 to create a Faculty of Liberal Arts, a School for Higher Indo-Chinese Studies, a Higher School for Pedagogy, etc. There were also beginnings of a School of Public Works and a Faculty of Science. The only two Faculties of the Hanoi University having a high standard and unquestioned durability and utility are those of Medicine and Law. In 1935 Robin eliminated all but those two schools.

The education of Annamite women is the most original contribution made by the French in the whole field. A native woman's status had already been expanded in practice beyond its narrow legal limits, as a wife and even more as a mother. But her education was nil except in aristocratic families where she was taught music, poetry, and the rules of chess. Beau's Committees in 1907 formally took up the problem for the first time. Annamite women needed above all practical training. They were among the worst housekeepers in the world, and infant mortality was enormous. Only later did the practical merge into theoretical education. The result has been a marvellously rapid and often premature emancipation. It is amusing to note that it is the most Occidentalized Annamite men who are the worst enemies of the education of their female compatriots.[1] The conservative tradition is too strong and, although the principle of women's freedom is accepted along with other Western ideas, when carried into practice there is

---

[1] Cf. Nguyen Thi Chinh's answer to a book by Tran Thieu Tu and Bui The Phuc, *Critique de la question féminine en pays d'Annam* (Saigon, 1932).

still a deep-dyed suspicion. Certainly a large part of Communism's popularity is due to the role it assigns to women. In Indo-China the feminist problem exists in embryo, but as yet the proportion of women who have had higher education is so small that the issue is almost wholly academic.

Professional and technical education has had an uphill struggle, in spite of state encouragement and the striking economic development of the colony. Manual labour introduced into the curriculum of elementary schools was the first attempt made to destroy the age-old Oriental prejudice. This amounted only to a training in viewpoint: a real apprenticeship is offered in institutions like the Professional School at Hué for both industry and commerce. This type school has been extended to the other countries and technical courses added to the regular school programmes. The Cambodian School of Arts is the most advanced of these vocational institutions. There are also more industrial courses: Saigon has a school to train Asiatic mechanicians. Both private industry and state aid combine to promote such training. That there is an increased interest in this phase of education is shown by the presence of four times as many students in these schools as twenty years ago. Yet, in 1931, their number only totalled two thousand —a very small percentage of the population.

French art instruction has had the worthy aim of saving Annamite art from itself. The very existence of this native art is problematical: it may be only a saddened and simplified version of its Chinese masters. The ornamentation is notably poor and the colours drab. Uncertainty and fear of the morrow is reflected in Annamite art, which was already suffering decadence before the French conquest. The first French effort was negative—to conserve what was left of the art of old Annam. This was done officially by the EFEO, and privately by groups like the *Société Franco-Annamite* and the *Amis du Vieux Hué*. On the positive side there was an early recognition of the dangers of European influences, notably in Mission teaching, dominating and extinguishing native art. Only two new art industries have been introduced by the French—that of lace-making and rug-making, both based on European models, for the export trade.

The first difficulty in restoring native arts has been to find appropriate teachers. Annamites have always suffered from a disdain of manual labour, and the artist in particular has had a low social and economic status. Evening courses at the *Société Artistique* and, on a bigger scale, the Beaux Arts School, aimed to train native teachers as a better medium than Europeans for effecting a renaissance of Annamite art. It was thought that the spirit of Oriental art could be retained and, at the same time, the European ideal of the observation of nature. Museums and Expositions have been very helpful not only in introducing those ideas, but in revealing the stages of their development. The 1910 Exposition showed the addition of perspective, movement, and chiaroscuro: that of 1902 revolutionized the embroidery industry of Hanoi. There was at the beginning a strong native reaction against idealization of the human figure, especially the female form, for Annamite art follows the Chinese in being dominated by the scenic aspects of nature.

The Hanoi Exposition of 1902 was a synthesis of such mutual misunderstandings. On the French jury which selected the pictures for exportation there was not one man who had ever lived in the Far East, and who might have gauged the horrified reaction of the Indo-Chinese to the goodly scattering of nudes. No attempt was made to understand what might interest an Oriental clientele or answer its needs. The Emperor of Annam was seen standing fascinated before a window display of dress shields. When the Annamites voted for their favourite picture they unanimously selected Rousseau's *Le Bœuf*. This familiar and bucolic subject was so realistically portrayed that they at once felt at home. Slavish copying of copies, or photographic reproductions, are the principal stumbling-blocks to Annamite progress in art. There is no point in having released the Annamite soul from servility to Chinese masters if it is only to fall into subjection to Western models. Unfortunately such subservience is only too congenial to the Annamite soul, and the problem of finding a market, which is always easier for stereotyped production, has encouraged their natural imitative bent.

The Annamite bourgeoisie, in adopting Western ways of living, has been prone to exhibit bad European taste. This clientele encourages cheap imitation of poorly selected Western objects. Catholicism, curiously enough, has had a notably cramping effect on developing native art traditions. Not only do they teach art from exclusively Western models, but conversions mean that fewer pagodas are built. All the art objects contained in pagodas, like wood sculpture, suffer in consequence. Fortunately new foreign as well as internal markets have been opened, only here there is competition with superior products from China and Japan. If the artisan's social and economic status has been improved, the rise in his salary and in the expense of materials has also increased the cost price. All the profit has thus been taken out of mother-of-pearl incrustation, formerly one of the finest Tonkinese products. The whole problem of art training is linked to the question of markets. The government cannot indefinitely subsidize the artists it has encouraged and trained to revive their country's arts, no matter how worthy such an aim may be in principle.

PRIVATE EDUCATION

Mission schools are by far the most important form of private education, but only since the War have they branched out into secondary education. The numerous seminaries for training the native clergy give neither vocational nor secondary education. A sprinkling of Malay, Burmese, and Chinese schools, notably the Franco-Chinese *lycée* at Cholon, with the group of Annamite vernacular schools complete the private school system. In 1924 all such institutions were placed under government supervision, which claims to confine itself to hygienic regulations and diploma requirements for teachers. In the Chinese schools there is an additional supervision designed to detect anti-French propaganda, though this is practically impossible in view of the linguistic difficulties. In 1930 there were enrolled in private native schools 45,211 pupils, and about 34,000 of these were in religious establishments. Chinese schools had 12,821 students. The total number of children receiving instruction in private schools was 60,151.

Anti-clericalism in the colony culminated in the increasing laicization of the school system under Beau, but in the Métropole feeling was far more rabid. In 1902 an association called the *Mission Laique* was founded to propagate lay education in the colonies. It sponsored the remarkable Jules Ferry Normal School whose restoration is being advocated nowadays. This school ran counter to the assimilationist current, for it gave special courses devoted to each individual colony. The War and rise of Communism finally conjured the spectre of the Machiavellian Mission; it was obviously futile to cultivate antagonism when there was room and need for all in the colony—and recognition of these factors led to a new co-operation in the educational field between Church and State.

So much agitation has been attendant upon these changes in educational theory and organization, that the fact that many Indo-Chinese receive no instruction at all has been forgotten. When Robin, in an official discourse in 1934–35, claimed that there were 397,723 students in the colony, he announced it as an 8 per cent increase over preceding years, and as caused by the spread of communal education. The number of Indo-Chinese children of school age would usually be arrived at by dividing, according to the European method, the total population—approximately 21,000,000—by seven. Half of the three millions thus estimated are boys, so that at even the most optimistic calculation less than a third of them receive an elementary education. In 1931 there were 40,000 girls receiving some degree of instruction—an even sadder statistic. Yet the budget shows an ever more honourable place allotted to education. In 1904 the percentage was 4·4 per cent, and in 1935 7·94 per cent was devoted to public instruction. This does not take into consideration the extraordinary total increase in budget expenditures.

Appropriate teachers and textbooks are still two perennial difficulties which are not yet solved. In creating a fifteen-volume series of textbooks (1924) in Annamite, Cambodian, and Laotian, the colony's educational service scored one of its greatest triumphs. The number of them sold—800,000 copies—testifies to their enormous success. A very low price makes them available to everyone, and their influence is far more widespread than that of the schools: twice as many copies have been sold as there are students in the colony. They aim to give the elements of Western culture accompanied by maps and charts in an easily comprehensible form. Sylvain Lévi compared the moral and intellectual revolution effected by these manuals to what the introduction of the daily paper accomplished for rural France:

One may say that Indo-Chinese students to-day have at their disposal a school equipment as complete and in some ways superior to that of French students, and at an unprecedentedly low price—50 centimes—and they are even given to those who cannot afford to pay for them.[1]

A series of textbooks for higher education is now being worked out.

When teachers in Indo-China are being criticized for their shortcomings it should be remembered that a totally new set of instructors for more than 300,000 children have had to be formed in a comparatively short time. Normal School courses have been increased, and a stream of pedagogic magazines and bulletins follow the teachers about, to perfect their work and to inform them of the most recent methods. The system of regular inspections tries to ascertain whether or not the teacher has profitably assimilated this knowledge lavished upon him. In 1935 there were 7,734 students in the colony's Normal Schools.

[1] S. Lévi, *Indochine* (Paris, 1931), Vol. II, p. 142.

The most recent educational formula leaves to the state the care of creating a number of model schools in which teachers are trained, of giving examinations, and of sending inspectors to keep their work up to standard. Elementary education is to be the concern of the communes and of private initiative, under government control. The vast majority of natives are to evolve culturally in their own orbit. A few of them, selected competitively, are to be given the chance to rise through the academic hierarchy to a higher education which, at the top, is the equivalent of the best which the West has to offer.

THE EXCHANGE OF IDEAS

The Press

The press in Indo-China has proved a far better medium for the exchange of ideas than has any other literary form. So far the books produced in Indo-China have been, almost without exception, the reaction of Frenchmen to the colony. To be salable on a remunerative scale, they must be written in a world language like French, whereas newspapers can be bought by many natives for whom books are prohibitively expensive. Moreover, through journalism, native writers can express themselves on a burning issue in their own language if they prefer, and for a public with the same tastes and zest for politics and gossip. These papers do not reach the masses, however, for the excellent reason that the great majority can neither read nor afford even that additional expenditure. Yet among the new native bourgeoisie public opinion is being formed by and through the press. The creation of such opinion, albeit restricted in value and in range, is entirely the product of contacts with the West.

Prior to the French conquest, the Court of Hué annually charged three mandarins with relating and commenting upon the events of each reign. To free them from opportunism or servility, these chronicles were placed in sealed bamboo tubes which were not to be broken until one hundred years later. This original idea created a form of retrospective press, an admirable historical document whose value lies not in its semi-legendary confusion, but in the commentaries made by qualified contemporaries. It cannot be said, however, to have effected or created contemporary opinion. News was spread to a very limited extent by the passage of *trams*, or imperial envoys, on their way to and from delivering state missives. There were so few markets and fairs that opinion was almost wholly confined to the commune. Scholars and mandarins had more chance for self-expression. In addition to forming secret societies where they discussed politics, officials often embodied severe criticism of government policy in their annual letter to the Emperor. At the monthly meeting in the Governor's residence, the mandarins had their only opportunity for common discussion of provincial affairs. The public, too, knowing the date of these sessions, was able to present its complaints, and in this mild way to exercise a minor control over abuses. Though the situation was in some ways analogous to that of France before Renaudet's Gazette (1630), the Annamite people were virtually mute and public opinion non-existent, or at best embryonic.

When the *Imprimérie Nationale* founded an annex at Saigon in 1879, the Indo-Chinese press was born. Its first manifestation were the bulletins of the Agricultural Committee, official documents, and the *Excursions et Reconnaissances*[1]—all naturally state-subsidized. When the *Courrier de Saigon* began publishing local news, along with state documents and vital statistics, the colony's first newspaper came into existence. The political press had a stormy début. *Le Gong*, founded by Peire in 1879, began a violent attack upon many of Saigon's Notables. Fines and a prison sentence sent its editor scurrying to Hong-Kong. This incident was symbolic of the future. Political newspapers in Indo-China have been numerous, virulent, and short-lived.[2]

The first printing press of Tonkin was a branch of the Cochin-Chinese Imprimérie (1883). Two years later Schneider's press was founded and prospered rapidly. Its most important publication was the *Avenir du Tonkin*, the colony's best and oldest newspaper. The early press of Tonkin was unspecialized; literary, economic, and political subjects came indiscriminately from the same font. The *Avenir* was the government paper until 1889. That same year the *Courrier d'Haiphong* and the *Indépendance Tonkinoise* were born. The *Revue Indochinoise* first appeared in 1893 and its high literary standard was set by its remarkable founder, Jules Boissière. Unfortunately the heavy cost temporarily forced it out of publication. Although its various incarnations have given it at different times a literary or a journalistic quality, it has always remained a brave and interesting experiment.

---

[1] *Excursions et Reconnaissances*, 25 vols. (Saigon, 1886).

[2] *Indépendant de Saigon* (1870–84), *Ere Nouvelle* (1879–82), *Journal de Saigon* (1880–84), *Saigonnais* (1883–88), *Unité Indochinoise* (1884–88), *Trompette* (1884–85), *Extrême Orient* (1886–87), *Lanterne Indochinoise* (October–November 1889), Longer lived were: *L'Indochinois* (founded 1887), *Courrier de Saigon* (1888), *Saigon Républicain* (1888), *Le Cochinchinois* (1888), *Progrès de Saigon* (1889).

The Indo-Chinese press is tri-lingual. The language of China still serves as a medium for Annamite scholars, and naturally, also, for the many Chinese living in the colony. It is not openly political, but bitter experience has made the government exercise a severe if not wholly effective censorship. Papers in *quoc ngu* have begun to appear in recent years[1], but the French press is by far the most important. More than three hundred papers appear in that language for the small public which the colony boasts. Pham Quynh's *Nam Phong* embodies in one periodical the colony's three journalistic languages, and symbolizes his desire to bridge the cultural gaps between the three countries.

In 1898 Doumer, characteristically, wanted to restrain the freedom of the Indo-Chinese press. He encountered little resistance from the few papers then extant. Doumer obtained powers for himself from the Métropole, by playing up the current Chinese unrest, in such a way that a simple edict could suspend a paper's publication. Unlike the French press, where the state's hand is stayed until after publication, methods in Indo-China are rather preventive, in that they require preliminary authorization to publish. The violence of the colony's press has provoked an endless series of decrees of such complexity that the Minister of the Colonies, in 1927, felt compelled to bring legal order out of this journalistic chaos.

The juridical régime to which the colony's press is subject was characterized by such confusion that laws not only differed from one country to another, but within the country according to the language of publication. Cochin-China's position is the most clean-cut. Saigon is under the French press law of 1881, and its papers have many traits in common with Parisian journalism. Elsewhere laws were fragmentary and often confusing, as shown by the contradictory interpretations given to them by different magistrates.

The Annamite or Chinese, desiring to found a paper, makes official demand of the administration which, in turn, proceeds to inform itself about the individual. Here arises the first difficulty, for the information received is bound to be arbitrary since there is no *état civil*, and enlightenment is only obtainable through a friend or a foe. Since the press in French enjoys a régime so much more liberal, an Asiatic often finds it simpler to hire a Frenchman as nominal editor, and then under cover of his nationality to write as he pleases. To prevent this evasion of

---

[1] Twenty-two periodicals, two religious weeklies, three pedagogic magazines, three official journals, three popular agricultural and scientific publications. The most important are the *Voix du Peuple* and *Nam Phong Revue*.

censorship, and to avoid complicated lawsuits, the government often counters by forbidding a printer to print the paper and functionaries to read it. Since invariably the paper has little capital, and inasmuch as the functionaries form the great majority of its subscribers, this has proved a very effective means of indirect control. The ungrateful task of censorship is performed by a group of linguistic Frenchmen with native assistants. Their work is complicated by the abundance and obscurity of the double meanings dear to Asiatic writers. Such was notoriously the case in 1908 when an incitation to revolt was disguised as an agricultural bulletin. This and similar blunders have made the censors unduly nervous, and in their zeal they have become ridiculous by crying rebellion at such simple phrases as *"la cloche qui reveille."* News of a factual but discouraging nature is also deleted, like the report of inundations or of regional uprisings.

A policy of reprisals is not exclusively a government monopoly. Indo-Chinese newspapers have flourished upon blackmail to such an extent that they have come to exercise in this way a form of private control. Annamite nationalists also turn the tables on French editors whose politics they find reactionary. Tirard of Haiphong, who founded the *Colon Français*, reproduced (December 18, 1925) in his paper an old military proclamation with his own commentaries. For this and a subsequent article he received numerous letters from Annamites filled with insults and even a threat of death if he persevered.[1]

A highly personal and violent tone characterizes the Indo-Chinese press. It has become the fashion for an aggrieved individual, usually a discharged functionary, to use his small capital to purchase a paper in which he can air his grievances.

Of dubious origin were *La Voix Libre* (1920), *L'Indochine, La Liberté, Le Populaire*, and, to a lesser extent, *Le Temps d'Asie*. Another publication of a highly personal character, but of a more general outlook, was the *Eveil Economique*, the darling of H. Cucherousset, who wrote under four pseudonyms excellent articles against the dangers of *étatisme* and the need for improving the colony's means of communication. He and Devilar in *L'Humanité Indochinoise* were among the journalists advocating freedom from harmful Parisian interference.

It is often hard to follow a paper's policy, for it changes hands and viewpoints with vertiginous rapidity. The *Dépêche* is used by Henri de Lachevrotière for his own ends, under guise of Fascist advocacy. Through years of journalism he has built up a highly personal clientele,

[1] Taittinger, Pierre, *Le Rêve Rouge* (Paris, 1930), p. 126.

mainly among the Hindu electorate, through whom he can support candidates of his choice. For example, Lachevrotière bought the *Impartiale* from C. Aymard, and in it he supported Outrey in his third campaign as deputy for Cochin-China. After successfully getting him elected, Lachevrotière sold the paper to the Octave Homberg group for 240,000 piastres, and Outrey had to find himself a new paper for the 1928 elections. Despite his promise to Homberg, Lachevrotière aided Outrey in amassing enough money to buy back the *Dépêche* which he had previously sold in 1924, after five years of electoral support. After Outrey was again safely elected in 1928, Lachevrotière bought up the entire paper, claiming that the ingrate Outrey had tried to oust him. This strategy proved profitable, for both gentlemen have subsequently flourished like the proverbial bay-trees. Outrey remains as perennial deputy, and the *Dépêche*, under Lachevrotière's magic touch, has become the most important paper in Cochin-China.

The fact that these papers are not subsidized, that for the most part they represent not public opinion but that of their owner, that they have few resources other than abuse, all accounts for their great number, violence, and short duration. Certain papers which owe their backing to big financial groups are much longer lived. For example, *L'Opinion*, which belongs to the Bank of Indo-China—which in turn represents the Parisian Banque de Paris et des Pays Bas—was long important. Eventually it was absorbed by the *Courrier Saigonnais*, owned by the influential Distilleries de l'Indochine. Likewise the *Avenir du Tonkin* belongs to the Paris Société des Missions Etrangères, and its success is the more striking as it deals little with politics. Unfortunately publications of high literary and aesthetic value have not survived for long. The *Pages Indochinoises* in the North and *Extrême Asie* for the South were both excellent periodicals, non-political, beautifully printed and illustrated, with contributors of distinction, yet they could not long stand the financial strain.

Despite their number, ephemeral duration, and marked individuality there are certain traits common to all the Indo-Chinese French press. On the whole these papers are highly conservative as regards native policy. Either they frankly represent vested interests, or a querulous opposition to government policy, or the functionary-colonist fear of native competition. They are read not for information but for their scandals and for the pleasure of hearing the government criticized. A widespread subscription to the big Paris dailies and monthlies supplements the reading of local news and gossip.

The native press has shown itself an apt pupil of its French colleagues, especially in its taste for political polemics in Cochin-China where its vocabulary of vituperation, and even its French style, is often superior. The Annamites' traditional respect for authority is not only extinct but its demise has been aggressively proclaimed. The native press in other Annamite countries is either non-existent or else confined to official or technical publications. In fact, it has been weakened by over-violence, for it specializes in destructive criticism. It has failed conspicuously in creating a constructive political and financial programme. It is true, however, that many native papers like the *Tribune Annamite* started mildly enough, but they became embittered in the early 1920's through the government's slowness in realizing Sarraut's promised reforms.

Sarraut had favoured the growth of a *quoc ngu* press in order to develop public opinion in the colony. At first he arranged for government subsidies to bring down the price of the papers to fit the average Annamite purse, but he was not permanently successful, for a native paper now costs three Annamite sous—a disproportionate sum when a coolie can dine for ten. Its price obviously places it only within bourgeois reach. This press was to be of mutual benefit. Not only would it create and influence native opinion, but keep the state informed as to mass reactions—in short, be a sensitive, reciprocally reflective intermediary between the governed and governing groups. Unfortunately the state now feels that it has nourished a serpent in its bosom, for the press has used its freedom to turn and rend its creator. It was but another example of the deformation of democratic institutions in a country whose government, by virtue of being a colony, was incompatible with the principles of 1789.

The Annamites have not been able to evaluate properly their press. Even the intelligentsia, educated according to Western ideas, have lacked the right background and have abused the journalistic medium. When Varenne was petitioned to loosen the press restrictions, he was favourably disposed to do so by his Socialistic principles, but he was almost immediately disillusioned by the mud-slinging polemics which he had unwittingly unleashed. In reality, it was a vicious circle: the native press lapsed rapidly from moderate to violent demands for political reforms. The French press, inherently conservative, became even more so through its alarm at the increasing virulence of the Annamite journalists. The uprisings of 1930-31 naturally made the government clamp down harder than ever on the press. The conservative French elements claimed that Yenbay was but the fulfilment of their gloomiest prophecies. But by 1935 Robin felt able to promise greater freedom to the press, but it was granted on the instalment plan, first to the periodical and then to the daily press. The proof that this was largely a nominal consolation to salve liberal opinion, was shown by his statement that he had to suppress only fourteen publications during this first year of "liberty."[1]

That censorship is irritating to the Annamites is undeniably true. How effective it may be, or how justifiable, is another matter. The conservatives complain that a few Annamites have constituted themselves political arbiters for which they have neither a mandate nor the authority, since they do not represent Annamite opinion but merely their own. It is also true that a detached and critical spirit on the part of the journalists is notably lacking. Annamite writers are enchanted to spread tidings of every governmental mistake without giving a corresponding publicity to its good works. If they started as "an ambitious minority" they have certainly swelled their ranks rapidly. Their attacks are usually violent and crude, largely because they are inebriated by their own words and are fairly immune from redress. The pseudonyms used by native journalists are an almost complete protection in a country where the *état civil* is in an embryonic state.

An interesting journalistic development is the fact that the solidarity of the Indo-Chinese press is broken not only along nationalistic lines, but more by individual jealousies. When one writer, either French or Annamite, gives birth to an original idea, there is a conspiracy of silence on the part of his colleagues to ignore his discovery, even if it is one of general utility. Such indirect censorship supplements official repressions, and the result is harmful to the public, which is often kept in ignorance of important events. The censorship of Chinese newspapers, for example, results in smuggling them into the colony, or the distortion of news from China by rumour and prejudice. This is even more harmfully true of local news. When the government suppresses "discouraging" events like news of inundations or rebellions, it also naturally inclines to cover up its own mistakes. The *Eveil Economique* claimed to be the only paper to inform the head of the Public Works Department that a certain bridge had collapsed in Laos—information which up to then his culpable subordinates had succeeded in keeping from him.

There has been so much denunciation of native journalists' incitations to violence that their beneficent influence has too often been ignored. The Annamite press has played an important role in politics, though it has not as yet developed into being a real social force. Some-

[1] *Discours du 3 décembre 1935 au Grand Conseil.*

times the benefit derived has been a by-product of personal grievances or interests. This was the case when De Monpezat publicized the evils of exporting labour to the Pacific Islands. The best case of benevolent press interference occurred in the Calendrier Affair. Here the liberal French and native press combined to denounce this attempt to create a monopoly of the port activities of Saigon-Cholon. Articles by Daguerches in *Vérité* and those of the *Tribune Indigène* dealt it a decisive blow. Another example of disinterested and effective journalism was Cucherousset's and Malpuech's campaign to give Laos an economic outlet. Too often, however, political scandals have been proclaimed for the pure pleasure of airing a grievance, or for personal gain. Under De Lanessan, the enmity of two of his best aides was fought out in the local press in the most discreditable language and bad taste. When the Mission wanted to get rid of Monet and his lay educational efforts, it cleverly attacked him in its paper, *L'Avenir du Tonkin*, on the ground that he was receiving subsidies from a foreign group. The most stirring and destructive of all press campaigns, however, was the widespread attack on Varenne by MM. Lachevrotière, Aymard, Cognacq, and Outrey.

The campaign which the Homberg and Outrey groups had so successfully conducted against Merlin in the *Depêche Coloniale* and the *Midi Colonial*, to show that he was letting Indo-China be ruined by Bolshevism, encouraged them with far more reason to take the same line with Varenne. When the native press was jubilant over Varenne's nomination, the conservative French press, as represented by the *Impartiale*, *L'Opinion* and the Franco-Hindu *Réveil Saigonnais*, took alarm at the prospect of Varenne's possibly paving the way for the colony's independence. They were outdone by the alarmist sheets, the *Midi Colonial* and *Liberté*, which proceeded to transmit a garbled account of Varenne's first speech. This, though later rectified, did much harm by alarming France. Cognacq, the reactionary Governor of Cochin-China, did everything to aid this group whose interests Varenne was undermining. Naturally, however, it was Varenne's native policy that the opposition attacked as his most vulnerable point, and one on which there was the most disagreement.

Two journalists, Nguyen An Ninh and Lam Hiep Chau, had written a eulogistic obituary of the revolutionist Pham Chu Trinh, which brought down on their paper the state's censure. Varenne asked for clemency, but the Prosecuting Attorney, Colonne, persevered in pronouncing an unnecessarily severe judgment. This obvious injustice as well as refusal to permit Annamite students to wear mourning for their patriot, led to the school strikes which the press opposition exploited, as evidence that the colony was being delivered over to Bolshevism.

What came to be known as the Affaire Bui Quang Chieu was the most important of all these indirect attacks on Varenne. Bui Quang Chieu was a functionary who was also founder of the paper *La Tribune Indigène*. In the course of a lecture tour in France, he had voiced the wishes of the Constitutionalist Party as well as a criticism of policies dear to Outrey and Lachevrotière, who at once denounced him as a Bolshevik. They had perhaps been made a little sensitive at that time by other Annamite articles exposing Cognacq's share in certain shady land transactions.

The occasion of Bui Quang Chieu's return to the colony was taken by both sides as a propitious moment for demonstrations. When the rival factions met on the wharf, the Annamites, through the publicity efforts of the *Echo Annamite*, were able to stage the bigger demonstration. The whole affair passed off in an orderly manner, yet Lachevrotière and his satellites denounced it as an Annamite revolt. It was certainly not through any lack of provocation on their part, and it is to the Annamites' credit that they refused to be stirred into rebellion.

This failure marked the end of the local press effort. The struggle was carried to the Métropole, where a Parliamentary decision paralysed those very forces in the colony which had called on Paris for aid in settling their personal grievances. It seemed at the time as if the forces of righteousness had triumphed. Cognacq retired in 1926, Colonne was recalled and Lachevrotière was temporarily out of journalism. One may truthfully say that if the Annamite journalists have not learned moderation and acquired a detachedly critical spirit, the responsibility can be laid at the door of their mentors.

Indo-Chinese Literature

Indo-China, at the crossroads of the two most brilliant civilizations of Asia, offers a peculiarly rich field for study of the Oriental mind. The obvious strangeness of life in the East was naturally what first occupied the attention of French writers, and for many years the inner life of the natives was thought to be beyond the Occidental grasp. It was only with trepidation that native culture was probed, either by poetical intuition or theoretical analysis. Such studies are handicapped from the outset. The French writer must approach his subject from the outside, and with a wholly foreign mentality. A native, describing his own people, has the immense advantage of writing from personal experience, but in turn he has trouble in expressing himself in a foreign language where he is never sure of conveying the appropriate shade of meaning. He cannot but feel hampered by his medium and this self-consciousness betrays itself in a certain stiffness of style. Indo-Chinese literature as yet has produced only a few noteworthy books, but it has, aside from its literary merits, significance as a record of the progressive attempt made by French and Annamites towards mutual understanding.

Annamites are notoriously poor at giving information about themselves. Theirs is a natural distrust which has historical justification. In any inquiry, the Annamite sees the Inquisitor. His natural secretiveness is complemented by hyper-sensitivity about any defects in his own people. He regards criticism of them as a reflection upon himself. When he describes his compatriots, it is as he would have them appear to the outsider rather than as they actually are. Like the colonials who refuse to recognize themselves in any unflattering portrait, the Annamite proclaims as false any book criticizing his fellow countrymen. Being on the defensive, he describes old Annam as a Terrestrial Paradise, and makes the French responsible for every subsequent flaw. Telling the truth has always been considered by the Annamites as poverty of wit. The docile facts are to be manipulated as best they may serve one's purposes. Answering what one's superiors would like to hear is surely the best way of advancing in the world. Truth is not absolute but relative, and personal success the only yardstick by which a man may be judged.

Frankness and sincerity are thus discouraged in the Annamite child as obstacles to his rise in life, so it is only natural that Annamite writers are found wanting in accurate objective information. Disinterestedness has never characterized their pursuit of learning. The coveted diploma was awarded to him whose memory could muster the longest number of quotations, and original thinking was deliberately discouraged. This conception of learning forged the long, philosophic digressions that still characterize Annamite style, and they prevent an Annamite novel from holding the reader's attention by pungent, terse phrasing, or by a stimulating plot. Even a novel like *Le Roman de Mlle. Lys*,[1] written in the purest French, clear and classical in style, suffers from boring digressions and from a lack of unity and direct observation.

Annamite literature in French, despite some pettish criticisms, shows a sure mastery of the language, but as yet the writing is too bookish, quite unrealistic and over-propagandist. Journalism here has been a

[1] Ng. Phan Lang.

most healthful corrective in curbing flowery and imagistic writing, as well as the moral tone to which even the best Annamites are prone. Annamite writers have perhaps been more successful in the field of translating French classics, although some of the irony and double meanings are sometimes either lost or miss fire. Yet it is in the field of interpreting the West to their compatriots, rather than their fellow countrymen to the West, that the Annamite writers have been most useful.

If these writers may be justly accused of lacking objectivity, the same criticism may be levelled, though not in the same way, at their more numerous French colleagues. Indo-China has not been French long enough to have produced a Kipling. Most of the books on the colony are the work of transients, not residents, for the very good reason that most colonials are money-makers and not artists. The feeling of impermanency, of regarding France as their home, of being suspended between two worlds, has militated against the production of a literature rooted in the colony: Indo-China has served writers far more as background for their own psychological experiences. This harmonizes with the cult of Metropolitan exoticism and its superficial romanticism, and it has created a rift between itself and the more realistic literature produced in the colony. There are, of course, exceptions, and some colonial writers, like Jean d'Esme, who know better, deliberately cater to Metropolitan tastes.

Poets have flourished in the colony not only because the scenes of native life and—literally—pipe dreams have fostered quaint charm, but more because exile and the climate have sharpened their sensibilities. The initial reaction to the country as a hostile land, bred a melancholy which is especially noticeable among the women poets. Their preoccupation with the external picturesque, or with their introspective broodings, has left little time for penetration of the native soul. Poetry is pre-eminently the work of transients absorbed by the outward aspects of colonial life. A notable exception is the work of René Crayssac, and possibly that of Alfred Droin.

Following the chronological output of colonial prose is an accurate weathervane to the degree and quality of French reactions to Indo-China. In the early days, the epic lives of Garnier and Rivière were reflected in an adventure literature which took either an heroic or an imaginative turn. Both men wrote extremely well. Garnier confined himself to recording sober facts and the reflections they inspired: Rivière—who was something of a dilettante—specialized in a charming

317

style. Their exploits inspired a host of narratives dominated by the physical and moral ordeal of the Tonkinese campaign. Though some of the best books on Annamite culture were written by officers like Luro, Philastre, and Diguet, the military in general hated the colony so much that the scant attention they paid to its inhabitants was blinded by prejudice. The perfidy of nature was matched by that of the Annamites. Even the gentle Khmers shared this universal disdain. The uncertainty of France's intentions, the fear lest their sacrifices be in vain, intensified their discouragement and fatigue. The result was a vicious circle: these very recitals of thirst and fever endured on the long marches under a tropical sun created Tonkin's sinister reputation in France, and were the very factors that made its fate hang in the balance. Theirs was the record of suffering and disillusionment in a country that did not live up to the French dream of an idealized Orient, rather than the expression of their desire to understand it. It became fashionable to say that the Annamites were the ugliest and most ignoble people in the Far East, who had neither an art nor a literature of their own.

The banditry with which the period was rife provided excellent material for a horror literature. Every Asiatic crime and cruelty, interspersed with the customary opium and *congaie* touches, was depicted in gory detail and with great success in France. If accurately described, the picture would have been sombre enough without playing up Primitive Passions and Mysterious Violence. Only when such stories were written by the master hand of a Boissière or a Pouvourville did the personal experience and knowledge of these authors make them valuable as records. What most French readers are apt to forget about Indo-China is that such accounts were accurate enough for their day but that now conditions have radically changed.

The difficulty which Occidental writers experience in understanding Oriental peoples, as well as the domination of the Romantic tradition, make them devote disproportionate attention to the exotic setting of their novels. With time, the charm of the country began to filter in. A small group of writers began to savour the romantic relics of the rapidly passing Annamite civilization, and in this way they became the apostles of Indo-Chinese culture to the French public. But the colony's regionalism has always been hard for foreigners to grasp, though it seems very pronounced to the natives. Tropical nature to some exiles remained permanently intractable: many felt its peculiar and potent charm, but it was never the refuge and the solace to which Occidentals are accustomed. France is a gentle country which offers stability and tranquillity in nature to the sensitive soul. Indo-China, on the other hand, is the land of extremes: wild and desolate mountain scenery alternate with the monotonous and drab rice-fields or the rampant tropical forest. Its restless and destructive vitality created a certain pleasure, but also a *malaise*. Man no longer seemed to count, he was too much at the mercy of uncontrollable forces.

With the growing ascendancy over these natural forces achieved by Western science, a new type of adventure literature was born. The mining prospector in the *brousse*, or the rubber planter, replaced the demoded bandit. The adventurer type slowly evolved away from the poor fellow living solely by his wits, to the strong man in love with living, dissatisfied with the narrow life of Europe. He had the iron hand in the velvet glove, imperiously dealing with an aggressive nature whose treachery was only outdone by the deceit of man. He was either the angelic apostle of European civilization to the benighted native, living ascetically a life of loving devotion, or a hulking brute who cultivated every vice and who loved to torture everything within his grasp, preferably natives. Such a hero had far greater appeal to the French public—all hearthside adventurers—than did the anguished and more realistic accounts of the first-comers.

The early novels for the most part unhesitatingly gave the centre of the stage to Europeans: natives were too enigmatic and too repugnant for men whose only knowledge of them was superficial observation. But the treatment of native characters nowadays has become the touch-stone by which contemporary colonial authors are judged. There is first the temptation to paint them like Europeans, so as to insure easy sales in the home market, for long and patient study is required, in addition to a certain cast of mind, to understand Annamite psychology. The assimilationist viewpoint is still so prevalent in France—that all men are spiritually akin despite a difference in skin pigment—that the first shock of disillusionment is apt to produce an equally extreme reaction confirming the impossibility of ever understanding Asiatics. It was obvious, however, that the mature artist might compromise by depicting those traits common to all humanity, along with the variations produced by a different set-up, both physical and moral.

With time, too, the colony seemed less hostile, and its natives took on charm by contagion. The allure of native women created a whole literature to itself. Cambodia and Laos inspired comparison with the Garden of Eden, and their inhabitants became the virtuous savages of eighteenth-century idealization. If the Annamites superficially appear wily and deceitful one should charitably remember the hard centuries of Chinese domination. If their conversation abounds in reticences, precautions, and indirect allusions, it is due to the fatal price exacted by frankness and sincerity. If their creative capacity seems dwarfed by their powers of assimilation, it was the result of a policy of suppression born of the state's fear of individual initiative.

This increased indulgence towards the native peoples, coming from a greater understanding of their life, was first clearly revealed in Nolly's *La Barque Annamite*[1]. This and his subsequent books pictured the poetic side of Annamite life, which he showed to be completely dominated by Confucianist morality and the cult of the dead. Jean Marquet in *De la Rizière à la Montagne*[2] continued and expanded this new trend. He was the first to write from inside Annamite life and not from the viewpoint of an exiled foreign observer. In portraying the native point of view his work has more insight, but is nevertheless akin to Pouvourville's *Annam Sanglant*.[3] Unlike him, however, Marquet wrote of the peasant, not the aristocrat-scholar who had not yet suffered the Occidental imprint. He showed the Oriental mind to be moved by things to which the Occidental is insensible—and reciprocally. The incomprehensible became natural and reasonable under his touch. The terrible cruelty of Asiatics was made more comprehensible when it was seen to be related to their tradition and laws, and it was part of that same aesthetic delight the Annamites took in inventing subtleties, for their own sake, in courteous and devious phrasing. Vendettas became a sacred duty when individuals had transgressed against the social order.

Since the family and commune took care of their own, no wonder that the Annamites had never developed any altruism. The Annamite was so hemmed in on every side by routine and misery that he was condemned from birth to be the victim of circumstance. Marquet's story showed his appreciation of the Annamite's subordination to society by having no central figure as its hero, but the group—the family and commune. This achievement epitomizes the renunciation of European psychology in approaching the Asiatic viewpoint. The Oriental cannot understand writing without a moral purpose, and it is the focus on the individual's emotional and spiritual development which is the barrier by which, up to now, Annamite literature has been sundered from the West.

[1] Nolly, Emile (Captain Detanger), (Paris, 1910).
[2] Marquet, Jean (Paris, 1928).
[3] Pouvourville, Albert de (Paris, 1898).

320

CHAPTER V

PEOPLES OF INDIAN CULTURE

"En moi est passé un peu de l'âme asiatique, et jamais plus je ne sentirai ni penserai en Européen." *Pujarniscle*

CAMBODIA

FOUNAN was the ancient name given to the Mekong valley, which includes modern Cambodia, Southern Laos, and Cochin-China. Like Champa, Founan was Indianized by successive waves of immigrants from India, which began before the time of Alexander the Great. Brahmans and merchants, bonzes and adventurers, they left India to become rich by colonizing these distant lands, bringing with them the culture and religion of their own country. Everywhere they founded principalities of varying importance, and in so doing they came into contact with the Khmers and Chams of Founan, and beyond. The Khmers, coming from the north-west, had displaced the Chams in the Mekong delta, a fertile land rich in hunting and fishing. There they organized the powerful kingdom known to the Chinese as Founan. The origins of that kingdom—ruled by the royal serpent race of Nagas —as well as its conversion to Brahmanism are shrouded in mystery and legend.

The first princes of Brahmanic caste were capable and cruel warriors. Warlike expeditions, as far as Malaya, alternated with palace revolutions thoughtfully engineered during their absence. Embassies were impartially sent to China and India, and modern experts think that the influence of the former was equal to and older than that of the latter. Certainly Chinese chronicles form the most valuable source for early Khmer history.[1] From the third to the twelfth centuries this kingdom was very powerful and covered probably twice the area of modern Cambodia, with a population of about four millions. Brahmanism was the official cult, but primitive religions survived among the people. In the fifth century a new intensive wave of Indianization profoundly modified the country's institutions. Closer relations were knit and maintained with the mother country, and the dynasty's origin proudly traced to Indian deities. Kambu, who gave his name to the country, became the founder of the sun race or Cambodians; no mean achievement for an anchorite.

[1] *Mémoires de Tacheou Ta Kouan* (translated by P. Pelliot, Bull. EFEO, 1902).

Succession to the throne was in practice if not in theory regulated by bloody combats, rival assassinations, and usurpations. Internal struggles and uprisings induced a period of weakness and relative obscurity in the late seventh century that paved the way for a series of Javanese invasions in the following century. The Javanese ravaged the peninsula, temporarily dominated Cambodia, and left a permanent imprint upon that country's art. The ninth century brought a new lease of vitality to Cambodia. Its institutions were modified, and it was probably at this time that the four *Samraps*, or royal houses, were created and the kingdom divided into fiefs. From this era dates the great building orgy. In the ninth century, Angkor was finally chosen as the kingdom's capital for its fertile fields and abundant water supply nearby. About A.D. 900, Angkor Thom and the temple of Bayon were finished. Draining the lakes, cutting down the forests, fashioning and transporting huge blocks of stone represented a colossal effort. If the Khmers were greater architects than builders—they never mastered the principle of the arch —their work showed a virile and original artistry. Three centuries of marvellous construction synchronized with a constant fighting of their neighbours and among themselves, and ended by exhausting the race's vitality.

An eleventh-century activity in building numerous religious establishments, both Brahman and Buddhist, was interrupted by an invasion of equally Indianized Chams. This was the signal for popular uprisings against the tyranny of the kings and Brahmans. Temples were destroyed; violent rebellion was crushed by an even bloodier repression. In the next century, the struggle with Champa was renewed as well as more peaceful relations with China. This was the last great building era. The country was exhausted and its power already waning before the rising stars of its former vassals, Siam and Annam. Cambodia's increasing weakness and reputation for wealth attracted the invaders who were, moreover, cut off from expansion in other directions. The Siamese were interrupted by periodic clashes with their Pegouan and Burmese neighbours, just as the Annamites, wedged in between the mountain and sea, had to drive out the Chams before they could come to grips with the Khmers.

In the fifteenth century Angkor's vulnerable position to Siamese attack compelled the first of many subsequent changes of capital. The Khmers moved first to Babour and then to Oudong, which remained their capital until the French developed Pnom-Penh. In the seventeenth century the Annamites were free to carry war into the heart of Cambodia whose kings they treated like vassals. Bien-hoa was colonized, and at Saigon the Annamites placed a viceroy to guard their new possessions and to organize their expansion along the gulf of Siam (1658–1758). Henceforth Cambodia was the miserable bone of contention between her aggressive neighbours. When it was not a prey to invasion the country was rent by civil war. For a century Cambodia wallowed in misery; agriculture became decadent, the countryside deserted, and traditions were forgotten. The Siamese invasions were the most disastrous, for they forcibly transplanted those Khmers whom they did not massacre, in order to people their own kingdom. Everything non-transportable was destroyed, as if it had been to the Siamese symbolic of the erstwhile greatness of their former masters. In the dry season, the Khmers fled before the Siamese advance, and during the rains they were at the mercy of a surprise attack by the Annamite fleet.

The Annamites were more deadly if not quite so barbarous. By using the same methods they had employed against the Chams they drove the Khmers out of the Mekong delta. Perhaps worse than the physical suffering they inflicted was the open contempt with which the Annamites treated, and still treat, the proud and sensitive Cambodians. It led to violent though spasmodic reprisals which were even more cruelly suppressed. By the end of the eighteenth century, at the time of the Tayson rebellion, the Annamites had conquered as far as the Grand Lac. The Siamese, profiting by Annam's preoccupation, at that time took over Battambang and Angkor. During the first half of the nineteenth century Cambodia managed to salvage the remnants of her country by playing off one enemy against the other, but in 1846 there was a general recognition of Khmer feudal subjection to both Annam and Siam. If France had not stepped in at this point and stopped Annam's westward expansion, there is little doubt but that Cambodia's absorption would soon have been completed. The Siamese were not finally checked until 1907, when they returned the two "lost" provinces to the Cambodian royal house.

Though few numerically, the Khmers are physically a very strong race. They live frugally, eat abstemiously, and bathe frequently. They are the living contradiction of *mens sana in corpore sano*, for their physical vigour has no counterpart in psychological vitality. They quail before authority and their fellow man, particularly the Annamites, but they are courageous before physical danger of an impersonal kind; for example, they are excellent boatmen in dangerous rapids. Their whole character is complicated by such contradictions. They have been variously and simultaneously described as gay, curious, naïve, fickle, formalistic, vain in their person and in their race, slow, patient, gentle, devoted, and lazy. They are naturally hospitable, yet their customs forbid receiving strangers into the home. Dr. Pannetier, a French doctor, often resented being kept waiting outside the house while the patient, who had urgently begged his coming, often at great inconvenience, leisurely finished his meal. The repast, as well as the home, has a sacred character. The Khmers have a comforting belief that even lightning will spare those who are eating.

In the same obliging way the Khmers are tolerant, though superstitious. Patting a child upon the head is unforgivable, a fact which some kindly French soldiers learned to their grief. Either through apathy or good nature, the Khmers are extraordinarily long-suffering —one of their kings called them buffaloes—yet their outbursts are terrible when they have been goaded beyond endurance. They can be unbelievably obstinate, yet outdo themselves in personal devotion. Their modesty is easily outraged by a display of the nude or of even cinema emotions, yet their literature is often crudely sensual. The Khmer character is the product of two forces: the Buddhistic conception of life and their historical past.

From childhood the Cambodian is nourished on a literature permeated with the miraculous. Fantastic visions of ancient splendour compensate for an unsatisfactory present. The supernatural constantly dominates frail humans. The chief preoccupation of these timid people is to consult omens and presages, propitiate the hostile spirits, and to conjure adversity by amulets and magic. Khmer superstition has not yet become formalized into rites, but nevertheless every act is regulated. For example, the head must always point to the South when one sleeps, for all other directions expose one to the dragons' revenge. Custom, code, and tradition combine to find ways of avoiding misfortune. All nature seems to them equally animated by fear and the desire to be ransomed from an evil destiny. Even the monkeys are thought to pay an annual tribute to the crocodiles at a fixed hour and place. As a result the country is a paradise for swindlers. One enterprising crook collected fairly recently a large sum on the ground that he was sent by the Japanese to collect taxes. The Chinese naturally are not to be outdone and they have one trick which repetition never makes less profitable: they circulate the most unlikely rumours which force down the price of paddy. Fundamentally it is not laziness or stupidity on the part of the Khmers, but a lack of self-confidence which only the habit of success can give. Inertia is their defence against physical violence, of which they have had only too much experience. Cambodian proverbs reveal the infinite despair of a conquered people resigned to the blows of fate:

If you are strong, make yourself feared: if weak, make yourself pitied.

The clemency of nature encourages a lack of foresight and perseverance, and also engenders a belief in the futility of effort. Living requires little exertion as the natural resources of the country are great and the population small. The Khmer can give himself up to his love of games and holidays. Temporary competition in games of skill is a form of voluntary and congenial activity unlike the monotony of routine work.

Buddhism still further disarms the Khmer by making him sentimental, mystic, and contemplative, and offers a refuge to his supersensitive and harassed soul. This earthly life is conceived as a series of incarnations, each regulated by the individual's actions in his previous existence. Life is a succession of ordeals inflicted on mankind to permit an appraisal of the soul's intrinsic worth. But the soul's real existence takes place outside of this world. In its terrestrial form the soul is deprived of memory and is delivered over to its natural inclinations. Living is thus an experiment according to which the soul expiates its sins in the appropriate heaven or hell assigned to it by divine justice, after which it undergoes a new life test. If it so chooses the soul may select the new form by which it will be incarnated, but this is a risky business. For if the choice falls above the soul's capacities, the errors inevitably committed entail painful expiation. When sufficient elevation has been attained, and the cycle is terminated in the monastic state, then the ordeal of incarnation becomes unnecessary. The basic concept is that each being finds a status appropriate to his inherent nobility. This breeds humility, resignation, and a fear of unpleasant reincarnations. Suicides are very rare: infanticide and abortion are unknown.

SOCIAL INSTITUTIONS

If the Khmer is quite inadequate at handling his own destiny, he is highly moral in his personal life and is in no sense, thanks to Buddhism, degenerate. As in Annam, the family is the basis of the social structure, but families live scattered over the countryside and not in towns or even villages. Marriage is not the imperious necessity that it is to Annamites, but is held in high honour. The celibate can only escape public opprobrium by becoming a bonze. Polygamy is legally instituted, but as ever

325

the poor are perforce monogamous. The law permits to the king eleven legitimate wives, and only three to his subjects, but the number of concubines is limited entirely by wealth. Though Khmer women leave the parental authority only for their husband's domination, they occupy an honoured position in the home. A wife may bring suit against her husband with the aid of any male relative available, and even be granted a divorce. No distinction is made between the sexes in the inheritance of property: succession is based on the rank of the mother. When they become adolescent Khmer girls "enter the shade," as it is euphoniously called, and lead chaste and retired lives. Like so many Oriental women they only begin to live when they become mothers. Children have great respect for their parents and this attitude is inculcated by tradition and law. Parental authority, though tempered by time, is still preponderate. The father controls all the family's possessions, and may even sell his children before they come of age.

The Khmers are divided into three social classes: freemen, serfs, and slaves. Freemen have full civil rights and liberties—to which they are violently attached—excepting what they owe as royal service, taxes, and *corvées*. All the male population between the ages of twenty-one and fifty owes to the state ninety days of labour a year. Boys and older men have lighter tasks; bonzes, Brahmans, and mandarins are exempt. Tax lists are based on a tri-annual census made by royal officials who travel throughout the provinces. Freemen must choose a patron among the mandarins of the capital: serfs as well as slaves are registered under the names of their masters.

The client-patron relationship grew up under the same conditions as did the mediaeval lord-vassal feudality in Europe. This curious and ancient organization had its uses in military campaigns and in the compulsory building dear to the Khmer kings, but its abuse led to numerous insurrections. Slaves formed an integral part of their master's family. Formerly they were absolute property, now they exist solely for debts and enjoy certain rights. Enslavement annuls the interest on their debt, but leaves the principal untouched. Their legal status is clearly defined: they owe respect, obedience, and service to the master and his family. His consent must be obtained for their marriage. Taking flight or bringing an unjust suit against their master entails severe punishment. On his side the master owes food and board to his slave: if he exceeds his rights or if the slave has been seriously maltreated, the latter may bring suit. Killing a slave is punishable by death. Nor can a master separate his slave's family. A slave may even change masters at any time if he can find another master willing to buy off his debt. The system is typically Cambodian in its leniency. The royal serfs are the descendants of great rebels or criminals whose death penalty was commuted to perpetual enslavement for themselves and their families. They are usually skilled workmen whose trade is passed down from father to son. These serfs are grouped in villages and placed under special officials and a unique régime. Serfs may own property under the same conditions as other Cambodians.

Khmer feudalism differs profoundly from Annamite society. The Cambodians have a sincere attachment to their hereditary lords, and they are knit together by the powerful ties of clan. Feudalism is fundamentally modified by religion and by the absolute power of the king, who can instantaneously reduce the power of his greatest vassals. The people's natural timidity and formalism have become crystallized by and into a hierarchized society, carefully policed. There is a great fear of and respect for authority and an inevitable traffic in influence. Etiquette and aesthetics form a part of their great love of ceremonies, which range from the family rite of cutting the adolescent's hair to the annual royal blessing of the waters. In its total lack of public opinion Cambodia is essentially a feudal country. The family group, or the hamlet, mark the limits of the average Khmer's spiritual and physical horizon. His inertia is complete, his lack of disinterested abstract curiosity total. Itinerant Chinese merchants form his sole link with the outside world.

POLITICAL ORGANIZATION

The theoretically absolute power of the king has been tempered by time, custom, and religion. The King of Cambodia is no figurehead. To his people he is the state without whom they can imagine no national existence. No matter how feeble or absurd he may personally be, the king is the object of a cult which makes his person sacred, his palace inviolable, and his word law. One may not address the king before being spoken to: his real name may never be enunciated, but only the one he selects to be known by. Only his first wives may awaken him, when state affairs press, by caressing his sacred feet. His harem is composed of three or four hundred ladies hierarchically ranked according to birth and to favour. The king may give away to courtiers those whose services he does not care to retain. Religion alone has authority over the king. He considers it a great honour to be the Protector of Buddhism, but in no way does he interfere with the priestly hierarchy. Fortunately for the French neither the king nor his people care that he should suffer the burdens of power so long as he retains its semblance.

The kingdom is divided into seven categories: the royal family; monks, both Brahmans and bonzes; distant relatives of the royal family; mandarins; freemen; serfs; and slaves. In addition there are the four *samraps*: the royal house; the house of the abdicated or second sovereign; the houses of the first prince and princess of the blood. The numerous officials of each *samrap* are picturesquely graded according to dignities: the highest, for example, has 10,000 dignities, a village chieftain about 500. As in Annam, the growth of a potentially dangerous aristocracy, in view of the quantity of royal offspring, is curtailed by law. After five generations descendants of royal blood lapse into a caste known as Brah Van and Prea Vongsa, a tactful title of nobility which carries with it no concrete privilege. Nor do the mandarins constitute a menace, for they are named and revoked at the king's pleasure. The only hereditary caste reminiscent of India which exists is made up of a few hundred families called Baku, of Brahmanic origin. In addition to certain picturesque duties, like wearing a special head-dress and guarding the sacred sword, they have real privileges in tax and *corvée* exemptions. They may be exiled for treason but cannot be executed.

The mandarins are a temporarily privileged group, about a thousand strong, whose organization is analogous to the Malayan. They are called the eyes, ears, and arms of the king, and are designated by title, not by name. The first group are the mandarins of the interior or of the crown, who have charge of the palace and of the army. The provincial, or mandarins of the exterior, were originally assigned to the five great provinces, but subsequent additions have expanded this group. The Phneak Ngear are another set of provincial mandarins who bought from the first group the privilege of judging certain lawsuits. The attributes of this group are variable. Since the Cambodian word for justice means "to sell," one can judge that the position is remunerative.

Sruk has been the traditional Khmer administrative division: Cambodia's numerous wars and dismemberments have modified the number, size, and importance of these provinces beyond all semblance of equality. A mandarin's position is determined by the province he governs: the border *sruk*, for example, entails extensive powers akin to mediaeval European marches. They have no fixed capital beyond where the governor happens to reside at the moment. Twice a year the mandarins must convene at the royal capital to swear their oath of allegiance. They have no fixed salary, but retain a certain proportion of the taxes and revenues from specified lands. This income as well as responsibility for public order, tax collection, *corvée* service, and military levies is shared with numerous subordinates. The *missi dominici* are a supplementary wheel in the provincial machinery. Formerly they were royal officers like Charlemagne's, assigned to temporary missions, but now they are a permanent and rival group to the mandarins. The constant abuse of their powers by the mandarinate necessitates such supervision by the central authority, even at the cost of duplicating services.

In theory taxes are the personal property of the king. They amount virtually to a tithe in Cambodia, where it is customary to tax only the products of the soil—principally rice. This tax is assessed annually at harvest time by an ambulatory committee which visits the warehouses and granaries designated by the local authorities. The committee then draws up a list of the sums owed by each taxpayer. In addition to the king's tithe proprietors have accessory taxes, usually paid in kind. An enormous number of traditions and local customs complicate tax collecting but they serve to moderate its arbitrary spirit. The giving and receiving of gifts according to rank is part of the extraordinary expenditures of, by, and for the mandarinate. The king shares with them and the winning party all legal fines. Commerce is almost impossible without the co-operation of the mandarins, the amount of which obviously depends upon the quality of the gifts.

Other revenues divided between the king and mandarins are an export and import tax, the rent of forest land, river banks, fisheries, a head tax on foreign merchants, the farms of opium, gaming, and the lotteries. Indirect taxes are only a recent innovation but they have proved lucrative. The Chinese pay taxes three times as large as the Khmers; but they enjoy in return profitable exemptions from *corvée* and military duty, and extra-territorial privileges. This is especially important for the army to which Cambodians owe limitless service under the aegis of their patrons, who may either lead them in person or turn them over to royal officers. The strength of this army cannot be measured in terms of firearms and discipline, but in the quantity of phials, magic formulae, and fetishes which fortify each gentle warrior. From top to bottom the country's administrative armour is riddled with corruption and superstition; every other consideration is subordinated to personal profit.

In the administration of justice Cambodian venality is most obvious and most harmful. By the time the French Protectorate was established it was so widespread that the high ideals of Cambodian law were seriously compromised. Khmer love of justice is renowned, and those kings famed for their equitable judgments are particularly venerated. Possibly this is due to the religio-philosophic origin of Cambodian law which is firmly rooted in Brahmanism and Buddhism, although there is a marked Chinese influence as well. In fact the codes are collections of royal edicts perpetually revised and reorganized by a medley of kings, bonzes, mandarins, and astrologers. The last of the important native revisions occurred in 1870 when a committee of lawyers submitted their work for approval to the king and an assembly of high dignitaries.

The confusion in the codes' organization, just like its repetitious and sententious character, well reflect the Cambodian mentality. A synthesis is very difficult to make because its general ideas are drowned in a mass of detail. The books into which the codes are divided begin by describing the creation of the world, the knowledge of good and evil, the laws of Manu, the qualities required of judges for the nine Hells and the slightly less numerous Heavens. Then follow etiquette rules for royal ceremonies, the privileges of religious bodies, the duties of the king's wives and councillors—all personally dictated by Buddha. There is a special emphasis on the qualities needed by those who govern.

On the surface Khmer laws are certainly barbarous. There are twenty-one ways of inflicting slow death. There is an eye-for-an-eye quality common to all primitives, and ferocious penalties quite inappropriate to the gentle and apathetic Khmers. It was Buddhism that tipped the scales on the side of mercy, and tempered in practice the primitive harshness of the law, especially in regard to slavery. Chinese influence is seen in the penalty of caning, and by the collective responsibility of the family and associates of the guilty person. As in all Oriental law there are important gaps from the Occidental viewpoint notably, a vagueness about ownership, *état civil*, and the relations between individuals, which custom and tradition must fill in. The Khmer law, like its Annamite neighbour, is essentially a penal code, and civil laws are confined to precepts taken from Indian statutes relative to loans, debts, and slavery. An exclusively agricultural people, their legislation never anticipated such a phenomenon, for example, as bankruptcy.

Inequality before the law is a striking feature of Cambodian as well as of Annamite legislation. Guilt and punishment are apportioned to the amount of damage done rather than to the guilty intent, and by the respective ranks of the culpable and injured parties. For example, it is more expensive to assault a married woman than a widow or a slave. Complicity is severely punished: it touches those who profit by crime, or those who have guilty knowledge of it and who do not either prevent or report it. Even landowners are partly responsible for such crimes as occur on their property. In spite of inequality before the law, women, slaves, and freemen are respectively inferior to men, freemen, and officials. There are, however, serious guarantees of individual liberty. A debt slave may bring suit against his master, daughters inherit equally with sons, the humblest citizen—at least in theory—may appeal to the king.

The minute provisions of Khmer law are not only a hopeless attempt to foresee every situation but a conscientious desire to forestall injustice. Far more than the individual's right society's interests are safeguarded, especially those of the king, who represents the nation against the encroachments of the bonzes and the feudality. Certain crimes against society are considered infamous and their punishment likewise, yet in the majority of cases, after the individual has expiated his guilt he is reinstated in society as of yore. The word "to judge" in Cambodian also means "to meet and to cleanse." Just as many years before the old moral penalities had become obsolete, so all punishments but the death penalty, enslavement, and property confiscation have been commuted to money payments. The judges, the accused, and the fisc all united to applaud this trend. It is the chains which a prisoner carries, not the fact of his imprisonment that denotes condemnation, but needy jailors are perennially susceptible to a softening of the heart effected by a few piastres.

Procedure is simple and swift. Anyone, even adolescents and slaves, may bring suit, the only exceptions are beggars and bonzes, who are classed with those having mental, physical, and moral deficiencies. The meticulously graded values attached to official witnesses' testimony is unfortunately undermined by the religious training of Cambodians, which makes them poor givers of evidence. Not only are they very gullible but they are loath to pass judgment on their fellow humans. But the oath has far greater importance for the Khmer than for the Annamite, for it is based on fear of supernatural revenge rather than upon a concept of personal honour.

The king is the supreme magistrate whose enormous powers are only limited by his conscience and tradition. His Ministers are his advisers, not judges, yet by special delegation of power they sometimes acted as a court of appeal—a tendency which has been encouraged by the French. As in mediaeval Europe royal justice has used the court of appeal to break the local power of the feudality, and to fill the treasury with reve-

331

nues. All courts judged both civil and criminal cases. The originally simple and effective procedure, like the moral and equitable basis of Khmer law, had long before the French Protectorate been distorted and undermined by a venality in which the fisc was the first to give the example to private profiteers throughout the whole system. Corruption, albeit of an amiable kind, characterized the Khmer feudality far more than it did the Annamite mandarinate.

KHMER CULTURE

The most characteristic manifestations of Khmer culture were inspired by religion. The penetration of Brahmanism and its sacred language Sanskrit into Cambodia probably date from the first century of the Christian era, and it maintained its ascendancy until the twelfth. Brahma, the absolute and universal, has incarnated himself as the creator; as Vishnu the preserver, and as Shiva the destroyer—three principles by which he permeates all nature. Worshippers usually select one of the trinity to whom to address their devotions, thereby automatically reducing the other two to secondary roles. In Cambodia it is above all the cult of Shiva, though the other two along with a host of minor deities are not without honour. The Brahmans, who have given to the country numerous kings, were never very scrupulous about caste. They were usually priests and scholars, though sometime artisans, highly avaricious of royal favours and donations. This caste also practised Buddhism, and it has survived as the Baku, or one hundred families, whom certain customs mark as a group apart.

The oldest inscription in Indo-China is in Sanskrit and is of Buddhistic inspiration. It shows the existence of an Indian colony in South Annam, as well as in Founan, by the second century. Buddhism, which has a strong missionary character, was probably imported into the peninsula by Indian merchants. From the end of the eighth century there is certain proof of the powerful expansion of Buddhism there, but of the complicated brand known as Mahayana, which came through Thibet and China, losing all semblance to the original doctrines on its way. It is essentially a transcendent conception of Buddha that multiplies his personality into a hierarchy of divinities who are, in their turn, surrounded by their emanations, the Boddhisattvas, and they too are encumbered by the most elaborate mythology. Malaya also at this period was emanating a Mahayanist Buddhism that manifested itself in the ninth century by the foundation of Buddhist monasteries in Cambodia.

Brahmanism maintained itself peacefully by its side, and its development paralleled that of India, where, in the eleventh century, the cult of Vishnu superseded that of Shiva. Simultaneously in Cambodia the temple of Bayon marks the highest glory of Buddhism and of its great warrior king, Jayavarman VII (1182–1201).

Purer Buddhism of the Singhalese or Hinayana variety filtered into Cambodia later through Siam, whither it had been carried from the south of India. This reform movement in Indo-China was probably responsible for Hinduism's failure to triumph over Buddhism as it had done in India. The masses were pleased by the change in religion which stopped the exhausting orgy of temple building. The tolerance and benign resignation of Buddhism was congenial to their character and offered spiritual stability in the midst of misfortunes. The search for peace of spirit and social tranquillity absorbed the Khmers, who were glad to lay down the burden of their glory.

The vehicle of the new Buddhism was Pali, and in that form it penetrated Laos as well. In both countries it became a deeply rooted national religion, though modified by outcroppings of ancient superstitions, but in Cambodia it had a much finer flowering. Monasteries offer a shelter to scholars and dispense elementary education. Vows are not eternal and there are few Cambodians who have not donned, for a few months at least, the yellow robes of the bonze. Though these bonzes are organized into a hierarchy, and the rules of monastic life are strict and numerous, the unity of Cambodian Buddhism is in marked contrast with the intricacy of Annamite ritual. Though the religion of the masses confines itself to offerings in the pagoda, the periods of fasting, meditation, and festivals, as well as the five rules for living, are observed alike by both laity and clergy. Bonzes enjoy great popular respect for their lives are of exemplary morality, but their scholarship is a thing of the past and superstition is rife, particularly in Laos where it has almost smothered out the fundamental concepts of Buddhism. If the bonzes' intellectual horizon is singularly limited, if they are essentially and passively preoccupied with their personal salvation, they are not fanatical and through their educational work and moral influence they are invaluable intermediaries with the Khmer people. Moreover they are, unlike most Orientals, hard workers, without any repugnance for manual labour. Politically they have observed a strict neutrality and do not compromise their dignity and detachment like their functionary compatriots. Buddhism has augmented the Khmer inclination to endow every act and object with supernatural meaning.

333

In all Khmer art forms the model is generally Indian as well as the subject-matter, save what is taken from Cambodia's legendary past. The whole country is filled with these sombre and burning ruins, of whose origin the modern Cambodians are inordinately proud but totally ignorant. They speak of these monuments in the most fanciful vein, preferring to attribute to them a supernatural construction rather than to search out the reality. Cambodia is certainly the richest art centre in the peninsula, for its aristocracy for many generations had as its preoccupation the building of temples, the accumulation of gold and of merit.

Khmer architecture, which flourished for eight centuries, is the most universally admired of Cambodian arts, and there is charm and originality in its *naïveté*. The earliest temples were constructed in wood, so that the Brahman monuments and the Buddhist builders who came after them, by using more durable materials have survived in greater quantity. Plan and perspective, designs of delicacy and richness have been the chief beauty of Khmer monuments, not the technical side of the construction, which was always their weak point. Their magnificent achievement represented an enormous drain on the country's resources and labour, for they were built with comparative rapidity. Many were left unfinished, perhaps because of the superstition that completion might provoke the death of their donor. As a by-product, sculpture and the goldsmith's art were highly developed as part of the Khmer love of delicate and harmonious ornamentation. Khmer architecture revealed a sudden splendour and an equally abrupt decadence. This was partly due to wars and partly to the influence of Buddhism, which was inherently hostile to the development of art and literature as it was to all forms which expressed personality.

The creators of literature, like the architects, were generally anonymous and were Court poets and bonzes. Perhaps it was just as well, for on the whole Khmer literature is monotonous and abounding in sententious sayings. It is partially derived from Chinese literature but wholly subordinated to Indian models, especially the Ramayana and the Jatakao, and recitals of the previous existences of Buddha. In addition there are translations of the sacred books, technical studies on medicine, astrology and magic, compilations of maxims, and above all versified novels. The last mentioned are variations of a type story dealing with a prosperous reign broken by Court intrigues which rend the royal family asunder. Deserving princes and princesses flee and are miraculously saved from death. They wander for long years and have adventures with other royal unfortunates. They encounter the Kinnari, or beautiful women with the feet of birds, also ogres and ogresses who are given to eating human flesh, and anchorites with infinite talent for self-transformation. Eventually they are reconciled to their parents and spend the rest of their days in the company of the various ladies they have amassed on their travels. Underneath this display of the fertile Khmer imagination, which loves to pile up incident upon incident, and complicate by the incessant intervention of the supernatural an essentially simple story, there is the belief that years of sufferings are indispensable to later happiness, especially when the hero is one of the innumerable incarnations of Buddha. Like the Annamites, the Khmers approve of the use of successful ruse on simple-minded people, and on this score the women come off much better than the men.

Fortunately the tropics are hard on such literary records and books were destroyed in a few years. At Angkor, nothing but the sites of the libraries are known. Only what was carved in stone has endured, though it is known that from the third century the Khmers had books and kept archives.[1] The oldest Khmer writing extant is dated A.D. 629. The calligraphers' work was excellent, whether they wrote in Sanskrit or in Khmer. Up to the eleventh century Sanskrit was used, and then came an abrupt change that shows the constant intellectual exchange and the sensitivity of Cambodia to India's tutelage. Two kinds of writing were used: one for the sacred books and the other for ordinary correspondence; yet to the Khmers the written word is venerated for its own sake because of its divine origin. The spoken language differs from Annamite or Chinese, and is much less difficult to learn. There are no tones, articles, or declensions, yet the construction is complicated. In everyday words the language is very rich, but in technical or metaphysical terms it has had to borrow from Pali, Sanskrit, or French. Poetry in particular has an extraneous vocabulary, full of archaic expressions that have no relation to the spoken language. These are used not to express emotion but to display erudition, so that the whole work is equally incomprehensible to scholars and to children. Much of the classic Khmer poetry is cherished for the moral sentiments in which it abounds. The drama is related to the novel in inspiration, as well as in plot and type characterization. It is really a pantomime ballet that lasts for days on end, and in which only the comic scenes are left to the actors' improvization and to the audience's understanding. The original Indian inspiration has been submerged by more recent Javanese and

[1] Groslier, G., *Recherches sur les Cambodgiens* (Paris, 1921), p. 1.

Siamese influences. Music is the inseparable companion of the theatre, where it is played during and between the acts. Singing is the most spontaneous medium for the dreamy and sentimental Khmer soul. The form is less rigid and their composition not confined to professional output. Though the love theme is monotonous, the improvisations are remarkable and beloved by all classes of the Khmers. Anonymous, like all Khmer art, it announces melodiously the futility of all achievement. Unfortunately the Khmers listen with such reverence and melting tenderness to what has been composed many years ago, that they prefer to play the old repertoire of about twenty-eight pieces, rather than to compose afresh their own.

Aside from these art forms connected with the theatre and architectural ornamentation, Khmer culture is mediocre and in no way comparable to the Siamese, which has fundamentally the same inspiration.

ECONOMY

Resources

The Mekong dominates Cambodian economy. It absorbs all tributaries and is incessantly changing its banks, thereby displacing houses and even villages. Yet the Khmer humility before its whims is based on that great river's essential benevolence, for every year it leaves a billion cubic metres of fertile alluvial soil. The Mekong is on its best behaviour in Cambodia and not impossibly torrential, as where it flows through Laos. The virgin forest is the second most important physical factor in the country. The heavily wooded mountains form an impenetrable citadel. If they afford Cambodia some geographical protection it is nevertheless true that the loss of seaports, which they now cut off, synchronized with the country's decline. They cut off human as well as commercial relations, and have contributed to an ingrown localism. Forests offer remarkable resources, which the French are trying to develop by protection and licensed exploitation in precious woods and fauna, yet much of them must be cut down before there is any economic progress in the country.

The psychological effect of the forest on human beings is another aspect of its importance. Even its silence is portentous: there is an intense life, an incessant and tumultuous activity. Hordes of ants on every branch; trees being eaten alive by insects—everywhere a large or miniature battlefield. Its climate is seasonless. Sunshine does not penetrate its lush foliage to indicate the time of day. Beside its vitality, human effort seems futile, its conquest foredoomed to failure. The forest is a formidable adversary which furthers defeatism, already too potent a factor in Khmer psychology.

The Grand Lac forms Cambodia's third most important resource, for it is one of the world's largest fish reservoirs. Floods and rains annually triple its surface, and its depth increases from two to fourteen metres. A vegetation conducive to fish fecundity is made by the waters flooding the surrounding forest land. A town springs into life every December at the beginning of the fishing season, whose polyglot population is made up of Malayans, Chinese, Annamites, and Khmers, with an elaborate tradition of rentals and sub-letting. When the waters retreat, the fish crowd into the shrunken lake and fall an easy prey to even the least adroit fishermen. The salt fish industry is enormously important because of local consumption and exportation. Yet there is much room for development.

The mineral resources of Cambodia offer no great prospects of wealth. Iron exists in the Moi country, where it is mined in limited quantities and by primitive methods. More variety is offered in stone. Limestone, of which there is a fair quantity, has been used in the building of Pnom-Penh. Sandstone is found at Kampot, where a curious tradition limits it as a family industry to the very small number of a hundred workers. In addition there is granite for road building, and marble at Pursat, which is hard to exploit profitably because of its inaccessibility and the lack of labour.

Animal husbandry has had some but could have more development in Cambodia. Buddhism discourages the eating of meat, so that exportation is its only future. This in turn depends on conditions in the world market, as Indo-China sadly learned through the closing down by tariff walls of the Philippine Islands and the recent prohibition of such imports into Malaya. Horses, buffaloes, elephants, pigs, chickens, and goats, as well as an assortment of wild animals, are evidence of what Cambodia might do in this field. The government has made some attempt at scientific cross-breeding but native indolence has retarded such experimentation. The Khmers' negligence is the cattle thieves' opportunity. Animals are let to wander about without care and without restraint. Their rapid multiplication—thoroughly haphazard—is offset by the ravages of epizootic to the complete indifference of their Cambodian owners.

The Khmers are primarily—if anything at all—an agricultural people. Their main crop is rice, of which there are two chief types and about

337

thirty varieties of each, then corn and sugar in the order of their importance. But the country is essentially one of *monoculture*—a danger for which the Khmers have only their indolence to blame. Only recently has an industrialized crop like rubber become important. As the climate is uniform throughout Cambodia, it is only the differences in soil and proximity to the Mekong that makes for the variety in crops.

The country produces more than it consumes and is consequently able to export fish, livestock, and rice. It has also a great future in cotton and rubber. Yet in spite of the country's potential and actual wealth, and the relatively small population, the Khmers are miserable. The thatch of Cambodia contrasts with the tiled roofs of her rich Cochin-Chinese neighbours. Fundamentally the Khmer is neither farmer, functionary, merchant, nor labourer, but an artisan whose innate aestheticism comes out in the fashioning and decoration of even the humblest tools. Khmer indolence and independence is both historical and natural, and has a good side in its docility. The climate aids and abets, and the abundance of nature is such that the Khmer can earn a livelihood by scratching the earth or dangling a fishline into the river. Their disdain of activity is genuine. They are perfectly willing to have the Chinese, the French, and even the Annamites control their country's economy.

Population

The population of Cambodia has been terribly decimated by foreign and internal strife. By the beginning of the twentieth century it had sunk to 1,200,000 and since then has only slowly increased. In the most recent census (1936) the Khmers formed only 50 per cent of the population in their capital, Pnom-Penh. The aborigines and immigrants numbered about half a million more. The indigenous peoples, vaguely related to the Khmers, lived peacefully beside them, yet without fusion. This attitude of indulgence is far from characterizing Khmer feeling for the Mois, the aborigines east of the Mekong, whom they pitilessly treat as savages and hunt as slaves. Chinese immigrants and half-breeds number about 100,000 and, unlike their status in Annam, they are more often farmers than merchants in Cambodia. No people could supplement another better than do the Chinese. To offset Khmer defects they offer thrift, perseverance, will-power, and a sense of hard realities. The Chinese may come to Cambodia as coolies but they do not remain such for long. They spring up any place where there is money to be made. They take possession of the soil pacifically: they impose nothing and make demands of no one. They intermarry with native women: they adopt local usages and customs, and what they change is done imperceptibly and inoffensively. They install themselves in the country, and if they lead the docile Khmer into debt they are also ever-present and ever-capable in the hour of need. In 1928 they made up a tenth of the country's population.

As much as they like the Chinese the Khmers dislike the Annamites. Historical reasons are not sufficient to explain this almost physical antipathy. The Khmers prefer to move away, even in their own country, rather than to share a village with immigrant Annamites. It is curious that the French, who stopped the military conquest of Cambodia by the Annamites, should have encouraged their immigration for economic necessity. The Annamites offer an almost perfect contrast with the Khmers. Their highly organized, decentralized commune offsets a centralized state and a capacity for expansion, whereas Cambodia is a disorganized Indian feudality whose absolute sovereign finds no opposition in the docile masses who are indifferent to public affairs. The Cambodians, much as they would like to, can offer no real resistance to the Annamites, much less to the Chinese, whom they like and admire. There are various unimportant minority groups: the Chams, for instance, who are merchants and fishermen, number about 50,000. The several thousand Malays, also Moslems and merchants, are allied by marriage as well as religion to the Chams. Siamese and Laotians also live peaceably in Cambodia, but rarely unite with the Khmers. The list is completed by that most nefarious of foreigners, the Indian *chetty*.

Labour

Shortage of labour is a clue to the problems of Cambodian economy, and the secret of the foreign infiltration which will probably complete the decline of the Khmers. It is not only their numerical deficiency in a country of potential wealth, but their lack of enterprise. The Khmers may suffer from famine, but they do nothing to remedy the dangers of *monoculture*. Grafting and fertilization are unknown to them, and they are, moreover, impervious to government exhortations and example. Their silks could be greatly improved by Chinese methods, but they never dream of adopting them. They use wood freely and never think of replacing the forests they have wantonly destroyed. Fundamentally there is no interest in working beyond bare subsistence needs. Labour is still a family affair and not that of individual workers. Large-scale cultivation before the plantation era was unknown in Cambodia.

339

Between Khmers the only labour contract is that of *métayage*, with all payments and advances in kind, not money. Even this form is very exceptional and confined to absentee officials farming their rice-fields. Independence is so firmly ingrained in the Khmer character that no contract on earth is strong enough to hold them if they feel moved to leave, which occurs when they have earned enough money for immediate needs. The absence of an *état civil* increases the difficulty of punishing the Khmers, who positively enjoy going to prison. Vagrancy is a race habit: whole villages decamp when the soil around them has become exhausted. Nature by her lavish abundance has taught the Khmers to be improvident. Gaming is another factor: in a single night they often dissipate a whole year's earnings.

There always remains requisitioned and penal labour, which is amply abused by French and native officials alike, but which is also notoriously inefficient. Seasonal labour from June to January is the least unreliable, and at best very scarce. Salaries are paid almost exclusively in paddy. Labour in payment of debts is customary, though impossible to estimate at its just proportion, and since the slave can never work off the principal of his debt, his servitude continues for life. Such labour is usually confined to the master's household, and is one way of getting round the servant problem in Cambodia. Khmer pride is often hurt in ways incomprehensible to the European, and this increases his natural nomadic tendencies. In brief, it is extremely difficult to get Cambodian labour and even harder to retain it. There is an instructive and amusing tale told of an enterprising Frenchman who, on a model philanthropic domain, bought a gramophone to entertain his workers. They were so effectively diverted that they left their work to listen all day to the records. The philanthropist was forced to retire from the enterprise, a wiser and a poorer man.

The Land Régime

In theory the king is so completely the owner of his country that the word sovereignty is confounded with that of property. Since it is to his interest that his lands should be worked, he permits his subjects to farm his kingdom and share with him its produce. The king's special rights of inheritance, when direct heirs are lacking, or after the land has been abandoned for three years, or in the confiscation of property for public or royal use without indemnity, all reveal his ancient rights. But in practice private property exists and is ardently defended as such by the Khmers. Taxes strike at the produce of the land, but not the land itself. As in Annam, this disparity between theory and actuality has led, understandably enough, to serious mistakes in the land concessions régime. With minor exceptions and without the usual formalities, private property exists as completely in Cambodia as in the West. When, at the outset, the French legally established private ownership, this astonished the Khmers, who indignantly thought that the French were trying to undermine their king's sovereign rights. It was not until 1909 that its formal establishment could be effected.

Much of the history of Annamite land ownership was repeated in Cambodia. There is, excepting Cochin-China, the same absence of middle-sized properties, the same indebtedness and lack of credit facilities other than usury for the small proprietor who is without reserves. The French banks show the same reluctance to extend credit in a country where property ownership does not offer sufficient guarantees, and whose officials are equally unreliable and unco-operative as guarantors of their poorer compatriots. Unlike the Annamite countries, however, there was and still is an enormous amount of fertile unoccupied land. Here again there was trouble in getting concessionnaires to exploit the lands they had lightly acquired until the post-War era, when the redlands of Cambodia became renowned for growing rubber.

Commerce

Cambodia has always been a commercial centre and the Chinese its perennial merchants. Khmer commercial ineptitude has thus been encouraged, and Cambodia's natural resources offer rich resources for Chinese needs: kingfisher feathers, rhinoceros' and buffaloes' horns, beeswax and spices were only a small part of the delicacies exported to Cathay. The Chinese, however, have never been in such complete control of this market that they could drive out all competition. The Malays enjoyed a certain amount of royal favour, and introduced into the country the *batiks* which modern Cambodians wear. This influence is reciprocal, for Khmer designs were copied to such good effect that they are found nowadays in Java. Indian commerce was formerly important, but few traces are now left except in the luxury industries and arts. Yet the Khmers had Indians to teach them how to make glass and weave cotton. Probably the Indians found the Chinese too firmly entrenched in the country to make competition profitable. The Siamese arrived too late—as merchants—in Cambodia to attain commercial importance, and the chronic state of wars after the thirteenth century was hardly conducive to mercantile exchange. The last two centuries

341

alone have witnessed a minor trade in articles for the Khmer aristocracy. Since the seventeenth century the Japanese have traded with Cambodia, furnishing firearms in return for animal and vegetable products.

The French developed an animal export trade with the Philippines only to have it crushed by the tariff. They also tried to improve the primitive methods which characterized all Cambodian output but without success. The Khmers cared not at all for improvement and wasted whatever money they made to the profit of the Chinese. Such industries as exist are in foreign hands. The Chinese have a cotton factory, also rice distilleries. Silk weaving and dyeing has been a Cambodian family industry for centuries, but it is swiftly disappearing through competition with the cheaper Chinese and Japanese silks. Boats are built and pottery is still being made by Cambodians for their own use. Work in precious metals and stones remains a fine tradition, though gradually being submerged by the new Occidental tastes of their erstwhile patrons.

THE FRENCH ADMINISTRATION IN CAMBODIA

In the mid-nineteenth century the age-old struggle between Annam and Siam for control of Cambodia seemed about to be resolved in favour of Siam, because Annam was so absorbed by her conflict with France. In 1859 Norodom succeeded to the Cambodian throne only to be dislodged in an uprising engineered by his ambitious brother Sivotha. He fled to Siam, bearing with him his crown, sword, and the royal seals. The Siamese restored him in 1862, with the result that they were more firmly entrenched than ever in power.

In an endeavour to throw off the ever-tightening hold of Siam, the Cambodian kings had begun in 1840 to make overtures to the French through their consul at Singapore. Ten years later a second attempt was made through a missionary. The French diplomat, Montigny, made the incomprehensible blunder of first approaching the King of Siam, with the result that he was not even granted an interview by the Cambodian king. When the Admirals were established at Saigon they tried to recover the ground France had lost by Siam's entering into friendly relations with Norodom. He, on his side, was delighted to fill the old Khmer role of playing off two dangerous rivals against each other, with France now taking Annam's former place. La Grandière made an exceptionally happy selection in Doudart de Lagrée as his representative and that of a government which had as yet nothing but the vaguest policy in Cambodia—one of watching closely a neighbouring country in which another foreign power was getting an uncomfortable ascendancy. As part of his unofficial mission Lagrée explored and studied the country, then almost totally unknown to Europeans. La Grandière, like his predecessors, visited Norodom, but on his own initiative he prepared a secret treaty which he got that wily king to sign in July 1863. This agreement was for a long time not known to Lagrée, but it was eventually ratified after some vacillation by the home government.

The Siamese, not to be outdone, put pressure in their turn on Norodom, who gave them a treaty which neutralized the concessions he had made to the French. This arrangement, which was published in the *Singapore Straits Times* on August 20, 1864, as having been signed the previous December, revealed a much stronger grip by the Siamese on Cambodian affairs. The issue was rather dramatically joined over the coronation ceremonies, which give, in the eyes of the people, legitimacy to the reigning prince. Lagrée prevented this coronation from taking place in the presence of the Siamese. Their subsequent efforts to dislodge Lagrée were unavailing. A second attempt to have Norodom go to Bangkok for his investiture was foiled by Lagrée's decisive action in occupying Oudong, the Khmer capital. Unfortunately for this newly enhanced French prestige, the Franco-Siamese treaty was signed in Paris at this time (1867) confirming the loss of Cambodia's two rich provinces, Battambang and Angkor. France promised not to annex Cambodia to Cochin-China, and the Siamese renounced tribute from Norodom.

A preliminary to further penetration was increased knowledge of the country, and this was one of the main objectives of Lagrée's exploration of the Mekong. Gradually efforts were made to get a more effective control over the country's internal organization. The 1863 treaty had given the French the right to do business and to acquire property in Cambodia, but there was no control over its internal administration, which remained completely independent. The numerous and increasing abuses of native officialdom, including the king who seemed to revel in capital punishments and unlimited extravagance, were covered by the French flag and moral responsibility. Banditry also was increasing, as did the slave trade. Public services existed only nominally and what roads there were, through lack of upkeep, defied traffic. Taxes continued to be farmed out to the ever-increasing profits of the Chinese and to the misery of the Khmer people, whose numbers dwindled steadily. As a mild beginning to reform, the French exacted the suppression of slavery (in 1877), the right to have a representative on the Ministerial

Council, and the registration of all contracts between the king and Europeans. What might have been an effective opening wedge remained a dead letter until the establishment of the civil government in Cochin-China.

The reorganization effected by Le Myre de Vilers and his successors was the first application in Cambodia of the Protectorate's hitherto purely theoretical powers of thirteen years' standing. French judicial control was increased at the expense of the Cambodian courts; measures were taken to suppress brigandage; fifty-seven provinces were compressed into eight, each headed by a French resident; Khmer functionaries' salaries were increased with the vain hope that this might cure their congenital venality.

Feeling that Le Myre had only made a beginning, Governor Thomson of Cochin-China chose an unfortunately violent way of dictating a new treaty. In the night of June 17th, he forced his way into the palace, awoke the sleeping king, and wrung from him a consent to important reforms which gave France control over the internal affairs of the country. This clumsily forced a delicate issue just at a time when Thomson was having his troubles with Annam. The heart of the difficulty, as always, was financial. King and people alike resented the French assessment and collection of taxes as derogatory to Norodom's sovereignty. The populace had already been upset by minor regulations curtailing their liberties, by the imposition of new taxes, and by giving priority to Annamites in the country. The movement, led by Prince Sivotha, began in January 1885 by an attack on the newly installed Residents, and lasted for eighteen months, inflicting serious losses on the French in both men and prestige. The territory over which their troops marched was a fifth the size of France. The country was largely unknown at the time, maps were almost non-existent, as also were means of communication, especially during the rainy season and through forest land. Lack of water, food, and all kinds of supplies made the ravages of sickness particularly heavy. Moreover, the Cambodian revolt stirred up a similar movement in Cochin-China. The military campaign was fortunately supplemented by diplomatic compromises on the part of the new governor, Filippini. He did not revise the treaty but modified it in application, leaving native officials in contact with the population and under a limited number of French Residents. When the situation was again altered, in 1897, it was at the request of Norodom himself, who either recognized the utility of the new measures proposed or the futility of opposing them.

The Protectorate ideal is identical for both Cambodia and Annam, but the institutions already existing in the two countries were not comparable. The Cambodian king was as despotic as an Indian rajah, naming and revoking candidates for office in a whimsical fashion that made the palace, and especially its harem, a hotbed of intrigue. The history of Cambodia is the history of its Court and a dull one at that. The only counterpoise to the king's authority is that of the bonzes, largely theoretical. The relation of sovereign to subject is reproduced everywhere throughout the country in the patron-client relationship. The system is inherently vicious because it cultivates a highly personal parasitism in which there is no vestige of public interest. Everywhere the arbitrary abuse of authority is triumphant.

It was only natural that Norodom did not relish French interference, which not only in theory interfered with his absolute powers, but was tactlessly applied by cutting his civil list. The history of the king's relations to the Protectorate after the 1884 treaty was that of a mediaeval prince trying to escape by Oriental wiles the powerful and tactless foreigners he had been forced to call to his aid. Only in 1897 was there a lessening of the tension between these two elements, through a compromise in which Doumer sought to give back to the king his prestige if not his power. The king was left master in his own palace with all the outward trappings of sovereignty, though carefully restricted as to range, because the Khmer people could not separate their national existence from that of their king. It mattered little to them—and a great deal to the Protectorate—that the reality of power lay in the hands of the Resident Superior. The whole country, with the exception of the king's private domain, came definitely under French control. The king was the only one displeased and even that could have been avoided. He was given a civil list of 1,200,000 francs, but he could not spend a sou of it without consulting his protectors. Besides paying palace officials and mandarins, taxes were forcibly extracted from him for the up-keep of Cambodia's dubious roads and gifts for charities in which he had no interest. He was told that he could order only so many bottles of champagne, and those must be of a particular brand. Next, European clothes were forced on the king and propaganda undertaken to make him see the joys of monogamy. The Resident Superior used the king's table to entertain his own guests and the king's purse when he was short of money. The stupidity of this needless alienation of Norodom's, and later of Sisowath's possible affections, was only matched by the contemporaneous treatment of the boy-Emperor of Annam.

Aside from tinkering with the king's sovereignty and private life, little was done that fundamentally altered the country's administration. In an effort to offset royal autocracy, communal organization was introduced into Cambodia at the same time that it was being destroyed in the Annamite countries. The Khmers could not grasp its purpose and were unprepared to utilize such an instrument. The prematurity of this change was shown by their refusal to accept the responsibility of the Notables' office, which was used solely to exploit the people under them.

The French failure to control effectively native officialdom is probably the most serious charge that can be brought against an otherwise successful Protectorate. Office-holding in Cambodia has still the character of a farm let out to the highest bidder—in other words, the best intriguer. Mandarins frankly announce the sum that their office has cost them. The literal translation of the Khmer word "to reign" is "the king eats his royalty," and as the king does so doth the busy functionary. What the Occidental calls abuse of power and graft is simply not understood by the Cambodians, who take it all as natural and inevitable. Certain important offices have no salaries at all and others are ridiculously underpaid. There are many Khmer judges who receive smaller wages than an Annamite cook—eighteen piastres a month. So it naturally follows that every functionary has but one guiding thought, to make the most out of his office in the quickest possible time, since its tenure, depending as it does on favour, is precarious. As in Annam, the coming of the French meant that the opportunities for money-making have increased, and the type of functionary is more of an opportunist than ever. The old-time official was venality incarnate, but his life of rustic simplicity had a patriarchal flavour that won him popular devotion.

The new official apes the French, is snobbishly distant from his people, and has along with his vices nothing like the moral and intellectual qualifications of his more benevolent predecessor. Village authorities are equally culpable, though forcibly restricted in their machinations. The people are too ignorant to protest, and it would be futile if they tried, for officials hang together when attacked, and the natives have no direct contact with the French administration. The presiding genius over all this pyramid of graft was the Minister of the Palace, who held office since 1898. With the king he was the only permanent among the many transient Residents Superior, and his powers steadily increased at the expense of both. Fundamentally the Protectorate was responsible for having raised this intermediary between itself and the people in an effort to keep the king from meddling in politics. And by 1912 his power and wealth were so great that the Resident Superior failed in an attempt to get rid of him.

The instability of the French Protectorate itself has made possible the continuation of the old administrative anarchy under an appearance of Occidental order. There have been fourteen Residents Superior in eighteen years—a characteristic of French colonization which prevents the effective pursuit of a stable policy. Moreover, the home government, nervous as always lest French opinion became hostile again, reiterates orders to its agents, *pas d'histoires*. The result is naturally the cult of the least effort, which is exeptionally easy in Cambodia where the indolence of the population is contagious and the climate enervating to Europeans. The practical outcome has been a stream of paper regulations that have remained a dead letter. The language requirements for functionaries, for example, were never seriously applied; the 1908 regulation of an *état civil* exists solely in theory and incidentally to fill native functionaries' pockets, for the natives have been made to pay for registering vital statistics. Minor reforms, as well as the abolition of corporal punishments, have never been carried out. Prisoners still wear chains regardless of decrees to the contrary. Every new regulation is a source of profit, as a timid and ignorant people like the Khmers positively invite abuse and domination. When the government tried to introduce representative assemblies in Cambodia to impress Metropolitan liberals, the people's misunderstanding of the measure was exploited by native officialdom as a new form of requisitioned labour.

Naturally taxes and *corvées* are most subject to serious abuse. The over-emphasis on fiscal success in French colonization is a dangerous partner to the graft of native officials. Taxes, as they are decreed, weigh heavily enough on the Khmers—they are the equivalent of a month's earnings—but they are augmented in proportion as native officials sense an individual's capacity to pay. It is dangerous to improve even the thatch on one's roof, for it will not go unnoticed by the official eye. As in Annam the population is ever on the edge of starvation. The natives' indolence and refusal to modernize their methods of cultivation are partly responsible; nevertheless it has always been imprudent to display too much ability. Nor have the benefits felt by the masses been commensurate with their sacrifices. A disproportionately large sum has been devoted to the costs of administration and too little been given to educational and economic development. A programme of public works related to Cambodia's needs, that would have attracted capital, has remained almost wholly in the realm of projects. Among the least essential constructions has been that of a palatial sanatorium for French officialdom. But perhaps it is the road building that caused the worst abuses to flourish. Khmers taken far from home have lacked the necessities of life and laboured far beyond their quota of days, impotent to prevent abuse, and not comprehending the utility of what they were suffering for. The Cambodian usually takes refuge in his poverty. Yet even the Khmer worm can turn, not often but viciously on the rare occasions when abuses have finally aroused to violence. The murder of the Resident Bardez is instructive as well as rare in Franco-Cambodian annals. The brutal tactlessness of this official who tried to collect taxes in a Khmer village on a religious holiday provoked his own demise.

Indirect taxes are as much of a blot on the escutcheon of Cambodian finance as in Annam. Generally the Khmer is neither an opium nor an alcohol addict, yet the government's measures to increase these sales have created a scandal in France. These vices have spread to the country districts, whereas formerly they were principally confined to the Chinese. Though the revenues increased as desired, there is something ironical in the widespread habit of using the cheaper opium dross which brings little benefit to the Treasury, and which has a disastrous effect on the population, as crime statistics show. Perhaps the forces of righteousness were discouraged by the failure to suppress the Gaming Farm. The Thirty-Six Animals is a form of lottery which is played all over Cambodia and has become a chronic disease with the Khmers. Its profits go to private individuals, principally the Chinese. Its effects are as noxious as before and they do not even benefit the treasury.

FRENCH JUSTICE IN CAMBODIA

Like its twin Protectorate Annam, justice in Cambodia remained longer untouched than in the directly administered countries. The first step was to extract Europeans from native justice, but not until 1891 was a mixed court instituted to judge cases between Cambodians and French. Because the Protectorate was so slow in getting under way—even Doumer feared to introduce the separation of powers—the dual system was perpetuated. Only gradually did the French take over cases between non-Khmer Asiatics. By 1897 native justice was left with only suits between Khmers. A limited organization of criminal and appeal courts was set up. In 1891 the Ministerial Council had replaced the former court of appeal, although this worked on the basis of an old Cambodian institution, and its development was quite contrary to the spirit of Khmer justice. Village and provincial courts were retained, but a Tribunal of First Instance was instituted at Pnom-Penh for cases considered too important for the local mandarins. To improve their knowledge, along with their standards of professional honesty, courses in judicial trainings were started for Khmer judges.

The War and a greater preoccupation with the Annamite countries postponed the inevitable separation of administrative and judicial powers in Cambodia until 1922, when the government allowed itself the luxury of a complete reorganization. Native provincial governors who had indiscriminately exercised all judicial powers were notoriously overworked and far from impartial. The network of courts set up in consequence resembled that of the other countries of the Union but was much less complete. A French magistrate keeps a centralized control over the whole system. One of the obvious results of this reform has been to decrease the number of courts. There are now only fourteen, whereas formerly there were fifty-one. This naturally means that litigants spend more time, money, and energy than heretofore. There is only one criminal court and one court of appeals for all Cambodia, and their control is in the hands of the French administration, which can consult any *dossier* of the civil courts it may desire. It is hard to reconcile those extraordinary powers with the treaty of 1863.

In revising the Khmer code the work accomplished by France bears comparison with what was done for Annamite legislation. In both countries France was confronted with a remarkably developed code which, nevertheless, lacked precision and any provision for dealing with modern conditions. Revision aimed to bring the traditional code into line with current life and yet retain sacred customs so as to mitigate the brutality of the change, to speed up the notoriously dilatory Khmer justice, and to curb the corruption of judges. In 1918 the Protectorate published thirty-nine ancient laws in the Khmer language. These were nothing more than a selection of old legal principles, omitting their barbaric penalties, but their form was so archaic that they were difficult to apply. Seven years later A. Leclerc published the Cambodian codes, but this was only a translation. In 1901 a committee was instituted to draw up a compromise code, but the result was not promulgated till 1911. In this severe penalties were decreed for acts touching French sovereignty, though there was a notable improvement in curbing judgments over-favourable to Europeans in their suits with natives and a severer application of the laws forbidding corporal punishments. The following year this code was re-studied and in 1920 it was applied. In 1927 a further judicial reorganization took place, and in 1929 still another change.

These numerous hesitations and revisions reveal the extraordinary delicacy and intricacy of the task. Though the harshness of the penalties was, in particular, greatly softened, it was almost impossible to control the judges' methods. Moreover, the French in an effort to be humanitarian had introduced the penalty of deportation to replace capital punishment, yet it was considered by the natives to be far more severe and hence almost never applied. Death with its possible improvement in•reincarnation status seemed infinitely preferable.

Though the code's frequent revisions have undoubtedly improved Cambodian justice, they have left untouched certain features which are perhaps incapable of amelioration. The pillory stand for witnesses has been abolished, but the Khmers cannot yet overcome their timidity in giving testimony in court and they are still afraid to report crimes lest it entail reprisals. Criminals in this way find protection everywhere and insecurity flourishes. Cambodian houses are particularly inflammable, and the constant effort to disguise what he possesses is due as much to the Khmer's fear of bandits' arson as it is to the fisc. All the numerous changes in the codes have fostered the feeling of general uncertainty and malaise. The Cambodians have compared the perpetual mutation in legislation to a newly sharpened sword placed in the hands of a blind man. But the greatest reproach that can be made against French justice in Cambodia is that it has not yet worked out a mechanism which protects the masses from exploitation by their unscrupulous compatriots.

It is still true that native judges administer the worst justice in Cambodia. The prisons are eloquent proof of this: they are so flimsy that only Khmers would not take the trouble to escape from them. Prisoners still wear chains, and even debt slaves continue to do heavy labour. Hygienic conditions are so bad that sickness is rife and the mortality astonishing. The French should have interfered more, especially when King Sisovath on coming to the throne in 1905 tried to change some of these conditions. Nor has any fundamental remedy been found to cure venality—that life-sized, supremely Asiatic vice. If the Protectorate were consistent with its principles the Ministers of State would be the first to serve prison sentences. Changes have taken place principally on the surface; underneath the condition of the masses is still much the same. The most insidious feature is their own attitude. They complain melodiously of abuses which they lift not one finger to remedy.

Until the mid-nineteenth century European knowledge of Annam was of the sketchiest, but it never reached the same depths as European ignorance of Cambodia and Laos. Cambodia, inaccessible and war-ridden, had been much less visited than Annam by missionaries and traders.

Bouillevaux was the first contemporary European who saw and described the Khmer monuments and attempted to study the history of that country. He took the trouble to learn both the Annamite and Khmer languages before embarking on his travels in 1850. The scientist, Henri Mouhot, is usually credited with rediscovering Angkor, and the lyrical description of these great ruins in his diary is one of the earliest and best-known accounts. Missionaries had long before known of its existence; the Portuguese in the sixteenth century had even visited it; Chinese annalists had written of it in the thirteenth century.

Mouhot's was a discovery only in the sense that it brought to Europe a realization of Cambodia's existence at a time when colonization was in the air. In addition to the work of Frenchmen there were three Englishmen and a German all travelling at about the same time in Cambodia. Lagrée's work, though far from being the earliest, was among the best scientific explorations. He made every effort to understand the Khmers; reading everything he could lay hands on, collecting old manuscripts, questioning bonzes and missionaries, and soliciting their aid in his research. Lagrée, perhaps more than any other precursor, drew Europe's attention to a new field for scholarship and paved the way for the later deciphering of Khmer inscriptions. The Lagrée Mission took a big stride ahead in the systematic exploration of Cambodia, which was carried to completion by the work of Pavie and his collaborators, and by Delaporte.

The next work to be done was that of interpretation. Aymonier was one of the first scholars to study historical writings. The official annals of Cambodia were translated, but it was found that these chronicles only went back to 1346. Prior to this only legends and stone inscriptions filled the void. Lagrée had recognized their documentary value and had a few of them translated by a bonze who, unfortunately, preferred to make serious mistakes rather than to admit himself no scholar. When Aymonier replaced Moura in 1879 as French representative in Cambodia, he brought to the study of that country's culture a remarkable language equipment, born of years of study. His previous deciphering of the inscriptions reproduced in Lagrée's book had led him to the conclusion that two languages had been successively used: Sanskrit and Khmer. Simultaneously in Europe, Professor Kern of Leyden, an Indian scholar, in translating some Sanskrit inscriptions that Harmand had collected, revealed beyond a doubt the existence of a Brahmanic cult of Siva, co-existent with Buddhism in Cambodia. But he also showed that old Buddhism had used Sanskrit, not Pali, as its written medium. Aymonier's studies in particular contradicted the current belief in the fabulous antiquity of Khmer monuments and thereby aroused considerable opposition. Nevertheless he succeeded in getting official support in 1887. From this time forth a stream of articles, inscriptions, and finally a monumental work on Cambodia from his pen wended their way back to France. The old Khmer civilization has exercised a fascination over many students, but modern Cambodia has comparatively few chroniclers.

The EFEO has done able work in restoring the innumerable ruins—notably that of Angkor—with which Cambodia is covered. The Royal Library at Pnom-Penh is another creation, the remarkable work of Suzanne Karpelès, who has overcome the bonzes' distrust of women to the extent of persuading them to entrust her with the most precious relics and manuscripts in their pagodas. The majority of the Library's readers are bonzes. Lectures, meetings, moving pictures and book exhibits are also organized there for their edification. A monthly review, *The Sun of Cambodia*, had 400 subscribers in 1928, only a year after it was founded. The publication of Khmer works and Buddhist subjects has had an enormous effect, as is shown by the sales. A recent edition of a collection of Buddhist texts, the Tripitaka, at great cost and effort, is one of the finest works of French colonization. It has provoked a veritable renaissance of Khmer intellectual life.

Just as education has been the great stumbling-block to mutual understanding in the Annamite countries, so in Cambodia it has been just the contrary—the bridge which has happily united the two diverse civilizations. The link so successfully used in Cambodia is the bonzes, whose immense moral influence over the Khmers has been utilized in effecting a reform in education.

Almost every Khmer youth spends some months of his life in the pagoda. He serves there both as disciple and servant to the bonzes. In former days the instruction he received was exclusively moral and religious—reading and writing maxims and versified novels. Literacy was even more widespread among the Khmers than the Annamites, and this is an extremely important factor in the formation of public opinion. Another very significant difference with Annam is the lack of connection between education and office-holding in Cambodia. There was never any higher education in Cambodia, and offices were allotted by favour and not through competitive examinations. China's proximity to Annam and the presence of so many Chinese in Indo-China did serve to keep alive her spiritual domination. Indian influence as well as Chinese was paramount in Cambodia, but for many centuries the spiritual isolation of the Khmers has been fairly complete. Cambodia's general situation was far simpler. Education can be used by the French as an instrument for teaching what they want the Khmers to learn, since it is not seized upon by ambitious natives, as it is with the Annamites, to reach positions that threaten French sovereignty.

It was Beau's *Conseil de Perfectionnement* that used its unerring judgment in deciding to work in the Cambodian language and through the existing pagoda schools. The memory of Cochin-China's failure was still green, and there was no desire to reproduce in Cambodia that premature destruction of an existing culture before anything had been devised to replace it. Once a general policy had been decided upon there remained serious difficulties in its application. In 1908, through a miscarriage of Beau's ideas, the bonzes were ignored and lay monitors sent to the pagoda schools. Only the pagoda itself and the children who regularly attended there were utilized, to the natural irritation of the bonzes. It was not until the general shake-up in 1924 that the Council's ideas were applied and with success. Tact was needed to win the indispensable co-operation of the bonzes, but they were eventually persuaded to take courses in pedagogy, use new textbooks and methods, and in general to add the elements of a scientific education to a curriculum that had hitherto specialized in the supernatural. So far it has been impossible to make much headway with women's education—a development of which the bonzes are very chary. Discreet efforts have resulted in some Franco-Cambodian schools for girls, which are, in this as well as in other respects, more liberal than the pagoda education. Higher education has paralleled the Franco-Annamite system in using as a basis the Pali language and literature on which to graft Western ideas. Various attempts to create a Pali school for bonzes, and even to send them to Paris, were unsuccessful, but some such training was essential, simply because there was no place to study Buddhist lore nearer than Bangkok. To fill in this need, as well as to extract the bonzes from undue Siamese influence, a Buddhist Institute was founded at the Cambodian capital, which already had a Royal Library. When a *lycée* was opened in 1935 at Pnom-Penh the educational system of Cambodia was finally given a framework, though it is not yet nearly so complete as in the Annamite countries.

French Revival of the Khmer Arts

The artistic heritage of the Khmers is so obviously great that its twentieth-century decadence has been particularly striking. The EFEO created in 1905 a museum for Khmer art prior to the thirteenth century, but its space was so limited that no new objects could be acquired. Two years later a Royal Factory was started, and in 1912 a School of Decorative Arts added to it. That the proper directing impetus was lacking was shown by the presence of only ten pupils five years after its founding, of which the oldest was sixteen years of age. The Factory's output had steadily declined, despite a quintupling of the tourist trade in those very years. An art section to the Professional School of Pnom-Penh had also been created but it only attracted Annamite pupils.

Albert Sarraut gave to his protégé, Georges Groslier, the task of resuscitating contemporary Khmer art. Groslier's study of the Cambodian art and character materialized in the form of a special programme for his new School of Cambodian Arts. He refused to adopt a ready-made art programme from France or from the Annamite countries. He believed that it was the lack of a clientele that was responsible for the decline in Khmer art, and in turn that that was due to Khmer passivity before the invasion of Western standards. Formerly all wealthy Cambodians had in their households, like the miniature courts of the Italian Renaissance, artisans, dancers, and musicians, but fifty years had sufficed to disperse these artists through the inroads made by bad Occidental art. The nine hundred pagodas of Cambodia suffered from the same malady. Instead of keeping their own artists they now bought paper flowers and Western bric-à-brac. By 1917 the king was almost the only Khmer left who kept his own *atelier*, but even the art produced there was decadent.

The Cambodian people, left to themselves, could not keep their

354

artistic traditions alive. Women who used to weave and dye cloth for their homes, the farmer who formerly decorated his house and even his tools, disappeared with surprising rapidity. Only the goldsmiths remained prosperous enough to practise their craft in its pure form. A rise in the cost of living had taken from the Khmer that slight surplus with which before he had indulged his artistic tastes. This made Groslier's task doubly hard, for it was almost impossible to find a Khmer who could teach the native arts. Westernism had been such a solvent of local artistic traditions that the whole people needed a re-education in their own culture.

After the War, buildings to serve as a museum and school were erected to illustrate and to house the best in the country's artistic past. The school's rapid growth showed a widespread popular response: there were eighty pupils in 1920, 165 in 1923, and the following year an annex was opened. The greatest problem after that of finding teachers was to make the Khmers submit to the essential discipline. Groslier placed royal artisans, chosen by the pupils themselves, at the head of the *atelier*. They taught as if they were in their own homes, using local materials and the traditional tools. The best stimulant to effort proved to be the Khmer pride in the past, and the example of their ancestors was held constantly before them. Khmer apathy and Westernization were not the only obstacles to overcome. French assimilationists wanted them to be taught in French and by French methods. Groslier insisted that the Khmer could not stand up under a system of competitive examinations, that they needed the constant stimulus of example, and discouragement of workshop laziness and intrigue. He was so successful in his methods that there was no disciplinary penalty imposed for seven years. Nor did any student take the vacation to which he was entitled.

Finding a clientele did not wholly solve the artisan's problems. A Khmer is too often so encouraged by a sale that he changes his work and leaves the school, thinking that he has nothing more to learn. A masterpiece in the old guild manner is made the requisite for a diploma—which consists of the school's official blessing and a kit of tools. The Khmer artisan is distrustful, non-enterprising, and vain. He is slow and will work only when he sees immediate results. His easy discouragement shows his lack of patience and perseverance. Being utterly without commercial sense he needs a middleman to make contacts with purchasers, usually nowadays a European, since Khmer taste has fallen so low. The school acts as such an intermediary, not only for its own students but for any artist, and in this way continues to exercise an artistic control. Even yet the Khmers do not wholly grasp the ideal of co-operation. The school's role is to keep up standards, both artistic and commercial; it considers its work that of a teacher until the Khmers themselves can take over its direction.

The Mission in Cambodia

Christianity was preached in Cambodia by the Portuguese Jesuits in the sixteenth century, but without much success. The Spanish, arriving in 1581, had better luck in making converts of some important members of the Court. One Dominican even obtained important concessions from a king whom he had helped in a successful revolt. This official tolerance did little to increase the body of the faithful. The Khmer kings were never persecutors, and it was not until an invasion of the King of Siam that one of the Mission churches was destroyed and its priests led away as prisoners. This episode was curiously paralleled in 1835 when, during the last Siamese invasion, a church of Pnom-Penh was burned down.

Two forces oppose the spread of Christianity in Cambodia: the hold of Buddhism on all classes of the people, and their economic situation. Recently the government became the official protector of Buddhism, and has set about to educate its bonzes. This has been a great blow to the Mission, which had capitalized the ignorance of the bonzes in its propaganda, for Mission prestige had already been undermined by anti-clericalism. Cao-daism, the regenerated form of national Buddhism, has very recently made such inroads that the government in alarm decreed that only two religions were permitted in Cambodia—Catholicism and Buddhism—thus ending an almost unprecedented history of tolerance.

The instability of the Annamites is mild in comparison with the chronic vagrancy of the Khmers. Not only was it caused by years of invasions and the primitive agricultural methods, but the country is eaten up by usury and creditors force debtors into frequent displacements. The Mission, as elsewhere, has led the way in giving employment and teaching new methods to increase production, but Khmer apathy has resisted their best efforts. It was too much trouble to drain a lake to create new rich land even though they were on the edge of starvation. There are no group conversions as in Annam: the work is accomplished individually. Moreover Khmer converts require constant attention lest they backslide. The women are the worst offenders: they keep their husbands in a perpetual procrastination in regard to assuring their salvation by baptism. Only recently the importation of planta-tion life has given a new fillip to their chronic instability.

FRENCH REACTION TO CAMBODIA

There is a certain type of Occidental for whom Cambodia has incom-parable charm. For those who like the mysterious and the solitary Northern Cambodia is full of folklore and genii; in the South it is more romantic and exotic. The contrast is striking between a glorious past, an insouciant and gay present, and a future—in all probability—disastrous. On the whole it is the past which has most attracted French-men. There are few books written on modern Cambodia compared with the host which have appeared on current Annamite problems.

The Khmer people are responsible for the spell that their country casts over foreigners. Their personality is pleasing, their character upright, and the women especially are beautiful to look upon. They exude an aesthetic tranquillity soothing to Western nerves, and they are not burdened with individuality. At the age of two, Khmers know their destiny and thereafter are never occupied with anything but their immediate concerns. Visible boundaries hem in their lives. They are inordinately proud of their past, but do nothing to revive it or even to learn about it. They bask in an atmosphere of credulous *naïveté* and this eventually effects the Westerner in their midst. His reasoning slowly loses a common-sense basis. He begins to sleep with his head to the south, to pay attention to native omens and unconsciously to pro-pitiate the spirits. Unlike learning Annamite customs, Cambodian life is contagious without effort. It is easier to slough off a superficial varnish of Western culture than to enter the complicated psychology of the Annamite mind. Roland Meyer's story of *Komlah* is that of a European who found the Khmers so overwhelmingly congenial that he gave his life to studying them. He became so steeped in Khmer life that he was dominated by what he had intended to master. In analysing the causes of their charming decadence his personality and will power were eaten away. In feeling so keenly their charm he absorbed the germs of their decadence. The unlimited devotion which the Khmer is capable of giving to those who know how to handle him is partially offset by the cloying docility of this perennially enslaved people. Despite their intelligence and obstinacy the Khmers are discouraging material with which to work, from the viewpoint of future development.

Many feel that it seems almost hopeless to patch up a decadent race which makes no move to help itself. They will never be able to equal their ancestors artistically, politically, or spiritually. Their economic future is more than dubious. They are doomed to disappear before the Annamite immigration. Of what use is an attempt to interfere with nature's selection of the fittest for survival?

NATIVE REACTION TO THE FRENCH PROTECTORATE

The core of the Khmer reaction to French control is the fact that the Protectorate was sought and not imposed, and this has eliminated all the psychological complications arising from the juxtaposition of victor and vanquished. An immediate and real protection was given to Cambodia from the encroachments of the Siamese and Annamites. When the two lost provinces were restored in 1907, French prestige was enormously enhanced and Khmer national pride vindicated. It is safe to prophesy that so long as their heritage remains, as well as its symbol, the royal power, the Khmers will be loyal to the Protectorate.

The king's sovereignty has been definitely tampered with and often in a stupidly tactless manner. This was partly due to uprushes of assimilationism, analogous to what happened in the Annamite countries, and partly to the personality of the Khmer kings. Norodom incarnated Oriental wiles and childishness in his reaction to the new Western influences. He adored every new gadget and he mixed them indiscriminately with Cambodian objects. He wore a series of semi-military uniforms studded with precious stones; his palaces were filled with mechanical toys; he had a statue of Napoleon III decapitated and his own sculptured head substituted—symbolic of the superimposing, without amalgamation, of one civilization upon another. His subjects naturally followed the royal example in so far as they were able. His Ministers took up bicycling with ardour until a new Resident Superior appeared with a motor-car, so they abandoned cycling and bought cars, only substituting gentle gongs for the raucous Klaxon. The king built a brick villa in the worst possible European taste, and they did likewise. An important by-product of this inrush of bad Occidentalism was the decline of the national Cambodian arts. An amusing picture of Norodom in 1881 has been left by Rivière when the king—then in his forty-seventh year and the father of only seventy-two offspring—visited him on board his warship. Norodom was enchanted with the twenty-one-gun salute, but even more by the portable roulette wheel the commandant had brought with him. The king spent such a delightful evening that he accepted without demur all the French demands. Under such casual auspices was the Protectorate launched.

His successor, King Sisowath, was invited to Marseille entirely because the Exposition of 1906 wanted to feature the Cambodian dancers, and the king would not let them go without him. The whole journey was significant. Sisowath first insisted that the ship follow the coast because the sea was rough. Fearing starvation in a foreign country he loaded the boat with edible livestock, and both on shipboard and in France he and his suite insisted on eating exclusively off gold plate.

Upon his arrival in France he was so pleased with the reception he received that he asked why the French of France were so much nicer than those in the colonies, and why so powerful a country should be unable to get back his lost provinces. Hurried from one reception to another he complained bitterly of having no time to rest. A hundred times a day he was vocally astonished by the seething activity of Marseille and begged to be told what sins these wretchedly busy people were expiating. He distributed 1,200 medals during his visit, and it was only with the greatest difficulty that he was prevented from giving one to the cook to whom he was spontaneously grateful. The king proved to be a general nuisance and was rather hastily returned to Cambodia, though he several times mentioned that he would prefer to stay longer.

The petty and incessant interference to which the king in his own country was subjected showed the total French incomprehension of his importance to his people. It was indeed hard to take a king seriously who said that he saw no use in building a certain road because he never expected to travel there, and whose idea of government in general was the gratification of his personal whims. But the Khmers were blindly devoted to their king no matter what he might be. The monarch's personal prestige was shown clearly during the War when the tottering Sisowath was able to calm a serious rebellion simply by asking his people to return to their homes.

Aside from a semi-religious loyalty to their king and a consciousness of their glorious past, the Khmers cannot be said to have produced a truly nationalist movement. Fatalism and a love of peace have made them prefer a secure, albeit foreign, protectorate to a struggle for dubious independence. There is no such thing as public opinion in Cambodia. The press is unknown there: just before the War an attempt to start a local paper there failed. Khmer nationalism, such as it is, has been up to now almost entirely passive. There are, of course, certain grounds for discontent.

The old Khmer-Annam struggle has been transferred from the political to the economic field. The small scattered Khmer population has neither the physical nor psychological force to resist the Annamite inroads, nor to develop its own country. Not that the Khmer is entirely without guile, for a disarming gentleness often covers up opportunism, but it is never aggressive like the Annamites'. The Khmer is so permeated with Buddhistic passivity and imaginative fantasy that he is no match for his more realistic neighbours who are coming to colonize the rich redlands of Cambodia. The Khmers want protection by the French from this new menace of their old enemy. But it is inherent in the nature of colonization for the country to be developed—if the French cannot use the local people then they must encourage those best qualified, even at the cost of destroying the indigenous population. Incidentally the name "protectorate" thus becomes a farce. Its irony would be greatly augmented if the Annamites brought with them the germs of Communism, that would destroy not only Khmer resistance, but French sovereignty as well.

The budget is fed almost exclusively by direct taxations. Indirect taxes are intermittent and irregular, depending too often on the degree of cordiality between the Governor-General and the Resident Superior of Cambodia rather than upon the country's needs. The tax on paddy, the oldest and most important of direct taxes, is based on produce and not on the land itself. Though it naturally has lent itself to fraud it was related directly to income. When this tax was supressed in 1924 and replaced by a land tax, all the defects of the old and none of its advantages were retained. Its essential unfairness is due to the lack of land surveying. Cambodia had no tax registers akin to the Annamite *diabo* by which even a vague accuracy might be approximated. More of the budget revenues should be allotted to medical and social service and to public works related to the country's needs and development.

On the administrative side the Khmers feel that France tends to govern Cambodia as if it were an annex of Cochin-China. Its needs are specialized and entirely different from those of Annamite countries. France inclines to send young and inexperienced functionaries to Cambodia, or those who have had experience without marked success in Annamite countries. Cambodia has been the Cinderella of the Union, and is neglected because the Khmers complain so much more gently than their aggressive Annamite neighbours.

In regard to the local administration the provincial Councils were suppressed in 1912, only to be restored, as in Annam, after the Yenbay

360

uprisings. In 1921 a further change occurred by which—though the village organization was retained—a new territorial unit called the *Khand* was created in the image of a French sub-prefecture. The idea was to effect a better control over the whole mandarinal hierarchy, but in reality all it succeeded in doing was to create more under-paid positions and needless confusion. It would have been sounder policy to have bettered the financial position of the old mandarinate and not simply created more officials to oppress the masses. The native Governor who topped the new hierarchy was theoretically a liaison officer with the French administration, but in actuality he became the Resident's hireling. The essence of the situation was the same as in the days of the *Affaire Iukanthor*—the Khmers wanted either effective control or complete independence.

On the social side, Leclere, a melancholy historian of native demoralization, estimated in 1902 that feminine morals had suffered badly. Formerly Khmer women were practically invisible, now they were far from inaccessible to Europeans. In 1892 there had been only five prostitutes in all Pnom-Penh: ten years later there were fifty. More divorces and fewer marriages indicated a general lessening of the grip of religion on Khmer life. Temples were less frequented; they were manned by fewer bonzes, who took orders for a shorter time, and who gave instructions to a declining number of pupils. Discipline and courtesy, especially to the old and to superiors, were markedly on the wane. This demoralization is very slight in comparison to the spiritual revolution experienced in Annamite countries. And there are definite ameliorations in their condition admitted by the Khmers themselves.

If the people are still exploited it is less now than formerly. A journalist was told by one Cambodian that nowadays rich people paid almost as many taxes as the poor. Some magicians and bandits have openly complained that they have had to seek other work since their professions are no longer lucrative. A slightly lesser degree of credulity means less sorcery and less servitude to genii. This undermining of superstition is due chiefly to the fine work of French doctors. Vaccination and hygienic care have tripled the kingdom's population. The Khmer peasant is better off economically than before, in spite of the higher cost of living and increasing exploitation by officials. Peace, the re-organization of native codes and justice, professional and modernized education, and new means of communication are all among these ameliorations. The Protectorate form has been strictly maintained: native civilization has been respected. Critics may well say that there is still an immense amount to be done, but the standard of judgment must always remain comparative. The French in Indo-China are between two fires. In the Annamite countries they are accused, and with reason, of having exercised too direct interference in native life; in Cambodia they are criticized, and with reason, for having interfered too little and left the old disorder under a superficial re-organization. One of the real bases of French success is intangible: the restoration of their national dignity in Khmer eyes through the maintenance of royal prestige, through the restoration of former boundaries, through the renaissance of Buddhist scholarship, and the revival of national arts. France's sins of omission pale beside the great accomplishment of having restored a nation's self-confidence.

In regard to personal contacts, the French and Khmers find each other mutually congenial, and each has left a strong imprint on the other. The refusal of the majority of French to study the Cambodian language and culture not only hurts the national pride of the sensitive Khmer but is a source of misunderstanding between two peoples. Although much of the worst side of colonials is the same as in Annamite countries, because inherent in the nature of colonization, the French on the whole are liked and admired by the Cambodians. What differences exist are of so fundamental a nature that they belong to racial Occidental-Oriental viewpoints and are not specifically Franco-Cambodian.

Their mental outlook is fundamentally opposed. To the Khmers everything has a moral foundation. This life must be led virtuously because it relates to future happiness and is not the European concern with immediate materialistic content. European life seems to them inconsistent: there is perpetual antithesis between virtue and vice, which, like poverty and wealth, pride and baseness, live together without apparent appreciation of their inconsistency. How can a European divorce public from private life and judge each by a different standard? A man cannot be impeccable in office who is immoral as a private individual. To the simple Cambodians the French are *yacks*, powerful but impious demons, condemned to exhaust themselves in diabolic works without ever discovering for themselves the secret of eternal happiness. It is a perpetual source of surprise to Khmers of all stations that men who have so much power and knowledge should lack simple goodness. Few Khmers have tried to get beyond this stage of gentle and plaintive query. Those Europeans who have tried to bridge the gap and to understand Khmer life have themselves been poisoned by its contagious decadence.

362

PEOPLES OF INDIAN CULTURE

LAOS

HISTORY AND ADMINISTRATION

Laos is a ribbon of a country stretching from Cambodia to the Yunnanese frontier, and entirely dominated by the Mekong River. That great waterway is so imperfect a means of communication that the geographic diversity of the country and its peoples has free rein. Laos is covered with *muongs* or totally independent village groups. They have only been united under either a powerful neighbouring state like Siam or Cambodia, or when the two strongest among them—the principalities of Luang-Prabang and Vientiane—had kings energetic enough to achieve a confederation.

The early period of Laotian history is that of confused invasions by the Javanese, Thibetans, Indians, and Mongols. The last-mentioned in the thirteenth century opened Laos to the tribes of South China, and to the long struggles of the indigenous Khas with the invaders, the most formidable of whom were the Thais, who arrived in the fourteenth century. This beginning of Laos's historic period was also that of the Thai Empire which, though it centred around the Menam Valley, spread over Siam, Northern Laos, and part of Yunnan and Burma. One able Thai, Phya Ngam, succeeded in carving a kingdom for himself out of the Laotian principalities, whose capital he established at Luang-Prabang. This remained the capital until the middle of the sixteenth century when it was abandoned for Vientiane. The Thai invasions finally succeeded in dispersing the Khas into small isolated groups.

Phya Ngam was related by marriage to the Khmer kings, and his reign marked the beginning of close relations between Cambodia and Laos. At Ngam's request Buddhist missionaries were sent to his kingdom and with them came Khmer workmen and scholars. The eastward expansion of this bellicose monarch brought him into contact with the Emperor of Annam, who made a boundary treaty with him, as did the King of Siam on the Western frontier. The peaceful period that followed was duly interrupted in 1478 by an invasion from Annam, now freed from Cham warfare. This war-like interlude was a strange lapse on the part of the gentle and amiable Laotians, whose pacific nature soon re-asserted itself by re-knitting friendly relations with their Eastern neighbours. The only shadow cast over this period was the slight religious intolerance of a pious Buddhist monarch who tried unsuccessfully to forbid the cult of Brahmanism in his domain.

The rise of Vientiane in the sixteenth century was due to its greater

363

proximity to Cambodia and Siam, and to its commercial prosperity. Cordial relations were maintained by the Prince of Vientiane with the now decadent Khmers, and with the King of Siam against Luang-Prabang and Burma. This alliance provoked three successive invasions on the part of the Burmese, who, though invariably victorious, were defeated by the country itself and forced eventually by famine and sickness to withdraw. The seventeenth century brought a period of needed peace both foreign and domestic. European travellers of the time have left accounts of the brilliance of contemporary Vientiane. The best narrative is by a Dutchman, Van Wusthoff, in 1641, who came to establish trade relations between Vientiane and Batavia, and it is corroborated by the accounts of two Jesuits, Martini and Marini.

Early in the eighteenth century a series of civil wars over succession to the throne brought this peaceful period to a bloody close. Annamite support of one candidate provoked a fatal rift between Vientiane and Luang-Prabang. These now mutually jealous principalities called in foreign support, to the inevitable annihilation of Laotian independence. Vientiane was totally eclipsed as a result and Luang-Prabang fell under the double tutelage of Annam and Siam.

When Luang-Prabang was an independent state, two kings, one for peace and one for war, headed its government. The former was the real ruler, and he could select as his successor any one of his direct heirs. Five Ministers were appointed by the king as his aides. There was also an assembly, the Séna, to which certain families automatically belonged by hereditary right. Land was divided into provinces and sub-divided into districts, each with an appropriate official taken from the five classes of mandarins. The people furnished requisitioned labour, soldiers for the army, and paid a head tax. Further revenues were brought in by opium, salt, and alcohol farms, by taxes on ivory and metals, and by tariff duties.

The Siamese naturally had a different organization for the lands which they successively conquered around the Mekong. The country was divided into *muongs* and subdivided into *menangs*, cantons, and villages (*bans*). A Siamese official, the Kha Luong, visited the provinces annually, as a sort of arbiter of disputes between the mandarins and the peoples, to collect taxes, and to see in general that the country ran smoothly. The Siamese left a remarkable amount of liberty to their Laotian subjects. Bangkok respected local institutions and customs, exacting only an annual tribute, military service and *corvées*, like a mediaeval feudal state. A governor, *chau-muong*, was named for life, but he could be recalled for neglect of his duties. He was responsible for taxes, order, and justice. A list of candidates to serve as provincial mandarins was sent to Bangkok for approval. The *kromakana*, or village mayors, were appointed locally from among the rich landowners, merchants, or citizens noted for their wisdom and virtue. All officials were required to have a spotless judicial past, and to take an annual oath of loyalty to the Siamese king. Land and head taxes were paid by the male population between the ages of eighteen and fifty according to lists drawn up on the basis of a tri-annual census. *Corvées* and taxes, in theory, were graded according to age, position, health, and poverty. The Chinese farmed indirect taxes with their usual acumen and profit.

The judicial organization was the weakest feature of Siamese rule. Judgments were arbitrary and confused, especially where national customs played no part. The venality of the judges, both mandarinal and village, was notorious. Cases could be dragged out indefinitely through the lifetime of several judges and at great expense to the litigants. Only those suits were settled quickly where the social and economic position of one party was definitely superior to that of its rival. Only those litigants who could furnish neither money nor guaranty of bail were put into prison. The principle of collective responsibility existed here as elsewhere in Indo-China. The chief judicial flaws were in the application of the law, and not in the code itself. The Siamese were remarkable for their use of native law wherever possible.

The two indigenous codes of Luang-Prabang and Vientiane have a gentle amiability that well reflects the character of their people, and which differentiates them from their neighbours. All penalties are commutable to money fines, and the severest is directed against adultery. Prison is agreeable enough, and the inmates wear flowers behind their ears. Crimes are few and capital punishment even rarer. Those condemned to death wear only a few more chains than the others. The code, in great detail, excuses everything that is remotely excusable. Hunger justifies one's eating another's provisions, and it is not punishable provided nothing is carried away—externally.

In the eighteenth and nineteenth centuries, Laos, like Cambodia, was the scene of Siamese and Annamite rivalry, interrupted by Annamite warfare with the Chams and Taysons, and the Siamese with the Burmese and Pegouans. At the time of the French conquest the Siamese had definitely the upper hand. They contented themselves with leaving nominal power to the King of Luang-Prabang and to the feudal chieftains, who governed Laotians *muongs* from father to son, and among whom they fostered rivalries. The Siamese, unfortunately, practised a policy which they had learned, to their sorrow, from the Burmese—that of forced expatriation. To populate their own provinces, depleted by warfare, the Siamese drained Laos of thousands of its inhabitants. The fact that the country thus became so much the less desirable to Annam was to them no minor consideration. The Annamites proceeded to annex the principality of Xieng-Khouang in retaliation. Siamese action was mainly inspired by the ideal of constituting a great Thai Empire. Such a policy involved consolidating their recent conquests on the left bank of the Mekong, and creating an hereditary fief at Bassac. Getting this hegemony recognized by their neighbours, notably the Annamites, was complicated enough without taking the newly-arrived French into consideration.

A series of invasions by the Chinese Hos was another factor in the situation. They came first in 1864, when civil war in Yunnan drove the famished refugees South. They came originally in scattered groups, but later organized themselves into armed bands which carried on regular brigandage. They had plenty of scope for their activities, since rival Laotian princes called upon their services only too frequently in their local conflicts.

The innumerable and systematic atrocities to which the Hos subjected the Laotians met with absolutely no resistance from them. The people simply fled at their approach, even from the capital Luang-Prabang. The Siamese made vague gestures of protection, but did nothing more than hasten their policy of wholesale deportations across the Mekong. Pavie, who happened to be in Luang-Prabang at the time[1], has left a moving description of this tragic exodus and of his own efforts to save the hopelessly be-muddled king. It was due almost entirely to Pavie that France began to interest herself in Laos's fate and to ruin—temporarily at least—Siam's dream of a Thai Empire.

France's 1883 treaty with Hué, and her pre-occupation with Tonkin, did not escape the notice of Siam. Backed by England, who saw in Laos a safe outlet for Siamese ambitions, Bangkok redoubled its efforts to get control of the lands belonging to the senile and insouciant king of Luang-Prabang. The Siamese expedition was prepared with such secrecy that De Kergaradec, the French envoy at Bangkok, only knew of it after the troops' departure. The Court of Hué, though feeling none too cordially towards the French, was not slow in pointing out this breach in Annam's sovereign rights in Laos, for which France was now

[1] Cf. above, p. 268.

responsible. A protest to Bangkok was necessarily vague because of the ill-defined rights of both Siam and Annam in the North, but it eventuated in the signing of a seven-years agreement between Siam and France on May 7, 1886. France profited by this arrangement to the extent of having a consul at Luang-Prabang and certain extra-territorial rights in Siam. The ratification of this treaty for the first time raised definitely the problem of Annamite-Siamese-Laotian frontiers. Pavie was dispatched again to gather the information necessary to drawing boundary lines in Upper Laos. He returned not only with the technical knowledge required, but with the conviction that the oppressed people of Luang-Prabang would relish a French Protectorate as a defence against Siamese encroachments and Hos invasions. His efforts led to the conclusion of an agreement on March 27, 1889, by which the Siamese were to stop the eastward march of their troops, evacuate the region of Cammon, where, however, a Siamese *khaluong* had a right to provisional residence, and the French to a military post at Napé.

As time went on the French claimed that the Siamese had fulfilled none of these conditions and were pushing steadily ahead in Laos. In proportion as these grievances piled up, the Metropolitan government was unwilling to take any action against Siam, especially as Tonkin was giving them quite enough trouble as it was. The English were simultaneously expanding in Upper Burma and in the Shan States, and getting ever nearer to Upper Laos. Not until 1889, when Pavie was given a semi-official mission and numerous collaborators to study the economic possibilities of the upper country, did France's interest there re-awaken. Despite Siamese opposition the mission was able to obtain precise and exhaustive information about the country, all the way from Yunnan to Cambodia, for the government and the newly formed French Commercial Syndicate of Upper Laos.

The fuse which set off the accumulating grievances against Siam was the suicide of the French consul at Luang-Prabang, worn out by his struggles with the Siamese. His death shocked the Chamber of Deputies into voting unanimously for action, which had also the Commercial Syndicate's backing and Pavie's documentation on which to act. The military campaign which followed in 1893 drove all the Siamese from the east bank of the Mekong, from Cambodia to Khemmaret. These operations against Siam centred around three points, but the most important was the naval demonstration at Pak Nam.[1] A treaty was subsequently concluded on the basis of the ultimatum which called

[1] Cf. above, p. 105.

for evacuation of the Mekong's left bank and indemnity for Siamese aggression. Siam found to her sorrow that too much faith had been placed in English backing and France's indifference and preoccupation with Tonkin. If in carrying out the evacuation clause Siam forced whole-sale deportations of the Laotians to her territory it was the final manifestation of her *drang nach Osten*.

Almost at the same time complications with England began to develop over her encroachments in the Shan States.[1] A commission was named in 1894 to study the problem, and Pavie headed the French delegation. Its work proved to be too slow for the English, who hastened matters by raising their flag at Muong Sing, despite Pavie's protests. New discussions and surveys resulted in another move on the part of the English, who this time occupied Tong-Muong-Sing. France seemed hopelessly weak and vacillating by contrast with England's strong action. While Pavie was engaged in this struggle Commandant Fournier was working on the South Chinese frontier, between the Black River and the Mekong. The treaty of Shimonoseki hastened the prompt solution of these frontier problems by an agreement that was favourable to the French and hostile to the British. This influenced the agreement signed between these two powers in May 1896, in which they renounced mutually aggression against Siam. England abandoned Muong Sing to France, thus giving the latter control of all the left bank of the Mekong from Yunnan to the Cambodian frontier.

Though the year 1893 marked the nominal occupation of Laos, it was not until three years later that the country was organized administratively as Upper and Lower Laos. This division remained purely theoretical and it was modified in 1899, when both sections were united under a single Resident Superior and a single budget. The local organization was left as it was found, only the upper stratum of offices was changed. In this the French were inspired by their Siamese predecessors, who had respected native institutions, and also by budgetary considerations. Thirteen French Commissars, aided by native officials and the inevitable interpreters, exercised all powers with a tranquil disregard of Montesquieu's principles. A native guard was adequate to perform police service among such a placid people. Revenues came from the usual head tax paid by the male population in money and in kind, and the commutation of *corvée* duty, licences for foreign merchants, and an export tax. There was no land tax and only a local levy on the products of the soil. The indirect tax on opium was harder to collect because certain

[1] Cf. above, p. 100.

368

tribes had always raised enough for their own needs. There was little increase in revenues despite the steady increase in population. The budget was poor and not properly drawn up, so it had to be regularly subsidized. Cochin-China, as usual, bore the brunt of this deficit.

As in Cambodia, the Laotian Protectorate was an immense success because it floated gently on top of the old native administration, giving an appearance of modernization to what had always existed and with which it did not interfere. The identical organization of all the *muongs* was a great help to the French. If the government of the Annamite countries erred on the side of over-direct administration, that of the Indianized countries was criticized as too superficial. Laos, it was said, had administrators but no administration. They collected taxes which had no accurate basis of assessment, received the semi-annual oath of functionary fidelity, and requisitioned labour and provisions. The native chieftains remained the real administrators, but no effort was made to select, train, and supervise the most able among them, or to give them regular salaries, and no longer let them take a percentage of the taxes and fines. Little was done, and that little was for the benefit of the few Europeans in the country.

Of the budget expenditures one per cent was allotted to road building, when paths were almost non-existent in Laos. Fifty per cent of the revenues was absorbed by the administration. A subsidy to the company that navigated the Mekong cost 350,000 francs: the total revenues were 600,000, and all for the occasional transportation of the hundred European residents and their mail. The Laotians were much too amiable and indolent to protest against this state of affairs. They were a charming people, who knew nothing of French civilization but the pleasure of paying taxes. They asked little and so they got little. If this were true of the Laotians it was even more so of the mountain peoples. The country was administered as if it were exclusively inhabited by Laotians. The codes, and the mandarins who applied them, were Laotian. The Provincial Council, long the sole representative organization, had no delegate from the mountaineers. Buddhists were given a monopoly of the education, though the Yaos were Confucianist and the Khas fetishists. The administration concentrated on the valley-bound Laotians and ignored the scattered mountain peoples, who differed radically in religion, language, and customs. The Meos's reaction to the Laotians was shown by the massacre of 1920.

The centralized administration of Laos was not only part of the French mania for simplification and uniformity, which for various reasons had reached Laos later than elsewhere, but was primarily stimulated by the economic importance of Laos's mines and town building in the post-war period. The modernization of Vientiane was especially notable, for it had been buried under the jungle, 400 kilometres from the sea, and on an almost unnavigable river. When the potential wealth of the country became evident, the administration began to veer away from the Protectorate ideal to direct government, making *tabula rasa* of native institutions. Some Hanoi officials took it into their heads to suppress the King of Luang-Prabang as an obstacle to transforming Laos into a *bona-fide* colony. Varenne had the good sense to recognize how much the Laotians venerated their king, and so he rescued his throne from the assimilationist peril. The Protectorate was saved, and to push Laos farther along the trail blazed by Annam and Cambodia, a native advisory assembly was given to the country in 1929, and a mixed Chamber of Agriculture and Commerce, both of which recently sent delegates to the *Grand Conseil*. The process can only fully develop when the rail and road network is completed—that administrative pipe-dream linking Laos to the rest of the Union—which in 1936 looked perilously near fulfilment. An unfortunate corollary is that the forty-year tariff freedom of Laos, a miracle in French colonization, died in 1932 with the growth of the Siamese and Indo-Chinese railroad construction.

Justice has followed in the wake of the Laotian administration. At first it was left almost untouched, with Laotian codes and magistrates, even for the mountain peoples. In 1900 the Resident Superior, Tournier, made a first tentative translation of some Laotian laws, but he found them so incomplete and so poorly organized that the work was temporarily abandoned. In 1908 Sallé, a Saigon magistrate, took up the task. Beginning with the kingdom of Luang-Prabang he promulgated three codes of civil and criminal law and procedure. Then new texts were discovered, which necessitated more study from 1917 to 1922, when another code was promulgated. It was this time very complete, in fact too complete for the type of judge who applied it. Simplification was needed for their understanding as well as for the illiterate masses. A modified version was put out in 1928, but the following year it was again changed. As in Cambodia and Annam, the problem of discovering, understanding, translating, re-organizing, and harmonizing native law with some basic principles of Western legislation is so delicate that it requires an enormous amount of time and experimentation.

The Resident Superior is at the head of native justice, which is administered by native magistrates under the control of French administrators. As yet there is no specialization of administrative and judicial powers, since magistrates are taken from the civil service. The general organization of the courts resembles that of the other countries of the Union. Unimportant cases are settled by the heads of the villages and cantons. Important suits are sent to the provincial courts, which are presided over by the administrative head of the province and native judges. A higher court judges appeals from the provincial courts and is placed under the Resident Superior, French, and native judges. Wholly French courts exist for European cases. Nowadays the code of Vientiane or of Luang-Prabang is applied to the Thai peoples and to certain Kha tribes; Burmese custom law to the Lus in Muong Sing; and their particular customs to the other ethnical groups—all under magistrates of their own people. The judgments of these courts are examined by the French authorities. This is not a useless precaution, as often the judges themselves are in a quandary about interpreting their laws and traditions. Moreover, the venality of these judges passes all understanding. If the native appears without offerings appropriate to his station and that of the judge, he is lost. Undoubtedly with time the specialization of magistrates, with guarantees in salary and promotion, will obviate the most flagrant of these evils.

POPULATION

The origin of the Laotian people is the object of much speculation. In all probability they were driven southward from Thibet and China in successive waves. They were and are to-day governed by petty chieftains and divided into families, each of which forms a community under the authority of the eldest son of its most ancient branch.

The people were simply divided into slaves and freemen. Of the former there were three kinds: slaves for debt, by sale, or by capture. Slave-trading used to be enormously profitable, for the offspring of slaves were born into perpetual slavery. In 1880 the King of Siam made a generous reform. The descendants of slaves were henceforth to be freemen, and it was made much easier for debt slaves to buy their freedom. No mention was made, however, of captured slaves, but severe penalties were meted out to men convicted of slave-trading. One of the first steps taken by the French was the abolition of the slave trade, despite its affecting important Laotian, Cambodian, Siamese, and even Burmese commercial interests. Next, debt slavery was attacked in 1896, and for this Tournier found an ingenious solution. Special attention

371

was paid to the Khas, who lived in a state of serfdom, and this provoked a series of revolts. Their enfranchisement was begun in 1898, and nowadays a form of patron-client relationship has been evolved, but the bond is easy. It is almost impossible to wipe the slate clean, for many of the slaves resist change, since it is an easier way of getting rid of a debt than by working as freemen.

RELIGION

Along with the first migrations from the North and West into Laos filtered the Vedic precepts and the laws of Manu. From 900 to 700 B.C. the more militant dogmas of Brahmanism began to appear, at the same time as the ancestral cult and innumerable auxiliary superstitions. About the thirteenth century Buddhism began to appear by different routes, but it is the Ceylonese variety, albeit profoundly modified, which has the largest number of Laotian followers. Chiefly because it rejects study and examination, this doctrine permits many superstitions to live side by side with it, embedded at varying depths in the popular consciousness. The kind of Buddhism practised by the Laotians and some Khas is almost entirely exempt from philosophic speculation. Bonzes recite prayers incomprehensible to themselves and to the people, but they must mark every social event. These ceremonies, a reverential attitude towards sacred places, a dash of animism, the ancestral cult, and a belief in Kharma, make up official Laotian religion. Some of this has been absorbed by the Yaos and Lus, Khas and Meos, each of whom has added their own assortment of superstitions. Laotian superstitions, too, are myriad. They attribute all evils to spirits—none other than their ancestors, who take delight in returning to earth expressly to torment their relatives. Hence the great power of sorcerers, who, incidentally, are rent by the greatest professional jealousy. All of this, with a smattering of Christian converts, form an ill-defined, uneasy pantheism, quite congenial to the Laotian soul.

Bonzes are organized into a clear-cut hierarchy, which is not exclusively masculine. They live in bonzeries, but in no sense form a class apart. Despite strict vows and penalties for lapses, their lives are not like their Khmer colleagues' examples of austerity and chastity. They perform useful, if not intensive, service as dispensers of a mild moral education, hospitality, and shelter to wandering unfortunates. The Laotian climate and character have prevailed over Buddha's principles, so it is not surprising that Buddhism has lost much of its prestige in Laos.

The Laotian tongue is very simple. It is mainly monosyllabic: the article is never used, and substantives are not declined. Profane literature includes historical works, chiefly the annals of Luang-Prabang as well as its codes of law, novels, and songs. There is a large sacred literature, a very small part of which has been translated from Pali into the vernacular. Their drama is akin to the Khmers' in length, costuming, and music. The themes are epic, religious, or bellicose history, love stories and legends, mostly taken from the Vedas, the Ramayana, and Mahabharata. Many Khmer and even Burmese plays, with a modern satirical tone, lend a cosmopolitan character to the Laotian repertoire. A kind of marionette theatre, analogous to the Javanese, exists as well.

MUSIC

There is almost no Westerner with soul so dead that he has not succumbed to the charms of Laotian music. The occasions for hearing it are multiple. Every festival and ceremony as well as impromptu meetings serve as excuse for a song fest. Their music has been lyrically described as "the purest manifestation of the Laotian soul"[1] and it even made Billotey forget "all the earth, those I love, and indeed myself."[2] The few instruments that exist, notably the *khène*, are of Malayan or Chinese origin. Both sexes share the honours as singers and improvisors. Songs are taken from poems which are the country's folklore, and the improvisations are recitatives either in Siamese or the vernacular. They are repeated like litanies, with a ritualistic intonation that requires much training as well as stamina, for these recitals often last twelve hours. Everything is grist to their improvising mill. The old is mixed with the new with a caustic verve and licence which is both crude and artistic. There is no method of notation, only memory and routine guide the musicians in selecting from their large repertoire. Unlike the Cambodians, the Laotians hold the dance in little honour. Only at certain fêtes do male dancers mimic like the Indians, and they are always accompanied by song. There are no professional dancers as in the royal and mandarinal palaces of Cambodia. The only *corps de ballet* that exists is at Luang-Prabang, and it is made up of little boys. Games of skill are much more pleasing to the Laotians. Boxing and wrestling, ball games,

[1] Le Boulanger, P., *Histoire du Laos Français* (Paris, 1930), p. 119.
[2] Billotey, P., *Sao-Keo* (Paris, 1930), p. 138.

and, above all, boat races take place at every festival, or as often as the Laotians can think of an excuse to have them. There is something in the temporary competitive and voluntary character of the effort required by games, as well as the chance to bet on the outcome, that makes such activity irresistible to the Laotians, who hate the routine drudgery of daily toil, which is inexplicably enough the Occidental ideal.

LAOTIAN ARTS

The seventeenth century was an era of peace that permitted the Laotian arts to flourish. The insouciance, which is a Laotian characteristic, explains the fragility of their innumerable monuments. In the South, Khmer influence predominates; in the North, Burmese. Under this double aegis temples, libraries, and reliquaries have been built by the Laotians without originality but always with grace and elegance. The pitiless tropical vegetation has strangled almost all of them; even the Vat Prakeo, which the French have tried to save, seems doomed to destruction. The wood sculpture is of gigantic proportions and fashioned in the expressionless attitude of the Buddhist liturgy. The painting, which consists of frescoes in the pagodas, was the work of foreign artists of whom the Laotians were only the pupils. It is in jewellery and the working of precious metals that the Laotians have shown their most inventive artistry. Like all Far Eastern peoples they are very clever at basketry and weaving.

THE ECONOMY OF LAOS

Laotian industry, if such it may be called, aims only to satisfy local needs. It is almost exclusively a family affair in which primitive tools are used with inevitably crude results. Only in precious metals and ivory or wood carving has Laos an industry that merits the name. Weaving and boat-building are also excellent, but as yet the output is confined to the artisan's personal wants.

When the French first occupied Laos, a number of investigations were undertaken to learn the country's commercial possibilities. The difficulties which the agents of the Commercial Syndicate encountered in the way of obstacles created by nature and by the Siamese, forced the government to grant it powers which gave a hybrid politico-commercial character to its activities. In spite of its semi-official support the Syndicate was doomed to failure, for a number of excellent reasons.

It was hampered by inadequate capital and knowledge of the country. Moreover, Upper Laos is an extremely unhealthy region, where even Asiatic merchants refused to go. The Syndicate's isolated efforts were concentrated on selling imports, which were more expensive than the Siamese and not so well adapted to the people's needs, and not on developing Laotian exports. The latter, to be sure, were food products, and hence very perishable. French industry simply did not produce articles essential to the Laotians, and what they sent to Laos was too high priced, not only as to original cost, but in heavy freight charges.

The Mekong was the only means of communication with Cochin-Chinese seaports. The subsidy accorded to the *Compagnie des Messa-géries Fluviales* to improve its navigation of the Mekong was too high for the colony's budget, yet inadequate for the work it had to do. Hundreds of thousands of francs were lost in acquiring a knowledge of these problems and in training a personnel. Mekong boats must reckon on three periods of navigation. In low water there are no less than eight trans-shipments between Pnom-Penh and Luang-Prabang, by rail and by road, both of which were expensive and difficult to build because of the shifting surface of the land. Mid-season is the best for navigation, since high water means contending with a terrible current. Laos is desperately in need of railroads, and it has fewer than any other country in the Union. Every Governor, from Doumer on, has had railroad projects, but they have always been laid aside for other works. The recent realization of Laos's mineral wealth through journalistic propaganda has been counteracted by the depression; yet once again there is promise to fill this crying need, notably Robin's impetus to road-building in 1935-6. Unless this is soon done, Laotian commerce will escape permanently to Bangkok. Contraband can never be controlled along the great watery frontier, and Siam's comparatively duty-free imports and cheap railroad and boat transportation will always have the advantage.

Labour

Labour, as is the case in so many tropical countries of great potential wealth, is the second greatest need. The Laotians' inadequacy, both numerically and psychologically, combined with the country's inaccessibility are almost insuperable obstacles to industrial or commercial progress. This was plainly seen when Laos's vast mineral wealth, especially in tin, attracted capitalist investment in the discreditable wave of mining speculation that spread over Indo-China in the late

1920's. The Laotians have no sense of time, and a thousand obstacles and superstitions interfere with the accomplishment of work at a fixed date. Their physical stamina is not proof against epidemics, especially those maladies brought from foreign countries. Whole villages displace themselves at the slightest provocation. One Laotian proverb says: "At the end of three days change your house; at the end of three years change your village." What started as a necessity to escape invaders or soil exhaustion has become a habit, and a means of escaping any regular irksome task. The ease with which the Laotians drift across the Mekong into Siamese territory makes the French authorities very loath to take strict measures with them. Moreover, the European residents themselves, who would normally be the motive force behind any change, succumb to the prevailing atmosphere of *su-su*, the Oriental equivalent of *dolce far niente*.

It is obvious that the future development of the country, as in Cambodia, cannot depend on any but imported labour. As ever, it is the prolific and industrious Chinese and Annamites who are flowing into Laos to the economic betterment of the land, but equally to the moral distress of its people. Middle Laos, from Savannakhet to Vientiane, is the region most subject to infiltration. Upper and Lower Laos will probably be cut apart by a wedge of foreign colonizers. The French cannot but favour this immigration. Laos is a terrestrial paradise offering an easy living, undisputed by the timid Laotians, to the miserable Annamites from the over-crowded Tonkinese delta. The Laotians, like the Khmers, prefer to withdraw rather than to struggle with their old enemies. A terse Laotian proverb crystallizes this ancient antagonism: "Dog and cat, Annamite and Laotian." In addition to taking their land and their women the Annamite has introduced vices like gaming and theft, and diseases like tuberculosis and syphilis. The contempt of the industrious and formalistic Annamite for the lazy and carefree Laotian is only matched by the latter's impotent hatred. Yet the evil is without remedy. Rich, unoccupied land will inevitably attract an industrious and prolific people like the Annamites, who are able and willing to do what Laotians cannot and will not do.

CONTACT OF IDEAS

The tempo of France's political and economic penetration of Laos has been so much slower than elsewhere in the peninsula that the intellectual counterpart inevitably lagged ever farther behind. Naturally, the first work accomplished was of a practical nature. Massie, of the Pavie Mission, wrote a dictionary in 1890–91, that included some 1,300 words, designed to aid French officials and merchants adrift in Thai countries. He found the language very simple, unlike the complexities of Annamite, and estimated only a year's study necessary for a relative mastery of it.

Laos has offered a rich field to scientists. Henri Mouhot was its first scientific explorer, and he was followed by others, chiefly zoologists. The Lagrée Mission continued this work, as did Dr. Harmand, who made a great collection there on his 1872–78 series of explorations. Pierre's work on the forest flora of Laos has been perhaps the greatest single scientific achievement.

Education

Much too small a sum has been allotted to education in the Laotian budget. Even elementary instruction is confined to the chief towns of the country and to the inadequate pagoda schools. Following the success of utilizing the Khmer bonzes as intermediaries, the French tried a similar policy in Laos with much less good fortune. To begin with, it gave the monopoly of education to the bonzes in a country not by any means wholly Buddhistic. The result has been that the mountain peoples remain quite illiterate. The French, in their love of simplification and uniformity, enjoy giving to a formula, which happened to succeed under one set of circumstances, an unjustifiably universal significance. As elsewhere in Indo-China, Laos has suffered from the assimilationist tendency to train natives for menial government service, as clerks and interpreters, by means of a French programme of studies that uproots its Asiatic victims spiritually from their setting. Only in Laos, through negligence or indifference on the part of both French and Laotians, this occurred much later. In 1928, however, Pasquier, on a tour in Laos, was horrified to hear a teacher expounding to his youthful pupils such irrelevant material as the French Wars of Religion.

In 1909, and again in 1912, efforts were made to renovate Laos's pagoda schools. The bonzes did respond to the government's appeal to come to its training schools, but they left as soon as they had received a little instruction, and took positions in the administration. The programmes proposed to them had been too advanced for both teachers and students. They lacked textbooks and equipment in general: control and supervision were entirely missing. The quality and prestige of Laotian bonzes was well below Cambodian standards, so it was impractical to count on the same degree of co-operation from them.

In 1931 the government reluctantly pulled itself together to remedy an admittedly bad situation. Certain provinces and certain bonzes were selected as fields for experimentation. An itinerant teacher was sent around to the pagoda schools to conduct model classes with a very simple programme, as a practical demonstration before the bonzes. Blackboards, textbooks, and chalk were doled out to these schools, which had heretofore lacked even such elementary equipment. Bonzes were asked to report semi-annually on the number and progress of their pupils. Slowly an examination was organized with a certificate, so as to set up some standard and to stimulate the sluggish Laotian zeal for knowledge. The problem of further training for bonzes is delicate. The idea of a small scale Normal School was again revived in 1932, and attempts were made to avoid some of the pitfalls which had doomed earlier experiments. The majority of bonzes still could not teach either reading or writing. They were less than half-hearted in falling in with the government's ideas, and would break training at the slightest provocation, thus automatically condemning their schools. The new courses are more modern in method, more prudent in application, and more successful in their results than the old, but it is too soon as yet to draw any conclusions about that elusive and infinitesimal effort known as Laotian education. Less than 300 schools teach fewer than 7,000 pupils in French Laos.

The Mission

In April 1881 two priests from the Society of Foreign Missions went to Oubone, where they found not a single native Christian. On a tour which they later made throughout Laos they found only four Christians in the whole country, two Siamese and two Annamites. When they began to evangelize Laos the current anarchy bred by the Ho invasions, Siamese deportations, and the perennial economic uncertainty was conducive to an encouraging number of conversions. With the establishment of the French, political security was assured, and the number of converts began visibly to decline. The ease of the early conversions had been misleading. Through centuries of persecution and uncertainty the Laotians have acquired a marked flair for success. They know to a fine point what earthly authorities it is worth their while to please. Moreover, the Laotians share the usual Asiatic indifference to dogma. One religion is as good to them as another, provided it does not upset the social structure. Catholic discipline is irksome too. The Laotians find the indissolubility and relative asceticism of a Christian marriage far less congenial than their traditional polyandry and polygamy. The missionaries have also vainly tried to induce them to clothe themselves more voluminously and to give up opium.

The Laotians have never been persecutors and they are hoplessly apathetic. Politely but interminably they put off conversion, on one flimsy excuse after another. Latin and their catechism are literally impossible for them to master. They seem to be paying attention, the missionaries complain, but their minds wander. Lack of roads and the unhealthiness of the country make it doubly hard for missionaries to press salvation upon them with sufficient regularity. Famines make the Laotians migrate, and they are naturally and historically nomadic. The Mission is not rich enough nor adequately staffed to offer them regular employment. Moreover, it would not be the same inducement to the Laotians that it is to the Annamites. One worthy Father wrote:

If the Laotian is not moved by fear, vexations, or lawsuits; if he is not shunned by everyone because of a hideous or incurable disease—he cannot bring himself without the greatest difficulty to study religion. He remains as quiet as a rat in his hole. He is neither hostile nor savage, but is simply a child who makes any excuse to put off his baptism.[1]

The static condition of the Laotian Mission moved the Society to change its policy. As in Annam, they are trying to appeal to all classes of the people through education, books, and medical care. The cult of *phi*, or evil spirits, is so deep-rooted in Laotians and so universally practised in cases of sickness, that Western science and social service can perhaps find there the most advantageous point for attacking native superstitions. Of course, here as elsewhere, they encounter the administration's jealous rivalry, but as yet in Laos penetration of any sort is so superficial that there is room for all comers. The government has recently dealt a blow to Mission prestige, as it did in Cambodia, by becoming the patron of Buddhism. Though recently founded, the Buddhist Institute in Luang-Prabang aims to train bonzes who formerly went to Bangkok for their instruction, as well as their investiture. This not only counteracts Siamese influence—and Bangkok has always been the lodestar of Laotian aspirations—but it is part of the French policy with Indianized peoples to revive their cultural heritage. In 1907 Tournier chose Vientiane to transform into a modern city, for he thought

[1] Société des Missions Etrangères: *Compte Rendu des Travaux* (Archives du Séminaire, Paris, 1900), pp. 249–50.

that it might attract all Laotians thither and away from Bangkok, the moral capital of the Thai people. It remains to be seen whether all these attempts will be successful.

The missionaries, even if they made little headway in conversions, enjoy great moral influence in Laos, especially among the mountain peoples, to whom they teach new methods of agriculture, in addition to their medical, educational, and Scriptural activities. These primitive peoples do not differentiate between spiritual and temporal authorities, and often use the missionary as intermediary with the administration. These regions are so remote, and their economic and political importance so obviously relegated to the future, that the Mission has not encountered there the anti-clerical opposition that existed for so long in Annamite countries.

The Contact of Peoples

In proportion, as the Laotian is the national group which has the least political and economic importance in Indo-China, so it is the country where the French find themselves most happy. Not that there are not some of the racial unpleasantnesses evidenced in a centre like Luang-Prabang, but in Laos the friction that seems inseparable from all colonization is at a minimum. The reaction to mutual contacts is the same as in Cambodia, but more intense in degree. For the rare Frenchman who sees in the Laotians a silly, lazy, and naïve people, there are hundreds who are charmed by their gentle affability and their aesthetic appearance. If they understand and like the Laotian character, there are no limits to the devotion they can inspire. But an offence to Laotian pride, albeit unconscious, or demands for sustained effort on their part, will meet with instantaneous defeat.

The effect which the French have had upon the Laotian people is as yet—perhaps because the economic exploitation is so dilatory there— very slight in comparison with the influence Laos has had upon the French. By contrast with the sombre inscrutability of the ambitious Annamites, the easy-going Laotian is infectiously gay. Suddenly it seems the simplest thing in the world to be happy. Laotian family life has an archaic simplicity. The country is an earthly paradise which offers a beauty and nourishment that demands no effort for its enjoyment. Partly it is because Buddhism has encouraged a life without violent desires, but it is also due to the climate which has conspired to reject effort and to encourage an immobile happiness. For the European, wearied with Western greed and strife, Laos seems to be the answer to all his problems. Laziness is an idle reproach in a land where work would obviously make one less rather than more content. In fact, Laos is in itself a passive reproach to the futility of Europe's bustling activity and soul-searchings. It is a museum-piece of earthly happiness, a reply to the West's gloomy disillusionment. Even the Civilizer, with all his utilitarian baggage, hesitates to trouble its idyllic calm. If Europeans are forced by a grudging nature to wrest a precarious living from it by irksome and boring toil, the Laotians have not had to submit to such indignity. They render lip-service to European superiority, because it is too much trouble to be impolite, but the Laotians do not believe in it. Nor does the European for long who lives in their amiable midst. Europe is well lost to gain a Laotian soul.

THE PRIMITIVE TRIBES

The economy of the primitive tribes of Indo-China is their only common denominator. Culturally they are divided into two distinct groups. The first is made up of Muongs, Thais, Lolos, Meos and Mans, most of whom live in Northern Tonkin. Theirs is an hierarchized, feudal organization under hereditary chieftains. The family is patriarchal and its religion a group not an individual affair, with the head of the family as its priest. Of this numerous and scattered group-type, all but the Thais are decadent. Chinese influence has almost wholly disappeared, as has their aristocratic origin. The second group is anarchical except where it has fallen under strong foreign influence. Their organization never progressed beyond mutually independent villages, with religion as an individual affair. This group is subdivided according to language and to family organization. The first division is matriarchal, and it includes Chams and related tribes, like the Jarai and Radé: the second comprises the Bahnar, Sedang, Rangao, and Stiengs, who are all patriarchal in type. These tribes are usually called Mois by the Annamites, Penongs by the Khmers, and Khas by the Laotians. Almost all of them live in the Annamite Range.

The Thais and their various subdivisions are the foundation tribes of the Northern Tonkinese and Laotian group. They form three-quarters of the population, and spend most of their time growing rice and performing their rites. The Annamites tried to undermine the feudal powers of these chieftains by fostering mutual rivalries, and by strongly impressing their culture upon them. The French find these direct and frank mountaineers refreshing after Annamite indifference and dissimulation. Even their extreme indolence is forgiven.

The Mans are the tribe next largest to the Thais, and they number about twenty thousand. They are related to the people whom the Chinese call Yaos, who live in South China. Theirs is a totem religion and family organization. They are nomads who live in the different mountain fastnesses, cultivating great mystery in regard to their customs. They are not related to the Thais, whom they detest, but they are greatly influenced by them. The Thais return the compliment by calling them a race of sorcerers. The French policy towards the Mans has been to try to attach them to the soil, and to educate them out of their destructive method of farming by *rays*.

The Lus are a Mongol people, pushed southward by successive invasions until they finally settled themselves in the Sip-Song-Panas. Though they are related to the Thai group, they are on a much lower economic level, but their literacy extends to the women of their tribes, and is remarkably widespread. Their religion is Buddhism, adulterated by spirit worship. Their social organization is strictly feudal, and their occupations hunting, smoking, and drinking.

The Meos live in the highest mountains, and in very dispersed groups throughout Northern Tonkin and Laos. Though related to their neighbours and to the tribes of South China, with whom they have cultural ties, they live in completely separate villages. The fact that they cannot acclimatize themselves to an altitude under 2,500 feet has saved them from absorption by surrounding peoples. Their social organization resembles that of the Lus. They are divided into nobles and peoples, and like them they are great animal breeders. They are also the greatest poppy growers of Tonkin. Like so many of these primitives they detest their neighbours, particularly the Chinese and Annamites, whom they call "men of paper." The Chinese, in turn, call them "ungovernable vermin," but the Annamites more kindly describe them as "sons of the untilled soil." The French have tried to attach them to the soil, to cure them of their nomadic and *ray* habits, and also to destroy the immense influence the sorcerers have over them. The Meo revolt of 1919 was stirred up by an inspired magician, Batchai, against their neighbours. Though not an important outbreak, guerilla warfare in such mountainous country was too risky a business to prolong. The most effective tactics used in suppressing the revolt was to encircle the affected region and reduce the villages by cutting off their rice supply, the nerve of war.

The Lolos are even less numerous, and live in isolated groups. They are to be found in the greatest numbers on the highest peaks near the Chinese frontier. They are nowadays the remnants of a formerly great people, driven out of Yunnan by the Chinese. They still live under hereditary chiefs and are extremely bellicose. They are not cordial to strangers, and are very avaricious. Merchants shun their country because of the frequent assassinations of any travellers suspected of having money, and because of their counterfeit activities which have reached the proportions of a tribal industry. They are a nomadic farmer people, with a religion mostly magic but with a Buddhistic flavour.

The Khas are descendants of the aborigines who mixed with the new arrivals to form a variety of secondary tribes, which are for ever sub-dividing, and which differ radically from one another. The amount of culture each tribe boasts depends on the degree of penetration to which Buddhism has attained. Each tribe is independent; each village a little republic. Their character differs enormously, according to the region and its degree of civilization. In the North the Khas resemble the Laotians, and are gentle and respectful, fearful and reserved, like all oppressed peoples. In the South they are far more independent and belligerent, given to slave-hunting, and slaves are the only article of exchange they have to offer. The French missionaries have great moral influence over these tribes, which they began to evangelize as more promising material than the Laotians and Khmers. The government and Mission have worked hand-in-hand when trying to suppress the slave trade and to develop them into an agricultural sedentary people. The Khas are a great potential force in the colony, and the state has recognized this by trying to improve their economic and moral status.

It is extremely hard for the government to deal coherently with these primitives. Not only are they physically inaccessible, and con-stantly changing residence, but they live widely scattered, kept apart by different languages, cultures, religions, and mutual antipathies. China has maltreated almost all of these peoples and driven them out without pity. Yet China is still their magnet. Their religion and philosophy are principally Chinese, and they perennially tend to be reabsorbed into South China. The government has tried to attach them to the soil, to create industries in a totally agricultural economy, and to destroy the nefarious power of their sorcerers by governing them directly through their own chieftains and no longer through the oppressive Annamite mandarins. In general they have welcomed French sovereignty. During the pacification they sided with the French and against the bandits in the interests of peace. Their great grievance against the government is the labour requisitioned for public works, notably road building. *Corvées* had also been exacted by the Annamites, and they are the indispensable preliminary to penetrating the difficult Northern hinterland, yet the tribes resent its legal use and abhor its frequent abuse. The population, small and scattered at best, is steadily declining, due to the inroads of alcohol and foreign diseases. All these factors explain the almost unavoidably superficial character of colonial action to date upon these tribes.

The primitive tribes of the Annamite Range, loosely grouped under the name of Mois, are less well known than those in the North. They are aggressively inaccessible, and differ radically among themselves according to the degree to which their environment has influenced them. Some of them are still independent. Three great Moi tribes live on the Darlac plateau. Of these the Radé are the most civilized and intelligent; the Jarai, the most powerful and bellicose. The Sedangs and Stiengs, despite strong resemblances, live far away from each other in independent villages.

The history of these peoples is a mystery. They have no traditions, no tombs, no altars. They suffered greatly as a buffer state during the Cham-Khmer wars, and that has been the most important single factor in their development. The Moi country served as a refuge for the vanquished according to the varying fortunes of war. After their permanent defeat the Chams came more and more to the Moi country, where they mixed with the tribes. All the Mois did not accept their arrival with equal docility. The Sedangs, for instance, were intractable and retired to the most distant mountain regions, and to this day they have remained the most independent and difficult to subjugate. The struggles between their neighbours were their safeguard, yet the sadness of their nomadic hunted lives is reflected in their songs and legends. They have been the victims of much injustice, and if their retaliations seem to be unjustifiably vicious, one must think of them in the light of the past. If the Mois take fright a whole village decamps with disconcerting rapidity. Inter-tribal rivalry takes up a good deal of their time. The victorious side takes as hostages the gongs and jars of its rivals.

Their agriculture is characterized by primitive and destructive methods. Only the great fertility of the soil permits them to survive at all. They have to supplement their miserable corn and rice crops by hunting and fishing. Commerce and industry, strictly speaking, do not exist. But the Mois do need certain articles like salt, wax, jars, gongs, and cloth, and in return they offer ironwork, pottery, and forest products. Jars and tomtoms are the most prized of Moi possessions. The older they are, the greater their value. Gongs of certain tones and jars several hundred years old bring fantastic prices. The bloody history of the Moi country, the insecurity of travel there, and the lack of roads—all militate against commercial development. They have distinctly limited capacities as merchants. They can scarcely count, they wear out buyers by interminable negotiations about every detail. Money until recently was unknown, so everything is subject to barter. Laziness is omnipotent, and pillage easier than regular work. The spirit of saving is both unknown and undesirable to the Moi. If the Mois have two successive years of good harvests, they use up the surplus in a series of village fêtes. The heavy eating universally indulged in at that time increases the tribal mortality appreciably. When the French tried to inculcate their speciality of thrift in these tribes, some of the chieftains took pains to explain how unsound an idea it was by this irrefutable argument:

If I create a reserve my elder brother, the white warrior, will take it from me to feed his escort. . . . If he does not, then my younger brothers my neighbours will come and seize it, so I am right in not storing things away.[1]

Abuse by Chinese and Annamite merchants is another important factor in Moi psychology. They have systematically exploited the Mois, who have indulged themselves in revenge whenever they could. The Annamite who has called these tribes "Mois" or barbarians thinks of them as his legitimate prey. He makes them pay in slavery for debts which they did not realize they had contracted, and the Mois would rather lose their lives than their independence. Bitter experience has made the Moi very chary of commercial dealings. His vanity, his love of display and gaudy apparel is perhaps the strongest counteracting force. But the merchants must remember that the different tribes have varying tastes. The Radé, for example, will accept only small beads coloured red, white, or blue. The Muongs will buy any coloured bead, but only white cloth. The French have fairly successfully tried to stop the Annamites' commercial exploitation, and road building has made more money circulate in the country and familiarized the Mois with this medium of exchange. Security is now also greater for merchants.

[1] Baudesson, Commandant, *Au Pays des Superstitions et des Rites* (Paris, 1932), p. 13.

By far the most important influence, however, has been the recent colonization of the Darlac plateau.

The Moi nation does not and never has existed. The social and administrative unit is the village, each independent and under its own hereditary chief for war, and in peace run by a council of old men chosen from among the free families. Contacts between Moi tribes are often friendly, and rivalry is confined largely to dress and ornamentation. For the outsider it is hard to recognize the differences, for they are all clothed in evangelical poverty—by a ray of sunlight, a rag, and a knife or axe to complete the costume. Languages are the greatest distinction between them, for they are mutually unintelligible because of the great number of dialects. Since the development of a language follows its people's cultural evolution, it is only through their rare contacts with foreigners that these dialects expand. Their linguistic divisions follow those of their neighbours—Polynesian, Khmer, or Burmese.

There are three social groups in each village: the chief's family, the free families, and slaves. The last-mentioned are the most numerous, but they are not badly off. Sorcerers enjoy high esteem, and they interfere constantly in all Moi activities—social, political, and judicial. Each family pays a tax in kind against future famine and towards the expense of communal fêtes. From three to sixty houses may make up a village, and they are easily and willingly abandoned in case of war or epidemic. It is in the Mois' passionate love of freedom and in the untrammelled power of their sorcerers that the dangerous germs of fanaticism lie.

Moi law upholds the strictest morality. Prevarication is a criminal offence punishable by exile or slavery. Much of their apparent injustice is caused by superstition and the perpetual warfare they have been forced to carry on. There is no formal justice, only arbitration by chieftains chosen by both parties. This would be fair enough if both litigants were of the same social class, which is rarely the case, and if the judge were honest, which is even rarer. All Mois are not equal before the law. What merits the death penalty for a slave means only enslavement for a freemen. Moi justice is essentially utilitarian and objective. An act is either good or bad solely in its relation to group welfare. Crimes against the individual are a mild indiscretion, punished with nothing like the severity exercised towards crimes against the state. Law is handed down by tradition, and applied with magic rites. Like all weak peoples, the Mois are vindictive. They will remember every

386

detail of an affront, and avenge themselves if it takes years of their lives. But even the joys of retaliation yield to laziness and gluttony. Killing one's blood enemy will be readily postponed if one happens to be invited to a feast.

Moi religion has no grandeur, only petty genii who are universally feared and propitiated. But there is no special cult at certain places, no priesthood, only sorcerers who interpret omens and conduct cruel sacrifices. The Moi imagination is not wholly concrete, but it has not the richness and force of its neighbours, the Chams or the Khmers.

The penetration of the Moi country has been remarkably slow considering that independent tribes still exist only 150 kilometres from Saigon. The lure of this ultimate frontier and its mysterious peoples has stimulated a number of explorers and scientists to visit these regions, with the government's consent and occasionally its aid. In 1880–81 Dr. Paul Neiss and Lieut. Septans were astonished by the timidity of the Mois, by their simple economy, and by their even simpler religion. They found that the French government was unknown to the Mois, even in the blessed form of taxes and *corvées*. Once a year an agent of the Forestry Service came to tell them that they must not use the *ray* method of cultivation, but he did not make them understand why. Neiss felt that the government should be more constructive in regard to Moi economy, and in particular save them from Annamite exploitation. Neiss was followed five years later by a medico-military expedition which conducted a minor exploration of three weeks' duration.

In 1888, two years after this expedition, occurred one of the most curious incidents in Indo-Chinese history—the reign of the free-lance king, Marie de Mayrena. This French adventurer bluffed the administration into authorizing his search in the Moi country for gold, and the missionaries into aiding his efforts. He entered into contact with the Moi tribes, made "treaties" with them, and formed them into a confederation of which he became the head. As in the case of so many sovereigns, it was a financial deficit that ruined Mayrena. He had even converted sceptical Parisians into believing in his kingdom, but he was undone by the international police, who, like the elephants, never forget.

Around the turn of the century there were some timid reconnoiterings of the Moi country by travellers and administrators. The government began to be ashamed of its lack of enterprise, so sent out a mission under Patté, who was foiled by the country's lack of roads and its reservoirs of malarial mosquitoes more than by its inhabitants. In 1909 Henri Maitre, the great explorer, began his methodical investigations, which continued until he was murdered by the Stiengs in 1914. He had specialized in the almost unknown Eastern region, nearest to Annam, but his work was left incomplete.

The Saigon-Nhatrang branch of the Transindochinois Railway only skirts that region, and it never did much to give it an outlet. Explorers who went unarmed to show their pacific and friendly intentions towards the Mois were killed by poisoned arrows or wandered for days in the forest to die of thirst. A project of Governor Krautheimer's in 1910 to carry out Doumer's idea of tapping the resources of the Moi country by a road through Baria province to the Mandarin Road, was allowed to lapse during the War. For eleven years the posts already occupied were maintained, but no further progress was made. It took the rubber boom of the 1920's to stimulate official and private efforts anew to penetrate the region. The government made several dramatic attempts by a military display, but more by road building, to win the fealty of the unsubjugated tribes. Though the Mois were attracted by the medical attentions and education offered, they were repelled by the labour requisitioned for road building.

The submission of these tribes has been spasmodic and unorganized. Annually some French soldier or functionary would be killed, an expedition would then be got up with some success, and the whole matter lapse until another incident provoked a repetition. French public opinion was so strongly opposed to drastic measures that the local government had to be deaf to appeals for military action. An attempt made just before the War to put an end to the despotism of the Moi chieftains and to abolish the slave trade was effective only in so far as it irritated the tribes who had already submitted. By removing authority from their chiefs the French were brought face to face with the population, who simply moved away—their traditional gesture of discontent. The shifting population resumed its nomadic life, which made them psychologically and physically impossible to govern, and which only increased their natural laziness and independence. Everyone agreed that means of communication were the best means of colonization, yet the Mois disliked road building intensely. Only their chieftains had any authority over them, and even that was a thing of the past, for the population had become scattered. There had to be a partial restitution of the chieftains' powers. Darlac was made into a province and administered by a Resident with a mixed Annamite and Moi

388

police force. An exotic form of revenue was supplied by an export tax on elephants—the sole resource. The administrator had not only to know the country and languages well, but to tour the district constantly to settle the disputes that were always arising. He had to be simultaneously engineer, architect, boat-builder, tax collector, magistrate, and labour bureau.

Pasquier may be said to have been the first to formulate a Moi policy. When he was Resident Superior of Annam, he sent out a letter on July 30, 1923, embodying his Moi programme. He inaugurated the annual oath of fidelity ceremony, and France's solemn promise of peace. Security, both physical and moral, was a prerequisite to winning the Mois' confidence. Annamites must be kept from exploiting the Mois; banditry must be suppressed; the slave trade destroyed, an effective medical service inaugurated; laws modified and codified; and educational facilities set up. Mois must be governed by their own chieftains under a watchful and well-informed French eye. The programme was excellent but, as ever in colonial enterprises, there were the obstacles of men and money. The Mois had a marked antipathy for the Annamites, who were the only teachers available. Instead of training them in their own traditions, they Annamitized the Moi children who swam into their ken. By 1926, however, there were 560 Moi children in school—a great achievement when measured by previous records. Of this reform Pasquier was the god, and the Resident Sabatier his prophet.

Land laws in the Moi country are the most difficult of all problems to solve. Sabatier was the able, bossy, humane, and energetic man who was sent to administer Darlac and its Mois, whom he knew and understood. He was determined that the Mois should evolve in the orbit of their own traditions, and that under the French aegis they should maintain their prized independence. Sabatier's method was enlightened paternalism. At the hospital which he built in his new capital, Ban-me-thuot, he fined sick Mois who had refused voluntarily to come there for treatment. He taught them new methods of agriculture and introduced new crops, like the courageous missionaries who had braved the Moi menace to found their Bahnar Mission. He gave them a written language, a *quoc ngu* transcription of their dialects. He reassembled their laws, wrote down their customs, and founded a model school. Realizing that boredom is one of the great plagues of primitive peoples, he organized and revived the traditional fesivals to distract them, incidentally creating a *corps de ballet* and musicians to keep alive the primitive dances and songs. In short, he did everything to stimulate and to defend their integrity as a group.

Unfortunately for his work, the plateau of Darlac was discovered to be a magnificent field for agricultural colonization. The Moi redlands became a synonym for wealth in rubber. In 1926, when the boom was at its height, the possibilities of Darlac were revealed. Sabatier made pathetic efforts to keep this country for the Mois, who, he knew, would be robbed of their soil and morally crushed by service as plantation labourers. Learning of the imminent arrival of a prospector, he had a bridge blown up that forced the man to return to Saigon, irritated and more determined than ever to force his way in. In fact, Sabatier paid for his temporary triumph by arousing the forces of finance against him, as well as against Varenne. He was called, in Parliamentary debate, a tyrant who had martyrized the natives. He was dismissed from his post and told to leave the country within twenty-four hours. In Paris he continued the struggle, aided by disinterested men like Dorgelès, and he was eventually reinstated in the administration, but never returned to Darlac.

It took the depression to defeat the powers of finance, but unfortunately by that time confidence in the French, which Sabatier had been at pains to build up in the Mois, was lost, and they had but one more cause for distrust of outsiders. Only the moral influence of the missionaries remained untarnished in Moi eyes. The attempts to create reserved zones for Mois were a failure. Large-scale dispossession was inevitable, for by 1932 there were 100,000,000 francs invested in Darlac. The Mois had, of course, "sold" their land, for sums far below its worth, and because selling for immediate though slight gain was easier than working in the rice-fields. Sabatier's efforts to protect the Mois from the consequences of their own laziness and ignorance were unavailing. Mois still prefer to live in abject misery rather than have to do any work that infringes on their liberties. In 1935 another punitive campaign was organized, and it looked as if the cycle of incident and expeditions had begun once more.

CHAPTER VI

REACTION TO FRENCH COLONIZATION OF INDO-CHINA

"Car l'important n'est pas d'avoir des colonies qui languissent et un
empire vaste qui périclite: c'est d'avoir semé ses idées dans le monde
et laissé des héritiers de son génie. La plus glorieuse colonie de l'Angleterre c'est encore les Etats-Unis. . . . Si ces colonies s'élevaient un jour
à la dignité de nations; si ces nations—filles de la nôtre—devaient
perpétuer notre renom sous d'autres cieux et dans d'autres âges, la
colonisation apparaîtrait alors parmi les peuples comme un merveilleux
moyen de rajeunissement, comme le plus puissant, le seul adversaire de
la décadence et la mort."   *Chailley-Bert*

THE MÉTROPOLE'S REACTION

CHANGE and diversity have characterized the political theories
applied by France to her colonies. The rapidity with which they
were rotated has been as much due to the contradictory policies inherited from preceding governments as to failure in their practical
working out. The pendulum has swung from the subjection favoured
by the *ancien régime* to the liberalism of the Revolution, and the resulting
compromise still suffers frem its inherent contradictions.

Policy for the colonies was moulded first by Richelieu and Colbert.
Because these statesmen attached so much importance to colonization,
free rein was not given to individual initiative. Monopoly and privilege
were the essence of the chartered companies they founded, and even
they were not free from state interference. Since colonization was
undertaken for the sole benefit of France, and since her king was the
source of all sovereignty, legislation emanated from the mother country.
Whenever the company's directors or the colonial government arrogated
to itself overweening power, the king pulled them up short with a heavy
legislative hand. The outcome eventually was the application of the
"Custom of Paris" as law, modified in practice by the royal edicts that
grew up by its side to form a special colonial code. The fact that colonial
governors also exercised certain legislative powers, delegated to them
as royal officers, made for considerable confusion. On the economic
side, the Colonial Pact, or the *exclusif*, had the triple aim of reserving
the colonial market to French producers, of developing the merchant
marine as the unique transportation link, and of supplying the Métropole with the raw materials appropriate to its needs. This unilateral
arrangement was given the misleading name of pact, though the

391

mother country was to receive all the benefits without any drain upon her resources.

Politically as well as economically the colonies were repeatedly sacrificed to the exigencies of treaty-making in Europe. Socially the *Code Noir* accentuated and crystallized the differences between colonials and natives, although the latter were to be instructed in the Faith, and slaves were recommended to the benevolence of their owners. The inevitable hostility of natives to colonials was taken for granted, so the problem of education, for example, was immensely simplified because it was entirely ignored. Complete passivity on the part of the natives was all that was asked of them.

A belief in the virtues of Rousseau's noble savage, and the contemporaneous attacks on economic monopoly by the Physiocrats, broke the ground before the Revolution's radical changes in colonial policy. The wave of nationalism which broke over France at that time neutralized the application of the Revolution's principles about natural liberties to the colonies, which should logically have brought about their independence. The only possible compromise was to integrate them into France and to endow them with the rights and responsibilities of citizenship. The equality and fraternity of all men naturally annihilated feelings of racial superiority and all economic barriers impeding a "commerce between brothers." The eighteenth-century taste for abstractions curbed practice to fit them. This was expressed by the phrase attributed to Robespierre: "Let the colonies perish rather than a principle." Slavery was abolished. Identical legislation was to serve for France and Greater France, despite complications of international or native law. The First Republic soon had its troubles with recalcitrant colonies, like Santo Domingo, when it refused to apply certain Metropolitan laws.

Under the Consulate and Empire there was naturally a vigorous reaction. Automatically legislation ceased to be identical for both France and the colonies. The paraphernalia of colonial self-government was swept away. Slavery and the Colonial Pact were restored. A special legislation sprang up in which was embodied the principle of the local executive's legislative competence, which still survives. No conscious theory marked this *volte face*. The Empire simply reflected the strong central power and a greater preoccupation with European conquest. More important was the indirect effect on the colonies of Napoleon's excessive centralization. To this day French expansionists bitterly attack him for having undermined France's faith in her colonizing abilities, the taste for distant exploits, and the saddling of her colonies with a rigid bureaucracy.

The colonial policy of the Restoration was dominated by a development of Bordeaux shipping, which unfortunately was short-lived because of the Bourbon refusal to trade with the revolted Spanish colonies. The struggle ended by maintaining the *exclusif*, as well as the principle of a special legislation for the colonies, although in practice the executive power continued to dominate unduly. The Charter of 1830 took into account the colonies' natural complaints at this intrusion upon their rights. Henceforth legislation was to be divided between Parliament, King, and Colonial Council. This division of power was somewhat vague. Parliament legislated by law in the most important cases; the king, by royal ordinance, for less vital matters; and the local council by decree for whatever was left over. More might have been made of this opportunity for greater colonial independence had not the local councils shown much recalcitrance along with incompetence in handling finances. The old colonies found themselves in growing opposition to the Métropole on the sugar issue and on slavery. These problems, and the acquisition of a new type colony like Algeria—which the July Monarch had inadvertently conquered—marked the formal demise of the *exclusif*. Under Guizot's influence and the development of steam navigation, a new conception of colonization was evolved. Colonies assumed a new military and commercial significance, which in the Far East began to supplement France's traditional interest in the Catholic Missions.

The confused policies which characterized the Second Empire marked definite albeit haphazard steps in the history of French colonization. Slavery and the Colonial Pact were abolished, in 1848 and 1861, in a rush of liberalism both economic and social. Cochin-China and Cambodia were acquired to satisfy the requirements of glory, both earthly and celestial. The *Sénatus Consulte* of 1854 gave a new legislative basis to the colonies, the principles of which outlived the Second Empire. This marked the definite ascendancy of the executive over the legislative power. Although theoretically Parliament still dominates, its intervention has now become exceptional. As if the situation were not already complicated enough, the Protectorate ideal was evolved by the Third Republic as the best compromise between its principles and the past. Native sovereignty was not officially destroyed, but neither was the field for Metropolitan legislative interference limited. Executive decrees have been its most usual form, since they are adaptable, supple, and swift, but they offer no guarantee of colonial rights. In addition, they violate the sacrosanct principle of the separation of powers on which French law is based. But the practical considerations have made the decree régime triumph over any theoretical objections. It has also the advantage of retaining the principle of legislation appropriate to each colony. On the other hand, there is the danger of instability and incoherence in being so arbitrary, and all the evils of excessive centralization. To offset this, certain representative bodies, like the *Conseil Supérieur des Colonies*, were created, but their function is purely advisory, and it is only lip-service to republican ideals.

The cross-breeding of the past with current exigencies has given Indo-China a mongrel judicial character. Cochin-China is a bona fide colony: Annam and Cambodia genuine protectorates: but Tonkin is a monster of public law, which falls into no known legal category. The French concessions of Hanoi, Haiphong, and Tourane are administered like colonies, though juridically they are Protectorates. Certain provinces of Cambodia—Battambang, Sisophon, and Siemreap—are *de jure* colonies but *de facto* Protectorates. The Kingdom of Luang-Prabang is in practice a Protectorate, but not legally recognized as such, whereas the former Kingdoms of Tran-ninh, Vientiane, and Bassac are factual colonies from the administrative viewpoint, but Protectorates before the law.

The confusion in the delegation of colonial legislative powers is matched only by their juridical set-up. Although legally illogical, the decrees issued by the head of the state constitute veritable laws in the colony. The contradictions and confusion are particularly felt in both factual and legal protectorates where there is an ill-defined division of sovereignty. Practical necessities have regularly triumphed over juridical scruples, but the general interests would be better served by a pruning and defining of this eternal duality in the sources and scope of law. In the confusion between the multiple legislators—Parliament, the President of the Republic, the Minister of the Colonies, the Governor-General of Indo-China and the local Governors—the *Conseil d'État* has tried to play the role of both arbiter and policeman, but the best work and will in the world cannot remedy the basic defects in the system. Though one may plead that it has not as yet prevented Indo-China's development, nor does such anarchy repel the Asiatic mind, yet from the viewpoints of political morality, juridical logic, and practical simplification, the régime of decrees and the juridical status of each country of the Union should be reformed.

Up to 1881 the Ministry of the Colonies was a branch of the Naval

394

Ministry, at which time it was transferred to the Ministry of Commerce. The next year it was restored to the Navy, where it remained until 1889, when for the second time it was shunted back to Commerce. This shuttling process was repeated in 1892 and 1893, and at last in 1894 it came to rest. The Colonies were finally awarded a Ministry of their own. The same uneasiness, however, was shown within its portals. From 1894 to 1930 there were no fewer than forty-six Colonial Ministers. As was natural with so many Ministers, and with the traditional grip in which Paris held the colonies, these men interfered constantly in colonial affairs. Ferry complained in vain that it was a real misfortune for a young colony to be at the end of the Ministerial wire.

A new country needs not only a consistent policy of broad outlines, but encouragement to find solutions for its particular problems. Distance not only creates misunderstandings, but ignorance. Yet Paris showed no common-sense appreciation of this, but intervened in the smallest details, and invariably in an obstructionist manner. The best-intentioned Ministers were too ignorant and too far away, too immersed in Parliamentary politics, and too transient. Their underlings were too narrowly devoted to accepted formulae, and too jealous of initiative on the part of the colonies. When Lyautey refused to await permission from France to build storehouses for rotting army supplies, he was denounced by officialdom, which preferred to lose a war rather than to break a regulation.[1] There was an amazing circular sent out in 1893 from France to the colonial governors prescribing the purchase of their supplies in France and indicating in what towns each commodity could be found, completely ignoring the fact that they could be more cheaply produced in the colony itself. The natural indolence of the Public Works service was encouraged by the cost and delays of getting their supplies perforce from France. De Lanessan and Doumer effectively won independence from intensive Ministerial supervision, but the Métropole's general economic policy is the same.

Ultimate responsibility can be laid at the door of French belief in the absolute value of theory. If an institution is good for France it has equal value in the colonies, or anywhere else in the world, for that matter. A classical love of uniformity and symmetry, as well as an education that is predominantly theoretical and humanistic, have made for over-simplified solutions to all problems, and an adherence to routine in their application. This tendency has been reinforced by the heavy stamp of Napoleonic bureaucracy. Moreover, there is im-

[1] Lyautey, H., *Lettres du Tonkin et de Madagascar* (Paris, 1921), p. 478.

patience to see the immediate effect of a theory's application. Twenty-four hours after a new system is inaugurated, Paris cables for news of the results. At the end of a week the Métropole is astounded to hear of no fundamental transformation. If a decisive triumph cannot be announced in a month's time, the newspapers declare the system a failure and the officials who applied it either dishonest or incompetent. And another theory is tried, antipodal to the first, with an entirely new batch of functionaries. No one imagines that patient experimentation over a period of time has anything to do with a theory's merits. There is no compromise possible, only a brusque *volte face*. This frame of mind is largely responsible for the frequent vacillations in French colonial policy, but there is the additional and important failure on the part of the French public to agree conclusively as to the merits of colonization.

With such a contradictory heritage, it is not surprising that the Third Republic has maintained no stable colonial policy. Although naturally favouring the Revolutionary egalitarian legacy, enough of the tenets of the *ancien régime* have survived to make France chary about treating natives as Frenchmen, by an education in the arts of peace and war, because their interests and those of France are inherently incompatible. In the economic sphere the tradition is more consistent, and so is the tariff policy which unites the colony to the mother country. Added to these factors were the circumstances under which Indo-China was acquired, and contemporaneous European politics also had an important influence on the outcome.

The Third Republic inherited an empire that in size and prosperity caricatured what had been lost in 1763 and 1815. Though there was pride in the colonial past, and a feeling that its glory had been tarnished only through governmental stupidity, yet there did exist simultaneously some doubt regarding French colonizing ability, which is betrayed by expansionist writers who protest too much France's imperial talents. Moreover, the geographical position of France has made for a policy of conquest both in Europe and overseas. In the 1870's the rise of Germany checked French expansion in Europe, and turned her energies and pride towards distant enterprises. Yet the Franco-Prussian War left both fears and the desire for *revanche*, which made many patriots oppose colonization on the ground that it drained away men and money which would weaken France on the Rhine. According to the Clemenceau-Broglie formula, a colonial expansionist was a traitor to the fatherland; according to the humanitarians, the noble savage was better off without the corrupting contact of civilization; according to the economists, colonies were an expensive and hollow mockery of their former empire—in short, colonization was not a national necessity but a dangerous mirage. There was no use in exposing France's slowly reviving self-confidence to another blow by renewing colonial failures. Cochin-China was the unwanted orphan of the Second Empire. Cambodia had thrown herself into French arms, but why deliberately stir up a hornets' nest by conquering Tonkin?

Jules Ferry was responsible almost single-handed for the conquest of Tonkin. Sincere conviction of the necessity for colonization, as well as adroit manipulation of home and foreign politics, were his only weapons. Ferry's principal appeal was based on economic grounds. The increase in European and American industrial competition, and the ensuing tariff war had created a rush for markets outside the protected zones of Europe. Tonkin would prove an excellent investment for French producers whose appetites were already whetted by the prospect of China's nearby markets. Moreover, the contemporary zest for colonies was shifting the balance of power in Europe. If France did not want to be hopelessly outdistanced she must actively anticipate the future. Colonies like Tonkin did not necessitate human but monetary expatriation, which meant an investment of superfluous capital and not the draining of men vital to home defence.

Ferry's theory was popularized by the able economist, Leroy-Beaulieu, and also impersonally aided by a simultaneous decline in French exports which gave body to Ferry's contentions. Ferry had far less difficulty in winning over the military element. Colonies offered new fields for their prowess, and their activities had been humiliatingly checkmated in Europe. The narratives of Lyautey and Galliéni show what those new opportunities could mean to adventurous spirits bored and restricted by the squirrel-cage routine of a provincial garrison town. Humanitarian motives, mixed with patriotism, further identified colonization with spreading abroad the benefits of French culture. By a clever use of circumstance and current psychology, Ferry succeeded in converting an anti-expansionist Parliament.

Parliamentary conversions are notoriously transient and uncertain. Dupré had been forced to disavow Garnier's action, and vacillation had marked both delta expeditions. When Rivière was killed and national honour was thought to be involved, the war in Tonkin took on such a sacred character that credits were voted by big majorities for fourteen months in the Chamber. But when the campaign dragged on for ten years it was felt to be unjustifiably homicidal. The opposition was based partly on sincere conviction of colonial warfare's wastefulness in men and money, which only immediate success and profits could justify, but also upon political opportunism. Unfortunately for the colony Tonkin became a party issue, a pawn in the struggle between the Moderate and Radical Republicans, and in general it was the rallying-cry for opponents of the Republic. At one time only three votes saved the Protectorate, but after that evacuation was not again seriously considered. France was willing to keep Tonkin, but reviled it, and Ferry was given the title *le Tonkinois* as a mark of general opprobrium. Even when the accurate report of the Langson defeat proved how unjustified had been the panicky vehemence that overthrew Ferry's Ministry, the unpopularity of Tonkin continued to be exploited by politicians. Nowadays it is the Extreme Left which uses the abuses of colonization as party ammunition. Native nationalists as well as Opposition leaders have appreciated the possibilities of heckling the Ministry even at moments when the colony's general welfare would have been better served by silence.

The office of Governor-General of Indo-China up to 1928 had been used as a political plum. It was awarded to a politician either to get rid of him during a critical period or as compensation for losing some higher office, or finally it has been used by the incumbent himself as a springboard to a more important position in France. De Lanessen was kept in Indo-China lest he return to become Minister of the Colonies. Doumer and Sarraut were accused by their opponents of having initiated an immediately effective but fundamentally unsound policy in the colony solely to promote their Metropolitan careers. The colony has offered sinecures—as was shown in the supposed dialogue of two deputies who had been appointed to lucrative positions in the Protectorate:

"Sometimes I wonder what we should have done if we had found nothing in Tonkin."
"Ah *dame!* we should have had to work."[1]

The coming of the civil government in Indo-China merely increased the quantity of dead wood from France's political wreckage. With the recent elevation of functionaries like Pasquier and Robin, there is promise of a Parliamentary change of heart, yet the appointment of Brévié indicated a return to the old trend. The principle of specialization in a particular colony has made headway in military circles and the magistracy. With more reason high administrative officials should be versed in local problems by training and by long experience. Just

[1] Bonnafont, L., *Notes d'un Tonkinois* (Hanoi, 1907), p. 20.

because a man like Merlin had been excellent in an African post, it was assumed with disastrous results that he would be an equally successful Governor of Indo-China. Promotion from within the ranks would not only stimulate the functionaries' zeal, but obviate the apprenticeship which every newcomer, no matter how brilliant, must serve. It would also have the advantage of loosening the grip which Parliament still has over its distant colony. Not content with disregarding the colony's needs in selecting its chief executive, Parliamentary selfishness and inconstancy is further exemplified by the frequency of its changes in policy. De Lanessan was recalled for having transgressed some minor ruling without regard for the confusion it would cause in Indo-China. The best of interim Governors have their terms needlessly prolonged. They can do nothing but mark time, and the uncertainty that ensues paralyses the colony's development. By the time the titular Governor has taken stock of the situation and settled down to apply his formula he is unceremoniously removed because he has offended some potentate in the colony or Paris, or because he has not immediately wrought miracles, or because there has been a change in the French political line-up. The percentage of misinformation aired in a Parliamentary debate reveals the deputies' ignorance of Indo-Chinese conditions and needs. Colonials may complain of Parliamentary interference, yet they deliberately brought it upon themselves to get rid of a Governor like Varenne. Until some policy is evolved in France or in Indo-China that is based on the colony's welfare and not on party selfishness, or the interests of powerful individuals, the same instability and wanton negligence will continue their malevolent reign until French sovereignty is hopelessly jeopardized.

The political and cultural assimilation of a colony was favoured by an overwhelming majority in the late nineteenth century. This involved the destruction of existing native institutions, and their replacement by those prevalent in France, with an inevitable substitution of language. It was believed that the mere knowledge of French would bring an insatiable thirst for French ideas and manufactures. The Colonial Congress of 1889–90 declared that language was the justification of colonization and the assurance of its permanence. After three generations of linguistic instruction,

when Paul de Koch and Alexandre Dumas, père, have stimulated the Annamites' interest, their ideals will be come French. When they have become prosperous they will buy our products. . . . They will be French and our equals.[1]

[1] Congrès Colonial National de 1889–90, E. Aymonier, *De l'Enseignemont en Indochine* (Paris, 1898), p. 336.

Language was to be the preliminary to a transplantation of French education that would eliminate the differences between races which are fundamentally if not apparently equal. So strong was this feeling that one speaker had to apologize for using the term "inferior races." The tenor of the Congress was shown by one of its formulated aims, "to form the colonies in our image in order to better them."[1] Economic and administrative assimilation were so taken for granted that they were not even discussed, nor was the possibility of any native contributions to French culture considered for a moment. It was assumed that the natives would eagerly turn from their own darkness to Occidental light. Leroy-Beaulieu declared that when the natives knew French better that they would willingly place themselves under French law and slough off their own legislation, now only temporarily tolerated.

Even before practice had proved the fallacy of these beliefs, a few dissenting voices were raised, notably those of Gustave le Bon and De Saussure. They insisted on the vital differences between races and the fatal consequences of transplanting foreign cultures. These men advocated an associationist policy, based on the existence of a colonial personality, the product of its own history and setting. Natives were not culturally a blank which would passively receive the imprint of a Western culture. In the equation of colonial policy, an X must henceforth be added for the unknown but no longer negligible quantity of colonial individuality.

Besides the writing of theorists, an enormous literature began to appear about 1900, both of actual and of fictionized experience, which further assailed assimilation on the grounds of practical failure. Annamite civilization might be from the abstract viewpoint not so good as the French, but it was admirably suited to the natives. Such a culture it would be neither possible nor desirable to destroy, yet it had undeniably been evolved for a world that no longer existed. By manipulation and by adapting it to modern life France would perform a valuable service. Assimilation was not only a failure but positively harmful, since it alienated the natives from the French, for it had destroyed and created nothing comparable in its place. The value of a people's culture was comparative, not intrinsic, and worthless when torn from its own setting. Men like Ajalbert and Bernard took pains to burst the bubble of French complacency or indifference. What mattered the economic transformation of a colony if the mother country

[1] Congrès Colonial National de 1889–90, E. Aymonier, *De l'Enseignemont en Indochine* (Paris, 1898), p. 246.

could not win the respect or gratitude of its people? If this were partly due to defects in the local administration, it was even more the fault of France's nagging interference, her lack of a consistent policy, and consideration for the colony's welfare. But above all it was premature to force on a young colony the burden of its own finances.

Prominent critics were not lacking in the first decade of the twentieth century. The 1900 International Sociological Congress reflected in its resolutions the changing tide of opinion. Colonization's aim was now

the physical well-being of the natives, and their moral and intellectual development, which can only be brought about by maintaining in principle the existing native institutions.

In April 1909 the Chamber of Deputies consummated this new development. Before passing to the order of the day they recorded their conviction

that the policy of association is necessary for the well-being of the populations and for the security of our possessions in the Far East; that in order to make it a reality, it is recognized that a change is necessary in the fiscal, judicial, and economic régime; that it is suitable to prepare gradually and wisely an advisory participation by the natives in public affairs.[1]

This official adoption of the association policy was indirectly due to a metamorphosis in the French attitude and directly to the 1908 uprisings in Annam.

Messimy, in his budget report of 1910, drew widespread attention to abuses in the colonial government. It was good to wash dirty linen in public provided it was effectively cleaned and not merely displayed. He laid responsibility frankly at the door of France's exaggerated fiscal policy and excessive centralization, which was mainly responsible for a disastrous native policy. Violette's report the following year again brought Indo-China into the limelight. He bared the colony's most vulnerable spots with judgments that were well intentioned but too absolute. France had destroyed everything in the colony and constructed nothing—which completely ignored the reforms that had been effected. He stirred up personal animosity by the violence and tactlessness of his denunciations: from the ground up everything must be reformed.

A better balanced criticism was that of Métin in his 1912 report. He made constructive comparisons with neighbouring countries, and

[1] Cammilli, B., *La Représéntation des Indigènes en Indochine* (Paris, 1914), p. 1.

suggested reforms that would not shake the whole structure. He also proposed ways to reduce the plethora of futile functionaries, to restore and purify the mandarinate, to increase the native advisory organizations, and to develop the country's resources. His report showed that Parliamentary committees were studying Indo-China seriously as a colony that had its own special problems. For the first time he foreshadowed the principle that upon the colony's well-being depends its value to the mother country. This idea appealed both to egoists and to humanitarians, and it gave the necessary driving force to a reform programme.

This metamorphosis of government policy was due not a little to the vague stirrings of contemporary French opinion. The exotic tradition has always been strong in French literature. It preceded and exceeded romanticism, and differed radically from colonial literature, in that it was and is wholly a Metropolitan product. Distant voyages with descriptions of picturesque peoples and their tropical setting, seen through the author's ever-present personality, have long been favourites with the home-loving French, who have preferred security to distant hazards.

Public Opinion

Indo-China, unlike Siam, enjoyed only a cursory vogue in France under Louis XVI. A head-dress *à l'Annamite* was evolved as an element of fashion, but those who wore it would have been hard pressed to tell where and what was Annam. Even nowadays all Orientals are Chinese to the French peasant, just as all white men and negroes are Occidentals to the Annamite. The diversity and cultures of the different peoples of Indo-China were not appreciated until long after the conquest. In 1861, when Cochin-China was first occupied, a renowned professor of the *Collège de France*[1] stated that with the possible exception of Burma the countries of the Indo-Chinese peninsula hardly deserved *"les regards de l'histoire."* Some historians of Siam, like the Abbé de Choisy, made scanty mention of the Khmers. But in the Far East it was China that stimulated imaginations in the seventeenth and eighteenth centuries, and set the pace and style for the exotic tradition that has been so strong a current in French thought.

It was not until the eighteenth century that one finds two small books inspired by Annam. Ignorance was felt to be no deterrent to

---

[1] Barthélemy Saint Hilaire.

using an Oriental country, in the *Lettres Persanes* manner, to criticize contemporary France. *Chinki, Histoire Cochinchinoise* (1768), was the story, with Physiocrat trimmings, of an honest man who was prevented from training his children to be worthy artisans by the red tape of the *ancien régime*. This and the second book, *Anecdotes Tonkinois* (1774), obeyed the exotic tradition which required all Oriental countries to be enchantingly lovely and peopled by men of idyllically simple tastes. A considerably larger percentage of accuracy was offered by the missionaries' reports, though they devoted an inordinate attention to the devil and his Oriental works. First came the Jesuits and Père Alexandre de Rhodes' masterly dictionary (1651), and then the Society of Foreign Missions with its bulletins of evangelical triumphs. Cambodia and Laos offered fewer converts and martyrdoms, so the faithful were regaled with fewer accounts of those countries.

The first real contact was furnished by the Annamite ambassadors sent by the Emperors Minh Mang and Tu Duc, who created momentary sensations in 1839 and 1863, when they toured French cities. The explorations of Mouhot, Pavie, Lagrée, and Dupuis which marked the closing years of the nineteenth century were the most important contributions to a knowledge of the new colony. The arrival of the Delaporte collection at the Trocadéro gave the French public a chance to see the concrete embodiment of an art they had known before only through reading.

The French press became mildly interested in the dispute between Dupuis and the family of Legrée for priority in the discovery of the Red River route. Newspaper polemics grew by leaps and bounds with the great public interest in Ferry's policy and war with China. Ferry himself complained of the press which spoke of the colonies only to deplore them, or who organized a conspiracy of silence when there was no evil to record. The big Paris dailies sent reporters to Tonkin when trouble broke out there, and they confirmed with joyous indignation the public's conviction that the war was Ferry's fault. A phrase that appeared in one paper, "You possess in Tonkin only the ground under your soldiers' feet," was used more than once as Parliamentary artillery. Papers gave publicity to exaggerated statements, as, for example, that Tonkin had cost France a billion francs and thirty-five thousand men. One wit called the expedition a *placement de père de famille*, another "The Panama of To-morrow." Public disapproval was fanned by press polemics to such a white heat that the government dared not reveal the truth about the campaign, and reiterated the statement that the colony was now thoroughly pacified. To give body to these declarations, and to calm public opinion, always nervous about the ascendancy of the military, the civil government was prematurely installed in the colony. When the statistics of the losses began to filter through to the public, there was an outbreak of indignation—and against the army. If the soldiers fell in ambush it was the fault of their officers, who stirred up trouble just to win promotion and decorations. Fundamentally it was the fault of a hostile public opinion that the campaign dragged on as it did. The government feared to send enough soldiers at one time, so only inadequate reinforcements dribbled through, and they had to be prematurely recalled just to soothe public opinion.

The reporters sent out by the Parisian papers were naturally more concerned with regaling the public with exciting stories than in ferreting out the truthful and dull facts. They were to a man discouraging about the ugly colony and its treacherous people. Their French public enjoyed the adventurous and exotic elements in their accounts, but the complicated character of colonial problems required more study than either the narrator or reader was willing to make. It was not until the administration of Doumer that official journalism was encouraged in order to inform public opinion with accuracy.

In the plethora of propaganda designed to encourage faith in the new colony, there were a few outstanding writers whose criticism penetrated the official façade. Colonel Bernard was a pioneer in this field. He pointed out that what prosperity existed in the colony was independent of French control, and that, all told, the country had a mediocre agriculture, an insignificant commerce, and a non-existent industry. Two articles in the *Revue de Paris* (1901) made Bernard's political fortune, and gave Doumer a blow from which he never recovered. His book was studied by Beau and his entourage on their way out to the colony, unfortunately to no tangible effect. Jung's books narrated the tribulations of the colonist who took the promise of official aid in good faith, only to encounter his most serious obtacles in the bureaucratic formalism of the administration. Jean Ajalbert was by far the most important of these debunking journalists, and he was the first to inform the French about Indo-China's reaction to Japan's victory over Russia. The results of his five years' residence in the colony are embodied in an excellent series of studies and novels, whose small editions demonstrate unfortunately that public interest was never commensurate with the importance of his criticism.

Claude Farrère's *Les Civilisés* had far greater vogue with less reason and worse consequences. The horrible picture he painted of colonial society, made up of the dregs of European failures, in conjunction with the more civilized Asiatics, whose nominal but not spiritual masters they were, confirmed the French public's worst suspicions about the moral bankruptcy of their colonies. This can be partly traced to the exotic tradition of the noble savage-native uncorrupted by so-called civilization, but it is also due to the inveterate bourgeois distrust of the adventurer. The French public is chronically prone to believe the worst about its own colonials and the best about its native subjects—a viewpoint that has been profitably exploited by journalists who proclaim that the colony is lost at the slightest disturbance.

The current of anti-colonial feeling, though it may take Protean forms, is still strong in France. After each native uprising—1908, 1913, 1930—it comes to light and denunciations abound. Partly it is an outcropping of Tonkin's old unpopularity, partly a feeling that colonies are a burden and a drain, and colonization a doubtful impertinence to peoples whose culture is rich in mellow wisdom. In time of war the distant colonies' defence would be difficult for France, and dubious from within by semi-loyal natives forces. Just before the War some French writers suggested exchanging Indo-China for Alsace-Lorraine and, only recently, as payment of the American debt. These proposals betrayed easy discouragement with colonial problems, and belies the Revolutionary concept of the colonies as an integral part of France. The colonies could be traded just like inanimate merchandise.

When it was proposed to place Indo-China at the head of all the French possessions in the Pacific for the greater convenience of France and to the financial detriment of the colony, there was widespread resentment in Indo-China at this new form of the old egoism. During the War there had come a sudden appreciation of Indo-China's great value as a reservoir of men and labourers, as well as a source of financial aid, which caused a change of front. With France's static birth-rate and her dependence on foreign countries for raw materials, the potential wealth of the colonies—especially "rich Indo-China"—seeped into the national consciousness. Sarraut's proposed colonial development scheme of 1921[1] reflected this new desire to tap colonial resources and a new conception of the French Empire as a whole.

The War had produced a wave of liberalism out of gratitude for the colonies' sacrifices for France, but unfortunately it also unleashed

[1] Sarraut, A., *La Mise en Valeur des Colonies Françaises* (Paris, 1923).

a prolonged era of Metropolitan selfishness. Tariff barriers were raised to reserve exclusively the colonial preserves for France. Bonds were drawn tighter in proportion to the Métropole's new appreciation of her colonies' value. Investors demanded increased protection for their capital. Indo-China's War contributions to the French military budget were so solacing that the Métropole graciously accepted them until the depression gave the colony a chance to plead off. Annamite troops, obviously against their will, were sent to police other French colonies. Indo-China's general budget in 1930 bore a 16 per cent subsidy of extraneous French enterprises in the Far East. No such sacrifice was asked of any other colony. It was no wonder that colonials demanded autonomy from Metropolitan interference, and native nationalists denounced France's turncoat liberalism.

Fortunately for Indo-China the post-War decade saw a simultaneous growth of liberalism in France. Grafted on to the old French distrust of colonials' laziness and oppressiveness was sincere gratitude and appreciation for the role played by the Indo-Chinese during the War, and a sympathetic interest in the Annamite national movement. The colonials were naturally the first to resent this attitude. A stream of journalists during the past decade has flowed through Indo-China, passing more or less hasty judgments of an uncomplimentary nature upon the French residents there. Not much progress has been marked since the early French belief that colonials lived either like savages in a hut, or wallowed in dissolute and luxurious idleness. Léon Werth's colonial ogre has been modernized, but he always acts the brute towards the aristocratic Annamites. Roland Dorgelès was the most embittering experience. Colonials felt that he had betrayed their hospitality by caricaturing them and the colony, as seen from a car window. Pierre Benoit's light-heated treatment of the Khmers was also duly resented, and with more reason the bleak picture of the seamy side of colonization which Andrée Viollis painted. A colonial review of Mme Chivas-Baron's *Folie Exotique*[1] ironically prophesied a great success with the Metropolitan public, though it might provoke old colonials to hearty laughter. Its author would probably be again crowned by the Academy because her story dwelt on the nonchalance and brutality of colonials as contrasted with the natives' primitive virtues.

The reading public in Indo-China is large and active. Any book that appears on the colony is avidly read and criticized. Though colonials are naturally more qualified than transient journalists to understand

---

[1] *Revue Indochinoise*, janvier-février, 1924.

their country's problems, their persistent refusal to acknowledge truth in adverse criticism does not create confidence in their impartiality. The home government in particular is suspicious of colonials' independence. The Parliamentary debates centring around Varenne showed less nervousness about a Governor who could always be recalled than a desire to curtail land concessions that might make colonials too independent. There was also a distinct feeling that colonials were responsible for the growing native unrest. In 1931 when Raynaud, then Minister of the Colonies, was sent to Indo-China to investigate the Yenbay uprisings, it was in the nature of a paternalistic gesture—more theatrical than effective—to show that the colonials were not the only power there.

Paris is obviously determined to tighten its control over the colony, loosened not only by the War but by the colonials themselves. Fortunately the renewal of this self-interested grip on Indo-China is partially neutralized by the realization that the colony's well-being is essential to its usefulness, that native grievances must be assuaged to insure their co-operation as labourers and protégés, that the colony's political and economic personality must be counted on in the formation of any policy—in short, that the moral conquest of the natives is the only safeguard against Communism and autonomy.

Up to a certain point modern exotic literature has followed a parallel development. An increasing appreciation of the differences between peoples has created a healthy humility and self-doubt, but has not destroyed a belief in the profound identity of all human beings. The current instability of Europe has found a steadying antidote in the immutable wisdom of Asia.

Public opinion in France still shows marked divergence from official policy. The government's perseverance in conquering Tonkin, in the face of hostile public opinion, was due to the idea of substituting immediate profits from their colony, by the conception of Indo-China as a long-term investment. This involved a series of loans to carry out a public works programme. Paris from the outset was, however, reluctant to involve its official credit, though individuals showed great confidence in the colony's future by over-subscribing the loans. The economic vitality shown by the colony during and after the War was so great that it caught up the Métropole in a contagion of confidence, and started an unprecedented era of financial speculation in the colony's natural resources. In fact this golden era of Indo-China was marked by such ignorance as to the nature of these resources as to ruin many of the investors. This was not in itself a reflection on the colony but on the greediness and gullibility of its would-be promoters. Small capitalists predominated among these investors, and they did not realize that the great financiers treated Indo-China as their own fief. It was, on the whole, a return to the old conception of the colony as existing for the benefit of the Métropole, a place where profits could and should be made with the minimum of effort. At present Metropolitan confidence has been sadly shaken, but the same spirit of speculation would be reborn at the slightest provocation, because it is inherent in French colonial psychology. Those who have persisted in the idea of the colony as a long-term investment and not a field for speculation, have in large measure retained their faith and their capital. In this double attitude towards the colony's wealth it is the government which has maintained the cautious investors' attitude, and the public which has vacillated between unreflecting enthusiasm and equally irrational despair.

If assimilation is old-fashioned as an administrative theory it has survived in a distorted form in the average Frenchman's attitude towards colonization. The French public is extraordinarily uninformed about its colonies, chiefly because it is not interested. This cannot be blamed on the lack of information facilities. Foreign observers have been struck by the excellence and quantity of French colonial periodicals. The Ministry of Public Instruction has created a chair of Indo-Chinese history and philology at the *Collège de France* and at the *Ecole des Hautes Etudes Orientales*. A committee on Indo-Chinese archaeology and the Colonial School are under the government's aegis. There is, too, the *Agence Economique de l'Indochine* in Paris and its excellent library. In 1876 a Society of Colonial Studies was founded in Paris; and in 1910 the Association of the French of Asia, which awards an annual prize for colonial literature and subsidizes the translation of books into French and *quoc ngu*. In 1925 the colonial government inaugurated a travelling art fellowship. Lecturers, both French and native, frequently discourse upon Indo-China.

Communications with the colony have in recent years been greatly increased. Tourist travel has been encouraged, and in 1929 Saigon was linked to Paris by an air route. In 1922 a supplementary steamship service plied between Bordeaux and Saigon, and two years later a new wireless station linked Indo-China to France. The greatest void is probably in the school programmes, which give little place to Indo-China. In higher education study is confined to Indo-Chinese philology and archaeology: in primary education, none at all: in secondary education, principally geography—and that none too accurate. The public's ignorance is less surprising than official errors. In a lecture at Marseille the Minister of the Colonies, Piétri, stated that there were five *lycées* in Indo-China for Annamites at a time when there were only two. The mistakes of lesser lights like deputies are more taken for granted. Colonial budgets are often voted in a single *séance*, interpellations are shortened, and the vote taken in the morning before an empty Chamber. The budget for the world's second largest empire is smaller than Belgium's colonial expenditures and less than half of Holland's.

The press is a slender reed of information on which to lean. Here, again, is the same vicious circle. The public is only interested in reading about colonial scandals which confirm their prejudices because they are uninformed, and they are uninformed because the papers print only sensational news about the colonies. This profound ignorance has both good and evil effects. It errs on the side of liberalism, but its credulity exposes the public to facile exploitation. The Parisian press aroused the public against Varenne, who had offended the financial powers by refusing to re-establish the gaming Farm. The *Comité de l'Industrie et du Commerce Indochinois*, representing investors of billions of francs in the colony, has a powerful Metropolitan press and lobby to form and sway public opinion. It was this group which opposed the investment of foreign capital in Indo-China at a time when French capital was unavailable. In a talk at the *Club du Faubourg* Varenne told a significant anecdote of his colonial career. He received a telegram from the Minister of the Colonies relative to certain outbreaks in Indo-China. Varenne replied that the country was so quiet that he could not report even a motor accident. It later transpired that these false rumours had been circulated to support a stock exchange operation. It was this same gullibility that unscrupulous speculators capitalized when they destroyed Indo-China's credit in the 1920's.

The anti-colonial prejudice that exists in France has made French public opinion a bar at which all colonial causes may be pleaded, or any cause, for that matter, provided it criticizes the government. French opinion has always been interested in foreign affairs provided that they have a tincture of republican idealism. Nowadays the French public is more opposed than ever, not only to the idea of a colonial war, but even to maintaining the present sovereignty by force of arms. Colonials and native nationalists alike profit by this attitude. During a local campaign in the Calendrier Affair[1] an appeal to Metropolitan opinion

[1] Cf. below, p. 314.

was effectively threatened as a means of breaking the monopolists. When Bazin was murdered in 1929, immediately an effort was made in the colony to cover up the labour conditions which had led to this assassination, but it did not prevent the telling articles of Robert Poulaine from appearing in *Le Temps*. It was early recognized that the only way of obtaining satisfaction and redress in the colony was by campaigning in France. In 1900 the *Affaire Iukanthor* was thrashed out in the French press through articles and revelations in the *Figaro* and the *Matin*. The press then made it impossible for the government to muzzle the whole affair.

The colonial press is nothing like so strong, because of its weak finances and censorship, and it cannot perform an analogous function for which its greater proximity and information facilities in the colony would seem to have marked it. Annamite nationalists have toured France, lecturing to sympathetic audiences on their compatriots' grievances. The spontaneity of French approval for any nationalist movement, even in their colonies, explains the government's anxiety to paint the Yenbay uprisings as a Communist plot—but even the Communists plead their cause at the bar of French opinion. In 1919 Nguyen-Ai-Quoc, the future leader of Indo-Chinese Communism, launched a bitter attack in *L'Humanité* against the colonial adminis-tration. Nguyen An-Ninh, editor of the gadfly paper, *La Cloche Fêlée*, thought it was useless to work through colonials for reform, but he did not despair of establishing relations with Metropolitan liberals. Appeals for clemency for the Yenbay prisoners were made in France. Louis Roubaud was sent by the *Petit Parisien* to investigate the situation. Two other journalists, René Vanlande and Andrée Viollis, contributed through their documentary reporting to the liberal cause. As in financial matters the public's ignorance is the dubious factor in its well-inten-tioned liberalism. Certain Communists admit to having falsified their photographs of colonials' brutality towards natives in order to re-inforce their propaganda. The majority of journalists who have made a living out of preaching colonization in France have no touchstone of accuracy derived from residence in the colony.

The *naïveté* of French liberalism has often made it the laughing-stock of those better informed on colonial affairs. Its weakness is senti-mentality, but it has also a fine humanitarian side which the more realistic viewpoint lacks. If there is a certain fatuous ignorance behind the liberals' belief that indigenous peoples are backward brothers who need only contact with French equality, fraternity, and—possibly—

liberty to perfect their primitive virtues, this essentially humanistic outlook has leavened the lump of colonial exploitation. Its common meeting ground with the official and financial viewpoints lies in the mutual conviction that an amelioration of native life must precede any profit realized by the mother country. This is no white man's burden, nor is there any crying over spilt milk. In the modern world it is inevitable that economic needs must triumph over theoretical considerations. Sooner or later Indo-China could not have avoided being drawn into the vortex of contemporary living. It only remains to make the period of adjustment as short and as painless as possible.

THE COLONIALS' REACTION

Reaction of French Colonials to Each Other

In trying to analyse the colonial type one must realize that colonial society is being constantly renewed by fresh blood from without, and that from within contact with the country and its people is continually transforming those long established in Indo-China, as well as newcomers. Despite its perpetual state of flux and evolution, colonial society has a certain homogeneity. The differences that exist are chronological rather than inherent, for all comers pass through three successive stages: the adventure period, followed by acclimatization, which merges eventually into the bourgeois phase.

The colonial vocation is a quality rarely encountered among the French. It is a composite made up of the teaching instinct, the spirit of adventure, love of the exotic, and the hope of finding an earthly paradise among primitive peoples of Golden Age virtues. An eminently bourgeois people like the French frown upon any career which is strong enough to break home ties. Love of the exotic has long been a tradition in France, but it has been largely reduced to fireside literature. Nevertheless, certain stalwart spirits have felt forcefully enough the desire for risk or wealth, and have re-acted strongly against the monotony of Europe to brave the unknown, perhaps disguising it to themselves under coating of some nobler motive. The potential colonial has probably exaggerated to himself the luminous skies, abundant flowers, and luscious fruits of the land of his desire. Many ardent youths have been stirred by an affinity with the Gorgeous East. Pierre Loti was aroused in childhood by pictures of glamorous Angkor. Such a contradiction in motives for expatriation, ranging from the youthful romanticism of the conquistador to the ruthless realism of the fortune-seeker, have produced a few interesting and many pitiful types. The extensive cemeteries of the colony bear eloquent testimony to the many youthful failures. The country presented too many psychological, climatic, and economic obstacles to permit more than a few outstanding successes.

Those who have come nowadays to be called colonial sharks had as their spiritual sires the soldiers of fortune who came with the army of occupation, or in its wake. The opening of a new land has always attracted men of eminently self-reliant qualities. They were picturesque, impenitent, and unruly. Neither the beauties of the landscape nor the culture of the East meant anything to them. They came to make their fortunes—all else was extraneous. It never occurred to them that they might learn something from the country. The natives were no more interesting than the scenery and important only as labour. If these men were egoistic and undisciplined, they were also alive and intelligent. Certain Governors realized their potential utility to the colony, despite their moral and intellectual inferiority. Others saw in them only unscrupulous adventurers, often guilty of inexcusable violence, a menace to the social order. This antipathy of the bourgeois for the adventurer was the basis of the functionary-colonist feud. The bourgeois elements triumphed in proportion as the colony grew in importance. Most of the conquistadors were tamed by the colony itself, rather than steam-rollered into submission by the representatives of law and order. They had to bow their heads and accept routine, and even ask for government jobs. In time they became as incapable of initiative as the meekest born functionary.

But the old distrust crops out from time to time. Rumours are still rife that certain colonists were forced to leave France because of their dark past. When colonials are guilty of hysteria or lawlessness there is an outburst of bourgeois disapproval or complacent cluckings about their doubtful origin. Yet these men had been willing to put up with hazards and discomforts, and to renounce a life of comfortable security as part of the colonial adventure. It was they who created the vital, generous, and liberal atmosphere which has not yet wholly disappeared under the rising tide of bourgeois principles. Many may still well mourn the day when economies were unheard of, and when the sight of a white woman—albeit a Marseille harlot—could cause a stampede in a Saigon café.

With the development of the colony's towns there grew an unmistakable air of French provincial life. The majority of colonials are functionaries or petty employees with prosaic middle-class ideals.

There is no European labouring class, no aristocracy, nor any *rentier* class. The resulting homogeneity is one of social circumstance and not of origin. Superficially cosmopolitan—for among others there is a large scattering of Corsicans—there is a certain spiritual affinity among colonials that can be traced to the fact that they are a handful of white men governing a majority of Asiatics. Once past Suez a sense of solidarity seizes upon the most disparate Europeans when they come face to face with the strangeness of Asia.

To the more introspective and sensitive man may come questionings and self-doubt, but the majority scurry to cover and find a collective security in a sense of racial superiority. An Englishman or a German becomes closer than a brother: even an Arab is more akin than the yellow man. There is a feeling of desolate isolation in this sea of yellow faces which to the newcomer look all alike. It is not so much inherent insolence that characterizes this group reaction as a need for protection, and the complacent belief that they must belong to a superior civilization just because they are in control. When vanity is individual it may be amusing, but when it is collective it becomes aggressive and dangerous. It is fundamentally a question of skin pigment, and national frontiers are effaced or non-existent in the native as well as European mind. When the Russians were defeated by the Japanese in 1905, so were the English and French in native eyes. If White Russians nowadays are forced to do coolie work in Manchuria, Europeans throughout Asia resentfully feel that their prestige as white men has suffered. Yet in Indo-China, while there have been manifestations—especially after a native uprising—this unity which is based on a minority's need for protection is encountered more rarely than among other Occidentals in the Far East.

Separatist forces among the French colonials are stronger than the cohesive factors. In addition to local rivalry the transplantation of Metropolitan factions—the civil-military dispute and anti-clericalism—have taken root in the colony. Even within these rival camps there are strong disruptive forces. In the army one corps looks down upon another; among the functionaries there is an incredible rivalry between the different departments. Traditional French individualism and its cult of criticism have flourished as never before in a new country, where competition is keener in proportion to the importance of opportunities. Calumny has become a terrible weapon with which to destroy rivals. Some newspapers exist solely on the proceeds of blackmail, which has risen to the status of a colonial institution. In 1888 the

Resident of Haiphong was forced to return to France because of a rumour that he had participated in the arms contraband. Later this was proved to be untrue, but a powerful group in Haiphong, whose interests he had successfully attacked, used this weapon to force his removal.

French travellers and residents have long noticed this noxious colonial disunity, engendered by an extraordinary atmosphere of distrust and gossip. Lyautey complained of the lack of *camaraderie* and presence of petty jealousy.[1] One traveller[2] found two Frenchmen living alone in an isolated district who could not see each other without quarrelling violently. If colonials complain that visitors criticize them, they have their own mutual disparagement to blame. There is much washing of dirty linen in public, but the colonials are surprised and hurt when their sayings and doings are recorded critically, and the colony earns the reputation of being a scandal factory. This is not true of the stranger in their midst. For him hospitality even under the most difficult circumstances is boundless. Among all their compatriots there is no one more universally disliked than the anchorite.

In the truly febrile tempo of social life the failure to entertain and to be entertained is equivalent to flouting the powers that be, and thereby failing to get ahead—the unforgivable colonial sin. He who lives unto himself is regarded with suspicion. It is rumoured that he smokes opium—a taste no longer tolerated among colonials. One may drink oneself to death, but this is regarded indulgently provided it is done in company. The newly disembarked are regarded with suspicion until they declare themselves one with the colonials, by joining in the social round and not giving voice to unorthodox ideas. Colonials who live in the *brousse* are with reason nervous about associating with their urban compatriots.

The climate has much to do with the universal exasperation and *ennui*, but it is hard to find a remedy. To win promotion or a fortune one must incessantly associate with one's compatriots, yet this very association breeds destructive criticism of the self-sufficient absentees. There is an absence of real spiritual unity. Colonial society refuses to recognize as leaders the bureaucracy imposed upon it from above, or to associate with the conquered native population beneath. Colonial society stagnates in sterile vanity and is indifferent to everything in the country which is not European. It has become fashionable to dampen

[1] Lyautey, H., *Lettres du Tonkin et de Madagascar* (Paris, 1921), p. 76.
[2] Billotey, P., *L'Indochine en Zigzags* (Paris, 1929), p. 219.

the enthusiasm of newcomers by being openly disdainful of everything in Indo-China; yet a Tonkinese is immediately at the throat of a Cochin-Chinese colonial who dares to criticize his country. Few realize how attached they have grown to Indo-China until they return to France, where perversely everything seems out of tune. Then, though they must admit that Indo-China is less beautiful than Europe and less colourful than the Midi, that its pagodas can never rival Gothic cathedrals, they must confess that the colony has for them an inexplicable and superior attraction.

Certain groups in the colony do pride themselves on their culture. An interest in and knowledge of the latest development in art, literature, and music exists, though less often encountered than abysmal ignorance, a stack of uncut books, or general indifference. The presence of the EFEO has made Hanoi an intellectual centre in the Far East, and leavened the lump of sordid fortune-seekers. There is to be found a delightful group who welcome newcomers, especially writers of talent, who are regarded with suspicion by other colonials. Nevertheless, many of the French of Hanoi have the same unpleasant characteristics of their more opulent compatriots in Saigon. Saigon has a theatre and so has Hanoi. An Annamite marvelling as to why he should be taxed for these performances can only be wilfully ignorant of their social if not cultural importance to the colonial French. Life is reduced to routine entertainments. The day's work and sleep are interrupted at five o'clock by a drive which has become traditional. By six o'clock everyone winds up at the usual café, where cards are played until dinner, at which one entertains or is entertained by the same people. This schedule calls for no reading or discussion of ideas. The fault does not lie in a lack of intelligence, only that it is confined to professional usage. If they had been strenuously cultured in France these colonials would feel the absence of spiritual nourishment in the colony, but the majority of them feel no such deprivation. Moreover, the colony offers distinct anti-cultural encouragement, excessive gossip, and alcohol, constant conviviality, brutalizing the natives, isolation, and depressed nerves, which are fed by a climate productive of general torpor and bad temper. The decadent, destructive atmosphere which encircles the white man in the Orient is contagious even for refined and sensitive people. The presence of new disruptive factors undermines what is left, and is completed by the absence of restraint and discipline. A gentleman in Europe degenerates in the East to the point of shouting at his servant that he is as stupid as ten thousand pigs for having served him the wrong dish. As Werth reiterated sadly,[1] the colonials are only a caricature of Europeans.

If common cultural cement is lacking, colonials have one great interest in common—the making of money. Indo-China at different times has known collective exaltations like the Klondike rush. Tonkin and Laos have had their mining fevers, and rubber speculation was rife in the South. The sudden and general prosperity of the colony accompanied by the sensational rise in the piastre led to unmeasured hopes, vertiginous expenditures, and general demoralization. Adventurers overnight became captains of industry. The sober traditions of bourgeois saving vanished in imprudent prodigality. The depression dealt them a deadly blow. Some felt it to be celestial retribution; others that it was a healthful purging of the colony. Men who had never enjoyed money, whose wives had always done their own housework, found in the colony a luxurious living which had a very demoralizing effect. Money became a god. Functionaries left secure positions in the administration for the first promising opening in business. They were astonished at native discontent. The work of these men was admirable in many ways, but it was 100 per cent materialistic. There was, however, on the whole, a pretty accurate reaping of what was sown.

In the early days new fortunes were amassed, and those came almost exclusively from the monopolies or public works contracts. Saigon was the first town to flourish and to assume an external coquetry that earned for it the felicitous title of Pearl of the Far East. It spared those newly disembarked the first pangs of homesickness, for they found themselves in an unmistakably French city. But nowhere was there a more brutal contrast between luxury and poverty than among the French residents there. Behind the brilliant façade was the stark misery of the white proletariat. The much advertised, easy, and liberal life in the colonies amounted to poverty for many of the petty employees, whose wives had to go to market in person to be jostled by the contemptuous native servants of their richer colleagues.

Hanoi, after a sickly and neglected childhood, began to rival Saigon after Doumer made it the seat of his government. The town was rapidly transformed under the rain of gold stimulated by Doumer's public works programme. In 1897 there were 23 French houses in Hanoi; in 1906 there were 631. Its growth was not hampered by the retrenchments under Beau, nor by a series of virulent typhoons soon after. Hanoi's proximity to Hongay's coal mines has marked it for an

[1] Werth, L., *Cochinchine* (Paris, 1926), p. 37.

industrial future. The residue of adventurers left by the military campaigns formed a nucleus of energetic unscrupulous men, some of whom became the country's foremost colonists. Tonkin was too over-populated and too mountainous to promise the same agricultural future as the South, but its abundance of labour and mines and its proximity to China offer at least equal opportunity.

Thousands of applicants in France wanted to sail the seven seas for the privilege of performing menial tasks in the colony at starvation wages. Natives could have lived handsomely on a salary that was misery for a European family. Certain comforts were essential to white people in the tropics. The price of living rose very rapidly: food and clothes trebled in cost. To be sure, there was a theatre and opera, but very few of the French colonials could afford to go. Much misery was real, but some was psychological. Enormous pressure was exercised to keep up to one's neighbours' standards of expenditure. Since all came to the colony as unknown quantities to each other, they were judged by the display they made. Ancestors counted for nothing in this new country, and in many cases had better be forgotten.

The facility with which credit was accorded to the colonials, especially by the Chinese, was one cause of their undoing. Rivalry among the women for the best display in clothes, jewels, houses, and motors has had an interestingly disruptive effect on family life. A novel by Mme Chivas-Baron[1] details the evolution of a simple French couple who became fired by ambition upon their arrival in the colony. The wife's extravagance leads to debts and to a lover who can supplement the modest earnings of her functionary-husband. He, in turn, becomes heavily indebted by gaming at the Club, to the neglect of his work, for which he is finally dismissed. This homely saga is the narrative of many disorientated colonials, who are demoralized in Indo-China by the greater freedom from social discipline and convention, by new wealth and habits of luxury. Although every white man is a petty lord in relation to the natives, there is a distinct hierarchy among themselves, based upon the success each has achieved, appraised in terms of money. The tropical climate which forces all growths has equally deformed Western conventions until a De Monpezat could dominate the colony and make the administration tremble. The picture has its good side: a forceful personality can break through conventions of class and economic traditions to make a fortune that will force his disgruntled rivals to forget his humble if not ignominious past. There is a vitality

[1] Chivas-Baron, C., *La Simple Histoire des Gaudraix* (Paris, 1923).

417

about the colonials which contrasts refreshingly with the bourgeois rigidity of society in a French provincial town. The informality of colonial life astonished an Englishman, Cunningham,[1] who found its freedom from artificial conventions a contrast with the English colonies. He saw the wives of prominent officials clothed in dressing-gowns walking through the streets of Saigon, and even into the hotel lobbies.

The advent of Frenchwomen to the colonies has been the decisive factor in purveying bourgeois ideals thither. In the early days few well-bred Frenchwomen were willing to go to the colonies. Their coming meant the resumption of French social life, which introduced more pleasure, more grace and refinement into the colony, but which also involved bourgeois conventions and—far more important—the cutting off of their husbands from a simpler life in contact with the natives. Though there were some Frenchmen who fell so completely a prey to the Oriental charms of their *congaies*, that all their female compatriots seemed well lost, the great majority found that *congaies* meant too many inconveniences and, in addition, bred a certain physical repugnance. It was a current saying that the newcomers might for a time surrender to the exotic, but that it was only a question of time and nostalgia before they would prefer a middle-aged compatriot to the loveliest and youngest of native women. Perhaps it was the sensing of rivals in native women that has made Frenchwomen so unfair to them. In every way they have tried to sever all connections with natives, except as servants. Part of this was due to the novelty of having a conquered people available as a permanent supply of domestic labour. Their disdain was reciprocated by the Annamites, many of whom refused to serve in households where there was a Frenchwoman. Though there are many sentimental stories of the women who gave up their comfortable lives in Paris to follow their husbands to the colonies, where they kept them pure from *congaies* and opium, at the sacrifice of life and health, there is more reality in those wives who complicate their husbands' existence by trying to reproduce their former existence and in refusing to adapt themselves to the colonies to the ruination of both their lives and dispositions. The Frenchwoman who interests herself in the natives and their culture, who becomes rooted in Indo-China, and who does not pine for France, and is willing to receive as an equal her former chambermaid after a successful marriage is a very rare phenomenon indeed.

[1] Cunningham, A., *Les Français au Tonkin et dans la Chine Méridionale* (Hanoi, 1903).

The French girl brought up in the colony is perforce a far more hybrid product. Newcomers register, with varying degrees of displeasure, that they are bolder and more independent than their Metropolitan contemporaries. The habit of ordering about non-resisting servants has given them too much the tone of command. It seems very easy for the white race to acquire the Oriental viewpoint about manual labour's demeaning qualities. Habits of helplessness, essentially based on the fear of losing prestige, fasten upon the colonial girl, who must call in a servant even to pick up something she has dropped on the floor. But the colony also makes them surer of themselves than the convent-trained Parisiennes. They learn early to mix with different kinds of people in a less strictly class-bound society. The transient population necessitates an interminable round of visits, but it is impossible to form permanent friendships. Girls must make an advantageous rapid-fire marriage among the floating population which places a premium on a good first impression. Habits of false luxury, superficial accomplishments, and the demoralizing custom of being waited upon—all make for a lack of perseverance, a rootlessness, and a restlessness from which many French women extract their daughters by sending them back to school in France. It is fundamentally the problem of too much leisure with no corresponding idea of utilizing it profitably. If the expatriated Frenchwoman has shown herself singularly unadaptable to colonial life, the French girl brought up in Indo-China, on the other hand, has been too prone to reflect its most glaring faults. The distaff side of the colonial partnership has shown a marked tendency to extremes and to exaggeration.

Colonials and the Administration

The establishment of the civil government destroyed the harmonious relations among the French in the colony. It introduced the civil-military struggle and the anti-clerical movement against the Mission. Though the latter has been almost completely conjured, the former still exists in an attenuated form. The civil element still suspects the military of wanting a dictatorship, and the military still believes that the civil are plotting to get back control of the frontier military zones. In the early days there were only a few colonists, and they badly needed state protection. With the pacification of the country they became more numerous and less dependent upon the government, and hence more critical of the state's sins of omission and commission.

The state's sins of commission can be summed up in the regular complaints of arbitrary action by high officials. Strong men like De Lanessan and Doumer aroused the hostility of colonials by their high-handed methods. Favouritism flourished; nothing could be obtained without servile flattery of those in power. Just because Cochin-China dissented from Doumer's federal policy, he indulged his rancour in disciplinary measures which aroused a strong regional feeling that has not yet wholly abated. This resentment on the part of Cochin-Chinese colonials has shown itself many times. In 1928 its Colonial Council twice refused to vote the budget, and they had previously done so in 1926. Cochin-China staged tumultuous manifestations during the depression to obtain a moratorium for planters' debts, to devaluate the piastre, and they even boycotted the state reception for Raynaud as a protest against the cut ordered in salaries. For years the colonials demanded some sort of representative body. The press and Chambers of Commerce and Agriculture were their only means of self-expression, and they were handicapped by inadequate funds and powers. Just because they could not muster an important lobby in Paris was no reason why the government should ignore their legitimate desires. Had not the state repeatedly asked for colonists to develop Indo-China? Yet when they patriotically responded to the appeal, nothing was done to aid them or even to take cognizance of their needs. It was a flagrant abuse of confidence. Not until 1928, when Pasquier created the *Grand Conseil*, did the colonists obtain satisfaction, and this was many years after representative institutions had been given to the native peoples.

In addition to the colonists' complaints about the lack of guarantee for their land concessions, and inadequate protection in their labour difficulties, they resented the state's irritating interference in non-essentials as much as they did its negligence. Moreover, taxes were arbitrarily increased and they varied so frequently that a colonist could never accurately budget his expenses from one year to another. When they complained to the administration they were either ignored or insulted. Functionaries formed the dominant element of the French population, and they controlled the few representative assemblies. In the colonists' eyes they represent the octopus-like administration, jealously trying to throttle any initiative other than its own. A local administrator can make the colonists' life miserable if he is so inclined. He has no interest in pleasing the colonist, only his superiors upon whom his promotion depends. When the colonist has the good fortune to find a congenial functionary he can be assured that the latter will not long remain in that particular office. Officials were shunted from one position to another just at a time when they were beginning to understand their district's particular problems. A functionary who had been specialized in Annamite countries might find himself suddenly transferred to Laos, either as a disciplinary measure or through sheer carelessness on the part of his superiors. The colonists sometimes organized themselves into groups, like the League of Cochin-Chinese Rice-growers, yet through internal dissension and impotence in the face of the all-powerful administration these attempts did not succeed in throwing off its paralysing grip.

Other methods have proved more effective in exercising pressure on the government—the local and Parisian press, crowd demonstrations, and Freemasonry. Many colonists have bought newspapers just to blackmail the administration. They feel that such an extraordinary weapon is justified since they have no other legal means for self-expression. Its power may be judged by the way in which the press disposed of MM. Merlin and Varenne. The prosperity of the 1920's created an extraordinary state of mind, especially in Saigon, which became a spoiled and pettish centre, and where any interference on the part of the state was sacrilege. If the colony had become wealthy overnight, it was due exclusively to the colonists' enterprise in spite of the handicap of *étatisme*.

Public opinion in Indo-China is still in an amorphous state. It slumbers for long periods, and shows at times a certain restlessness, but is rarely completely aroused. After the native uprisings in 1908 and 1913, and when the Détham roamed at large near Hanoi, the colonials made themselves ridiculous by pleading that the ladies of the town were not sufficiently protected. At different times it was said that General Pennequin, or Sarraut, Sabatier, Varenne, and Pasquier, had delivered the colony over to the current enemy—bandits or Bolshevists. After Yenbay, public hysteria demanded barbaric punishment of the rebels, and even of passive manifestants. When public opinion is aroused from its slumbers it is usually at the wrong time, when measures of public utility are being enacted. Saigon rioted when the budget forced salary cuts, or when the Bank of Indo-China refused to grant exceptional clemency in individual cases. Undisciplined and selfish, colonials who have participated in the colony's prosperity refuse to share its adversity. Gossip is ever rife; calumny has been given the status of an institution. Personal interests triumph over a sense of social welfare. In short, public opinion in Indo-China, as yet, is capricious, egoistic, and destructively immature.

Freemasonry

Freemasonry has never attained the heights of influence in Indo-China that it enjoyed in France. In 1886, after Bert's death, the Masonic League of Hanoi was founded. By 1905 the Masons had flourished sufficiently to build a new temple upon land given them by their brother, Governor Beau. For many years the importance of the Masons ebbed and flowed according to the favours granted them by the upper administration. While it was true that many granted were Masons, most of them, like Doumer, Klobukowsky, and Merlin, were influenced by other considerations to such an extent that they were considered backsliders by their more ardent colleagues. Lodges exist in all the chief cities of the colony, but the Tonkinese Fraternity has from the outset been the most important. At Hanoi they have founded a library and a recreation hall for natives, where courses in French are given. In 1901 they printed a Masonic newspaper, *l'Indochine Républicaine.*

In estimating Freemasonry's influence on official policy in Indo-China, one is faced with serious gaps in documentation. Moreover, the subject is so fraught with feeling and reticences that the historian is reduced to accepting either its evaluation by the Masons themselves or the appraisal of their enemies. Aside from mutual aid, the Masonic work in the colony has been directed to undermining the Mission's influence, and to formulating a native policy which would reconcile the principles of Masonry with the exigencies of France's position as the colonizing power. After Yenbay the Tonkinese Masons were prompted to a searching of conscience and a stock-taking of their activities and responsibilities in regard to natives. They embodied the result of their reflections in a pamphlet sent to their brothers in Paris which might

perhaps aid in absolving the Tonkinese Lodge and the Indo-Chinese Lodges, in general, from the unjust discredit which for some time has fallen upon them.[1]

The expression of this hope reveals their awareness of Metropolitan criticism that colonial Masonry had allowed colonial psychology to dominate the traditional Masonic sentiments towards their brothers, the Annamites. Many critics had pointed out the curious fact that

[1] Fraternité Tonkinoise, La, *Du Rôle des Missions Catholiques en Indochine* (Hanoi, 1900).

radical organizations, like the Masonic Leagues and the *Ligue des Droits de l'Homme*, had in Indo-China taken on an unmistakably conservative cast.

Before the War the Masons had largely confined their activities to getting solidly established in the colony, and to the distribution of tracts and copies of the *Rights of Man* to the native peoples. In 1923 an inquiry into the Mission's activities was made. The following year a report was written on the subject of education in the colony, and a lecture given to show the superiority of lay over religious instruction. In 1924 the principle of admitting natives into Lodges was formulated, and the Masons later rallied to Brother Varenne's project to admit Annamites to government office. Among their social and economic studies the Masons reported to the government on agricultural credit, the Eurasian problem, labour legislation, secret societies, Buddhism, and Franco-Annamite relations.

The tone of these reports is distinctly more liberal than the average colonial opinion, but far more conservative than its Metropolitan equivalent: the framework of French sovereignty in the colony must be maintained even at the cost of republican principles. The Masons claim to have always preferred association to assimilation as administrative policy. Annamites were to be educated to fill an increasingly important role in their country's government, but the proportion and tempo of this participation was to be decided by the sovereign power.

Violent seizure of power was decried: all must be in accord with the Protectorate principle. Too Western an education, too much naturalization and freedom of the press are dangerous weapons. Sedition must be severely punished, for the Annamites are born plotters. The representation of Indo-China in Parliament is undesirable, but eventually a bi-cameral representative government would be viewed favourably for the colony. The lack of professional conscience, however, an inclination to violence and arrogance, a preference for theoretical as against utilitarian education—all make the Annamite intelligentsia dangerous. The illiterate masses are even less prepared for universal suffrage. The electorate should be based on ability and not on money or position: with the Annamite's evolution it will be progressively enlarged.

There is no need to pursue further this reluctant liberalism. Like the Protectorate ideal, after which it was fashioned, it is inherently contradictory. What is admitted in principle is denied by practice. The fact that Masonic policy accords so exactly with the recent government action suggests either a direct influence or a natural harmony of ideals. The latter explanation seems to correspond better to the inconspicuous position of Masonry in the colony. Conditions in Indo-China, unlike those of France, have never been propitious for its development.

Colonials' criticism of the government is so often petulant and destructive that it is hard to ascertain their positive desiderata. Protection—that blanket term—is one of their strongest claims. This means increased protection against physical insecurity, ranging from pests and inundations to a more general police protection of colonials' lives and property. They also want more legal guarantees. The French code has not replaced Annamite legislation in the sense of giving the same protection to those in power, and this is as true of Chinese bankrupts as it is of runaway coolies.

What the colonials really want is aid without interference. They would like the state to supply them with regular, cheap labour and not inquire into their disposal of it. They would also like tariff protection for colonial products, and direct aid to planters in trouble. They want a reduction of the tax burden, more long-term agricultural credit facilities, and an economical administration that would devote itself to a public works programme and to carrying out a *stable* policy on which planters could count.

Most of the old Tonkinese colonials are disappearing, either worn out by their labours or forced by discouragement to return to France. Life has been so difficult that few young men are coming forward to replace them. This decline in colonists preceded the depression, and can be traced to deep-rooted causes. Failures might in many cases have been avoided by agricultural experimental stations conducted with perseverance according to a systematic plan. Instead of this one official would try an experiment in coffee growing and then neglect it for another scheme, such as planting cotton in arid land. Funds were lacking just at a time when an experiment was beginning to have value. The men in charge changed as often as the ideas, and the budget outdid them both in mutations. Private enterprises have had to experiment at their own expense, since the official work was never consistently enough carried out to be serviceable. Colonists have had to learn for themselves, and often at disastrous cost, what would profitably be grown in certain regions. The government's role, according to the colonists, should be that of a passive policeman, the disinterested experimental scientist, the altruistic and understanding banker, the financier of public works, the contact mechanism for supplying labour.

The Métropole and the Colonials

From 1886 to 1926, a period of forty years, there have been fifty-two transmissions of power in Indo-China. No commercial house, let alone a colony, could stand so many successive upheavals. They are the more serious since there has never been applied to the colony any consistent policy—each new Governor has brought his own. Moreover, the choice of Governor-General has been dictated by political exigencies and not suitability to the colony. Cochin-China has been equally unstable: there have been 38 changes in forty years, with interim Governors lasting longer than the titular incumbents. Tonkin has had 31 Residents Superior in the same period; Annam 32; Cambodia 22; and Laos 17 in thirty years. It is hard to find an adequate reason for the long delays in appointing Governors and the short terms they are allowed to fill. The colony has reproached the Métropole often for this negligence, which paralyses needlessly its development. There was only recently a long delay of eight months in naming Varenne's successor. The five-year interval taken by the Métropole for the ratification of the 1930 treaty with China is cited as another example of Paris's criminal neglect. When the Franco-Siamese treaty was signed in 1893, many colonials felt that France had failed them in refusing to assume the hegemony of the Indo-Chinese peninsula.

The War brought this whole problem to the fore. Irritation at the selfishness of French tariff ties, at the wanton disregard of the colony's welfare in treaty-making and selection of Governors, was augmented by remembrance of the help the colony had given to the mother country in time of stress. Indo-China's contribution to France's military budget—amounting to 150,000,000 francs in 1929—was rewarded by a threat to sacrifice Indo-China in the post-War bargaining on the altar of international debts. The colony's prosperity during the War, by contrast with France, and her post-War isolation, reinforced the colony's self-sufficiency. By the complete or partial cutting off of cable communication with France, and also of the Trans-Siberian Railway and steamship services, the independentist movement grew among the French of the colony. Since Indo-China made no financial demands on France, Paris should have no directing hand in the colony's policies. The home government knew nothing about Indo-China—and even less the French public—where ignorant interference had invariably proved harmful. The simultaneous growth of Indo-China's diplomatic personality in the Far East made her feel a part of the Pacific community to which she was already united by natural economy. The rise in the piastre and the success of Long's local loan ushered in a decade of unparalleled prosperity which did not a little to increase the colony's separatist desires. Colonials resented hotly the appearance of Parisian journalists, who returned their hospitality by describing them as unnatural brutes or as caricatures of Europeans. Writers spent a few weeks in the country and the inevitable book appeared in due course, whose sales were apportioned to the colonial scandals it revealed. Undoubtedly there were many inaccurate and foolish statements therein, but colonials refused to admit any of the unpleasant truths that were proclaimed. Resentment was at white heat over Dorgelès' comments on the Hongay coal mines and at Madame Viollis' revelations of prison conditions. Colonials might be at each others' throats, but they naturally resented being criticized and judged by transient reporters. It was but another form of the mother country's nagging interference.

Two factors evident in the later 1920's counteracted this independentist movement. Aggrieved colonials and natives alike found it convenient and effective to appeal to Metropolitan opinion. When the Socialist deputy Varenne stirred up the colonial hornets' nest, the President of the Saigon Chamber of Commerce departed post-haste for France to obtain his recall. Simultaneously two Annamite nationalists toured France on behalf of their oppressed compatriots. And curiously enough both factions found partial satisfaction. A glimmering of common sense revealed to all but fanatics that there were too many elements of strife within the colony to be safely freed from France's control.

The depression was, however, the decisive factor in reuniting France to her wayward colony. The government might nail Indo-China's piastre to the gold franc, and tariff assimilation might still be voted by the deputies, but it took the hard realities of a declining world market to drive home to colonials the value of the mother country. When Far Eastern tariff walls closed down on Indo-China, the colony could still sell her rice, corn, and rubber to France. The Métropole could and did guarantee a loan that permitted the continuation of the public works and consequently the colony's development. Arrogant and spendthrift in the days of her prosperity, the prodigal colony has returned to the parental fold in adversity. While the Métropole's welcome has not included any killing of the fatted calf, for the French wheat growers are openly hostile, yet France has stood by her colony in the hour of need. It is possible, however, that the new orientation towards the Far East given by Robin may have come just in time.

426

Reaction of Colonials to the Country

Nostalgia is, in one way or another, symptomatic of the beginning and end of colonial life. The homesickness for France felt by the newly disembarked is later almost always experienced by the old colonial on leaving the colony which has become his home. There are many functionaries, notably in Cambodia and Laos, who have let years slip by without taking their furloughs. Wherever he is, the colonial will regret the country he has left, for him the reality has never the same charms as his imagination. He is morally and physically uprooted; he belongs neither to the Western nor Eastern world. The first leave is spent with pleasure in France, but the satisfaction of returning to the colony is almost equal. On his second absence he is astounded to find France drab and its people colourless: he dreams of rice-fields and tropical forests while walking the boulevards of Paris. The third leave is voluntarily shortened, and the next time he decides never again to leave the colony which has taken full possession of his soul and body. This transformation does not come swiftly nor inevitably, but there is no Frenchman who has lived long in Indo-China who does not bear to some degree its physical or spiritual imprint.

Adaptation to colonial life may be almost wholly destructive, both to physical and mental health. For many years Indo-China was but a vast cemetery for the French, and this haunting fear of death has long underlain colonial thought. The slightest imprudence in the way of living undermines the body and the viewpoint. This is partly due to the numerous readjustments required by biennial repatriations. The colony's climate is peculiarly fever-productive. Martyrs to malaria look as if they were suffering the eternal flames—the effect on the spectator is perhaps more depressing than on the victim himself.

Originally part of the prevalent ill-health was due to defective living conditions. This was notably true of the army, which was not prepared for the campaign. The survivors were prematurely aged, and not only was their health destroyed but confidence in their work and in the future of the country. Many of the officers who participated in the conquest have left accounts of their sufferings. The military strategy they retail is too involved and too technical to follow easily, but the narrative of their hardships is moving and heroic. The exhausting climate, fatigue, and privations are the *leitmotif*. Descriptions of soldiers covered with mud trying to drag heavy artillery over slippery dykes recur constantly. The unpopularity of Tonkin in France was only augmented by such recitals: Indo-China became in the popular imagination a murderous country which killed its white victims by fever or boredom.

Eventually it was realized that an Occidental could adapt himself physically to the colony by a new way of living. This was a very hard lesson for Frenchmen to learn, for they regard their way of living as the universal model. But Indo-China has forced on them a new routine. In food, for instance, the staple of a French meal is bread and meat. Wheat must be imported in tins from France or Australia, which makes it invariably expensive and variably digestible. Beef is available locally and of good quality; veal and mutton, however, are very mediocre. The country offers better chicken, pork, eggs, vegetables, and fruit. One of the hardest lessons has been the emphasis on adaptability and simplicity. Yielding to the temptation of serving a variety of courses, as in France, has had disastrous results. Pure water is greatly appreciated in the colony. Moderation in eating and drinking and a stricter adherence to the native diet is forced on the Occidental. The climate makes for long siestas and inactivity; though in recent years there has been a healthful emphasis on sport, the arrival of the motor-car has almost offset its good effects.

In addition to the work of the Sanitation Service, the Pasteur Institute's fight against malaria, the creation of mountain health stations, mark the most important strides in preventive measures. It is a convenience for the colonials and a saving for the government to be spared frequent repatriations. It permits keeping families together, and this obviates some of the resulting social complications. Unfortunately, this fundamentally sound idea was not intelligently pursued.

In 1897 Dr. Yersin cited the existence of the plateau of Lang Bieng and his suggestion was favourably seconded by the Europeans who had gone there. Doumer, acting on the report that its climate was like Nice, decided without further ado or research to build a sanatorium and railroad there. Nothing was really known about it. A luxury hotel was constructed, only to be abandoned during the War. A similar mistake was made with Baria in Cochin-China. Cap Saint Jacques was long used for fever patients until it was proved to be one of the most malaria-ridden regions. Far better was Tam Dao in Tonkin, within easy reach of Hanoi, and it has been positively remunerative to the Protectorate that built it. Dalat's future is still uncertain. Originally roads were traced, and a monumental hotel begun there: villas were started and then abandoned. A school, a garrison, and a railroad were envisaged, so as to make Dalat a summer capital like Simla. Recently the idea has been resumed but not definitively, but the completion of the Trans-indochinois railroad has revived interest in it as a federal capital. Cambodia's Popokvil has suffered from a similar caprice. The idea of using it as a health station was first proposed in 1911, but it took ten years of official reports and pushing to get action on it. Suddenly, in 1917, the reputation of Popokvil spread miraculously and everyone wanted to see it. As if spurred by remorse the government wasted innumerable piastres and human lives in a frenzy to rush through a route there. Prisons were emptied to supply the needed labour. In two years a road, 30 kilometres long, rising through forested mountains to an altitude of 1,050 metres, was finished.

Indo-China is a drainer of energies. If for a short time it stimulates unduly, it is the forced growth characteristic of the tropics. The reaction is all the swifter, for in the long run the colony is inhospitable to Europeans. They must return periodically to France for new blood and new strength—yet these reiterated re-adaptations constitute a drain in themselves.

The moral isolation experienced by the colonial is more destructive than the physical depletion, yet partially its consequence. The form that it takes depends on the mental baggage brought along by the young colonial. If his love of the exotic has a romantic flavour, his disillusionment may be brusque and severe. The ardour of the first-comers to Tonkin was dampened by the sadness of the country. At first the climate and the people were definitely repellent. A reddish ochre coloured everything with the discouraging possessiveness of all dull things, unconscious of their ugliness. Its immensity was without grandeur, the eternal rice-fields and endless dykes were exasperatingly monotonous. Hundreds and hundreds of dirty ragged coolies, more beasts than men, accompanied the army. Their pillaging of the towns and villages was a nightmare. When they were punished they deserted and were replaced by swarms of lamentably identical coolies, guilty of the same horrors. Where were the fruits and flowers of that land of golden sunshine which they had fondly pictured as Tonkin?

The same sense of isolation and despair was felt perhaps more keenly by the pioneer colonists who went along into the *brousse*. The tropical forest has an uncanny effect upon the Occidental. Many have testified to the demoralizing and terror-inspiring solitude of a night in the *brousse*. Everything is so alive, nothing rests, and one can even hear the grass growing. The homesickness this land inspired was the more cruel since parts of the country were reminiscent of France.

Alfred Droin, the poet, compared the Red River plain to the *landes* of Brittany. Newcomers, especially in the early days, were very susceptible: in 1881 there was a veritable epidemic of suicides. Insanity is notably more frequent among Europeans than among Asiatics, and in Asia more than in their native lands. The easy morality of the colony is partly responsible, yet what drives many a colonial to *congaies*, gaming, or opium, is fundamentally nostalgia.

Indo-China has been a great destroyer of homes. In the early days there were long separations. The native women who were willing to become the *congaies* of Europeans were not representative of the best of their country. In rare cases the mutual repugnance remained overwhelmingly strong, but usually physical need and the ensuing bondage of affection completed the European's downfall. When Frenchwomen began coming to the colony, the dangers were increased rather than diminished because of their singular inadaptability. *Celles qui s'ennuyaient avec application* could imagine no existence away from France without languishing. Servants were nagged into leaving, for most Frenchwomen were possessed by the idea that all natives were thieves. Fearful of fever, they had an equal horror of sunshine, and would go out swathed in veils or with the curtains of the cars perpetually drawn. They were defeated by the colony's strangeness and discomforts. Undermined by self-pity they exasperated their friends and husbands with the recital of their woes. Another type of dislocated *foyer* was caused by the taste for luxury which colonial life stimulated. The lack of real occupation and the intense rivalry in display led many women to take rich lovers. Other homes were broken up involuntarily by ill health which compelled the wife and children to return to France. The exceptional Frenchwoman was able to adapt herself to the colony and to enjoy it, but in most cases Indo-China has proven a solvent of French family life.

Opium and alcohol, according to temperament, were the principal creators of oblivion for the disillusioned colonial. The more sensitive took to opium and the pleasures of the imagination, whereas the more social-minded and those of coarser fibre preferred the more active lethe of alcohol. The effect on European and Oriental was quite contrary: natives are used to opium in small quantities,[1] whereas alcohol for them is dangerous in proportion as the consumer is primitive. For the European the reverse is true, yet this "terrible poison" of opium

---

[1] 70 per cent of the Chinese; 30 per cent of the mountain tribes; 1 to 2 per cent of the Annamites.

has been subjected to literary as well as actual abuse. Opium can be an agreeable stimulant, helpful to the health if moderately used. But such moderation requires great force of character, particularly difficult for a solitary man in the *brousse*. Moreover, opium is an individual and refined vice, unlike alcohol, which brutalizes not only the drinker but makes him a social menace and the transmitter of a weakened physique to his children.

Opium has created a vast literature of which the best exponent in Indo-China was the incomparable Jules Boissière. Europeans are fascinated by the analysis of their reactions under the drug. Opium's stimulation is highly gratifying:

I hear breathing beings whom I cannot see. I see insects on rafters far away from me. I remember events which happened to me long ago, and which I have never since recalled—all this comes over me ardent and overwhelming.[1]

Contrary to the renunciation of self advocated by Buddhism, opium creates a dream world patterned after one's inmost desires. The European addict usually begins it harmlessly enough, as a cure for ill health, nostalgia, or boredom. Almost imperceptibly the dose is doubled. Opium was a form of nineteenth-century literary snobbery that attracted emulation by the curious. Its appeal was universal: the aesthete had his ivory and jade pipe, and the coolie found forgetfulness in a sordid den. For many years it was supposed that opium held all colonials in its noxious enchantment. Nowadays the tendency is to ridicule the reputation it has acquired. It is undeniable that love of exotic drama has led to absurd exaggeration of its evils, yet opium may have two destructive effects: it can undermine the health, and its over-use creates an artificial paradise which forms too painful a contrast with prosaic daily living. This may mean the tyranny of habit, the renunciation of responsibility, the paralysis of the will and desire for action. Yet careful usage that does not form a habit may be beneficial nervously and physically.

By way of contrast with these destructive and negative forms of escape from the colony a vigorous life of action is a far more creative form of reaction. For all its brutality and sordid deception, the first Europeans felt a certain exaltation. War seemed pardonable for the grandeur of the instincts it awakened; it aroused the brute in man, it

[1] Bonnetain, Paul, *L'Opium* (Paris, 1909), p. 139.

might be the formidable revenge of the animal on the spirit, but for a moment at least it made the conqueror into a superman.

To those less brutally introduced into the colony, there came after the first shock, a physical flowering and awakening. It was a slow process. Indo-China had neither the stunning beauty of the Alps nor the obvious loveliness of the Midi, yet its enchantment worked obscurely in the blood, like the slow but fatal intoxication of opium. The senses of white men were overwhelmed by the great heat, but they still responded to the imperious vitality in everything about them. The tropical fires consumed the weak fibre of Occidentals, yet irresistibly attracted them by its barbaric pushing force. This awakening of the senses increased the love of living and also the fear of death. New feelings, unsuspected resources were discovered and brought to life by contact with this overwhelming nature and by these strangely different Orientals. Emotions became more intense—the good as well as the bad. The colony was for some men, exasperated by the routine of bourgeois existence, a stimulating escape. It meant the return to a more real set of values and away from the artificiality of social conventions and the machine age.

In Cambodia and Laos the transition was particularly easy to a simple life amid peoples whose Rousseau-like virtues harmonized with eighteenth-century traditions. There was a repose in the force and majesty of nature: the timelessness of this contemplative life was uninterrupted save for monthly letters from France. The sense of profound peace, the comforting happiness that comes from the absence of violent emotions, the relaxing conviction that nothing exists beyond the eye's horizon—all have made a particular appeal to world-weary Europeans. Yet those who have responded most completely to this siren appeal have found it fraught with danger. The European surrenders his action-loving soul to Oriental contemplation at the cost of his will. He cannot renounce his European heritage without a despairing sense of atrophy. Like other growths forced by the tropics, the premature awakening of the senses, or the spell cast by its charm, is broken by a swift inner collapse. Destruction follows expansion; in the end the Occidental fibre deteriorates and the spirit crumbles away just as certain textiles are rotted in the tropical climate. Too great love of the exotic victimizes the Westerner, like the slavish love of perverse things. Even if he escapes, the European has been fundamentally transformed. He is doomed to everlasting discontent; the West seems to him pallid and he is irresistibly drawn back to what has destroyed him.

Those who do not surrender to the passive charm of the East may find there expression of their new love of living in the conquest of the country and its people. This may take the unpleasant form of a thirst for gold and the pursuit of intensely material forms of satisfaction. Luxury must be maintained at any cost and rivals beaten down by dishonest methods. Only old age, which comes prematurely in the tropics, and the fear of death cannot be conjured. Elsewhere the defeat which the Occidental has inflicted on nature is so complete that his arrogance knows no bounds. He is at pains to annihilate even the vestiges of his erstwhile enemy—the forest and wild animals—in an orgy of destruction which is ultimately his undoing. The inevitable pride of the white man in the Orient is swollen by his sense of achievement under terrible handicaps. In its best form the Occidental may become absorbed in his world: he wants to build bridges, roads, and cities. His is the satisfaction of tangible results; the material conquest of the country becomes his goal and ideal. Yet he can never rest, for an abandoned road or village within a few years is so overgrown by the virgin forest that it is almost unrecognizable. There can be no material immortality, no permanent physical accomplishment in the tropics, without a perpetual struggle which ultimately wears out the individual. As elsewhere in the Orient the early intense satisfaction in achievement is doomed to ultimate defeat.

The moral conquest of the natives is the ambition of another type of colonial—the missionary, doctor, teacher, and magistrate—who more subtly affirm the omnipotence of Western reason and individualism. This assumption of superiority is the more galling since it underlies and permeates, perhaps unconsciously, even their most altruistic actions. The satisfactions of these workers may be less immediate and less intense than those of the men of action, yet they are more profound and enduring wherever they have succeeded in imposing their sense of moral order. The victory is harder won. The whole technique of approach to a people of so different a culture and psychology must be built up from the very foundations. The path to understanding is full of material and psychological obstacles. The young missionary sent into the *brousse*, who must fight the sense of moral isolation and accept physical adjustments, who must learn the language and customs of a people whom he must first teach to have confidence in him and then to believe in his mission—his life is symbolic of the profundity of a faith which combats such hardships, and of the undramatic quality of his heroism.

FRENCH INDO-CHINA

Reaction of Colonials to the Natives

Discouragement with the country and disillusionment in the exotic charms of its people characterized almost without exception the reaction of the first French in Indo-China. Men of such varied temperaments as Bourde, Bonnetain, Dutreuil, and Lyautey found the Annamites, from top to bottom of the social scale, totally unheroic, lacking in virility, essentially servile, incapable of spiritual growth. The case was hopeless: the modern Annamite was only the degenerate débris of a race formerly great but now foundering beyond redemption. Physically he was repellent, his face bestial, hideous, and petrified with idiocy.[1] The aristocratic Louis de Carné felt an unconquerable repugnance for his Khmer companions though they were all of royal blood.[2] None of the Indo-Chinese could compare with the colourful and artistic Hindus, or had the dramatic beauty of the Arabs.[3]

Later, when the French had recovered from their initial disappointment and found an aristocratic elegance in these people, even their most ardent admirers could not help reflecting upon the extraordinary combination of refinement and dirt. They were like carved ivory buried in grime. They might wash frequently, but in muddy water; they burned incense at the ancestral altar yet reeked of decayed fish; the children were covered with sores, yet even the poorest of them wore silver necklaces; they put on exquisitely embroidered tunics, yet at even the greatest ceremonials gave unmistakable evidence of being vermin-ridden.

Unfortunately, the first unfavourable impressions were only strengthened by association with the interpreter-servant class of Annamites, and to this day for the majority of colonials they constitute their sole contact with that people. They are either unaware or forget that such Annamites are the dregs of native society, isolated from the restraining discipline of communal and family life, and so they are peculiarly subject to the disintegrating effects of European contact. The conversation of Frenchwomen in Indo-China is largely devoted to the misdeameanours of their servants—chiefly their thefts and lightning-like escapes. The shocks given to European households by their servants have often been narrated, but nowhere more amusingly than by Madame Vassal.[4] At the end of her first month's residence all her linen had disap-

[1] Lefebre, Paul, *Faces Jaunes* (Paris, 1886), p. 54.
[2] De Carné, Louis, *Voyage en Indochine* (Paris, 1872), pp. 5–6.
[3] Lyautey, H., *Lettres du Tonkin et de Madagascar* (Paris, 1921), p. 81.
[4] Vassal, G. M., *Mes Trois Ans D'Annam* (Paris, 1911), p. 36.

peared or was in rags. She found that the special cloths designed for glassware had been devoted to cleaning shoes or serving as turbans. The rest had been sold or mislaid. All the food provisions disappeared with the same haste as the linen. Meals were very expensive, despite the cheapness of food in the market. Eventually Madame Vassal discovered the co-operative system between her cook and that of a neighbour: each cooked meals for both families on alternate days. Dishes were washed cheerfully in the drinking-water well. A table that was ostensibly for dish washing and cleaning silver was used for a couch.

Annamites simplify every operation by using as few utensils as possible. They will not use a corkscrew so long as they have teeth, or a shovel where their fingers could serve. Madame Vassal's cook used his manly chest on which to roll potato croquettes. Servants, like other Orientals who dislike routine work, ask for periodic leaves of absence. They appear in a white turban with the announcement that their mother has died. When the same process is repeated a few weeks later, the uninformed European calls them liars, not realizing that a mother's demise is the Oriental equivalent for the Occidental office-boy's permission to attend his grandmother's funeral. The frequent recurrence of stories of this nature is apt to make one forget that, in general, the Annamites make excellent servants. They are very observing, assimilate rapidly, are clever with their hands, and astonish newcomers by the excellence of the meals and service. But the natural French impatience is augmented by a trying climate and linguistic misunderstandings. The colonials who have a vast retinue leave their servants with more leisure than they are accustomed to, with naturally disastrous results on a none too strong moral fibre. For the servant who steals, there are others who have become so invaluable to their masters that they are taken back to France with them.

The ignorance or indifference of colonials to native culture is largely attributable to laziness. The Annamite language, to be sure, is one of the most difficult extant, and few are willing to make the effort to overcome this first barrier. The majority of civil and military residents have a restricted cultural outlook at best, and for the most part it never occurs to them that the country is anything but a place of exile to be endured just to make a fortune. The first soldiers roamed through the towns looking suspiciously at the native food which they never dreamed of eating. Even the fruit and rice cakes were suspect. Of cautious peasant stock, these men distrusted the Yellow Race on principle and made fun of whatever was different or strange. But was throwing paper in tombs any more absurd than refusing to sit thirteen at table? They were totally unaware of the profound side of native culture. Hué was only a mass of broken-down buildings: its emperor just a backward school-boy. There was a more aggressive turn to this non-appreciation of Annamite civilization. Many of these soldiers earned for themselves the name of colonial apaches by their cruel violence towards native coolies and shopkeepers. Their attacks were not confined to the natives and for a time they practised profitable holdups on Europeans as well.[1]

Frequency of contacts and the will to understand are the indispensable preliminaries to a study of any foreign culture. Most colonials are not brutes or Machiavellian schemers trying systematically to oppress the native population. For them the native problem does not exist, because they think of them only in terms of labour. The most liberal theorists are often the last men willing to expatriate themselves to apply their ideas. This also applies to functionaries who, though they do not accumulate fortunes so rapidly, are nevertheless attracted to the colonies by the larger salaries offered there. The perennial charm which office-holding has for the French is shown by the great number of applicants for even the most humble positions in the colony. The desire for such a form of security has been even more pronounced since the depression. The lower ranks of officialdom are notoriously more hostile to a liberal native policy than the upper—undoubtedly because of their greater fear of native competition. The *bloc* of anti-liberal opinion, made up of the vast majority of functionaries and colonists, is almost impossible to overcome. The majority of the French residents in Indo-China are functionaries—that is, transients in the colony who, having assured positions, naturally favour a policy of domination. They must refuse to see virtues in the Annamite civilization and intelligentsia, as the price of their continued survival in the colony. Their hostile obstinacy is a greater stumbling-block than either indifference or laziness to mutual understanding.

Another group of fear-ridden conservatives are the Frenchwomen who have come to the colony. Often the *congaie*, "the sleeping dictionary," was an excellent medium for learning the native people and their language, and her gradual elimination has been harmful to better inter-racial understanding. The desire felt by Frenchwomen to undermine a rival influence and to find compensation for exile by creating a second France has reduced the contacts between the races. Before they came there was a more primitive social life, and the lack of diversions

---

[1] Ajalbert, J., *Les Destinées de L'Indochine* (Paris, 1909), p. 60.

made the French seek out natives as a way of passing the time. But natives in a salon add nothing to the world of fashion, with their blackened teeth, bare feet, and betel-reddened mouths. Women who are unused to having servants in France abuse their new status by treating all natives as inferiors, ignoring the traditional hierarchy among them. With some notable exceptions Frenchwomen have formed themselves into a wedge between their men and the native population.

The motor-car, impersonal as it is, has become another means of reducing contacts. The administrator who used to take a week to inspect his province on horseback, conversing with the village Notables in the evening hours, was able to learn their grievances in this way and their viewpoint. Now in a car he can cover his territory in a day. And he has no longer time for idle conversation. The increase in bureaucratic red tape has tied him to his desk and away from his people. The motor-car gives him the means of yielding to the rising pressure of office work, and spares him some of the fatigue engendered by an energy-draining climate.

The men who first studied Annamite culture seriously naturally approached the problem from a French viewpoint. Many students found Annamite justice arbitrary, property poorly divided, and above all the sacrifice of the individual to the group revolted their individualistic upbringing. It was no wonder that compatriots of Victor Hugo, who proclaimed that he would not sacrifice a child to save a whole people, believed that the Annamites were subject to an incredibly oppressive régime. The assimilationists, with generous if ignorant idealism, wanted to share with their Oriental brothers French institutions and ideas that would with time eradicate the superficial differences between them, and fashion the Annamite after the French image. Initial misunderstandings were only natural in view of the obstacles in language and different outlooks. And the Annamite intelligentsia were sulking in their tents and not making any effort to enlighten the Western barbarians. Each interpreted everything in the light of his own culture without appreciation of the other viewpoint. The French who distributed copies of the *Rights of Man*, who abolished the *lays* to superiors, who refused with righteous indignation the traditional gifts tendered by their subordinates as attempts to corrupt their republican integrity, were insulting the Annamites or making themselves absurd with the best intentions in the world. It took many years for both sides to appreciate the necessity of ridding themselves of their particular mental set-up before understanding each other.

To the important though negative handicap of infrequent contacts may be added the most ominous of all forms of Oriental-Occidental misunderstanding—the white man's assumption of superiority. Almost inevitably this feeling settles over the Occidental, no matter how liberal his viewpoint may have been in his own country. Idealistic young Frenchmen have come to the colony longing to play Cyrano to the oppressed natives, brutalized by his compatriots. He is often disillusioned upon arrival. Old colonials tell him condescendingly that he will outgrow such notions, or he may have an experience that confirms their worst prophecies. Try as he would, Jules Boissière could find no profoundly learned and disdainful bonze who would instruct in the secrets of the East one benighted Occidental who burned to drink of his wisdom. In addition to the discouragement afforded by a difficult language and a profoundly different culture, it was even more disillusioning not to find a qualified teacher, and to feel that all one had amassed is but arid and banal. If further study proves Annamite civilization rewarding, almost all scholars agree that they are at first disappointed by its dull mediocrity. The totally inaccurate and romanticized cult of exoticism that prevails in France is largely responsible for these early disillusionments. The amount of perseverance and discipline required to master even the technique for understanding the East has given birth to the legend of Asiatic impenetrability. This is the solution encouraged not only by laziness but by the attraction which the very mystery of the East has exercised over the Western mind. Understanding Asia would probably lessen its charm for Europe. The obstacles to penetrating Eastern thought are real enough without deliberately swathing it in thicker veils. The Orient does nothing to further Western understanding, but even opposes it by the force of inertia and ridicule.

For the few who are disappointed, there are the many more who are immediately ripe for that state of mind known as the *esprit colon*. This unhappy attitude is an aggressive composite of smugness, laziness, fear, and racial prejudice. Though colonial society is less class-bound than in France, it is an aristocracy in its relations to the natives, a return to the feudal régime. According to this philosophy the most miserable white man is above the best native. This attitude is further encouraged by the average native acceptance of inferiority. They understand the Europeans' presence in the colony only in terms of the latter's leadership. When the European treats the Annamite as an equal the latter responds by treating the European as an inferior. Under these circumstances, the champion of egalitarian principles feels his ardour dampened. If under the *ancien régime* the good side of feudal morality was reflected in *noblesse oblige*, there is no corresponding benevolence to mitigate colonial arrogance. A human tendency to abuse power is augmented by a difficult climate and by the fact that the aristocracy is a minority fastened by force upon a numerically superior and potentially hostile mass of different nationality. The obscure menace of revolt makes for colonial solidarity. Fear creates injustice in an unequitable leniency towards Europeans and no mercy shown to native delinquents in their conflicts with them. In racial prejudice there is an admixture of physical repugnance on both sides, and the isolation in which it results may be further strengthened by a fear of going native —essentially the instinct of self-preservation. This narrow pride emphasizes those very differences which mark racial groups, and long residence in the colony only accentuates this barrier. If the natives accept, without visible protest, domination on these terms, they are despised, for the weak are necessarily wrong. Their hostility, which the colonial feels, further alienates him. This attitude is more characteristic of the English colonies. British visitors have expressed this viewpoint, and were astonished to see French soldiers commanded by an Annamite officer, and to hear that a touch of colour in a Frenchman is thought to make him the more interesting.

The fundamental reproach made by the conservative colonial is simply that the Oriental is not a European. It is so easy to be swept along by the tide of prejudice, especially when the advantages are all one way. Feeling superior is very comfortable. The evolution of the young colony has been so uncertain and its growth so spasmodic that it is natural that expatriated idealism should be weak and its moral orientation fluctuating and unstable. Power is very heady in a climate like Indo-China's, especially when dealing with a people who have no redress and where there is no counterpoise in public opinion. And the Annamites are the first to give an example of brutality to their compatriots. All this means moral anarchy under an appearance of order. What happens in the colony could never occur among the same people if they were in France. There is certainly a refreshing outlet for one's emotions, and in the colony one can give vent to one's irritation with impunity. Colonials lose the habit of being contradicted; the existence of a conquered people under their orders is a perpetual flattery to their pride. The native intelligentsia is a nightmare to this colonial: he regards every liberal measure as the opening wedge to Communism. Flagrant examples of colonials' brutality go unpunished, or are even rewarded, as was the case with Darles in Tuyen Quang. This, however, is not calculated to soothe the feelings of the native nationalists.

The colony has created a new type of being whom the liberal Frenchman from France refuses to acknowledge as a compatriot. Werth saw even a missionary strike a rickshaw coolie, and a priest oust natives by blows from the places reserved for Europeans in the Hanoi cathedral. To the European who claims to find justification in the Annamite character for the use of brute force as the sole means of insuring comprehension, one may reply that times have changed radically. In 1895, a soldier who killed an Annamite had to pay 50 francs—enough to cover his victim's funeral expenses. Nowadays the military authorities enforce punishment of violence if a complaint is lodged by a native.

This does not ensure equal treatment, but it marks a nearer approximation to it. Those who visited the colony after the War claim to have noticed a marked diminution in brutality. One remembers Sarraut's circular forbidding colonials to strike natives. Though brutality is definitely waning it is a change of heart that the colonial needs. To him the native is a perpetual minor: he fails to notice his evolution or denies it through fear of competition, because he is out of touch with native thought. He is still the conqueror dominating a vanquished people. Unfortunately just at a time when assimilationists were getting discouraged about their liberal theories, and were relapsing into a belief that the two races were too different for effective co-operation, the intelligentsia who had evolved through contact with Western ideas began to resent the use of force and to demand instruction from the West which they had formerly scorned. Each group was being forced by the shock of the first disillusioning contact into the position formerly occupied by the other.

For the many colonials who felt an unquestioning superiority there was a corresponding, though smaller, group who realized that Annamite culture had been mellow at a time when France was still under the Franks. For those who felt drawn to Annamite civilization to the point of adopting native life and thought for their own, nothing in the West could ever again satisfy them. Europeans—especially in the colony—were awkward parvenus, the Annamites the epitome of aristocratic grace and finesse. The life of even the humblest Annamite seemed infinitely artistic. They might appear to be doing nothing but they were not unoccupied. They relished time, pure time, for its own sake, and were distracted by it. A city like Hué, with its River of Perfumes, came to symbolize the fascination exercised over admiring Europeans. By contrast with the outbursts of the red-faced choleric colonial the impassive and fragile Asiatic gave an admirable example of self-control. All his training has gone into this self-discipline. What the Oriental lacks in positive accomplishments in the external world he atones for in passive endurance and mastery of himself. This is partly due to a less highly developed nervous system, and also to his religious belief in the transiency of this life, yet the invariable stoicism with which he endures suffering, and even the imminent prospect of death, never fails to impress the European.

The two most salient characteristics of Annamite culture, in the eyes of its European students, were the group's obliteration of the individual, and the domination of the living by the dead. Impersonality and hierarchy were everywhere supreme; cemented and re-enforced by rites that gave Oriental society a stability and immutability that both attracts and repels the Occidental. If natives are wisely unmoved by the element of fashion in life they are, unfortunately, equally impervious to spiritual adaptation. Under this seemingly solid shield the Oriental is a mass of puzzling contradictions. Centuries of oppression and training have made him both puerile and wise, prudent and naïve, bold and timid, realistic and abstract. He may be amazingly self-controlled in the face of suffering and adversity, but prosperity makes him unsupportably arrogant, without perseverance in the face of unforeseen obstacles. When thrown off the routine to which he has been trained, and away from his accustomed external restraints, the Oriental shows an uncontrolled emotionalism that outdoes the West. Immutability gives the illusion of solid security, but it has taken only a few years of contact with a dynamic social order to slough off what had for centuries seemed to represent the sum total of wisdom, and to reveal underneath a dangerous capacity for hysteria.

At the time when the Annamite intelligentsia were beginning to disinter their heads from the sand, and to view Occidental culture with a wondering and envious eye, the West was experiencing a crisis of self-doubt. Not only in France, where writers and politicians were taking pains to dwell on the failures of French colonization, but in Indo-China individuals began to look with suspicion on the changes being wrought by the machine. Issues which had seemed clear-cut at the outset became hopelessly confused. Were the men they were fighting bandits or patriots? Could Annamite nationalism be an assertion of the sacred principles of '89? Had not France's civilizing mission possibly miscarried, or perhaps the Annamites had been happier under their old régime? Material betterment had given birth to the Annamite bourgeoisie, who were a peculiarly destructive product. The increase in crime and violence, the dissolution of the family and commune, were of ominous significance. Not that anything could be done to prevent this progressive decline, and these idle reflections were a form of "spilt-milk" thinking, but the thoughtful Frenchman could not help questioning the value of what he had offered to replace what he had thoughtlessly destroyed.

It was an undeniably healthy sign provided that it prefaced a re-modelling of colonial psychology, but there was a fatal and simultaneous tendency to brand all effort as futile. Were not the differences between peoples too profound to be bridged, and Occidental philanthropy at best an impertinent blunder? This form of fatalism, so foreign to the West, was but one of the profound effects Oriental thinking was having on the conqueror.

The Effect upon Colonials of Indo-China and its Peoples

Not only does the colony transform Europeans physiologically, but there is a spiritual metamorphosis as well. Orientalists are only a small group consciously studying native culture, whereas the vast majority of colonials are unaware of the effect native life has upon them. But it is none the less real because they deny it or are even unaware of the change it has brought about in themselves.

By contrast with those whose activities are stimulated by colonial life there are some Frenchmen who become impregnated with Eastern philosophy. The Buddhist ideal which eliminates regret and desire, the anonymity of Asiatic life, the belief that the perfect formulae of living have long ago been discovered and comfortably embodied in its static society, are especially attractive to Occidentals whose natural zest for action has been exhausted by a personal cataclysm or the World War. The Oriental absorption in the moment, relegating the past to obli-vion and the future to care for itself, its smiling and graceful resignation to fate, is seductive to Occidentals given to melancholic musing. The Asiatic pitilessness for others is also agreeably contagious. One of the causes for the joyous exaltation felt by a European in the East is that he has been delivered from the burden of compassion. Abstention from sharing the suffering of others accounts for the callousness which charac-terizes many colonials. The atrophy of the will and sensibilities is accompanied by a form of moral anaemia.

The gamut of Occidental emotions is chameleon to its Oriental counterpart, and is often transformed thereby beyond recognition. In a country where all are newcomers without common ties and traditions, competition is more bitter and men less scrupulous. If friendship has degenerated into mutual exploitation, called doing business together, then love is reduced to pleasure and profit. Native women have no souls in the Occidental sense; so long have they been subordinated to the group that they have become type-women without personality of their own. This automatically reduces their lovers to a corresponding male type who have, in taking them, purchased their freedom from love in the Western sense.

The charm of absolute possession is enhanced by an aesthetic appeal. The *congaies'* miniature bodies, their exquisitely modelled hands and feet, have an elegance and grace that is part of the heritage of their civilization. Asiatic beauty resides principally in the carriage and gestures which is antipodal to the Western cult of energy. It makes the European seem clumsy and boorish by comparison. An Occidental may win a *congaie* without effort, beauty, or intelligence. The egoistic man expands complacently. He is perennially charmed by the obedience, discretion, and detailed attention with which he is surrounded by the delightful creature whom he owns.

Habit, however, is apt to prove too strong for him. Eventually he surrounds her with the aura of Western love, and from that day begins to lose his footing. Soon the supple slave becomes the task-mistress. She sees that her lover cannot get along without her. Sulking proves a successful weapon and is effectively repeated. Though the *congaie* may be illiterate her powers of observation are phenomenal. She knows her lover's salary and which are his important papers. She holds the keys to all the doors and orders about the servants. A European lover is humiliating for a native woman and she must take a lover of her own race—usually one of her master's servants—to retain her self-respect. Her family eventually comes to live in the house: confusion, dirt, and noise then reign supreme. The arrival of progeny supplies the finishing touch and the European's servitude is now complete. Soon the *congaie's* charm and grace have been destroyed by that premature ageing characteristic of Eastern women.

The frequency of this procedure has created a new verb in the French language to express the male servitude: *encongayer*. All over Indo-China Frenchmen, inspired by the false sentimentality of Madame Butterfly, transpose Western emotions to an Eastern setting and allow themselves to be ensnared. It is not only dangerous to them as individuals, but for their work. Hierarchy is so powerfully ingrained that a *congaie* automatically takes on the rank of her lover, and if he is influential she may acquire a proportionate hold over those who do business with him, and no one may approach him without appropriate gifts to her. Frenchwomen have been unnecessarily unfair to their Asiatic rivals: it is unjust to judge them apart from their setting. They have no reason to love their European masters who take them and then abandon them. Money is the sum and substance of their attraction, and the European whose vanity leads him to think that his *congaie* is the exception to the rule of infidelity only makes himself ridiculous. The European Don Juan's code of male morality has found its supreme revenge in the Oriental woman.

The *congaie* whose weeping for her dead or departed lover is graded according to the effect it has upon spectators, among whom may be a potential substitute, is far nearer the reality than Loti's Madame Chrysanthème. If one understands the position of women in Annamite society one is no longer shocked by their passivity and limitations. Their perpetual submission to the will of others, their indifference to passion, their importance, based entirely on their son-bearing activities —all have reduced their role to that of dray-horses and mothers, catering to masculine needs. The aristocratic native woman is a recluse whom the European never sees, so generalizing about all Annamite women from his own *congaie* is not only a profound insult to them but a source of grave error. The *congaie* has undeniably good qualities: her business capacities are well above native men's, her passion for gaming at least equal, and her need for ornamentation superior—hence her European lover must see that she does not secretly deplete his exchequer. A *congaie* is an excellent institution if kept in her place. If she has the defects of courtesans the world over, she has exceptional charms. She removes the complications from love, but a false transposition of European idealism transforms her into a nuisance and a danger.

Frenchwomen have not experienced to the same degree an attraction towards Annamite men. The racial charm of native women seems effeminate when seen in their male compatriots: their diminutive physique and long hair do not make for attractive virility. In the colony there is too much racial prejudice, and too few Frenchwomen, numerically, who have a wide choice among their own kind. Yet in France the success of Annamite students with Frenchwomen is notable. The exotic tradition, as well as Oriental courtesy, has made a vast impression on the hurried West. The poorest Annamite can write a poem or present a flower with aristocratic grace. Mixed with other reactions is a certain maternal instinct that wants to atone for the treatment of Annamites as racial inferiors. The vanity that makes the European fatuously proclaim his *congaie* uniquely loyal to him is akin to that of the Frenchwoman who believes her Annamite lover when he tells her that he is a mandarin's son.

Of this type of mixed marriage the couples who remain in France are faced with no exceptional problems: their happiness seems to be sealed according to the husband's capacity for absorption into his wife's milieu. But quite the contrary applies to the Frenchwomen taken back to the colony by their Annamite husbands. During the War a number of such unions were made despite everything the authorities could do to discourage them. Whenever possible photographs were taken of the fiancé's home, swarming with naked children in intimate barnyard surroundings, and sent to the prospective bride. Annamites marry very young, so that a French wife would encounter complications with a predecessor and probable successors, if she had no children. The physical adjustment to a totally different way of living, in addition to the psychological adaptation to an anti-individualistic social unit dominated by ritual, would be enough to shatter a more than ordinarily united couple. The Asiatic husband tends to be increasingly absorbed into his milieu, and his French wife isolated in a strange and often hostile environment, which eventually defeats them both. Fundamentally it is too different a conception of marriage: for the Annamite it is not a union of individuals but the perpetuation of the family and its social traditions.

Eurasians

Immediately after the conquest, upper-class Annamites gave their daughters to the French invaders, under the impression that these unions would be regarded as legitimate marriages. But when they found that these women were abandoned resourceless when their husbands returned to France,they naturally refused to allow any more such unions. In many countries white blood enhances a native's prestige, but the Annamites, with their immense pride of race, are not so obsequious. The régime of the *petite épouse* followed the brusque termination of marriages with good families, and lasted till the coming of Frenchwomen to the colony. In general, repugnance rather than attraction was felt towards these lower-class native women, but this was offset by physical need, the desire for a comfortable home, loneliness and boredom, and the convenience of having an intermediary with the native population. These women cannot be classed as prostitutes, the more able among them have even attained to a definite status and prestige. Occasionally among the French permanently resident in the colony there were legal marriages, but this was not true of functionaries and other transients. Despite affection, the father often does not legitimatize his children. Economic reasons or the desire to marry later in France prevents his taking them back when he goes, so he abandons them to their native mother, leaving with her some money for their support, which usually disappears as soon as he does. This amounts to virtual abandonment—understandable but also blameworthy. It is less hard on the mother, who can usually form another liaison, than on the children who are left without economic or legal support.

Eurasians enjoy the unpleasant reputation among Europeans of having retained only the vices of both races. From the outset they encounter these wounding prejudices. Some families refuse to send their children to schools which receive Eurasians. When admitted they are exposed to insults such as being called *sale métis* by their companions. Much of this hostility can be traced to the Frenchwomen's hatred of their *congaie* rivals. There are, of course, courageous exceptions, but as a rule French society is closed to the half-breed.

The native attitude is quite as hostile as the French. This is partly due to the Eurasian's contempt for his mother's people, which is more bitter than that of the whitest Aryan. They naturally retaliate by mocking him: he is a stranger in his own country. He becomes ashamed even of his mother. The hatred of both peoples is embittering and inspires him to revenge, particularly upon his father's people who refuse him admission as an equal. Knowing the native language and customs he may esily become the leader of a rebellion: he is the source of perpetual social and political *malaise*. If the Eurasian is a woman her lot is easier, for her status may be resolved by a marriage, which absorbs her definitely into one group or the other. More often, however, her career ends in prostitution.

For boys there are few professional openings. For many years the army, excepting the Foreign Legion, was closed to them. If perchance the Eurasian should be financially successful his native family cling to him like leeches and drag him down. If it is hard for him to make headway professionally, it is even harder to create for himself a social milieu. His aspirations and efforts naturally tend towards his acceptance as wholly French, for in this lies every social and professional advantage

Up to 1928 the legislator showed no concern for the status of the Eurasian who was not legitimatized by his father. They were classed as either French subjects or protégés, a status very inferior to that of French citizens—socially, professionally, and financially. Their military service was performed as natives. The first progress was made in 1912, when an Eurasian was authorized to establish his paternity as a preliminary to acquiring French citizenship. Decrees followed facilitating naturalization, but they were insufficient. Impoverished Eurasians were unable to take advantage of the law, which involved a long and costly procedure. In 1926 the Hanoi Court of Appeal took the important step of reversing previous decisions and declaring the Franco-Annamite to be a French citizen. This decree was confirmed two years later, and is of considerable social and economic import. It removes the chief obstacle to the admission of Eurasians to French society, since they may be declared French during their minority. They are admitted to schools and professions on an equal footing. This spares not only untold humiliations, but also extracts the Eurasian from the often harmful influence of his mother and her family. Important as this decree is, it has not wholly solved the Eurasian problem, which is essentially one of an education that will give them a mentality that conforms to their new legal status.

For many years the moral and social aspects of the Eurasian problem were neglected. A scientist, Colonel Bonifacy, was the first to recognize its significance and to conduct, in 1910, an inquiry into the psychology of the Tonkinese Eurasian. Various periodicals, the *Revue Indo-Chinoise* in 1913, and the *Revue du Pacifique* in 1931, have pursued the same line of investigation. The subject has also received a fair amount of literary treatment, for it has obvious emotional value, but most writers feel a definite antipathy in addition to the delicacy and complications offered by the study of half-breeds.

Writers are unanimous in attributing to the Eurasian certain moral defects, notably a pride that degenerates into touchiness or arrogance, a disdain of manual labour that might betray his native origin, and a retention of injuries and humiliations that leads to ultimate revenge. The Eurasian experiences simultaneously a hatred and attraction for things French. Their intellectual level is invariably high, perhaps due to a forced canalizing of their energies into achievements that will vindicate their racial origin. The worst of these defects disappear when

447

the Eurasian is definitely absorbed by one race or the other, so that resolving the problem is more educational and social than eugenic. It is an evasion of the issue to send Eurasians to France, where the prevailing exotic tradition has given Orientals a glamour that insures hospitable reception. But to begin with, this is impossible on a large enough scale to settle the problem, aside from anything else. The place for Eurasians seems definitely to be in the colony provided that they can be formed into a serviceable link between the two people whose blood runs in their veins. They need social roots and emotional stability—such as the Sino-Annamite half-breeds have. Private charity, one of the most commendable of the early Mission enterprises, is excellent so far as it goes, but its alleviation is necessarily temporary, and does not prevent the Eurasians from forming a class apart. The state recently has recognized its responsibility by subsidizing these private institutions, but modifying the legal status of Eurasians has been a far greater contribution.

NATIVE REACTION TO CONTACTS WITH FRENCH COLONIALS

When the Court of Annam sent ambassadors to Paris in 1893 they took with them a letter for the French President, in which the character representing Annam was placed so as to dominate that of France, thus reducing the latter to the position of a vassal state. This insult was characteristically Oriental. The fact that the French failed to grasp its significance did not prevent the Annamites from relishing their insolence. The Annamite language abounds in insults and compliments but it takes an expert to appreciate the shades of irony under the respectful exterior. The Chinese domination of Annam is responsible for this characteristic, which is based on the fear of openly expressing contempt for those who are superiors by force of arms, and disdain for the Western Barbarian as inherently inferior to the Chinese.

It was natural that the Scholar class, impregnated with Chinese culture, should add disdain of the West to their resentment of the French destruction of the mandarinate, of which they were the mainstay. They regarded as traitors any who were willing to co-operate with the conquerors—which made it impossible for the French to find good native officials. This hostility extended to the French language and even to *quoc ngu*. An Annamite mandarin who wanted to learn French dared not do so openly. Ignoring the ignoble present by burying oneself in the past, through study and meditation mixed with opium and tea, harmonized with the cultural ideals of this group. If the lower classes were unable to indulge themselves so agreeably, the harsh necessity for daily toil and daily rites absorbed all their energies and effected an equal insulation. Immersed in the past or absorbed by current material preoccupations, the great majority of Annamites lived for many years without real contact with their conquerors.

The hostility of the intelligentsia was matched by the superstitious fear of the masses. Even obvious differences in external appearance frightened them. The French were not like other men. The stiff way in which the soldiers marched led the *nhaqués* to conclude that they had no knee joints. But the awe they inspired by feats of arms did not convince the natives of their innate superiority. This was illustrated by the speech of a mandarin at the funeral of a French officer:

You are a curious personage. You have curly hair, a nose which stands out˙ You ride horseback, and whistle for your dog to follow you. You place bottles on your table for ornaments, and plant grass in your courtyard. Despite your military talents, you have succeeded in getting yourself killed. How sorry I am for you.[1]

To the majority of Annamites, excepting those in the towns, all Europeans look alike, and their prestige rises and falls collectively. Yet in 1905 a curiously double reaction was produced by the Japanese victory over Russia. Western science took on new lustre because Japan had used Occidental methods, but Europeans themselves inspired less awe, because it was thought that anyone could master their machines and beat them at their own game. The Annamites shared this belief. They stormed the gates of the new Hanoi University with renewed self-confidence, yet simultaneously they resented the presence of the purveyors of these now desirable ideas. Pride of race has from the outset dominated Franco-Annamite relations, but most Westerners forget that the vanity of the Oriental at least equals if not exceeds that of the Occidental.

The Annamites have adapted themselves to Westernisms with astonishing facility. Their powers of assimilation are remarkable. Even detractors of their moral qualities admit that they can be readily trained into making splendid cooks and mechanics. They have adopted Western clothing, though not always in the best taste, and Western sports, though they formerly despised bodily exercise. Many observers claim that this Annamite transformation is purely imitative and superficial.

[1] Pham Quynh. *L'Evolution Intellectuelle et Morale des Annamites* (Paris, 1922), p. 15.

One writer walking through an Annamite cemetery on All Saints' Day questioned a child whom he found there. The astonishing response was made in pidgin French:

Pas l'école aujourd'hui . . . moi même chose français, moi gratter papa.[1]

For those Annamites who adopt bourgeois lives unfalteringly through parvenu snobbery, many more have selected certain French customs, including the language, but modified them almost beyond recognition. The Annamite, with his diverse mental set-up, cannot grasp the ideas behind Western culture, despite assimilationist dreams, and what he takes over purely externally, he necessarily distorts. Many customs are definitely antipathetic or comical to them. The soldiers who used to fondle native babies were not considered genial fellows but ogres who lived on a diet of children. Their feeling for the dead gives the Annamites a profound horror of surgery. Doctors have the greatest difficulty in persuading native women to submit to medical examinations. In general, it may be said that the Annamite has adopted what appealed to his vanity or what did not run counter to his traditions. The Annamites' insistence upon treatment finely graded to his rank and that of his interlocutor has been a great obstacle. If the Frenchman treats him unjustly as an inferior, he is insulted beyond repair; but if the snub is unconscious he disregards the intention and considers it a deliberate injury. The Annamite envoys at Paris noted with incredible minutiae the quantity and quality of deference shown them, yet they could not understand French decorum which imposed silence as a mark of respect upon the funeral procession of Thanh Thai's mother. The obvious sterility of this preoccupation with hierarchic observance does not prevent its playing an important role in Franco-Annamite relations.

So striking are the temperamental resemblances, that one English traveller in Indo-China called the Annamites the French of the Far East. Le Myre de Vilers also pointed out this similarity. Both are, as a people, brave, industrious, intelligent, gay, ironic, *frondeur*, desirous to be educated and to be functionaries.[2] Unfortunately the resemblance is more striking as regards defects. The peasants, in particular, are alike in addiction to craft and avarice, and feel the same need for living in dirt and discomfort. Perhaps their very similarity makes for friction, but more likely it is a different evaluation of their mutual qualities. To the Annamite, European virtues are tenacity, initiative, *sangfroid*,

[1] Ajalbert, J., *Les Destinées de L'Indochine* (Paris, 1909), p. 26.
[2] Le Myre de Vilers, *Les Institutions Civiles de la Cochinchine* (Paris, 1908), p. 36.

and the ability to discern truth in a mass of lies, not humanitarianism or integrity. Timidity, *naïveté*, and humility are the supreme Western vices. They despise one who gives an order as if he were asking a service, or the man who does a task which he might get someone else to do for him. A scandal was created in the early days by French soldiers who were seen washing their own clothes. An Annamite prisoner, if he can, will hire a coolie to carry his bundles for him. The humanitarian gesture of dispensing the natives with corporal punishments and *lays* costs the French enormous prestige. So does the display of anger and impatience, dear to the French heart, for it runs counter to the Chinese element of self-control. A man is important in proportion to the display he makes, regardless of the qualities of his soul. When an Annamite ceases to admit outwardly his inferiority, he no longer feels respect; he has no experience in expressing spontaneous emotion. The criticisms which the French lavish upon each other and their institutions not only sharpen the Annamites' capacity for irony but undermine his respect for what can be criticized with impunity. Success is the supreme touchstone: it is the symbol of celestial approval; it is idealized at the cost of every other standard. Fundamentally it is the cause of Oriental acceptance of Occidental supremacy. If France had not been victorious in the World War it is no exaggeration to say that she would never have been able to keep Indo-China.

Oriental pride is the great uneasy factor in any acceptance of Western supremacy, and it is felt most keenly by the upper classes, who are weighed down by the knowledge that they are the heirs of a great civilization. Being so sensitive to the marks of respect, they are constantly being outraged by the French who, often unconsciously and sometimes deliberately, humiliate them. They do not take into consideration a natural ignorance of native customs, a different viewpoint, or good intentions—everything is subordinate to the external results. French officials often fail to show the proper respect, *tutoyer* the high mandarins, are over-familiar through *bonhomie* as well as condescension, and wound Annamites by going straight to the point in conversation instead of respecting the traditional form of a devious approach. The necessity for using interpreters has increased the opportunities for misunderstanding, partly involuntary and partly—when profitable—intentional.

When the insult is deliberate, as is too often the case in colonies where the white man feels himself a god, the Annamites' already sizeable inferiority complex is enlarged. The French seem unable to compromise between an exaggeratedly favourable and an unjustifiably unfavourable attitude towards the natives. The Annamites are very sensitive to injustice and will not be put off with indulgence or pity—which they find equally insulting. The whole relationship is dominated by the enforced proximity of conquered with conqueror.

Brutality characterized far more the early days of colonization than the post-war period, yet it is only within the last ten years that French writers have begun to publicize the fact. During the pacification the treatment of French prisoners by both Annamites and Chinese was anything but gentle, and their cruelty engendered reciprocal brutality. A rebirth of this violence recurred with the industrialization of the colony, when the usual capital-labour struggle was aggravated by the race problem. Léon Werth is the historian of abuse on the French side, especially in the master-servant relationship, and his book makes sorry reading. He records the anger of Annamites at the presumption of the Occidental barbarians in mistreating a people more civilized than themselves. Unfortunately it is the petty official—*la mentalité sous-off*, of which there are legion—who casts terror wherever he goes. At word of his coming whole villages are deserted. He is regarded as a carnivorous and alcoholic brute, and his servants inspire even greater fear and hatred. He either does not thank the Notables at all for their gifts, or in such a way that it diminishes their prestige. All breathe a sigh of relief when he has passed on to make the life of another village miserable, by threats of fines and imprisonment.

But in condemning, and rightly, the brutality of the white race towards men who have no recourse against their caprice, one must not forget that the example was first given by the Annamites themselves. The most ardent native nationalist cannot but admit that the worst exploiter of the Annamite is his own countrymen. This is true throughout the whole economic scale, from the rich landowner who evicts the poor farmer to the plantation foreman who physically and morally abuses the men under him, and like the jailers even use torture to elicit money. No Westerner could equal the atrocious cruelty that characterized the Communist uprising. Those Annamites who resent so bitterly the disdain with which they are treated by the French, forget their own history. They wiped out the Chams and were in the process of cruelly exterminating the Khmers and Laotians at the time of the conquest. They despise these nations, as they do the Hindus and Africans, as inferior peoples. They have been the ruthless exploiters of primitive tribes like the Mois. This trait in the Annamite character as well as their deification of success-at-any-price, makes their denunciation of French race-pride hypocritical. The only difference—and it is an important one—is that the Annamites are not purveyors of the principles of '89, nor do they have to reconcile their former attempts at colonization with a civilizing mission. But one is forced to conclude that it is not their humanitarianism but their pride which the French have offended, and both sides have been busier pointing out the weak spots in the other's armour than in taking active measures to remedy the situation.

The Annamite reaction to French racial discrimination is partly in the Oriental tradition and partly a new phenomenon. Apathy is a great and congenial weapon, whose efficacy has been proven in India. Polite inertia is an invincible means of dampening enthusiasm and exasperates Western nerves. The French have consistently found that the apparent acceptance of their projects did not guarantee in any way their execution. The mandarins have means of exercising pressure upon their fellow countrymen that no one else disposes of, and these indispensable intermediaries can block with bland courtesy any measure they choose to boycott. This is part and parcel of the distinction made by the Annamites between the physical force at the disposal of the French and the moral authority which is the exclusive prerogative of the mandarinate.

Annamites have made a miserable failure of opposing force by force. Their psychology is fundamentally responsible. The Chinese taught them to disdain physical prowess, but simultaneously forced them to accept their domination. Ruse and irony, the weapons of the weak, have been inculcated into their character. Annamite literature features the small animal who, by his cunning wiles, triumphs over brute force. Any method is justified if it succeeds. The resulting lack of sincerity and respect for the truth is not bemoaned by the Annamites, excepting by the more Occidentalized.[1] It has its roots in the Annamite upbringing: parents, by blows and slaps, are the executioners rather than the educators of their children. They urge the teacher similarly to "correct" their pupils. The child, already small and timid, is easily fashioned by these methods into a hypocrite and a liar. Oriental courtesy is essentially a lie: it is based on the desire to maintain harmony at the cost of truth. Those in authority have the habit of promising rewards or threatening punishments which do not materialize, so that the child soon learns the disparity between word and deed. Diplomas are awarded to him whose memory is the longest, and not to the student

[1] Vu-Tam-Tap, *De la Sincérité chez les Annamites* (Hanoi, 1924).

whose penetration of truth is the deepest. A lie is only a crime when it is a blunder.

Such tactics are at best only negative. Something more positive is required in dealing with a Western people. This realization did not come to the Annamites very early, nor all at once, but it has been the most original and constructive result of the French conquest. It took a long time for the Annamites to get over the humiliation of being vanquished, but the example of China and Japan helped to blaze the trail. Injured national pride was not the only incentive for learning from the Westerner the means of fighting him. A whole new world was being opened to this isolated people. The intelligentsia were the first to perceive the foolishness of keeping their heads buried in the sand. But even the masses are slowly realizing that here is an enormously important new element in their lives towards which they must formulate an attitude. This reaction was a process of varying degrees of slowness, and inevitably it produced a rift in the hitherto harmonious Annamite society.

The first phase of this reaction was destructive self-doubt. As time went on and the impious foreigners were not ousted by Heaven's wrath, certain natives began to wonder if something had not been rotten in the state of Annam. Possibly fatuous pride had covered serious internal weakness. Hard reality had shown the local genii impotent to combat the Western gods. Perhaps exaggerated respect for Chinese civilization had been another cause of their failure, and in the subsequent release of the Annamite soul from servility to the Chinese, the French have permitted the rebirth of a national culture. The change at first presented itself as a simple and practical exchange of old gods for new, for the ramifications of this transformation, which broke Annamite spiritual solidarity, were not immediately apparent. From the French viewpoint the discord thus engendered automatically made their task of dividing and ruling far easier.

French action was from the start both conscious and unconscious. Assimilationist policy further hastened the dissolution of Annamite traditions, begun by native self-doubt. Everything in a fixed and immobile society was tampered with—justice, education, family, and communal authority. If, in this, a definite policy had been sustained, the Annamites would have more easily adapted themselves, but France's mixed motives and confused political situation made for anything but stability. The colonial pendulum swung back and forth between contrary sets of theories, and even the officials who applied them. This universal uncertainty generated a *malaise* among natives who are constitutionally opposed to change. Nothing, however, was done about it and passive resentment was not sufficient to stem the tide. Curiously enough, the most important phase of the ensuing destruction was involuntary. It was true that traditional education and institutions had been wilfully destroyed, but the dissolution of the moral bases on which Annamite society was erected was an involuntary result of their contact with Western individualism and science. The French had aimed to destroy a state within a state and its dubiously loyal officialdom, but not the socio-religious framework which held the people together.

The whole transformation was, at best, premature. In a country where the standard of literacy had always been high, the vast majority of children were left totally without instruction. The worst void lay in the failure to give a substitute for Confucianist ethics. Annamite docility to authority, that had for centuries made them so easy to govern, was in consequence destroyed. Confucius' precepts had subordinated the individual to the group, but its discipline was external and not self-imposed by the individual will. So when this morality was no longer taught in the schools, when changes in legislation permitted children to bring suit against their parents, when the commune's privileges were replaced by increased burdens—then Annamite individualism was born automatically through the relaxation of external restraints. The rush of individualism to the Annamite head has made them resentful of any authority at all. The destructive forces which the French unwittingly released by removing the moral check have proved to be a boomerang. A government without the sanction of Heaven, that can be attacked in the courts and the press, is no longer respected. Annamites who have studied the West's struggles for political liberty are quick to use this most vulnerable spot in the armour of French colonization to demand civil rights for themselves. The *immediate* effect of obliterating the traditions was totally destructive. When they crumbled away there was no internal substitute to help the Annamites to appraise and check their new-found impulses.

Demoralization was everywhere apparent. It was most in evidence among those directly in contact with the conqueror—the servants and interpreters—who found the vices of their masters much more contagious than their virtues. In old Annam the commune had so circumscribed its inmates that only the scum of village undesirables had left its paternal protection for the questionable freedom of a vagabond's life. The French conquest had multiplied the number of these outcasts

455

by giving a new lure to town life and by a greater laxity in the law. Anticipating governmental action as a solvent of traditional restraints these men sloughed off their old discipline and lived as they pleased and could from day to day. Thefts were more frequent and delinquents went unpunished in a country which lacked legal means of identification. Insolence grew apace in a people which had always been renowned for their intricate courtesy. This intensified laxness among the Annamite lower classes and earned for the servants of Saigon their present undesirable reputation.

Linguistic barriers and the elimination of the old mandarinate caused the rise of a group of enterprising native interpreters whose ethical standards were no better, only more decorous, than those of the servant class. Outward appearances might be better sustained, but their covert venality knew no bounds. Gratuitous service never characterized Annamite officialdom, but in the old days it was tempered by Confucianist idealism and an *esprit de corps*. Interpreters were particularly noxious in the law courts, yet everywhere it was they who controlled contacts between the people and the administration. Their ill-gotten gains waxed larger through usurious investments which still further contributed to their leech-like grip on the masses, who had for them none of the awed respect that had been lavished upon the old mandarinate.

If the Annamite government had proven no trustworthy bulwark against the Occidental invader, the foreign substitute inspired far more fear than respect. Demoralization and destruction characterized the long and painful adolescence of Annamite individualism. It took time and a mental revolution to build up out of the vacillation between disheartening self-doubt and a slavish imitation of the West some welding of the durable in the old with what was adapted to Oriental needs in the new. In this the Annamites were psychologically hampered by their own and French race pride, and by a congenital tendency to imitate rather than to create. It was inevitable that they would mould what they took over from the West to their own needs and distort it so grossly that the bones of the early assimilationists must have turned over wretchedly in their graves.

NATIVE REACTION TO THE MACHINE

The supremacy of the West in Asiatic eyes is symbolized by the machine. Partly because it is an inanimate object, obedient to the will of Oriental and Occidental alike, and partly because it means a control of nature which has always been master in the East, the machine has been the link and the stimulus to understanding between the two civilizations. But the machine represents processes of thought antipodal to the Annamite mind. A vague animism endows all objects with the same quality of life, and this belief—characteristic of all primitives—has survived longer in Annam because typhoons and droughts have annually reminded man of his impotence. Imbued with Chinese philosophy the Annamite has turned away from the unequal combat with nature and concentrated upon the control of himself. Disaster and sickness force him, as the price of survival, to propitiate the angry spirits by rites and magic, but for the most part the Annamite accepts natural phenomena as fixed and final. The misery of the Annamite people testifies to the failure of their attempts, even though Confucianism may have succeeded in creating a harmonious and tranquil society impervious to physical achievements and discomfort.

Western science on the other hand has directed attention upon what may be measured, counted, and controlled in space and time, and has concentrated upon those aspects of experience that lend themselves to objective observation, to the neglect of the organic world. The subjective—intuition and feeling—has been dismissed as unreal, and sensory reactions have been intensified. This is in its way as great a deformation of experience as that practised by the Annamites, who treat society and nature as fixed elements. Because the West has increasingly succeeded in controlling nature and amassing wealth, it has become as arrogant of its powers as the Confucianist scholars who believed in the absolute and definitive truth as found in the classic books. Just as the Occident is too prone to believe that all change marks progress, so the Annamite in his conceited rigidity finds perpetual adjustments to changing circumstances a sign of decadence. The scientific method differs from the magic which the Annamite practices in being the result of disinterested and extensive observation, rather than the solicitation by means of potent formulae of immediate favours through the inter-vention of the spirit world.

The machine has brought to the Annamite a clearer consciousness of the external world. The use of spectacles, microscopes, mirrors, and windows has brought fresh and clear-cut impressions of objective phenomena. It has brought a corresponding change in viewpoint: an Annamite who realizes that he can learn the predictable rules by which the universe is governed has a foundation for dispassionate criticism of himself and of society. Formerly the eye was turned inward: the ideal was meditative leisure and opium reverie. The machine rudely intruded upon this introspective world, causing a rift between man and matter. Curiosity about the life around them was a novelty for the Annamites. When the first French boats appeared off the shores of Annam, the provincial governor was informed of the presence of a sea monster vomiting smoke. It never occurred to the mandarin to go out and look at it. Instead he turned to his books, recollecting that in a previous age a similar crocodile had been persuaded not to destroy the town only by propitiating sacrifices.

The machine made Annamites realize that there was more in this world than ever dreamed of by Chinese philosophers. The Annamite delegates sent to the Paris Exposition by Thanh Thai gave evidence in their reports of a new curiosity. Minute observation of the railroad tunnels and bridges; of the arrival and departure of trains on a predictable schedule; the eternal counting of the number of doors, gates, and rivers; the price of land per hectare—all were recorded. If these men showed new powers of observation they also betrayed the Annamite weakness of not distinguishing between the categories of objects classified. They were constantly distracted by a thousand irrelevant details. War workers, who became excellent mechanics, showed a childish love for machinery, and could be disciplined by being kept away from their machines, which they loved to take apart just for the pleasure of seeing the wheels go round. Aeroplanes make a vast impression and enhance the white man's prestige, though the primitive peoples, who live close to the supernatural, are less astonished than the more evolved Annamites. King Norodom's palace had the most amazing collection of mechanical gadgets: he was astonished by the French Resident's annoyance when he had been made unsuspectingly to sit on a music box shaped like a chair.

For the few who feel the direct imprint of the machine, the changes it has wrought in their external world are obvious to all the natives. The farmer who had always precariously balanced himself on a bamboo bridge, and who can now take himself and his cart safely across a steel structure, appreciates the difference. Bridges, railroads, and highways knit rural districts together and break down the commune's isolation, formerly its pride and defence. The French are great city builders, and in a country which prior to their coming knew no large groupings of population. The conquest of climatic and topographical conditions involved in constructing a town like Saigon are striking to a people who never before were conscious of bringing order out of mental or physical chaos. The idea of imposing upon the violence of nature obedience to the human will was entirely novel: the land and nature had hitherto always dominated Annamite life.

The law for generations bound Annamites to the soil in order to colonize the empire. Ritual for the ancestral tombs further strengthened these ties; when necessity forced their land's sale it was only on condition of repurchase. An Annamite leaves his natal village but to return. This love of the land is not idealistic, though religious. It is materialistic but profoundly impressive, for it creates that mysterious tranquillity which attracts the European to Asia. The Annamite peasant, bent over the land in which are his gods and his ancestors, feels a harmonious union with it all his life, and in death he becomes part of it. This peasant has no individuality: each worker is like his companions, and all resemble their predecessors and successors in this anonymous and earthy cult.

The French were naturally unconscious of intrusion on this sacred soil. When the natives returned after the pacification to find their land in the possession of foreigners they became embittered by the sacrilege. If their fear of the mountains had been less great the problem might have been resolved by developing those untenanted regions. But in opening new territory in the South to native labour French colonization has given to the Annamites a new attitude towards the land. New crops, markets, and scientific methods have made this vast cemetery into a source of wealth. The old fear of digging canals or foundations lest the land dragon's claws be scraped, or of running wires above the imperial tombs, has been forgotten in the ensuing benefits. Spirits which could not destroy sacrilegious constructions, like the Pont Doumer, lost their prestige and worshippers. The French have been great de-sanctifiers of the soil, and it has meant a release of the Annamites' soul and body, even if it has also increased their arrogance and materialism.

If the machine has deprived the land of much of its sacred and life-giving quality for the Annamite, it has added to his own sense of power over it. The machine has tapped sources of wealth which the Annamites never dreamed they owned. The worthless black dust of Hongay has turned that placid village into a mining town to which the Chinese, always the barometer of prosperity, have come in droves. Ambition for personal possessions and power has replaced the Confucianist ideal of group harmony through high thinking and plain living. Sumptuary laws forbade wealth and display, even in mandarinal dwellings.

If by chance one amassed wealth, one did not go on working for the sheer pleasure of accumulating money, nor step out of one's accepted hierarchic rank. Climate was an additional factor in arresting work beyond one's needs, and those needs were few. But it has taken only the prospect of riches, the introduction of the element of fashion, the opportunity of making a display superior to one's neighbours, for the machine to play into the hands of that Annamite arch-vice—vanity. When parasols, the former symbol of rank, could be bought by anyone, everyone automatically became a mandarin. This was a windfall to French umbrella manufacturers, who foresaw the realization of that old dream of the colony as an expanding body of consumers. It looked as if the release of the Annamite soul from drudgery and abject servitude to nature had been replaced only by service to Annamite vanity. Happiness is no longer measured in terms of social virtues, yet in all this wave of crass materialism the Annamites have acquired a joy of living, a sense of well-being in this world which they have never before known. The rising cost of living and increase in taxation have gone far to counteract the benefits experienced, but a change in viewpoint has occurred beyond the tally of immediate debit and credit.

The new orientation of the Annamite mind has taken a dangerous turn. If the machine has made man like a god in giving him a sense of power the Annamite has not escaped the Olympian weakness of arrogance. Because he can control the machine—and the Annamites make excellent mechanics—he thinks himself the equal of its inventor. The scientific method, the years of persevering toil, the austere self-discipline and professional integrity involved in the creation of the machine, are unappreciated and overlooked by the fatuous Oriental. The machine to him is neither more nor less than a superior bit of magic which can be mastered like any secret formula. The vital difference in outlook between East and West that made it possible only for the latter to experience the Industrial Revolution is ignored by the Annamite, who does not see beyond immediate effects, nor the fact that he too can pull levers and press buttons. And this attitude is by no means confined to the economic field.

The machine is so new to the colony that the labour problems it has brought are as yet embryonic. Ritual had long cast the Annamites into a mould with a discipline of regular habits. For centuries the Annamites had performed certain rites at specified times which gave them a mechanized routine akin to that of industry. Living intimately in large family groups under arbitrary paternal authority requires unquestioning conformity. Rice-fields demand indefatigable labour under difficult conditions, though the work is seasonal and spasmodic with no premium on long-sustained effort. Annamites, despite their Sinicized contempt for force have always been fighters, and the new enforcement of military training disciplines them to barrack life. All these factors are extremely important in having for long trained Annamites to the methodical routine required in handling machines. Timed work, contracts, and payments inculcate the sin of wasted time and the virtues of thrift and foresight, of which the Annamites were formerly quite innocent.

Games of chance have for Orientals an irresistible fascination. For the majority they are the sole diversion and opportunity to indulge their taste for risk. A lifetime's toil in the East succeeds at most in staving off starvation. Gaming is thus the sole means of escaping the common lot of misery by the sudden acquisition of wealth. If this is a serious weakness from the viewpoint of bourgeois saving it is also a perennial inducement to work. It is grist to the factory system through its discipline of fear and famine, though this is less true of Southern Indo-China, where subsistence is far easier. The Annamite is patient, skilful, and sober, though he has little sense of time in pushing through his work. Lack of the creative urge and exceptional assimilative powers make him docile in service to the machine.

Mines need a type of labour that contrasts with the peasant's sober plodding. It is irregular and uncertain as to results, but it appeals to the gaming instinct since its rewards are disproportionate to the amount of skill and work involved. Though Annamites find farming in a typhoon-ridden country has much the same element of chance, yet they hate mining. Part of their dislike is due to fear of disturbing the mountain genii, and part to the heavy mortality of mining, but chiefly because such work requires brute force and an unflinching assault upon a resisting nature alien to Annamite taste. From the industrial viewpoint the over-population of Tonkin, with its annual increase of 80,000, where most of the accessible mines are located, is a fortunate coincidence. The extraordinary fecundity of the Annamite people promises a permanent and abundant supply of cheap labour, but as yet the natives' attachment to the soil is the chief cause of labour's instability.

The recent rapid growth of industry has given the country, however, certain traits of capitalism and has increased the labouring class. In 1931 there were 221,052 workers in Indo-China, of whom a third were in agricultural enterprises; about 40 per cent in commerce and industry and 24 per cent in mines.[1] The government, tentatively in 1918 and seriously in 1927, stepped in to regulate conditions in the hiring and treatment of labourers with a minutia which the planters loudly deplored. The state's care of the Indo-Chinese worker is legally superior to that of France and other Far Eastern countries, even Japan, and is undeniably in advance of the social status of the workers. The government replies to its critics that such measures are only temporary and that free labour is expected to replace contract labour through the completion of the railway system. If there have been blunders in detail, which are natural enough when a foreign code is bodily transplanted, the government's measures have commendably anticipated the worst problems. The method may be artificial, but it has been effective, especially since the depression has eased the strain occasioned by a forced growth.

Among its provisions the state organized in 1930 a Conciliation Committee, and later auxiliary bureaux to settle labour disputes, and this arbitration has been successful in certain cases. The right to strike has been strictly confined to certain circumstances, and here enters the colonial factor, for there is fear not only of labour's instability, but of Communism as well. It is true that each year the number of strikes has dwindled. The first strike occurred in November, 1922, in Cholon after the wages of dyers had been reduced. From 1922 to 1925 there were twenty-five strikes, and a steady decline after the new 1927 legislation. Most of them show a certain confusion of political and economic motives. Trade unions, analogous to those of Japan and India, do not exist in the colony. The vast majority are still agricultural labourers with little tendency to group themselves. The isolation from home and family which has been forced upon the worker is not intentional but is, nevertheless, significant in uprooting him from old ties, and in making him unstable and ripe for propagandists. This is particularly true of the women, who have been taken out of the home and absorbed into the factory system and urban living.

A Communist memorandum issued in 1928 by the Revolutionary Party stated that there were individual capitalists in Indo-China but no capitalistic class. Nor had the labourers developed any class consciousness. As yet they are too dispersed throughout the country: the biggest factory in Tonkin employs only 5,000 workers, and these are unskilled and unorganized. A small native bourgeoisie exists but there

[1] Dumarest, A., *La Formation des Classes Sociales en Pays Annamites* (Lyon, 1935), p. 61.

is to date no clear-cut capital-labour problem, for the whole situation is dwarfed by the colonial issue. The capitalists are still elmost exclusively French, and the workers in the main Annamites, with a sprinkling of Javanese and Chinese. Local nationalism and Chinese communism complicate the labour situation, of which as yet only the vaguest outlines are discernible.

Before the coming of the French, social classes did not exist in Annam. The population was principally peasants from which sprang the mandarinate, with a few artisans, and an even smaller nobility in Hué without influence or privilege. Poverty was only a question of degree. Commerce was in the hands of the Chinese; there were no big properties, no industry, and hence no means of acquiring wealth. Post-War French colonization has created a bourgeoisie, albeit restricted in number and quality, and a labouring class. Even the artisan has now become a wage-earner. The growth of *latifundia* has been possible only in the under-populated South, where communal lands do not cut across and dominate rural property as they do in the North. In addition to being absentee landlords with attendant evils for their tenants, these native bourgeois are rapacious usurers and speculators rather than planters. Their standard of living is higher than that of their compatriots, but the depression has been severe for them, for they and their property are heavily indebted, and they have lived far beyond their means. This group is swelled by the intellectuals, composed of functionaries, French-educated Annamites, and those in the liberal professions. The lower *bourgeoisie* is drawn from the artisan group, clerks, and secretaries. More and more this whole class is adopting French customs. Rice, native clothes and furniture are beginning to disappear from their lives. The unemployment brought on by the depression has accentuated the nascent class consciousness. That the proletariat feels the inherent enmity is shown by the amount of damage done to native bourgeois property during the 1931 uprisings.

The new-born proletariat and bourgeoisie have naturally clashed with the communal and family groups and have contributed heavily to their dissolution. Caste never existed in Indo-China, and if hierarchy was ingrained, it was not on a class basis, for the upper ranks were never closed. There is, on the face of it, something artificial about the sudden appearance of a class war in the colony, as if it were part of the baggage of imported Western ideas. The Annamite Notables and mandarins have always used their positions to exploit the poor peasant, and their will and capacity to do so has increased with the new means at their disposal. The government is the only bulwark of the masses' defence, and is a co-operative link between the two. The new social classes are the product and the problem of French colonization.

The Annamite bourgeoisie are principally landed proprietors, but there are a certain number of native industrialists and merchants. Indo-China has always been overwhelmingly agricultural. Before the conquest there were very few native industries and those of a family order. In 1906 a French writer was able to enumerate twenty-six objects of native manufacture—principally mother-of-pearl incrustations, wood carving, and lacquer, but they were in decadence long before the French came. Other industries, like salt, were ruined by the monopolies: copper, cloth, and iron objects were killed by European and Japanese competition. Weaving, pottery, brick-making are inferior to the Chinese production and only for family use, but they could be enormously improved by new methods. Modern businesses which are mainly in native hands are auto and river traffic, printing presses, tile factories, and cabinet-making.

The French were without doubt responsible for the Annamites' interest in commerce, for up to their coming it had been lodged without protest in Chinese hands. The great majority of Annamites raised enough for their scant needs, foreign commerce was forbidden, communications non-existent, and the natives seemed to realize their inability to compete with those most brilliant of all merchants, their former masters. Psychological obstacles as well as inexperience have handicapped Annamites in their attempts to assault the Chinese commercial monopoly. Foresight and thrift are virtues whose cultivation Annamite insecurity never permitted, and whose lack prevents their undertaking large-scale enterprises. Annamite stockholders have a propensity for withdrawing their money at short notice from an investment that does not give immediate profits. In addition to the fact that little Annamite capital is available, they understand only two uses for money: to bury it in the family jar or jewels, or to lend it at usurious rates. An Annamite's interests almost never go beyond his commune's gates, so the incessant travel required for commercial knowledge and sales is antipathetic to him. He does not concern himself with improvements and infinitely prefers routine. Annamites cannot differentiate between commercial ability and crookery. History is full of their quarrels, and of no instance of prolonged co-operation. Annamites thrive on lawsuits and mutual theft. The women are superior in commerce to the men, but both are puerilely addicted to small-scale robbery. In sacks of corn, Annamite peasants mix sand, and to rubber they add stones and earth to increase its weight. It is hard to identify the guilty persons, but such methods alienate purchasers and in the end defeat their purpose. Annamites are concerned with immediate gain and are unsurpassed at tricking the individual rival, but they lack the experience and acumen of the Chinese for large-scale enterprises, and above all their solidarity.

The individual Annamite artist may be very skilled, although uncreative, but he suffers from the disrepute in which manual labour is held in the East. Moreover, he can never estimate a piece of work accurately, either in foretelling the amount of material needed or the time required, or a reasonable profit. Artisans fix a price at random and then find it wrong. An order is never filled in the time they set. They haven't enough money to buy the basic materials so must ask for a deposit, and usually wear out the customer by repeating the process. They then have recourse to the usurer, whose exorbitant charges absorb all the profit. Trying to recoup their losses by gaming, they lose everything and go bankrupt. The artisan chronically labours under the delusion that his client is in desperate need of the object ordered, so that he can safely make an enormous profit—an excellent way of killing trade. He is apt to give up when confronted with difficulties. This lack of commercial ability goes back to historical causes, and the immediate and disproportionate profit ideal has been set up by usury.

The first formal evidence of the new Annamite interest in commerce dates back to Gilbert Chieu, who promised to teach his compatriots the secrets of Western trade success. In the post-War period the anti-Chinese commercial movement, in 1919 and later in 1927, took on a distinctly nationalist flavour. Annamites were so indebted to the Chinese and so inferior to them as business men that, despite the violence of the outbreaks, the Chinese soon had the upper hand. They did not abuse their advantage, however, for by that time Southern China had become a less desirable place for the Chinese to return to. In 1926 *La Société Annamite de Crédit* was founded with a modest capital, and this was the first attempt to create an Annamite bank. Though the experiment has not been a great success Annamites are beginning to replace some of the Chinese *compradores*. The French, who have been recently alienated by Chinese bankruptcy and accountancy methods, are beginning to feel that they have neglected the economic education of their protégés.[1] This is undoubtedly true, but

[1] There is only one Annamite department store in Hanoi, Vu Van An.

no magic wand can be waved over Annamites to endow them with mercantile skill. Experience and training are needed, but even more a changed psychology and an appreciation of professional integrity.

The government, serving as intermediary between the two hitherto water-tight compartments, is now encouraging Franco-Annamite financial co-operation. It has long been a complaint of the Annamite bourgeoisie that whereas they have been docile about subscribing to the state's loans they have never been permitted to share in the profits of French colonial enterprises. To which the colonials reply that the Annamite bourgeoisie, in addition to being overbearing and self-important, have not the requisite knowledge. And when they are trained the natives forsake commerce for government jobs. They point to the case of one Annamite for whom the administration had cleared the way to directing an important enterprise. He was ruined by his innumerable family, the members of which are ever prone to fasten themselves leech-like upon any relative whose financial prospects are bright, and thus kill the goose before it can lay even the first golden egg. The depression has done little to solve the impasse, but for the present the problem is in abeyance. Though the Annamite bourgeoisie have not the virtues of the European middle classes, the creation of social groups based on wealth is for better or worse the product of Western colonization.

NATIVE REACTION TO FRENCH CULTURE

The scientific side of Western culture has been more easily assimilated by the Annamites than any other. Not that they esteem science above literature. On the contrary, for them the great man is the poet and moralist. But the machine represents to them the sole unqualified justification for the Western claim to superiority. It belongs to the universal world of the senses and does not require for its understanding a special background. Science has an inter-racial common denominator: it is realistic and concrete, it is utilitarian and immediately profitable. The prodigious Annamite memory can grasp and retain its formulae, if not the point of view that made such discoveries possible. Literature is a much more indigenous product. It is the fruit of a people's experience and their attitude towards life.

The divergence between two racial cultures is nowhere more clearly shown than in the Annamite reaction to Western education. Chinese instruction was thoroughly utilitarian. Although the child absorbed a complete system of ethics, as part of the paraphernalia of learning, he continues to study not in order to expand his viewpoint by new knowledge, but to win honours that lead to high government positions. The European ideal of disinterested scholarship is incomprehensible to the Annamite, who regards knowledge as no dynamic growth based on study and experience, but as a vast memorizing of texts which embody the sum total of knowledge. When the Annamites demanded more educational facilities they meant more administrative openings. It is true that the earliest schools in the colony trained interpreters and that the French *agrégation* is the equivalent of a teaching position for life, nevertheless, it was not true of the colony's educational system as a whole, and the deception felt by the frustrated Annamite students is shown by the number who have joined the revolutionary ranks. Those who have received diplomas and positions are almost equally undesirable. Their arrogance is unbearable, and they have acquired no humility from a realization of the immensity of knowledge. This attitude towards education has been an important factor in alienating liberal opinion in France. The Academician Brieux was touched by the Annamites' wish for education, but only recently has it been realized that those very Annamites who have been most generously educated lead the anti-French agitation.

Annamites who have made sacrifices to send their children to French schools find them changed: the old respect and courtesy have become impudence and conceit. The patriarchal system and the gods who supported it have been shattered. The culture of the Occident has brought the individual out in relief from his social background. Here the missionary and functionary have joined hands. The glory of God and of the Third Republic were thought to be equally served by encouraging Annamite individualism. The results have discouraged those who encouraged it most. The educated Annamites have not received the recognition or positions to which they feel themselves entitled, and they are hopelessly uprooted from their own setting without being transplanted into Western culture. Their parents have undermined their own authority and have lost their children in trying to fit them for a new world that has come too suddenly upon them. The French have alternately reproached themselves with parsimony in fulfilling their cultural obligations towards their protégés, and at the same time of having given them the desire and the means of driving out their foreign conquerors. The deception has been universal, but it is too late to turn back.

The Confucianist ideal of self-control and self-effacement has, in

one generation, been swamped in the rising tide of individualism. At
first the Annamites were horrified by the outbursts of feeling to which
the French gave vent, and even more by the self-analysis and cult of
sensibility inherent in French culture. The classic drama, for example,
to the Annamites did not mean moderation and reason, but the exaltation of the emotions. As is natural with emotional adolescence, the
Annamites have developed sentimentality, a love of rant and bombast,
and of the sensational. In political reading they love the fiery passages
of Rousseau. An investigation of sales in Tonkin bookshops shows a
love for French romantic writers, ranging from Dumas to Victor Mar-
guerite, and of detective stories. The modern sentimental Chinese
novel also has great success with the Annamites, and it has created for
them an unreal and fantastic world. Even the poor buy books entitled
On the Ocean of Love and *Where, Then, Is Thy Promise?* To counteract
this rush of sentimentality to the heart the government has subsidized
translations of the soberer Western classics.

The utilitarian aspect of the Annamites' interest in education is partly
the result of being cut off from Chinese classics and partly the desire
to profit by the new opportunities. When the missionaries invented and
propagated *quoc ngu* they were trying to burn Annam's bridges with
Confucianism in order to leave a virginal mind, ready to receive the
imprint of Christianity. By destroying respect for the traditional authority they unloosed—much to their surprise—a critical spirit which was
no more docile to Catholic than to Chinese doctrine. *Quoc ngu* became
the symbolic bridge over which the Annamites have passed from the
old to the new. It is an instrument by which the native who has perseverance and a textbook may acquire literacy and a veneer of Occidentalism within a few months, but it is not a subtle medium for thought.
Some natives have not been willing to make even this small effort.
When in 1906 *quoc ngu* schools were opened the Annamites at first
co-operated eagerly, thinking that it meant the beginning of a new era
of wealth. But the lack of immediate advantages—always in terms of
government jobs—as well as the necessity of paying the teacher, soon
chilled their enthusiasm so that few pupils were left. Those who persevered and rose in the world felt that there was nothing left for them to
learn.

The old type of Annamite scholar whose life was devoted to the
pleasures of learning, and who dreamed and discussed philosophy,
agreeably lying on a mat in his garden, had been abolished to give place
to an upstart go-getter. The old scholar was stagnant, complacent,

contemptuous of manual labour, and quite out of touch with the practical world, but he made an art of living. He was bound to disappear because he was an anachronism, but his successor is far less sympathetic, for he has lost the best in the old and acquired only the worst of the new. Western culture in Annamite hands is deformed, just as the French language is distorted by their pronunciation. Both the language and ideas are hybrid. Annamites learn to live like Occidentals, dress like them, and repeat what they say. But though they can be trained in analysis, they are inept at synthesis and grasp of general ideas—even the most brilliant among them. Just as in the economic sphere they are extraordinarily subtle in serving their own immediate interests but inadequate in large-scale enterprises, so in the realm of ideas they are incoherent and clumsy when handling the abstract. Assimilation and memorizing rather than criticism and creation are, up to the present, their forte. They have evolved marvellously in a short period, but they have accumulated emotions more quickly than their ability to appraise or utilize them. They are suffering from an indigestion of Western culture. Time alone will reveal whether they or the superficial learning they have acquired will be the master. In the future they may be constructive, but up to now the destructive side has triumphed.

Altruism is conspicuously absent from Oriental psychology, and the Annamite mentality is not propitious for the propagation of Christianity. The family and commune are responsible for their own, and not the individual, beyond membership in those two groups. In fact, to some Annamites pity, charity, and benevolence are effeminate emotions. A European does good for the comfortable feeling it gives him—more for the satisfaction of his vanity than for its efficacy. From the Buddhist viewpoint the emotional effect either on oneself or on others is incidental: one should do good, if at all, without knowing or caring to know how it is received, or whether the recipient is undeserving or otherwise, with the sole desire of remedying universal injustice. Charity that ends with the family and village harmonizes with the provincialism of old Annam. The universality of Christianity is inconceivable to men whose religion is that of their village gods. It does not necessitate public spirit—a complete void in the Annamite character. One who occupies himself with general welfare is suspected of neglecting a more imperious duty to his family. Christianity for the Annamite has been a disruptive force cutting across the closest of his ties. The highly localized character of Annamite life, encouraged and enforced by religion and law, has been a primary cause of their immaturity as a people, both politically and emotionally.

Honour, like altruism, is an individualistic conception. Only superficially is it akin to Oriental "face." In "face" there is more vanity, and it depends upon the amount of concrete authority and prestige a man can muster either through his position or personality. Honour arose out of the European's need for making himself respected, even when he could count on nothing but his own character. When honour degenerates into touchiness, as in the practice of duelling, for instance, it becomes more akin to "face." But there is always an essential difference, for the Oriental has no concept of personal dignity. He is insolent in good fortune and obsequious in misfortune. Honour, a subjective ideal, depends entirely upon its owner: "face," being objective, can be destroyed or created by the attitude of other people.

Honour and altruism alike seem to the Annamites both droll and stupid. The servant who says of his master: "*Monsieur beaucoup bon, Monsieur beaucoup bête,*" sums up the Oriental's viewpoint. In a society where there is no middle ground between being a sheep or a wolf— and one is a sheep only when one cannot become a wolf—voluntary abstention from preying upon the weak is incomprehensible.

Proselytizing to the native intelligentsia is but another proof of European discourtesy. The assumption of superiority inherent in the assimilationist idea is part and parcel of missionary work. Christianity with its confusing and metaphysical preoccupations has not the ordered clarity of Chinese philosophy, and seems in consequence an inferior superstition. Differences in dogma are not striking enough, nor the Catholic liturgy sufficiently aesthetic to lure the cultured classes. Annamite religion is essentially practical, whereas Catholicism is based on revelation. These considerations pale beside the important obstacle— that Catholicism runs counter to the social and political fabric of Annamite society. Catholicism, with its concern for the individual soul, subordinates society's interests to its salvation. Even more, Protestantism, by making the individual conscience the supreme arbiter, undermines the religious sanction Confucius gives to society and the state. Polygamy and the ancestral cult are but two illustrations of the irreconcilable differences between the Christian and Confucianist outlook. Hierarchy, firmly ingrained in the Annamite soul, finds satisfaction in graded religions: Confucianist doctrines for those who can appreciate its subtleties, and a profoundly modified Buddhist-Taoist practice for the masses. In short, the Annamites are satisfied with a religion which

470

they are used to and which confirms their socio-political order. The only advantages which conversion offers in their eyes are material. Hence in studying the problem one must differentiate between abstract Christian ideals and Mission practice.

The rising materialism of the Annamites, a consequence of the French conquest, was regarded by the Mission as both an obstacle and an aid to conversions.

> With the rich it is the burning desire to become even richer; with the poor it is the sharp prick of necessity which is increasing with the ever heavier public burdens. The spirit of insubordination, of absolute liberty, of disdain for good traditions, disorganizes families and perverts individuals. Any pretext is good enough for a young man to leave home. Married couples abandon each other without a thought for their children. Even our Christians do not escape this epidemic of insubordination and vagrancy. . . .[1]

Like the administration with whom it had co-operated to destroy the traditional culture the Mission found that it had simultaneously demolished moral discipline and respect for authority—Confucianist and otherwise. On the other hand the current materialism was a two-edged sword. It might work to Mission advantage. Preoccupation with the things of this world was not wholly due to preference but to necessity. The prevalent misery of the masses is a *leitmotif* that runs through Mission reports. It caused seasonal displacements for work and this neutralized any effect the missionaries might have by lives of self-abnegation, toil, and even martyrdom. To make any headway at all the Mission had to adapt itself and make it worth the Annamites' while to convert themselves—not a high plane of appeal but an effective one. The Mission held a privileged position as landowner, dating from the pre-conquest period. Rice-fields would tempt the land-loving Annamite as nothing else. The missionary, too, could be a good friend at court, and a powerful intermediary with the administration.

Many Annamite families pride themselves on having been converted to Christianity at the time of the conquest, and incidentally of having thus laid the basis of their fortunes. If some of them were later massacred by the mandarins as French partisans, if subsequently the survivors' hopes of being treated as a privileged group were deceived, nevertheless many had profited by their perspicacity to see at an early stage which way the wind blew. Conversion statistics reflect accurately the Mission's influence, notably after security was assured and anti-clericalism influenced the government, and show that there was a vast

[1] *Société des Missions-Etrangères; Compte Rendu des Travaux* (Paris, 1907), p. 200.

decline in conversions. Spring and Fall pastoral visits, exhortations to attend Mass, inquiries into absences—all show the native Christians' constant need for stimulus to piety and tendency to backslide. It is curious that the Mission has in itself and in its converts deliberately encouraged greed and materialism as a means of spiritual salvation.

Efforts to adapt Christian doctrine have been frowned upon by the Church. A Papal Bull forbade assimilating the ancestral cult to Purgatorial dogma. An experienced missionary,[1] recognizing the difference in native mentality, concocted a new Paradise to suit variegated Annamite tastes. He found that sitting on the right hand of God was too vague a formula to stimulate Annamite ambition. The tortures of Hell were far more comprehensible. To make a Paradise to match, he filled it with fruit trees, cock-fights, plenty of good food, gaming houses, and libraries. But his superiors, safely tucked away in Rome, where they were too remote to understand and too enmeshed in theory, removed this dangerous missionary to another field. This inelasticity and rigidity of the Church has cost it many a convert, and forced the Mission into a colonial career of temporal possessions.

Not only were many French colonials not attractive exemplars of Christian virtues, but the type of Annamite who forsook all to acquire rice-fields was of so low a social and moral fibre that he alienated the best of his compatriots from Christianity. Whole villages had to turn Catholic to avoid the moral and physical isolation that individual conversions would have entailed. When converts came to claim their share of the family heritage the ensuing struggles made the Mission hated and feared. The mandarinate, since the pre-conquest days, had persecuted the Mission and the feeling was later enforced by their privileged position. Since the War the Mission has made an effort to improve the quality of its converts, to attract the indifferent, and to propitiate the hostile. Secondary education, newspapers, lectures, organizations like the *Jeunesse Catholique* and the *Cercle Annamite des Etudes Catholiques* have succeeded in attracting a certain number, but the influence of Communism has made many of the young Annamites incurably hostile.

Communist hatred of the Mission is not based solely on its dislike of Christianity *per se*, but on the economic role it plays in the colony. Natives working Mission property are depicted as serfs in the usurious stranglehold of the Mission. They point to the nefarious role played by the Mission during the conquest, when it aided the French against Annamite patriots. Similarly they claim that during the 1931 uprising

[1] Monet, P., *Les Jauniers* (Paris, 1931), p. 116.

the Mission betrayed secrets of the confessional and delivered over Annamite nationalists to the scaffold, and that it used this occasion to take revenge on those villages which had refused to be converted. The Mission is so much disliked that it has become the target for contradictory attacks: the Communists hate it for being the government's ally, and the government in turn fears the Mission as a state within a state because of its influence over the natives. The Communists have an additional grievance in the resistance which native Christians have shown to the siren voice of Moscow. On both sides the uprisings covered revenge for a multitude of old grudges.

Nor has nationalism spared the bosom of the Church. Even at the time of Japan's victory there were not only fewer converts but fewer candidates for clerical ordination. Now the formation of a native priesthood is the primary preoccupation of the Society of Foreign Missions: the conversion of the infidel is but secondary. This is especially important as the War and anti-clerical laws have cut down the number of French missionaries sent out from France. Though the native clergy had a most honourable record during the era of persecutions, nevertheless the Society has shown a marked reluctance to promote Annamites in the ecclesiastical hierarchy. They have accepted the idea in principle, but in practice the French missionaries cling to the top positions. Right after the War the Annamite clergy showed a marked spirit of insubordination, paralleling the general nationalist movement. In 1922 a scandal broke out over the treatment of native priests supposed to be implicated in the theft of a French missionary's possessions. The following year a native priest at Chaudon murdered a French missionary, and the Bishop of Pnom-Penh was accused of muzzling all complaints and the evidence of discontent. During the Emperor Khai Dinh's trip to Paris, an Annamite priest succeeded in presenting to the Vatican the native clergy's demands for equality of status with the French missionaries. In January 1926 an encyclical letter, *Rerum Ecclesia*, tactfully rendered homage to missionary devotion in Indo-China, but recalled to them the duty of Christian charity in making native priests their collaborators. A Papal Legate was sent to Hanoi as evidence of Rome's watchful care. Further steps taken by the Annamite clergy led to the nomination of a remarkable native bishop, Père Six, who was given the diocese of Phat Diem. In 1925 a second native bishop was named. Père Six had had a splendid record during the heroic period[1] and after the French conquest he was made *curé* at Phat Diem,

[1] Olichon, Mgr., *Le Baron de Phat Diem* (Poitiers, 1931).

a parish formed by alluvial deposits in the Red River. His remarkable organizing ability was shown not only among his parishioners but by the building of dykes and a cathedral in the Annamite style, with only the resources of his followers. Men like Joffre and Lyautey visited him and many came to ask his advice. The court of Hué, his erstwhile prosecutor, now made him honorary Minister of Rites. He was named Baron of Phat Diem, he was made Officer of the Legion of Honour, and, as crowning glory, 40,000 people attended his funeral. His life is an illustration of the Mission thesis that Christianity is the best bridge which can span the abyss between Oriental and Occidental cultures.

It is not coincidence that the religious movement, both within and without the Church, took on a nationalist tincture. The self-assertion of the Annamite clergy synchronized with the birth of a new politico-religious sect in Cochin-China called Caodaism in 1926. On the religious side it has an eclectic character—a reform version of Buddhism which includes Taoist and Catholic dogmas. It is a compromise between the old and the new, a reconciliation of Eastern and Western concepts. Its guiding deity is a spirit named Cao-Dai, whose Pope was an extremely able Annamite named Le-Van Trung. The headquarters is at Tayninh, where a pagoda has been constructed, manned by a priesthood, nourished by a domain of rice-fields and flanked by a village, school, printing press, and weavers' looms. There is a Ghandiesque flavour about creating a community which is economically self-sufficient. At first the government, true to its policy of protecting native religions, encouraged the movement, but its enormous growth, its close-knit organization, its clandestine meetings, and the presence of dubious characters, in government eyes, among its disciples soon made the state nervous. It might be Communism masquerading as religion, and there was an undeniable similarity between the two organizations. It has also created a hitherto unknown fanaticism in the colony: the spirit of Cao-Dai can save the Indo-Chinese who have lost their independence as punishment for their sins. Nationalists and Caodaists use to good effect the plea for liberty of conscience, and claim that the state's persecution— the mild Pasquier was particularly virulent—of this religion is unjustified. The King of Cambodia has abolished Caodaism from his realm and now only tolerates Buddhism and Catholicism. The Mission's attitude has received official approbation. The death of Le-Van Trung in 1935 coincides with the freedom recently granted to this cult by Robin.

The Mission which encouraged the conquest has been, on the whole, a loser by it. If it no longer suffers persecution and has become a great temporal power, the Mission has lost influence—though now without bitterness—to the administration which has absorbed all but its spiritual functions. Its converts and missionaries have not increased, and many of its compatriots openly flout its ideals. From without it is threatened by Communism and Caodaism, and from within by nationalist insubordination. Stalemated in every direction the Mission's eye has been forced to turn inward, to care for its own, and to attempt the conversion of primitive tribes. The native reaction to the Mission has been very realistic. Around the small nucleus of sincere conversions there has been a cloud of converts through self-interest. With the decline of Mission power and the opening of new and more profitable fields the Annamites have turned away from the Mission, and put pressure to bear on the more powerful administration to win certain concrete aims in this world. It is even doubtful whether the Mission influence is responsible for the one constructive indigenous religious movement among the Annamites—Caodaism.

NATIVE NATIONALISM

Although the most far-reaching transformation of native life has resulted from the involuntary absorption of Western ideas, French action in the three fields of politics, education, and Missions was consciously directed towards modifying native life. Annamite nationalism may trace its roots to the Chinese-dominated past, but even after independence was achieved, regionalism and communal loyalties atrophied its development. Prolonged contact was needed with the nationalistic West to quicken it to life. Though France naturally never wanted an indigenous nationalist movement to destroy her colonial sovereignty, French institutions are so impregnated with the ideals of 1789 that they unconsciously fostered in the Indo-Chinese the principles of political liberty.

In 1862 the French Admiral at Saigon received the following proclamation:

All the inhabitants of Gocong (Cochin-China) make this declaration: in losing the government of our sovereign, we are as desolate as children who have lost father and mother. Your country belongs to the Western seas: ours to the Eastern. As the horse differs from the buffalo, so do we differ from you in language, writing, and customs. Gratitude attaches us to our emperor:

we will avenge the injuries inflicted on him and will die for him. The conflict will be long, but we are acting in accordance with the laws of Heaven, and our cause must triumph. . . .[1]

These were not vain words, the Admiral commented. Never did a people prolong their resistance in such great distress.

Unfortunately for the future reputation of Annamite nationalism its pure heroism was mixed with the dross of piracy and brigandage. The issue became hopelessly confused: the French confounded patriot with pirate, mandarins confounded all native Christians with French partisans, Chinese soldiers sent by their government to Tonkin turned private bandits once in the country. Less cruelty, deceit, and disunity on the Annamite side, and more understanding and clemency on the part of the French, could have cut the struggle short. As the French conquered province after province, the Annamites more and more took refuge in passive isolation. Instead of uniting on some plan of resistance they burned incense before the ancestral altar, trusting in the spirits to deliver them.

Typical of this attitude was the experience of the first Frenchman to visit the Hué palace. Wandering through a maze of gardens and passages he was finally led to a room, where he saw the Emperor Tu-Duc on his knees before a bamboo partition. For only a brief moment this screen was rolled up to reveal the aged Empress in her yellow robes, her face like old ivory. This was the supreme and ineffectual concession old Annam made to the sacrilege of European curiosity and the new order. A rare exception was the great mandarin, Phan Thanh Quang, who appreciated the reality of the conquest. To save what was left of the provinces he administered he made peace with the French, but to punish himself for being the instrument of the inevitable he committed suicide in the miserable hut which had been his home even in the days of his grandeur. Few of the old Annamites had his vision and his courage: if they could not oppose the West they were determined to ignore it.

The financial burdens, characteristic of the Doumer era, awakened the native masses to a consciousness of their collective misery. They were ripe for the growing wave of excitement that flooded Asia as a result of the Sino-Japanese War, the Boxer Rebellion, the occupation of the Philippines, the Japanese victory over Russia, and the Chinese Revolution. In 1906 occurred the first reaction to Asiatic unrest of the Indo-Chinese—the Gilbert Chieu conspiracy. From Japan Prince Cuong De wrote letters in blood to urge his compatriots to prepare themselves to

[1] Garros, G., *Forceries Humaines* (Paris, 1926), p. 83.

476

drive out the Western barbarians. This movement was essentially Chinese in its anti-foreign motivation, and eminently Annamite in that it was embroiled in discreditable financial difficulties from the outset. A *cahier des doléances* of the Young Annamites, presented to Governor Clémentel at about the same time, is more constructive in its aim. It protested principally against the Franco-Russian alliance and the arbitrary arrests of innocent Annamites, later exiled to the Poulo Condore penitentiary. This protest was only temporarily effective, for the pre-War period known as the Era of Plots saw severe repressions of these outbreaks. A new conspiracy was announced daily: colonials in a panic demanded "protection," and denounced the liberal policies of Beau, Klobukowsky, and Sarraut as responsible.

While these uprisings were evidence of popular discontent, a more constructive criticism of the government than throwing bombs and cutting hair was to be found in the letters of two mandarins, Tran Ba Loe and Phan Chau Trinh.[1] The former attacked France's assimilationist policy in a report he had been asked to make on a new state project. His chief criticism was directed against the new mandarinate installed by the French, especially their arbitrary and extortionate methods. Phan Chau Trinh's letter to the Resident Superior of Tonkin was unsolicited and was the first native effort to inform a high official directly of the country's misery. He blamed the growing abyss between French and Annamites upon the former's disdain for the latter, and neglect of their duties as colonizers. The new mandarins profited by this estrangement to indulge their vanity and their cruelty, while their predecessors were absorbed in a futile regret of the past. If the upper class had lost all its dignity the masses were crushed by taxes and misery, and the country was relapsing into a state of semi-barbarism. If Phan Chau Trinh did not spare the French he was far harder on his own people. They had only themselves to blame. If the Emperor had studied how to improve his country, if the upper classes had done something besides amuse themselves, if commerce and industry had been developed, their energies would not have been absorbed by sterile civil wars. It would be futile to throw off the French yoke. Another master, perhaps worse, was inevitable, given the country's inherent weaknesses. France should stay, but take up her colonizing task more scrupulously. The author of this courageous letter was condemned to death by the Court of Hué, but Klobukowsky commuted this penalty.

[1] Tran Ba Loe, *Excursions et Reconnaisances*, vol. 2 (Saigon, 1880), p. 148. *Bulletin Efeo* (Hanoi, 1907), p. 166.

A more Machiavellian counsellor, though to largely the same effect, was Hoang-Cao-Khai, former viceroy of Tonkin.[1] He advised his compatriots to learn all they could from the French. A premature attempt to break away was foredoomed to failure: Japan might be a more permanent and harsher master than France. Learn of the West and lie low for a hundred years, then Annam will be ready for autonomy. Like Phan Chau Trinh he blamed the fatuous stagnancy of old Annam for the conquest, nor had the upper classes learned anything by this failure. In 1876 the most brilliant reply to the question asked at the Hué examinations: "Was Japan right in turning to Western methods?" was in the negative, on the grounds that it meant an eventual return to barbarism.

It was China, Annam's perennial teacher, who gave the Annamites confidence in the West. Though Japan had been victor, the reforms which China instituted in 1900 influenced much more the Annamite intelligentsia. The writings of the Chinese reformers, Kang and Liang, stirred the Indo-Chinese to read European books, chiefly the eighteenth-century philosophers. They even took on Chinese names: Rousseau became Lu, and Montesquieu Manh. Revolutionary ideas buzzed in every Annamite head. France was reproached with having denied her heritage by keeping her protégés in ignorance. This was the first time that the Annamite intelligentsia admitted that the West had any grounds for superiority.

Japan, after her 1905 victory, became the champion of the Yellow Races and drew Annamites to study there as well as in China. It was appropriate that Prince Coung De should have directed his conspiracy from Nippon. A change in the Annamite viewpoint was evidenced at the opening of the new Hanoi University. Beau realized that if they had no facilities in the colony Annamite students would go abroad where foreign influences might be subversive. The closing of the University, as part of the reaction to the 1908 uprisings, disillusioned the native élite who were just beginning to have confidence in Western culture. Their disappointment was shown in the resolutions formulated by the Permanent Annamite Mission at Paris in 1908: more and better education was asked even before improvements in the colony's economy. It was unfortunate that at the very time the Annamites were eager to learn of the West France was beginning to retract and regret the generosity of the earlier period. The Annamites were still preoccupied with the *malaise* which contact with the West inspired in them. They

[1] Hoang-Cao-Khai, *Revue Indo-Chinoise* (February 1910).

contented themselves with citing abuses for the French to reform, but they did not yet think of taking matters into their own hands by demanding political rights. This was essentially the attitude that dominated the pre-War period. Learning, not revolution, was the byword of the great majority before 1914.

The first reaction in Indo-China to the War was surprise at Europe's suicide, and panic on the part of all the population. Crops were sold at any price just to get rid of bank-notes. This painful impression was increased by the first War news, but the clamping down of censorship and word of the Marne victory reassured the public. Annamite tradition believes that success is the mark of Heaven's approval, so that the ultimate victory strengthened French prestige by religious sanction. Japan's entry into the War on the Allied side was not only comforting but it removed any hope of enlisting Japanese support of an Annamite uprising.

That Sarraut's liberal policy antedated the War was an important factor in keeping the country quiet. More important was the stimulus given by the War to the colony's economy. The piastre rose steadily, and with it the standard of living. Ties with France were loosened psychologically and economically, and Indo-China began to acquire a place all her own in the Far East. Not that the country was entirely quiet, but what incidents occurred were of a local rather than a general character.

The attempted escape of the Emperor Duy Than, the uprising of Quang Nghi, and the attack on the prison of Saigon, were the most dramatic occurrences. A few military columns manœuvred in Upper Tonkin, where the unrest was happily attributed to German propaganda in nearby Yunnan and Siam. The most discreditable War incident took place in 1917, when the militia of Thai Nguyen revolted, attacked the garrison, and devastated the province. The population, exasperated by the criminal behaviour of the Resident, Darles, resisted for two months. The subsequent investigation revealed terrible conditions in his charnel house of a penitentiary, and his sanction of torture of the prisoners who had offended him. Despite the Court of Saigon's recognition of his guilt he was fined just 200 francs and given a lucrative position by the reactionary colonials led by Governor Cognacq, after his withdrawal from the administration.

The War Department in 1915 tried for the first time importing forty-four trained Annamite workers to France to serve in the Aviation School at Marseille. The experiment proved so successful that throughout the year 4,000 workers came to France. The original year's contracts were prolonged and the workers placed under military discipline. Workers received the local French wage, though the government withheld a portion to indemnify the cost of clothing and transportation. There was no trouble with the first recruits who came from Indo-Chinese towns where they were used to contact with Europeans, but later, peasants were sent, timid, suspicious, and unprepared for their new life. Bonuses were given to stimulate zeal: part of their salary was extracted and sent back to the workers' families; glowing letters were reproduced in the colony's papers. The kind of work was given Annamites in which they could see results almost immediately. Paternalistic attempts were made to counteract the Annamites' natural melancholia, aggravated by homesickness: reading-rooms, lectures and lessons in French, theatricals, etc.

By 1918 there were about 100,000 Annamites in France, half of whom were workers, The military authorities had at first been chary about using Annamite soldiers at the Front, but after Verdun they were forced to spare the French troops. First mixed detachments, then all-Annamite regiments were created—the Cambodians were placed with the Senegalese and not with the Annamites. The valiant behaviour of these troops was evident at their first engagement in 1917 at Chemin-les-Dames. The qualities they revealed were courage, intelligence, endurance, discipline, resignation, avarice, and a zeal for military decorations. The greatest difficulty lay in their concern for ritual burial.

If these soldiers had been volunteers in reality as well as in name their sacrifice would have been less tragic, but colonial recruiters used reprehensible methods and violence. There had been lamentable scenes in the villages and stations where these miserable "volunteers" were herded together and put under military guard. Some even jumped overboard from the transport ships in a pathetic effort to escape back home. Money contributions suffered from the same abuse, but in that case the damage was not so vital. The sacrifice demanded was far beyond the colony's strength. The War did not concern the Indo-Chinese. France had promised to protect them, but this contract was unilateral. Despite the assimilationist theory the Annamites had not been morally assimilated. Their participation in the War was nothing more nor less than forced labour. Nor were the liberal promises France made to the colonies in her hour of need fulfilled. The native discontent that piled up in the post-War decade was only a fitting retribution.

Indo-China's marked prosperity and isolation during the War increased the feeling of self-confidence and independence on the part of colonials and natives alike. Sarraut's liberal policy stimulated native ambitions: workers and soldiers returning from France brought with them new ideas and influences. The tempo of the colony's development was, in consequence, enormously accelerated, and very soon evidence of this forced growth became apparent. Trends and defects which might otherwise have made themselves felt only slowly and uncertainly sprang up overnight and demanded immediate solutions.

The colony's relations with its former master, China, have ever been the touchstone of its metamorphoses. In 1919 a fishwives' street brawl developed into an Annamite boycott of the Chinese. Its ineffectuality was due to the Chinese control of the economic situation, not to any lack of driving emotions on the part of the Annamites, for whom the boycott assumed almost national proportions. This negative form of nationalism was supplemented three years later by a very positive element from the same source—communism *à la Cantonaise*. Although Annamite wartime workers had been influenced by French communistic ideas, communism in its pure form has little appeal for a people so in love with the soil. Regionalism is another factor which has militated against its spread, but communism grafted on to post-War nationalism took root in Indo-China with amazing rapidity.

Tonkin and North Annam, by their historical development, economic setting, and proximity to China, are the regions naturally marked out for nationalism's finest flowering. Chinese culture is most deeply-rooted and self-conscious in the North. The long struggle of the Macs, Les, Nguyens, and Taysons has bred in the Tonkinese a contempt for their Southern compatriots. Hué was far away, and the viceroy in Tonkin did not enjoy his master's religious authority. These differences in outlook between the different Annamite countries have been aggravated by the varied administrative policies of the French. Nationalism, therefore, has taken a different form in each Annamite country: in Cochin-China it has become an electoral struggle in the worst demagogic taste: in Annam it is dynastic: and in Tonkin primarily economic and cultural. Unlike the Japanese Mikado the Occidentalized Emperor Bao Dai is not the focus of the national movement—he is regarded as too useless and expensive—except in Annam, where an artificial loyalty has been created among those Annamites dependent on Court patronage. The peasant's awed veneration for the sacred invisible Emperor has been largely dissipated by his prolonged residence in France, and by seeing him drive his own car daily out to the golf links or tennis courts.

The age-old, piecemeal patriotism of the masses still stops at the portals of their commune. A really national patriotism can only rise from the ashes of communal society and the communal gods.

The Scholar party of old irreconcilables continues to exist but not to flourish. The nationalists are the young men whose political adherence is Western in concept, shading all the way from constitutional monarchy to complete autonomy. But they are all working on the foundation of the old secret societies dear to the Oriental heart which existed under the Chinese and Annamite emperors and which continue to offer organized resistance to whatever government is in power. They are made up of magical, religious, and profane elements, attracting the credulous by their mysterious glamour, and affording those of independent and rebellious calibre the only outlet in a society of otherwise crushing rigidity and formalism. Circumstances either bring out their potentialities or force them into the background, but from time immemorial these secret organizations have been the mechanism by which all Annamite social and political movements have become effective. The Annamites were the cultural offspring of China in their contempt for foreigners. They lumped in an aggressive disdain cultured Khmers, amiable Laotians, and primitive Mois. For the Chinése "uncle" they feel an admiration mingled with hatred for past injuries and present competition. Towards the Hindu they feel the arrogance of the Aryan for coloured peoples. The masses are little affected by such considerations since they know nothing of the world beyond the village community, but the hardness of their lives makes them susceptible to any propaganda by which they have nothing to lose and everything to gain. Vinh, the greatest famine province, is ever the first to revolt. The contrast with the easy life of Europeans in the colony, and the birth of a new class consciousness among natives adds to the ferment of discontent. The old enemies—flood, famine, and the extortions of officials and usurers—have intensified these grievances by the higher cost of living.

The native intelligentsia have special complaints which supplement the more universal economic discontent: their ambitions have been frustrated. Their flirtations with higher education have been checked both in the colony and in France. The desire to learn of the West, as evidenced by the birth of native opinion, did not spring from disinterested motives. It was partly forced on them, coming from the Japanese-inspired ambition to beat the West at its own game, or to secure a position which would bring security and prestige for life. To be sure, there was an unanswerable contradiction in French policy. A native press and opinion were deliberately created and simultaneously stifled: traditional education was destroyed and its substitute inadequate in both quality and quantity. Naturalization was a requisite to professional promotion, but it was grudgingly given and it uprooted the native from his setting. The Annamites could not appreciate the complications of French colonial tradition. They felt that France took back with one hand what had been given with the other. Oriental pride is dangerous dynamite. A personal slight may make an Annamite into a revolutionary leader. Nguyen Thai Hoc, founder of the Annamite Nationalist Party, as a young man addressed numerous reform projects to the Governor General, who failed even to acknowledge their receipt. One is reminded of Madame Rolland.

The average Annamite who does not encounter these obstacles to his rise in the world has other grievances against the administration. There is, for instance, inequality of treatment before the law. The same crime committed by an Annamite and a Frenchman is given a totally disparate verdict. To begin with, there is not enough guarantee of justice for natives in the composition of the Courts. In recent years there has been a certain improvement in severity shown towards Europeans guilty of aggression towards natives, but a fundamentally unfair discrimination remains. The average Annamite complains of a lack of security. Though he cannot deny that peace is far better preserved than formerly, thefts and brigandage have not ceased. He wanted for many years, and has finally achieved, a new codification of the law, the abolition of debt imprisonment, access to the Bar, the regularization of concessions—all political liberties sanctioned by the Revolution of '89. There still remains, however, to have the régime of the *indigènat* and the Criminal Commission abolished—in both of which the interests of the colonizing power still triumph over abstract justice. The average native needs more protection from the extortions of native officials and usurers; more stability in the administration, both as regards policy and functionaries; and less red tape and formalities that consume time and money. The Annamite is already too prone to routine without having his slight bent towards initiative curtailed by incessant bureaucratic interference.

Military service is forced labour for the average native, who is always a civilian at heart. From two to four years of continuous service contrast with the intermittent three-month periods of the old Annamite government. Barracks routine differs unpleasantly from their family life, nor is the old custom retained of exempting soldiers' families from taxation. Natives show the greatest zeal in escaping this draft— about 5,000 recruits annually—and the village Notables are naturally anxious to palm off their worst elements. False identity papers, bribery, and desertions testify to its unpopularity. Well-to-do families can buy off their sons, but poor peasants have no recourse but to submit. Originally little was done to win the devotion of these unwilling recruits but with time indemnities and pensions were paid to the wounded and to bereaved families; leaves of absence, decorations, and promotions became more available. Annamites now form ninety-five per cent of the native army, and since the War are considered excellent military material. The necessity for saving French soldiers has benefited the status of the native soldiers. The French troops form one-third of the peace-time forces by the 1926 reform, and it is now possible for Anna-mites to become officers. Yenbay provoked another reform in a more careful selection and training of French officers. The communist policy of winning over the army is a trump card for those Annamites who ask for shorter service, higher pay, no foreign service, and rice fields for the families of drafted men.

Criticism of administrative policy does not confine itself to demanding redress from personal injustice and arbitrary decisions, but it extends among the intelligentsia to the state's public works programmes. Nationalist leaders point to those suitable and necessary public works which have been left undone and which would enhance French pres-tige and revenues enormously. Waste, the lack of foresight, and poorly selected undertakings have pointlessly dispersed the unconsulted tax-payers' money. The widening of an avenue in Hué caused the displace-ment of 6,000 tombs without indemnity to those whose religious beliefs had been violated and for whom there was no commensurate benefit. Waste has also characterized the numerous official "missions" which drain the budget. Taxpayers near starvation can hardly find it imperative to know that the Muong flute has six holes, whereas the Siamese has only two. Raynaud's visit cost Indo-China huge sums that could have been better expended fighting famine in North Annam. The Colonial Exposition of 1931 cost so many millions that the state never dared to publish the exact sum. Wanton extravagance rather than dishonesty has been the rule in Indo-China's expenditures—coloniza-tion's detractors to the contrary. There have been the monopolies contracts, and the usual government graft, but the functionary corps has maintained a higher standard in integrity than ability. The native complaint is essentially that public utility is not the yardstick of expenditures, and that the Indo-Chinese who are industrious and miserable must perforce support many purely French interests. When the colony sent money to succour the inundated regions of Southern France the gesture was not reciprocated for the devastated provinces of Nam Binh. It is a clear perversion of the colonization ideal when the benefits are unilateral and the colony must drain itself for a sovereign state that was not of its choosing.

In the Protectorate theory there is inherent the principle of a progressive native participation in the colony's government, but the protecting state is to judge what time is propitious to withdraw its guiding hand. When the French claim that the natives have neither the appropriate training or experience to direct their own destinies the Annamites complain that they have no chance of acquiring either. The education and civil liberties dispensed to the Annamites are but a caricature of their Occidental prototypes. Such native grievances and desires have been expressed in various forms, both active and literary, but never better than in the *Cahier des Voeux* presented to Varenne. In this connection it is interesting to note that the *Cahier* sent to the Minister of the Colonies in 1936 by 300 Cochin-Chinese embodies substantially the same resolutions as those presented to Varenne and Raynaud. Puerile violence is but one of the many obstacles in the way of understanding native opinion—if such a thing exists in Indo-China. One point shines clearly through the haze of uncertainty: the Annamites have definitely turned their backs on Chinese culture in favour of Western science. If France will not teach them they will go elsewhere to learn it.

In the new nationalism that has invaded Indo-China there are destructive forces which have not yet been conjured. To begin with, nationalism is confined to the Annamite countries which frankly would treat Khmers and Laotians, not to mention the primitive tribes, as subject peoples. Secondly, even Annamite nationalists cannot agree among themselves. The leaders have shown both a divergence in viewpoint and a mutual jealousy that has undermined their co-operation. They can unite in disliking their subjection to the French rule but they cannot come to any agreement on a constructive programme. The younger generation of nationalists, for example, dislike and are heartily disliked by the older generation, which feels that it has paid for the privileges which the younger men are enjoying without effort and without gratitude. Fundamentally there is a lack of public spirit in Annam which has reasonable historical explanations, but which cripples the whole movement. Mismanagement of funds has from the outset discredited nationalist parties. This, as well as prudent selfishness, may explain why the Annamites, who claim they would sacrifice everything for patriotic ideals, do not contribute voluntarily to the movement. The Annamite bourgeoisie is rich and selfish. Often it is wounded vanity that has pushed the Annamite into the nationalist party, and no great movement can be built upon such shifting emotional sand. Violence and dishonesty, which extends to the deliberate falsification of reports, have gone far towards alienating liberal sympathizers in France.

Not all the nationalist parties are revolutionary. The Tonkinese Party of Pham Quynh and the Constitutionalist Party of Bui Quang Chieu want reforms along democratic lines rather than a violent break with France. In 1925 a secret society called the Revolutionary Party of Young Annam (Tan-Viet-Cach-Manh-Bang) was founded in North Annam among the small bourgeoisie of nationalist sentiments. It never grew beyond the organizing stage before most of its members were absorbed into the communist party. The roots of this party went way back to a group called Phuc Viet, the Restoration of Annam, formed in the Poulo Condore penitentiary among the prisoners from the 1908 outbreaks. It was an old-time revolutionary group in the Chinese manner, linked to the exiled Pham Boi Chau, but it went quiescently underground when the Chieu conspiracy was betrayed to the government. In the post-War period it was revived through an alliance between the Siamese and Chinese revolutionaries, but it was more moderate and methodically organized than of yore. In fact it was too mild to please the revolutionary element, who leaned more and more to Cantonese communism.

The party, which took the name of Vietnam-Cach-Manh-Bang in 1926, thus contained two increasingly divergent elements—the nationalists and communists. The failure of Pham Quynh at about this time to win governmental approval of his moderate reform programme sent many of the neutral members into the revolutionary camp, and made the Cantonese influence predominate. The period which followed was one of preparation and organization: it was the era of strikes and manifestations. The leaders' mutual jealousy, as well as their failure to fuse the two opposing camps, proved fatal. When trouble broke out in Canton, in 1929, the Annamites felt generally that the Cantonese communists had deceived and exploited them. The leaders became discouraged, the party lost strength and influence, and finally died when the communists broke away at the end of 1929. The moderate elements hesitated to denounce their communist ex-colleagues lest they themselves became involved, but their erstwhile comrades did not hesitate to denounce them to the police, and with their arrest in 1930 the party came officially to an end.

The Nationalist Annamite Party (Viet Nam Quoc Dan Dong) is Tonkinese. In view of the regional feeling its origin made it impossible for this group to unite with the party in Annam. The more realistic temperament of the Tonkinese has made their revolutionary attempts more formidable, though it has never formed a large group numerically —only 1,500 members out of a population of eight millions. This party is the replica of the Canton Kuomintang, founded by Sun Yat-sen. In 1927 two brothers founded a publishing house in Hanoi, with the double aim of making money and of spreading revolutionary ideas. Youth characterized the members of this party: not one of them was over 30 years old. Many of the students who had been excluded from schools for their participation in the 1925–26 strikes formed excellent revolutionary material. From the outset this was a terrorist group. Propaganda was addressed to students, employees, and, above all, to the army. Women were also affiliated and thus given one of their first opportunities for self-expression. Foreign aid was solicited. In 1928 a group visited Siam to link forces with kindred organizations there. But this attempt was a conspicuous failure, not only there but in Southern China and Cambodia and the other Annamite countries as well. Finally in 1930 they successfully established relations with the Cantonese and Yunnanese groups.

In January, 1929, the party made a first unsuccessful attempt to kill Pasquier, and a month later succeeded in murdering Bazin, head of the Labour Recruiting Bureau. This took place on the eve of the Annamite New Year, so the revolver shots were not heard above the explosion of firecrackers. A letter was pinned to Bazin's body denouncing in violent terms the crimes which had led to his execution. It was subsequently in making arrests that the police for the first time got their clue to this party's existence. They were astonished to learn that fifty per cent of its members were in government service, and that its leader, who escaped arrest, was a former school teacher whose record was not of the most spotless. The party, however, survived largely intact, but in a reorganized form. Members had been too well known to each other, and so, in order to prevent betrayals identity henceforth was to be kept strictly secret. Traitors were executed with dramatic flourishes for its effect upon members and upon the country at large. A few accidents in the preparation of arms and ammunition in December, 1929, led the police to discover 700 bombs. More important was the party's method of filling its depleted treasury by acts of banditry which also helped the police in tracking them down. The police got so hot on their trail that the party decided prematurely to launch their programme from the preparatory state to that of action. Their efforts were concentrated upon the troops which garrisoned Yenbay, because this post controlled the Red River valley, and simultaneously action could be concerted with the Yunnanese party.

On the morning of February 10, 1930, a dispatch from Hanoi startled the French public with the news that the native soldiers had mutinied at Yenbay the night before and had killed some of their French officers. A warning had been received but it was disregarded. The murders were particularly brutal, but the rebels were either frightened by the morning light or by the resistance offered them, for at dawn they returned to their barracks in good order. The days that followed were marked by violent outbreaks all over the colony. At Hanoi bombs were thrown at the Commissariat; a policeman on the Pont Doumer was wounded; the sub-prefect of Vinhbao was assassinated. Simultaneously in widely separated regions in the three Annamite countries long lines of insurgents marched to the Resident's home to present their grievances. Most of these manifestants were unarmed, and they marched in impressive silence. Unfortunately the Residents and militia became nervous, and after giving repeated orders and warnings to disperse, they opened fire on the crowd. At about the same time 700 match workers at Benthuy attempted to burn down their factory, and this could not be attributed to economic grievances as they had just received a rise in wages. The simultaneousness of these manifestations betrayed a unity of direction. Thousands of peasants participated in these movements, which spread all through the Annamite countries.

Some of the party leaders tracked by the police took refuge in the Tonkinese village of Coam, where they tortured the local officials and sought to rally their forces. An aeroplane attack finally succeeded not only in dislodging them but in killing 200 of the innocent villagers. As in old Annam the tearing down of Coam's bamboo barricade was the official consummation of its disgrace. A little later the party leader, Le Huu Canh, and remnants of his followers were arrested in the midst of new preparations to kill Pasquier. The perennial need for money, and the use of blackmail to get it, had given them away to the police. Wholesale arrests followed throughout 1930–31. In Yunnan a number of attempts were made to reconstruct the party, but they failed through lack of leaders. In 1933 the party died as an organized group: the only influence that has survived is indirect.

Louis Roubaud, the journalist sent by the *Petit Parisien* to investigate the situation, talked with the imprisoned leaders of this party. He found that they had concerned themselves almost exclusively with Yenbay, under the delusion that that uprising would have been the fuse to set off the whole country. There was a conspicuous absence of organizing ability. The revolutionary movement showed itself capable of isolated acts of terrorism and manifestations, but it was weak in arousing the masses because its programme and methods were too much the work of the intelligentsia. The pacific mass demonstrations were the only activities of which the Moscow communists approved, for they capitalized the Oriental force of inertia and proved to European imperialists their dependence upon native labour.

In 1931, when the Communist Party was at its height, six years after its birth in Indo-China, it numbered 1,500 members with 100,000 affiliated peasants. Nguyen-Ai-Quoc was its founder, mentor, and saviour. Recognizing the Annamites' love of property and their patriarchal family system, as well as the numerical and intellectual weakness of the proletariat, he planned first to assure Annam's independence under a democratic bourgeois régime and then, by a second step, to integrate it into the Soviet Union.

Nguyen-Ai-Quoc, born in 1892 in a province of Annam where the revolutionary tradition was strong, from his earliest childhood resented the servility of the mandarinate—of which his father was a member—to the French. He left home at the age of seventeen and worked his way around the world on a French ship. In Paris he practised different trades, lived an austere life, bought books with his savings, and affiliated himself with the French communists. Compassion for his oppressed compatriots stirred his imagination, and was the dynamic ideal lodged in a frail body. At the end of the War, he drew up a list of Annamite desiderata and sent it to the Versailles treaty-makers. He founded in Paris the Intercolonial Union of Coloured Peoples. In 1920 he attended the Communist Congress at Tours, where he cast his vote in favour of the Third Internationale. He founded a newspaper in 1922 in which to denounce the abuses of French imperialism. His work harmonized with the new trend in Bolshevik policy which, after 1923, determined to attack European countries through their colonies and to establish an *entente* with Sun Yat-sen. That same year Nguyen-Ai-Quoc went to Moscow where he remained for some time studying revolutionary methods and associating with Soviet leaders who esteemed him for his remarkable intelligence. When thoroughly prepared he was sent to Canton, where he founded a branch of the League for Oppressed People, and—much more important—the Association of Revolutionary Annamite Youth: the first communist cell for Annamites in China. While working with Borodine in the adjacent province of Kwang Tung, Nguyen-Ai-Quoc was feverishly active in writing and circulating violently anti-colonial tracts in Indo-China and France.

Canton had long been the Mecca of Indo-China's communists. Every year on June 19 homage is rendered there to the Tonkinese student who, in 1934, threw a bomb at Governor Merlin. His tomb has become a pilgrimage shrine for Annamite youth, always under the influence of the dead, who have built up the customary legend around the bones of their patriot-hero. More constructive was the instruction offered to young Annamites at the politico-military school of Whampoa, founded at Canton by Borodine to prepare leaders for the world communist revolution. Russian, Chinese, and Annamite professors offered both theoretical and practical education in propaganda and revolutionary technique. The orientation Nguyen-Ai-Quoc gave to its programme was nationalistic rather than communistic, which he regarded as a subsequent stage. The Whampoa School formally expressed the aspirations of the nationalist-communist group: a reduction of the fiscal burden, especially in years of bad harvest; suppression of extra-legal jurisdiction; division of the alluvial lands and abandoned rice-fields among the neighbouring peasants; and no recruiting of soldiers and coolies for foreign service.

In 1927, when the outlook for Cantonese communism was brightest, the attack directed against it by the Right Wing of the Kuomintang forced Borodine and Nguyen-Ai-Quoc to seek refuge in Russia. Here the latter was officially given the mission of founding Indo-Chinese communism. His prospects were brightened almost at once by the *entente* which his followers in Canton had managed to reach with the new authorities there, on condition that they would confine their activities to attacking French imperialism. By that time 250 Annamites had received revolutionary training abroad, and the great majority of them had returned to the colony, where they had garnered about 1,000 partisans. Each country had its committee which propagandized the

working class, but in the North the movement found supporters principally among the intelligentsia. All the key positions were held by men
trained in Canton.

On May 1, 1929, when the annual meeting of the Indo-Chinese
communists took place in Hongkong, the three delegates from Tonkin
electrified the congress by proposing reforms along purer Marxist-
Lenin lines, and away from the Annamite nationalistic trend. The
conservative element, called bourgeois by the Marxists, broke away in
fright and formed their own party, which now made the third communist
group in Indo-China. Each flirted with the Third Internationale for
recognition, but Moscow showed great reluctance to select any one of
them for official investiture, and urged Nguyen-Ai-Quoc to reunite the
groups, whose mutual denunciations were purely destructive. All were
agreed that he was the only possible leader, so a delegation was sent to
him in Siam, where he was working on revolutionary propaganda. In
spite of his bad health he accepted the task and transferred the party's
headquarters from Bangkok to Haiphong and thence to Saigon. Though
Moscow gave its blessing and a monthly subsidy of 5,000 francs to the
now united party, Nguyen-Ai-Quoc cannily held in his own hands the
key to Russian support. This arrangement had the advantage of secrecy,
but the drawback of isolating the party both financially and morally
after its leader's arrest. This took place at Hongkong on June 6, 1931,
through the co-operation of the British police. He was cared for in
prison with a devotion that can only be attributed to the fear that his
death—for he was very sick with tuberculosis—would give him the
crowning glory of martyrdom.

Nguyen-Ai-Quoc, however, had had time to give his party an organization along Muscovite lines of village cells and town and cantonal
sections which sent delegates to the directing central committee.
Many groups were worked upon—factory hands, functionaries, peasants, and students of both sexes. This man, mystic and ascetic that he
was, not only was a remarkable organizer but he could raise money
from the wary and miserable Annamites. His policy of anonymity of
leadership and discipline has been strictly maintained: in some cells
the romantic oath in blood was still in vogue. Russia showed its continued interest in her willingness to educate promising Annamite material, and about one hundred Annamites have taken advantage of this
opportunity. Moscow's influence has been decidedly one of restraint.
It has formally disapproved of terrorism in Indo-China, and preferred
tracts, strikes, and meetings as methods of fostering the strength of the

young party. Nationalism is still to be the means of arriving at communism, and their prevalent misery exploited as a method of arousing the
masses.

The brutality of the French suppression of the communist movement
has been severely criticized both in the colony and in France. The
government claimed as justification that the Red Terror, already guilty
of torturing its enemies, would have unleashed an orgy of crime and
cruelty only possible among Orientals. In assembling the evidence of
communist brutality in 1930–31 the Indo-Chinese police stated that
the slightest success would have had an incalculable effect upon the
masses, who believe that Heaven thus selects one side for approval,
and upon possible foreign supporters. So-called preventive measures
have always the disadvantage of depending for their justification upon
hypothesis, which can be used by both sides with equal conviction.
Certainly the evidence brought forward at the grotesque trial of the
Foreign Legionnaires was damaging to the administration, and to
Robin in particular, who had encouraged their brutality. If, as the light
penalty they were given indicated, it was unjust to punish soldiers who
were only carrying out orders, it was criminally negligent to have
simultaneously exonerated those in high positions who were responsible.

Acting on the assumption that communism was not a mass movement the police have concentrated on the arrest of its leaders. The
party's secret organization here proved effective. Not only were incrimi-
nating documents unavailable but native official co-operation, through
collusion or fear, as well as proximity to the frontiers, complicated the
search. Despite their numerical inadequacy the Indo-Chinese police
did a remarkable work. A country larger than France with over twenty
million inhabitants, most of whom were unidentifiable, is policed by
only 341 French agents. The rapidity with which they had to act—and
most of the 1930 plots were aired in time—inevitably resulted in much
injustice. Though it was natives who applied the time-honoured methods
of the Annamite government for producing evidence the French public
was horrified by this use of torture, with the knowledge, if not the
actual participation, of French officials. The Third Degree, fashionable
among Occidental police, may be no better, but it is less obviously
brutal. Andrée Viollis's *Indochine SOS*, though in many ways uninformed, reproduced with photographic honesty what she saw of the
terrible prison conditions, the arbitrary injustice, and wholesale arrests
of the ignorant and innocent. The whole colony was honeycombed
with spies, and denunciations became a profitable duty. It is hard to

get at the exact figures since both sides obviously exaggerate. The communists claim that for the murder of six French soldiers two years of terror spread over twenty million people. Thousands were killed and still more thousands languish in prison. Official figures total the executions at less than a score, and state that subsequent measures of clemency have virtually emptied the prisons. The present Minister of the Colonies, Moutet, in 1936 examined the cases of 1,871 political prisoners and 68·25 per cent were granted commutations of sentence. The two penitentiaries of the colony enjoy a sinister reputation because of the frightful lack of hygiene and care. Thirty of the 200 political prisoners sent to Son La prison in February, 1933, died within less than a year.

Though many communist leaders escaped abroad, calm was restored by 1932. That same year an attempt to reconstitute the party failed, as it did again some months later. The most recent tracts which have been found show a slight change in attitude. They advocate less violence because in the past it has facilitated police investigations. They are now more prudent; both from the viewpoint of self-preservation and the desire to establish connections with Moscow, which has consistently disapproved of their violence. The Third Internationale is, for its part, still interested in Indo-China, as evidenced by statements of the leaders in July, 1935. Propaganda is being directed by Moscow's *Bureau d'Orient*, whose headquarters are at Longtcheou, near the Tonkin frontier. Arrests have been made in the Cao-Bang region during 1935–6, and it is known that cells are re-forming in the North. It is probably only a question of time before a new attempt will be made, though there has also been a marked liberalism in French policy and the depression has complicated the whole problem.

Ineffective organization, mismanagement of party funds, mutual jealousy on the part of leaders, who are perennially tending to split off and form new groups of their own, are minor and transient obstacles compared with the important communist-nationalist issue. Moscow and the Annamite extremists are unwilling to sanction any form of bourgeois-nationalist government, even provisionally, whereas the mass of the Annamites are stirred to patriotism only by appeals couched in terms of ownership of the soil.

Nationalism is undeniably the Occident's gift to Indo-China. It is the sole creative indigenous movement to which contact with a Western nation has given birth. Without the leaven of nationalism the Annamites reaction to the French conquest might have degenerated into a cult of the past. France has welded five disparate countries into a political and economic unit which would never have been achieved independently. Whether or not Annamite nationalism could be so expanded and modified as to take in incipient Laotian and Cambodian national consciousness is problematical, and at present seems very unlikely. The Annamites have caught fire from the West politically and economically, far more than they have culturally.

It is idle speculation to debate whether or not the Annamites were better off spiritually before the French conquest. Sooner or later they would have been forcibly drawn into the modern world, and in the sense that it was inevitable, French colonization is beyond good and evil. When and if Indo-China emerges as a real nation, it will bear upon it the imprint of French culture—not in the pure form imagined by the assimilationists—but in a hybrid version, whose modifications were made by its transplantation to an exotic setting. French institutions themselves have not been sufficiently affected by contact with Annamite culture to change, except in a subtle evolution of viewpoint on the part of colonials resident in the colony. Save in the economic sphere the balance sheet of French Indo-China up to now has registered on both sides more destructive than constructive change.

BIBLIOGRAPHY

ABADIE, M. *Les Races du Haut-Tonkin* (Paris, 1924).

ABEL DES MICHELS (trad.). *Les Annales Impériales de l'Annam* (Paris, 1889).

ABEL, M. H. *Solution Pratique de la Question de Cochinchine* (Paris, 1864).

Académie des Sciences Coloniales: *Compte Rendu* (Paris, 1922, to date).

    Annales (Paris, 1925, to date).

Affaires de Chine et du Tonkin, 1884–85 (Paris, 1885).

L'Affaire du Tonkin: Histoire Diplomatique par un Diplomat (1882–85) (Paris, 1885).

Les Agriculteurs Tonkinois à M. le Ministre des Colonies Raynaud (Hanoi, 1931).

AJALBERT, J. *Les Destinées de l'Indochine* (Paris, 1909).

    L'Indochine par les Français (Paris, 1931).

    L'Indochine en Péril (Paris, 1906).

    Les Nuages sur l'Indochine (Paris, 1912).

    Raffin Su-Su (Paris, 1930).

    Sao Van Di (Paris, 1934).

ALBERTI, J. B. *L'Indochine d'Autrefois et d'Aujourd'hui* (Paris, 1934).

D'ALLENJOYE, C. *Un Apôtre Français au Tonkin: Mgr. Puginier* (Paris, 1896).

ANDRÉ-CUEL, G. *Jonque Immobile* (Paris, 1926).

Anecdotes Chinoises, Japonoises, Siamoises, Tonquinoises (Paris, 1774).

ANGOULVANT, G. *Etapes Asiatiques* (Paris, 1930).

Les Annales Politiques et Littéraires: Numéro Spécial, *L'Indochine Française*, Janvier, 1928.

ANTONINI, P. *L'Annam, Le Tonkin, et l'Intervention de la France en Extrême Orient* (Paris, 1890).

Appel à la Société des Nations pour le Droit du Peuple Annamite à disposer de lui-même (Paris, 1926).

ARCHIMBAUD, L. *L'Enseignement Indigène en Indo-Chine* (*Revue du Pacifique*, 15 janvier, 1932).

ARMENGAUD, CAPT. *Lang-son* (Paris, 1901).

Assemblée Nationale: *Compte Rendu des Séances du Sénat et de la Chambre des Députés et les Documents Parlementaires.*

AURILLAC, H. *Cochinchine* (Paris, 1870).

AYMONIER, E. *Le Cambodge*, 3 vols. (Paris, 1900).

    La Langue Française et l'Enseignement en Indochine (Paris, 1890).

    Notice sur le Cambodge (Paris, 1875).

BAILLE, F. *Souvenirs d'Annam* (1886–90), (Paris, 1890).

BARBANNEAU, M. *Etude sur l'Organisation Judiciaire en l'Indochine* (Paris, 1906).

BARBIÉ DU BOCAGE, M. V-A. *Bibliographie Annamite* (Paris, 1867).

BARRÉ, LÉON. *De L'Influence Française au Royaume des Khmers* (*Annales de la Société d'Emulation des Vosges*, 1902).

DE LA BARRIÈRE, LÉOPOLD PALLU. *L'Expédition de Cochinchine en 1861* (Paris, 1888).

BARTHÉLEMY, MARQUIS DE. *Au Pays Moi* (Paris, 1904).
 En Indo-Chine (1894–95), (Paris, 1899).
 En Indo-Chine (1896–97), (Paris, 1901).
 Mon Vieil Annam; Ses Hommes (Paris, 1927).
     Ses Bêtes (Paris, 1930).
BAUDESSON, COMM. *Au Pays des Superstitions et des Rites* (Paris, 1932).
BAUDOIN, M. J. *Le Cambodge Pendant et Après la Grande Guerre* (Pnom-Penh, 1927).
BAUDRAIS, G. *Le Politique Coloniale Française en Indochine* (Paris, 1920).
BEAU, P. *Situation de l'Indochine* (1902–07), (Saigon, 1908).
BÉNARD, CH. *Au Service de l'Indochine* (Paris, 1931).
BENIGNE, PÈRE. *Vingt Ans en Annam* (Paris, 1884).
BERJOAN, A. *Le Siam et les Accords Franco-Siamois* (Paris, 1927).
BERNANOSE, M. *Les Arts Décoratifs au Tonkin* (Paris, 1922).
BERNARD, F. *L'Indochine: Erreurs et Dangers* (Paris, 1901).
BERNARD, P. *Le Problème Economique Indochinois* (Paris, 1934).
BILLOTEY, P. *L'Indochine en Zigzags* (Paris, 1929).
 Sao-Kéo ou le Bonheur Immobile (Paris, 1930).
BLANCHET, A. *Nicole et Ramsès* (Paris, 1919).
BLAQUIÈRE, H. *Le Sphinx Indochinois* (1927–30) (Saigon, 1930).
BOISSIÈRE, J. *Fumeurs d'Opium* (Paris, 1909).
 Propos d'un Intoxiqué (Paris, 1908).
BONNAFONT, L. *Trente Ans de Tonkin* (Paris, 1923).
 Les Ressources du Tonkin (Hanoi, 1910).
 Notes d'un Tonkinois (Hanoi, 1907).
BONNETAIN, P. *L'Extrême Orient* (Paris, 1887).
 L'Opium (Paris, 1909).
 Au Tonkin (Paris, 1887).
BORIE, J. *Le Métayage et la Colonisation Agricole au Tonkin* (Paris, 1906).
BOUDET, P. ET BOURGEOIS, R. *Bibliographie de L'Indochine Française.*
 Vol. I. 1913–26 (Hanoi, 1929).
 Vol. II. 1927–29 (Hanoi, 1932).
 Vol. III. 1930 (Hanoi, 1933).
BOUDET, P., ET MASON, A. *Iconographie Historique de l'Indochine Française* (Paris, 1931).
BOUDILLON, A. *Le Régime de la Propriété Foncière en Indochine* (Paris, 1915).
 La Réforme du Régime de la Propriété Foncière en Indochine (Hanoi, 1927).
BOUILLEVAUX, M. C-E. *Voyage dans l'Indochine* (Paris, 1858).
BOUINAIS, A., ET PAULUS, A. *La France en Indo-Chine* (Paris, 1892).
 L'Indochine Contemporaine (Paris, 1885).
 La Cochinchine Contemporaine (Paris, 1884).
LE BOULANGER, P. *Histoire du Laos Français* (Paris, 1930).
BOULÉ, E. *La Rénovation des Ecoles de Pagodes au Laos* (*Bulletin Général de l'Instruction Publique*, 1933).
BOURDE, P. *De Paris au Tonkin* (Paris, 1885).
BOUVIER, R. *La Crise en Indo-Chine* (Marseille, 1933).
 Thi Cau (Paris, 1932).

496

BIBLIOGRAPHY

BRAEMER, P. *Dix Années de Recherches Agricoles au Tonkin* (Hanoi, 1932).

BRENIER, H. *Les Ressources de l'Indochine* (Melun, 1917).

Essai d'Atlas Statistique de l'Indochine Française (Hanoi, 1914).

BRIEUX, E. *Voyage aux Indes et en Indochine* (Paris, 1926).

BRIFFAUT, C. *La Cité Annamite.* 3 vols. (Paris, 1909–12).

BUI QUANG CHIEU. *France d'Asie* (Toulouse, 1925).

BUI THANH VAN. *La Tour du Monde par un Annamite* (Hué, 1929).

BUI TUONG CHIEU. *La Polygamie dans le Droit Annamite* (Paris, 1933).

CABATON, A. *L'Indochine* (Paris, 1932).

Cahier des Voeux Annamites (Saigon, 1925).

DU CAILLAUD, F. R. *Histoire de l'Intervention Française au Tong-King de 1872 à 1874* (Paris, 1880).

Campagnes Glorieuses du Règne de Napoleon III (Paris, 1863).

CARLOTTI, A-L. *De l'Application faite en Cochinchine du Principe de la Séparation des Autorités Administratives et Judiciaires* (Paris, 1903).

CARNÉ, L. DE. *Voyage en Indo-Chine* (Paris, 1872).

CARPEAUX, L. *Chasse aux Pirates* (Paris, 1913).

CASSON, P. *Etude sur la Situation Militaire de l'Indochine* (Paris, 1906).

CASTEX, R. *Jaunes contre Blancs* (Paris, 1905).

CENDRIEUX, J. *François Phuoc, Métis* (Paris, 1929).

CHAIGNEAU, M. D. *Souvenirs de Hué* (Paris, 1867).

CHAILLEY-BERT, J. *Paul Bert au Tonkin* (Paris, 1887).

La Colonisation de l'Indochine (Paris, 1892).

L'Education et les Colonies (Paris, 1898).

CHAUTEMPS, M. *Le Vagabondage en Pays Annamite* (Paris, 1908).

CHIVAS-BARON, MME. C. *Confidences de Métisse* (Paris, 1927).

Folie Exotique (Paris, 1924).

La Simple Histoire des Gaudraix (Paris, 1923).

CLAVEL, DR. *L'Assistance Médicale Indigène en Indo-Chine* (Paris, 1908).

COCHINCHINE FRANÇAISE: *Excursions et Reconnaissances,* 25 vols. (Saigon, 1886).

COLAS, R. *Les Relations Commerciales entre la France et l'Indochine* (Paris, 1933).

Conférences Publiques sur L'Indochine, faites à l'Ecole Coloniale (Paris, 1904–14).

Congrès Colonial National, 1889–90: *Recueil des Délibérations,* Compte Rendu en Trois Volumes (1890).

Congrès International de Sociologie Coloniale: *Rapports et Procès-Verbaux,* 2 vols. (Paris, 1900).

Congrès Colonial de Marseille: *Compte Rendu et Rapports,* 2 vols. (1906).

Conseil de Gouvernement: *Discours des Gouverneurs-Généraux* (Hanoi, 1911–13; 1922–28).

Conseil de Gouvernement: *Rapports* (Hanoi, 1923–29).

CORDIER, G. *Littérature Annamite* (Hanoi, 1914).

CORDIER, H. *Bibliotheca Indosinica,* 4 vols. (Hanoi, 1912–15).

La Reprise des Relations de la France avec l'Annam sous la Restoration (Leide, 1903).

A Narrative of the Recent Events in Tongking (Shanghai, 1875).

497

COULET, G. *L'Organisation Matérielle du Théatre Populaire chez les Annamites* (Saigon, 1926).
　Les Sociétés Secrètes en Terre d'Annam (Saigon, 1926).
COUSSET, A., ET RUEL, H. *Douze Mois chez les Sauvages du Laos* (Paris, 1898).
CROUZET, P. *Education in the French Colonies* (Yearbook of the International Institute of Teachers College for 1931).
CULTRU, P. *Histoire de la Cochinchine Française* (Paris, 1910).
CUNNINGHAM, A. *Les Français au Tonkin et dans la Chine Méridionale* (Hanoi, 1903).
CURY, L. *La Société Annamite* (Paris, 1910).
DAGUERCHES, H. *Le Kilomètre 83* (Paris, 1913).
DANGUY, H. *Le Nouveau Visage de la Cochinchine* (Saigon, 1929).
DARRAS, M. *Le Nouveau Code Civil du Tonkin* (Paris, 1934).
DARTIGUENAVE, H. *L'Evolution Indigène en Indochine* (Cantho, 1924).
DAUSSE, M. *La Civilisation Annamite et le Protectorat Français* (Bordeaux,1919).
DECAUX, F. *Les Pouvoirs du Gouverneur Général de l'Indochine* (Lille, 1919).
DELAHAYE, V. *La Plaine des Joncs* (Rennes, 1928).
DELAMARRE, E. *L'Emigration et l'Immigration Ouvrière en Indochine* (Hanoi, 1931).
DENNERY, E. *Foules d'Asie* (Paris, 1930).
DESCHAMPS, R. *La Main d'Œuvre en Indochine* (Poitiers, 1908).
DETAY, A. *Les Sociétés Commerciales Indigènes en Indochine* (Paris, 1932).
DEVILAR, C. *Comment on perd une Colonie* (Paris, 1927).
DIGUET, E. *Les Annamites* (Paris, 1906).
DOAN VINH THUAN. *La France d'Asie et son Avenir* (Paris, 1909).
DORGELÈS, R. *Sur la Route Mandarine* (Paris, 1929).
DORSENNE, J. *Faudra-t-il Evacuer l'Indochine?* (Paris, 1932).
DOUDART DE LAGRÉE. *Lettres d'un Précurseur* (Paris, 1886).
DOUMER, P. *L'Indochine Française* (Paris, 1930).
　Situation de l'Indo-Chine (1897–1901), Hanoi, 1902).
DOUTRE, A. *Politique Indigène en Indochine* (Paris, 1907).
DREVET, C. *Les Annamites Chez Eux* (Paris, 1928).
DUBREUIL, R. *De la Condition des Chinois et de leur Rôle Economique en Indochine* (Bar-sur-Seine, 1910).
DUFRESNE, M. *Binh-Yen* (Hanoi, 1918).
DUMAREST, A. *La Formation des Classes Sociales en Pays Annamites* (Lyon, 1935).
DUMOUTIER, G. *Les Chants et les Traditions Populaires Annamites* (Paris, 1890).
　Essais sur les Tonkinois (Hanoi, 1908).
　Les Symboles, les Emblèmes et les Accessoires du Culte chez les Annamites (Paris, 1891).
DUONG VAN GAO. *L'Indochine pendant la Guerre de 1914–18* (Paris, 1925).
DUPRÉ, J. *De l'Assimilation des Indigènes aux Nationaux* (Montpellier, 1913).
DUPUIS, J. *Les Origines de la Question du Tonkin* (Paris, 1896).
　L'Ouverture du Fleuve Rouge (Paris, 1879).
　Le Tonkin de 1872 à 1886 (Paris, 1910).
　Le Tonkin et l'Intervention Française (Paris, 1898).

BIBLIOGRAPHY

DURTAIN, L. *Dieux Blancs, Hommes Jaunes* (Paris, 1930).

DUTREB, M. *L'Amiral Dupré et la Conquête du Tonkin* (Paris, 1924).

ESSARTS, LANGLOIS DES. *Etude sur la Main d'Œuvre en Indochine* (Paris, 1907).

Exposition Coloniale Nationale de Marseille: *Comte Rendu et Rapports*, 2 vols. (Marseille, 1922).

FAMIN, COMM. P. *Au Tonkin et sur la Frontière du Kwang-si* (Paris, 1895).

FARRÈRE, CLAUDE. *Les Civilisés* (Paris, 1901).

FERRY, J. *Le Tonkin et la Mère-Patrie* (Paris, 1890).

FERRY, R. *Le Régime Douanier de l'Indo-Chine* (Paris, 1912).

LE FÈVRE, G. *Démolisseurs et Batisseurs* (Paris, 1927).

    L'Epopée du Caoutchouc (Paris, 1927).

FINOT, L. *Les Etudes Indochinoises* (Paris, 1908).

    Sur Quelques Traditions Indochinoises (Paris, 1911).

FONTAINE, A. R. *Essai de Politique Indigène en Indochine* (Paris, 1926).

FOURNIER, C. *Homme Jaune et Femme Blanche* (Paris, 1931).

La Fraternité Tonkinoise: Du Rôle des Missions Catholiques en Indochine (Hanoi, 1900).

GALEMBERT, J. *Les Administrations et les Services Publics Indochinois* (Hanoi 1924).

GALLIÉNI, GENERAL. *Trois Colonnes au Tonkin* (Paris, 1899).

GARNIER, F. *Voyage d'Exploration en Indochine*, 2 vols. (Paris, 1873).

GARROS, G. *Forceries Humaines: L'Indochine Litigieuse* (Paris, 1926).

GIRAN, P. *Psychologie du Peuple Annamite* (Paris, 1904).

    De l'Education des Races (Paris, 1913).

    Magie et Réligion Annamites (Paris, 1912).

GIRAULT, A. *Principes de Colonisation et de Législation Coloniale* (Paris, 1895).

GOURDON, H. *L'Indochine* (Paris, 1931).

GOUROU, P. *Le Tonkin* (Hanoi, 1931).

GRALL, DR. C. *Hygiène Coloniale Appliquée* (Paris, 1908).

GREVERATH, A. *L'Agriculture en Indo-Chine* (Paris, 1900).

GROSLIER, G. *La Reprise des Arts Khmers* (*Revue de Paris*, 15 nov., 1925).

    Le Retour à l'Argile (Paris, 1929).

    La Route du Plus Fort (Paris, 1925).

    Recherches sur les Cambodgiens (Paris, 1921).

HENRY, YVES. *Economie Agricole de l'Indochine* (Hanoi, 1932).

HESS, J. *L'Affaire Iukanthor* (Paris, 1900).

HUYNH XUAN CANH. *Le Crédit Indochinois* (Paris, 1929).

Indochine Française: Exposition Coloniale Internationale, Paris, 1931.

    L'Organisation de la Justice en Indochine (Hanoi, 1930).

    Les Services Militaires en Indochine (Hanoi, 1931).

    Administration des Douanes et des Régies en Indochine (Hanoi, 1930).

    Inspection Générale des Mines et de l'Industrie (Hanoi, 1930).

    Documents Officiels (Paris, 1931).

    L'Annam (Hanoi, 1931).

    La Cochinchine (Hanoi, 1931).

    Le Tonkin (Hanoi, 1931).

    Le Laos (Hanoi, 1931).

Indochine Française (*continued*):
> *Le Cambodge* (Hanoi, 1931).
> *Le Service de l'Instruction Publique en Indochine en* 1930 (Hanoi, 1930).
> *Le Centre de Formation Professionelle de Hué* (Hanoi, 1931).
> *L'Industrie Minérale en Indochine* (Hanoi, 1931).

Institut Colonial International: *Compte Rendu* (Bruxelles, 1895).

JACNAL JEAN, *Mémoires de S. E. Huynh Condit Dan Tuong* (Hanoi, 1926).

JAMMES, H-L. *Au Pays Annamite* (Paris, 1898).
> *Souvenirs du Pays d'Annam* (Paris, 1900).

JEANSELME, E. *Etude sur la Lèpre dans la Péninsule Indochinoise* (Paris, 1900).

JOLEAUD-BARRAL. *La Colonisation Française en Annam et au Tonkin* (Paris, 1899).

JUNG, E. *Histoire d'un Colon* (Paris, 1903).
> *La Vérité sur l'Indochine* (Paris, 1902).
> *La Vie Européenne au Tonkin* (Paris, 1901).

La Mission Lyonnaise d'Exploration Commerciale en Chine (Lyon, 1898).

DE LANESSAN, L. *L'Indochine Française* (Paris, 1889).
> *Les Missions et leur Protectorat* (Paris, 1907).
> *La Colonisation Française en Indo-Chine* (Paris, 1895).

LANGLET, E. *Le Peuple Annamite* (Paris, 1913).

LAUNAY, A. *Histoire de la Mission de Cochinchine* (1658–1823) (Paris, 1923).
> *Mgr. Retord et le Tonkin Catholique* (Paris, 1919).

LE BRETON, H. *Le Budget et l'Instruction Publique en Indochine* (Hué, 1932).
> *Le Problème Scolaire au Pays d'Annam* (Hué, 1932).

LEBEL, G. *Deux Aspects de l'Evolution du Protectorat Français en Annam-Tonkin* (Paris, 1932).

LEBEL, R. *Histoire de la Littérature Coloniale en France* (Paris, 1931).

LECHESNE, P. *Indo-Chine* (Paris, 1907).

LECLÈRE, A. *Recherches sur la Législation Criminelle et la Procédure des Cambodgiens* (Paris, 1894).
> *Les Livres Sacrés du Cambodge* (Paris, 1906).
> *Contes Laotiennes et Contes Cambodgiennes* (Paris, 1903).
> *De la Démoralisation des Conquis par les Conquérants et des Conquérants par les Conquis* (Paris, 1902).

LECLERC, J. *De l'Evolution et du Developpement des Institutions Annamites et Cambodgiennes sous l'Influence Française* (Rennes, 1923).

LEFÈVRE-PORTALIS, P. *Chansons et Fêtes du Laos* (Paris, 1896).

LEHAULT, P. *La France et L'Angleterre en Asie*, vol. I (Paris, 1892).

LEJEUNE, C. *Régime de la Propriété Foncière en Pays Annamite* (Paris, 1904).

LEMIRE, C. *Cochinchine Française* (Paris, 1884).
> *Les Cinq Pays de l'Indochine Française* (Angers, 1899).
> *Les Codes Comparés de l'Annam, du Tonkin et du Laos* (*Mémoires de l'Académie d'Arras*, 1912).

LEUBA, J. *L'Aile de Feu* (Paris, 1920).
> *Frick en Exil* (Paris, 1923).
> *La Brève Lumière* (Paris, 1930).

LE VAN DINH. *Le Culte des Ancêtres en Droit Annamite* (Paris, 1934).

LE VAN KIM. *Les Travaux Publics en Indochine* (Paris, 1926).

LÉVI, SYLVAIN (ed.). *Indochine*, 2 vols. (Paris, 1931).

LOGE MAÇONNIQUE: La Fraternité Tonkinoise. *Nos Vues et Notre Action en Matière de Politique Indigène* (Hanoi, 1930).

LOIR, M. *L'Escadre de l'Amiral Courbet* (Paris, 1894).

LORION, DR. L. *Criminalité et Médicine Judiciaire en Cochinchine* (Lyon, 1887).

LURO, E. *Le Pays d'Annam* (Paris, 1878).

  Cours d'Administration Annamite (Saigon, 1875).

LY BINH HUE. *Le Régime des Concessions Domaniales en Indochine* (Paris, 1931).

LYAUTEY, H. *Lettres du Tonkin et de Madagascar* (Paris, 1921).

MAITRE, H. *Les Régions Moi du Sud Indo-Chinois* (Paris, 1909).

MALLERET, L. *L'Exotisme Indochinois dans la Littérature Française depuis 1860* (Paris, 1934).

DE MAROLLES, VICE-AMIRAL. *La Dernière Campagne du Commandant Rivière* (Paris, 1932).

MARQUET, J. *La Jaune et le Blanc* (Paris, 1927).

  Lettres d'Annamite (Hanoi, 1929).

  De la Rizière à la Montagne (Paris, 1928).

  Du Village à la Cité (Paris, 1931?).

MARTINET, J. *Une Fleuve de Sang* (Paris, 1931).

MASPÉRO, G. *Un Empire Colonial Français: l'Indochine*, 2 vols. (Paris, 1929).

MASSON, A. *Hanoi Pendant la Période Héroique* (Paris, 1929).

MATHIEU, E. *Evolution Intellectuelle et Sociale des Annamites sous L'Influence Française* (Saigon, 1930).

MAYBON, A. *L'Indochine* (Paris, 1931).

MAYBON, C. B. *Histoire Moderne du Pays d'Annam* (1592–1820) (Paris, 1919).

MESSIMY, A. *Notre Œuvre Coloniale* (Paris, 1910).

MÉTIN, A. *L'Indochine et l'Opinion* (Paris, 1916).

MEYER, R. *Saramani, Danseuse Cambodgienne* (Paris, 1932).

  Le Laos (Hanoi, 1931).

  Komlah: Visions d'Asie (Paris, 1930).

MONET, PAUL. *Annamites, au Travail* (Saigon, 1926).

  Entre Deux Feux (Paris, 1928).

  Français et Annamites (Paris, 1925).

  Les Jauniers (Paris, 1931).

MONOD, G. H. *Légendes Cambodgiennes* (Paris, 1922).

MONTAIGUT, D. DE. *La Colonisation Française dans l'Est de la Cochinchine* (Limoges, 1929).

MOREL, J. *Les Concessions de Terres au Tonkin* (Paris, 1912).

MORICE, J. *Les Accords Commerciaux entre l'Indochine et le Japon* (Paris, 1933).

MOUHOT, H. *Voyages dans les Royaumes de Siam* (Paris, 1868).

MUNIER, P. *Les Poètes Français d'Indochine* (Hanoi, 1932).

LE MYRE DE VILERS. *Les Institutions Civiles de la Cochinchine* (Paris, 1908).

NETON, A. *L'Indochine et son Avenir Economique* (Paris, 1904).

NGANN MANN TCHE LUO. *Mémoires sur l'Annam* (Pékin, 1896).

NGO VI LIEU. *Les Œuvres Complémentaires de l'Ecole en Indochine* (Hanoi, 1929).

  La Société d'Enseignement Mutuel du Tonkin (Hanoi, 1930).

NGUYEN AN NINH. *La France en Indochine* (Paris, 1925).

NGUYEN AI QUOC. *Le Procès de la Colonisation Française* (Paris, 1926).

NGUYEN KHAC VE. *Les Institutions Représentatives des Interêts des Habitants de l'Indochine* (Paris, 1922).
La Naturalisation Française en Indochine (Paris, 1921).

NGUYEN MANH TONG. *L'Individu dans le Vieille Cité Annamite* (Montpellier, 1932).

NGUYEN THANH KHIET. *La Cochinchine Française* (Montpellier, 1915).

NGUYEN THI CHINH. *Critique de la Question Féminine en Pays d'Annam* (Saigon, 1932).

NGUYEN TRONG HIEP. *Paris, Capitale de la France* (Hanoi, 1897).

NGUYEN VAN NGHI. *Etude Economique sur la Cochinchine Française et sur l'Infiltration Chinoise* (Montpellier, 1920).

NGUYEN VAN NHO. *Souvenirs d'Un Etudiant* (Hanoi, 1923).

NGUYEN XUAN GIAC. *Le Régime Economique de la Cochinchine* (Paris, 1920).

NICOLAS, P. *Le Rôle des Missionnaires Religieux en Indochine* (Paris, 1893).

NOGUÈS, GÉNÉRAL. *De la Tranchée de Reims à la Brousse Tonkinoise* (Paris, 1924).

NOLLY, E. *Hien le Maboul* (Paris, 1908).
La Barque Annamite (Paris, 1910).

NORMAN, C. B. *Tonkin, or France in the Far East* (London, 1884).

NORMAND, R. C. *Lettres du Tonkin* (Paris, 1886).

NORODOM, R. *L'Evolution de la Médicine au Cambodge* (Paris, 1929).

OLICHON, MGR. *Le Baron de Phat Diem* (Poitiers, 1931).

ORY, P. *La Commune Annamite au Tonkin* (Paris, 1894).

PANNETIER, DR. *Au Cambodge* (Saigon, 1918).
Au Coeur du Pays Khmer (Saigon, 1916).

PARGORIE, L. *Le Problème Monétaire en Indochine* (Paris, 1933).

PARIS, C. *La Maçonnerie Indochinoise* (Hanoi, 1909).
Le Colon et l'Administration (Paris, 1896).

PASQUIER, P. *La Politique de la France en Indochine* (Paris, 1928).
L'Annam d'Autrefois (Paris, 1930).

PATTÉ, P. *Hinterland Moi* (Paris, 1906).

PAVIE, A. *A la Conquête des Coeurs* (Paris, 1921).
Mission Pavie: *Explorations de l'Indochine* (1879–95) (Paris, 1879).
   Géographie et Voyages, 7 vols. (Paris, 1900–19).
   Etudes Diverses, 3 vols. (Paris, 1898).

PEROZ, E. *France et Japon en Indochine* (Paris, 1906).
Hors les Chemins Battus (Paris, 1908).

PETIT, R. *La Monarchie Annamite* (Paris, 1931).

PHAM QUYNH. *Lettre Ouverte à S.E. le Ministre des Colonies* (Hanoi, 1932).
L'Evolution Intellectuelle et Morale des Annamites (Paris, 1922).
La Poésie Annamite (Hanoi, 1931).

La Politique Indigène en Cochinchine depuis la Conquête jusqu'en 1905 (Saigon, 1905).

POSTEL, R. *A Travers la Cochinchine* (Paris, 1887).

BIBLIOGRAPHY

POUVOURVILLE, A. DE. *Deux Années de Lutte* (Paris, 1892).
    Griffes Rouges sur L'Asie (Paris, 1933).
    L'Asie Française (Paris, 1911).
    Dans les Seize Chaus (Paris, 1895).
    Le Cinquième Bonheur (Paris, 1921).
    La Défense de l'Indochine et la Politique d'Association (Paris, 1905).
    L'Annamite (Paris, 1932).
    La Greffe (Paris, 1923).
    Etudes Coloniales (Paris, 1894).
    La Question d'Extrême Orient (Paris, 1900).
    Le Maître des Sentences (Paris, 1899).
    Le Tonkin Actuel (Paris, 1891).
    L'Annam Sanglant (Paris, 1912).
POUYANNE, A. A. *L'Hydraulique Agricole en Tonkin* (Hanoi, 1931).
    Les Travaux Publics en Indochine (Hanoi, 1925).
PUJARNISCLE, E. *Le Bonze et le Pirate* (Paris, 1929).
GOUVERNEMENT GÉNÉRAL DE L'INDOCHINE. *Question des Affaires Politiques*, 5 vols. (Hanoi, 1933).
RECOULY, R. *Pistes, Fleuves et Jungles* (Paris, 1932).
RÉMY, E. *Monographie du Cadastre en Indochine* (Hanoi, 1931).
RHINS, J. L. D. *Le Royaume d'Annam et les Annamites* (Paris, 1889).
ROBEQUAIN, C. *L'Indochine Française* (Paris, 1935).
RONDET-SAINT, M. *Dans Notre Empire Jaune* (Paris, 1917).
ROUBAUD, L. *Vietnam* (Paris, 1931).
SABATIER, L. *Palabre du Serment au Darlac* (Hanoi, 1930).
SALAUN, L. *L'Indochine* (Paris, 1903).
SARRAUT, A. *La Mise en Valeur des Colonies Françaises* (Paris, 1923).
SAUMONT, J. B. *L'Œuvre de Klobukowski en Indochine* (Hanoi, 1910).
DE SAUSSURE, L. *Psychologie de la Colonisation Française* (Paris, 1899).
Les Scandales de l'Agriculture en Indochine (Saigon, 1932).
SCHREINER, A. *Les Institutions Annamites en Basse Cochinchine*, 3 vols. (Saigon, 1900–02).
SCHULTZ, Y. *Dans la Griffe des Jauniers* (Paris, 1931).
SCOTT, J. G. *France and Tongking* (London, 1885).
DE SEMALLÉ, COMTE. *Quatre Ans à Pékin* (1880–84) (Paris, 1934).
SÉNÈQUE, CAPT. *Luttes et Combats sur la Frontière de Chine* (Paris, 1906).
SEPTANS, A. *Les Commencements de l'Indochine Française* (Paris, 1887).
SILVESTRE, J. *Considérations sur l'Etude du Droit Annamite* (Paris, 1901).
    L'Empire d'Annam et le Peuple Annamite (Paris, 1889).
SIMONI, H. *Le Rôle du Capital dans la Mise en Valeur de l'Indochine* (Paris, 1929).
Société Académique Indochinoise de France: *Mèmoires de . . .* (1877–78), 2 vols. (Paris, 1879).
Société des Missions Etrangères: *Compte Rendu des Travaux* (Paris, 1900– to date).
STAR, J. *Tonkinades* (Paris, 1902).
SUIGNARD, J. *Les Services Civiles de l'Indochine* (Paris, 1931).

TAITTINGER, P. *Le Rêve Rouge* (Paris, 1930).

TALON, VITAL. *Le Régime Douanier de l'Indochine* (Paris, 1932).

TANTET, V. *Inventaire Sommaire de la Correspondance Générale de la Cochin-chine* (1686–1863) (Paris, 1905).

TEDRAL, P. *La France devant le Pacifique* (Paris, 1926).

DE TENEUILLE, A., ET TRUONG DINH TRI. *Ba-Dam* (Paris, 1930).

DE TESSAN, F. *Dans l'Asie qui s'Eveille* (Paris, 1922).

TESTON, E., ET PERCHERON, M. *L'Indochine Moderne* (Paris, 1931).

THANH NGUYEN HANH. *Coutumes et Constitution de la Famille Annamite Bulletin de la Société Académique Indochinoise*, 1882).

TOUZET, A. *L'Economie Indochinoise et la Grande Crise Universelle* (Paris, 1934).
   Théorie du Régime Législatif Indochinois (Paris, 1932).

TRAN VAN CHUONG. *L'Esprit du Droit Sino-Annamite* (Paris, 1922).

Travaux du Comité Maçonnique d'Etudes Franco-Annamite, 4 vols. (Saigon, 1927).

Un An de Terreur et de Lutte Revolutionnaire en Indochine (Courbevoie, 1931).

VALAT, CHARLES. *L'Indochine Actuelle et son Avenir* (Hanoi, 1924).

VANLANDE, R. *L'Indochine sous la Menace Communiste* (Paris, 1930).

VAN RAVESCHOT. *Les Inséparables du Progrès: La Franc-Maçonnerie au Tonkin* (Paris, 1906).

VARET, P. *Les Dieux qui Meurent* (Paris, 1932).

VASSAL, G. *Mes Trois Ans d'Annam* (Paris, 1911).
   Mon Séjour au Tonkin et au Yunnan (Paris, 1928).

VIAL, P. *L'Instruction Publique en Cochinchine* (Paris, 1872).
   L'Annam et le Tonkin (Paris, 1886).
   Les Premières Années de la Cochinchine, 2 vols. (Paris, 1874).

VIGNON, L. *Un Programme de Politique Coloniale* (Paris, 1919).

VILLARD, E. *Etudes sur la Littérature Annamite* (Saigon, 1882).

VIOLLIS, A. *Indochine S.O.S.* (Paris, 1935).

VIVIÈS, A. *Les Timoniers* (Nice, 1926).
   Le Limon (Paris, 1926).
   L'Ame de la Cochinchine (Saigon, 1924).

VUONG QUANG NHUONG. *Des Conflits des Lois en Indochine* (Paris, 1930).

VU TAM TAP. *De la Sincérité chez les Annamites* (Hanoi, 1924).

WERTH, L. *Cochinchine* (Paris, 1926).

WILD, H. *Le Conquérant* (Paris, 1925).
   L'Autre Race (Paris, 1930).
   Les Chiens Aboient (Paris, 1926).
   Dans les Replis du Dragon.

YANN, L. *Croquis Tonkinois* (Hanoi, 1889).

BIBLIOGRAPHY

PERIODICALS

Asie Française.
Bulletin de l'Agence Générale des Colonies (Agence Economique de L'Indo-
    chine).
Bulletin de l'Ecole Française d'Extrême Orient.
Bulletin de la Société Académique Indochinoise.
Bulletin de la Société de Géographie.
Bulletin de la Société d'Enseignement Mutuel du Tonkin.
Bulletin des Amis du Vieux Hué.
Bulletin Economique de l'Indochine.
Depèche Coloniale Illustrée.
Eveil Economique de l'Indochine.
Extrême Asie.
Monde Colonial Illustré.
Pages Indochinoises.
Questions Diplomatiques et Coloniales.
Revue d'Asie.
Revue Economique d'Extrême Orient.
Revue de l'Extrême Orient.
Revue de l'Histoire des Colonies Françaises.
Revue Indigène.
Revue Indochinoise.
Revue Maritime et Coloniale.
Revue du Pacifique.
Société des Missions Etrangères de Paris: Bulletin.

INDEX